The American Journalism History Reader

The American Journalism History Reader presents important primary texts—research and essays about journalism from all stages of the history of the American press—alongside key works of journalism history and criticism. The Reader aims to place journalism history in its theoretical context, to familiarize the reader with essential works of, and about, journalism, and to chart the development of the field.

The Reader is divided into four parts, each of which combines classic sources and contemporary insights. The first part introduces various theories of journalism and media history, and it is followed by parts discussing the 18th, 19th, and 20th centuries respectively. Each part begins with a critical introduction, which establishes the social and political environment in which the media developed to highlight the ideological issues behind the historical period. The volume includes work by:

Gerald J. Baldasty
Erik Barnouw
Silas Bent
Margaret A. Blanchard
Stephen Botein
Walt Brown
Eric Burns
James W. Carey
Michael L. Carlebach
Daniel J. Czitrom
Robert Darnton
Hazel Dicken-Garcia
Benjamin Franklin
Frederic Hudson
Will Irwin
Hank Klibanoff

Daniel J. Leab
Alfred McClung Lee
H.L. Mencken
John Nerone
Allan Nevins
Robert E. Park
Gene Roberts
Ishbel Ross
Dan Schiller
Michael Schudson
George Seldes
Jeffery A. Smith
David R. Spencer
Oswald Garrison Villard
Talcott Williams

Bonnie Brennen is the Nieman Professor of Journalism at Marquette University. She is author of *For the Record: An Oral History of Rochester, New York Newsworkers* and co-editor, with Hanno Hardt, of two books, *Picturing the Past: Media, History, and Photography* and *Newsworkers: Toward a History of the Rank and File*.

Hanno Hardt is Professor Emeritus of Communication and Journalism and Mass Communication at the University of Iowa. He is currently Professor of Communication Studies at the University of Ljubljana in Slovenia. His many books include: *Myths for the Masses: An Essay on Mass Communication*; *Social Theories of the Press*; *Picturing the Past: Media, History, and Photography* (edited, with Bonnie Brennen); *Newsworkers: Toward a History of the Rank and File* (edited, with Bonnie Brennen); and *Critical Communication Studies: Essays on Communication, History and Theory in America*, also published by Routledge. His most recent book is *Slovenci. Traces of the Real* published by the Scientific Research Center, National Academy of Arts and Sciences in Ljubljana, 2010.

The American Journalism History Reader

Critical and Primary Texts

Edited by

Bonnie Brennen and Hanno Hardt

Routledge
Taylor & Francis Group

NEW YORK AND LONDON

First published 2011
by Routledge
711 Third Avenue, New York, NY 10017

Simultaneously published in the UK
by Routledge
2 Park Square, Milton Park, Abingdon, Oxon OX14 4RN

Routledge is an imprint of the Taylor & Francis Group, an informa business

Typeset in Perpetua and Bell Gothic by
RefineCatch Limited, Bungay, Suffolk, UK

Library of Congress Cataloging in Publication Data
The American journalism history reader : critical and primary texts / edited by Bonnie Brennen and Hanno
Hardt.
p. cm.
Includes bibliographical reference and index.
1. Journalism—United States—History. I. Brennen, Bonnie. II. Hardt Hanno.
PN4855.A44 2010
071'.309—dc22
2010014324

ISBN13: 978–0–415–80186–7 (hbk)
ISBN13: 978–0–415–80187–4 (pbk)

Contents

Acknowledgments

Chapter 1: Allan Nevins (1959). American Journalism and Its Historical Treatment. *Journalism Quarterly*, 36(4): 411–22, 519.

Chapter 2: James W. Carey (1974). The Problem of Journalism History. *Journalism History*, 1(1): 3–5. 27.

Chapter 3: Margaret A. Blanchard (1999). The Ossification of Journalism History: A Challenge for the Twenty-First Century. *Journalism History*, 25(3): 107–12.

Chapter 4: John Nerone (1993). Theory and History. *Communication Theory*, 3(2): 148–57.

Chapter 5: Michael Schudson (1987). A Revolution in Historiography? *Critical Studies in Mass Communication* (December): 405–8.

Chapter 6: Benjamin Franklin (1730) [Randolph Goodman (ed.)]. *An Apology for Printers*, 3–16. Camarillo, CA: Acropolis Books Ltd.

Chapter 7: Frederic Hudson (1873). The Fourth Epoch 1783–1832. In *Journalism in the United States from 1690–1872*, 141–57. New York and Evanston: J. & J. Harper Editions.

Chapter 8: Stephen Botein (1980). Printers and the American Revolution. In *The Press & the American Revolution*, 11–57. Worcester: American Antiquarian Society.

Chapter 9: Jeffery A. Smith (1988). The Colonial Journalist: Good Humour'd Unless Provok'd. In *Printers and Press Freedom: The Ideology of Early American Journalism*, 95–107, 202–6. New York and Oxford: Oxford University Press.

Chapter 10: Walt Brown (1995). The Federal Era III: Scissors, Paste, and Ink. In *John Adams and the American Press: Politics and Journalism at the Birth of the Republic*, 39–49, 161–5. Jefferson, NC and London: McFarland & Company, Inc.

Chapter 11: Eric Burns (2006). The End of the Beginning. In *Infamous Scribblers: The Founding Fathers and the Rowdy Beginnings of American Journalism*, 20–33, 414–15. New York: Public Affairs.

Chapter 12: H.L. Mencken (1924). Reflections on Journalism. In *A Second Mencken Chrestomathy*, 357–60. New York: Alfred A Knopf.

Chapter 13: Robert E. Park (1922). The Immigrant Press and Assimilation. In *The*

Immigrant Press and its Control, 49–88. New York and London: Harper & Brothers Publishers.

Chapter 14: Ishbel Ross (1936). Front-Page Girl. In *Ladies of the Press: The Story of Women in Journalism by an Insider*, 1–13. New York and London: Harper & Brothers Publishers.

Chapter 15: Alfred McClung Lee (1937). The Editorial Staff. In *The Daily Newspaper in America: The Evolution of a Social Instrument*, 603–41. New York: The Macmillan Company.

Chapter 16: James W. Carey (1989). Technology and Ideology: The Case of the Telegraph. In *Communication as Culture: Essays on Media and Society*, 201–31. London, Sydney and Wellington: Unwin Hyman.

Chapter 17: Hazel Dicken-Garcia (1989). Changes in News during the Nineteenth Century. In *Journalistic Standards in Nineteenth-Century America*, 63–96. Madison, WI: The University of Wisconsin Press.

Chapter 18: Michael L. Carlebach (1992). Paper Prints for the Masses. In *The Origins of Photojournalism in America*, 43–61. Washington and London: Smithsonian Institution Press.

Chapter 19: Gerald J. Baldasty (1992). American Political Parties and the Press. In *The Commercialization of News in the Nineteenth Century*, 11–35. Madison, WI: The University of Wisconsin Press.

Chapter 20: Robert Darnton (1975). Writing News and Telling Stories. *Daedalus*, 104(2): 175–94.

Chapter 21: Will Irwin (1911). The Reporter and the News. In *The American Newspaper*, Jan–July: 38–42.

Chapter 22: Talcott Williams (1925). Pay and Pecuniary Reward. In *The Newspaperman*, 145–76. New York: Charles Scribner's Sons.

Chapter 23: George Seldes (1938). The House of Lords. In *Lords of the Press*, 3–19. New York: Julian Messner, Inc.

Chapter 24: Silas Bent (1939). A Neglected Story. In *Newspaper Crusaders: A Neglected Story*, 3–19. New York: McGraw-Hill Book Company.

Chapter 25: Oswald Garrison Villard (1944). The Disappearing Daily. In *The Disappearing Daily: Chapters in American Newspaper Evolution*, 3–29. New York: Alfred A. Knopf.

Chapter 26: Erik Barnouw (1966). Voices. In *A Tower in Babel: A History of Broadcasting in the United States to 1933*, 7–38. New York: Oxford University Press.

Chapter 27: Daniel J. Leab (1970). The Beginnings. In *A Union of Individuals: The Formation of the American Newspaper Guild, 1933–1936*, 33–65, 294–9. New York: Columbia University Press.

Chapter 28: Dan Schiller (1981). Democracy and the News. In *Objectivity and the News: The Public and the Rise of Commercial Journalism*, 179–97. Philadelphia: University of Pennsylvania Press.

Chapter 29: Daniel J. Czitrom (1982). Dialectical Tensions in the American Media, Past and Future. In *Media and the American Mind: From Morse to McLuhan*, 183–96, 224–5. Chapel Hill, NC: University of North Carolina Press.

Chapter 30: David R. Spencer (2007). Fact and Fiction. In *The Yellow Journalism: The Press and America's Emergence as a World Power*, 95–12, 239–40. Evanston, IL: Northwestern University Press.

Chapter 31: Gene Roberts and Hank Klibanoff (2006). "A Fighting Press". In *The Race Beat: The Press, the Civil Rights Struggle, and the Awakening of a Nation*, 12–23, 415–17. New York: Alfred A. Knopf.

BONNIE BRENNEN AND HANNO HARDT

GENERAL INTRODUCTION

IN THE 21ST CENTURY, THE FIELD of American journalism is undergoing major economic and conceptual challenges and changes and the journalism that emerges in the years to come is bound to be a very different practice.

Yet, it is important that an understanding of the role and function of journalism throughout the history of American society inform any discussion about the future of journalism. To know the history of the press is to understand the challenges faced by previous generations, which have struggled to reassess the nature of journalism and its place in society. The history of American journalism provides the foundation for understanding not only its public mission since the beginning of the nation, but also its practices and the ways historians have defined and described them over the centuries.

The writing of American journalism history constitutes an exercise in tracing, describing, and reinforcing ideas about the press as a pivotal force in society, indispensable for producing social cohesion, asserting cultural identity, and upholding the principles of democracy. As a result, journalism history often focuses on the role and function of the media as societal institutions and the production of their institutional persona as a symbol of freedom of expression. From this perspective, journalism history becomes a continuing discourse with references to a reality by which American society lives.

This collection of readings provides the basis for appreciating the position of journalism in the public life of the United States and contains an historically grounded argument for the future of journalism in a democracy. Throughout the centuries, journalism historians have reinforced the importance of the press as a vital institution in the life of a democratic society, and have constructed a view of journalism as a vigorous and consistent force working in the interest of the public. It has been a vision of the press that had been shaped by the presence of the First Amendment and its implications for individuals, and their relations to the major institutions of society. Implicit in this view has been the centrality of communication as a social process through which society accumulates knowledge, acts on information, and moves forward in a constructive manner, while the press emerges as an institution of social control and moral guidance.

Consequently, this collection becomes an exercise in remembering, and a relevant source of reflection on the explanatory power of history. Its cumulative influence produces a definition of the American press which is closely identified with democratic ideals and an entrepreneurial spirit, resulting in an institutional expression of collective freedom and individual enterprise which, in turn, yields an example of the workings of a capitalist model of public communication.

The American Journalism History Reader introduces a series of significant texts that place journalism history in its theoretical context, familiarize readers with original texts, and expose the construction of media history. The history of media, like any other history, is an intellectual construct, embedded in the social and political currents of respective periods. Therefore, readers will experience not only the specific concerns of individual authors regarding the development of printing, newspapers, magazines, and electronic media, but will also gain an understanding of the increasing complexity of constructing an American journalism history.

In contrast to other collections of readings, this volume combines originality of texts and chronology of authorship together with a larger cultural context of doing media history, which results in an intellectually rigorous and comprehensive understanding of the meaning of a uniquely American history of journalism. This volume provides the basic literature for courses in media history, offers itself as a resource for social or cultural historians with an interest in media history, and serves as a primary reader for students of communication and media history.

The American Journalism History Reader is divided into four parts, beginning with pertinent examples of 20th-century historiography which showcase American journalism history as ideologically constructed narratives embedded in specific social, cultural, economic, and political conditions. Part Two of the Reader, "The Age of Public Enlightenment," focuses on discussions of journalism in the 18th century and before. It begins with "An Apology for Printers" by Benjamin Franklin, an essay first published in 1730, which addresses issues of censorship that remain central today. H.L. Mencken's "Reflections of Journalism" introduces Part Three, "The Age of Universal Literacy," which discusses journalism during the 19th century. Mencken's essay, first published in 1924, takes aim at the proliferation of tabloid papers, and questions the role of newspapers in American society. Robert Darnton's personal account, "Writing News and Telling Stories" leads off Part Four, "The Age of Information," which addresses the myriad changes in the construction of American journalism during the 20th century.

Each part of the Reader is placed in context by an introduction, which establishes the environment in which the media developed, and is followed by the respective selections of original (reprinted) texts. Rather than selecting brief excerpts from previously published work, this collection reprints complete essays and chapters so that readers may get a sense of the ideological grounding of these authors and their writing style, as well as an understanding of the social and cultural contexts relevant to the respective publications. The collection also includes bibliographical information regarding all references together with an additional listing of relevant contributions to the writing of American journalism history. Ultimately it is our hope that *The American Journalism History Reader* provides readers not only with an appreciation for the centrality of journalism history but also with the background for understanding contemporary challenges facing the field of journalism.

Historiography

INTRODUCTION TO PART ONE

HISTORIOGRAPHY, OR MORE PRECISELY, THE HISTORY of historical writing, beginning with Henri Lancelot Voisin de la Popelinière's *Histoire des Histoires* in 1599 (republished by Fayard in Paris, 1989) gained popularity in the 20th century and has become a measure of understanding history as a narrative, subject to ideological, cultural or political visions of the historian, rather than as a definitive, value-free and objective statement of past events.

Thus, historical writing is based on the collection and accumulation of records and the process of writing, components that are imbedded in a social, cultural and political context and framed by time and place. The result is an explanation of events that have shaped individuals and institutions and that informs a contemporary understanding of the world. Such an historical explanation is rooted in the nature of individuals and their practices as well as in recognition that ideologies permeate history itself. It is, therefore, essentially different from an explanation of physical phenomena. Historians are interested not in the repetitions (or laws) of nature, but in happenings as unique events. These theoretical insights have produced a distinct methodology, which allows historians to reconstruct actions or practices in order to create a sense of the past.

The writing of journalism history began with the invention and development of technical means of communication, such as printing, as a narrowly conceived narrative of publishers/craftsmen and the political rise of the press as a "fourth branch of government." These efforts relied by and large on the intellectual effort of publishers, followed by those teaching journalism, who had a strong interest in the historical roots of American journalism. The resulting national inventory contains the story of the origins and developments of the press as products of individual enterprise across geographically distinct regions. The earliest examples constitute a biographical approach to understanding journalism history as a story of institution-building with a tendency to isolate the historical processes of evolving communication in society from their embeddedness in the social, political, economic or cultural environments. The result has been a series of factual accounts supported by periodization and a strong sense of place. For instance, the lack of a national press resulted in a regional focus, such as in *The History of Printing in America* (1810) by Isaiah Thomas, whose work stands at the beginning of historical accounts related to printing and newspapers in the United States, with strong roots in the pursuit of biographically and geographically specific information.

Following these developments, journalism history has drawn on an evolutionary model of history, perfected during the 20th century, whose linearity produces an orthodoxy of historical research, reinforced by a rigid adherence to the myth of realism. The latter focuses on perpetuating original claims about the position of media in modern society and their economically determined stature as institutional voices in a given ideological context. As such, journalism typically emerges as part of the commercial landscape strengthened by constitutional guarantees.

Since its beginnings, the writing of American journalism history has been produced as a distinct subfield of historical studies, and has been located on the periphery of the intellectual domain of social or cultural historians. Indeed, journalism history typically lacked the intellectual roots in a rich professional discourse regarding the form and nature of history, and, therefore, rarely participated in contemplating questions of fact and fiction, or myth and reality, which had been well recognized issues of those engaged in shaping historical explanations of the world.

Therefore, contemporary journalism history, not unlike most institutional histories, operates in the margins of a considerably larger field of social history, despite the rising acknowledgment of communication as a fundamental social process and the cultural and political impact of media structures on society. The impact of new ideological perspectives with the rise of cultural studies, specifically, was followed by a new appreciation of social history as an empowering explanation of the present. Yet, journalism history as a decontextualized reconstruction of the past has relied primarily on reporting the rise and fall of institutions and their ruling editors and publishers, reminiscent of a narrowly executed, 19th century neo-Rankean history, which concentrated on describing the activities of the leading forces in society.

These observations are reflected in the selections below; the latter represent major historiographical writings in the field of journalism history. In their critique of American journalism history, they also constitute an historical account of historiography as a scholarly endeavor among journalism historians. The rising critical thought about journalism history is reminiscent of the work of James Harvey Robinson, whose turn to a "new history" at the beginning of the 20th century called for a broader approach to history as a process rather than as a product to better serve the present. Progressive historians, such as Charles A. Beard or Carl Becker, had even suggested that faith rather than scientific objectivity would help recover the past, relying on the strength of American exceptionalism.

Hence, contemporary voices have called for repositioning the writing of media history in the social and political context of society. Thus, while Allan Nevins, one of America's leading social historians, had engaged journalism historians in a critique of their work a generation ago (1959), James Carey inspired an internal critique of doing journalism history 15 years later. His writing came at a time when social historians in the United States had been engaged in rethinking the role and function of a social history, especially in the context of the civil rights movement and projects that focus on the lives of ordinary people. By then journalism history had become a key to understanding the role of the press in the making of society along with a multi-disciplinary approach to historical interpretation.

Indeed, the earlier writings on American journalism had rarely acknowledged relations to other disciplines, such as its proximity to the social sciences, or the social or cultural embeddedness of media and the variety of sources that are available to reconstruct the complexity of media development in a societal setting. The current rise of the citizen-journalist, with the arrival of personal communication devices and their potential for sharing observations and ideas, contains the potential of changes in the traditional definition of journalism and offers a relevant example of a shifting understanding of a history of journalism.

Furthermore, the historical process of mass communication has broken down the traditional boundaries between journalism and literature with serious consequences for the writing of history. One is reminded of Norman Mailer's *The Armies of the Night: History as a Novel, the Novel as History* in 1968 or of the introduction of the New Journalism at the same time. These are creative efforts to capture the structures of feeling in a subjective and dynamic manner, surrounded by an atmosphere of multiple knowledges and truths when the writing of journalism history becomes an exercise in recovering experiences while discovering the potential of a cultural narrative that establishes the relations of institutions and people and the emerging meanings of journalism in the public sphere. Art, not unlike the social sciences, is a different way of seeing the world.

As a result, there has been a widening recognition among media historians that any conceptualization of media history in the tradition of social and cultural history must become increasingly important as a source of knowledge at a time when the rising scholarly recognition of communication processes as central to a variety of disciplines could well result in further marginalizing any writing of conventional journalism histories.

Furthermore, historical practice involves the experiences and expressions of culture; it engages the human actors in their relations to social, political and economic institutions, and provides a rationale for ways of doing and being in society. Social theories are the product of historical practice within a cultural setting, while history is more than the reconstruction of the past; it is the experience of its effects and an articulation of its confrontation with the present. When social theory is viewed separate from history, any doctrinaire practice of journalism history remains a study in conformism, where the dangers of compartmentalizing and impeding the growth of ideas seems greatest when it becomes institutionalized either in textbooks and classroom teaching or in organizations.

The presence of critical responses to the existing repertoire of journalism history, as suggested by the readings below, is an important contribution to understanding the importance of doing media history. They also reflect the intensity of the scholarly turn to larger issues at the site of history with their return to previous narratives of media history. The works of Daniel J. Czitrom, *Media and the American Mind: From Morse to McLuhan* (1983), and Paul Starr, *The Creation of the Media: Political Origins of*

Modern Communications (2004), for instance, are appropriate examples of defining the character of communication in America and tracing the development of media in a political atmosphere that differed from European experiences by moving away from specialization and, therefore, compartmentalization to pursue developments across periods and disciplines.

The historiography of American journalism as a scholarly interest has remained a modest intellectual effort alongside the considerable body of historiographical work in the United States, especially since the mid-20th century. Nevertheless, writing about journalism history as an act of self-reflection or as a critique of doing history, offers an important insight into how media historians have constructed history, disclosing the ideological roots of their understanding of the role and function of journalism in society, and exposing the ideology of journalism history itself. A return to the text of history, therefore, becomes a recurrent obligation for those wanting to understand the present. Given new theoretical impulses, advanced by cultural and critical communication studies in the presence of a rapidly changing media environment with practical consequences for journalism, questions such as what is journalism history, how is it constructed, and what should it include, remain relevant issues for contemporary journalism historians to address.

Chapter 1

ALLAN NEVINS

AMERICAN JOURNALISM AND
ITS HISTORICAL TREATMENT

E VERYONE WILL AGREE THAT SINCE THE days of Benjamin Franklin the
American press has made a more interesting, variegated and important record than
that of any other nation. But how should that record be written? As a chapter in our
culture? As a striking part of American business enterprise? Or in relation to the
working of democratic government? The answer is, of course, in all three lights; but
there can be no question that the third is the most significant.

Early in 1959 the International Press Institute in Zurich published a study of *The
Press in Authoritarian Countries* which every journalist and historian should read. It
showed how much of the world's press, from Russia to the Dominican Republic and
Indonesia, is in chains. It demonstrated how fatal to healthy journalism are authoritarian
controls; in Santo Domingo, for example, the total circulation of all newspapers is
below 75,000. It brought out clear evidence that in all totalitarian lands educated
people feel a deep thirst for a press which can freely tell the truth. In short, the report
made it plain that a vigorous democracy and a vigorous free journalism have the closest
interrelationships, so that one cannot exist without the other. This interdependence is
the central theme in the history of the press in any free country.

During the last century a series of memorable phrases were invented to characterize the role of the press in good government. A regent of sovereigns, a tutor of nations,
said Napoleon I. Edmund Burke's remark that journalism is the Fourth Estate was given
popular currency by Carlyle's *French Revolution*. Carlyle himself said that journalists had
become the true kings and clergy, and that newspaper dynasties had replaced the
Tudors and the Hapsburgs. Norman Angell termed newspapers the chief witnesses
upon whose evidence the daily judgments of men on public affairs are based.

One of the most emphatic statements of the social and governmental importance
of the press can be found in the defense which Italian Fascism made of its laws for
controlling the press. The state manages the public schools, said the Fascists, so that they
may always teach patriotism. Newspapers are "schools for character, lecture rooms for
daily teaching, pulpits for preaching"; hence they also must be tightly controlled. But

the Fascists forgot the truth reiterated by the International Press Institute, that a tightly controlled press is a dead press.

Journalism can be the best single instrument of democratic self-government, informing the mind, enlightening the conscience and freeing the spirit of intelligent citizens. It can also be a mortal foe of modern democracy, and that sometimes in subtle ways. Only history can place the achievements and shortcomings of the newspapers of any land in full and fair perspective. Sound historical works on the press and its leaders are as important to the United States as sound works on presidents and cabinet officers, generals and admirals, inventors and industrialists. This branch of history should be expert, incisive and candid—as sternly critical for recent periods, especially as our histories of Second World War campaigns, written by Bradley, Montgomery and Alanbrooke, as unflinching as the assessments of Munich and Pearl Harbor, as outspoken as the best estimates of Stanley Baldwin and Herbert Hoover. Of such history we have as yet the barest beginning.

We cannot take much comfort from the fact that poor as our journalistic history is, it is better than that of any other nation. No history of German journalism in the last generation, for reasons which need no statement, has yet been written. For reasons quite different, no respectable history of modern French journalism has ever been published. The greater newspapers of Paris—*Le Temps, Le Moniteur, Le Matin, Figaro*, and so on—are each so closely identified with specific economic or political groups, or with some compelling individual, that any historian who approached them would find himself dealing with the ruling regime, the group or a prominent leader. A history of the mid-19th century *Moniteur* is only a history of Napoleon III, and a history of *l'Homme Libre*, later *l'Homme Enchainé*, is but a history of Clemenceau.

Even the history of British journalism has been less ably covered than ours. It is in some respects the most distinguished press record, running from Daniel Defoe to Sir William Haley, in the world. One unmatched mountain-peak of historical achievement, the five-volume study of the London *Times* by Stanley Morison and others, fittingly commemorates the work of the most powerful single newspaper. But beyond this the historians have done little, particularly for the last century. It is unfortunate that so illustrious a journal as the Manchester *Guardian* is represented in our libraries by nothing but a slight 200-page sketch, and so important a paper as the London *Telegraph and Morning Post* by nothing at all.

But the deficiencies of other lands cannot be made an excuse for our own, for we have greater advantages and larger responsibilities than European countries. Our democracy is preeminently a newspaper-reading public. Since Jacksonian days every foreign visitor has noted our devotion to daily and weekly publications. Nor is our journalism dominated, as in Britain and France, by a few great centers, for it is spread from the Penobscot to the Pacific. Local and regional pride is enlisted behind many of our newspapers to an extent impossible in Western Europe. Far more money is invested in and spent by our press than in and by that of any other land. Journalism in America is more highly professionalized than in any but a few other countries.

Why, then, do we have so little good history that the number of volumes which can be termed excellent can be counted on the fingers of two hands? Assuming that the history of the press is better worth writing here than elsewhere, for we have more of it and have it more powerfully; assuming also that it must be expert and objective, or it is not worth writing at all, what can we do to improve its scope and quality? Paul Lazarsfeld wrote in *Journalism Quarterly* in 1948: "If there is one institutional disease to which the media of mass communication seem particularly subject, it is a nervous reaction to criticism." The best cure for this sensitivity is more good history of slashing honesty.

The thinness and unevenness of work in this field is largely explained by one simple fact: the fact that, as Thackeray said in *Pendennis*, "All the world is in the newspaper." The files are replete with entertaining detail on a thousand topics, from wars to women, from music to murders. How easy, the amateur says, to fill a volume with amusement and instruction. Actually, the superabundance of jumbled, disparate and mainly trivial details in the files place on the writer a burden of assortment and synthesis under which most men break down.

Compare the task of the biographer of a newspaper with that of the biographer of such a public figure as William Jennings Bryan. The author of a life of Bryan has to relate him to the history of his times—and ours; but only to the history of politics, for apart from a few unhappy episodes like his enlistment in the battle of fundamentalism against evolution, Bryan was merely a political animal; and even in politics only a restricted number of issues, of which currency and imperialism were the chief, need be considered. But the man who writes the history of a great newspaper for the same period has to take cognizance of a thousand subjects from the poetry corner to corners in wheat. If he does not fix on the right principles of selection and synthesis he might as well throw himself into the nearest vat of printer's ink.

When we add that most histories of individual newspapers are prepared with an eye to pious commemoration, or profitable promotion; that the veteran reporter who, if well trained, would today make the best historian, usually lacks any training whatever; and that the writer is subject to covert pressures, ranging from loss of his job to threats of libel suits, and too often yields to them by evasion if not mendacity, then we can understand why such histories are in general poor.

The tasks of selection and synthesis, and the even greater task of finding matter of real historical novelty, are complicated by the universal failure of American newspapers to preserve any data on two subjects of cardinal importance① the method of getting news, and② the facts behind the news. Practically no effort is made in our editorial offices to get and keep such material.

The unapproached distinction of Stanley Morison's five volumes on the London *Times* lies in two facts. The first is that for much more than a century the *Times* has been an integral and important part of the political structure of Great Britain. Its news and its editorial comment have in general been carefully coordinated, and have at most times been handled with an earnest sense of responsibility. While the paper has admitted some trivia to its columns① its whole emphasis has been on important public affairs treated with an eye to the best interests of Britain. To guide this treatment, the editors have for long periods been in close touch with 10 Downing Street. Thus when Morison came to write his history, he found the task of selecting the material already largely accomplished.

The *Times* itself had selected what was most important, had lifted it to a proper plane, and had given it the right emphasis. To give one example out of many, the Berlin Conference of 1878, from which Disraeli brought back peace with honor, was covered for the *Times* by the fabulously expert Paris correspondent M. De Blowitz; he kept in close touch with the editor Thomas Chenery, who had just succeeded Delane, and with the chief owner, John Walter III; they in turn maintained close relations with the Foreign

Office. Morison could feel sure that what the *Times* had reported, and what Chenery had said in his leaders, was history of a specially significant type. ②

The second reason for the distinction of Morison's volumes is that the *Times* kept an unrivaled archive of the news behind the news. De Blowitz, writing to Walter and Chenery, gave the secret history of many episodes and conversations which it was impossible to print, and they told much that now adds color and life to the narrative. Not infrequently the editors, governed by a cautious sense of high responsibility, suppressed perfectly truthful dispatches that it seemed indiscreet to print, and they went into the archives. So did significant letters from a great number of men in public and private life. The *Times*, we may recall, scooped all other newspapers on the text of the Treaty of Berlin, which De Blowitz's assistant, Donald Mackenzie Wallace, carried from Berlin to Brussels sewed in the lining of his coat, and thence telegraphed to London. But the *Times* was quite capable of suppressing a scoop if Disraeli or Gladstone or Salisbury wished it; and then it lay undiscovered until Morison levied upon it for his history.

Most American newspapers have some intimacy with the stream of events, even though it is on a small scale. They deal with affairs for their city or state as the London *Times* dealt with affairs on the national and international level. The difficulty is that they do not bring to them, in most instances, any high sense of responsibility; and this handicaps the historian. They could keep an archive, if they were not too careless or indolent. Any newspaper could ask its best reporters to write memoranda on significant bits of what Thomas Hart Benton in his *Thirty Years' View* called inside history—more important, he said, than external history. Any editor who spent 15 minutes a week dictating his own confidential memorandum or diary would soon have a record priceless to the future historian. An office diary identifying the author of all unsigned articles of note should be an essential part of the machinery of every daily—and comment could be added.

Why are archives not kept? ① Hurry, ② lack of space, ③ preoccupation with crowding daily tasks, are excuses that seldom have much validity. What is needed is a sense that the newspaper is history beyond the day. My own special activities once led me to search carefully the offices of the New York *Evening Post*, New York *Herald* (before its merger with the *Tribune*) and New York *World* for archival material. They were practically bare. Readers of my life of Grover Cleveland will see that I did discover in the *World* morgue one paper of importance. After the dramatic battle in 1893 over the repeal of the Sherman Silver Purchase Act, which opened an irreparable breach between the President and the party majority in Congress, the Washington correspondent of the *World* wrote a confidential history of the struggle as he had seen it from the lobbies of the capitol and the offices of members. This was all.

Lunching with Arthur Sulzberger and some of the editors of the New York *Times* three years ago, I called their attention to the value of an archive preserving confidential materials. Mr. Sulzberger then and there gave instructions to have such an archive formed; but whether these directions were ever carried out I do not know.

In an effort to escape the difficulties of selection and synthesis from the hodgepodge material in the ordinary newspaper file, writers have resorted to two expedients which on a casual view appear legitimate, but which too often lead to an abdication of their proper function. The first expedient is the adoption of a biographical approach, so that the record is treated in terms of a few prominent men. The New York *Sun* becomes personified in Dana, the Springfield *Republican* in Samuel Bowles, the Chicago *Tribune* in

Joseph Medill. This is proper for that part of our journalistic history dominated by great editors, but for that part alone. It is this particular segment of our journalistic annals that has thus far been most efficiently treated. The biographies of Horace Greeley by James Parton, Glyndon Van Deusen, William H. Hale and others, of Samuel Bowles by George S. Merriam, of Dana by James Grant Wilson, of Henry J. Raymond by Francis Brown, of Bryant by Parke Godwin, of Henry Watterson by Joseph Wall and of George William Curtis by Gordon Milne, taken together, provide an adequate impression of the work of the editorial thunderers. Yet large gaps exist. Greeley deserves a really thorough two-volume biography; Joseph Pulitzer merits a much better-informed and less superficial life than Don C. Seitz gave him; and Edwin L. Godkin should long ago have been rescued from the incredibly ill-organized, helter-skelter chronicle written by Rollo Ogden. Nevertheless, by and large, our great editorial personalities have been amply displayed. We can readily discover how the most powerful captains of the press applied their talents to the problems of the day, where their judgment erred, and what they accomplished. This is the simplest element in newspaper history, the most dignified and impressive, and with a proper use of quotation, the most pungent. A dehumanized page on the treatment the New York press gave the great Hungarian patriot, Kossuth, is now but palidly interesting. But a page on the banquet to Kossuth in 1850 at which Bryant presided, Henry J. Raymond was the principal speaker and Greeley was an enthusiastic participant, cannot but be fascinating.

The other expedient used in simplifying the vast melange of material in a newspaper file is the related device of emphasizing opinion at the expense of reporting, views at the expense of news. This, too, is legitimate for the period when opinion was the chief staple of a great newspaper, as it assuredly was for a long generation in the middle of the 19th century. But it becomes a painful distortion when we reach the modern era in which news reigns paramount over opinion. Contrast the *Tribune* of Greeley's day with the New York *Times* as Adolph S. Ochs developed it after 1896. Greeley's chief concern was with the shaping of public policy by a daily page of informed, positive and sometimes eloquent editorials, and he marshaled his news, his special articles and even the letters to the editor to support his page. To Ochs, news—full, honest, objective, clean news—was the heart and soul of the *Times*; he would have dispensed with the editorial page with a relatively minor pang, and always kept it to a minor role.

It is ironic that at the very time the far-reaching revolution which minimized opinion and exalted the news was taking place, historians of journalism busied themselves with the views of the great editor and neglected the news-gatherers. American reporting has become the most enterprising, the frankest and most courageous and the most humanly appealing, though not the best written, in the world. It is much more tough-minded and skeptical than British reporting, much more objective than French. Yet where can we find a narrative which tells just when and why the change took place? In general terms, it is well treated in the admirable histories of journalism by Frank Luther Mott, and by Edwin Emery and Henry Ladd Smith, but they have no space for explanatory detail and telling examples. It is in relation to this change that we most need a thorough analytical biography of Ochs. The task of writing one was first entrusted to Claude G. Bowers, who, working in far-off Chile, failed so completely that the family never used his book; it was then undertaken by Gerald W. Johnson, whose readable volume is deficient in research—especially that kind of research which drains the memories of all surviving associates. It is chiefly with reference to influence on news-gathering that we need a better biography of Pulitzer than that of Don C. Seitz, whose main interest lay in the counting-room. No one can run through the sheafs of telegrams and memoranda in Pulitzer's papers at Columbia without discerning that he was a true genius both in ferreting out news, and in creating it.

If historians must use the biographical approach, it is effective managing editors rather than brilliant editorial writers who since 1900 most deserve their attention. Lord Bryce in *Modern Democracy* remarks that civic opinion is better instructed in America than in Continental Europe because of better news: "the publicity given by the newspapers to all that passes in the political field." Walter Lippmann has said that the greatest successes of present-day journalism lie in "the objective, orderly, and comprehensive presentation of the news." But I know of only one incisive study of an eminent managing editor, James W. Markham's *Bovard of the Post-Dispatch*. This paints a living portrait of an arrogant man who made his newspaper a force for the betterment of St. Louis and Missouri; who taught his best reporters, including Raymond P. Brandt, Paul Y. Anderson and Marquis Childs, to get not only the facts but the truth behind the facts.

We lack an adequate book about an even more distinguished managing editor, Carr Van Anda. More than Bovard, Van Anda saw how complex the truth is, and realized that to discover it a great newspaper must have not simply a slick skill in reporting surface news, but a patient, scientific-minded exploration, by well educated specialists, of intricate situations. An event is a force momentarily made visible. The good news specialist must look for the force behind the event, as something to be explored, measured and analyzed.

It is through the news pages, special features and the exploratory work of labor specialists, educational specialists, sports specialists, economic specialists and others that the best newspapers today exercise leadership. But where is the historical record of this change? A reader may go through a long shelfful of books searching for light on news-gathering and news-analysis, and end in despair. Sam Acheson's history of the Dallas *News*, for example, entitled *35,000 Days in Texas*, is primarily concerned with editorial positions on local, national and international issues since 1842. We learn of the newspaper's attitudes toward Texas banking laws and Ma Ferguson, the Grover Cleveland and Woodrow Wilson campaigns, and the Spanish War; but we find no discussion of news-gathering in connection with these or other subjects. Archer Shaw's *The Plain Dealer* offers two 10-page sections on news, one of which sketches wartime reporting, but the record of the *Plain Dealer*'s valiant fight for Tom L. Johnson's crusades, which earned Johnson's special thanks, is written in editorial terms. Joseph E. Chamberlain's *The Boston Transcript: A History of Its First Hundred Years*, is similarly disappointing. He tells well such stories as that of the skinflint manager William Durant, the most picturesque of the *Transcript*'s heads, who consistently opposed raising the wages of employees on the ground that more money would demoralize them. The one memorable item on news policy in the *Transcript* history records that in the excited days of Jackson and Nullification, the editors invited the public to visit the office and read the news they had not printed. Thomas E. Dabney's book on the New Orleans *Times-Picayune, One Hundred Great Years*, is a waterless Sahara so far as the treatment of news-gathering goes.

It is refreshing to list a few shining exceptions to this category of failure. The general histories by Mott, and by Emery and Smith, give excellent running accounts of progress in news-gathering, and such books as Leo Rosten's *The Washington Correspondents* and Douglass Cater's recent *The Fourth Branch of Government*, while not history, contain many historical preceptions and episodes. The best of all our newspaper chronicles, Meyer

Berger's volume on the New York *Times*, is the work of a skilled reporter. It deals thoroughly and expertly with the method, development and outstanding achievements of news-gathering, especially during the last half-century. With an important story to tell, Berger relates it so brilliantly, in fact, that we hesitate to add one critical reservation: his book is written in pure journalese, undiluted by a touch of stylistic elegance. It had an able preceding volume to surpass, Elmer Davis's; but that, while in better English, is more largely concerned with the editorial conduct of the *Times*. Erwin D. Canham's history of the *Christian Science Monitor, Commitment to Freedom*, has the balance that we would anticipate from its author. John P. Young's *Journalism in California*, a volume concerned generally with San Francisco and specifically with the *Chronicle*, is spasmodically strong in its analysis of reporting, and in relating the *Chronicle* to the social milieu. Young analyzes the news in its historical and social context, discusses such topics as the effect of high telegraph charges on conciseness, and investigates the truth of the *Morning Call's* statement that San Francisco reporting in the early decades was "beneath contempt," concluding that this was because newspapermen were untrained in observation.

The sparkling volume by Gerald Johnson, H. L. Mencken and others on the *Sunpapers of Baltimore* does partial justice to news, almost equating it with opinion. Across the continent Dana Marshall's *Newspaper Story: Fifty Years of the Oregon Journal*, the work of a reporter and special writer who became head of the editorial page, carefully relates the development of news to the growth of Portland. Here the paper and community appear inseparably wedded, serving each other, and all the crusades in which the *Journal* played a part, from campaigns for better mayors to campaigns for better milk, can be found in some detail. We may find material of value on newsgathering in such dissimilar books as James Weber Linn's life of James Keeley, the greatest of Chicago managing editors, who found zest in a hundred exploits, from his personal chase of a murderer through the swamps of Arkansas to his chase of Senator William Lorimer through the swamps of Chicago politics; Ralph E. Dyer's *News for an Empire*, revolving about the Spokane *Spokesman-Review*; and J. Cutler Andrews's study of the Pittsburg *Post-Gazette*, which discusses reporters and illustrators along with editors and circulation managers.

Of course it can be said that the greatest reporters tell their own stories most entertainingly, as they have done from the time George Wilkins Kendall of the New Orleans *Picayune* penned his narrative of the *Texas Santa Fe Expedition* in 1844 to Herbert L. Matthews's *Education of a Correspondent* more than a century later. What newspaperman cannot learn a hundred lessons from the second book of Lincoln Steffens's *Autobiography*, with two hundred pages on a newspaper reporter's work in the days of Boss Croker, Jacob Riis and Police Commissioner Roosevelt?

But systematic history holds a larger usefulness. The reporting of the Civil War by American correspondents has at last been comprehensively analyzed by trained historians, Louis Starr of Columbia University, Bernard A. Weisberger of Antioch College, Emmet Crozier, and J. Cutler Andrews of the Pennsylvania College for Women. Mr. Andrews is a product of Arthur M. Schlesinger's Harvard seminar. So is J. Eugene Smith, whose *One Hundred Years of the Hartford Courant* is the most skilfully planned of all newspaper histories. Similarly, Harry Baehr's capable book on *The New York Tribune since the Civil War*, with a sound account of the way in which the line was held against sensational news in yellow-press days, Candace Stone's treatment of *Dana and the Sun* and Joseph Wall's life of Watterson, three exceptionally good books, were products of a Columbia graduate seminar.

If newspaper history is marred by thinness and spottiness, and over-emphasis on editorial personalities and opinion as distinguished from reporters and news, it has one still more glaring fault. Taken as a whole, it is deplorably uncritical and some of it is dishonest. With too few exceptions, the authors wrote like kept hacks. In their silences they imitate some present-day attitudes of the press itself. Newspapers have long been accused by such observers as Oswald Garrison Villard and Walter Lippmann of refusing to criticize themselves, or each other, or journalism in general. An excessive regard for press comity estops each journal from speaking ill of others, or from noting even egregious blunders and offenses. Many newspapers are unwilling to print intelligence about libel suits against their contemporaries. Most offices have sacred cows stabled somewhere, but the greatest sacred cow is journalism itself. Yet bad as <u>newspaper</u> practice is, some press historians go further; they gloss over blunders, <u>defend misinterpretations</u> and injustices, and sweep glaring omissions and lost opportunities under the bed.

Why? Theoretically, ① the veteran newspaperman is a hardboiled, toughminded writer, ready in pursuit of truth to cut his own mother's throat. Actually, in historical vein, he often writes like a mawkish sentimentalist, or a party wheelhorse at convention time recalling the greatness of James G. Blaine. We have mentioned one reason, the promotional origin of many histories. ② Another reason is that employees fall in love with their paper; they awaken every morning saying to themselves (to paraphrase H. J. Massingham), "I wonder how the dear old slut is this morning? Damn the hussy! I must do something for her." Knowing her sins, they love her too much to expose them. ③ A third reason is that all ephemeral media, like the stage, the ballet, the motion pictures or the circus, become invested with a romantic aura and encrusted with legends. As a result, the typical newspaper historian is a *laudator tempus acti*, who hangs nothing but spotless linen on the line.

This is easy, because the newspaper reflects light from so many facets; it so often gets on both sides of important issues—and if a third side existed, would get on that; and it can so easily be quoted out of context. The America-Firster attitudes of the Chicago *Tribune* just before Pearl Harbor, and the defense of Joseph McCarthy by the Hearst press, were foolish and immoral, but any agile newspaper historian could find quotations to prove that they embodied a profound patriotism. Of course most historical dishonesties are on a minor scale, and can be labelled simply special pleading; still, they are dishonesties. It was dishonest of me in the *Evening Post* history to suppress the bitter quarrel between the owner, Villard, and the editor, Rollo Ogden, both then living and both hypersensitive. It was dishonest of Elmer Davis to treat Charles R. Miller's *Times* editorial of September 16, 1918, urging unconditional acceptance of the Austro-Hungarian proposal for a non-binding discussion of peace terms, as shrewd and judicious, though Woodrow Wilson's wiser treatment of the proposal showed that Miller was guilty of a deplorable *gaffe*. We can read Frank M. O'Brien's book on the New York *Sun* without the slightest realization of the harm wrought by Dana's cynical defense of Tammany, hatred of civil service reform, spasms of jingoism and constant demands for the annexation of Cuba and Canada. Henry Adams tells us that he could have found a place on Dana's staff, but he knew that he could never please himself and Dana too, for "with the best intentions he must always fail as a blackguard, and a strong dash of blackguardism was life to the *Sun*." To grasp the blackguardism, a reader must drop O'Brien and read Candace Stone's book.

The history of the London *Times* by Morison and others is in general unflinchingly honest. It tells everything, for example, about the libelous *Times* accusations against

Charles Stewart Parnell, based on forged letters, and about the ruinous penalty; for the ensuing suit cost the *Times* almost £200,000. But even this admirable history has been accused by no less a person than Lord Beaverbrook of flinching at the full truth when it deals with the abdication of Edward VIII. This story is told in an appendix to the final volume.

Morison makes it plain that the *Times* was one of the principal agents in compelling the abdication. Indeed, its editor, Geoffrey Dawson, a man of formidable intellectual and personal force, stood next to Prime Minister Stanley Baldwin in the unseating of Edward VIII. Dawson was one of the first men in Britain to learn of the King's love affair. Horrified, he set out on what Beaverbrook calls a "propaganda canvass" of public men. The king offered Baldwin a plan for a morganatic marriage, by which he would take a wife but not a queen. The prime minister notified Geoffrey Dawson of this before he consulted the Cabinet, or the heads of the great dominions, and the puritanical editor was again horrified. He at once began a tremendous campaign in the *Times* upon the importance of keeping the Crown completely free from any taint of personal scandal; and according to Beaverbrook, he published one article which was innocent on its surface, but which carried "wounding and malicious innuendo." At the outset public opinion in Britain had been heavily on the side of the king and his proposal. Dawson and the *Times* swayed it in the opposite direction, until on a foggy December night the Duke of Windsor boarded the destroyer *Fury* for a French port. No reader of Morison's pages can doubt that he has told the story with general accuracy, making plain the vital part played by the *Times*. But according to Lord Beaverbrook, he did not make it plain that Dawson had used unfair weapons.

Our newspaper historians have not told the truth about the external pressures which have so often colored news and opinion. Murat Halstead remarked to the Wisconsin Press Association in 1889 that he saw no objection if readers should "find out that the advertiser occasionally dictates the editorials." "No objection at all to that," rejoined E. L. Godkin; "the objection is when they don't find it out." Direct advertiser-dictation has largely disappeared; but the treatment of news is still prostituted, all over the map, to the acquisition of larger and more vulgar bodies of readers, so that circulation managers may go to advertisers and boast of the clientele which their paper reaches. Historians have failed to emphasize properly the stupid conservatism of most of the press, its blind attachment to the status quo, and especially the economic status quo. Franklin D. Roosevelt in 1938 remarked on this reactionary hostility to change, saying of the papers using the Associated Press or United Press services that he estimated "85 percent of them have been inculcating fear in this country during the past year." He was quite right; the newspapers, themselves business enterprises, have repeatedly been too responsive to business in opposition to needed change.

Press historians rightly make much of Paul Y. Anderson's part in remorselessly following the oil scandals under Harding to the doors of the Republican National Committee, but they say little of the general inertia and complacency of newspapers in Harding's day. They say even less about the callous indifference of most metropolitan newspapers to depressed economic groups, such as the farmers, miners and textile workers, during the boom of the 1920s. Mr. Dyar in *News for an Empire* quotes the statement which President Truman made in Spokane in 1948 about the *Spokesman-Review*: "This paper and the Chicago *Tribune* are the worst in the United States." But he does not explain the sins of omission and commission which led to this outburst.

Long ago Dr. Johnson spoke of the debasing effects of great conflicts upon press ethics: "In wartime a people only want to hear two things—good of themselves, and evil of the enemy. And I know not what is more to be feared after a war, streets full of soldiers who have learned to rob, or garrets full of scribblers who have learned to lie." But we still lack a full *exposé* of the effects of the First and Second World Wars on the hysterical and irresponsible parts of the American press.

We have numerous accounts of the more blatant indecencies of yellow journalism, with special attention to such episodes as the Spanish War. As Matthew Arnold said long ago, sensational papers offer "the best means to efface and kill in a whole nation the discipline of respect, the feeling for what is elevated." The blatant indecencies, however, often do less harm than those of a subtle, insidious kind. A recent book by Judge Irwin D. Davidson and Richard Gehman, entitled *The Jury Is Still Out*, explores at length the murder of a crippled New York boy, Michael Farmer, by a street gang. Not the least important part of the book analyzes the contribution to social disorder steadily made by the gutter press. Honest depiction of the immense but hidden harm long done by sensational journalism is much needed in every section of the country. The extent to which lurid reporting under slanted headlines has interfered with the administration of justice in the courts offers another problem which the historian could profitably explore.

Much could also be said of various requirements, as yet badly met, in the history of newspapers as business institutions, for their financial record bears on their stability and their independence. Most newspaper histories neglect even a partial account of circulation revenue, advertising revenue, profits and losses, because records are wanting, or secrecy is desired, or such matters seem dull. It is curious, for example, that after Ochs's original purchase, the financial history of the New York *Times* is almost entirely omitted from Meyer Berger's otherwise complete narrative. When I wrote the history of the *Evening Post* I found no financial records anterior to 1900, and few later; the Villard family had some, which were not open to me.

Far more important than this, however, is a proper treatment of the public service function of newspapers. It is of the first importance, now that so many cities have but one newspaper, that historians study the question whether a correlation can be traced between a good newspaper and a well-governed community, a bad paper and a badly managed community. Was the Boston of James Curley what it was partly because Boston newspapers (the *Monitor* excluded) were so wretched? Was Louisville a specially healthy city because of the public spirit of the *Courier-Journal*? Mayors come and go, but a newspaper is a continuing institution.

No subject is of more importance than this to the political scientist, the sociologist, the general historian—and the aspiring young newspaperman. The best young men and women enter the profession because they hope to make not only better newspapers, but better towns and cities. Many evidences point to the fact disclosed by Columbia University's examination of the young people who attend its Scholastic Press Convention each year. They state that they know that journalism seems less attractive than law; medicine, engineering, science or even university teaching; as a profession it is low in pay, low in amenities, low in social prestige. But they believe they can play a more direct and fruitful part in community improvement through newspaper work than through any other calling. Their first task, of course, is to improve the newspapers, and it is discouraging to see how little our fast-multiplying schools of journalism have thus far done for such betterment. The theory of Dean Luxon of North Carolina that 50 years is too short a time to measure their effect is rather cold comfort. But ambitious young entrants have their eyes fixed on the greater goal of service to town, or city, or state; and every history which can tell a story of such service will give them inspiration.

What, then, are the principal requirements to be satisfied if we are to have the adequate histories of journalistic effort that we now lack? They are implied in what I have already said, and may be summarized under a few headings.

(1) First, it is of cardinal importance that the newspaper has a history worth honest research and honest writing. That, alas, can not be said of most dailies in the United States. Mere size and power are not proper criteria. We can say of a number of prominent dailies that they should not have histories because a really veracious record would be impossible, and even a counterfeit record would be repellent or painful. But every good journal is worth a history, which will benefit the paper, the community and the nation.

(2) Second, every newspaper which deems its record worthy of commemoration should keep an archive. This means that some member of its staff should learn the rudiments of archival method; that an elementary office diary should be kept; that editors and reporters should be encouraged to make memoranda, save significant in-letters, and keep carbons of important out-letters; and that in general, some record be made both of the methods of news-gathering, and of the untold truth behind the news. The problem of room for an archive can sometimes be solved by the cooperation of the nearest historical society or library.

(3) In the third place, the choice of a writer should not be left to chance or impulse. It will of course depend on circumstances. A history written as promotion is better than no history at all, but the promotional motive should be secondary. A writer selected within the office, and particularly in the newsroom, will be more expert than an outsider; an outsider will be more objective. Any writer should make the fullest use of oral reminiscences. The advice of a good college or university department of history can be obtained more readily than most newspapermen suppose, and will be more valuable than they generally believe. University teachers write badly, but they have a sense of organization, and they will see aspects of the subject that newspapermen may miss.

(4) In the fourth place, this association, it seems to me, could make one important contribution to the systematic cultivation of press history in the United States. It might do something to improve current newspaper practice, and a great deal to guide future historians, if every five years it published a critical review, by regions, of the attitudes and activities of the principal newspapers. One committee in each region—that is, in say 10 areas of the country—could be made responsible for the critical evaluations. The members of this association, holding close relations with the principal newspapermen of their states, regularly reading the important journals, and possessing a keen critical sense of what is good and bad in journalism, could provide this review more easily and expertly than anyone else. Such a quinquennial volume, written with verve and penetration, would be accepted by any publisher, and would be sure of a large sale. Money needed to support the research and pay the essayists could readily be obtained from one of several foundations. As these volumes grew across the shelf, their impact on journalism, and their value to historians, sociologists, economists and students of government would grow too.

(5) Finally, the historian should hang over his desk an amended version of the motto with which Joseph Pulitzer adorned his newsrooms: Honesty, Accuracy, Honesty.

JAMES W. CAREY

THE PROBLEM OF JOURNALISM
HISTORY

THE STUDY OF JOURNALISM HISTORY REMAINS something of an embarrassment. Can it be justified as a form of knowledge, an entry in the curriculum, an activity to which one can usefully devote his professional life? By our behavior we answer the questions affirmatively and yet a doubt remains. Each generation of journalism historians has been dissatisfied with the nature of our knowledge and the forms of our presentation. Writing in a short-lived newsletter, *Coronto*, about 1950, Theodore Peterson argued:

> . . . in many schools and departments of journalism, history of journalism is the least rewarding course in the curriculum. The reasons are various. One is that all too often history is the orphan, or at least the grubby little cousin, who must depend on charity for its care and feeding. Young instructors teach it from sufferance; senior faculty members teach it because they have worked up an adequate set of notes that it's a shame to waste. They drone about the dull, dead past and somnolent students cache away a store of names, dates, and places to see them through the cheerless examination season.

Peterson finally concluded that the trouble was not intrinsic to the subject matter, but in the way journalism historians had handled their materials. He argued Frank Luther Mott had laid down a solid factual foundation for the field and that we now needed "interpretive studies utilizing the factual information about the press, per se, that Mott and his predecessors have given us." Peterson in *Magazines in the Twentieth Century* and Edwin Emery in *The Press and America* have attempted just that: building an interpretation on the raw data using, I think it is fair to say, Ralph Casey's elucidation of the great impersonal forces affecting the press as the spine of their story.

Despite these achievements, and there are others that might be cited, the thought remains that our subject matter has not been domesticated or, to invert the metaphor, has been so tamed that all vitality has been drained from the enterprise. It has recently been argued that journalism history is dull and unimaginative, excessively trivial in the problems chosen for study, oppressively chronological, divorced from the major current of contemporary historiography, and needlessly preoccupied with the production of biographies of editors and publishers. As in 1950, the persistent apathy of student response to historical studies is offered as proof of the criticism.

There is truth in all these charges, though I think they often mistake the fish story for the fish. For example, student response to history, not just journalism history, has been in decline. This is because the American sense of history has always been lamentably thin and students are drawn, for reasons de Tocqueville recognized, to the more abstract and generalizing social sciences. Our major response to this must be to accept a challenge: the major problem with American social thought is its scientific and ahistorical character and our dual task remains a thoroughgoing critique of the behavioral sciences and the permeation of our studies and our students' thought with historical consciousness.

Furthermore, the existing critiques of journalism history are superficial; they fail to get at a deeper set of historiographical problems. For example, we have defined our craft both too narrowly and too modestly and, therefore, constricted the range of problems we study and the claims we make for our knowledge. We have, in general, failed to base our work on an adequate sense of historical time, and we have likewise ignored the most fruitful research of modern historians that might serve as the basis of fresh interpretations of our subject matter.

I cannot here deal with all these problems; such treatment I have reserved for a longer work in progress. However, one paradoxical issue can be treated; namely, that the most fundamental failing in journalism history is but the reverse of our success. Our field has been dominated by one implicit paradigm of interpretation—an interpretation I will call, following Herbert Butterfield, a whig interpretation of journalism history. This interpretation, which is absorbed in the invisible culture of graduate school, has so exclusively dominated the field that we do not even have, to mention the most obvious example, a thoroughgoing Marxist interpretation of press history.

Herbert Butterfield used the notion of a whig interpretation of history to describe the marriage of the doctrine of progress with the idea of history. The whig interpretation of journalism history, to put it all too briefly, views journalism history as the slow, steady expansion of freedom and knowledge from the political press to the commercial press, the setbacks into sensationalism and yellow journalism, the forward thrust into muckraking and social responsibility. Sometimes written in classical terms as the expansion of individual rights, sometimes in modern terms as growth of the public's right to know, the entire story is framed by those large impersonal faces buffeting the press: industrialization, urbanization and mass democracy.

The problem with this interpretation, and the endless studies and biographies executed within its frame, is simply that it is exhausted; it has done its intellectual work. One more history written against the background of the whig interpretation would not be wrong—just redundant.

Much journalism history is now devoted to proving the indubitable. In art the solemn reproduction of the achievements of the past is called academicism. And that is the term which describes much journalism history. It is not that the whig interpretation was wrong or failed to teach us anything, but it is moribund and to pursue it further is to guarantee dead ends and the solemn reproduction of the achieved. Our historians are so set on this interpretation that they largely rewrite one another adding a literary cupola here, a vaulted arch there, but fail to look at the evidence anew and afresh. We are suffering from what, in another context, Morris Janowitz has called "the dead hand of competence."

Our studies need to be ventilated, then, by fresh perspectives and new interpretations even more than by additional data. I would like to suggest that such a ventilation might occur by developing the cultural history of journalism. In fact, I take the absence of any systematic cultural history of journalism to be the major deficiency in our teaching and research.

I place an emphasis on cultural history because I think we should consider anew the objectives of our historical effort and the materials of our craft. We often think of our efforts as aimed at reconstructing the events, actions, institutions and organizations of the past. We wish to know when a particular newspaper was founded, the progression of its editors and editorial policies, when and how particular technology was innovated and diffused, when particular judicial decisions or legislative acts affecting the press were promulgated, under what circumstance and with what effect. There are innumerable such studies which knitted together into a general history create that documentary record known as journalism history. This documentary record when subject to certain rules of interpretation, forms the positive content of the discipline: an interpreted record, of the events and actions of the past. This is, in general, what we choose to remember of the past.

However, there is another dimension of the past, related to this documentary record, but not simply derivable from it. This dimension we can call cultural and illustrate it with an artlessly simple example drawn from John William Ward.

The documentary record of military history includes an attempt to determine, for example, how, when and under what circumstances Caesar crossed the Rubicon. But this is not the only dimension of that event and, for many purposes, not the most important dimension either. The cultural history of that event is an attempt to reconstruct what Caesar felt in crossing the Rubicon: the particular constellation of attitudes, emotions, motives and expectations that were experienced in that act.[1] To verify that Caesar crossed the Rubicon is to say nothing of the significance of the event, a significance which derived from Caesar's defiance of a convention giving Republican law authority over the soldiers of the state.

Cultural history is not concerned merely with events but with the thought within them. Cultural history is, in this sense, the study of consciousness in the past.[2] As such, it derives from three assumptions: first, that consciousness has a history; second, that as Charles Cooley never tired of arguing, the solid facts of society are the imaginations men have of one another and third, that while the actions of men illustrate in a general way a certain uniformity across time and space, the imaginations behind such actions illustrate a considerably wider variety. Most people make love and war, have children and die, are educated and work, constrained by the physical limits of biology, nature and technology. But for us to understand these events we must penetrate beyond mere appearance to the structure of imagination that gives them their significance. If most men march off to war, they do so in the grip of quite different imaginations: some march to recover holy lands for their God, others to protect their nations from foreign devils, others reluctantly and sullenly as the exploited slaves of an imperial power. The facts of warfare give none of this information directly, but the significance of military action lies in how it is imagined.

The task of cultural history, then, is this recovery of past forms of imagination, of historical consciousness. The objective is not merely to recover articulate ideas or what psychologists nowadays call cognitions but rather the entire "structure of feeling" "The most difficult thing to get hold of, in studying any past period, is this felt sense of the quality of life at a particular time and place: a sense of the ways in which the particular activities combined into a way of thinking and living."[3] We want to show, in short, how action made sense from the standpoint of historical actors: how did it feel to live and act in a particular period of human history?

How does all this relate to journalism history? Our failure to develop the cultural history of journalism has led us to exclude from our literature any serious attention to what I believe is the central historical story we have to tell, namely the history of reporting. We have legal histories of the press, institutional histories, technological histories, even some economic history of the press. But the history of reporting remains not only unwritten but largely unconceived. The central story in journalism has been largely banished from our remembrance of things past.

Prior—both logically and chronologically—to journalism being an institution, or business, or a set of rights, or a body of technology, journalism is a cultural act, a literary act. The technology of journalism existed prior to news or newspapers. Journalism is essentially a state of consciousness, a way of apprehending, of experiencing the world. The central idea in journalism history is the "idea of a report" and the changing notions of what has been taken to be an adequate report of the world. Because we are a news saturated people it may seem strange to argue that the desire to know, understand and experience the world by getting news or reports about it is really a rather strange appetite. But it is less obtuse to suggest that there is a vast difference between what is taken to be an adequate report of the world by those who queue up before Tom Wolfe and the new journalism versus those readers wholly satisfied with the New York Times. In fact our failure to understand journalism as a cultural form has left us virtually bereft of intelligent commentary on the "new journalism."

The central and as yet unwritten history of journalism is the history of the idea of a report: its emergence among a certain group of people as a desirable form of rendering reality, its changing fortunes, definitions and redefinitions over time (that is, the creation and disappearance of successive stylistic waves of reporting), and eventually, I suppose, its disappearance or radical reduction as an aspect of human consciousness.

I call this a cultural history for the following reason. By culture I merely mean the organization of social experience in the consciousness of men manifested in symbolic action. Journalism is then a particular symbolic form, a highly particular type of consciousness, a particular organization of social experience. This form of consciousness can only be grasped by its history and by comparing it to older forms of consciousness (mythic, religious) which it partially displaced and with other forms with which it emerged and has interacted—the scientific report, the essay and aesthetic realism.

When we grasp the history of journalism, we grasp one form of human imagination, one form—shared by writer and reader—in which reality has entered consciousness in an aesthetically satisfying way. When we study changes in journalism over time, we are grasping a significant portion of the changes that have taken place in modern consciousness since the Enlightenment. But to do this we must temporarily put aside our received views of what journalism is and examine it afresh as a cultural form, a literary act, parallel to the novel, the essay and the scientific report. Like these other works journalism is a creative and imaginative work, a symbolic strategy; journalism sizes up situations, names their elements and names them in a way that contains an attitude toward them. Journalism provides what Kenneth Burke calls strategies for situations—"strategies for selecting enemies and allies, for socializing losses, for warding off evil eye, for purification, propitiation and desanctification, consolation, and vengeance, admonition and exhortation, implicit commands or instructions of one sort or another." Journalism provides audiences with models for action and feeling, with ways to size up situations and it shares these qualities with all literary acts.

Journalism is not only literary art; it is industrial art. Stylistic devices such as, for example, the inverted pyramid, the 5 W lead, and associated techniques are as much a product of industrialization as tin cans. The methods, procedures and canons of journalism were developed not only to satisfy the demands of the profession but to meet the needs of industry to turn out a mass produced commodity. These canons are enshrined in the profession as rules of news selection judgment, and writing. Yet they are more than mere rules of communication. They are, like the methods of the novelists, determiners of what can be written and in what way. In this sense the techniques of journalism define what is considered to be real: what can be written about and how it can be understood. From the standpoint of the audience the techniques of journalism determine what the audience can think—the range of what is taken to be real on a given day. If something happens that cannot be packaged by the industrial formula, then, in a fundamental sense, it has not happened; it cannot be brought to the attention of the audience or can be presented only in distorted fashion.

When we study the history of journalism we are principally studying a way in which men in the past have grasped reality. We are searching out the intersection of journalistic style and vocabulary, created systems of meaning, and standards of reality shared by writer and audience. We are trying to root out a portion of the history of consciousness.

Journalism as a cultural form is not fixed and unchanging, journalism has changed as it has reflected and reconstituted human consciousness. Journalism not only reveals the structure of feeling of previous eras, it is the structure of feeling of past eras or at least significant portions of it.

For example, my colleague Albert Kreiling has tried to show how the history of the Black press is much more than the documentary record of Black papers and editors, successes and failures, or quarrels among Black editors and writers. He has tried to describe the Black press, first and foremost, as a record of Black consciousness—its origins and transformation—in modern times. We do not study the Black press because it passively reflects Black consciousness; the press is not merely a source of data about Black social history. Black consciousness is forged in, it exists in the Black press: the arena where Black consciousness is created and controlled by canons of Black journalism. It is not the only place of course: one need not derogate art, pulpit and politics to show that Black journalism does not passively reflect Black consciousness. To study the history of the Black press or any other press is to recover the consciousness of men in the past and to relate that record to the present.

There is, however, another and better explored side to the cultural history of the press. The press is itself an expression of human consciousness. Whether we think of the press as an institution, a set of legal prerogatives regarding expression or a body of technology, it is, first of all an expression of a certain ethos, temper or imagination. The press embodies a structure of feeling derived from the past and as this underlying structure of feeling changes, the press itself is altered. The press should be viewed as the embodiment of consciousness. Our histories in turn must unpack how a general cultural consciousness becomes institutionalized in procedures for news gathering and reporting, forms of press organization, and definitions of rights and freedom.

We have made some progress here for we have realized that any understanding of the freedom and rights of journalists must take into account the changing fortunes of general legal consciousness identified by terms such as natural law, legal realism and sociological jurisprudence.

That body of literature often called "four theories of the press" has also attempted to show how general patterns of consciousness identified by political handles such as liberalism and marxism have been institutionalized into specific patterns of press organization, news performance, and definitions of freedom and rights. However, this work has never gone far enough, either historically or comparatively, and suffers from an overly intellectualistic cast. It has not shown how forms of consciousness shared in narrow intellectual circles have become generally shared and how they have been altered in this process of democratization.

The cultural history of journalism would attempt to capture that reflexive process wherein modern consciousness has been created by the symbolic form known as the report and how in turn modern consciousness finds institutionalized expression as journalism.

Our major calling is to look at journalism as a text which said something about something to someone: to grasp the form of consciousness, the imaginations, the interpretations of reality journalism has contained. When we do this the presumed dullness and triviality of our subject matter evaporates and we are left with an important corner of the most vital human odyssey: the story of the growth and transformation of the human mind as formed and expressed by one of the most significant forms in which the mind has conceived and expressed itself during the last three hundred years—the journalistic report.

Notes

1.   John William Ward, *Red, White and Blue*, New York: Oxford University Press, pp. 4–5.
2.   To do this requires we overcome the prejudice against consciousness as an historical fact: A useful place to begin this task is with Erich Naumann's *The Origins and History of Consciousness*, New York: Pantheon Books, 1954.
3.   Raymond Williams, *The Long Revolution*, New York: Harper and Row, 1966, p. 47.

Chapter 3

MARGARET A. BLANCHARD

THE OSSIFICATION OF
JOURNALISM HISTORY
A Challenge for the Twenty-First Century

RECENT YEARS HAVE SEEN AN INCREASE in the number of articles criticizing our particular subfield of history. James W. Carey, perhaps, started this critical examination by terming "the study of journalism history . . . an embarrassment." The problem, he wrote twenty-five years ago, rests in the fact that "we have defined our craft too narrowly and too modestly and, therefore, constricted the range of problems we study and the claims we make for our knowledge."[1]

Carey's criticism unleashed the pens of other scholars who undertook to analyze the problems of journalism history and to offer solutions to those difficulties. Joseph P. McKerns, for instance, argued that the problem with journalism history was its over reliance on "progressive history."[2] Garth Jowett called for scholars to study "the importance of communication as a force for historical change."[3] And David Paul Nord pled for "journalism history," defining that as broader than newspaper history.[4] The argument over what journalism history is—or should be—has gone on for years. These articles have tried to categorize journalism history in various ways, have sought to bring the knowledge base of other disciplines into journalism history, or have urged further specialization within the field.[5] These articles have brought many of the best journalism historians into the fray, with each one offering a solution to a problem that is hard to define and harder yet to solve.

Such a plethora of criticism almost naturally leads to substantial concerns about the status of our field, especially as we enter the twenty-first century. Fundamentally, my concern always ends up at the same question: Will journalism history survive the challenges of the twenty-first century or will our subfield stand immobile in the face of these challenges, ossify, and die? I know it sounds strange to mix history and the future, but the two seem inextricably linked.

When any discipline is subjected to so much criticism and offered so much advice, its practitioners may well find it much more difficult to move in any direction. Indeed, journalism historians may feel that no matter what they do, the action will be criticized by someone. Consequently, our tendency is to ossify our positions—to stand immobile, to go with what we understand, to further limit our horizons by rigid definitions of what scholarship is and, indeed, of what history is.

One reason to tackle this subject again, however, may be the consequences of what might happen if we do not do so. At stake may be the development and loyalty of a new generation of journalism historians. This new generation—whose members are currently well along in their doctoral studies or are recent graduates—is increasingly eager to apply new ideas and new approaches to journalism history research projects. These scholars see great possibilities in melding theoretical constructs and research approaches from feminist studies, critical studies, and other disciplines as they approach their work, and they envision a broader field of study that encompasses a variety of media—including motion pictures, television and radio entertainment, books, and visual displays as well as traditional news-related topics, at the very least. The insights that these and other approaches allow them to reach about how such a variety of media both reflected and shaped American life over the years are substantial, and these newer scholars should be congratulated for their efforts.

But their efforts face a tremendous barrier—one that may force them to abandon their efforts at innovation in an attempt to survive in the academic world. The obstacle, of course, is the need to obtain an academic position in the first place and the need to earn tenure and promotion thereafter. The reason that this is an obstacle, quite frankly, is that those of us who tend the gates for conference presentation and journal publication often are not terribly hospitable to new approaches to journalism history.

Granted, some of the studies exploring new ways to research our history are not well done and should be rejected on those grounds alone. We should never abandon our demands for solid research with original sources, careful thinking, and precise writing. Well-done studies, however, often run into trouble because they stray too far from acceptable (traditional) topics for journalism history or from acceptable (traditional) research methodology.

Some journalism historians would argue that there have been changes in the field already and that new scholars (and some old ones as well) should be content with the evolutionary nature of change in the field. Indeed, some aspects of journalism history have changed. A preliminary study prepared by Alf Pratte and J.R. Rush of Brigham Young University, for example, showed that 26 percent of the papers presented at the American Journalism Historians Association conference from 1982 to 1997 focused on minority or women's history or biographical studies. Thirty-one percent of the articles published in *American Journalism* during the same time period focused on the same three topics.[6] The two scholars told the 1998 AJHA conference that further work needed to be done to refine the study, and it will be interesting to discover how many of those papers or articles on women and minorities also fall into the biographical studies area, either biographies of people or institutions. Changing subject matter slightly within the overall field of journalism history while maintaining traditional research methodologies may be more acceptable than changing the subject matter too substantially or applying research methods that differ too substantially from the norm.

Faced with the blunt reality of what is acceptable for progress in your career and what forms your research and theoretical interests, many new scholars may well opt for traditional and acceptable rather than innovative. I can't say that I blame them, but it does hurt my spirit of scholarly adventure when I hear students and new graduates talk about giving up their scholarly interests to earn points for employment or tenure or trying to figure out how to adapt their interests so that they include just the right amount of "journalism history" in their research studies to appeal to judges and reviewers. Such decisions to withdraw from the forefront of the struggle to change the field can only stultify our field, or indeed lead to an ossification of our discipline. There will be no progress. And perhaps there will be no life in our field either.

Some people would argue our field cannot develop, cannot evidence either life or progress because it is isolated from the mainstream of historical research and because it finds itself trapped in a journalism and mass communication program. David Paul Nord, for instance, has written on this point, attributing some of our stultification, which is more likely my interpretation than his, to that separation.[7] Nord, who has worked closely with the historical profession through his relationship with the Organization of American Historians and the *Journal of American History*, has also argued that journalism historians have things to teach the traditional history profession as well, noting especially the insider knowledge about how the field works that we could contribute to traditional historical interpretations.[8]

Some of our colleagues in journalism and mass communication may see our placement as a detriment to our development as historians. And some of our colleagues may indeed find it distasteful to be joined in programs that also include individuals with strong social science research interests. But our placement within journalism and mass communication programs could benefit our development as historians, for scholars may easily borrow from other research disciplines within the academic offerings made in those programs to enrich research methodologies and approaches.

Indeed the program in which I teach already does have a certain amount of blending across areas. Our dissertation proposal format seems to borrow heavily from the format used by our colleagues in social science, for we require substantial literature reviews, justifications, research questions, and methodology statements in our proposals. When colleagues from the history department across campus participate in our dissertations, they accept our format for proposals but tell us that the format is far different from those presented in history. But for us to live in a department filled with more people who claim allegiance to the social sciences than to the humanities, such compromises are vital to maintaining happy colleagues, students, and committees.

In addition the Ph.D. program in which I teach allows students to take up to one-half of their course work outside of the School of Journalism and Mass Communication. Here future scholars learn how to approach the same question in many different ways. Here they learn that other fields, including History Department history, see research differently than their advisers and colleagues in journalism and mass communication. These experiences make it difficult to explain to young scholars why our historical work is so tradition bound, so limited in scope, so frozen in time.

My Ph.D. program also requires students to take half of their course work within the School of Journalism and Mass Communication. That is eight courses. And we only offer two graduate-level courses in journalism history. Consequently, the history students that I advise take other journalism and mass communication courses, and they want to meld historical methodology with research methods from other courses, particularly those from theory and qualitative methods courses. We find that the results coming from such a mixture are challenging and insightful, but I often worry about how judges and reviewers will accept such amalgamations. My concern continues as students wish to leave the traditional confines of journalism history in order to study topics not so closely tied to news, news dissemination, and news organizations.

I have three primary concerns here, one of which focuses on the definition of the field and one of which focuses on how the field is studied. My students and I wrestle regularly with the term journalism history. "Journalism History." "Journalism History?" "Journalism History!" That's what we study, but what does it mean? How much do we have to have about "journalism" in a paper or article before it is considered "journalism history?" Is journalism history doing a paper that discusses how newspapers covered a certain topic? This type of research, it seems to me, focuses more on the product and less on its production. Or must journalism history come from the inside out? Must student work focus more on production and the people who do that production than on the product produced? And if so, why?

After twenty-five-plus years of looking at conference paper and article evaluations, I have decided that "journalism history" is a terribly restrictive term. "Journalism history" research, it seems, must deal with the news media from the inside only. "Journalism history" is most often an insider's history rather than an outsider's story that shows us, for instance, how news coverage influenced the way in which society would discuss the problem being reported.

In addition, "journalism history" certainly does not include all media forms. Film and books are definitely not included in "journalism history," which is strange given that most of our journalism and mass communication classes now deal with "mass media," which for teachers using introductory texts includes radio, television, books, advertising, comic strips, motion pictures, news, entertainment, and so on. Students in these other courses also discuss how these forms interact with one another and with society, topics that should be of interest to historians. Many in this new generation of scholars often seem far more interested in how the news is reported and what impact that reporting had on society than anything else. Or they are interested in how various media forms treat certain subjects. Such interests ultimately may be a problem for them careerwise.

Nor does "journalism history" include the entertainment aspects of the media although entertainment is introduced to mass media students both in introductory courses and mass media and society courses and despite the fact that the entertainment aspects of media often seem to have a greater effect on society than news reporting. I have colleagues where I teach, for instance, who study how the entertainment media influence the development of gender identification. Following that development historically could be fascinating and illuminating and would attract many members of this new generation of scholars.

Sometimes "journalism history" does not include analyses of how coverage of certain events or groups influence the growth, development, and acceptance of those groups in society. For some reason, judges and reviewers often consider such research as research about the groups or issue (a sociological subject) rather than on the medium itself. How this conclusion is reached is a mystery to me, because media and society interact rather than exist in splendid isolation, but I've seen this result come back too many times in judges' comments or reviewers' notes to assume that such reactions are flukes. Some scholars in our field could possibly say that such historical studies may fit into the agenda-setting literature in which researchers study how the media tell their audiences what sorts of things they should think about. Trying to trace this phenomenon historically seems important for an understanding of the way in which our media and our society developed.

Logically, to me, "journalism history" for the twenty-first century should become Mass Media History. It should look more broadly at the role of all media in society—at how the media are run, what they disseminate to the community at large, what impact the message has on the consumer and the society, and how the consumer in return influences the medium.

This is where many of our younger scholars want to focus. They want to break the traditional boundaries that restrict their research efforts by pre-existing definitions of journalism history that in turn limit their research largely to studying the news and how news organizations grew. These younger scholars know that all forms of the media are important due to the influence they exert on society, and they don't appreciate being prevented from engaging in such studies by scholarly standards that may no longer be as relevant as they once were. (Granted their unwillingness to pursue their research interests often is due more to the problems inherent in getting their material accepted than any other issue.)

Second, I am concerned about restrictions on methodological approaches. Perhaps we as journalism historians are too rigid in what we deem acceptable methodologically. I'm not suggesting by any means that our reliance on primary sources, good research, good thinking, and clear writing be abandoned in favor of gibberish and opinion. I do think, however, that we need to broaden our horizons as to what research approach will yield the most accurate pictures of our mediated world.

Some of my concerns here stem from a growing trend among my students in particular to mesh disciplines and research methodologies. Many of them want to combine mass communications theory with mass communications history. They are particularly interested in combining framing theory with media history to try to determine how media reporting influenced the development of American perceptions of that issue.

Other students want to use the communications studies technique of discourse analysis to look at the way in which information is presented. Still others want to study images, a growing field in some disciplines but one that still has to win great acceptance in media history. And still others want to use some quantitative approaches to gathering information—particularly in the sampling area, which allows them to use a wider range of original materials and to get away from providing us with history according to the *New York Times*.

But many of these newer scholars worry about pursuing broader methodologies or indeed broader media bases because they fear the reaction of reviewers. I hear more and more young scholars in our discipline wonder how to research and write to please the judges. Once they decide what they believe is the magic formula in terms of winning acceptance, they revise their research agendas to meet that description. Such a curtailing of intellectual curiosity leads to a lack of original thinking and growth in the field. It leads, as noted above, to stagnation. One of the reasons that history continues to grow and prosper as a profession is that scholars are willing to challenge the presumptions of earlier historians and to use new techniques to explore new subjects.

Some of this reaction by the keepers of the "acceptable" journalism history gates may be due to the fact that we don't know these new techniques ourselves and don't know really how to evaluate their use. I find myself constantly scrambling to keep up. But professors also can learn, and perhaps we need to set up some sessions at our annual meetings to teach us how to use and evaluate new methodologies insofar as historical research is concerned. Such discussions certainly could enliven proceedings as well as breathe some new life into our small corner of history.

We must, however, acknowledge that we have achieved a professional comfort level in journalism history. As the historical profession continues to approach diverse ways of research, journalism historians tend to find far more comfort in the old way of doing research and interpreting the boundaries of our field. We set comfortable boundaries; we understand what we are doing when we judge for presentation or publication. Moving into film, books, entertainment as subjects for research is a totally different matter—and one for apprehension. As is dealing with those who use different method-ologies. Honestly speaking, we want to be like the History Department historians in a limited way—as long as it does not include looking at new approaches to research in our field.

We also need to develop some new methodologies. We need to learn how to launch historical studies of various media forms, especially in the entertainment field. If we don't want impressionistic articles on these media forms, we need to establish exactly what we do want and explain carefully how we want those research problems handled. What is an acceptable way to study media-based images, for example? Other disciplines have studied this field; we could adapt their work to our field.

Third, I am concerned about the dated nature of the way in which we categorize and analyze our field. I admire the work that David Sloan has done in explaining the various schools of historical thought and how they have influenced our history; indeed, I teach some of his historiography in my graduate history class.[9] But I also know that discussions of historiography among our colleagues in the history department are far more expan-sive and intellectually challenging than the discussions we have about our field. History department historians have not let the type of categorization used in our field—Whig, Progressive, Consensus—become the central focus of their work as we have in our efforts to explore our organizational patterns. Rather than spending time categorizing history, our colleagues in history departments have sought to find new and better ways to study our past. For a while their work focused on areas that we still spend some time in—intellectual history, cultural history, etc. Many of our colleagues in the history department have more recently been studying how issues of race, class, and gender have influenced the growth of the United States. These subjects also attract our students.

To me, it seems that our history colleagues find the issues of the day that could use historical illumination and develop ways to study such issues. Instead of our taking this approach, we more often lag behind insofar as we develop ways to look at and analyze the growing media world and its impact on society. I must confess to being far more interested in such research topics than in papers about an obscure newspaper of 200 years ago that no one else has heard about before this particular research effort. Granted there are some reasons to write about such a newspaper, but more often the reason the newspaper has stayed obscure is that it deserves to be obscure. I think our students are tired of reading about and studying historical literature that still writes the record in journalism history. It is time for some assessment of that record and of that research in order to consider whether new questions and research approaches to journalism history will offer greater insights than our current approaches have.

Now, you might ask, why has she bothered to spend her time thinking such thoughts? Doesn't she have something else to do? Well, my students have necessitated such pondering. I see a new generation of history students out there—ones who are not content with the approaches and forms of study that are so familiar to us. They are interested in history because of the depth that the subject allows in terms of research and treatment, because of the intellectual processes needed to deal with such subjects, and because they think and write beautifully. I'm simply afraid that we might lose an outstanding generation of scholars if we don't find a way to make them welcome in our field. If these students go off to other departments—history departments, for example or American studies or communication studies—or into other fields within mass communication research, our discipline will be the worse for it. That's why I consider what might be done.

In conclusion, then, I would suggest that for our field to remain viable and attractive to scholars in the twenty-first century, "journalism historians" must start to talk about the dimensions of the field and how it should develop. We should devote sessions at our annual meetings to such discussions or debates. Among the topics that should be on the agenda are:

- Should we have a broader definition of what "Journalism History" is—a definition that will include more media forms as well as entertainment?
- Should we develop broader approaches to methodology—ones that will allow the evolution of new and different ways to rigorously analyze gathered data?
- Should we find a way to categorize our work more creatively and to develop techniques to productively integrate what we all do into a more enlightening picture of media and society over time?
- Should we learn these new approaches ourselves so that we can evaluate work that uses research methodologies that we are not well acquainted with or that look at media forms that are equally unfamiliar?
- Should we develop standards for evaluating such research?

The goal here is not to turn traditional historical work on journalistic topics upside down but to find a way to make it comfortable to both the new scholars and those of us who have been around awhile. Even more important is the goal that we should learn as much about our field as possible and should adopt and adapt whatever tools are necessary to carry out that mission.

Notes

1. James W. Carey, "The Problem of Journalism History," *Journalism History* 1 (Spring 1974):4.
2. Joseph P. McKerns, "The Limits of Progressive Journalism History," *Journalism History* 4 (Autumn 1977):88. McKerns defined Progressive history as the reliance on "the conflict between 'good' and 'evil'."
3. Garth S. Jowett, "Toward a History of Communication," *Journalism History* 2 (1975):34. His call was for a study of what essentially is interpersonal communication rather than mass communication.
4. David Paul Nord, "A Plea for *Journalism* History," *Journalism History* 15 (Spring 1988):8.
5. Donald Lewis Shaw and Sylvia L. Zack, "Rethinking Journalism History," *Journalism History* 14(Winter 1987): 111–17. See also Michael Emery, "The Writing of American Journalism History," *Journalism History* 10 (Autumn/ Winter 1983):38–43; Marion Marzolf, "towards a holistic approach: American Studies—Ideas for Media Historians?" *Journalism History* 5:1 (Spring 1978):1, 13–16; Catherine L. Covert, "Journalism History and Women's Experience: A Problem in Conceptual Change," Journalism History 8:1 (Spring 1981):2–6.
6. Alf Pratte and J.R. Rush, "Significant Data—Triviality or Relevance?" Study presented at the 1998 American Journalism Historians Association conference, Louisville, Kentucky.

7.   David Paul Nord, "A Diverse Field Needs a Diversity of Approaches," *American Journalism* 10 (Summer-Fall 1993):26.

8.   David Paul Nord, "WHAT WE CAN DO FOR THEM: Journalism History and the History Profession," *Journalism History* 9:2 (Summer 1982):56–8, 60.

9.   Wm. David Sloan, "Journalism History," in *History of the Mass Media in the United States*, ed. Margaret A. Blanchard, Chicago and London: Fitzroy Dearborn, 1998, 290–1; James Startt, "Historiography and the Media Historian," *American Journalism* 10:3–4 (Summer-Fall 1993): 17–25 provides a good overview for beginning historians.

Chapter 4

JOHN NERONE

THEORY AND HISTORY

HISTORIANS ARE FREQUENTLY CRITICIZED FOR PAYING too little attention to theory. This criticism is certainly justified, though it is often ill-informed. On the level of conscious argument, historians are wary and dismissive of theory in one sense—as "covering law"—but have often embraced theory in another sense—as "grand narrative"—and are somewhat receptive to theory in a third sense—as methodology. Yet, on the level of practice, historians put theory aside in the explication of sources, and adopt as an (unattainable) ideal the telling of the past in its own terms. This leads to a common mentality that is instinctively hostile to theory and its latinate vocabularies.

Communications historians are less likely to share the instincts and practices of the bulk of the historical profession. But, while claiming in some cases a greater theoretical sophistication, and while sharing an agenda with various styles of communications research, communications historians often ignore the work of cognate historians. This allows them to advance grand narratives in a way that most historians now disavow.

This article begins with a discussion of the development of the historical profession and its distaste for theory. It then outlines the crisis of professional history of the past few decades, dwelling on a few of the historiographical issues that arose during that crisis. It then contrasts this to the situation of communications historians.

History Versus Theory

Part of the craft culture of professional historians is a scorn for theory and theorists. Historians conceive of themselves as blue-collar workers who mine archives and craft narratives. They think of their work as concrete and deride the scholars of the abstract. They joke, punning on Veblen, about the leisure of the theory class.

Historians' scorn for theory has a history itself. History as a discipline and a profession was formed in the 19th century as a subset of a broader array of historical thought. Put another way, professional historians colonized a wide continent of historical thinking and entrenched themselves against attacks from other colonists—"speculative" or "philosophical" or "evolutionary" notions of history—and from aboriginal barbarians—the popular memory. Historians excluded popular memory by emphasizing objectivity and critical analysis of documents and denying the political import of their own narratives. At the same time, on the other frontier, they excluded other historical thinkers (Hegel, Marx, Spencer, Comte, Darwin) by developing an explicit set of rules of argument and evidence and an implicit rejection of overarching theory and deductive method (Nisbet, 1969).[1]

The terrain of professional history, in separating itself from the rest of history-land (and all of the other human sciences), declared itself to be the land of "factual narrative." Both terms in this formulation are significant for the formation of a professional mentality. "Factual" means that historical inquiry ideally must proceed from *facta*: the smallest units of "things done," which can presumably be established as empirically verifiable on the basis of a critical reading of documentary records. The facts, when ascertained through proper procedures, will form a narrative, and the narrative will speak for itself, presenting the past as it actually happened, usually with some moral import (the "judgment of history").

Historians, thus, have (almost) always presented the past in story form. Without exploring the issue too deeply, it will suffice to acknowledge that time is the central dimension of historical knowledge, and that what historians seek to do is to present an account of persistence and change *within identities* over time. This means that historical knowledge will tend to assume narrative form.

The narrativity of historical knowledge separates it from other kinds of knowledge. Narratives are true in as much as they describe what actually happened with fidelity. This means that the truth of a narrative is singular. Theoretical knowledge, on the other hand, is generally understood as being true in as much as it describes (or predicts) a broad range of phenomena. Put another way, narrative knowledge is thought of as true in its uniqueness, while theoretical knowledge is thought of as true in its generality. This distinction has been codified in academic tradition as that between the idiographic and the nomothetic disciplines. In this schema, history is the paragon idiographic discipline, while physics is the ultimate nomothetic discipline. (This is a convenient if spurious division, one created for historical or social reasons to explain an existing or developing division of labor. Still, there is no question that the distinction exists in the minds of historians and other scholars, and for the time being it will be useful to continue thinking in terms of this distinction.)

In the context of the idiographic/nomothetic distinction, narratives add up while theories divide. One takes narrative data and piles them up to form bigger narratives, but the big narratives do not dissolve the little ones, and, in fact, the smallest narratives always seem the most real, because they are always the most demonstrable and the most concrete. This is why history always seems to return to biography. Theories, however, are always more real than the data from which they are derived. Theories, in explaining phenomena, also explain them away—they are no longer important, because their quantum of truth has been appropriated by the theory that explains them. Theories present their truth as predictive power, which is to say that their truth is their future, while their past is of strictly historical interest.

But if historians aren't theorists, can history really be a human *science*? Does the disclaiming of nomothetic power involve also renouncing any pretensions to scientific authority? Does the narrativity of historical knowledge make it an art rather than a science? Is the stance of the historian subjective rather than objective?

The process of narrativization is, of course, dicey as science. First, when historians encounter the sources, they are already narrativized in some form. So in the process of ascertaining the facts historians must actively denarrativize the sources. Then, in the process of letting the facts speak for themselves, historians must again actively narrativize the facts. Naturally, all of this denarrativizing and renarrativizing involves more than empirical science. And historians have always recognized this, since they have always known that, while History may not change, histories go out of currency very quickly. Common sense among historians has always maintained that history is part art and historians part artist.

Still, historians insist upon the empirical core of their discipline and have developed practices of argument and intersubjective verifiability. If history is a science, then it must develop knowledge beyond the individual work and the individual historian. How does historical knowledge develop, and how do historians settle their arguments? The fundamental techniques are, first, a critique of the sources, and second, the telling of a more detailed narrative. So, for instance, Charles Beard (1913) argued that the U.S. Constitution was constructed to further the economic interests of its framers. Forrest McDonald (1958) rebutted him by showing that he misused sources describing the personal holdings of the framers. But Lee Benson (1960) rebutted McDonald by describing a different formation of economic interests—essentially, telling a more nuanced story. From another angle, Linda Grant DePauw (1966) critiqued McDonald's description of the delegates to New York's ratifying convention, moving the narrative from a federal to a state level, and inviting in the process at least 12 other state-level narratives. On any question, historians will commence this process of telling smaller and smaller stories. In the process, the first story—Beard's, in this case—which was big enough to actually sound like a theory, will have been qualified and annotated to the point where its explanatory and predictive power will seem negligible. At the same time, everyone but the specialists will have lost interest. The big stories, of course, have a way of recurring—thus Fresia (1988) has restated Beard, just as Fukuyama (1992) has restated Hegel and Acton. The specialists groan at the thought of running over that ground again, and lament the stupidity of a populace that has not learned the pointlessness of telling these big stories.[1]

The process of narrative conflict resolution, no matter what its real value in establishing significant truths, performs two very useful purposes for historians. First, it allows them to claim scientific status because it establishes intersubjective verifiability. Second, it excludes both the barbarians (i.e., the public) and other colonizers (i.e., the theorists) from what has been claimed as history-land.

This sounds like a rather naked move to stake a claim to a monopoly of historical knowledge. But historians justify this move in two ways. The first is the need to eliminate falsehoods from the field of historical representations. It is impossible to follow the methods of professional history and conclude, for example, that the Holocaust did not occur. This negative function alone makes historical inquiry important. But historians have also aspired to a second, positive justification. There is a traditional horizon to historical knowledge. It is hoped that when enough solid little stories have been told they can be piled up into a singularly true grand narrative—a mighty cathedral of History built up of all the bricks of histories. Upon completion of the cathedral, History will be able to speak with the force of theory. Until then all theorizing will be premature and inappropriate. Good historians will be brickmakers, blue-collar workers who despise the leisure of the theory class.

The Disappearance of the Cathedral of Knowledge

Sadly, fewer and fewer historians ever hope to worship in the completed cathedral of knowledge (Novick, 1988). This is not for any shortage of bricks. Quite the contrary, there are altogether too many bricks. What is lacking is an architect. But, unlike other buildings, the cathedral of knowledge will not allow its architect to choose the building materials. Every brick that does not readily crumble must be used. As the bricks multiply, and as they assume new and strange shapes, the date of completion recedes into the distance. Meanwhile, heterodox architects have commenced building other cathedrals, less grand but no less solid. These architects angrily cast aside some bricks while they fight over others. A sad parable indeed.

How did this state of affairs come about? Among professional historians in the United States and parts of western Europe, it seems that several different processes, all flourishing in the period from the mid-1960s through the 1970s, effectively dismantled an already incomplete synthesis of historical knowledge.

First, the politics of professional history was called into question. Outside the profession, activists angrily questioned the assumptions and biases of "received histories," with their tendency to celebrate the achievements of public life and to ignore the histories of groups traditionally excluded from the public on grounds of race, class, or gender. Inside the profession, these questions were accented with the anger of intergenerational hostility. The result was a movement to write history "from the bottom up," to write the history of the excluded and "inarticulate," and to draw attention to the politics of history.

Second, the public seemed to lose interest in the works of professional historians. Quaintly put, the social histories of the 1960s and 1970s were histories *of* the people but neither *by* nor *for* the people. Moreover, these histories did not readily yield big narratives, the kind that a reading public might enjoy. Historians might rightly value a book on family structure in colonial Andover, Massachusetts (Greven, 1970), for instance, but who in the Book-of-the-Month Club will take note?

But the proliferation of monographs on smaller and smaller subjects was (is?) structurally determined by the internal economics of the historical profession. The 1970s-era overproduction of Ph.D.s resulted in increased demand for faculty positions and hence a rise in the price of hiring and tenure, which in turn led to an increase in the production of monographs. Whether one looks upon this efflorescence of material as triumph or tragedy, it must be admitted that no grand narrative can contain it. No architect can use all these bricks.

Historians began to notice that the hope of achieving a grand narrative was never really well founded in the first place. The disappearance of grand narrative left historians without a basis for claiming meaning in their histories. A growing number of historians have taken to borrowing theories from other social and behavioral sciences to plug the gap, but the profession as a whole remains shy. In practice, it is still the empirical work that is thought to give a history merit. Sound research can save a theoretically naive work, but no amount of conceptual sophistication will protect a historian who gets dates wrong.

Historians and the Rest of the Academy

The demise of the dream of grand narrative was poorly timed. Just as historians were losing hope that their monographic work would produce a meaningful synthesis, other social scientists began to emphasize the historical dimension of social theory. The gap between "idiographic" and "nomothetic" disciplines has begun to disappear.

This rapprochment involves nothing less than an entirely new way of conceiving of theory. Theory in the social sciences is less often conceived in terms of the positive sciences and more often in terms of historical and social context. Such theories cannot be abstracted from the concrete and specific. In effect, such theories become virtual narratives (Abrams, 1980). This process is most clearly evident, I think, in contemporary marxism. Marxist theorists have always emphasized the historical, of course, and a large proportion of Marx's key texts are, in fact, histories—his accounts of French history in the *Eighteenth Brumaire* and *Class Struggles in France*, for instance, and the chapters on primitive accumulation in volume 1 of *Capital*. But for decades these texts were read as exercises in theory application. The true science of marxist history, it was thought, was the working out of certain necessary laws. Few academic marxists now credit economic determinism, which has been denounced as "economism" (Gramsci, 1971) and "essentialism" (Laclau & Mouffe, 1985, among others), and most characterize the economistic passages in Marx himself as being alien "incrustations of nineteenth-century positivism."

But if theory is not law—cannot be abstracted from concrete particular situations and has little predictive power—then what is theory? Why, what else but narrative? Theory is a big story that can be used to give more meaning to a lot of little stories. To reverse a familiar formula, a qualitative difference has become a quantitative one. Where once history and theory were thought of as two different species, now they seem genetically identical—though theory is considerably bigger. This rapprochement between history and theory has not yet been translated into a new set of practices for professional historians, who continue to produce by mining archives and to argue by telling more detailed stories while renouncing the "speculative."[2] But the move to "theory in the concrete" or "theory in context" ideally offers an answer to the problem posed by the disappearance of grand narrative. For if the individual historian can no longer expect a sublime architect to fashion one's work into a divine cathedral, then mustn't the historian become an architect, if only in a humble way?

At this point Becker's (1935) relativism becomes relevant again. Becker argues that, since historians cannot capture the past entire, they will always be representing it in fragments to an audience that has its own practical concerns. Historians are essentially mythmakers.

Historians have rejected Becker on two grounds. One is the assertion that the basic task of the historian is—and should be—political. It is obvious that, as a subject taught in schools, imprisoned in museums, and displayed on national holidays, history has always been a politicized field. But historians have always insisted that their work has to withstand scrutiny on grounds other than politics, and most have felt that this means disavowing a political agenda themselves. The collapse of grand narrative has put the politics of history writing back at the center of attention, however, because it underlines the absence of a real empirical determinant for undertaking any particular historical project.

The second ground for rejecting Becker is his challenge to the privileged status of the historian in constructing accounts of the past. Everyone, after all, constructs a version of history; everyone uses historical methods; thus everyone is his or her own historian. Becker underscored the necessary inability of the historical profession to maintain a monopoly and hence to create something that could be called a science.

This leaves us with historians who are mainly storytellers. But professional historians must be storytellers with a difference, in that they do consciously and hence perversely what others do automatically.

Storytelling is itself a matter of theoretical concern. And in fact the most lively sort of theory writing among historians and philosophers of history today is literary-critical (LaCapra, 1985; White, 1973, 1978, 1987). Oddly, this particular kind of theory seems to escape the historians' instinctual labeling as speculative and is rather contrasted to speculative philosophies of history as analytic. Still, historians resist categorization as mere writers of mere texts, insisting on the basis of common sense that they are doing much more substantial work.

History, Theory, and the History of Communication

Much of the theoretical distress of professional historians has escaped the attention of communications historians. Communications historians retain a tendency toward grand narrative that other historians have renounced in embarrassment. Moreover, work in communications history is fragmented among various styles, each with its own grand narrative. Among all the styles there is a general lack of concern with the collapse of grand narrative; meanwhile, from style to style, there is a general lack of recognition that contradictory grand narratives are being employed. A few selective examples will demonstrate these two points.

U.S. journalism history has traditionally used a whiggish grand narrative. The rise of an independent "fourth estate" has been traced through stages of growth—the penny press, the yellow press, muckraking, and so on—marked by the integration of news media into an economy based on commodity exchange (Bleyer, 1927; Emery & Emery, 1988; Mott, 1962). Recent histories, while assuming a critical stance toward this history, have also adopted the basic contours of that grand narrative (Schiller, 1981; Schudson, 1978). More than a few scholars have written in criticism of this grand narrative (McKerns, 1977; Nerone, 1987), but monographic literature is still generally produced within the narrative, usually with the expectation of being a brick in the cathedral-building process.

Another grand narrative is embodied in the work of Innis (1951), McLuhan (1962), Ong (1982), and others. Here the narrative hinges on the transitions from technological stages: orality to literacy to print to electronic communication. This grand narrative, totalizing along the dimension of communicative systems, resembles nothing more than the stages of development posed by the 19th-century thinkers that professional historians gradually disenfranchised (Heyer, 1988).

Yet a third grand narrative pivots on a moment of industrialization in the 19th century. This moment, whether sketched with homage to Weber (Beniger, 1986) or to Marx (Lears, 1983; Thompson, 1964; Williams, 1961), projects a narrative of the rise of modernity, individualism, corporate structure, the managerial state, and mass culture, usually with a sub-textual critique of the oppressiveness of the modern system.

Historians of communications rarely bring these conflicting narratives into contact with each other. From time to time, an attentive practitioner will call into question the implied meanings of this or that grand narrative, but rarely will the followers of McLuhan, say, clash with the epigoni of Emery and Emery or the devotees of Raymond Williams.

There is an organizational reason for this lack of cross-narrative controversy. The followers of each grand narrative (and more might be mentioned: the history of the book, literary history, the history of freedom of the press, feminist scholarship, and the history of the public sphere each projects its own grand narrative) operate within a relatively insulated institutional framework: Journalism historians belong to AEJMC and AJHA and publish in *Journalism Quarterly* and *American Journalism*; their work is little noted nor long remembered by scholars in cultural studies, who are nevertheless increasingly attentive to historical study, nor by McLuhanites, who congregate in the various divisions of ICA.

If the lack of cross-narrative controversy suggests that the various styles of communications history are relatively autonomous from each other, one should not conclude that communications historians operate in a void. While the different styles rarely communicate with each other, still they are in constant conversation with positions and movements within the broader study of communications. Thus, journalism history corresponds with other styles of studying journalism and neglects, for the most part, developments in literary history.

In some cases, this sort of insulation from other histories permits communications histories to adopt an alien agenda. A prominent example here is the work of Neil Postman (1986), which is frankly tied to a polemic about the state of contemporary American culture. In cases like this, historical work becomes a simple crutch for a lame argument to lean on.[3]

The fragmentation of communications history reflects and reinforces the fragmentation of the field of communications. At root are not just institutional factors (mentioned above) but also a glaring intellectual void, namely the absence of a shared definition of the object of study. In this essay, I have used the term "communications" and "communications history," both of which are chosen among many alternatives, most prominently "media," "communication" (without the "s"), and "mass communication." Moreover, each of these terms can be defined in different ways. Take "media" for example. Journalism historians use the term to refer to a specific set of institutional actors—the *New York Times*, for instance, and CBS. But McLuhan and others also use the term to refer to technologies of communication—print or the spoken word. Many ambiguities result, not least of which is the confusion over whether the word "media" is singular or plural.

Dispelling such ambiguity requires an effort at formulating the fundamental terms that define the object of communications history. Such an effort would come naturally from an end to isolation for communications historians and the clash of grand narratives it would entail.

This is where the crisis in professional history is instructive. There the collapse of grand narrative has had contradictory effects. One legacy is a corrosive agnosticism about "the meaning of history," whether as an object or a process of inquiry; to the true believer, history will always hereafter be an exercise in frustration.

But the decline of grand narrative has also opened up possibilities for new histories and new voices that were earlier not to be hoped for. Among other things, the past few decades have seen a real renaissance in the history of previously neglected groups, people, and venues, and a rare window of opportunity for vigorous theoretical debate among historians. Communications history can only benefit from such an opening up.

But two problems loom. One comes from the field of communications generally, where interest in, among other things, marxism, feminism, and cultural studies has prompted new interest in historical work. But the hoped-for history tends to be, alas, a grand narrative. Will the theoretical interest in history lose patience with the buzzing ambiguity, the multiplicity, the sheer endlessness of historical work? Will communications scholars demand cartoon histories and simple moral tales?

The second problem is more frightening. As communications historians engage in the clash of narratives, will they discover that they really are not studying the same things? Will it turn out that the existing institutional dispersion of communications history is actually rooted in the field of study? Will it turn out that there really is no such thing as communications history? Will all our study turn into context with no center? And what might that mean for the field of communications generally?

Notes

1. This is not because early professional historians were allergic to romantic ideas of national character or Hegel-like speculations about the course of history as the progress of liberty. See, for instance, Krieger (1977) and White (1973). More important than attitude or ideas in excluding "theory" at this stage was the institutionalization of a set of practices in historical argument, which always turned disputes away from theory and toward "the facts" or "the sources."

2. Historians, though, often use theory in a "taxonomic" way: not to make generalizable truth claims but to classify situations. Thus, concepts like "hegemony" (Lears, 1983, 1985) and "bureaucracy" have been borrowed from Gramsci and Weber to illuminate some aspects of specific situations through an act of classification. More than a few historians have used "bureaucracy" as a unifying theme for discussions of industrialization and progressivism, for instance (Hawley, 1979; Wiebe, 1967). But in identifying a process as bureaucratic, these historians are neither confirming a set of hypotheses that Weber proposed nor applying a set of "laws of bureaucracy" to a specific situation. Rather, they are identifying a dimension of similarity among diverse phenomena—railroads and temperance reform, for instance. This discovered or asserted similarity on the plane of bureaucratic organization does not effect a reduction of the two instances to each other; on the contrary, by identifying a similar dimension, the historian is simply making a move toward a more textured explanation of each instance *on its own terms*. That is why even an infinite number of "bureaucratic" histories of industrialization or progressivism will not resolve the long debate between Weber and Marx.

3. I borrow the characterization of historical research as a crutch from James Beniger, who applied that metaphor to his own work, though not in an especially critical tone, in comments at the ICA convention in Dublin, June, 1990.

References

Abrams, P. (1980). "History, sociology, historical sociology". *Past + Present*, 87, 3–16.

Beard, C. A. (1913). *An economic interpretation of the Constitution of the United States*. New York: Macmillan.

Becker, C. L. (1935). Everyman his own historian. In *Everyman his own historian: Essays on history and politics* (pp. 233–55). New York: F. S. Crofts.

Beniger, J. R. (1986). *The control revolution: Technological and economic origins of the information society.* Cambridge, MA: Harvard University Press.

Benson, L. (1960). *Turner and Beard: American historical writing reconsidered.* Glencoe, IL: Free Press.

Bleyer, W. G. (1927). *Main currents in the history of American journalism.* Boston: Houghton Mifflin.

De Pauw, L. G. (1966). *The eleventh pillar: New York state and the federal constitution.* Ithaca, NY: Cornell University Press.

Emery, E., & Emery, M. B. (1988). *The press and America: An interpretive history of the mass media* (4th ed.). Englewood Cliffs, NJ: Prentice-Hall.

Fresia, G. J. (1988). *Toward an American revolution: Exposing the constitution and other illusions.* Boston: South End Press.

Fukayama, F. (1992). *The end of history and the last man.* New York: Free Press.

Gramsci, A. (1971). Some theoretical and practical aspects of economism. In Q. Hoare and R. W. Smith (Eds. & Trans.), *Selections from the prison notebooks of Antonio Gramsci* (pp. 158–68). New York: International Publishers.

Greven, P. J. (1970). *Four generations: Population, land, and family in colonial Andover, Massachusetts.* Ithaca: Cornell University Press.

Hawley, E. W. (1979). *The great war and the search for a modern order: A history of the American people and their institutions.* New York: St. Martin's.

Heyer, P. (1988). *Communications and history: Theories of media, knowledge, and civilization.* New York: Greenwood Press.

Innis, H. A. (1951). *The bias of communication.* Toronto: University of Toronto Press.

Krieger, L. (1977). *Ranke: The meaning of history.* Chicago: University of Chicago Press.

LaCapra, D. (1985). *History and criticism.* Ithaca, NY: Cornell University Press.

Laclau, E., & Mouffe, C. (1985). *Hegemony and socialist strategy: Towards a radical democratic politics* (W. Moore & P. Commack, Trans.). London: Verso.

Lears, T. J. J. (1983). From salvation to self-realization: Advertising and the therapeutic roots of the consumer culture, 1880–1930. In R. W. Fox & T. J. J. Lears (Eds.), *The culture of consumption* (pp. 2–38). New York: Pantheon.

Lears, T. J. J. (1985). "The concept of cultural hegemony: Problems and possibilities". *American Historical Review, 90,* 567–93.

McDonald, F. (1958). *We the People.* Chicago: University of Chicago Press.

McKerns, J. P. (1977). "The limits of progressive journalism history". *Journalism History, 4,* 88–92.

McLuhan, M. (1962). *The Gutenberg galaxy: The making of typographic man.* Toronto: University of Toronto Press.

Mott, F. L. (1962). *American journalism* (3rd ed.). New York: Macmillan.

Nerone, J. C. (1987). "The mythology of the penny press". *Critical Studies in Mass Communication, 4,* 376–404.

Nisbet, R. A. (1969). *Social change and history: Aspects of the Western theory of development.* New York: Oxford University Press.

Novick, P. (1988). *That noble dream: The "objectivity question" and the American historical profession.* Cambridge: Cambridge University Press.

Ong, W. J. (1982). *Orality and literacy: The technologizing of the word.* London: Methuen.

Postman, N. (1986). *Amusing ourselves to death: Public discourse in the age of show business.* New York: Penguin.

Schiller, D. (1981). *Objectivity and the news: The public and the rise of commercial journalism.* Philadelphia: Temple University Press.

Schudson, M. (1978). *Discovering the news: A social history of American newspapers.* New York: Basic Books.

Thompson, E. P. (1964). *The making of the English working class.* New York: Pantheon.

White, H. V. (1973). *Metahistory: The historical imagination in nineteenth-century Europe.* Baltimore: Johns Hopkins University Press.

White, H. V. (1978). *Tropics of discourse: Essays in cultural criticism*. Baltimore: Johns Hopkins University Press.

White, H. V. (1987). *The content of the form: Narrative discourse and historical representation*. Baltimore: Johns Hopkins University Press.

Wiebe, R. H. (1967). *The search for order: 1877–1920*. New York: Hill & Wang.

Williams, R. (1961). *The long revolution*. London: Chatto & Windus.

Chapter 5

MICHAEL SCHUDSON

A REVOLUTION IN HISTORIOGRAPHY?

JOHN NERONE HAS WRITTEN AND INTERESTING and exasperating essay. It is full of points well taken, even a few at my own expense. I think Nerone makes a contribution to emphasize that cash sales rather than single issue sales may have been the more important economic innovation of the penny papers; to remind us that daily newspapers still competed with weekly and twice or thrice weekly publications; to point out (though David Eason [1984] did so more convincingly) how difficult it is to know what "classes" read what papers in the 1830s; to argue against some historians (though in concert with my own position) that modern professional efforts at "objectivity" should not be read back into the penny press; and most of all, in my view, to argue persuasively that previous historians have not properly characterized what was new, or not so new, in the nonpartisanism of the penny papers.

All this is laudable. Unfortunately, Nerone's article is as amply supplied with errors as with insight, major misrepresentations based on a framework of analysis that is wildly wrong. I will take up the most substantial misunderstandings and then try to suggest what might have been done more profitably and what might yet be done in studying the history of the American news media.

Nerone claims that the concept of the penny papers, or the "mythology" as he insists on calling it, has served as a significant legitimating factor for contemporary journalism. ("The mythology of the penny press exerts a significant inertia on attitudes toward the modern newspaper" [p. 401].) He offers not a shred of evidence for this. And I cannot think of much evidence that would support the point. When I began my own research on the history of American newspapers 13 years ago, I had never even heard of James Gordon Bennett. How often do journalists speak the name of Bennett or Benjamin Day or even Henry Raymond even in their most ceremonial and self-congratulatory addresses? Zenger, yes. Franklin, yes. Horace Greeley, on occasion, but the reference is usually to his strong political opinions, not to his role as proprietor of a cheap commercial paper. Nerone absurdly overrates the power of journalism historians' attention to the penny press as a factor in the legitimation of contemporary journalism.

Journalists do not legitimate themselves with reference to the penny papers that served large numbers of readers. They trace their history most of all to the First Amendment. They believe today's press earned its democratic spurs not by selling lots of copies cheaply but by criticizing governmental authority boldly.

The only journalist I know about who ever gave much thought to James Gordon Bennett is Walter Lippmann. Lippmann (1931, pp. 435–37) saw Bennett as initiating a commercial revolution in the press that, with all the sins it gave rise to, nonetheless opened the only road to a politically free and independent press. Not that Lippmann was satisfied with Bennett's revolution; he looked toward a second revolution in the press, one that would give journalists a new professional standing and free them to pursue the truth dispassionately. Lippmann's position is a kind of legitimation of the press. But with friends like this, who needs enemies? Lippmann remains, on balance, an astringent critic of the press and its pretensions.

I do not deny that journalism history as it used to be taught in journalism schools, and probably still is taught in many places, is designed to legitimate the structure and values of the contemporary press. I do doubt that this has had a far-reaching effect. It is better to say that in the conventional journalism history course, one of the courses where the fullest airing of alternative and challenging and demythologizing views of the press might be expected, such views have failed to get much attention.

Nerone makes a second error in assimilating the work of revisionist historians like Alexander Saxton, Dan Schiller, and me to the work of "mainstream" journalism historians such as Frank Luther Mott or the Emerys. He is right that the revisionists (or "new social historians" as Eason [1984] puts it) borrowed, perhaps too uncritically, the concept of the penny press from the mainstream historians. This does not make us all of a piece. My own work does not try to (and does not inadvertently achieve) a legitimation of contemporary journalism or even of its ideals, although I think this fairly describes the work of some of the standard textbook histories. On the contrary, my work examines historically a chief legitimating system within journalism itself, the concept of objectivity, and demythologizes it. My work, Schiller's and Saxton's as well though in different ways, and more recent work (Carey, 1987; Nord, 1986) seriously questions whether professionalization in journalism has been progress toward a democratic journalism. This profoundly separates revisionism from the conventional textbook historians of journalism whose work it tried to revise.

(I am much closer to Schiller and Saxton than to Mott and the Emerys but there are important debates among us, too, particularly about the class basis of the penny papers. I find my own insistence on the penny press as part of a middle class movement needs reconsideration in the light of Schiller's and Saxton's work. At the same time, however, the connection of the strongest and most lasting penny papers to what looks like a middle class public seems to me still a phenomenon of enormous importance. James Gordon Bennett's special pride in the *Herald*'s coverage of the stock market and his rhetorically colorful efforts to distinguish his paper from other cheap papers as well as from the six-penny dailies seems to me some provisional evidence that Bennett was reaching for readers from a middling segment of the population.)

Nerone's blurring of conventional historians and revisionists leads to the glaring distortion that we all emphasize "daring" editors or "notorious or dramatic newspapers and editors" and that we all have organized facts around an "heroic narrative". This bizarrely misstates the intention and, I think, achievement of the revisionists. In the history Nerone would have us write, the innovations of the penny press will be seen to be "functions of forces external to the papers themselves rather than the result of unique personal initiative" (p. 377). I agree. Nerone's suggestion that "instead of looking at newspapers as independent actors in the historical arena, we should look for the long-term broad-based social and cultural developments behind them" (p. 402) is a perfectly apt description of *Discovering the News*.

Nerone's contribution is to chip away at the clear edges of an historical ideal type, to remind us that "the penny press" is a reification (along with, I would note, "the Jacksonian Era," "the Founding Fathers," "the Great Awakening," "the abolitionist movement," and a variety of other still useable concepts), that it never represented all of journalism or even the majority of newspapers (I am not sure anyone claimed otherwise), or that it emerged full-blown on a September day in 1833 in New York and instantly transformed all of journalism for all time. Fine. But even Nerone agrees that the penny papers "stand out as discontinuous, they have a character that is not simply the product of evolutionary forces". He adds that Bennett and Greeley "were more than just servants of historical processes; they were also agents of change, and there is more than a little truth to the common view that they were not only the most influential but also the best newspapermen of their age" (p. 402). This admission flies in the face of the rhetoric of the 46 manuscript pages that precede it. Is the glass half empty or half full? You do not correct grossly distended claims by denying, in a conclusion, that they are really true; you make them more carefully in the first place.

Nerone's essay helps call attention to errors of emphasis in my work and the work of others, but I think it falls far short of offering new directions for research. Nerone does little to advance the history of American journalism here (and does a bit to set it back), although he draws in this work on a detailed knowledge of early nineteenth century Cincinnati newspapers he discusses much more fully in his dissertation, a work I admire. His most novel suggestion, that one study the typical rather than the unusual newspaper, is not helpful. If you write the history of science, it is important to know what typical science was in whatever period concerns you. Or if you write political history, it is important to know what typical political life was like. Still, there is plenty of justification for the science historian to be especially curious about Newton or Einstein and the social forces surrounding science at the revolutionary moments we associate with these giants. There is plenty of rationale for writing more books about Jackson or Lincoln than about an obscure Albany ward boss or a long forgotten Tennessee Congressman. Some individuals and institutions loom larger than others in their long-term influence; ordinarily these same individuals and institutions loom larger in their own day, too (Gregor Mendel, notwithstanding).

I think we can do better in suggesting directions for research in the history of newspapers. I would offer two suggestions. First, I think we have still scarcely scratched the surface of questions regarding the relationship of newspapers to democratic politics. One of Nerone's most powerful observations is that the partisanship of the elite press of the late 1820s was not a feature of longstanding but a break from papers' neutral stance during the years before the second party system was established. Ronald Formisano (1983, p. 122) points out that Massachusetts papers in the "Era of Good Feeling" stressed their neutrality by printing the state tickets of both parties. A history of the press as an agent of political communication should be integrated with a history of political parties, themselves agents of political communication and political life.

The penny press was a force for democratization in American culture, but a democratization of the peculiar sort that the market-place provides. Critics of a market-based society rightly point out that equality before the forces of the market is a severely crippled model of democratic society, but this is not to say that the market-place has not been subversive, and in an egalitarian direction, of a deferential and hierarchical social establishment. There are other models of democracy and other models of how newspapers might fit into and encourage democratic politics. David Nord (1986) has nicely made this point in a brief, provocative essay on William Lloyd Garrison. In this, he follows a historiographical lead taken by Michael Katz (1971) in educational history 16 years ago, arguing the importance of studying not only the models of social organization and cultural ideals that have triumphed over time, but equally those models and those ideals that fell by the wayside but that might still provide guidance for our own thinking today.

Second, I think there is much to be gained by studying the newspaper as a text and a cultural form. Most histories of journalism examine the newspaper text for "bias" but fail to understand the newspaper as a cultural text. What is the difference? The search for bias presumes that the newspaper can and should be a "mirror" of the real world. Much contemporary literary theory denies that we can really operate on this assumption and that any literary genre, news or novel or epic poem, has to be read on its own terms, has to be understood as a social and linguistic construction operating according to its own rules, in dialogue not only with the "real world" but with literary conventions and traditions. Looking at the newspaper in this way, as a text, requires a kind of closeness to the material that, I think, can be very revealing (however painstaking it may be).

I offer a work of my own (1982) as an example here. I studied a shift from chrono-logical stories in the newspaper to summary lead stories in reporting the President's annual State of the Union message. I found some very interesting changes in the form of the news story and in what a reporter bothered to mention in a news report. Bias was not the only and not the primary matter of interest; the changing form of the story revealed fundamental assumptions journalists made about politics, about news, and about their own function in society. And these assumptions were common to papers whether they relied on telegraphic transmission of the news or not: my study sheds some doubt on historiographic positions that attribute to the telegraph the primary responsibility for the changing nature of journalism in the late nineteenth century. I think the approach I took in this study to the newspaper as text, while scarcely unique, is still relatively rare. One of the problems with the history of newspapers, I would suggest, is that historians of journalism do not yet know how to read newspapers as texts or do not know that this is even a possibility. (Thomas Leonard's *Power of the Press* [1986] is a distinguished exception and a perceptive and provocative contribution to the journalism history literature.)

I am not altogether disenchanted with Nerone's suggestions for a better history of the news media. I agree with him that the world of journalism is wider than traditional histories, and much revisionist history, have credited it, and that we should keep in mind the powerful religious press of the nineteenth century, the black press, the foreign language press, the political reform press, the enormous variety of the news media in the United States past and present. At the same time, part of the analysis of journalism should be a study of relations of dominance and influence within journalism. *In These Times*, while an excellent weekly news magazine, does not have the reach of *Time*, nor is it cited so often, nor do institutions of memory make it easy for it to be cited in the future (the *Reader's Guide to Periodical Literature*, for instance, does not index it). New York newspapers and New York-based national television circulate much more in Cincinnati than Cincinnati news media circulate in New York (and there was a similar disparity in 1835). Variety is one thing, but leadership and trend-setting and, if you will, cultural hegemony is something else and just as essential a part of the field for media historians to examine. There will be better histories of journalism when there is a better social science theory of power and a social science theory of culture, and a theory of the mutual relations of culture and power. There will be better histories of journalism when historians incorporate these larger issues more self-consciously in their own work as they arrive, in the first place, at questions worth asking of the past.

References

Carey, J. W. (1987, March–April). "The press and the public discourse". *The Center Magazine*, pp. 4–16.

Eason, D. L. (1984). "The new social history of the newspaper". *Communication Research, 11*, 141–51.

Formisano, R. P. (1983). *The transformation of political culture: Massachusetts parties, 1790s–1840s.* New York: Oxford University Press.

Katz, M. (1971). *Class, bureaucracy, and schools.* New York: Praeger.

Leonard, T. C. (1986). *The power of the press: The birth of American political reporting.* New York: Oxford University Press.

Lippmann, W. (1931). "Two revolutions in the American press". *Yale Review, 20*, 433–41.

Nord, D. P. (1986). "Tocqueville, Garrison and the perfection of journalism". *Journalism History, 13,* 56–63.

Schudson, M. (1982). "The politics of narrative form: The emergence of news conventions in print and television". *Daedalus, 11*, 97–112.

PART TWO

Age of Public Enlightenment

INTRODUCTION TO PART TWO

THE DEVELOPMENT OF JOURNALISM IN THE United States is framed by the Enlightenment thinking of 18th-century intellectuals who sought to break the bonds of oppression and ignorance as they fought for the distribution of power, wealth and education. Benjamin Franklin, Thomas Jefferson, Thomas Paine among others wished to extend government participation and they envisioned the press as a means of breaking the monopoly of knowledge held by the elite.

While the growth of independent journalism in the colonies got off to a slow start, by 1721, colonial newspapers like the *New-England Courant* included foreign and domestic news and commentary and began to report on and critique government activities. Colonial newspapers also regularly printed ship sailings, posted lost and found articles, advertised help wanted and a variety of merchandise for sale including slaves. As Willard Grosvenor Bleyer notes in *Main Currents in the History of American Journalism* (1927, p. 72), "Sometimes a small wood-cut depicting a man running was used in advertisements of runaway negro slaves or white indentured servants."

Benjamin Franklin's refashioning of the *Pennsylvania Gazette* in 1729 turned a dull broadsheet into an entertaining newspaper, which contained visually appealing advertising and news of consequence that was said to impact colonists' lives. Franklin also financed print shops in other colonies creating a printing network that began to disseminate news and information. In 1758, Franklin and William Hunter, as deputy postmasters general for the colonies codified the practice of exchanging newspapers postage-free among printers. Such a policy allowed printers to share news and information throughout the colonies. After the adoption of the U.S. Constitution, the Post Office Act of 1792 formalized the free paper exchange practice, further encouraging the sharing of news and information throughout the country.

Colonial newspapers targeted educated, white Anglo-Saxon male property owners. Charles E. Clark in "The Newspapers of Provincial America" (1991, p. 387) suggests that colonial newspapers sought to narrow "the cultural gap between the learned and the merely literate and the information gap between the privileged and the merely competent." During the 18th century, women and minorities were politically invisible and were not considered worthy of inclusion in any discussion of political, economic or social rights.

In 1735 John Peter Zenger criticized the colonial governor in his newspaper, the *New York Weekly Journal* and was arrested for seditious libel. During his eight months of imprisonment, Zenger's wife Anna continued to publish the *Journal*. At trial Zenger's lawyer, Andrew Hamilton, argued that individuals must be free to speak and write the truth—even if it criticizes the government. Zenger was acquitted and for the first time truth became a defense for publishing criticism. Printers throughout the colonies retold this important legal precedent: the Zenger story and the case became a symbol of American's developing consciousness regarding the importance of a free press.

By the middle of the 18th century, colonial newspapers took the lead in the fight for American independence: writers, editors and printers reported on political and economic pressures placed on the colonies by the English Crown, and the influence of the press in colonial life grew. Pamphlets from this era provided evidence of a conspiracy by members of the parliament to deny and undermine the rights of colonists as British subjects. Whether or not the conspiracy actually existed is not clear but, according to Bernard Bailyn in *The Ideological Origins of the American Revolution* (1992), pamphlet writers and colonists believed it to be true and they responded to the perceived threat.

During the Revolutionary War period, the press played a fundamental role, championing independence, encouraging colonists to support the war effort and accept their new identity as American citizens, and helping to unify the colonies into a single nation. While the American Revolution was primarily engineered through wealthy members of the colonial ruling class, laborers, merchants and farmers bought into the consensus-building rhetoric of the Revolution, supporting military service and the distribution of land. The American Revolution created the opportunity for African Americans to begin challenging their role in society. Howard Zinn, in *A People's History of the United States* (1990), maintains that African Americans looked to the Declaration of Independence for guidance, petitioning Congress and state legislatures to abolish slavery and to give African Americans equal rights.

Immediately following the end of the American Revolution, newspaper editors and printers recognized the weaknesses of the Articles of Confederation and they began to support efforts to create a new form of federal government. The Constitution, proposed by the Constitutional Convention, was printed in every newspaper in the country and editorial columns discussed its merits. Of the hundreds of articles published in support of the Constitution, a series of 85 essays by Alexander Hamilton, James Madison and John Jay, "The Federalist Papers," originally printed in the *New York Independent Journal* from October 1787 to April 1788, were the most widely republished. The insightful essays argued for a strong federal government and Constitution to protect citizens' liberty, dignity, and happiness. Those opposed to the Constitution were known as Anti-Federalists and they feared that the new federal government would take power and rights from the states and the people. Ultimately, all but 12 newspapers supported the ratification of the Constitution.

As the nation's new government emerged, the battle between a strong federal government and states' rights intensified and a political party system began to take shape. Both Federalists and Anti-Federalists envisioned the press as instrumental to their efforts to gain political dominance and influence public opinion. Legislators expected newspapers to represent the differing political, economic, and class interests and they assumed that issues given a "fair hearing" by "right thinking men" would result in "self evident" policies and opinions.

Newspaper publishers participated in the political battles, resulting in opinion and argument frequently dominating news coverage. Politicians supported newspapers that favored their agenda and attempted to quash newspapers that were critical of their policies. The press gained political importance because of the position it occupied as the main source for the distribution of news and opinion. Political parties often provided money to start new papers or modernize existing newspapers. Urban newspapers possessed important circulation lists and were the only medium capable of consistently informing the general public at this time. Newspaper readers studied each issue, thoroughly reading each article and sharing information with others in their community. The prominence of newspapers encouraged their tremendous growth, not only in power but also in numbers. According to William David Sloan and James D. Startt in *The Media in America* (1996), in 1783 there were 35 newspapers in the nation, which were all published weekly; by 1790, 83 weekly and eight daily newspapers existed; by 1800 there were 234 newspapers, 24 of which were dailies and by 1833 there were 1,200 daily and weekly newspapers published in urban areas as well as on the frontier.

Throughout the 18th century, most newspapers functioned as job-printing operations. Printer-publishers wrote editorial and news articles, oversaw circulation and served as typesetters, pressmen and advertising managers. The emergence of the newspaper as the spokesperson of a political party required writers with the ability to craft thoughtful political argument and, by the end of the century, editors who wrote opinion pieces and oversaw newspaper content occupied prestigious positions on many of the newspapers.

As a partisan press rose to prominence in the United States, politicians, publishers and general citizens alike maintained that the press was crucial to the success of the political system and they felt that its overriding purpose was to serve a particular political cause or party. Newspapers offered readers a mixture of news, opinion, advertising and political commentary that was inspired by politicians and political leaders. Frederic Hudson in *Journalism in the United States from 1690 to 1872* (1873/1968, p. 142) notes that during this era, editors and publishers understood that "independence of opinion and expression, outside of party, was political and financial ruin."

During the 1780s and 1790s Federalists were in power, controlling the government, the mail and most newspapers. By the end of the century, under the leadership of Thomas Jefferson, the Anti-Federalist or Republican movement gained strength in its opposition to a strong central government. Sympathetic newspapers ran articles accusing governmental officials of bribery, theft and treachery. Federalists viewed Republicans as "dishonest," "vile," "merciless" and "ungodly," and they considered the Jefferson-led opposition to government policy illegitimate, and possibly even treasonous. They responded with the passage of the 1798 Sedition Act, which made it a crime to speak or publish anything considered false, scandalous or malicious about the U.S. government or its officers. David Paul Nord in "Newspapers and American Nationhood, 1776–1826" (1991, p. 401) explains that "Nearly every opposition newspaper suffered under the 'reign of terror,' as Jefferson called it," which instead of limiting dissent resulted in increased partisanship in the American press.

Chapter 6

BENJAMIN FRANKLIN

AN APOLOGY FOR PRINTERS

BEING FREQUENTLY CENSURED AND CONDEMNED BY different persons for printing things which they say ought not to be printed, I have sometimes thought it might be necessary to make a standing apology for myself, and publish it once a year, to be read upon all occasions of that nature. Much business has hitherto hindered the execution of this design; but having very lately given extraordinary offence by printing an advertisement with a certain N.B. at the end of it, I find an apology more particularly requisite at this juncture, though it happens when I have not yet leisure to write such a thing in the proper form, and can only in a loose manner throw those considerations together which should have been the substance of it.

I request all who are angry with me on the account of printing things they don't like, calmly to consider these following particulars:

1. That the opinions of men are almost as various as their faces; an observation general enough to become a common proverb, *So many men so many minds*;
2. That the business of printing has chiefly to do with men's opinions; most things that are printed tending to promote some, or oppose others;
3. That hence arises the peculiar unhappiness of that business, which other callings are no way liable to; they who follow printing being scarce able to do anything in their way of getting a living, which shall not probably give offence to some, and perhaps to many; whereas the smith, the shoemaker, the carpenter, or the man of any other trade, may work indifferently for people of all persuasions, without offending any of them; and the merchant may buy and sell with Jews, Turks, heretics and infidels of all sorts, and get money by every one of them, without giving offence to the most orthodox, of any sort; or suffering the least censure or ill-will on the account from any man whatever;
4. That it is as unreasonable in any one man or set of men to expect to be pleased with everything that is printed, as to think that nobody ought to be pleased but themselves;

5.   Printers are educated in the belief, that when men differ in opinion, both sides ought equally to have the advantage of being heard by the public; and that when truth and error have fair play, the former is always an overmatch for the latter. Hence they cheerfully serve all contending writers that pay them well, without regarding on which side they are of the question in dispute;

6.   Being thus continually employed in serving both parties, printers naturally acquire a vast unconcernedness as to the right or wrong opinions contained in what they print; regarding it only as the matter of their daily labor. They print things full of spleen and animosity, with the utmost calmness and indifference, and without the least ill-will to the persons reflected on, who nevertheless unjustly think the printer as much their enemy as the author, and join both together in their resentment;

7.   That it is unreasonable to imagine printers approve of everything they print, and to censure them on any particular thing accordingly; since in the way of their business they print such great variety of things opposite and contradictory. It is likewise as unreasonable what some assert, "That printers ought not to print anything but what they approve;" since if all of that business should make such a resolution, and abide by it, an end would thereby be put to free writing, and the world would afterwards have nothing to read but what happened to be the opinions of printers;

8.   That if all printers were determined not to print anything till they were sure it would offend nobody, there would be very little printed;

9.   That if they sometimes print vicious or silly things not worth reading, it may not be because they approve such things themselves, but because the people are so viciously and corruptly educated that good things are not encouraged. I have known a very numerous impression of Robin Hood's songs go off in this province at 2 s. per book, in less than a twelvemonth; when a small quantity of David's Psalms (an excellent version) has lain upon my hands above twice the time;

10.   That notwithstanding what might be urged in behalf of a man's being allowed to do in the way of his business whatever he is paid for, yet printers do continually discourage the printing of great numbers of bad things, and stifle them in the birth. I myself have constantly refused to print anything that might countenance vice, or promote immorality; though by complying in such cases with the corrupt taste of the majority I might have got much money. I have also always refused to print such things as might do real injury to any person, how much soever I have been solicited, and tempted with offers of great pay; and how much soever I have by refusing got the ill-will of those who would have employed me. I have hitherto fallen under the resentment of large bodies of men, for refusing absolutely to print any of their party or personal reflections. In this manner I have made myself many enemies, and the constant fatigue of denying is almost insupportable. But the public being unacquainted with all this, whenever the poor printer happens either through ignorance or much persuasion, to do anything that is generally thought worthy of blame, he meets with no more friendship or favor on the above account, than if there were no merit in it at all. Thus, as Waller says,

> Poets lose half the praise they would have got
> Were it but known what they discreetly blot;

yet are censured for every bad line found in their works with the utmost severity.

I come now to the particular case of the N. B. above-mentioned, about which there has been more clamor against me, than ever before on any other account.

In the hurry of other business an advertisement was brought to me to be printed. It signified that such a ship lying at such a wharf would sail for Barbados in such a time, and that freighters and passengers might agree with the captain at such a place. So far is what's common; but at the bottom this odd thing was added, "N. B. No Sea-hens nor Black Gowns will be admitted on any terms." I printed it, and received my money; and the advertisement was stuck up round the town as usual. I had not so much curiosity at that time as to enquire the meaning of it, nor did I in the least imagine it would give so much offence. Several good men are very angry with me on this occasion. They are pleased to say I have too much sense to do such things ignorantly, that if they were printers they would not have done such a thing on any consideration, that it could proceed from nothing but my abundant malice against religion and the clergy. They therefore declare they will not take any more of my papers, nor have any further dealings with me, but will hinder me of all the custom they can. All this is very hard!

I believe it had been better if I had refused to print the said advertisement. However, it's done, and cannot be revoked. I have only the following few particulars to offer, some of them in my behalf, by way of mitigation, and some not much to the purpose; but I desire none of them may be read when the reader is not in a very good humor:

1. That I really did it without the least malice, and imagined the N. B. was placed there only to make the advertisement stared at, and more generally read;
2. That I never saw the word Seahens before in my life; nor have I yet asked the meaning of it. And though I had certainly known that Black Gowns in that place signified the clergy of the Church of England, yet I have that confidence in the generous good temper of such of them as I know, as to be well satisfied such a trifling mention of their habit gives them no disturbance;
3. That most of the clergy in this and the neighboring provinces, are my customers, and some of them my very good friends; and I must be very malicious, indeed, or very stupid, to print this thing for a small profit, if I had thought it would have given them just cause of offence;
4. That if I had much malice against the clergy, and withal much sense, it's strange I never write or talk against the clergy myself. Some have observed that it's a fruitful topic, and the easiest to be witty upon of all others; yet I appeal to the public that I am never guilty this way, and to all my acquaintances as to my conversation;
5. That if a man of sense had malice enough to desire to injure the clergy, this is the most foolish thing he could possibly contrive for that purpose;
6. That I got five shillings by it;
7. That none who are angry with me would have given me so much to let it alone;
8. That if all the people of different opinions in this province would engage to give me as much for not printing things they don't like, as I can get by printing them, I should probably live a very easy life; and if all printers were everywhere so dealt by, there would be very little printed;
9. That I am obliged to all who take my paper, and am willing to think they do it out of mere friendship. I only desire they would think the same when I deal with

them. I thank those who leave off, that they have taken it so long. But I beg they would not endeavor to dissuade others, for that will look like malice;

10. That it's impossible any man should know what he would do if he were a printer;

11. That notwithstanding the rashness and inexperience of youth, which is most likely to be prevailed upon to do things that ought not to be done, yet I have avoided printing such things as usually give offence either to church or state, more than any printer that has followed the business in this province before;

12. And lastly, that I have printed above a thousand advertisements which made not the least mention of *Sea-hens* or *Black Gowns*; and this being the first offence, I have the more reason to expect forgiveness.

I take leave to conclude with an old fable, which some of my readers have heard before, and some have not:

"A certain well-meaning man and his son were travelling towards a market town with an ass which they had to sell. The road was bad, and the old man therefore rode, but the son went afoot. The first passerby they met asked the father if he was not ashamed to ride by himself, and suffer the poor lad to wade along through the mire; this induced him to take up his son behind him. He had not travelled far, when he met others, who said, they are two unmerciful lubbers to get both on the back of that poor ass in such a deep road. Upon this the old man got off, and let his son ride alone. The next they met called the lad a graceless, rascally young jackanapes, to ride in that manner through the dirt, while his aged father trudged along on foot; and they said the old man was a fool for suffering it. He then bid his son come down, and walk with him, and they travelled on leading the ass by the halter, till they met another company, who called them a couple of senseless blockheads, for going both on foot in such a dirty way, when they had an empty ass with them, which they might ride upon. The old man could bear it no longer. 'My son,' said he, 'it grieves me much that we cannot please all these people. Let me throw the ass over the next bridge, and be no further troubled with him.'"

Had the old man been seen acting this last resolution, he would probably have been called a fool for troubling himself about the different opinions of all that were pleased to find fault with him. Therefore, though I have a temper almost as complying as his, I intend not to imitate him in this last particular. I consider the variety of humors among men, and despair of pleasing everybody; yet I shall not therefore leave off printing. I shall continue my business. I shall not burn my press and melt my letters.

[handwritten: deport immigrants]

[handwritten: history focused, the colonial era Talks about the Colonial Alien and sedition Laws, The party press, the stamp Tax]

FREDERIC HUDSON

[handwritten: Partison press]

THE FOURTH EPOCH 1783–1832

[handwritten: period of time in history marked by notable events or particular characteristics]

THE PRINTER AND THE PRESS HAVE ceased to be martyrs in England and America. The time when journalists were dragged through the streets to Tyburn, or had their ears cut off as with Prynne, or put in the pillory as with Defoe, or had their papers burned by the common hangman as with Zenger, has passed with the Anglo-Saxon race. Occasionally, it is true, by the blunders and passions of those in power, as in the enactment of the Alien and Sedition laws in 1798, in the suspension of the *New York World* and *Journal of Commerce* in 1864, and in the arrest of Samuel Bowles, of the *Springfield Republican*, in New York in 1868, there is a glimmering of the despotism of the seventeenth and eighteenth centuries. But this is all. Such mistakes as these are not likely to be repeated on this side of the Atlantic.

After numerous persecutions of the Press in England, more freedom began to dawn on journalism there; and in the great struggle for the abolition of the stamp duty, which originated in an effort to muzzle the Press in 1712, the journalists of Great Britain made rapid progress in acquiring their rights. This struggle began in 1828, and ended, for a time, in 1836, in a reduction of the tax from fourpence to one penny, and its final abolition in 1871. But in obtaining this result there were nearly a thousand prosecutions, imprisonments, and fines for selling unstamped publications. So decisive a victory was only finally achieved after a fierce contest, and through the early exertions of Hetherington, the cheap journalist, aided by such men as Hume, Grote, Bulwer, Birkbeck, Cobden, and others, at a later day.

There was now greater latitude in the United States. Some of the best intellects of the country continued their contributions to the newspapers in the organization of society, of parties, of politics, of literature, and of religion. It was necessary to place the nation on a solid foundation. Newspapers were necessary to accomplish this desirable result. Scarcely had the echo of the last hostile gun of the Revolution died away when the country became divided into two great political camps, with newspapers as their needle-guns, and pamphlets as their chassepôts. Journalism, however, had not yet become a profession. It was a power with the people, but it was managed by ambitious political chiefs, as armies are manœuvred by their generals. It was, during these fifty years, a Party Press. It had more enterprise, more reading matter, more advertisements, more originality, but its views and opinions on public affairs were the inspiration of politicians and statesmen. Editors were free of prisons; they were in no danger of having their ears cut off; they could fight duels; they had their legal rights; they felt their power in all elections, and in all great questions that agitated the public mind, but they were bound to party. Independence of opinion and expression, outside of party, was political and financial ruin. But the world was moving, and its soul was marching on.

When the independence of the United States was acknowledged in 1783, the people, solid and compact during the war, began to disintegrate, and, from a grand Revolutionary Party, with one sublime object in view, formed themselves into two political parties. Each was a safety-valve to the country; each was honest and patriotic in its purposes, but each entertained different views on the policy and form of government deemed best for the republic. With the close of the Revolution, fought out on military principles, the organization of the nation and its political progress and improvement were to be arranged and settled by lesser contests and revolutions, which would take place every four years, and peacefully accomplish their objects and purposes at the ballot-box. This was the course of things during this epoch.

The remarkable events in our national history, nowhere else so splendidly achieved as on this continent, were results obtained by the political leaders and political parties through the Press. Thus the pen became "mightier than the sword." But the people had not acquired, any more than the newspaper, their full freedom of thought and action, for they had become, in the heats and passions of political campaigns, strong partisans. Through the light of time, however, and with the spread of that great national school-book, the Newspaper, the masses have become educated to think and act more independently.

In the organization of parties after the Revolution, one was called the Federalist, under the lead of Alexander Hamilton, and the other the Republican, under the guidance of Thomas Jefferson. The term Democrat was then applied to the Republicans as one of reproach. In retaliation, the term Aristocrat was given to the Federalists. The names of the parties were changed in 1824. The Republicans, in the campaign resulting in the election of John Quincy Adams, accepted the name of Democrat, and the party has ever since been known as such, with a few local distinctions, such as Hard Shells, Soft Shells, Barn-burners, Hard-fisted, Locofocos, Tammanyites, Huge Paws, etc. The Federalists also changed their name to National Republicans, and since then the opposition party to the democracy has gone through several revolutions and changes. It has been known since 1789 as Federalist, National Republican, and Whig, and since the Fremont campaign of 1856 it has assumed the original name of the Democratic Party, and fought its political battles as Republicans. Splits, in certain localities, have taken independent names, such as Conservatives and Silver Grays in New York—Nathaniel P. Talmadge at the head of one, and Millard Fillmore the representative man of the other. Attempts have been made to rally the masses under the names of popular candidates, without, however, much success. Adams men and Jackson men were known, but the titles remained only for an election. There were Hard-Cider and Log-Cabin Whigs in the Harrison campaign, but "principles, not men," seemed to be the governing idea of the people.

One day Dr. Nehemiah Niles, our charge d'affaires to Sardinia, was in Vienna, and had an interview with the venerable Metternich. "If I lived in the United States," said

Metternich, "I would be a Locofoco." "Why so?" asked Dr. Niles. "Why?" continued the prime minister; "because that is the party of your people; their interests are democratic, and the people govern the nation. I am in favor of absolutism here. One is as necessary to America as the other is to Austria." Wise old diplomat! Swept away in the revolution of 1848, he died before Sadowa semi-liberalized the absolutism of the Hapsburg empire.

On the conclusion of peace North America was under the government of the Articles of Confederation which had been adopted by the colonies, and which went into operation on the 2nd of March, 1781. It was demonstrated, after the war was over, that this form of government was too weak and too defective to build a great and powerful nation upon, leading to serious confusion in the intercourse and commerce of the several states. This experience resulted in the calling of a Convention, which met in Philadelphia on the 25th of May, 1787, and gave the world, on the 17th of September of that year, the present Constitution of the United States. In the political contest growing out of the immature condition of the nation from 1783 to the final adoption of the Constitution, the first two parties, the Federalists and Anti-Federalists, came into existence. It was during this period of public excitement and popular agitation that the newspapers were arrayed on either side, and it was in this important and vital political conflict that the Party Press had its origin in the United States.

Of those papers that passed through the fire of the Revolution and entered the new political arena, the *New York Journal*, the *New York Packet*, the *Massachusetts Spy*, the *Boston Gazette*, the *Newport Mercury*, the *Connecticut Courant*, the *Maryland Gazette*, the *Boston Independent Chronicle*, the *Salem Gazette*, the *New Hampshire Gazette*, the *Pennsylvania Gazette*, the *Pennsylvania Journal*, were the most prominent. Other journals were soon established, and many of the most distinguished men who have since held high positions started in political life and distinction with these papers.

The several New York journals which were removed from that city during its occupancy by the British troops were returned to their old quarters on the conclusion of peace. Among others was the *New York Journal*, published by John Holt. It was now named the *Independent Gazette, or the New York Journal revived*. In the following January it was printed on new and handsome Bourgeois type, and issued twice a week. Holt died before the end of the year, and the paper passed into the hands of Elizabeth Holt, his widow. Holt was a man of ardent feelings, a High-Churchman, a good writer, and a firm Whig. Soon after his death his widow printed a memorial of him on cards for distribution among her friends. It was as follows:

> A due tribute to the memory of JOHN HOLT, printer to this State; a native
> of Virginia; who patiently obeyed Death's awful summons, on the 30th of
> January 1784, in the 64th year of his age. To say that his family lament
> him, is needless; that his friends bewail him, useless; that all regret him,
> unnecessary; for, that he merited every esteem, is certain. The tongue of
> slander cannot say less, though justice might say more. In token of sincere
> affection, his disconsolate widow hath caused this memorial to be erected.

Mrs. Holt continued the *Journal* till 1785, but it was published only once a week. Eleazar Oswald, a kinsman of Mrs. Holt, who had been a colonel in the American army, conducted the paper for her from 1785 to 1786, after which Oswald printed it in his own name, Mrs. Holt receiving a proportion of the profits. In January, 1787, Mrs. Holt and Oswald sold the *Journal* and their printing establishment to Thomas Greenleaf. Oswald died in September, 1795.

Soon after Greenleaf took possession of the *Journal* he made the establishment the foundation of two papers. The paper intended for city circulation was called *The New York Journal and Daily Patriotic Register;* the other, with the same title, was published weekly, on Thursday, for the country. The titles of these papers were afterward altered; the daily was called *The Argus,* or *Greenleaf's New Daily Advertiser;* and *Greenleaf's New York Journal and Patriotic Register* was published twice a week. When the two great political parties were forming, the measures of Washington's administration were attacked with virulence in Greenleaf's paper. It was, in fact, the first Democratic organ in the country.

Thomas Greenleaf was born in Abington, Massachusetts, and learned to set type of Isaiah Thomas. He was the son of Joseph Greenleaf, who was a printer in Boston in 1774. The *Journal and Argus* were published by Greenleaf in New York till 1798, when he died of yellow fever, at the age of forty-two. He was a good printer, enterprising, and of an amiable character. He was elected one of the sachems of the Tammany Society in 1789. He had been an editor on the *Independent Chronicle,* of Boston, prior to 1787. That paper, on the 24th of September, 1798, in noticing his death, said:

> He was a steady, uniform, zealous supporter of the Rights of Humanity; a warm friend to civil and religious liberty, unawed by persecution or prosecution, both of which it has, not unfrequently, been his lot to experience. He loved his country; and if, at any time, as Editor of this paper, he dipped his pen in gall, and exercised it with unusual severity, it was occasioned by that strong abhorrence he felt against political apostacy, and the fervor of his wishes to preserve the Constitution from encroachment.

Mrs. Greenleaf, his widow, published both the daily and semi-weekly papers for some time, but finally disposed of the establishment to James Cheetham, an Englishman, who altered the titles of both papers; the daily to the *American Citizen,* and the semi-weekly to the *American Watchman.*

These papers flourished from 1801 to 1810. They were edited with marked ability by Cheetham, who acted with that portion of the Democratic party of which George Clinton, De Witt Clinton, and Judge Spencer were leaders, in opposition to Aaron Burr. Violent quarrels took place between the Van Nesses, Swartwouts, Matthew L. Davis, and other friends of Colonel Burr on one side, and Cheetham, Richard Riker, afterward Recorder of New York, De Witt Clinton, and Judge Spencer on the other. Several duels took place. On one occasion, Matthew L. Davis sallied forth in Wall Street with pistol in hand, expecting to be constrained to shoot Cheetham at sight. The latter, however, kept out of the way of Davis, and the affair ended without bloodshed. In 1803 Colonel Burr instituted a suit against Cheetham for libel, growing out of the Presidential election in the House of Representatives in 1801, which created considerable excitement. There were some able writers for Cheetham's paper, and he always stood high with his section of the Democratic party as a ready writer and skillful tactician. He wrote a life of Thomas Paine, which was distasteful to Paine's followers. In opposing the embargo the *Citizen* declined, and ceased to be the organ of the Republican or Democratic Party the year previous to Cheetham's death.

Cheetham was not a professional printer, but he was an able editor, and acquired great distinction as a writer. Occasionally the vigor and pungency of his style caused his productions to be compared with the letters of Junius, which were long considered a model for political writers here as well as in England. But Junius was not alone his model. Dr. Francis, who was with him when he died, thus described his death-bed scene:

> He had removed with his family to a country residence, some three miles from the city, in the summer of 1809.——Within a few days after he exposed himself to malaria, by walking uncovered by his hat, through the fields, under a burning September sun. He was struck with a complication of ills: fever, congestion of the brain, and great cerebral distress. The malignancy of his case soon foretold to his physician the impossibility of his recovery. Being at that time a student of medicine, I was requested to watch him; on the second day of his malady, his fever raging higher, he betrayed a disturbed intellect. On the night of the third day, raving mania set in. Incoherently he called his family around him: addressed his sons as to their peculiar avocations for life: giving advice to one ever to be temperate in all things: upon another urging the importance of know-ledge. After midnight he became much worse, and ungovernable. With herculean strength he now raised himself from his pillow: with eyes of meteoric fierceness, he grasped his bed covering, and in a most vehement but rapid articulation, exclaimed to his sons, "Boys, study Bolingbroke for style, and Locke for sentiment." He spoke no more. In a moment life had departed.

The personal appearance of Cheetham was remarkable: tall and athletic. None of his political difficulties ever made him a principal in an actual duel, but in 1804 he challenged William Coleman, of the *Evening Post*. Mutual friends interfered, preventing a meeting, which, however, resulted in a duel, in which Cheetham was a second. This remarkable affair of honor we shall fully describe in our sketch of the *Post*. Mrs. Cheetham died about the same time that her husband departed this life. We believe that his orphan daughter, a very beautiful girl, was sent to Norwich, Connecticut, for education, after the death of her parents.

The *New York Packet*, published by Samuel Loudon, returned to New York with the others. Shortly after its publication was changed from a weekly to a daily, and was continued for several years. It was called, as late as 1793, the *Diary, or Loudon's Register*. In the number of February 12 of that year it contained the following dramatic advertisement:

T H E A T R E.

By the OLD AMERICAN COMPANY
THIS EVENING, the 12th of February,
A   C O M E D Y,
CALLED, THE
R O A D   T O   R U I N.
To which will be added,
A   C O M I C   O P E R A,
called, the

R   O   M   P   ;
Or, A Cure for the SPLEEN.

PLACES in the BOXES may be had of Mr. *Faulkner*, at the Box Office from *Ten* to *Twelve* A.M. and on the Days of Performance from *t hre* to *five*, P. M. where also Tickets may be had, and at Mr. Gaine's book-ftore at the Bible in Hanover-Square.

The Doors will be opened at a quarter of an hour after Five, and the Curtain drawn up precifely at a quarter of an hour after Six o'clock.

BOX 8s.   PIT 6s.   GALLERY 4s.

VIVAT RESPUBLICA.

On the 12th of February, 1869, there were four columns of advertisements of theatres and other places of public amusement in the *New York Herald*, and there were twenty-three theatres open nightly in that city. One religiously inclined would say that the Road to Ruin was an open thoroughfare in 1869 in that metropolis.

The *Packet* was the political opponent of the *Journal*, and strongly advocated the Federal side, and the adoption of the Constitution. Loudon was an elder in the Scotch Seceders' Church in New York. He lived to an advanced age. Several years previous to his death he had retired from business.

The most influential and enterprising paper in Massachusetts after the Revolution was the *Massachusetts Centinel and the Republican Journal*, started as a semi-weekly by Warden and Russell in 1784, and managed for forty-two years by Major Benjamin Russell, who was the master-spirit of the establishment. Its first number was issued on the 24th of March. It was, after the war, what the *Spy* and *Gazette* were before the war—the popular guide in Massachusetts. Major Russell learned the art of printing in the office of Isaiah Thomas, and served six months in the Continental Army as a substitute for Thomas. He was one of the guard at the execution of André. The *Centinel* was immediately recognized as a good newspaper, and its proprietors endeavored to keep up with the progress of the times. It was established at an important period in the world's history: when Europe was being remapped and reorganized by revolutions and Napoleon's victories, and this country moulded into a great republic.

Major Russell, with the true instinct of a journalist, made politics and the interests of the merchant and mechanic the standard matter of his paper. But he did not lose sight of literature. Nearly all of Goldsmith's poems, the narrative of Cook's voyages, Cunningham's Pastorals, and portions of Cowper, Gray, and other British poets, were published by him. Original poetry also found a place in his columns. The *Centinel* was in favor of protection to all domestic manufactures. The British factors and agents made great efforts to establish themselves in the United States. Having lost the country, they endeavored to save the trade. Several public meetings were held in Boston to deliberate on the subject. One, of merchants and mechanics, was held in Faneuil Hall in 1785, when it was voted, as many opposed to the extravagance of our day and the course of England during the late rebellion, would have voted in 1863–4,

> That we do pledge our honor, that we will not directly or indirectly, pur-
> chase any goods of, or have any commercial connections whatever, with,
> such British merchants, agents, or factors, as are now residing among us,
> or may hereafter arrive; and that we will not let, or sell, any warehouse,

shop, house, or any other place, for the sale of such goods, nor will we
employ any persons, who will assist said merchants, factors, or agents,
by trucks, carts, barrows, or labor, (except in the reshipment of their
merchandize) but will *discountenance* all such persons, who shall in any way
advise, or in the least degree help or support such merchants, factors,
or agents, in the prosecution of their business; *as we conceive all such British
importations are calculated to drain us of our currency, and have a direct tendency
to impoverish this country*.

These meetings and these appeals had very little more effect then than they would
now have. Fashion was more potent.

The *Centinel* also opposed the return of the refugees. Other papers favored their
restoration to political and property rights, because other states, more liberal than
Massachusetts, would allow their return, and reap the advantages of their property and
industry. Some of the newspaper paragraphs on this subject, which we have lately seen
in regard to the Southern rebels, remind one of those published eighty-five years ago.
The *Centinel*, in August, 1784, said:

However the principles of common benevolence, and the desire of curing
the calamities of our fellow citizens, might operate in favor of an act of
amnesty and naturalization to the ill-fated body of men, the refugees; yet
the antipathies nurtured during the war have taken so deep a root, as will,
we are apprehensive, be very difficult to remove.

In our sketch of the *Gazette*, the course of the venerable Edes in regard to the threats
against the editor of the *Centinel* is noticed. In the latter paper of January 19th, 1785, the
assault, then anticipated, was made on Major Russell, which is thus *naively* paragraphed:

A few days since we were requested to publish a small performance on the
institution of the Sans Souci. After carefully perusing it, and perceiving it
to be only intended to display the dangerous tendency of that society, not
the vehicle of personal abuse, (as has been too common) we determined to
publish it and advertised our intentions of so doing. This roused the passions
of those who conceived themselves deserving the lash of satire, and urged
them to endeavour to suppress it in embryo. A variety of injuries was
threatened us, if we persisted in our determination of publishing it. In
the afternoon of Saturday we were waited upon by Mr. Samuel Jarvis, who
desired to speak with one of us in another apartment; being attended
thither, he demanded to know whether or not we intended publishing "A
Farce," and being answered in the affirmative, exclaimed, "By God, I'll kill
you if you do," and endeavored to put his threat into execution, *but found
his efforts inadequate to the task*.

In the political contests of those days the newspapers were frequently more violent
in coarse invective and ribaldry than even in our modern political campaigns. With an
exception here and there, an improvement in this respect, as well as in many others,
affecting the character and dignity of the Press of America, has certainly taken place.
When the local Stamp Act of 1785 was passed, the *Centinel* was quite tame on the

subject. Major Russell thought the tax on newspapers injudicious, but was really in favor of the tax on advertisements!

Shay's rebellion was denounced, but the great feature of the *Centinel* was its course in favor of the acceptance of the Federal Constitution by the people. From the adoption of this instrument in National Convention till its adoption in State Conventions, the *Centinel* kept up a constant fire in its favor. One is reminded, in reading its paragraphs and illustrations, of the energy and persistency of the *New York Herald* in carrying through an important measure in after years. Meetings of mechanics, a series of them indeed, were held in Boston by the influence of Major Russell, to represent their sentiments to the State Convention, then in session, and the petition from this class which was submitted on that occasion turned the scale, said John Hancock, in favor of the Constitution. The *Centinel* announced with great enthusiasm, as the news came in, the fact of the ratification of the Constitution by the several states. According to Russell, little Delaware was the first, and he based large hopes on the result in this small state. He said:

> The State of Delaware being the first to adopt, ratify, and confirm the American Constitution, argues well. It is a good maxim, which inculcates the practice of '*entering at the little end of the horn;*'—as, at every step we take, our circle is increased, and our basis progressively growing broader and broader.

Delaware was the eighth state; New Jersey was the first.

The Massachusetts Convention met in an old church, on the spot where William Ellery Channing afterward preached, in Federal Street. Its proceedings were reported by Russell. He thus describes his own labors and a scene in the Convention:

> I had never studied stenography, nor was there any person then in Boston that understood reporting. The presiding officer of the Convention sat in the Deacon's seat, under the pulpit. I took the pulpit for my reporting desk, and a very good one it was. I succeeded well enough in this my first effort to give a tolerably fair report in my next paper; but the puritanical notions had not entirely faded away, and I was voted out of the pulpit. A stand was fitted up for me in another place, and I proceeded with my reports, generally to the acceptance of the Convention. The doubts that still existed as to whether enough of the states would come into the compact as to make the constitution binding, made the proceedings of the Convention intensely interesting. When the news arrived of the acceptance of it by the State of Virginia, there was a most extraordinary outbreak of rejoicing. It seemed as if the meeting-house would burst with the acclamation.

On the adoption of the Constitution there were celebrations every where. When it was evident that a sufficient number of states had voted in its favor, New York had a grand pageant. This was on the 23d of July, 1788. There was, of course, a procession. All the trades turned out in costume. Among the others, numerously represented, were the printers, bookbinders, stationers, and all those connected with the Press. They marched in this order, with the other trades and professions:

THE PRESS SECTION.
Marshals.
Hugh Gaine of the *Gazette*.
Samuel Loudon of the *Register*,
on horseback.

The standard was alternately supported by Messrs. Bryce, Carroll, Harrison and Purdy.

A handsome stage, drawn by four horses.

Upon the stage, the federal printing-press complete; cases, and other typographical implements, with pressmen and compositors at work. During the procession, many hundred copies of a song and an ode, adapted to the occasion, were struck off, and distributed, by Messrs. A. M'Lean and J. Russel, among the multitude. A small flag on the top of the press, on which was inscribed the word "Publius," in gold letters. Mr. John Loudon, representing a herald, mounted on the back of the press, dressed in a flowing robe, and a cap, on which were written the words, "The Liberty of the Press;" with a brazen trumpet in the right hand, proclaiming, "The epocha of Liberty and Justice," pending from the mouth of the trumpet. In the left hand, a parchment scroll, representing the new constitution.

The master Printers, Booksellers and Bookbinders, with their journeymen and apprentices, four abreast, following the stage.

Description of the Standard.

Fame, blowing her trumpet, and supporting the medallion of his excellency Doctor Franklin; Liberty attending, holding her cap over his head; the electric fluid darting from below; on the upper corner, the union flag, and Stationers' arms; and below, the Bible and federal constitution, representing the religious and civil constitution of our country.

Mottos,

1st. "*Ars artium omnium conservatrix.*"

2d. "May the liberty of the Press be inviolably preserved, as the palladium of the constitution, and the centinel of freedom."

Surrounding the medallion of his excellency Doctor Franklin, the following words:

"Where liberty dwells, there is my country."

With the adoption of the Constitution the Federal Party considered itself fully organized, and prepared to sit *en permanence* over the destinies of the nation. On the inauguration of Washington and Adams, the Boston *Centinel* formally announced the death of the Anti-Federalists after the following manner:

Notwithstanding the medical exertions of a *celebrated Physician*—the prescriptions of three *gubernatorial* Esculapians—and the endeavors of the whole fraternity of *State Quacks* and *Mountebanks* to prolong its existence—in convulsions the most violent—in contortions and wreathings the most painful, on *Wednesday* last, finished its wicked career,

The Genius *of* Antifederalism.

It was born in August, 1787—was aged 17 months. Though thus cut off in its childhood, it still lived to do much mischief; and to have grown so detestable, that even its friends—its foster-parents, shewed the utmost resentment whenever called by its name: It has, however expired, a striking instance of the truth of the adage,—"*The wicked shall not live half their days.*"

On WEDNESDAY, MARCH 4th, the funeral obsequies will be consummated—when a GRAND PROCESSION will be formed.

ORDER OF THE PROCESSION.
The DEMON of REBELLION,
drawn in a flaming Car, by *Ignorance, Knavery*, and *Idleness*.
DANIEL SH-YS, and JOHN FR-NKLIN,
armed with *levelers* in their right, and halters in their left hands.
DAY, SHATTUCK, &c. &c. their followers, two and two, each with
caps and *bells*.
Several "*great men*" their abettors, in *disguise*.
CHIEF PHYSICIAN—

Supporters,	The BODY	Supporters,
Injustice,		Knavery,
Abuse,		Defamation,
Prevarication,		Falsehood.

His SATANIC MAJESTY—Chief Mourner.
His standard—motto—"*The prop of my
Empire is fallen.*"
A KNOW-YE Rhode-Islander—and a *pine-barren* Carolinian, in
sackcloth, with brazen helmets—crest "*A Highwayman
robbing by law*," motto—" 'Tis power which
sanctifies a crime."
A cart drawn by *Fraud*—with Paper-Money, Tender-Laws, &c.
the sides painted, "*Be it enacted*," &c.
The GODDESS of DISCORD—in weepers.
—In her right hand a torch expiring—in her left a bloody
sword broken.
BENEDICT ARNOLD, SILAS DEANE, &c. with swords embossed,
"*In '75 we were right.*"
A standard, motto, "*Birds of a feather flock together.*"
Hon. PATRICK H-NRY, of Virginia,
Bearing a scroll, with the words, "*In the creation of* TWO
Confederacies are all my hopes of greatness."
His Excel. G. CL-NT-N, Esq.
In both hands a Purse, tied up. The words thereon,
"*If New-York loses the Impost, I lose thee.*"
The GENIUS of IMBECILITY,
In a car—painted on both sides with hieroglyphicks. "*A ship rotting in the
harbor.—An English Crow picking the Eagle's eyes out—the Eagle asleep; his talons
cut—an American fort, with English colors—a rusty sword—a broken plough-
share—starving mechanics—broken merchants, &c.*"

200 Wrongheads, two and two
"While we're in, let's keep in."
A WOLF, covered with the golden fleece of a LAMB, marked
4000l. per ann.
The Geniuses of the Philad. Gazetteer—New-York Journal—
Boston Gazette, &c. in their original *blackness;*
"The days of our years are evil and few."
A cart, with antifederal Pamphlets, Essays, Protests, &c. in reams,
marked *"waste-paper."*
GALEN and the Junto—two and two.
The GODDESS of POVERTY—in tatters—
"Follow me, my sons," she cries,
"We do," each scribbler replies.
A dray with stumps of pens, broken inkstands, &c.
Antifederal Scribblers, in dishabille, two and two, chaunting the
following lines:—*Who will close the Procession.*

There was a singular prediction of the recent rebellion in the Virginia scroll borne by Patrick Henry in this imaginary procession.

On the 16th of June, 1790, the name of the paper was changed to *Columbian Centinel.* Very few of the journals of the last century continued long under one title. Some of the newspapers had as many *aliases* as an English nobleman. Major Russell and Isaiah Thomas were ever inventing some new title or some new device for their figure-heads. In the progress of the republic, and in the progress of journalism, the broader views of Russell suggested the more comprehensive name of *Columbian Centinel*, and so it was thereafter called. It became more national in its character. It was strongly in favor of Washington, Adams, and Hamilton. It was full of Federalism and patriotism. On one occasion Russell printed all the public laws gratuitously. When called upon for his bill, he sent it to the State Department receipted. "This must not be," said Washington on learning the fact. "When Mr. Russell offered to publish the laws without pay, we were poor. It was a generous offer. We are now able to pay our debts. This is a debt of honor, and must be discharged." Shortly after, a check for seven thousand dollars was sent to Major Russell.

The "war of editors," which began in England in 1645, and in America in 1719, continued at this period of our history. Wherever and whenever two newspapers come in competition in politics, circulation, or advertisements, there is a fight. Such was the case with the *Centinel* and *Chronicle* in 1790–3, and such is the case with the *Times*, and *Tribune*, and *World*, and *Sun* now. There was a disgraceful scene in Faneuil Hall and on 'Change in 1793 between Major Russell and Benjamin Austin, Jr., of the *Chronicle.* Austin publicly, in Faneuil Hall, called his opponent "such a fellow as Ben Russell." Shortly after, Russell met Austin on 'Change, and spat in his face. There was an action for damages, and the jury awarded Austin twenty shillings.

The Citizen-king of France in 1830, Louis Philippe, was an exile in Boston, teaching school there, in 1793–4. Talleyrand was also in that city at that time. They often visited the office of the *Centinel*, especially on the arrival of news from Europe. In return for the privilege of looking over the *Moniteur*, Louis Philippe presented an Atlas to Russell, then a rare book in the colonies, and it was by the aid of the maps thus obtained that he was enabled to make his compilations of the movements of the armies on the Continent of Europe so clear and comprehensive that the reader could easily trace the operations of Napoleon and his opponents in all the great battles of the Empire. In this way the *Centinel* acquired a high reputation throughout the country.

In the Presidential contest of 1796, the *Centinel*, true to its party, although Federalism began to show evident signs of weakness, advocated the claim of John Adams. The aggressions of the French on our commerce were the irritating and exciting topics. Adams was elected. But the Democratic Party began its real existence in that contest, and secured the office of Vice-president for Jefferson. It was at the instigation of Russell that the Federalists of Massachusetts wore the black cockade. In the *Centinel* of July 4, 1798, it was strongly recommended:

> It has been repeatedly recommended, that our citizens wear in their hats on the day of Independence, the American Cockade, (which is a *Rose*, composed of black ribbon, with a white button, or fastening) and that the Ladies should add to the attraction of their dress (the Ladies' cockade should be a *white rose*,) this symbol of their attachment to the government, which cherishes and protects them—either on their breasts or in their bonnets. The measure is innocent; but the effect will be highly important. It will add cement to the *Union*, which so generally and so happily exists. Every cockade will be another edition of the *Declaration of Independence*, and the demonstration of it, by this national emblem now, will be as highly laudable as the display of the immortal instrument of 1776 was then: Those who signed the Address to the President are pledged to display this evidence of it to the world—and they may be assured, that the influence of their example in this measure will be productive of as great good, as the influence of their names was on the paper. All those, who have not had opportunity to sign the address, and who feel themselves Independent Americans, cannot hesitate to show by some outward mark, that they love their country better than any other in the world; this mark ought to be the black cockade. The Ladies, we understand, are universally in favor of the measure; and if they lead, who will not follow?

This suggestion arose from the order of Adet, which had previously appeared in the Philadelphia *Aurora*, for all Frenchmen in the United States to wear the tri-colored cockade. In the heat of political excitement many Americans wore the same emblem. After the appearance of the above, the *Centinel* said:

> The Jacobins have the impudence to say, that the people of Boston were really divided, and they give as a proof, that not more than half of them wear the American Cockade. This being the case, let every Bostonian, attached to the constitution and government of the United States, immediately mount the COCKADE, and swear that he will not relinquish it, until the infamous projects of the external and internal enemies of our country shall be destroyed.

Again Russell came to the rescue of the black cockade:

> The Cockade is generally worn by every class of citizens in almost every town in the United States. It is considered as a token of patriotism and

union. It will enliven our commencement at Cambridge this day. It will receive the smiles and approbation of the Fair Daughters of Columbia; and will convince the Gallic spies, now in our country, that we are not a divided people.

It appears that William Cobbett, although in the interests of the Federalists, had hit Russell several times in the columns of the *Porcupine*, then published in Philadelphia. In reply, the *Centinel* said:

* * * * * * COBBETT was never encouraged and supported by the Federalists as a solid, judicious writer in their cause; but was kept merely to hunt Jacobinic *foxes, skunks*, and *serpents*. The Federalists found the Jacobins had the *Aurora, Argus*, and *Chronicle*, through which they ejected their mud, filth, and venom, and attacked and blackened the best characters the world ever boasted; and they perceived that these vermin were not to be operated on by reason or decency. It was therefore thought *necessary* that the opposite party should keep, and *feed* a *suitable beast* to hunt down these *skunks* and *foxes*; and *"the fretful Porcupine"* was selected for this business. This imported, or transported beast has been kept as gentlemen keep a fierce *bull Dog*, to guard his house and property against thieves, Jacobins and Frenchmen, and as such he has been a good and faithful dog, and has been *fed* and caressed accordingly. * * * * * *

In the next great political contest, which resulted in the overthrow of the Federal party and the election of Thomas Jefferson, the *Centinel*, and many of the Federalists of Massachusetts, declared in favor of Aaron Burr. On the 4th of March, 1801, Major Russell published an epitaph for the tombstone of his party under the head of

Monumental Inscription.

"That life is long which answers Life's great end."

YESTERDAY EXPIRED,
Deeply regretted by MILLIONS of grateful Americans,
And by *all* GOOD MEN,
The F E D E R A L A D M I N I S T R A T I O N
Of the
GOVERNMENT of the *United States;*
Animated by
A WASHINGTON, an ADAMS;—a HAMILTON, KNOX,
PICKERING, WOLCOTT, M'HENRY, MARSHALL,
STODDERT and DEXTER.
Æt. 12 years.

Its death was occasioned by the
Secret Arts and Open Violence,
Of Foreign and Domestic Demagogues:
Notwithstanding its whole Life

> Was devoted to the Performance of every Duty
> to promote
> The UNION, CREDIT, PEACE, PROSPERITY,
> HONOR, and
> FELICITY of its COUNTRY.

The remainder of the inscription is very long, and gives an elaborate epitome of the political history of the United States for the previous twelve years, showing how much good the Federalists accomplished for the country. It ends by saying

> The "Sun of Federalism is set for ever."
> *"Oh shame, where is thy blush?"*

The *Centinel* opposed all the measures of Jefferson and Madison, and strongly denounced the war with England. With Russell originated, during Madison's administration, that famous political term "Gerrymandering." The incident is thus related by Buckingham:

> In 1811, when Mr. Gerry was governor of the commonwealth, the Legislature made a new division of the districts for the election of representatives to Congress. Both branches had then a democratic majority. For the purpose of securing a democratic representative, an absurd and singular arrangement of towns in the county of Essex was made to compose a district. Russell took a map of the county, and designated by a particular coloring the towns thus selected. He then hung the map on the wall of his editorial closet. One day, Gilbert Stuart, the celebrated painter, looked at the map, and said the towns, which Russell had thus distinguished, formed a picture resembling some monstrous animal. He took a pencil, and, with a few touches, added what might be supposed to represent claws. "There," said Stuart, "that will do for a salamander." Russell, who was busy with his pen, looked up at the hideous figure, and exclaimed, "Salamander! call it Gerrymander." The word became a proverb, and, for many years, was in popular use among the Federalists as a term of reproach to the democratic Legislature, which had distinguished itself by this act of political turpitude. An engraving of the "Gerrymander" was made, and hawked about the State, which had some effect in annoying the democratic party.

De Witt Clinton was the Federal candidate, in opposition to Madison, for the presidency in 1812. The *Centinel* gave him a very weak support. On the election of Monroe in 1816–17, the "era of good feelings," a phrase which also originated with Russell, commenced, and the Federalists were no longer known as a party. The *Centinel* began then to lose its hold upon the public. It had changed its name by adding "American Federalist" to the principal title. It advocated the election of John Quincy Adams in 1824, and his reelection in 1828. With the incoming of the Democratic Party again under the lead of Andrew Jackson, the influence of the *Centinel* became still less potential. In November, 1828, Russell sold the establishment to Adams and Hudson, and, with a farewell banquet given him at the Exchange Coffee-house by the editors and printers of Boston, he retired to private life.

In 1830 the *New England Palladium*, and in 1836 the *Boston Gazette*, were merged with the *Centinel*. In 1840 the *Centinel* disappeared in the embrace of the *Boston Daily Advertiser*.

That Methuselah of newspapers, the *New Hampshire Gazette*, started in the last, lives through this, and runs through all our epochs. After the death of Daniel Fowle the establishment passed into the hands of two of his apprentices, John Melcher and George Jerry Osborne, in 1785. Shortly after Osborne retired, and Melcher carried it on till February 9, 1802, when he sold the establishment to Nathaniel S. and Washington Pierce. The Pierces began to print the *Gazette* February 9, 1802, when they changed its politics from Federal to Republican, or Democratic, as it would now be called. They, in connection with Benjamin Hill and Samuel Gardner, published it till May 21, 1805, when they sold it to William Weeks. Up to this time little or no editorial writing had appeared in the paper, except a little political matter at certain seasons. The scissors did most of the work. The news and selected matter were all that was expected. Mr. Weeks wrote more than his predecessors, and remained editor more than four years of a stormy period, and until December 14, 1813, when he was succeeded by Beck and Foster. This firm continued the publication till it was dissolved by the death of David C. Foster, which occurred in 1823. From that time to 1834 Gideon Beck was the publisher. He then admitted Albert Greenleaf as a partner, and published it with him till July 14, 1835, when Mr. Beck finally left the business.

In conducting their paper and managing their business, Beck and Foster were industrious and successful. Both of them were members of the Legislature of the state, and the decease of Mr. Foster was felt to be a public loss. On the 14th of July, 1835, the imprint bore the names of Thomas B. Laighton and Abner Greenleaf, Jr.; from 1836 to 1841 the name of A. Greenleaf, Jr. On the 15th of June, 1841, it was changed to Virgin and Moses, who published it to 1843, when Virgin left, and S. W. Moses appears as publisher. In 1844 Abner Greenleaf is named as editor; then A. Greenleaf and Son, editors. The year closed without any imprint whatever, and the paper was published without any during the year 1845–6. Abner Greenleaf died in September, 1869, aged eighty-three. In 1847 the *N. H. Gazette and Republican Union* was published by William P. Hill, who began in March, and remained till August 13, 1850, when he was succeeded by Gideon Rundlett. The present publisher, Edward N. Fuller, commenced in March, 1852. Several of these numerous editors were men of talent and energy; but the sudden and frequent changes of conductors and printers have operated against the profit of the proprietors.

The *Connecticut Courant*, which became the property of Hudson and Goodwin in 1779, was printed by them till November 21, 1815, when George Goodwin and Sons appeared as printers. That interval of excitement and anxiety between the peace with Great Britain of 1783 and the practical operation of the new Constitution in 1789 is vividly outlined in the files of the *Courant*, and the beneficent influence of Washington's administrations clearly traced through its columns. It was a supporter of Washington and Adams. The paper remained in the hands of the Goodwin family until September 12, 1836. When the last Goodwin retired in that year he was eighty years of age, and had been in the establishment, as apprentice, journeyman, and owner, for seventy years! In 1836 the concern passed into the hands of John L. Boswell, and was published by him until January 1, 1850, when William Faxon was associated, and the paper appeared in the name of Boswell and Faxon until the 1st of January, 1855, when it passed into the hands of Thomas M. Day. It appeared in the sole name of Mr. Day until the 1st of January, 1857, when A. N. Clark was taken in, and the paper appeared in the names of Day and Clark. In 1865 the firm was again changed, and the paper published by A. N. Clark and Company.

Chapter 8

Colonial habits
Franklin, how the
Stamp Act affected
Printers. Printr
Proffesson

STEPHEN BOTEIN*

PRINTERS AND THE AMERICAN REVOLUTION

1. Introduction

AMONG THE MISCELLANEOUS MATERIAL THAT ISAIAH THOMAS appended to his exhaustive *History of Printing in America* was a list of more than 350 American newspapers published in 1810. All but approximately 50 were classified according to political affiliation, Federalist or Republican.[1]

Reflected in this information was a powerful new trend in American journalism. As the Reverend Samuel Miller had observed at the start of the century, the newspapers of republican America were "immense moral and political engines" that advanced opinions as well as reported occurrences.[2] The press had become capable at once of greater good and more serious mischief, depending on the perspective of readers, than in the colonial period. To a nostalgic conservative like James Fenimore Cooper, writing from the vantage point of midcentury, this seemed to be a development as inevitable as it was ruinous. Not the least of the evils to undermine the island paradise that Cooper imagined in *The Crater* was the press. "Fortunately," in the happy early days of Cooper's fictional community, "there was yet no newspaper, a species of luxury which, like the gallows, comes in only as a society advances to the corrupt condition; or which, if it happens to precede it a little, is very soon to conduct it there." Eventually, after a newspaper had been introduced, this utopian experiment collapsed.[3]

It was almost as if Cooper meant to confirm or vindicate the fearful predictions of British authorities in the very infancy of American society. In a declaration of 1671 that has won him much historical notoriety, Gov. William Berkeley of Virginia had been moved to "thank God" that his colony lacked a press—which he associated with "disobedience," "heresy," "sects," and "libels against the best government."[4] For almost a

* The author wishes to thank Michael T. Gilmore, Christopher M. Jedrey, and Harriet N. Ritvo for valuable criticism and suggestions.

century, Berkeley's alarm had appeared unjustified. In Virginia and the other mainland British colonies of the eighteenth century, it proved difficult to prevent the establishment of printing houses, many of which published newspapers; but these were normally innocent of controversial matter. By the time Isaiah Thomas wrote his *History*, however, virulent political partisanship had become characteristic of American journalism.

Drawing on the personal experience of its author, that pioneering chronicle focused knowingly on the crucial period and process of transformation. Although the political press of the early nineteenth century was a product of contemporary party conflicts, the origins of controversial journalism in America could be traced back to the decade of Revolutionary turmoil that preceded Independence. In the changing business and political strategies of printers, who ran the eighteenth-century press, were registered the circumstances that accounted for the new partisan practices. Revealingly, as an aside in his bitter narrative of the "American Rebellion," the loyalist Peter Oliver had called the art of printing "black," adding that Benjamin Franklin—for one—had made it "much blacker."[5] Many others were of the opinion, at the time, that the behavior of the trade as a whole had aggravated divisiveness and violence, thus hastening the movement of events toward war. Printers, reported one Pennsylvanian at the outset of the crisis, "almost without exception, stuffed their papers weekly . . . with the *most inflammatory pieces* they could procure, and *excluded every thing that tended to cool the minds of the people*."[6] However exaggerated, this pointed quite accurately to those who were responsible for the unprecedented level of partisan controversy in American journalism during the Revolutionary years.

Throughout, too, Benjamin Franklin played a central part, as Oliver understood. It was a part more characteristically ambiguous, however, than angry loyalist feelings would allow. Franklin's career and reputation as a printer were illustrative of traditional practices in the colonial trade as well as the new patterns that emerged in the Revolution. By examining not only printers as a group but the curiously complicated role of Franklin as their most prominent "brother type," it is possible to appreciate some of the larger forces reshaping the public forum of a provincial society convulsed by political crisis. It is possible, furthermore, to understand how that crisis ultimately reshaped the self-imagery, or "occupational ideology,"[7] of the printing trade. For it was the figure of Franklin, already legendary, that loomed most impressively in the rhetorical efforts of American printers after Independence to affirm and honor the contribution of the press to the Revolutionary movement. Appropriately or not, he became the symbol of a new identity that they formulated for themselves in the new republic. This identity they would continue to promote even in the face of contrary realities, as they struggled with deteriorating business conditions in the early decades of the next century.

2. Colonial Habits

It was Franklin's custom, in later years, to speak fondly of the craft that he had practiced as a young man but abandoned in middle age. For one of his grandsons, he predicted, printing might be "something to depend on," an independent source of income that happened to have been "the original Occupation of his Grandfather." Meanwhile, at Passy, "Benjamin Franklin, Printer," would amuse himself with a private press, in emulation of aristocracy.[8]

If the inverted snobbery of this ritual pleased Franklin, it was pardonable. That the most illustrious American of the eighteenth century was also a printer, at least by training, seemed incongruous by European norms. Franklin's remarkable career can only be appreciated in the distinctive context of American social and economic realities, particularly as found in the conditions of the colonial printing trade. Despite limitations on the status that printers could claim in the social hierarchy, the circumstances of the American trade encouraged upward mobility. Probably Franklin could never have achieved his most spectacular successes in the face of the harsh business realities that increasingly threatened the self-esteem of the printing fraternity in London.[9]

By the middle of the eighteenth century, it was no longer common for printers in the capital city of the empire to function as the major entrepreneurs of the publishing business; for the most part, others had usurped that lucrative and influential role. Initially, printers had controlled the principal stages of production in the English book world. Because they alone could actually put a manuscript into print, they were able to demand the exclusive right to profit by its sale. But as the book business grew and required more capital, in response to an expanding middle-class market for print, its separate stages of manufacture and distribution became more specialized. The book-seller, who dealt in the craftsman's product, emerged as the person who laid out capital in a publishing enterprise and then gathered in the benefits.[10] As early as 1663, a dissident group of printers launched an unsuccessful rebellion against the booksellers who dominated the Stationers' Company in London. Protesting that they were now "yok'd to the Booksellers," who once were "but as an Appendix to the Printers," the insurgents charged that their rivals had grown "bulkie and numerous" from the "several other Trades" that they had absorbed and were "much enriched by Printers impoverishment."[11]

A few printers in eighteenth-century London—among them William Strahan, Franklin's friend and correspondent—ran large businesses that generated sufficient profit to permit investment in copyright, with which they might hope to "emancipate them-selves from the Slavery in which the Booksellers held them."[12] But they were exceptional figures. To most of their brethren in the trade, the times seemed hard. In 1750 an eccentric master printer named Jacob Ilive—whom Franklin had known, and remembered for his bizarre religious speculations—addressed a general meeting of the trade in London. "Where is the Man," he declaimed, "be he *Divine, Astronomer, Mathematician, Lawyer, Physician*, or what else, who is not beholden to Us?" What a "great Pity," he lamented, that printers "do not meet with an *adequate Encouragement*, suitable to the Labour and Pains they take in the Exercise of it"; but this verifies the old Proverb, "*That true Merit seldom or never meets with its Reward.*" It is certain "from the present Situation of Affairs," he concluded, "that in *Our Case*, it never CAN, nor ever WILL."[13]

The difficulty was not simply a matter of economics. Many of the first European printers had been accomplished scholars, and this distant heritage seems to have shaped the ambitions of eighteenth-century London printers like Ilive. As their economic importance diminished, so did the credibility of their original reputation as men of independent intellect and learning. The dissident printers of 1663, lamenting their subservience to booksellers, had given early voice to what would later be a common anxiety among London's printers—that they would be considered mere manual laborers. In England, the dissidents said, printers "have so light an esteem" that they fail to "finde like respect or care with the meanest of Occupations." Specifically, they complained of an argument used against them by booksellers in the internal struggles of the Stationers' Company. The printers were "the Mechanick part of the Company," it ran, "and so unfit to rule." By way of contrast, reported the insurgents, printers in France "*are above Mechanicks, and live in the suburbs of Learning.*"[14] At stake were traditions that had sustained the pride and prestige of the English trade. Despite isolated literary achievements by members of the fraternity eager to establish credentials that would distinguish them from the ordinary run of skilled workers, printers as a group failed to make these traditions plausible in eighteenth-century London.[15]

Pre-Revolutionary American printers had some reason to hope that they might rank higher in general public esteem, despite prevailing social conventions to the contrary. Theirs was a delicately ambiguous role, however, the strengths and weaknesses of which were determined to a great extent by the structure of business life in an underdeveloped colonial economy.

Compared with the larger printing offices of London, even the most successful firms in the American colonies were modest enterprises. The decisive difference between American printers and those at the top of the London trade was that the former seldom had occasion or incentive to print books of substantial size, because demand for such items in the colonies was unsteady and oriented toward English products.[16] As a result, colonial printers could not expect to prosper from their craft alone, and poverty was often more than a remote contingency.

In order to compensate for limited printing business, however, it was the normal policy of a colonial printer to expand the scope of his work to include enterprises that were no longer or never had been associated with the craft in London. Like printers in provincial England, perhaps their closest counterparts, printers in the colonies participated in a relatively unspecialized trade that reflected the conditions of an inadequate market.[17] Although they lacked the volume of printing business engrossed by major figures in the London trade, they were in practice far from simple mechanics. The very slenderness of the living that they might expect to earn from their skill led them to diversify and thus play more varied roles in their communities than was customary for their brethren in London.

Colonial printers usually sold whatever they could get their hands on. It was not extraordinary to find a general store appended to a printing house; available there, along with the usual selection of dry goods and other imports, might be a wide assortment of the best books that the mother country had to offer. Not only was the colonial printer often a bookseller as well, unlike a printer in London, but quite possibly he also owned and edited a newspaper, which was a convenient place for him to advertise his various wares and insert himself into the intimate daily dealings of his town. Otherwise, too, printers in America were habitually at the center of things. Many staffed the colonial post office; some were clerks in the governments for which they printed laws and currency. By the sum of such activity, a colonial printer might well become a prominent man, unavoidably involved in a broad range of local affairs.[18]

Yet if prominent, he was also vulnerable, enjoying no more status—based conventionally on his occupation—than a printer in the mother country. However lofty his aspirations or diversified his business, it was inescapable that a colonial printer had been brought up to work with his hands. Isaiah Thomas neatly summed up the problem in a capsule memoir of Franklin's nephew, Benjamin Mecom. "He was handsomely dressed," recalled Thomas, "wore a powdered bob wig, ruffles and gloves; gentlemanlike appendages which the printers of that day did not assume—and, thus apparelled, would often assist, for an hour, at the press."[19] In the colonies, as in both London and the provinces, printers had to face the hard, discouraging fact that in the eyes of many neighbors, especially those who claimed to be "gentlemen," they were by training mechanics, without full legitimacy as men of independent intellect and creed.

The discrepancy here between social convention and occupational reality was ironical but easily ignored. One reason Franklin had chosen to be a printer, rather than a soapmaker like his father, was to satisfy his "Bookish Inclination." And certainly his own experience confirmed the advice he gave William Strahan in 1754, as Strahan's oldest son was learning the business in London. "If, with the Trade," Franklin wrote, "you give him a good deal of Reading and Knowledge of Books, and teach him to express himself well on all Occasions in Writing, it may be of very great Advantage to him as a Printer."[20] Although Franklin cited "some Instances" in England to prove his point, it was more frequently the colonial printer, so often a newspaper editor too, who needed and acquired literary facility. More plausibly than their brethren in London, whose work had felt the impact of specialization, printers in America might still take pride in the intellectual dimensions of their craft. Nevertheless, conventional social prejudices tended to persist. A colonial printer was not commonly expected to possess a mind of his own, and this expectation was likely to undercut whatever efforts he made to influence his neighbors.[21]

Even Franklin, perhaps the finest prose writer in the colonies, could not hope to transcend effortlessly the prevailing public image of his occupation. In 1740, when a lawyer in Philadelphia proposed to edit *The American Magazine* for Franklin's chief competitor in the printing trade, Franklin responded to the challenge by claiming that the scheme was originally his; the scornful reply was that Franklin's involvement in the periodical had never been projected "in any other capacity than that of a *meer* Printer."[22] Before the decade was over, Franklin had decided to disengage from work that ultimately impeded realization of the very ambitions it stimulated. A managing partner "took off my Hands all Care of the Printing-Office," he wrote in his *Autobiography*. Thus released, "I had secur'd Leisure during the rest of my Life, for Philosophical Studies and Amusements."[23] Only after ceasing to practice his craft could Franklin become a scientist and statesman.

Thus released, too, Franklin was no longer as vulnerable as he had been to the pressures of powerful men and competing interests in his community. A further weakness in the position of the colonial printer, working as he did an underdeveloped local market where he needed all the business he could get, was that he had to take pains to please all customers at all times. As often in the English provinces, but not in London, a printer in America might face no competition but still have few clients, because local demand for his product was apt to be slight. Usually unable to rely for a living on the favor of any one group among his neighbors, including those who wielded political power, a colonial printer by custom labored to serve diverse interests in his community. Unlike London, where large profits were sometimes to be had by making partisan commitments to one well-financed faction or another, colonial America was a place for printers to be studiously impartial.[24]

Upon occasion they explained and justified this trade strategy in elevated terms, professing devotion to "liberty of the press," as they chose to understand that phrase.[25] A press was "free," in this formulation, only if it was "open to all parties." A printer, in other words, should offer everyone the "liberty" of his press, without favoring one set of opinions over the rest. Whatever the social utility may have been of equalizing access to every colonial press, printers were attracted to the principle because it suited their business interests to serve all customers. Often they frankly admitted as much, in language that ignored the traditional learned pretensions of the English trade; at times, indeed, they sought to take rhetorical advantage of their conventional social standing as mechanics. "Governour, it is my imploy, my trade and calling," Pennsylvania's first printer had argued in 1689, finding himself in trouble for printing an unauthorized edition of the colony's charter, "and that by wch I get my living, to print; and if I may not print such things as come to my hand, which are innocent, I cannot live." Printing, he insisted, was "a manufacture of the nation," not an instrument of faith or ideology.[26]

By far the best known and most sustained colonial argument for an impartial press was Franklin's "Apology for Printers," first published in a 1731 issue of the *Pennsylvania Gazette*, after the wording of an advertising handbill produced in his shop had given offense to the local clergy. "Printers are educated in the Belief," Franklin insisted, "that when Men differ in Opinion, both Sides ought equally to have the Advantage of being heard by the Publick." Here was a principle consistent with advanced eighteenth-century doctrines of the public good, defined in terms of free competition by individuals or interests, but Franklin was quick to ground such considerations in business pragmatism. Printers "chearfully serve all contending Writers that pay them well" he explained, "without regarding on which Side they are of the Question in Dispute."[27] This was precisely the modest, self-denying role—so exclusively "mechanical"—that some members of the trade in London found disagreeable. Although literary craft traditions seemingly accorded more with reality in the colonies than in the mother country, Franklin's "Apology" offered on behalf of printers a formulation of principles usefully congruent with the trade strategies required by an underdeveloped economy. One man's right to be heard might be another man's employment.

The chief difficulty, as Franklin knew well, was to persuade one's neighbors to recognize the legitimacy of this strategy. It might be acceptable enough in normal circumstances, but in times of bitter controversy—when powerful men in the community turned to print to gain advantage in their quarrels with one another—its usefulness became less certain. Because "the Business of Printing has chiefly to do with Mens Opinions," Franklin observed, printers had to live with "the peculiar Unhappiness" of "being scarce able to do anything in their way of getting a Living, which shall not probably give Offence to some and perhaps to many."[28] Possibly because disharmony in the public forum was at odds with traditional norms of political behavior, many colonists still held a printer responsible for the sentiments he set in type and seem to have been unprepared to tolerate him if, caught in the middle of intense conflict, he wished to publish both sides.

When attitudes polarized, a printer sometimes had to work for a single faction; otherwise he might antagonize everyone. That this solution might be at least briefly lucrative, as well as unavoidable, is evident from the experience of such printers as John Peter Zenger and Franklin's brother James. Publications like the *New-York Weekly Journal* and the *New-England Courant* reflected temporary calculations by their printers that more was to be gained and little could be lost in periods of political turmoil if they abandoned neutrality and served those who insisted on and were willing to pay for partisanship. In quieter times Zenger or James Franklin might hope to maintain the "liberty" of their presses to different opinions, but this was a policy that did not always promise to be advantageous for a printer, especially if he were less than fully established in the trade. To pursue it rigorously could subject him to severe and contrary pressures when the political scene became agitated.[29]

To avoid trouble, the potential for which was greatest in the conduct of a news-paper, probably it was best in the long run to abstain from publishing polemics altogether, or as much as possible. Frequently, therefore, printers would qualify their dedication to the principle of an "open press" not by expressing veiled partiality to any one side but by trying to exclude the more censorious effusions of all parties. The result was not receptivity but even-handed aversion to diverse and forceful opinions. Although in his "Apology" Franklin wished to persuade people to tolerate the publication of polemical matter without blaming its printer, he also affirmed that printers did "con-tinually discourage the Printing of great Numbers of bad Things, and stifle them in the Birth." Returning to the subject in his *Autobiography*, he was even more emphatic. "In the Conduct of my Newspaper," he recalled, "I carefully excluded all Libelling and Personal Abuse."[30]

Pre-Revolutionary trade habits of neutrality, it seems, did not always promote that disputatious "liberty of the press" advocated by such libertarian authors as Trenchard and Gordon. Instead, sometimes citing Addison, colonial printers repeatedly indicated their reluctance to open their presses—their newspapers especially—wide enough to allow a full range of controversial matter into the public forum.[31] Most commonly, by filling the columns of their papers with anecdotal news of European war and diplomacy, colonial printers tried to avoid becoming embroiled in local struggles. Accordingly, the contents of most colonial papers were unrelievedly bland—"*dull and flat*," as James Franklin would tacitly concede in a late subdued phase of his career.[32]

If it is true that the political language and thought of pre-Revolutionary America were often curiously unrevealing, highly sensitive perhaps to the shared concerns of local elites but not to the issues that made for divisions among both powerful and common people, the trade strategies of printers may have been partially responsible. Unaccustomed to a politics in which partisan activity was fully legitimate, they acted in such a way as to retard the development of a public forum where conflicts could be thoroughly and continuously articulated. Only during the prolonged crisis of the Revolutionary period did printers as a group begin to act in ways that promoted a politics directly expressive of tension and dissent.

3. Franklin and His Friends

In the first major political contest of the Revolutionary years, the controversy over the Stamp Act, colonial printers had a substantial economic interest. David Ramsay was later to suggest that printers, never lacking in "attention to the profits of their profes-sion," had united to oppose legislation that "threatened a great diminution" of their income as well as an abridgement of American liberty.[33] At the time the act was passed, Franklin—serving as a colonial agent in London—realized immediately that it would place a heavy economic burden on his former profession. "I think it will affect the Printers more than anybody," he wrote early in 1765 to his managing partner in Philadelphia, "as a Sterling Halfpenny Stamp on every Half Sheet of a Newspaper, and Two shillings Sterling on every Advertisement, will go near to knock up one Half of both. There is also Fourpence Sterling on every Almanack."[34]

There was ample precedent in England for taxing printed matter, novel as it was of Parliament to apply such a plan to the empire. For over half a century, a stamp tax had been in force in the mother country, and the system was not generally regarded as intolerable.[35] It had caused occasional distress in the provinces, however, and previous experience with local stamp duties in New York and Massachusetts had suggested that a tax on paper, payable by the printer in advance, might damage the colonial trade. Like their provincial brethren, but unlike publishers in London, printers in the colonies sold mostly on credit, some of which inevitably turned out to be bad. Understandably, then, they were fearful that much of the new tax could not be passed on to their customers.[36]

The first reaction of David Hall, Franklin's Philadelphia partner, was that it might not be worthwhile to continue the *Pennsylvania Gazette* at all. "The Case betwixt you and us, with respect to News Papers," Hall explained to William Strahan in London, "is very different—your Hawkers are ready to take yours all off, and pay the Ready Money for them." James Parker, a key Franklin associate in New York, predicted that his days in the trade were numbered, since "the fatal *Black-Act*" with its "killing Stamp" would surely turn printing into a business of "very little Consequence."[37]

No doubt this was unduly alarmist; both Franklin and Strahan tried to encourage Hall with a variety of optimistic suggestions.[38] But by the beginning of summer it was apparent that the dimensions of the problem had changed. Well before they had the opportunity to formulate business strategies that would minimize the threat of the Stamp Act to their livelihoods, printers in the colonies were faced with the more urgent challenge of coping with unprecedented political turbulence. For some—often "the more opulent," as Isaiah Thomas recalled[39]—traditional habits of political caution prevailed; among the hesitant were Franklin's associates in the trade. Such was the magnitude of the transatlantic crisis, however, that their customary business strategies failed to provide reliable guidelines for behavior.

David Hall, for one, had never been inclined to meddle rashly in controversy; but this instinct, so often useful in the past, seemed inappropriate or even imprudent in the radically altered circumstances. In June 1765, he reported to Franklin with some bewilderment that the *Gazette*'s customers were already "leaving off fast" in anticipation of the Stamp Act. For the most part, it was not that they lacked the extra shillings; it was a question of principle. Their resolution, Hall said, was "not to pay any thing towards that Tax they can possibly avoid; and News Papers, they tell me, they can, and will, do without." Evidently uncertain himself as to the constitutional implications of the new law, Hall perceived the temper of the colonies with apprehension. "In short," he observed privately, "the whole Continent are discontented with the Law, think their Liberties and Privileges, as Englishmen, are lost, and seem, many of them, almost desperate.—What the Consequences will be, God only knows." Hall's own fear was that there would be "a great deal of Mischief."[40]

Unquestionably, considered from the perspective of his trade, the Stamp Act was a "horrid Law" that would "knock up" most printers in America. But Hall was in no hurry to oppose it publicly. From the first, he told Franklin, exaggerating somewhat, "all of the Papers on the Continent, ours excepted, were full of Spirited Papers against the Stamp Law, and . . . because, I did not publish those Papers likewise, I . . . got a great Deal of Ill-will." Hall had hoped to ride out the storm, but after a while came to realize that he had been "much mistaken" as to his proper course of action. The *Gazette*'s silence, zealous patriots warned, would injure the cause of the people. "And, I have been told by many," Hall explained, "that our Interest will certainly suffer by it." It would be best "to humour them in some Publications, as they seem to insist so much upon it." Yet he hesitated to rush into the fray, "the Risk being so great" if he pursued a course of outright defiance.[41] Eventually, like many of his colonial brethren, he made the most of a disagreeable situation by publishing his paper without his name on it. Uneasily and with circumspection, he became and would remain a patriot—less ardent than his chief business rival, William Bradford III, but forthright enough at least to avoid being accused of Toryism.[42]

Further to the south, Charleston's Peter Timothy was even more circuitous in his response to the issues of the Revolutionary period. Since he was an official in the imperial postal system, his loyalties were suspect from the very beginning of the crisis. Naturally, he abhorred "Grenville's hellish Idea of the Stamp-Act," but he was reluctant to join the resistance movement. Acting in concert with most of his southern brethren, he elected to suspend his *Gazette* temporarily rather than to continue publication in overt disregard of the new law. Furthermore, he declined "to direct, support and engage in the most violent Opposition"—so he later explained to Franklin, a former business associate—and this thoroughly "exasperated every Body." The result was that within a short time he found himself reduced from "the most *popular*" to "the most *unpopular* Man in the Province." Especially humiliating was the decision of local patriots to help Charles Crouch, his brother-in-law and once his apprentice, to set up a new *South-Carolina Gazette* that would represent the cause of American liberty more boldly than either Timothy's or the even more timorous *Gazette* of Robert Wells. For a time, Crouch's paper prospered, as its warm criticism of the Stamp Act attracted patriot readers. Having missed his chance, Timothy seemed unable to restore his credit with the more hot-blooded spirits of Charleston. "Ruduced [*sic*] to this situation," he advised Franklin in 1768, "I have not been myself since Nov. 1765. Nor shall I recover, unless I quit the Post-Office when some other Occasion offers to distinguish myself in the Cause of America."[43]

When opportunity next beckoned, Timothy was somewhat more alert to the perils of hesitation. In 1770 he distinguished himself as the only southern printer to mark the Boston Massacre with black newspaper borders. Just the year before, however, he had printed William Henry Drayton's caustic criticisms of the non-importation agreement in force at Charleston, and as late as 1772 his interest in politics seemed to lapse. He had "suffered, by never being lukewarm in any Cause," he told Franklin then, and so—his eyes "almost worn out"—he was prepared to accept a comfortable retirement post in the British imperial administration. As it happened, nothing was immediately forthcoming, and soon afterward Timothy's patriotic ardor revived, carrying him to the prestigious peak of his lengthy career. In the following years, as he proudly informed Franklin in 1777, he was "continually in Motion," as secretary to the second Provincial Congress and a member of various political committees. Briefly imprisoned by the British in 1780, he died two years later, assured of his reputation as a patriot.[44] To reach that point, however, had required a long and somewhat roundabout journey.

For James Parker—temporarily in New Jersey when the Stamp Act passed, having left his New York office under the management of a Virginian named John Holt—even a lukewarm commitment was to be avoided. Much as he loathed the new tax, he could not seriously contemplate resistance. Sometimes, he wrote to Franklin in June 1765, "the true Old English Spirit of Liberty will rise within me, yet as there is a Necessity to acquiesce in the Chains laid on me, I endeavour at a patient Resignation." Fortunately, it appeared, he was at a distance from the arena of conflict—"or perhaps the Impetuosity of my Temper would have plunged me deep one way or the other." Impetuous or not, he plainly had no stomach for popular agitation and disorder. As tensions mounted in the fall of 1765, it seemed to him that the people were "running

Mad," and would speedily bring "an End to all Government" by their "dreadful Commotions."[45]

The next year, returning to New York, Parker continued to lament the insubordinate "Spirit of Independence" that inflamed the populace. He had moved back at the urging of Franklin, who wanted him there to serve more effectively as general comptroller of the colonial post office; as an additional incentive to relocate, Franklin provided a minor customs post in the city. Predictably, like Peter Timothy in Charleston, Parker soon became implicated in the bitter political divisions of the time. The Sons of Liberty, he told Franklin, "carry all before them." Their favorite printer, John Holt, was emboldened to harass Parker by refusing to relinquish management of the New York office, although Parker was unquestionably its sole proprietor. Eventually Holt yielded the title of Parker's old paper, the *New-York Gazette*, renaming his own after John Peter Zenger's famed *Journal*, but Parker was still obliged to "launch into Business" anew, without his former clientele and even some of his office equipment.[46]

Most damaging was the decline that his political reputation had suffered in the course of the previous year. "Mr. *Holt*," he noted in a bitter broadside, "seems to insinuate . . . that in the late Troubles I was no Friend to Liberty." This was probably unfair of Holt, but Parker's public record was indeed ambiguous. In spite of his antipathy to the Stamp Act, he had done what he could to insure compliance with the law, evidently considering this to be the unavoidable duty of a royal official. One consequence, apparently, was "a little Sour Looking, and perhaps some Contempt." More serious was the widespread feeling, nurtured carefully by Holt, that Parker's crown offices—his customs appointment in particular—had compromised his personal integrity. In 1768, the customs job may well have cost him the patronage of the New York Assembly.[47]

Evidently it was difficult for Parker to abandon the old trade ways and plunge into controversy with enough zeal to please the emerging leadership of the patriot movement. John Holt had no trouble outmaneuvering his former employer and business associate. In 1768 Parker's fortunes rose as he began to run the "American Whig" essays of the Livingstonian party in his *Gazette*; within a short time he had gained more than 200 new subscribers, while losing only 70 Anglicans. Holt quickly pirated the series, though, and it became doubtful whether Parker's recently acquired customers would stay with him. Once again, late in 1769, he chose to try his hand at polemical politics by printing an anonymous broadside libel written by Alexander McDougall; then, threatened with a legal proceeding and dismissal from the post office, he backed down and identified the author. Not long afterward Parker died, having made a few last-minute efforts to atone for this treachery by publishing on behalf of McDougall's cause.[48]

Perhaps this indicated where his true sympathies lay; possibly he was in the process of beginning to commit himself aggressively—as Timothy would—to the Revolutionary position. Nevertheless, considered as a whole, Parker's politics in the crucial years after passage of the Stamp Act had been unhappily inconsistent. No American printer had been more vehement in his criticism of colonial stamp duties than Parker, but his perceptions of economic self-interest had not made him into a Son of Liberty. The lasting strength of old trade ways, in spite of new political realities, was revealed in Parker's continuing attempts to shun conflict long after it might have been apparent that this strategy was unwise. By trying to avoid one kind of trouble, Parker invited another.

One reason Hall, Timothy, and Parker were unequipped to deal with the abnormal pressures of a Revolutionary situation was Franklin, their long-time patron and associate in the trade. More than anyone else, even while on assignment as a colonial agent in London, he could claim influence among American printers; over the years, especially south of New England, he had accumulated business connections that to some observers looked dangerously like a transatlantic propaganda network. "Depend upon my doing every Thing in this Affair for the Printers and Papermakers," he had promised Hall at the time of the Stamp Act, "as zealously as if I were still to be concerned in the Business."[49] Unfortunately for those who followed his cues, Franklin's political judgment at the beginning of the Revolutionary crisis was unsure, not least because at some level of consciousness—despite his retirement from active business life—he remained a colonial printer. His practice of imperial politics represented with curious exaggeration the habitual trade policy of neutrality, elevated to the sphere of statecraft. Much has been written of Franklin's passion for conciliation and his extraordinary diplomatic skill; interpretations based on political and even psychoanalytic theory have been suggested. Viewed from a different perspective, however, Franklin's public behavior in London during the period before Independence may be understood as an extension of the business and political strategies that he and his brethren in the colonial trade had followed for decades preceding the Revolutionary crisis.[50]

Thus, as an agent, he tried to act the part not of an advocate but of a reporter—an "impartial historian of American facts and opinions." With some of the instinctive distaste for controversy that characterized newspaper publishers in the colonies, Franklin also set out to mute transatlantic political debate. "At the same time that we Americans wish not to be judged of, in the gross by particular papers written by anonymous scribblers and published in the colonies," he wrote to his son in 1767, "it would be well if we could avoid falling into the same mistake in America of judging of ministers here by the libels printed against them." His self-assigned task was not only to report impartially the arguments of both sides, each to the other, but also to discount all extreme, offensive statements of opinion—"to extenuate matters a little," as he explained.[51]

If in the past this approach to imperial affairs had worked well, it was ill suited for a period of intense political turmoil. Hoping to please both his colonial employers and British officialdom, Franklin found it difficult to satisfy either side. It "has often happened to me," he wrote shortly after his subtle involvement in the Hutchinson letters uproar had been exposed, "that while I have been thought here too much of an American, I have in America been deem'd too much of an Englishman."[52] Both compromised and compromising, Franklin played a role in London—so typical in its essentials of a colonial printer—that diminished his credibility with patriots as well as English officials, and therefore reduced his usefulness to long-time associates like Hall, Timothy, and Parker.

Most troublesome to patriots was the lingering memory of his initial acquiescence in the Stamp Act. With pardonable ambivalence, Hall wrote that he wished his famous partner could have provided daily counsel "on the Spot" instead of three thousand miles away. Yet, added Hall, "I should be afraid of your Safety, as the Spirit of the People is so violent against every One, they think has the least concern with the Stamp Law, and they have imbibed the Notion, that you had a Hand, in the framing of it." Nowhere were the distortions of Franklin's outlook more evident than in the congratulations he conveyed to Hall for trying to exclude criticism of the Stamp Act from the *Pennsylvania Gazette*. "Nothing has done America more Hurt here," he explained, "than those kind of Writings; so that I should have been equally averse to printing them if I had held no Office under the Crown."[53]

Whether or not Franklin really was "a dangerous Person," as John Holt would later complain in private to a fellow printer, it was plain enough—within the trade as well as without—that in the early years of the imperial crisis he lacked his usually shrewd sense of political direction. His decision to abandon the middle ground and espouse the colonial cause was gradual and far from enthusiastic. "I assure you," he wrote in 1772 in answer to Peter Timothy's request for a job, "it is not in my Power to procure you that Post you mention or any other, whatever my Wishes may be for your Prosperity." His explanation reflected resignation more than patriot ardor. "I am now thought here too much an American," he pointed out, "to have any Interest of the kind." Ultimately, like Timothy but on a much grander scale, Franklin emerged from the Revolutionary turmoil with honor, even glory; but this happened at least in part because in 1774 the British ministry moved against him so heavy-handedly for his complicity in the Hutchinson affair.[54] Until then, still the colonial printer, he had persisted in his reluctance to engage in overt partisan politics, continuing perilously late to value the benefits of official British patronage.

4. Reluctant Partisans

Similar doubts and hesitation were characteristic of other colonial printers, although they were not as close to Franklin as Hall, Timothy, or Parker. Unused to the violently polarizing effects of a Revolutionary conflict, they tried to temporize, often to their eventual regret. Willingly or not, sooner or later most printers in the colonies gave up neutrality to choose sides. More than twice as many, it appears, opted for the patriots as for the Tories. No exact count is possible, however, since some switched parties and others were so tepid in their commitments as to elude meaningful classification.[55] Reluctant to advertise themselves as full-fledged partisans, many printers tried in public to claim the middle of the road, steering one way or another only when obliged.

Some, like Franklin and his associates, managed in the end to establish themselves convincingly as patriots. In North Carolina, for example, James Davis and Adam Boyd were able to take a patriot line while continuing to avoid excessive partisanship, as were James Adams in Delaware and Jonas Green in Maryland.[56] Outside the southern colonies, however, this was less usual, on account of competition from more energetically patriot presses. For a patriot printer who wished seriously to persist in the old ways, the most effective solution may have been that adopted by the Fleet brothers, Thomas, Jr., and John, who published Boston's *Evening-Post*. Although it was known that their personal sympathies lay with the American cause, their policy as printers was to maintain at least a semblance of impartiality. According to one querulous Tory, the Fleets restricted comments by pro-American "Dirtcasters" to "the Holes and Corners and other private Purlieus" of their paper, whereas "all the Pages and Columns" of the fiery *Boston Gazette* were filled with inflammatory propaganda against the mother country. As late as the early months of 1775, the Fleet brothers were still promising that the *Evening-Post* would be "conducted with the utmost Freedom and Impartiality," and would always, "as usual, be open for the Insertion of all Pieces that shall tend to amuse or instruct, or to the promoting of useful Knowledge and the general Good of Mankind." The next month, they published a letter from a self-styled moderate commending their editorial policy, and another—on the duty of obedience—that hailed their "well known impartiality." A week later, without prior notice, the last issue of the *Evening-Post* appeared, with a brief note from the printers explaining that they had decided to suspend publication until matters were "in a more settled State." Since matters only became more unsettled, the *Evening-Post* never revived. Without sacrificing other printing business, the Fleets were thus able to remain faithful to old trade ways in a stridently patriot community.[57]

More commonly, however, lukewarm Toryism became the only realistic option for a printer determined to stay neutral in the face of strenuous patriot pressures. Georgia's James Johnston, for one, veered inconsistently as he responded to both threats and incentives; eventually, because he was not enough a patriot, he became a Tory, was declared by patriots to be guilty of treason, and was banished. Among other printers who were forced by this logic to back slowly into Toryism were such prominent figures as Robert Wells of Charleston and Boston's Richard Draper. Strict political neutrality, which had never been easy to achieve in a time of conflict, became highly implausible during a revolution. In 1775, Philadelphia's James Humphreys, Jr., founded the *Pennsylvania Ledger* with the naively stated intention of keeping it authentically open to all sides. When this proved futile, he became known by default as a Tory. "The impartiality of the Ledger," Isaiah Thomas commented laconically, "did not comport with the temper of the times."[58]

How Revolutionary pressures within the printing trade could transform an uneasy patriot into an uneasy Tory was revealed painfully in the careers of Daniel and Robert Fowle, in New Hampshire. Perhaps because of his previous unhappy involvement in a "famous Cause" of New England's political history, Daniel Fowle was disinclined to make a firm commitment in the Revolutionary crisis. Although he associated himself with Wilkes to support the longstanding lawsuit that he had brought after his false imprisonment by the Massachusetts House in 1754, for allegedly printing the notorious *Monster of Monsters*, otherwise his deportment reflected habits of prudence befitting a public printer who also served as a magistrate. His *New-Hampshire Gazette*, which he conducted with his nephew Robert, "was not remarkable in its political features," according to Isaiah Thomas. If "its general complexion was favorable to the cause of the country," mild patriotism was not enough in time of stress. "Some zealous whigs," Thomas recalled, "who thought the Fowles were too timid in the cause of liberty, or their press too much under the influence of the officers of the crown," encouraged one Thomas Furber to establish the *Portsmouth Mercury* early in 1765. Although the upstart paper began with a customarily cautious promise "to print Nothing that may have the least Tendency to subvert Good Order," it went on to assert that "neither Opposition, arbitrary Power, or publick Injuries" would be "screen'd from the Knowledge of the People, whose Liberties are dearer to them than their Lives."[59]

Furber himself proved so disappointingly prudent that the Fowles were able to outdo him in patriot spirit by the end of the Stamp Act controversy, but in the long run their *Gazette* was still insufficiently partisan. In 1772 Benjamin Edes and John Gill, printers of the *Boston Gazette*, accused Robert Fowle of scheming to obtain a customs house appointment—a charge that Fowle merely dismissed as "premature and founded in a Mistake." Furthermore, he told his readers, it was "more honorable to hold any Post under the Government, than to spend his Time in libelling and railing at the Rulers of the People," as Edes and Gill did. Two years later, following the neutral logic of pre-Revolutionary printers, the *New-Hampshire Gazette* reprinted the opposing views of "Novanglus" and "Massachusettensis" in parallel columns, along with advice from the printers that people "*read both Sides with an impartial Mind*." Daniel Fowle was subsequently reprimanded by the New Hampshire legislature for his willingness to publish an argument against American independence; Robert, less fortunate, came to be known unequivocally as a Tory and was forced to flee, eventually finding consolation as a British pensioner.[60]

Most Tory printers waited as long as they dared before abandoning fully the trade principle of neutrality. This was especially so in Boston, where patriot feeling was a stern discouragement to those interested in printing for the cause of crown and Parliament. Because Richard Draper was insufficiently enthusiastic in his attachment to the mother country, despite his appointment as printer to the governor and king, it was necessary for Thomas Hutchinson and his friends to cast about for more adventurous figures in the trade. To find the right men proved difficult. John Green and Joseph Russell, in business together since 1755 and printers to the Assembly, were apparently prepared to risk the displeasure of patriots and accept the lucrative contract that Governor Bernard secured for them in 1767, to serve the New Board of Customs Commissioners in Boston. It also seems that when John Dickinson's *Farmer's Letters* first attracted local notice, partisans of the mother country privately urged Green and Russell "by no means to print the same." Heeding this advice, they promptly fell out of favor with the House of Representatives and most of their former clientele. "Mind, Green, who will get most at the winding up of Affairs," Bernard supposedly said by way of cajolery, "Edes and Gill or you."[61] This was not enough to reassure the anxious partners, however, so Massachusetts Tories were forced to seek out other printers.

John Mein and his partner John Fleeming, recent immigrants from Scotland, had been quick to serialize the *Farmer's Letters* in their *Boston Chronicle*, professing eagerness that the paper "always, when any dispute claims general attention, give both sides of the question, if they can be obtained." But evidently the prospect of customs patronage persuaded them instead to try specializing in "the partial Praise of a Party," as Edes and Gill scornfully explained. Mein, it seems, was altogether too choleric to survive in Boston. After exposing local violators of the non-importation agreement, assaulting John Gill, and drawing a pistol on a hostile mob, he hastily made his way to England, where he became a hack writer for the North ministry. Left behind, his associate Fleeming struggled on for a time, only to be supplanted by a new Tory team consisting of two young printers—John Hicks, formerly an apprentice of Green and Russell, and Nathaniel Mills, who had been trained by Fleeming. Hicks, who originally had been something of a patriot, was said to have been involved creditably in the circumstances of the Boston Massacre. But, observed Isaiah Thomas, "Interest too often biasses the human mind." Although his own father was killed by English troops at the very beginning of the Revolutionary War, Hicks became a Tory.[62]

To the south, only New York offered Tories adequate printing facilities. By 1774, according to an indignant out-of-town newspaper reader, Hugh Gaine and James Rivington were brazenly publishing anyone who would "sneer at, and deduct from the merit of the most ascertained and sacred Patriots." Nevertheless, both printers persisted in justifying themselves in accordance with traditional trade rhetoric. "Gaine," Isaiah Thomas would recall, "seemed desirous to side with the successful party; but, not knowing which would eventually prevail, he seems to have been unstable in his politics." Perhaps because of his previous connections with New York's Anglican community, his *Mercury* appeared to be leaning in the direction of Toryism by the early 1770s, but not irrevocably so. Nor was Rivington's bias especially obvious when in 1773 he began to publish his highly successful *Gazetteer*. Promising to avoid "acrimonious Censures on any

Society or Class of Men," Rivington announced that it was his goal to be "as generally useful and amusing as possible." In the circumstances, this would have required remarkable diplomatic talent. "When so many Persons of a vast Variety of Views and Inclinations are to be satisfied," the *Gazetteer* conceded in a shrewder vein, "it must often happen, that what is highly agreeable to some, will be equally disagreeable to others."[63]

What stamped both Gaine and Rivington as Tory sympathizers by 1774 was not so much their public political sentiments as their apparent determination to maintain the traditional neutrality of the trade. In contrast to Philadelphia's patriot printers, who were said to refuse to publish the Tory viewpoint because of their "unaccountable delicacy," Gaine and Rivington claimed to understand what a "free press" should be. The "TRUE SONS OF LIBERTY," Rivington suggested in his *Gazetteer*, were those who printed without showing partiality. A few issues later, he quoted with approval an article from a London newspaper that caustically described the efforts of American patriots to abridge "freedom of the press" by preventing printers from "daring to publish on both sides." Fortunately, noted Rivington, there were some courageous souls who could withstand such pressure. "The printer of a newspaper," he declared, "ought to be neutral in all cases where his own press is employed." He himself would definitely publish all views in his paper, and also all pamphlets submitted to him, "whether of the Whig or Tory flavour."[64]

Privately, too, Rivington did his best to resist a premature commitment to Toryism, despite his own personal and business ties to the mother country, from which he had emigrated a decade earlier. In 1774 he assured Philadelphia's Charles Thomson that he would listen to the latter's "excellent moral Counsell" against antagonizing patriot colonists, and would be careful to "give no more offence on the score of Impurity." Most certainly, he would be happy to publish the opinions of American partisans in Philadelphia—"and I will use every endeavor to please all my patrons." Through Henry Knox, his Boston correspondent, he also seems to have tried to let John Hancock know that he had meant no harm whatsoever, but had acted merely out of "a necessity," in publishing a letter critical of his conduct. Any appropriate reply, he indicated, would be graciously received and promptly put into print.[65]

That this was an untenable strategy to follow in an era of revolution was tacitly conceded by Rivington in a *Gazetteer* of December 1774, which presented a brief poetic summary of the printer's plight:

> Dares the poor man impartial be,
> He's doom'd to want and infamy.

A week later, a correspondent commended Rivington for following the policy of "a true whig," by remaining "open to all doctrines," but admitted that this could be accomplished "only at the hazard of your fortune and your Life." Circumstances were forcing Rivington to become a partisan. Toryism, after all, might bring its own rewards, which Isaiah Thomas considered "sufficiently apparent" to be left unspecified. Circulating rumors mentioned the sum of £500 as a possible incentive. A boycott was organized against Rivington, and he was hanged in effigy; angry patriots went so far as to threaten his personal safety.[66]

Well into 1775, however, both he and Gaine were still equivocating. Much to the irritation of Lieutenant Governor Golden, Gaine refused to include in his *Mercury* a Tory account of what had happened at Lexington and Concord, and Rivington—who in March had begun to serialize Burke's "Speech on American Taxation"—published two contradictory narratives. For a time, the latter even seemed to make his peace with some of the local patriots. Agreeing that he had "given great Offence to the Colonies," Rivington vowed publicly to make amends, explaining that he had been acting simply in deference to his notions of "the Liberty of the Press" and his "duty as a Printer." Having conformed, he was exonerated by the Provincial Congress, only to lose all of his equipment to a destructive mob, apparently unimpressed by his show of penance. In 1776, he returned to England; Gaine, just before English troops occupied the city, left for Newark.[67]

Both would be back, though. Eventually, war—and the comforting presence of the British army—brought vacillating printers like Gaine and Rivington into the Tory ranks. Once there, they had little choice but to declare their loyalties with a forthrightness that their brethren of an earlier day would have considered most unbusinesslike. Gaine, it seems, deliberated and finally decided that "the strongest party" was encamped in New York; accordingly, he recrossed the Hudson and resumed trade there. Then, in October 1777, Rivington "surprised almost every Body," as Gaine recorded in his journal, by reestablishing himself in the city with new equipment and the title of King's Printer. Plainly, this was bad news for Gaine, although he professed to welcome it; soon he had to take second place to Rivington. Always, Rivington announced in a new version of the *Gazetteer* brought out under the royal arms, he had labored "to keep up and strengthen our Connection with the Mother Country, and to promote a proper Subordination to the Supreme Authority of the British Empire." He hoped that "his former Friends" would recall his services and patronize his office. Having belatedly discovered a firm sense of political principle underlying his previous conduct, Rivington proceeded to make the most of it.[68]

Like Gaine and Rivington, other printers in the colonies moved along the same circuitous route to Toryism, becoming unequivocally onesided printers as much from military circumstance as from political principle or connection. Such camp followers in the trade included John Howe, the Robertson brothers, Mills and Hicks, and James Humphreys, Jr. Once they had made their decisions, they could not easily retrace their steps. No one "can wish more ardently than myself for a peace with America," wrote John Hicks from Charleston in 1782, "but rather than Great Britain should Stoop to acknowledge ye independency of this country I would sacrafice every farthing of my property & then my Person to oppose them." Having been forced to leave Boston, Hicks had tried his hand at a number of different printing jobs and then—after being reunited with his partner Mills, who had spent two intervening years in England—he had opened a luxury import shop in British-controlled South Carolina. By the close of 1782, as the two men told their London supplier, they could only "dread" a parliamentary surrender to American demands.[69]

In the end, like several of their fellow craftsmen who had come to favor the cause of the mother country, Mills and Hicks moved to Nova Scotia.[70] Toryism had been a gamble for them, and they had lost. More generally, traditional trade strategies had proven ineffective in Revolutionary conditions, incapable of protecting and sustaining those American printers who had tried to maintain the "freedom" of their presses to Tory points of view.

5. New Commitments

As the prospects of some colonial printers became uncertain after 1765, with passage of the Stamp Act, those of others looked brighter. Seemingly, what was required was a knack for exploiting the political situation. Benjamin Mecom, Franklin's nephew, was as quick as anyone to see the possibilities of the crisis, although—as always—he lacked the talent to achieve success. Despite the economic burden that the new stamp duties threatened to place on printers, he proposed to establish a newspaper of his own. This was to be a staunchly patriot revival of the *Connecticut Gazette*, aimed at zealous Whigs in New Haven. Rival printers soon moved into town and took away his business by putting out a superior paper, but Mecom had acted in terms of the same strategy followed by Charleston's Charles Crouch and New Hampshire's Thomas Furber, in trying to profit from the partisan fervor of the moment.[71] Especially for a printer of middling prosperity or less, the crisis could be interpreted as an opportunity to get ahead, by riding the waves of political emotion.

Correctly or not, many colonial printers appear to have made optimistic business calculations in response to the political troubles of the 1760s and 1770s, disregarding the economic discouragements first of the Stamp Act and later of the tax on paper included in the Townshend Act.[72] Before war physically disrupted the colonies, the Revolutionary period was a time of expansion in the American printing trade. From 1763 to 1775 the number of master printers at work in colonial America increased from forty-seven to eighty-two, while the number of newspapers that they published doubled, from twenty-one in 1763 to forty-two in 1775.[73] Conditions were such that many men in the trade were ready to try their luck and reach for entrepreneurial success. At least to some, however, it seemed that success was not to be achieved by following traditional routes. The vicissitudes of transatlantic conflict, non-importation in particular, constricted the profits that printers could expect to derive from such allied enterprises as imported books and stationery. At the same time, newspaper circulation increased markedly, reflecting the heightened polemical temperature of colonial journalism. In the circumstances, it was natural enough for some printers to conclude that partisan commitments might prove advantageous. Although it is unclear whether or to what extent purely political printing grew to become a significant business of its own during the Revolutionary years, it was obvious that the political loyalties of printers could be crucial in determining who would be their customers, or readers, and who would not.[74]

Compared with their Tory brethren, many patriot printers saw reason to react to the Revolutionary crisis by making early and relatively unambiguous political moves, accompanied by ardent expressions of high constitutional principle. Their cause, after all, was generally popular—hence likely to be profitable as well. Although some decorated their newspapers with variations on the slogan "Open to ALL Parties, but Influenced by NONE," this was now an empty gesture recalling a policy no longer relevant to the realities of American political controversy.[75]

Despite the persistence of conventional rhetoric, there was emerging a rudimentary alternative to the familiar trade understanding of "liberty of the press." Some of the inevitable verbal confusion accompanying this shift in meaning was evident in an issue of the *Pennsylvania Journal* that appeared in September 1766. Its printers, William Bradford III and his son Thomas, came forward to answer a harsh attack by the local stamp distributor, John Hughes, provoked by their exposé of his political correspondence. In threatening to start a lawsuit, they claimed, Hughes was trying "to demolish the liberty of the Press." But what precisely was that? Although the elder Bradford was a leading Son of Liberty and his paper had firmly opposed the Stamp Act, the Bradfords went on to recite a customary trade refrain. "We are only the printers of a free and impartial paper," they argued, "and we challenge Mr. Hughes and the world, to convict us of partiality in this respect, or of even an inclination to restrain the freedom of the press in any instance." Then, abruptly, they altered their emphasis. "We can appeal to North-America not only for our impartiality as printers," they said, "but also for the great advantages derived to us very lately from the unrestrained liberty, which every Briton claims of communicating his sentiments to the public thro' the channel of the press. What would have become of the liberties of the British Colonies in North-America, if Mr. Hughes's calls on Great Britain had been heard, to restrain the printers here from publishing, what he is pleased to stile *inflammatory pieces?*" Here was a subtle indication that "freedom" might become a word without implications of political neutrality. Like Zenger's paper in an earlier day, the *Pennsylvania Journal* could be considered "free" because it made a stand for "liberty" against the supposedly tyrannical designs of those in power.[76]

A similar distinction was suggested that same year by developments in Virginia. Alexander Purdie was naturally anxious to reassure readers that his new *Virginia Gazette*—unlike its "closed" predecessor—would be "as free as any publick press upon the continent," ready to publish the views even of those parties at odds with the authorities for whom he was official printer. But impartiality was not what would satisfy "some of the hot Burgesses," as Governor Fauquier called them, so William Rind was procured to print a second *Virginia Gazette*. This impressed Thomas Jefferson as truly a "free paper." Although its masthead bore a motto making the familiar promise of openness to all sides, Rind's practical understanding of "freedom" differed from Purdie's. Anticipating in his first issue what would later become more obvious, Rind hinted that he was particularly "free" from the influence of Tories, and highly receptive to patriot viewpoints. In publishing a piece of propaganda put out by the local Sons of Liberty, he also printed their monitory suggestion that by so doing he would give "an early Instance" of his determination to conduct his press with due respect for principles of freedom.[77]

One further indication of a new trade ethic came in 1774, when John Holt chose to respond to accusations in Rivington's *Gazetteer* that the fiery partisanship of his *New-York Journal* was "a flagrant perversion" of "Liberty of the Press." Was he a biased printer, "wholly employed in prosecuting Party Designs"? Holt's reply was not strictly a denial. He was indeed trying "to make the people in general sensible of their just Rights," and to warn them of "the great Danger of losing them." Had he sold himself to those able to offer the most? The ministry, noted Holt, "could bid higher than any Body else, nor are they without Mercenaries even more contemptible than myself"—a jab at Rivington. If "the Public in general" was what the words "highest Bidder" meant, added Holt, then to be sure he was guilty as charged. In fact, just recently his patriot editorial line had brought the *Journal* more than 200 new subscribers. Nevertheless, unwilling to leave the subject on that note of self-interest, Holt proceeded to emphasize a different set of motives; he was himself personally devoted to the American cause. "In short," he concluded, "I have endeavoured to propagate such political Principles . . . as I shall always freely risk my Life to defend." Disingenuous or not, this was a statement that would have been unthinkable for a colonial printer before the Revolutionary era.[78]

Although the old standards and assumptions of the colonial printing fraternity were losing their force, the process of change was uneven and individuals pursued unclear or contradictory objectives. An instructive case is that of Isaiah Thomas, whose original contribution to the American cause was neither prompt nor enthusiastic. Recalling the first appearance of his *Massachusetts Spy* in 1770, he later explained that he had intended the Boston paper to "be free to both parties, which then agitated the country, and, impartially, lay before the public their respective communications." He soon found, however, that "this ground could not be maintained" in the passionate atmosphere of the period. For a few weeks, in accordance with a policy of "openness" proclaimed in its masthead, the *Spy* published some opinion favorable to the claims of the mother country, but not enough to satisfy hard-line Tories in the vicinity. As a result, they turned against Thomas, boycotted his paper, and used the powers of imperial officialdom to harass him. Supported by John Hancock, Joseph Greenleaf, and others whose politics were warm, Thomas with reluctance converted the *Spy* into a stridently one-sided organ of opinion. In "a general commotion of the state," one of his correspondents observed in 1771, "there should be *no neuters*." Though unavoidable and seemingly much to the advantage of the *Spy*, the circulation of which soon exceeded that of any other New England paper, this policy was not altogether to Thomas's liking. The next year, he contemplated abandoning the high road of patriotism in Boston and moving to the West Indies. Because a printer in Boston "must be either of one party or the other (he cannot please both)," he wrote to an acquaintance in Bermuda, "he must therefore incur the censure and displeasure of the opposite party." And "to incur the censure and displeasure of any party or persons, though carressed and encouraged by others," he added, "is disagreeable to me."[79]

Very gradually, despite such uncertainties of purpose and practice, there arose from the Revolutionary experience a revised understanding of what it was to be an American printer. Responding to and perhaps also promoting a new belief that sharply antagonistic opinions might properly be articulated in the public forum, printers in America began to discard their neutral trade rhetoric, in order to behave aggressively and unapologetically as partisans. At the same time, reflecting the more intense ideological content of Revolutionary politics, American printers began to revive the ancient trade refrain of their English forebears. Once again it was insisted that printers were not mere "mechanics" but men of independent intellect and principle.[80]

That this new understanding agreed with the spirit of the time is apparent from the response of patriot wits to the conduct of printers who sided with the mother country. Whether or not their motives were any more mercenary than those of their patriot brethren, Tory printers could not devise a rationale for their business strategies that drew effectively on the prevailing popular creed of "liberty." As one Philadelphian observed in 1774, it was difficult for anyone to print a Tory sentiment without exposing himself to the charge that he had been subsidized by the Treasury in London. Rivington, in particular, was the object of vicious diatribe. He was "not actuated by any Principles" but worked simply as "a tool" of officialdom, in implicit contrast to dedicated patriot printers. "I am . . . literally hired"—so went one parody of his position—"to wage open war with Truth, Honour and Justice." According to a "MIRROR for a PRINTER," submitted in 1774 to John Holt's *Journal* by an anonymous local poet, Rivington operated

> Without one grain of *honest* sense,
> One virtuous view, or *just* pretence

To patriotic flame;
Without a patriotic heart or mind.[81]

Most vulnerable to such satire were those Tory printers who, loath to go into exile, managed to rehabilitate themselves after their cause had failed. Rivington was perhaps acting as a double-spy by 1781, whereby he may have earned permission to remain in New York and carry on his trade after the war. By means of skillful but less desperate footwork, Hugh Gaine was able to rescue his reputation and stay on. Elsewhere, Georgia's James Johnston and Pennsylvania's Benjamin Towne were also able to negotiate abrupt reversals. Towne's political loyalties were more spectacularly erratic than those of any other colonial printer. Originally associated with Joseph Galloway and his friends, he later became a stout Whig and drove James Humphreys, Jr., from Philadelphia by prematurely branding him a Tory. Once British troops had taken over the city, Towne switched sides—and was promptly attained as a traitor by the patriots. After Philadelphia had been retaken, he changed his colors again, and succeeded in escaping prosecution.[82]

New York's two outstanding examples of unpunished fickleness inspired Philip Freneau to compose biting doggerel. "As matters have gone," he had Hugh Gaine say of his initial decision to join the Tories,

it was plainly a blunder,
But *then* I expected the whigs must knock under,
And I always adhere to the sword that is longest,
And stick to the party that's like to be strongest.

A comparable calculation underlay Rivington's subsequent desertion of King George:

On the very same day that his army went hence,
I ceas'd to tell lies for the sake of his pence;
And what was the reason—the true one is best;
I worship no suns that decline to the west;
In this I resemble a Turk or a Moor,
The day star ascending I prostrate adore.[83]

Lack of principle, it seems, was the major offense committed by these two men, and the charge itself was a sign that expectations concerning the responsibilities of American printers were being reshaped by the Revolutionary conflict.

This change was revealed strikingly in John Witherspoon's prose satire upon Benjamin Towne's last political conversion. Towne's conduct, according to Witherspoon, was due to nothing more than "desire for gain," since he was utterly indifferent to the content of what he published. "I never was, nor ever pretended to be a man of character, repute or dignity," conceded Witherspoon's lampoon version of the capricious Philadelphia printer. Echoing a pre-Revolutionary formula of the American trade, Witherspoon had Towne explain that he was "neither Whig nor Tory, but a printer."[84] The disarmingly self-deprecatory style of Franklin's "Apology" had become the stuff of satire.

There would still be printers—New Jersey's Isaac Collins, for one—who continued to follow the traditional strategy, claiming that they hoped to please as many people as possible even during the most heated political struggles. For some, on the other hand, it became almost obligatory to assert their own principles. In 1770, when William Goddard wrote and published a lengthy defense of his stormy partnership with Joseph Galloway and Thomas Wharton, the old role and the new were balanced uneasily. In 1766, soon after printing an emphatically patriot *Constitutional Courant* in Woodbridge, New Jersey, Goddard had showed up in Philadelphia—"on speculation," as he put it. As it turned out, he was "misled" by Galloway's promises of support into forming an unnatural alliance with men whom he later came to regard as "enemies to their country." Explaining his decision to strike out on a more independent path, Goddard relied in part on trade custom. It was his policy, he said, to act "in the most impartial and just manner" in order to promote his own interest "without becoming a party in any disputes." Being implacable party men, Galloway and Wharton would not permit their printer to be true to the traditions of his craft. At the same time, Goddard offered another, less conventional apology for quarreling with his employers. Against Galloway's wishes, he had printed Dickinson's *Farmer's Letters* because he thought "they deserved the serious attention of all *North-America*." Apparently this initiative took his partners by surprise. "Mr. *Galloway*," Goddard remembered, "ridiculed my notions about liberty and the rights of mankind."[85]

Such ridicule was understandable enough. Unlike the European founders of their craft, printers in colonial America had neither professed nor been expected to have notions of any sort; they were supposed to make and sell their product indifferently, to suit this or that customer. During and after the Revolution, expectations came to differ. It was in the war years, for example, that the printer of Hartford's *Courant*, George Goodwin, first explicitly identified himself as an "editor." In Massachusetts, glossing over his reluctance to deviate from neutral trade policies, Isaiah Thomas subsequently insisted that he had given the *Spy* "a fixed character" consistent with his own patriot beliefs.[86]

In 1785, when the state of Massachusetts attempted to raise a revenue for itself by imposing stamp duties, the printing trade was piously indignant. The new tax, it was said, would lead to "the ruin of a set of artisans" whose exertions in the Revolutionary movement should have guaranteed them "a more liberal fate." Thomas's paper registered special outrage. "Generous Reader," it made a point of stressing, "the services rendered by the SPY to the Publick, were not for the sake of sordid gain, but from *Principle*."[87]

Late in the century, Benjamin Edes—a former Son of Liberty—would conjure up an image of himself standing forth as "an undaunted Centinel in those times which 'tried men's souls' . . ., when the hope of gain could not be considered as the lure to pretended Patriotism." However self-serving, his words did reflect the new rhetoric of ideological commitment that had entered the trade during the Revolutionary years. With that commitment went pride. The newspapers of colonial America, John Holt told Samuel Adams in 1776, had first received "Notice of the tyrannical Designs formed against America," and generated a response "sufficient to repel them."[88]

When Virginia's Governor Dunmore seized the patriot Norfolk press of John Holt's son, in 1775, there was an appropriate echo of the past in the words with which he justified the action. Thus would be suppressed "the means of poisoning the minds of the people," and arousing "the spirit of rebellion and sedition."[89] More than 100 years had passed since Governor Berkeley had warned of the disastrous consequences that would accompany the introduction of printing into Virginia. Alarmist as Berkeley's reaction had been, it had pointed to a distant future. For much of the eighteenth century American printers had followed business and political strategies that impeded the flow of diverse and dissident opinion into the public forum. But during the Revolutionary years the trade adapted to a new politics of controversy. By so doing, printers seemed assured of recognition as major figures in the political life of the republic. Presiding over a press transformed by the pressures of the Revolution, they would be free to report basic conflicts and disputes as well as remote "occurrences"; they would be expected not only to register events but to make and modify them.

6. '76 In Retrospect

Long after Independence, as the machinery of the new American party system came to be elaborated at both national and state levels, printers continued to express satisfaction at the expanding importance of the press. Newspapers "exert a controlling influence on public opinion, and decide almost all questions of a public nature," boasted one Boston printer before a gathering of his brethren in the third decade of the new century. Partisan journalism was a well-established feature of American politics.[90]

Undeniably powerful as the press had become, however, this was not to say that nineteenth-century American printers had succeeded in realizing the promise of the role fashioned for them during the Revolutionary years. Gradually, in a sequence of developments that in some respects resembled what had happened to the London trade more than a century before, printers in republican America had to withdraw from entrepreneurial activities previously associated with their craft skills. The trend in American publishing—accelerated by the introduction of costly new technology that opened up larger markets—was toward specialization. A "publisher" with capital would hire printers and others to produce the goods he wished to sell.[91] An exceptionally enterprising printer like Isaiah Thomas could count himself among the ranks of leading publishers, much as the London printer William Strahan had done in the eighteenth century, by investing capital in copyright and book production. But it soon came to appear that only in the "yet almost uncorrupted West" could the average printer still realistically plan to build the diversified business and act the prominent part in his community characteristic of the trade in colonial days. So, early in the century, one New Yorker with "utopian expectations" reportedly resolved to go west "to give elevation to the art of Printing." Remaining in the settled sections of the country, a printer might well have to relinquish his hopes of becoming a publisher as well.[92]

From the perspective of most printers, unprepared and unwilling to adjust to such changes, the conditions of the trade had deteriorated alarmingly. Like other artisans of the period, they turned to verse and song at their fraternal gatherings to share and perhaps alleviate their experiences of hardship. Pervading the folklore of post-Revolutionary American printers, whose "sorrows, sufferings, cares and strife" followed them "like their shadows . . . through life," was a bitter sense of economic ruin. "Sheriff," went one seriocomic poem,

> . . . spare that press;
> Touch not a single type;
> Don't put me in distress,
> To stick to me through life.

'Tis all in all to me;
If lost, what shall I do?
Then why not let it be,
Oh, sheriff, boo hoo hoo.[93]

For journeymen, grievances multiplied early in the century and soon prompted organized protest. Their wages were said to be lagging behind those of other mechanics; new machinery seemed to threaten some jobs, while employers tried to cut costs by hiring foreign or inadequately trained native labor. According to one estimate of 1809, the situation in New York was so bleak that nearly half of those who completed their apprenticeships as printers were forced eventually to abandon their trade altogether and look for other kinds of work. Chief among the villains, as journeymen in Philadelphia viewed matters about the same time, were "the gang of pettifogging master printers," whose dedication to the welfare of the trade as a whole was appreciably less heartfelt than their individual desires for gain.[94]

Over time, the intensity of this particular antagonism seems to have subsided, to be replaced by a broader range of complaint with which many employers as well as employees in the trade could sympathize. Again and again, most regularly in the 1830s, public expressions of protest focused not on exploitation of journeymen by master printers but on exploitation of the entire craft by outside entrepreneurs. Such people, "speculating on the labor of printers," were out to reduce everyone in the trade to poverty, according to some contemporaries. Perhaps most damaging to the traditional craft pride of American printers, long accustomed to function as newspaper proprietors, was the appearance of "professional" or "hireling" editors, who worked under contract to entrepreneurial publishers. Usually these new editors were lawyers. By midcentury, it had become rare for a printer in an urban center to edit a paper of his own.[95]

Like their English brethren of a previous era, many American printers in the early nineteenth century declined to accept passively the implications of the new economic order. Summoning up legends of learned Europeans in the trade, they began to affirm with an insistence unknown before in America that printers had contributed significantly and uniquely to the progress of western civilization. The art of printing, according to one of its New York practitioners in 1801, "is the parent of every other"— "an Art, the adoption of which has, in some degree, banished baleful superstition from the world, and in its stead reason and philosophy have found sanctuary in the mind of man." Another New York printer some years later called it "an art truly divine," without which the human intellect forever "might have slumbered in the lap of ignorance."[96]

The irony beneath this fulsome oratory, applied specifically to the situation of American printers, was obliquely acknowledged in the wordplay of one printer's song:

Though I'm not skill'd in Greek or Latin lore,
Nor ancient Hebrew in days of yore,
With due submission I inform my betters,
That I can boast I am a man of *letters*.

But others in the trade were less inclined to admit so humorously the discrepancy between their intellectual aspirations and reality. In the glorious career of Benjamin

Franklin, above all, they found inspiration. As one printer in Boston chose to interpret the biographical facts, Franklin had made of printing "the instrument of his own fame," rising through his craft to become "a scholar, statesman, and philosopher." Despite discouraging trade conditions, Franklin's successors had only to follow in his footsteps to redeem their fraternal heritage. "The next in rank," continued the same Boston printer, ". . . is ISAIAH THOMAS."[97]

Thomas, indeed, emulated "learned" European predecessors not only by writing his *History* but by founding the American Antiquarian Society. His natural successor was Boston's Joseph Buckingham, whose career epitomized the post-Revolutionary sensibilities of the trade. Born just a few years after Independence, he had been impressed as a young man with the "dignity and importance" of printing a newspaper, and so determined to learn the craft. Like Franklin, he read voraciously, stressing grammar in his self-education. "I foresaw that it would be useful to me, as a printer," he later explained, "but indispensable as an editor,—a profession, to which I looked forward as the consummation of my ambition." From the beginning, he recalled, "I found it difficult to repress my aspirations to display my intellectual as well as my industrial and mechanical abilities." Eventually, having satisfied himself by building a reputation as a journalist with a mind of his own, he assumed "the character and pursuits of a scholar" to edit a sequel to Thomas's *History*, a two-volume historical anthology called *Specimens of Newspaper Literature*, published in 1850.[98]

Other American printers, too, refused to limit their intellectual prerogatives and be demoted to mere mechanics. In 1808, Boston's Society of Printers—of which Buckingham was a leading member—went so far as to change its name to the Faustus Society, because the old name was "too narrow and confined to embrace the higher branches of our profession, which are not *mechanical*, nor bounded by rules, but which soar to improvements as valuable to science and humanity as those which have immortalized the discovery of Faustus." The New-York Typographical Society, for its part, included men of recognizable "intellectual, moral, and social worth," not least its one-time president Peter Force, later an active antiquarian and editor of historical documents.[99]

"I have heard old journeymen claim that it was a Profession," William Dean Howells wrote of printing at the very end of the century, "and ought to rank with the learned professions." Himself the son of a printer, Howells remembered well one youth who had entered his father's shop "with the wish to be a printer because Franklin had been one, and with the intent of making the office his University." Such purposefulness may not have been uncommon in the nineteenth-century trade. "Let it not be to any a subject of special wonder," announced the preface to a mid-century collection of literature written by printers, "that they who have so often assisted in ushering into the world the productions of others should now in turn venture to originate ideas of their own, and appear before the public in the ambitious character of Authors." In fact, several of the century's most distinguished American writers—Walt Whitman and Mark Twain as well as Howells among them—had worked as young men in printing shops.[100]

Some notable political personalities, too, began their careers as members of the trade, often entering politics through journalism. "Printers should never lose sight of the dignity of their profession," observed a members of the fraternity, "for the most eminent men have embraced it." One was the Republican politician Thurlow Weed, who made a point in his memoirs of emphasizing that several of his journeymen acquaintances in the trade had been endowed with "decided literary taste and acquire-ments." Another was Horace Greeley, for whom entry into the trade had marked the beginning of his escape from the *mindless monotonous drudgery*" of farming. Governors, legislators, diplomats, mayors—printers were pleased to record that among their brethren were occupants of the highest offices in the land.[101]

These of course were uncommon men, but ordinary printers could and did also claim a place of special importance in public life. Out of their Revolutionary heritage, they tried to assert a role less prominent but perhaps ultimately more rewarding. "Among the gloriously congenial effects, produced by the ART OF PRINTING," declaimed a patriotic speaker in 1802 at the Boston Franklin Association, "no one is so conspicuous on the roll of fame, as the FOURTH OF JULY, 1776!" Throughout the early decades of the nineteenth century, similar sentiments were repeatedly expressed by printers before assemblages of their brethren. According to the prize-winning ode at a July 4th celebration of the New-York Typographical Society in 1811,

> . . . Heaven decreed
> That Columbia be freed,
> And *Printing* and valour accomplish'd the deed.
> The banner of war was by Justice unfurl'd,
> And Freedom by Printing proclaim'd to the world.[102]

It was in this self-congratulatory spirit that at one banquet of printers a toast was offered to the Declaration of Independence—"From the *Press* of Franklin and Com-pany." As late as 1834, a grandson of the famed patriot printer William Bradford III could argue feelingly that his father, the printer Thomas Bradford, was entitled to a Revolutionary war pension because publication of the *Pennsylvania Journal* had been "*of more value to the cause of American freedom than if he had for six years commanded a regiment in the field*." Isaiah Thomas probably did more than anyone else to sustain such affirm-ations, having labored over his hagiographical *History* to demonstrate as fully as possible that the press "had a powerful influence in producing the revolution."[103]

Faithful to the relatively recent political traditions of the trade, it was understand-able if a printer in the new republic should want to refer hyperbolically to the press as "one of the most deadly engines of destruction that can possibly be arrayed against the encroachments of despotic power." Especially in America, where newspapers were so widespread as to be considered among "the necessaries of life," printers had awesome public responsibilities. Since a "free press" was "the people's surest safeguard," it was vitally important for printers to "support the right, and wrong attack"—and "tweak the despot's nose."[104]

As custodians of the public welfare, too, printers could hope to make an unusually forceful case in protesting the very economic conditions that had conspired to diminish their livelihoods and undermine their social standing. The narrow interests of the trade, it seemed, were linked to the well-being of the larger American public. For if printers were the "natural guardians" of a free press, it was their duty as citizens and the duty of the general citizenry as well to resist usurpation by "hireling editors," subservient to combinations of wealthy individuals. To retain control of the press, thereby preserving its integrity, would require of printers much the same degree of "jealous regard and sleepless vigilance" that had marked their Revolutionary forebears—the generation memorialized by Isaiah Thomas.[105]

Appropriately, "independence" was a key word in the vocabulary of socioeconomic complaint by printers in early nineteenth-century America. As with other struggling mechanics at the time, *independence* signified desirable conditions of work and unoppressive structures of economic life; most emphatically for printers, the word also brought to mind crucial political experiences of a previous era. In 1826, at the Franklin Typographical Society in Boston, current aspirations and historical memories mingled revealingly in an elaborate toast:

> *Getting under weigh*—the good ship *Typographical*, Captain *Franklin*, with a *true hearted crew, bound on a voyage* of *charity, sailing* in the *current of public opinion*, with *favourable breezes*, and taking the correct *course of truth, honesty*, and *sobriety*; keeping out of the *calm latitudes* of *idleness* and *gulph* of *intemperance*; avoiding the *rocks* of *dissipation*; *steering clear* of the *shoals* of *poverty*, and *touching* at the *port* of *benevolence*, may she *finally arrive* in *safety*, in the *harbour* of INDEPENDENCE.[106]

They have been called "intellectuals of the working class." Whatever the merits of that designation, printers in early nineteenth-century Europe joined the ideological vanguard of the first workingmen's movements. That this was so in America as well, despite the bland politics of the eighteenth-century trade, reflected the strong impact of the Revolution upon their occupational identity.[107]

Historical ironies aside, which might have been grimly pleasurable to a loyalist like Peter Oliver, it was peculiarly fitting that in 1856 the 150th anniversary of Benjamin Franklin's birth should have been celebrated in the city of Boston by a huge self-assertive parade of patriotic mechanics, in which the printing fraternity was separated from most other groups of mechanics by being designated one of the "mechanical professions."[108] Franklin himself had been more of a mechanic than sometimes he had cared to admit, and less of a Revolutionary; for American printers by the middle of the nineteenth century, the meaning of both experiences had been redefined, and fused symbolically in his name.

Notes

1   Isaiah Thomas, *The History of Printing in America*, 2 vols. (Worcester, Mass., 1810), 2: 517–52; citations throughout are to the original version of this work, but see also Marcus A. McCorison's 1-volume annotated Imprint Society Edition (Barre, Mass., 1970).

2. Quoted in Thomas, *History of Printing*, 2: 403. Earlier, according to Miller, newspapers had been mostly restricted to "mere statement of *facts*."

3. James Fenimore Cooper, *The Crater*, ed. Thomas Philbrick (Cambridge, Mass., 1962), pp. 374–75, 432–38.

4. Thomas, *History of Printing*, 2: 139.

5. *Peter Oliver's Origin & Progress of the American Rebellion*, ed. Douglass Adair and John A. Schutz (San Marino, Calif., 1963), p. 79.

6. John Hughes to Stamp Office Commissioners, Oct. 12, 1765, as reprinted in *Pennsylvania Journal*, Sept. 4, 1766; appointed to the office of stamp distributor in Philadelphia, Hughes was unable to put the new Stamp Act into practice.

7. By "occupational ideology" is meant the general system of values and beliefs espoused by printers, arising out of but not limited to trade activities. See Vernon K. Dibble, "Occupations and Ideologies," *American Journal of Sociology* 68 (1962–63): 229–41.

8. Franklin to Richard Bache, Nov. 11, 1784, *The Writings of Benjamin Franklin*, ed. Albert Henry Smyth, 10 vols. (New York, 1907), 9: 278–9; Franklin to Madame Brillon, Apr. 19, 1788, ibid., pp. 643–45; John Clyde Oswald, *Benjamin Franklin, Printer* (Garden City, N.Y., 1917), chap. 15.

9. For more elaborate documentation of what follows, in part 2, see Stephen Botein, " 'Meer Mechanics' and an Open Press: The Business and Political Strategies of Colonial American Printers," *Perspectives in American History* 9 (1975): 130–211.

10. Marjorie Plant, *The English Book Trade: An Economic History of the Making and Sale of Books*, 2d ed. (London, 1965), pp. 59–62, and see generally A. S. Collins, *Authorship in the Days of Johnson* (London, 1927).

11. *A Brief Discourse Concerning Printing and Printers* (London, 1663), pp. 4–5; Cyprian Blagden, *The Stationers' Company: A History, 1403–1959* (Cambridge, Mass., 1960), pp. 147–8.

12. Strahan to David Hall, July 15, 1771, Miscellaneous Collections, Historical Society of Pennsylvania, Philadelphia, and see generally J. A. Cochrane, *Dr. Johnson's Printer: The Life of William Strahan* (Cambridge, Mass., 1964).

13. *The Papers of Benjamin Franklin*, ed. Leonard W. Labaree et al. (New Haven, 1959–), 17: 315–16n. (hereafter cited as *Franklin Papers*); *The Speech of Mr Jacob Ilive to His Brethren the Master-Printers* (London, 1750), pp. 4, 6–7.

14. Plant, *English Book Trade*, p. 32; *Brief Discourse*, pp. 18, 15, 23.

15. Samuel Richardson, author of *Pamela*, was the most celebrated literary printer in the mother country; see William M. Sale, Jr., *Samuel Richardson: Master Printer* (Ithaca, N.Y., 1950). A less ambitious figure was Samuel Palmer, an employer of Franklin and author of *The General History of Printing* (London, 1732).

16. "All publications of consequence, in point of size and expence," wrote an English observer as late as 1789, "are executed in Europe." *Bibliotheca Americana* (London, 1789), p. 14.

17. On provincial English printers, see Geoffrey Alan Cranfield, *The Development of the Provincial Newspaper, 1700–1760* (Oxford, 1962); Roy M. Wiles, *Freshest Advices: Early Provincial Newspapers in England* (Columbus, Ohio, 1965).

18. The best general account of the American trade is still Lawrence C. Wroth, *The Colonial Printer*, 2d ed. (Portland, Me., 1938); on diversity of enterprise, see esp. chap. 9.

19. Thomas, *History of Printing*, 1: 351.

20. *The Autobiography of Benjamin Franklin*, ed. Leonard W. Labaree et al. (New Haven, 1964), p. 58; Franklin to Strahan, Nov. 4, 1754, *Franklin Papers*, 5: 439–40.

21. Thus, in 1753, when Hugh Gaine attempted to defend himself against opponents of his *New-York Mercury*, he felt compelled to apologize for his audacity. It was a departure, he conceded, "to appear in print in any other Manner, than what merely pertains to the Station of Life in which I am placed." *New-York Mercury*, Sept. 3, 1753.

22. *American Weekly Mercury*, Nov. 20, 1740. The literary dimension of Franklin's printing career is discussed in James A. Sappenfield, *A Sweet Instruction: Franklin's Journalism as a Literary Apprenticeship* (Carbondale, Ill., 1973).

23. *Autobiography of Franklin*, pp. 195–6.

24. See Cranfield, *Development of the Provincial Newspaper*, p. 118; Wiles, *Freshest Advices*, pp. 33–4, 292. The London pattern is illustrated in Sale, *Samuel Richardson*, pp. 54–9, and treated more generally in Laurence Hanson, *Government and the Press, 1695–1763* (London, 1936).

25. The literature on liberty of expression in the colonies is vast but mainly tangential to the point here, since most of what has been written does not take into account the perspectives of printers. A useful overview of some general issues raised by the secondary literature may be found in Leonard W. Levy's preface to the paperback edition of his *Legacy of Suppression*, published as *Freedom of Speech and Press in Early American History: Legacy of Suppression* (New York, 1963). For a view that differs from what follows, see Lawrence H. Leder, *Liberty and Authority in Early American Political Ideology, 1689–1763* (Chicago, 1968), chap. 1.

26. John William Wallace, *An Address Delivered at the Celebration . . . of the Two Hundredth Birth Day of Mr. William Bradford* (Albany, N.Y., 1863), pp. 49–52.

27. *Pennsylvania Gazette*, June 10, 1731. Whether or how a newspaper contributor was expected to pay is unclear, but the possibility was certainly contemplated in the well-known "Stage Coach" metaphor to which Franklin referred in his autobiography. (Anyone willing to pay had "a Right to a Place." *Autobiography of Franklin*, p. 175.) On the other hand, there is no

evidence to suggest that in practice printers of colonial newspapers routinely received payments from contributors or that they gave weight to the prospect of such payments in their business calculations. (Accusations that they did were rarely made before the Revolutionary period.) By accepting or rejecting controversial articles, they figured that they might gain or lose subscribers or—and this was doubtless more important—other kinds of printing business.

28. *Pennsylvania Gazette*, June 10, 1731.
29. See generally Livingston Rutherford, *John Peter Zenger, His Press, His Trial, and a Bibliography of Zenger Imprints* (New York, 1904); Harold Lester Dean, "The *New-England Courant*, 1721–1726: A Chapter in the History of American Culture" (Ph.D diss., Brown University, 1943).
30. *Pennsylvania Gazette*, June 10, 1731; *Autobiography of Franklin*, p. 165. From one point of view, James Morton Smith, *William and Mary Quarterly*, 3d ser. 20 (1963): 157–9, is probably correct in arguing that in practice—regardless of prevailing legal doctrine—there was considerable freedom in the American colonies from official coercion of the press. Self-censorship on the basis of business strategy, however, made the colonial press far less "radical" than Gary B. Nash suggests in "The Transformation of Urban Politics, 1700–1765," *Journal of American History* 60 (1973–74): 606, 616–18.
31. On the influence of political writers like Trenchard and Gordon, see Gary Huxford, "The English Libertarian Tradition in the Colonial Newspaper," *Journalism Quarterly* 45 (1968): 677–86, but the argument there ignores an important contrary tradition; see, for example, Elizabeth Christine Cook, *Literary Influences in Colonial Newspapers, 1705–1750* (New York, 1912), p. 125.
32. The convenience of foreign news has been noted with regard to the provincial English press by Cranfield, *Development of the Provincial Newspaper*, p. 67; the point applies equally well to America. *Rhode-Island Gazette*, Nov. 23, 1732.
33. Ramsay's observations were cited approvingly by Arthur M. Schlesinger, *Prelude to Independence: The Newspaper War on Britain, 1764–1776* (New York, 1958), which greatly elaborated on the theme; a more recent discussion along the same lines is provided by Francis G. Walett, "The Impact of the Stamp Act on the Colonial Press," in Donovan H. Bond and W. Reynolds McLeod, eds., *Newsletters to Newspapers: Eighteenth-Century Journalism* (Morgantown, W.Va., 1977), pp. 157–69. An abbreviated version of the analysis that follows, through part 5, appeared in Botein, " 'Meer Mechanics' and an Open Press," pp. 211–25.
34. Franklin to David Hall, Feb. 14, 1765, *Franklin Papers*, 12: 65–7.
35. On English experience, which suggested that the "vent" of newspapers depended less upon price than upon "circumstances of the times exciting more or less curiosity," see Frederick S. Siebert, "Taxes on Publications in England in the Eighteenth Century," *Journalism Quarterly* 21 (1944): 12–24; Edward Hughes, "The English Stamp Duties, 1664–1774," *English Historical Review* 56 (1951): 234–64.
36. On the problems of printers in provincial England, see Cranfield, *Development of the Provincial Newspaper*, pp. 44–7, 237–40; Wiles, *Freshest Advices*, pp. 98–103. Colonial experience is discussed by Mack Thompson, "Massachusetts and New York Stamp Acts," *William and Mary Quarterly*, 3d ser. 26 (1969): 253–8. The distress of printers in Massachusetts is mentioned by Thomas, *History of Printing*, 2: 186n, 232, 238–41. The effects of similar legislation in New York, "like to a killing Frost," were vividly described at the time in a printer's broadside; "James Parker *versus* New York Province," ed. Beverly McAnear, *New York History* 22 (1941): 321–2, 326–8, 330n. Parker's reaction to the new parliamentary statute, illustrated below, was perhaps predictable.
37. Hall to Strahan, May 19, 1765, David Hall Papers, American Philosophical Society, Philadelphia; Parker to Franklin, Apr. 25, June 14, 1765, *Franklin Papers*, 12: 111–13, 174–6.
38. Their basic assumption was that Hall would be able to add the tax to his prices and inaugurate a policy of payment in advance. Franklin to Hall, June 8, 1765, *Franklin Papers*, 12: 170–2; Strahan to Hall, July 8, 1765, David Hall Papers.
39. Thomas, *History of Printing*, 2: 189.
40. Hall to Franklin, June 20, 1765, *Franklin Papers*, 12: 188–9; Hall to Strahan, Sept. 6, 1765, David Hall Papers.

41. Hall to Strahan, Sept. 19, 1765, David Hall Papers. Hall to Franklin, Sept. 6, Oct. 14, 1765, *Franklin Papers*, 12: 255–9, 319–21. See generally Robert D. Harlan, "David Hall and the Stamp Act," *Papers of the Bibliographical Society of America* 61 (1967): 13–37.

42. Schlesinger, *Prelude to Independence*, pp. 77–8.

43. Timothy to Franklin, Sept. 3, 1768, *Franklin Papers*, 15: 199–203; Hennig Cohen, *The South Carolina Gazette, 1732–1775* (Columbia, S.C., 1953), p. 142; Schlesinger, *Prelude to Independence*, pp. 78–9; Thomas, *History of Printing*, 2: 160–1, 370–1.

44. Cohen, *South Carolina Gazette*, pp. 13, 244–7; Schlesinger, *Prelude to Independence*, pp. 126–7. Timothy to Franklin, Aug. 24, 1772, *Franklin Papers*, 19: 283–5; June 12, 1777, in "The Correspondence of Peter Timothy, Printer of Charlestown, with Benjamin Franklin," ed. Douglas C. McMurtrie, *South Carolina Historical and Genealogical Magazine* 35 (1934): 128–9.

45. Parker to Franklin, June 14, Sept. 22, Oct. 10, Nov. 6, 1765, *Franklin Papers*, 12: 174–6, 274–7, 308–10, 355. Parker's eagerness to avoid trouble may have been heightened as a result of his apparently inadvertent connection with the notorious *Constitutional Courant*, an extraordinary one-issue journal of radical propaganda that William Goddard—then associated with John Holt—seems to have printed on Parker's press at Woodbridge, presumably without Parker's permission. See ibid., pp. 287–8n, and Ward L. Miner, *William Goddard, Newspaperman* (Durham, N.C., 1962), pp. 50–2. Schlesinger, *Prelude to Independence*, p. 111, misleadingly groups Parker with Holt as "devoted patriots."

46. Parker to Franklin, June 11, May 6, Oct. 25, 1766, *Franklin Papers*, 13: 300–312, 262–6, 472–6.

47. Beverly McAnear, "James Parker *versus* John Holt," *Proceedings of the New Jersey Historical Society* 59 (1941): 88–95, 199. Parker to Franklin, Sept. 11, Oct. 11, 1766, *Franklin Papers*, 13: 409–13, 454–9; Jan. 21, 1768, ibid., 15: 27–8.

48. Parker to Franklin, April 18, 1768, ibid., 15: 100–2; May 30, 1769, ibid., 16: 137–40. Thomas, *History of Printing*, 2: 479–83; Schlesinger, *Prelude to Independence*, pp. 114–15.

49. Franklin to Hall, June 8, 1765, *Franklin Papers*, 12: 170–2. The charge that Franklin used his trade connections for political advantage became especially pointed as a result of his role in the Hutchinson letters controversy. *Writings of Franklin*, 6: 286–8, and see more generally *Benjamin Franklin's Letters to the Press*, ed. Verner W. Crane (Chapel Hill, 1950).

50. See, for example, Gerald Stourzh, *Benjamin Franklin and American Foreign Policy* (Chicago, 1954); Richard Bushman, "On the Uses of Psychology: Conflict and Conciliation in Benjamin Franklin," *History and Theory* 5 (1966): 227–40. Another interpretation of Franklin's outlook as a printer—which does not take into account the habits of a provincial tradesman—is to be found in Lewis T. Simpson, "The Printer as a Man of Letters: Franklin and the Symbolism of the Third Realm," in J. A. Leo Lemay, ed., *The Oldest Revolutionary: Essays on Benjamin Franklin*, (Philadelphia, 1976), pp. 3–20.

51. *Franklin's Letters to the Press*, p. xxxvii. Benjamin Franklin to William Franklin, Nov. 25, Dec. 29, 1767, *Franklin Papers*, 14: 322–6, 349–51.

52. *Writings of Franklin*, 6: 260. This observation appeared in an apologetic tract of 1774 that went unpublished during his lifetime. To English radicals like Thomas Hollis, too, Franklin was a "doubtful Character." See, for example, Franklin to Thomas Brand Hollis, Oct. 5, 1783, ibid., 9: 103–5.

53. Hall to Franklin, Sept. 6, 1765, *Franklin Papers*, 12: 255–9; Franklin to Hall, Sept. 14, 1765, ibid., 12: 267–8. Indeed, Franklin's custom of publishing softened versions of his opinions in London—which were then reprinted in colonial newspapers—was especially damaging to his reputation at home; see ibid., p. 207n. Of course, his position at the head of the colonial post office and the political ambitions of his son also complicated his role in London.

54. Miner, *William Goddard*, pp. 163–4; Franklin to Timothy, Nov. 3, 1772, *Franklin Papers*, 19: 362; and see David Freeman Hawke, *Franklin* (New York, 1976), chaps. 29–30.

55. Sidney Kobre, *The Development of the Colonial Newspaper* (Pittsburgh, 1944), pp. 147–8, lists 39 newspapers as patriot, 18 as Tory—which is probably as useful a ratio as any, since it was mainly by the contents of their papers that colonial printers signalled their loyalties.

56. Charles Christopher Crittenden, *North Carolina Newspapers before 1790* (Chapel Hill, 1928), pp. 36–8; D. L. Hawkins, "James Adams, The First Printer of Delaware," *Papers of the*

Bibliographical Society of America 28 (1934): 45–6; David K. Skaggs, "Editorial Policies of the *Maryland Gazette*, 1765–1783," *Maryland Historical Magazine* 59 (1964): 346.

57. Thomas, *History of Printing*, 2: 333–4; Schlesinger, *Prelude to Independence*, p. 93; *Boston Evening-Post*, Mar. 6, Apr. 10, 17, 24, 1775. Mary Ann Yodelis, *Who Paid the Piper? Publishing Economics in Boston, 1763–1775* (Lexington, Ky., 1975), pp. 11–13, indicates that the Fleets' general printing business did not suffer especially before the outbreak of war; it was their newspaper that was vulnerable.

58. Alexander A. Lawrence, *James Johnston: Georgia's First Printer* (Savannah, 1956), pp. 10–22; Philip Davidson, *Propaganda and the American Revolution, 1763–1783* (Chapel Hill, 1941), pp. 304–7; Thomas, *History of Printing*, 2: 333–4.

59. Clyde Augustus Duniway, *The Development of Freedom of the Press in Massachusetts* (New York, 1906), p. 172; Thomas, *History of Printing*, 2: 281–4, 1: 434.

60. Ibid., 2: 283–4; *New-Hampshire Gazette*, Nov. 20, 1772; Schlesinger, *Prelude to Independence*, p. 221; Ralph H. Brown, "New Hampshire Editors Win the War," *New England Quarterly* 12 (1939): 35–51.

61. Thomas, *History of Printing*, 1: 347–8; O. M. Dickerson, "British Control of American Newspapers on the Eve of the Revolution," *New England Quarterly* 24 (1951): 455–9.

62. Joseph T. Buckingham, *Specimens of Newspaper Literature*, 2 vols. (Boston, 1850), 1: 213; John E. Alden, "John Mein: Scourge of Patriots," *Publications of the Colonial Society of Massachusetts* 34 (1937–42): 582–3, and 571–99 in general; "The Letter-Book of Mills & Hicks," ed. Robert Earle Moody and Charles Christopher Crittenden, *North Carolina Historical Review* 14 (1937): 39–41; Thomas, *History of Printing*, 1: 389–91.

63. *Pennsylvania Journal*, Oct. 19, 1774. Thomas, *History of Printing*, 2: 300; *The Journals of Hugh Gaine, Printer*, ed. Paul Leicester Ford, 2 vols. (New York, 1902), 1: 51–2; *Rivington's New-York Gazetteer*, Apr. 22, 1773. Rivington's goals may have been quite conventional at the outset. According to Thomas, *History of Printing*, 2: 315–16, no American paper was "better printed, or more copiously furnished with foreign intelligence" than the *Gazetteer*.

64. *New-York Gazette; and the Weekly Mercury* (the formal title of Gaine's paper after 1768), July 25, 1774; *Rivington's New-York Gazetleer*, July 14, Aug. 11, Dec. 8, 1774.

65. Rivington to Thomson, June 24, 1774, Bradford Papers, Historical Society of Pennsylvania, Philadelphia; Rivington to Knox, Apr. 20, 1774, in "Henry Knox, Bookseller," *Proceedings of the Massachusetts Historical Society* 61 (1927–28): 279–81. See generally Leroy Hewlett, "James Rivington, Loyalist Printer, Publisher, and Bookseller of the American Revolution, 1724–1802" (Ph.D. diss., University of Michigan, 1958), chap. 2.

66. *Rivington's New-York Gazetteer*, Dec. 8, 15, 1774; Thomas, *History of Printing*, 2: 113; Hewlett, "James Rivington," chap. 3. Further information about Rivington, for these and subsequent years, may be found in *Rivington's New York Newspaper: Excerpts from a Loyalist Press, 1773–1783*, Collections of the New-York Historical Society, vol. 84 (New York, 1973), pp. 1–27; Robert M. Ours, "James Rivington: Another Viewpoint," in Bond and McLeod, eds., *Newsletters to Newspapers*, pp. 219–33.

67. *Journals of Hugh Gaine*, 1: 52, and see generally Alfred Lawrence Lorenz, *Hugh Gaine: A Colonial Printer-Editor's Odyssey to Loyalism* (Carbondale, Ill., 1972), chaps. 6–10. *Rivington's New-York Gazetteer*, Mar. 16, 23, Apr. 27, June 1, May 4, 1775.

68. Thomas, *History of Printing*, 2: 103–4; *Journals of Hugh Gaine*, 2: 50; *Rivington's New-York Gazette*, Oct. 13, 1777 (title varied afterward); Hewlett, "James Rivington," chap. 4.

69. Schlesinger, *Prelude to Independence*, pp. 291–2. Hicks to Thomas Dickenson, Jr., May 27, 1782, in "Letter-Book of Mills & Hicks," p. 62; Mills and Hicks to Champion and Dickenson, Dec. 9, 1782, ibid., pp. 68–9; and see ibid., pp. 41–4.

70. Schlesinger, *Prelude to Independence*, pp. 257–8.

71. Ibid., p. 75, and see James Parker to Benjamin Franklin, Dec. 24, 1767, *Franklin Papers*, 14: 345–8. It was a sign of Parker's own political obtuseness that he failed to appreciate Mecom's reasons for undertaking the project.

72. Schlesinger, *Prelude to Independence*, p. 86, and Wroth, *Colonial Printer*, pp. 142–3, present the paper duties as onerous for the trade, but there is no evidence to suggest that printers perceived a serious economic threat. See, for example, Robert D. Harlan, "David Hall and the Townshend Acts," *Papers of the Bibliographical Society of America* 68 (1974): 19–38.

73. Figures for printers are based on Charles Frederick Heartman, *Checklist of Printers in the*

United States from Stephen Daye to the Close of the War of Independence (New York, 1915), which derives from a variety of standard bibliographical sources. As far as possible, Heartman has been corrected in the light of more accurate available information. Figures for newspapers are from Davidson, *Propaganda*, p. 225.

74. See, for example, Harlan, "David Hall and the Townshend Acts," pp. 31–7; Schlesinger, *Prelude to Independence*, appendix A. Peter J. Parker, "The Philadelphia Printer: A Study of an Eighteenth-Century Businessman," *Business History Review* 40 (1966): 38; but cf. Yodelis, *Who Paid the Piper?*, pp. 19–23, 42–3, and passim, where it is suggested that the volume of purely political printing business did not become large enough to be the only or decisive consideration. It should be noted, too, that calculations made by patriot printers before 1776 would not necessarily assure them of success in the turbulent years that followed Independence.

75. Schlesinger, *Prelude to Independence*, pp. 137, 165, gives examples of the old trade rhetoric that may have reflected confusion during a period in which habits were being altered; see also Davidson, *Propaganda*, p. 304.

76. *Pennsylvania Journal*, Sept. 11, 1766, and see John William Wallace, *An Old Philadelphian: Colonel William Bradford, the Patriot Printer of 1776* (Philadelphia, 1884), chap. 13.

77. Thomas, *History of Printing*, 2: 146; *Virginia Gazette* (Purdie), Mar. 28, Nov. 6, 1766; Schlesinger, *Prelude to Independence*, p. 79; *Virginia Gazette* (Rind), May 16, 1766.

78. *Rivington's New-York Gazetteer*, Aug. 11, 1774; *New-York Journal*, Aug. 18, 1774.

79. Thomas, *History of Printing*, 1: 378–9, 2: 250; Buckingham, *Specimens of Newspaper Literature*, 1: 232–3; William Coolidge Lane, "The Printer of the Harvard Theses of 1771," *Publications of the Colonial Society of Massachusetts* 26 (1924–26): 9; Thomas to (Joseph Dill?), Mar. 18, 1772, Isaiah Thomas Papers, American Antiquarian Society, Worcester, Mass.; Clifford K. Shipton, *Isaiah Thomas: Printer, Patriot, and Philanthropist, 1749–1831* (Rochester, N.Y., 1948), chap. 2.

80. How gradual and uncertain the process of change would be is evident from Dwight L. Teeter, Jr., "Decent Animadversions: Notes Toward a History of Free Press Theory," in Bond and McLeod, eds., *Newsletters to Newspapers*, pp. 237–45. Like most Americans for a long time to come, printers were inclined and expected to justify partisanship in terms of the general public interest. It should be understood, of course, that printers were not the only occupational group to show the effects of politicization during the years of Revolutionary crisis; see, for example, Charles S. Olton, *Artisans for Independence: Philadelphia Mechanics and the American Revolution* (Syracuse, N.Y., 1975). As custodians of the press, however, their trade response to Revolutionary conditions had unique impact on the nature of American public discourse.

81. *Rivington's New-York Gazetteer*, Sept. 2, 1774; "To the Publick" (New York, Nov. 16, 1774); *Pennsylvania Journal*, Mar. 8, 1775; *New-York Journal*, Sept. 15, 1774.

82. Charles M. Thomas, "The Publication of Newspapers during the American Revolution," *Journalism Quarterly* 9 (1932): 372; Catherine Snell Crary, "The Tory and the Spy: The Double Life of James Rivington," *William and Mary Quarterly*, 3d ser. 16 (1959): 61–72; *Journals of Hugh Gaine*, 1: 63–4; Lawrence, *James Johnston*, pp. 24–7; Dwight L. Teeter, Jr., "Benjamin Towne: The Precarious Career of a Persistent Printer," *Pennsylvania Magazine of History and Biography* 89 (1965): 316–24.

83. Freneau's poems are reproduced in Thomas, *History of Printing*, 2: 483–95.

84. Ibid., pp. 453–8: "The Humble Confession, Declaration, Recantation, and Apology of Benjamin Towne, Printer in Philadelphia."

85. Richard F. Hixson, *Isaac Collins: A Quaker Printer in Eighteenth-Century America* (New Brunswick, N.J., 1968), pp. 97–8; William Goddard, *The Partnership: or the History of the Rise and Progress of the Pennsylvania Chronicle &c* (Philadelphia, 1770), pp. 5, 8–9, 16, 17, and see generally Miner, *William Goddard*, chaps. 4–5, 7.

86. J. Eugene Smith, *One Hundred Years of Hartford's Courant* (New Haven, 1949), p. 15; Thomas, *History of Printing*, 1: 379.

87. Duniway, *Development of Freedom of the Press*, p. 136n; Buckingham, *Specimens of Newspaper Literature*, 1: 241–2.

88. Rollo G. Silver, "Benjamin Edes, Trumpeter of Sedition," *Papers of the Bibliographical Society of America* 47 (1953): 265; Holt to Adams, Jan. 29, 1776, in Victor Hugo Paltsits, *John Holt,*

Printer and Postmaster, Some Facts and Documents Relating to His Career (New York, 1920), pp. 10–15.

89. Paltsits, *John Holt*, p. 10.

90. Jefferson Clark, *Address Delivered at the Anniversary Celebration of the Franklin Typographical Society* (Boston, 1826), p. 14. On the development of partisan journalism at the beginning of the nineteenth century, see generally Donald H. Stewart, *The Opposition Press of the Federalist Period* (Albany, N.Y., 1969), chap. 1.

91. See, for example, Rollo G. Silver, *The American Printer, 1787–1825* (Charlottesville, 1967), pp. 40–62; Milton W. Hamilton, *The Country Printer, New York State, 1785–1830* (New York, 1936), p. 46; Ethelbert Stewart, *A Documentary History of the Early Organizations of Printers* (Indianapolis, 1907), pp. 5–41. Of course, this trend in publishing was one element in a more general process of industrialization that affected other American craftsmen in the first half of the nineteenth century.

92. Shipton, *Isaiah Thomas*, chap. 4; Stewart, *Documentary History*, p. 134; David Bruce, "Recollections of New York City" (c. 1810), Miscellaneous Manuscripts, New-York Historical Society, New York, N.Y.

93. Robert S. Coffin, *The Printer and Several Other Poems* (Boston, 1817), p. vii; *A Collection of Songs of the American Press and Other Poems Relating to the Art of Printing*, ed. Charles Munsell (Albany, N.Y., 1868), p. 45.

94. Stewart, *Documentary History*, pp. 11, 28–9, 43, 21, 14.

95. Ibid., pp. 59 and n, 131–32; Hamilton, *Country Printer*, pp. 150–1.

96. John Clough, *An Address . . . before the Franklin Typographical Association* (New York, 1801), pp. 10–11; Adoniram Chandler, *An Oration, Delivered before the New-York Typographical Society* (New York, 1816), p. 9.

97. *Collection of Songs of the American Press*, p. 113; John Russell, *An Address, Presented to the Members of the Faustus Association* (Boston, 1808), pp. 20–1.

98. Shipton, *Isaiah Thomas*, chap. 6; Thomas, *History of Printing*, 1: 10, had undertaken his chronicle of the trade despite a feeling that the task might have been better performed by "some person distinguished for literature." Joseph T. Buckingham, *Personal Memoirs and Recollections of Editorial Life*, 2 vols. (Boston, 1852), 1: 21, 27–8, 53.

99. Silver, *American Printer*, p. 88; *Autobiography of Thurlow Weed*, ed. Harriet A. Weed (Boston, 1883), p. 58.

100. William Dean Howells, *The Country Printer* (Norwood, Mass., 1919), p. 36; *Voices of the Press; A Collection of Sketches, Essays, and Poems, by Practical Printers*, ed. James J. Brenton (New York, 1850), p. iii. The link between printing and authorship remained, of course, journalism; see S. M. Lipset, M. A. Trow, and J. S. Coleman, *Union Democracy: The Internal Politics of the International Typographical Union* (Glencoe, Ill., 1956), pp. 29–30, where the role of printers editing the modern labor press is noted.

101. Charles Turrell, "Longevity of American Printers," in *The Typographical Miscellany*, ed. Joel Munsell (Albany, N.Y., 1850), pp. 82–3; *Autobiography of Thurlow Weed*, p. 44; Horace Greeley, *Recollections of a Busy Life* (New York, 1868), pp. 60–1.

102. William Burdick, *An Oration on the Nature and Effects of the Art of Printing* (Boston, 1802), p. 20; Asbridge, *Oration*, p. 26. Other groups of mechanics continued to celebrate the Revolution, but without as specific a sense of participation; see Howard B. Rock, "The American Revolution and the Mechanics of New York City: One Generation Later," *New York History* 52 (1976): 367–82. The 4th of July, of course, was the favored occasion for expressing such sentiments.

103. Clark, *Address*, p. 21; Thomas Bradford, Jr., to Samuel McKean, May 7, 1834, Bradford Manuscripts, Historical Society of Pennsylvania, Philadelphia; Thomas, *History of Printing*, 1: 15.

104. Asbridge, *Oration*, p. 12; Clark, *Address*, p. 14; *Collection of Songs of the American Press*, p. 21.

105. Stewart, *Documentary History*, pp. 147–8.

106. Clark, *Address*, p. 22. On the relationship of the American and Industrial Revolutions, see generally Alan Dawley, *Class and Community: The Industrial Revolution in Lynn* (Cambridge, Mass., 1976).

107. Lipset et al., *Union Democracy*, p. 30.

108. *Memorial of the Inauguration of the Statue of Franklin* (Boston, 1857), pp. 146–87.

Chapter 9

JEFFERY A. SMITH

THE COLONIAL JOURNALIST
Good Humour'd Unless Provok'd

IN THE SUMMER OF 1798, AT the height of the Sedition Act frenzy, Samuel Smith, a Republican congressman from Maryland, cut out a newspaper article and mailed it to Vice President Thomas Jefferson. The article accused Jefferson of having recently been "*closeted*" with several people, including the editor of the Philadelphia *Aurora*, Benjamin Franklin Bache, who was then awaiting trial for seditious libel. Noting that his movements were watched by his political opponents, Jefferson wrote to Smith that Bache, the country's most militant Republican journalist, was a man of ability and of principles favorable to liberty and the American form of government. "Mr. Bache has another claim on my respect," Jefferson added, "as being the grandson of Dr. Franklin, the greatest man & ornament of the age and country in which he lived."[1]

Jefferson frequently used hyperbole, but his assessment of Benjamin Franklin, who had been dead for eight years, was a reasonable one. In addition to his many contributions to science, literature, and everyday life, Franklin was a prominent participant in virtually all of the major American political developments of his time. He, along with Jefferson, stood at the pinnacle of the American Enlightenment. During their public careers, however, both Franklin and Jefferson were denounced in print as being weak, devious, immoral, and incompetent. Neither ultimately wished to see personal attacks go unpunished, but both believed that free expression, whatever its difficulties, was essential for maintaining a free and uncorrupted government.

Jefferson and Franklin, both poor speakers, relied heavily on their superb writing to account for their actions and explain their ideas. Both indulged in righteous anger but generally avoided purely scurrilous remarks about individual political opponents. Still, their approaches to political communication differed. Jefferson, although he understood the power of the press and declared that it would be the "engine" in his party's drive for power in 1800, confined himself almost exclusively to the relatively aloof activities of producing public documents and private letters. Franklin, on the other hand, was a printer by trade and not above the tasks and risks of competitive journalism. His writing ability, he observed in his autobiography, was "of great Use to me in the Course of my Life, and was a principle Means of my Advancement."[2]

Franklin, along with his relatives and business associates who were printers, pursued vigorous journalism at an early point in the development of the American press. They also demonstrated that libertarian press theory could be easier to defend in principle than to put into practice. They found that assertive journalism enraged powerful individuals and that personal libel flowed all too readily from the pens of writers. Efforts to promulgate Enlightenment ideals could lapse into mere propaganda and personality contests. Yet early American journalism operated at a level of sagaciousness and intensity that made it all but impossible to restrain.

I

Benjamin Franklin had an early introduction to disputes over freedom of expression. Raised in Boston, where defamation suits and licensing controversies had already been occurring for decades before his birth in 1706, he was able to witness repeated attempts to suppress the opinions of church and government factions. One of the pieces he read in his youth was *A Looking Glass for the Times* which was written in 1676 by his grandfather, Peter Folger, to castigate the Massachusetts Puritans for persecuting religious sects. Folger, who was a Baptist living on the island of Nantucket, congratulated himself in the work for not being a libeller, but admitted his surprise that his polemic had been able to "pass the Press." Folger's plea for tolerance impressed his grandson as having been "written with a good deal of Decent Plainness & manly Freedom."[3] Anxious to develop his own skill as a writer, Franklin managed to achieve a clear, self-confident prose style during his youth, but found that decency was difficult to maintain and that strong opinions were not always appreciated.

At the age of twelve, Benjamin Franklin had both a "Bookish Inclination" and a "Hankering for the Sea," as he recalled in his memoirs. His Puritan father, Josiah, who had already lost one son at sea, did not want him to become a sailor. He took Benjamin on walks through Boston to observe tradesmen at work and to find an occupation that would keep an intellectually curious boy on dry land. Benjamin was at length apprenticed to his twenty-one-year-old brother James, a printer who had recently returned from his own apprenticeship in England. Benjamin quickly demonstrated proficiency in the work, but the two older Franklins were soon at odds in advising him about writing. James encouraged him to write news ballads for the two of them to print. Hawking the first one in the streets, Benjamin was proud to see that copies sold well. Josiah, who was giving his son suggestions on style, nevertheless ridiculed the verses and warned him that poets were generally beggars. Franklin, who regarded his father as a man of sound judgment, then began to practice writing prose with the *Spectator* as his model. He was, he later remembered, "extremely ambitious" to become "a tolerable English Writer."[4]

James Franklin, meanwhile, was using a brash, entrepreneurial spirit he had acquired in England to compete with Boston's five other printers. In 1719 he helped postmaster William Brooker start the *Boston Gazette*, the second continuously published newspaper in Boston and the second in the American colonies. A new postmaster, Philip Musgrave, took over the newspaper in 1720 and chose another printer, Samuel Kneeland. Undaunted by this turn of events, Franklin started his own newspaper, the *New-England Courant*, in 1721. In addition to titillating its readers with stories of crime and sex, the

Courant accused Musgrave of being inept and dishonest as postmaster. The paper also spewed forth abuse of local Puritan clergymen—Increase and Cotton Mather in particular—for advocating inoculation during an outbreak of smallpox. While charging the ministers with recklessly encouraging a dangerous medical procedure, the *Courant's* writers depicted Musgrave as a "Butter-headed Churl" who stole money from letters and made himself an "Intolerable Grievance which the People Groan under." A policy statement in the second issue of the paper had promised that nothing would be published reflecting on the clergy or government or lacking in "Decency or good Manners." The next item, however, was a piece of black humor on "A Project for reducing the Eastern Indians by *Inoculation*."[5]

A writer in Boston's oldest newspaper, the *News-Letter*, found the *Courant* "full freighted with Nonsense, Unmannerliness, Railery, Prophaneness, Immorality, Arrogancy, Calumnies, Lyes, Contradictions, and what not, all tending to Quarrels and Divisions, and to Debauch and Corrupt the Minds and Manners of New England." Using a reference to an outlawed group of devil worshippers in England, a defender of the ministers used Musgrave's *Gazette* to portray Franklin's correspondents as "the *Hell-Fire Club* of Boston." In an announcement in the *Gazette*, Rev. Increase Mather warned the public not to read the "Wicked Paper" and lamented the absence of effective restraints. "I can well remember when the Civil Government could have taken an effectual Course to suppress such a *Cursed Libel!*" he fumed.[6]

James Franklin could remain serene in the face of such outbursts because the government appeared incapable of controlling the press as Mather had so bluntly suggested. Licensing, a formality largely disregarded by Boston printers for years, no longer seemed a threat. On March 15, 1721, Governor Samuel Shute reminded the General Court that the king had given him authority to license publications and asked the legislators for a law to use against "Factious & Scandalous papers." The House, which cared little for the governor or his prerogatives, refused to comply, citing the "innumerable inconveniencies and dangerous Circumstances this People might Labour under in a little time."[7]

The Council, which agreed with the governor on the need for a press law, was meanwhile finding it foolish to depend on the courts. In February the Council had ordered the attorney general to prosecute bookseller Benjamin Gray for publishing a pamphlet on currency problems in the colony. Acting in contempt of the Council, Gray advertised that he sold "all" recent pamphlets and in May a grand jury refused to indict him. During the episode James Franklin printed and Gray sold Daniel Defoe's *News From the Moon*, a masterful burlesque of public officials attempting to punish their critics.[8]

After he started publishing the *New-England Courant* later in 1721, Franklin had the opportunity to spell out some of the principles of libertarian press theory. He calmly dismissed complaints about his newspaper's editorial content, saying that he practiced a lawful trade and that he and his correspondents had a right to speak out in self-defense. "And the Law of Nature, not only *allows*, but *obliges* every Man to defend himself against his Enemies, how great and good soever they may appear," he declared. For good measure, he reprinted recently published essays by Trenchard and Gordon's Cato on freedom of expression and on the need for the people to jealously guard their liberties. Cato defined libel as writing that hurt particular persons, without doing good to the public, and stated that governments were instituted for the people. The exposing of public misdeeds, Cato told the readers of the *Courant*, could never be a libel.[9]

Although he printed little in favor of the *Courant*'s adversaries, Franklin continually maintained that he was an impartial editor who was simply "publishing the different Opinions of Men." This, he insisted, was the only reasonable policy. "Even Errors made publick, and afterwards publickly expos'd," he wrote, "less endanger the Constitution of Church or State, than when they are (without Opposition) industriously propagated in private Conversation." In an essay on the proper role of an editor, one of his contributors, a Mr. Gardner, praised Franklin for his courage and impartiality and told him that no newspaper publisher could please everyone. "Indeed the whole managery of such an Affair, requires the greatest Prudence imaginable," he said. "A Man had need exercise as much Caution, as if he were to fall between the perilous Rocks of Scilly and the fatal Quick-sands of Carabdis, that so he may keep the middle Channel between all Parties, and only press either Side to pursue the publick Interest, at least preferrably to their private Prospects."[10]

James Franklin thus set out to be a champion of free expression and of the people's interests and as long as he crusaded against smallpox inoculation, he had a safe issue. When the epidemic erupted in the summer of 1721, the Massachusetts House, Boston's town selectmen, and all but one of the city's physicians had gone on record opposing the practice. As half of the city's 12,000 residents contracted the disease and more than 800 died, Franklin cheerfully reported his subscription gains. He warned the Mathers, who were busy condemning the paper, that he could say of the *Courant* and himself what a Connecticut trader once said of his onions: "*The more they are curs'd, the more they will grow.*" Rumors being spread that the government was about to suppress the paper, Franklin observed, only brought in new customers with "an Itch after the Novelty of the Subject that should cause such a Report."[11]

The editor's only serious bout with remorse came when he printed a story by John Checkley, a militant Anglican who was one of the *Courant*'s initial contributors. Checkley charged that one of the writers defending the ministers, Reverend Thomas Walter, a nephew of Cotton Mather, was inspired by rum and entertained in the bed of "two Sisters, of not the best Reputation in the World." After a scolding from his own pastors, Franklin announced he would accept no more of Checkley's articles and promised to publish in the future only pieces that were "innocently Diverting" and "free from malicious Reflections." Franklin's resolution did not last long, however. In subsequent months, as the smallpox epidemic took its toll and finally ended early in 1722, Franklin published essays recalling the ministers' participation in the Salem witchcraft trials and employing vicious wit to depict the Mathers as deranged hypocrites. Cotton Mather confronted James Franklin in the street at one point and lectured him on the consequences of serving the Devil. Franklin reported the incident in the *Courant* and stated that he was acting only as an impartial printer and was inviting pieces written with "Freedom, Sense and Moderation."[12]

II

Benjamin Franklin imbibed the spirit of the *Courant* writers and in 1722 became one of its contributors. From April through October, the sixteen-year-old apprentice published fourteen comic and often bitingly satirical letters on Harvard, hoop-petticoats, funeral elegies, drunkenness, and other topics. Signing his essays with the pen name "Silence Dogood" and placing them under the door of the printing house at night, he had the satisfaction of hearing the Hell-Fire Club praise the pieces without knowing who wrote them. When he revealed his authorship, the *Courant*'s writers expressed their admiration. In the second Dogood letter, Benjamin followed the paper's editorial slant by proclaiming himself "a mortal Enemy to arbitrary Government & unlimited Power" and saying that he had a natural inclination and ability for criticizing others. "I speak this by Way of Warning to all such whose Offences shall come under my Cognizance," he told his readers, "for I never intend to wrap my Talent in a Napkin." Franklin did not plan to be always severe, however. He was, he explained, "good-humour'd" unless "first provok'd."[13]

Franklin did proceed in a jocular tone until a serious provocation actually occurred in the summer of 1722. At the time of the colony's spring elections, the *Courant* had needled particular candidates for attempting to intimidate or improperly influence voters. James Franklin had also published a pointed but anonymous pamphlet advising the public to elect representatives who could remain uncorrupted, revive the economy, and support freedom of the press against misguided efforts by some members of the Council to restrict it. Such impertinence did not go unnoticed. When, in June, a *Courant* news item sarcastically announced that the Massachusetts government was ready to dispatch a ship to pursue a band of pirates "sometime this Month, if Wind and Weather permit," the Council summoned James Franklin to its chambers. The editor, as he later admitted, acted with "Indiscretion & Indecency" before the legislators, and both houses agreed to imprison him until the end of the session for breach of legislative privilege. Benjamin Franklin was also questioned, but, as he recalled in his autobiography, "did not give them any Satisfaction." While the older Franklin was confined, the Council took note of the *Courant*'s insults "boldly Reflecting" on the government, churches, and college and voted to place the publication under the censorship of the secretary of the province. The House, which had its own conflicts with the Council and with Governor Shute's administration, rejected the measure.[14]

During the month that James Franklin was in jail, his younger brother took charge of the *Courant*. Benjamin wrote in his memoirs that he "resented a good deal" the legislature's action and "made bold to give our Rulers some Rubs." Benjamin began cautiously, however, by inventing a cool, urbane, and curiously revealing persona for himself as editor. "Janus" described himself as a lover of truth who sought desirable knowledge and avoided extremes in conversation and behavior. "I converse with all sorts of Persons," Franklin wrote, "and know how to adapt my Discourse to the Company I am in, be it Serious, Comical, or anything else; for I can screw my self into as many Shapes as there are different Opinions amongst Men." Observing that he often joked and that some of his female companions considered him a fool, a sharp fellow, or a wag, the maturing Franklin stated that he had arrived at "such a firm and equal Temper of mind" that he could hear good and bad opinions about himself and value or despise them as he pleased.[15]

Janus, who purported to "appear in the Town towards the Dusk of the Evening, to make Observations," was perhaps too mysterious and self-conscious a version of Addison and Steele's Mr. Spectator to be an immediate success in Boston. To deal with the legislators and others the *Courant* had angered, Franklin reverted to his Silence Dogood pseudonym and issued a policy statement saying the *Courant* did not attempt to please everyone and would look with "Pity and Contempt" on those who reproached it while it promoted virtue and worthy actions. Mrs. Dogood used a lengthy quotation from Trenchard and Gordon's Cato to respond to the jailing of the *Courant*'s publisher. Cato contended that officials were only trustees of the people and that freedom of expression was essential to free government. The only limit on this liberty, Cato said, was where one individual injured the right of another. Dogood's next essay roundly condemned hypocrisy in religion and government. James Franklin appreciated his brother's efforts, but Benjamin found that others—apparently including his father—"began to consider me in an unfavourable Light, as a young Genius that had a Turn for Libelling and Satyr."[16]

Once James Franklin was released, he took his case to his readers. He published statements pointing out that he had been denied due process of law and questioning the authority of a provincial government to imitate Parliament by using breach of legislative privilege. He also printed a poem supposedly *"Thrust into the Grate by an unknown Hand"* which decried his paper as seditious and defamatory and complained that the *Courant* was "prais'd and priz'd by some above the Bible." In response, James Franklin claimed he never published anything to affront the government, but he then asked if it was "a greater Crime in some Men to discover a Fault, than for others to commit it." Franklin brought his arguments to a conclusion in September with a long, front-page poem parodying his appearance before the Council and ridiculing its members for their reaction to honest criticism. "Some Crime . . . You are afraid should thus be shown," the verse said, "And to your injur'd Country known."[17]

A second confrontation with the legislature occurred when the *Courant* of January 14, 1723, carried a slashing essay on Puritan pretentiousness as well as brusque letters advising the House on how to conduct itself in its relations with the governor. Citing the paper's habit of mocking religion and affronting the government, both houses of the legislature voted to forbid James Franklin to publish the *Courant* without the prior approval of the secretary of the province. Franklin disregarded the order—which passed the House by only one vote—and placed in his next issue a psalm from the Bible which began:[18]

> O Thou whose Justice reigns on high,
> And makes th' Oppressor cease,
> Behold how envious Sinners try
> To vex and break my Peace!
> The Sons of Violence and Lies
> Join to devour me, Lord;
> But as my hourly Dangers rise
> My Refuge is thy Word.

The Council issued an order for his arrest, but the undersheriff reported back the same day that he had been unable to find Franklin during a "Diligent Search." The *Courant,* however, continued to appear and to convey its indignation. In the first *Courant* published while the printer was in hiding, Franklin was given a ludicrous set of rules on how to be "pleasant and agreeable" and was wryly cautioned that he should neither condemn any persons nor risk damnation by resisting rulers who governed by divine right. He was also told to pay particular attention to Boston's emerging political machine—those "Men of Power and Influence" who were "scoffingly call'd, *The CANVAS CLUB.*" Letters in the following issue noted that Franklin had broken no law and was being punished without an opportunity to defend himself. One of the correspondents addressed Judge Samuel Sewall, a member of the Council, and reminded the public of his role in the Salem witchcraft trials. "If this *Printer* has transgress'd any Law," the writer said, "he ought to have been presented by a Grand Jury, and a fair Tryal brought on." In Philadelphia, Andrew Bradford's *American Weekly Mercury* commented that the Massachusetts legislators appeared to be "oppressors and bigots."[19]

When James Franklin reappeared in early February, he was required to post a one-year, £100 bond, and his case was scheduled for grand jury action. Acting on the advice of his Hell-Fire Club, the editor took the precaution of changing the name of the printer of the *Courant* to Benjamin Franklin, so that he would not be guilty of further infractions of the legislature's order that James Franklin not print the paper without permission. The younger brother, who considered the change of name a "very flimsy Scheme," was accordingly released from his apprenticeship, but was required to sign new, secret indentures. The nominal editor then proceeded to announce that his brother had quit the paper and that Janus, a man of good temper and sound judgment, had taken over. "No generous and impartial Person then can blame the present Undertaking, which is designed purely for the Diversion and Merriment of the Reader," Benjamin wrote. "Pieces of Pleasancy and Mirth have a secret Charm in them to allay the Heats and Tumors of our Spirits, and to make a Man forget his restless Resentments." In the same issue was a notice concerning advertisements which stated that the circulation of the *Courant* was "far greater" than its competitors and that it was "more generally read by a vast Number of Borrowers."[20]

For several months, the *Courant* did confine itself to witty essays and poems addressed to Janus. Not until the week that the grand jury was to decide on Franklin's case did the paper make another play for public support. Three of the four pages of the issue of May 6, 1723, were devoted to a letter from "PHILO-DICAIOS" which defended the printer. The correspondent objected to the wording of the legislature's order and showed how the procedures used against Franklin had not allowed him due process of law. He then offered a hypothetical dialogue between a barrister and a juryman on the subject of whether a bishop who complained about instances of judicial misconduct should be indicted on the charge of having uttered false and scandalous words about government and the administration of justice. The juryman stated flatly that he would pronounce the bishop not guilty and that the words in themselves were "not Criminal, nor reflecting on any particulars." The barrister agreed and remarked that the situation was like that of the Spanish Inquisition when Protestants were dressed in garments painted with devils. Innocent men should not be condemned, the barrister said, "for Words or Matters harmless in themselves, and possibly very well intended, but only rendered *Criminal* by being thus hideously dressed up, and wrested with some far-fetch'd, forced and odious Construction."[21]

The next issue of the *New-England Courant* was able to report that the grand jury had refused to indict James Franklin for violating the legislature's order. Franklin did not bother to comment on his victory, but did insert a news item from a London paper which he thought would be "entertaining" for his readers. Appearing with a Boston dateline, the story gave an account of the legislative proceedings against Franklin and said that the author of the *Courant* was believed to be a member of the "diabolical Society" known as the Hell-Fire Club.[22]

III

While employed at his brother's printing house, Benjamin Franklin learned the advantages of being able to manipulate appearances, to maintain composure, and to argue shrewdly and boldly in journalistic confrontations. Schooled in radical Whig doctrine, he spent his free hours reading works of logic, deism, and philosophy. Through his reading he became a "real Doubter" in religion and a vegetarian. He also began to use the Socratic method "continually" and "grew very artful & expert in drawing People even of superior Knowledge into Concessions the Consequences of which they did not foresee, entangling them in Difficulties out of which they could not extricate themselves. . . ."[23]

Franklin's quickly developing talents and intellectual positions served him well enough as Silence Dogood and Janus, but at the same time he saw his relationship with his master and others deteriorate. James Franklin, who concluded that Benjamin's successes had made him vain, sometimes struck his younger brother for being insolent. With only a covert apprenticeship agreement holding him, Benjamin made up his mind to go to another printer, but neither his father nor his brother would let him. After considering that he had made himself "a little obnoxious, to the governing Party" and had been "pointed at with Horror by good People, as an Infidel or Atheist," Benjamin decided to run away from Boston, where he thought he would be likely to get into "Scrapes" like the "arbitrary Proceedings" against his brother. He sold some of his books for money and boarded a ship for New York, the nearest city with a printer. Not finding a job there, he went on to Philadelphia, where he found work in the printing shop of Samuel Keimer. In the September 30, 1723, issue of the *New-England Courant*, an advertisement said: "James Franklin, Printer in Queen Street, wants a likely lad for an Apprentice."[24]

James Franklin published the *Courant* for three more years, but without further success. He continued to print droll essays and verse and to identify Janus as the editor and Benjamin Franklin as the printer. The amount of original material declined, however, and the number of advertisements was never satisfactory. From time to time the paper reported on press freedom issues as they arose in England and America, and letters occasionally made economic or political comments, but correspondents often settled into protracted literary and religious bickering. Although Janus at one point asked the participants in a religious debate to "suspend their red hot Zeal," Franklin sometimes allowed the tone of the *Courant* to sink to mere invective. Still presenting himself as an innocent, impartial printer, he professed a casual attitude toward personal defamation, something he had promised to avoid during the inoculation controversy. Detraction should be heeded if true, Franklin said, and could be ignored if it was not. "As no man is accounted guilty in the Law till he is Found so upon Tryal," he maintained, "so all Reports are to be look'd upon as false, till they are prov'd otherwise."[25]

Facing depressed economic conditions in Boston, James Franklin discontinued the *Courant* in 1726 and prepared to leave for Newport, Rhode Island, a city half the size of Boston, but without any printer. Before leaving Boston, Franklin composed and published a verse pamphlet titled *The Life and Death of Old Father Janus, The Vile Author of the Late Wicked Courant*. He explained in the poem that he might have been considered a "Public Pest" and a "thriftless Fool," but had felt the necessity of pleading for truth, justice, liberty, and common sense even if the paper's "pois'nous Arrows" made enemies. "With your own Rules your Practice interfer'd," he admitted to himself. At the end, he wrote:[26]

> Thus, vext with Fleas, the *Fox* to save his Blood,
> Contrives Deliv'rance from some neighb'ring Flood:

> Softly he sails from Shore, then gently dives,
> And on a Woolly Ark, the rav'nous Vermin leaves.

With its relatively high degree of freedom, Rhode Island had long served as a refuge from Puritan theocracy. After arriving in Newport, James Franklin celebrated the liberty of his new home in a poem on the ghost of Samuel Gorton, a Rhode Island religious and political radical who had been banished from Massachusetts ninety years before. He also printed the colony laws, religious tracts, and his own "Poor Robin" almanacs, a publication of lively and sometimes coarse humor which took a facetious approach to astrology and served as a model for his brother's "Poor Richard." As Poor Robin, Franklin spoke out against partisanship and damage to personal reputation:[27]

> The Faults of my friend I'd scorn to expose,
> And detest private Scandal, tho' cast on my Foes. . . .
> No Man's Person I hate, tho' his Conduct I blame.
> I can censure a Vice without stabbing a Name.
> To no Party I'm Slave; in no Squabble I join,
> Nor damn the Opinion that differs from mine.

The subject of attacks on private character also came up in the *Rhode-Island Gazette*, another forum for wit and occasional political commentary which Franklin published for eight months beginning on September 27, 1732. Correspondents in the first issues of the short-lived paper repeatedly disavowed any patience with the defamation of individual reputations. One recommended that Franklin provide plain discussions of the "true Principles of Liberty" and reject both *"Personal Scandal"* and the "insipid Affectation of fine Writing and Politeness, that has made some Folks so ridiculous." Accordingly, in a poem in a subsequent issue, "Will Rusty" lamented:[28]

> HE that to *Wit* has no pretence,
> May lawfully make use of *Sense:*
> Yet *Sense* offends as much as Wit,
> If any Mark it chance to hit. . . .

A week after Will Rusty's performance, Franklin apologized for publishing a newspaper that was too often *"dull and flat"* and blamed his health and the newness of the undertaking. "Self Interest, which is at the Bottom of most of the Actions of Life (altho' gilded over with other Pretences) prompted me to exceed my Brother Newswriters in every Point," he said of his efforts to start the paper. He said he still intended to "soar a little higher" and *"lay open the Malignity and Folly of several Practices that are very Prevalent."*[29]

A notice in the *Gazette* of January 11, 1733, asking for more punctual payments and more subscriptions apparently went unheeded, however, and the paper was discontinued by the end of May. Benjamin Franklin, who was becoming established as a printer in Philadelphia, visited Newport in the autumn and had a "cordial and affectionate" meeting with his brother. "He was fast declining in his Health," Benjamin wrote in his memoirs, "and requested of me that in case of his Death which he apprehended not far distant, I would take home his Son, then but 10 Years of Age, and bring him up to the Printing Business." James Franklin died on his thirty-eighth birthday, February 4, 1735. His widow, Ann, and their two daughters continued to operate the press. His son, James Franklin, Jr., after completing an apprenticeship with his uncle in Philadelphia, returned to Rhode Island where in 1758 he founded the *Newport Mercury,* which he published until his death in 1762. Samuel Hall, a printer who married one of Ann Franklin's daughters and received financial help from Benjamin Franklin, took over the *Mercury* and eventually became one of the most notable patriot editors of the American Revolution.[30]

Notes

1. TJ to Samuel Smith, August 22, 1798, in Jefferson, *Works*, 8: 443.
2. TJ to JM, February 5, 1799, in Jefferson, *Works*, 9: 34; *Autobiography*, p. 12. Jefferson admired the easy prose of Franklin as well as that of Thomas Paine. TJ to Francis Eppes, January 19, 1821, in Jefferson, *Works*, 12: 195. On Franklin's view of the problems and potential of communication, see Philip D. Beidler, "The 'Author' of Franklin's *Autobiography*," *Early American Literature* 16 (Autumn 1981–1982): 257–69.
3. Peter Folger, *A Looking Glass for the Times, or the Former Spirit of New England Revived in This Generation* (n.p., 1725), pp. 14, 15; *Autobiography*, p. 6. Folger's *Looking Glass* may have been circulated only in manuscript before 1725 since no printed copy before this date can be found. On Folger and other critics of prevailing practices and opinions in Massachusetts, see Leo P. Bradley, Jr., "The Press and the Declension of Boston Orthodoxy, 1674–1724" (M.A. thesis, University of Washington, 1977).
4. *Autobiography*, pp. 8, 10, 11, 12, 14; Albert Furtwangler, "Franklin's Apprenticeship and the *Spectator*," *New England Quarterly* 52 (September 1979): 377–96. In his almanac, Franklin paid tribute to Joseph Addison, one of the authors of the *Spectator*, as the man whose "writings have contributed more to the improvement of the minds of the British nation, and polishing their manners, than those of any other English pen whatever." *Poor Richard, Improved*, 1748, in *PBF*, 3: 254.
5. *NEC*, August 14, 1721; January 22, 1722. On James Franklin, see Jeffery A. Smith, "James Franklin and Freedom of the Press in Massachusetts and Rhode Island, 1717–1735," paper presented at the annual convention of the Association for Education in Journalism, East Lansing, Michigan, August 11, 1981; Jeffery A. Smith, "James Franklin," in Perry J. Ashley, ed., *American Newspaper Journalists: 1690–1872* (Detroit: Gale Research Co., 1985), pp. 212–18. On the *Courant* and its contributors, see Worthington C. Ford, "Franklin's *New-England Courant*," Massachusetts Historical Society *Proceedings* 57 (April 1924): 336–53; Arthur B. Tourtellot, *Benjamin Franklin, The Shaping of Genius, The Boston Years* (Garden City, N.Y.: Doubleday & Co., 1977), pp. 233–310.
6. *BNL*, August 28, 1721; *BG*, January 15, 29, 1722. On the activities of the Hell-Fire Club in England, see *NEC*, February 12, 1722.
7. General Court Records, Massachusetts Archives, Boston, Massachusetts, 11, p. 113; *BNL*, April 3, 1721. On the conflicts in Massachusetts politics at this time, see Thomas Hutchinson, *The History of the Colony and Province of Massachsetts-Bay*, ed. Lawrence Shaw Mayo, 3 vols. (Cambridge: Harvard University Press, 1936), 2: 174–208; G. B. Warden, *Boston, 1689–1776* (Boston: Little, Brown & Co., 1970), pp. 80–99; William Pencak, *War, Politics, & Revolution in Provincial Massachusetts* (Boston: Northeastern University Press, 1981), pp. 61–80.
8. Bradley, "The Press and the Declension of Boston Orthodoxy," pp. 111–16; Clyde A. Duniway, *The Development of Freedom of the Press in Massachusetts* (New York: Longmans, Green, & Co., 1906), pp. 93–6; [Daniel Defoe], *News from the Moon, A Review of the State of the British Nation* ([Boston: James Franklin, 1721]); *BNL*, March 6, 1721; *BG*, March 6, 13, 1721.
9. *NEC*, September 11, December 4, 1721. For other essays by James Franklin, see, e.g., *NEC*, September 4, 1721; January 22, February 5, 12, 1722. For other essays by Cato, see, e.g., *NEC*, October 9, 16, 23, 30, 1721. On the *Courant* as a dispenser of radical Whig ideology,

see T. H. Breen, *The Character of the Good Ruler, A Study of Puritan Political Ideas in New-England, 1630–1730* (New Haven: Yale University Press, 1970), pp. 261–9.

10.   *NEC*, November 20, December 4, 1721.

11.   John B. Blake, "The Inoculation Controversy in Boston: 1721–1722," *New England Quarterly* 25 (December 1952): 489–506; C. Edward Wilson, "The Boston Inoculation Controversy: A Revisionist Interpretation," *Journalism History* 7 (Spring 1980): 16–19, 40; *NEC*, December 4, 1721; January 22, February 5, 1722.

12.   *NEC*, August 21, September 4, December 4, 1721; Kenneth Silverman, *The Life and Times of Cotton Mather* (New York: Harper & Row, 1984), pp. 336–63. James Franklin's commitment to Puritan beliefs is open to question, but he may have attended either the theologically moderate Old South Church or the more liberal Brattle Street Church, Cotton and Increase Mather were copastors of the conservative Second Church. For *Courant* attacks on the Mathers, see, in particular, *NEC*, August 7, November 6, December 4, 1721; January 22, February 5, 12, May 21, 1722. See also, *A Friendly Debate; Or, a Dialogue between Rusticus and Academicus About the Late Performance of Academicus* (Boston: Printed by J. Franklin, 1722). For an example of a Mather reply, see *A Vindication of the Ministers of Boston, From the Abuses & Scandals, Lately Cast Upon Them, in Diverse Printed Papers* (Boston: Printed by B. Green, 1722).

13.   *Autobiography*, pp. 17–18; *NEC*, April 16, 1722; Bruce Granger, *American Essay Serials From Franklin to Irving* (Knoxville: University of Tennessee Press, 1978), pp. 15–24.

14.   *NEC*, March 26, April 9, 30, May 7, 14, 28, June 11, 1722; *English Advice to the Freeholders, & c. of the Province of Massachusetts-Bay* (Boston: Printed by James Franklin, 1722); General Court Records, 11, pp. 319–20; 370; *Autobiography*, p. 19. The title of the election pamphlet appears to have been taken from a spirited British polemic comparing Whigs and Tories, [Francis Atterbury], *English Advice, to the Freeholders of England* (n.p., 1714).

15.   *Autobiography*, p. 19; *NEC*, June 18, 1722. This unsigned essay is ignored in the Franklin *Papers*, but it clearly seems to be the product of his pen and to foreshadow the Silence Dogood essay of September 24, 1722, on *"Night-Walkers."* Janus reappears in a BF essay published in the *Courant* of February 11, 1723. On Janus, the Roman god with two faces, see *NEC*, August 19, 1723. When Janus was introduced the second time, the *Courant*—perhaps in a reference to James and Benjamin Franklin—describes its editor as having two faces and as being able to "look two ways at once." *NEC*, February 11, 1723.

16.   *NEC*, June 18, July 2, 9, 23, 1722; *Autobiography*, pp. 19, 31.

17.   *NEC*, July 16, 30, August 27, September 17, 1722.

18.   *NEC*, January 14, 21, 1723; General Court Records, 11, pp. 491, 493.

19.   Council Records, Massachusetts Archives, Boston, Massachusetts, 7, pp. 452–3; Suffolk County Court Files, Boston, Massachusetts, 146, No. 16480; *NEC* January 28, February 4, 1723; *AWM*, February 26, 1723. On Boston politics, see G. B. Warden, "The Caucus and Democracy in Colonial Boston," *New England Quarterly* 43 (March 1970): 19–33; Gary B. Nash, *The Urban Crucible*, pp. 80–8, 139–40.

20.   *Autobiography*, p. 19; *NEC* February 11, 1723. Thomas Fleet, a Boston printer who was a member of the Hell-Fire Club and later a dauntless though impartial newspaper publisher, was one of two persons who put up £50 for Franklin's bond. Records of the General Session of the Peace, Suffolk County, Boston, Massachusetts, 1719–1725, p. 186.

21.   *NEC*, May 6, 1723.

22.   *NEC*, May 13, 1723. Records of the Superior Court of Judicature, Boston, Massachusetts, 1721–1725, p. 119. Documents related to both of James Franklin's cases are reprinted in Duniway, *The Development of Freedom of the Press in Massachusetts*, pp. 163–6.

23.   *Autobiography*, pp. 14–16.

24.   *Autobiography*, pp. 18, 19, 20–27; *NEC* September 30, 1723.

25.   *NEC*, March 16, November 9, 1724. For the *Courant*'s coverage of the Massachusetts prosecution of John Checkley for libel, see *NEC*, June 8, 15, July 20, December 7, 1724. For an extract from a British paper criticizing the flexibility of seditious libel law, see *NEC*, July 20, 1724. For an example of a complaint about personal scurrility in the *Courant*, see *NEC*, September 2, 1723.

26.   [James Franklin], *The Life and Death of Old Father Janus. . . .* (Boston: Printed by James Franklin, 1726), pp. 2–5, 7. On the economic conditions in Boston, see Warden, *Boston*, p. 81. For a description of Newport at this time, see Edwin S. Gaustad, *George Berkeley in*

America (New Haven: Yale University Press, 1979), pp. 1–13. Franklin did die without a large estate. Appraisers set the total at £163. Samuel Wickham and Josias Lyndon, "Inventory of the Estate of James Franklin," May 5, 1735, Town Council Book, Newport Historical Society, Newport, Rhode Island, 7, pp. 236–8.

27.   Carl Bridenbaugh, *Fat Mutton and Liberty of Conscience: Society in Rhode Island, 1636–1690* (Providence: Brown University Press, 1974); Lawrence L. Lowther, "Rhode Island Colonial Government, 1732" (Ph.D. dissertation, University of Washington, 1964); [James Franklin], *Mr. Samuel Gorton's Ghost: Or, The Spirit of Persecution Represented in the Similitude of a Dream* (Newport, R.I.: Printed by James Franklin, 1728); "Samuell Gorton, New England Fire-brand," *New England Quarterly* 7 (September 1934): 405–44; Philip F. Gura, "The Radical Ideology of Samuel Gorton: New Light on the Relation of English to American Puritanism," *WMQ,* 3rd ser., 36 (January 1979): 78–100; Philip F. Gura, "Samuel Gorton and Religious Radicalism in England, 1644–1648," *WMQ,* 3rd ser., 40 (January 1983): 121–4; John E. Alden, *Rhode Island Imprints, 1727–1800* (New York: R. R. Bowker Co. for the Bibliographical Society of America, 1949), pp. 1–13; Clarence S. Brigham, "James Franklin and the Beginnings of Printing in Rhode Island," Massachusetts Historical Society *Proceedings* 65 (March 1936): 538–44; [James Franklin], *The Rhode-Island Almanack for 1734* (Newport, R.I.: Printed by James Franklin, 1734). "Poor Robin" had been the pen name of William Winstanley, a highly successful seventeenth-century almanac maker whose work was suppressed when it first appeared in 1662. See Thomas, *Religion and the Decline of Magic*, pp. 335–6; Capp, *English Almanacs*, pp. 39–40, 123–7, 385. Poor Robin's poem was taken from verse which appeared in the *SCG*, January 8, 1732, and *PG*, November 16, 1733.

28.   *RIG*, October 18, 25, November 8, 16, 1732.

29.   *RIG*, November 23, 1732.

30.   *RIG*, January 11, 1733, *Autobiography*, pp. 98–9; Isaiah Thomas, *The History of Printing in America*, ed. Marcus A. McCorison (New York: Weathervane Books, 1970), pp. 176–8, 315–17; 325–6; BF to Jane Mecom, January 13, 1772, in *PBF*, 19: 28. Hall, who apparently never settled his debt to BF, left Newport in 1768 to start the *Essex Gazette* in Salem, Massachusetts. For an example of a defense of press freedom in his paper, one in which a correspondent quoted Cato and complained about officials turning legitimate criticisms into "arguments against you as *disturbers of the peace*, and *movers of sedition in the state*," see *EG*, May 7, 1771.

Chapter 10

WALT BROWN

THE FEDERAL ERA III
Scissors, Paste, and Ink

A Free press would soon destroy the most gloomy despotism.
—George Clinton, *An Oration,*
Delivered on the Fourth of July, 1798

MORTON BORDEN, WRITING ON THE DIFFERENCES between America in the revolutionary period and America under the Federalists, has commented: "the age of blood had passed, [and was] replaced by that of ink." But the ink of the 1790s, like much of the revolutionary ardor, was generated primarily in Philadelphia and was exported, in an era of tediously slow communications, to the remainder of the country. Philadelphia newspapers amounted to a wire service "in an era of scissors and paste journalism" because editors in the outlying states were satisfied to reprint recently arrived news from Philadelphia. Frank L. Mott has depicted the first quarter of the nineteenth century as "a kind of Dark Ages of Journalism"; if 1801–1825 was indeed the Dark Ages, then Federalist and Republican editors were the Vandals and Huns whose editorial barbarism brought on the journalistic darkness.[1]

Having viewed in the two previous chapters the frenzy of the era, we need now to delineate what newspapers were and what they were not, as well as to explain how they were subject to and contributors toward the passions of the era. In addition, brief sketches of the careers of some of the more influential editors will be provided.

A consensus was established by the leading figures of the Federalist age that the contemporary press was extremely licentious and lacking in ability to provide accurate information to the general public; modern historians have opted to accept that consensus wholeheartedly. In 1793, Washington wrote to a friend: "Sequestered you say you are, from the World, and know little of what is transacting in it but from newspapers. I regret this exceedingly."[2] John Jay later wrote Pickering, "Many of our presses are licentious in the extreme, and there is little reason to presume that regard to propriety will restrain *such* parties." Federalist editor John Ward Fenno wrote that

"The newspapers of America are admirably calculated to keep the country in a continual state of insurrection and revolution."[3] Fenno also offered the strongest overall indictment of journals and editors when he complained: "The American newspapers are the most base, false, servile, and venal publications that ever polluted the fountains of society—their editors are the most ignorant, mercenary automatons that ever were moved by the continually rustling wires of sordid mercantile avarice."[4]

Historians have concurred on the low intrinsic value of the press of the Federalist years. Allan Nevins, agreeing with Henry Adams, viewed "the infant press of the country, about 1800, as simply a storehouse of political calumny." Other historians have found the press to be "a mass of crimination and recrimination," "lively and intensely personal," and "the most violent and vituperative that was to appear in a century and a half of American history."[5] There is a historiographical debate whether Federalist polemics were more or less dignified than those of their opponents, but the partisanship, the political propaganda, and the electioneering of many (but not all) of the sheets of both parties of the Federalist period are common historical themes.[6] Another theme is the willingness of editors to use violent abuse and to indulge in personalities and name-calling. Marshall Smelser has shown that the early Republican attacks on "Publicola" prove that abuse of leading figures became commonplace early in the era.[7] Even though one author saw the period as the "Golden Age of American political writing," it is more accurate to say that "The invective displayed in this newspaper war certainly debased the standards of journalism."[8]

It is time to consider what the "standards of journalism" were during this period. Primarily, what we consider a newspaper did not exist in the Federalist period, except for a few trade-oriented mercantile sheets which bear a very slight resemblance in form to today's *Wall Street Journal*. The politically oriented Federalist-era newspapers were generally one sheet, folded in half to create a four-page effect. They contained foreign news, domestic events, local gossip, abusive columns resembling editorials, letters to the editor, and "entertaining scraps" (which included everything from bad jokes to obituaries to marriages). Finally, advertisements took up a greater or lesser amount of room, depending on the volume of commerce in the area or the amount of politics the printer wished to include in a given issue. The newspapers lacked features we take for granted today—banner headlines, photos, comics, television listings, and horoscopes—and they also lacked objectivity and decorum. Trade journals such as the *Pennsylvania Packet* featured more objective reporting than the political sheets, but politics became a factor in trade as the Anglo-French war cut deeply into American commerce. Other newspapers, such as the Philadelphia *Minerva*, printed literary tidbits, lonely hearts columns, anecdotes, amours, and some incredibly soporific vignettes. This style of publication had little to fear either from the Anglo-French war or from the Sedition Act.[9]

Journalism in the 1790s depended on scissors and paste. In the absence of news-gathering services, rural editors reprinted news from the capital or from a nearby urban center, which undoubtedly had gotten its news from Philadelphia. This technique virtually guaranteed a uniformity in the political news printed by each faction. It also had the tremendous advantage of repetition, because when editors printed the same scandal or canard repeatedly, it became easier to believe. One sheet noted: "JACOBIN INFAMY . . . Every slander that is published in one Jacobin paper is republished in all the rest, and nine tenths of them go uncontradicted." Occasionally, there was no news to report in Philadelphia, as Bache once admitted, "not even so much as a piece of private abuse to grace a paper." But lack of news in Philadelphia meant that other editors also lacked news; one Vermont editor printed an apology for the lack of news in the past week because no papers had arrived from New York or Boston.[10]

As tenuous as this practice of reprinting Philadelphia reportage was, the situation only worsened when rural editors went out on their own because they frequently mistook bombast for rhetoric and mistook doggerel for poetry. Poetry, at least, improved in the 1790s; Federalists were willing to print Freneau's poetry—it was only the man and his politics they detested.[11]

Newspapers kept the public's attention for several reasons. National politics and local gossip had an intrinsic entertainment value, then as now. In addition, a population that was 95 percent rural required some workable form of communication, and newspapers were the only medium then. Sunday papers or papers oriented toward science had not yet appeared. In the meantime, politics, commercial information, and literary pieces were able to answer the public's need for information and grew in sophistication as time passed.[12]

Newspaper titles were as widely copied as were their contents. Between 1704 and 1820, "Gazette" (by definition, "a kind of official record") appeared in the titles of 488 newspapers. "Advertiser" appeared in 440, "Herald" in 115, "Journal" in 114, "Intelligencer" in 104, "Register" in 86, "Republican" in 77, "Chronicle," in 75, "Patriot" in 57, "Centinel" or "Sentinel" in 56, and "Courier" in 45.[13]

One issue of a newspaper was printed in 1690, but the paper was suppressed for reasons best known to the English Crown at the time. The *Boston News-Letter*, begun in 1704, was the first regular sheet to appear. By 1760, the press had taken the form it would maintain for the next five decades and became hotly involved in the revolutionary agitation. Between the Treaty of Paris in 1783 and Jefferson's inauguration in 1801, 450 newspapers and 75 magazines were founded. Some newspapers existed only briefly, but at least a few had some significance. Magazines, on the other hand, were not in sufficient demand to make them an economic success. Among newspapers in 1790, there were 70 weeklies, 10 semiweeklies, three triweeklies, and eight dailies, a daily being a Monday to Saturday press run. Ten years later, there were 178 weeklies, 29 semiweeklies, three triweeklies, and 24 dailies. In 1810, there were 302 weeklies, and there were 422 in 1820. Philadelphia had 12 newspapers as early as mid-1791, but only Fenno's *Gazette of the United States* had any national influence. The spread of newspapers was due in large measure to the extraordinary freedom enjoyed by the press in the years immediately following the American Revolution and also to the extreme unwillingness of government, at least at the outset, to interfere with an obvious First Amendment guarantee, even when it was suspected that such guarantee was being used as a cover for slander. The growth in newspaper circulation was also a direct response to the ongoing inland march of the population.[14] For a complete breakdown of the newspapers as they existed during the presidency of John Adams, refer to Table 10.1.

In terms of circulation, the *Boston Columbian Centinel* led all rivals with 4,000. *Porcupine's Gazette* averaged about 2,000 per issue, the equal of any British daily, and was matched by the Walpole, New Hampshire, *Farmer's Weekly Museum*, the finest country newspaper of its era. The *Aurora* was close behind with 1,700 copies per press run. A subscription to a daily cost $6 to $10 per year, while a weekly or semiweekly cost between $1.50 and $5 yearly. Frontier sheets ran about $4 to $5 per year. Average newspaper circulation in the decade 1790–1800 was between 600 and 700 and determined cost and wages. A journeyman printer usually earned about $6 per

Table 10.1 Newspapers in the United States by state and political affiliation 1797–1801

State	Total	F	I-F	N	I-D	D	LP	JA
Connecticut	23	11	5	3	3	1	2	4
Delaware	4	1	1	0	1	1	0	0
District of Columbia	8	2	0	3	2	1	0	0
Georgia	6	1	4	0	1	0	2	1
Kentucky	6	0	0	1	1	4	0	0
Maine (part of Mass.)	9	7	2	0	0	0	1	0
Maryland	14	1	5	3	3	2	2	1
Massachusetts	34	19	4	4	3	4	3	0
Mississippi (terr.)	1	1	0	0	0	0	0	0
New Hampshire	20	14	4	1	0	1	3	0
New Jersey	11	6	1	1	0	3	0	3
New York	53	19	6	13	4	11	10	1
North Carolina	14	6	3	3	1	1	2	0
Ohio (terr.)	3	0	0	2	0	1	0	0
Pennsylvania	50	16	6	11	3	14	4	1
Rhode Island	8	4	2	0	0	2	0	0
South Carolina	9	2	1	4	2	0	0	0
Tennessee	5	1	1	2	1	0	0	0
Vermont	12	2	5	2	1	2	2	0
Virginia	24	6	1	4	3	10	0	0
West Virginia (part of Va.)	4	0	1	1	1	1	0	0
Total	318	119	52	58	30	59	31	11

Sources: Donald H. Stewart, *The Opposition Press of the Federalist Period* (Albany: State University of New York Press, 1969), pp. 867–93; Clarence L. Brigham, *History and Bibliography of American Newspapers, 1690–1820,* 2 vols. (Worcester, Mass., American Antiquarian Society, 1947); findings confirmed where possible by the author's research.

Total — The number of newspapers in the state, published for any part of the period from late 1796 to mid-1801
F — Federalist
I-F — Independently-Federalist
N — Neutral, doubtful, or of a literary nature
I-D — Independently Democratic-Republican
D — Democratic-Republican
LP — Devoted little space to politics
JA — Believed to have existed for the duration of John Adams's term, March 1797 to March 1801

week, plus $.25 for each 1,000 ems of composition, in a job noted for long hours, hard work, and grime.[15] Advertising was the chief source of revenue, and ads drew the readers' attention to newly published books, ship arrivals and departures, lotteries, rewards for runaway slaves, rooms to let, and jobs for hire. A large amount of advertising space was devoted to medicines claimed to be capable of curing everything from coughs to social diseases.[16] Editors frequently had trouble collecting the subscription fees and were willing to take goods or food in lieu of cash. One editor, evidently addicted to politics, issued an urgent appeal in 1800: "Never did Mr. ADAMS want to hold his seat—Nor did ever the Republicans want to turn him out of it, than at this crisis, the editor of the *AMERICAN* wants the payment of the monies due to him." Lastly, although papers were passed around "until dog-eared" and each copy was often read by several people, it is still an open question whether readers took political news as seriously as did the editors who wrote it. While the average citizen did not eat, sleep, and drink politics, as did Bache or Fenno, the early journals nevertheless provided information and opinion of value to citizens in their daily pursuits and at election time.[17]

Franklin printed the first cartoon in 1754, but cartoons were still scarce as late as the Federalist years. In their absence, woodcuts of horses, ships, and slaves, as well as patriotic symbols such as flags, eagles, drums, or anchors occasionally broke the monotony of words. Citizens wrote letters to the editor, but Philip Freneau is credited with the introduction of "the extract of a letter" technique, a device which allowed him to print a letter he had written to himself, while giving the reader the impression that it came from a concerned citizen.[18] Printers usually operated bookstores along with their newspapers because the running of a newspaper could become a lonely and profitless business if the anticipated ship did not arrive from Philadelphia. The position of editor began to emerge in the 1790s, although some newspapers remained one-person operations. In the latter cases, the editor also sold ads and subscriptions and served as typesetter and delivery boy. Editorials in the pure form as we know them rarely appeared as such because opinion was essentially propagandized directly into the news. Styles changed with editors: "Bache criticized men rather than measures, while to Duane the policy rather than the man was the object of attack." There were several women editors at this time because women sometimes took over the printing business at the death of their husbands. Margaret Bache and Ann Greenleaf edited two of the most prominent sheets.[19]

There were a few foreign language journals which lasted briefly. French sheets, such as the daily Philadelphia *Courier Français* were reserved, but German language papers in Pennsylvania were so strongly Jeffersonian that the Federalists were forced to respond in kind with the *Deutsche Porcupein* in 1797.[20]

Rumors were stock-in-trade. The heading "Important-If-True" was commonplace, while the *Massachusetts Mercury* ran a regular column entitled "Rumors from Europe." Once a rumor was printed in one paper, however, it became public domain and spread through reprints as if it were true. In this way, six New England newspapers printed the "news" of Napoleon's death (supposedly in December 1798) between March 6 and 13, 1799.[21]

Newspapers faced several problems. The first was limited to Democratic-Republican sheets and arose from Federalist control of the Post Office. Federalist sheets were often politically franked, while opposition papers were secretly suppressed by Federalist postmasters. The second problem was nonpartisan: editors of both factions were forced to abandon shop in Philadelphia during fever outbreaks, and when Philadelphia was not turning out news, the remainder of the nation's editors were left to survive on their aforementioned limited talents. A third problem was the time lag in reporting news. The delay in printing foreign news, such as Napoleon's alleged passing, could run into months, as noted above. Domestic news, more easily routed yet still slow, was hampered by bad roads and inclement weather. John Adams's inaugural address was printed under the date March 4, 1797, in Philadelphia and was printed as late as March 28 in New Hampshire. Adams's message to the special session of Congress in May 1797 was printed between May 17 and 29, depending on the distance between source and press.[22]

Government printing contracts were sought by editors, and that explains at least some of the partisanship of the press, which apparently even extended to disease. Federalist editors blamed the yellow fever on a French ship, the *Marseilles*, while the opposition blamed a British bottom, the *Arethusa*. Fisher Ames, in a eulogy on John

Fenno, commented, "No printer was ever so *correct* in his politics." One German language paper, the *Readinger Adler*, claimed to be "unpartisan," but it was an empty claim.[23]

Perhaps the best index to partisanship is the reportage on commerce raiding. Federalist newspapers were conspicuous for columns which noted "French Fraternity," "French Depredations," or, in the candor of Cobbett, "French Piracies." Bache showed the way to Democratic-Republican editors by printing a regular column sarcastically titled "EVIDENCES OF BRITISH AMITY," which was usually copied verbatim by sympathetic printers.[24]

Charles Warren has written: "It was with the newspaper editors . . . on both sides, that a climax of rancorous and venomous abuse was reached."[25] Before noting this abuse, however, an introduction of the more noteworthy editors is in order. Many were foreign in origin, as were many of the plain folk for whom they wrote. Federalists were quick to lament the foreign origins of some editors, although Cobbett was as much an alien as any of the editors the Federalists disliked. Modern historians have echoed Federalist sentiments on the alien urge to become a journalist. Harold Weisberger portrays the editors as "gentlemen," although he cites Adams's comments that editors were "vagabonds, fugitives from a bailiff, a pillory, or a halter in Europe."[26]

On April 15, 1789, before Washington left Mount Vernon to be inaugurated, John Fenno launched the *Gazette of the United States* "to hold up the people's own government, in a favorable point of light—and . . . by every exertion, to endear the GENERAL GOVERNMENT TO THE PEOPLE." Fenno ironically shared a birthday with his opposite number, Benjamin Franklin Bache, and the two men died four days apart from the fever in Philadelphia in 1798. Fenno received badly needed financial help from Federalists, which caused him to think of himself as the editor of a "court journal." Philip Freneau, in a satire on Adams and Fenno entitled "Pomposo and his Printer," accused Adams of being the moving force behind Fenno, and a few historians have agreed with Freneau. Adams later strongly denied aiding Fenno in any way. Fenno's death was mourned by Federalists, who hoped for a continuance of his policies from his son, John Ward Fenno.[27]

Benjamin Franklin Bache, "gadfly to the Federalist party," began the *Aurora* on October 1, 1790. In the following eight years, he established himself as a master of journalistic scurrility. Despite a mild beginning, his peak years were distinguished for frequent strong calumnies, biting invective, and occasional weak judgment. He must also have been very dedicated, because he lacked the kind of financial support that Fenno could draw upon and he lost an estimated $14,700 in eight years as an editor. After Bache's death, his widow continued the paper briefly on her own. She then turned the editorship over to her second husband, William Duane, whose publishing talents made him the defendant in 60 libel suits by 1806.[28]

Bache was ably abetted and forwarded in his career by Philip Freneau, once described as "more Jeffersonian than Jefferson." Freneau had been Madison's roommate at Princeton and had invested in a ship (ironically, the *Aurora*) to fight Britain during the American Revolution, but he spent much of the Revolution aboard a British prison ship, watching many of his comrades die. While those circumstances explain his Anglophobia, his position as a Philadelphia journalist was made possible by an offer of a clerkship in Jefferson's State Department, which provided a $250 yearly salary and sufficient free time to do as he pleased. Jefferson's precise role in Freneau's decision to become an editor is still unresolved. Nevertheless, Freneau began the *National Gazette* on October 21, 1791, and slowly but surely began to attack Federalist canons and leaders one by one or en masse. Although the paper did have a literary merit equal to Freneau's widely recognized prose talent, it was more oriented toward vituperation: "All of Freneau's formidable literary talent was devoted to the cause of destroying Hamilton's good name." Freneau's *National Gazette* ceased publication in 1793, a victim of the fever and subscriber apathy. Freneau then went on to found the *Jersey Chronicle*, which lasted from May 2, 1795, to April 30, 1796; in 1797 he served as editor of the New York *Time Piece*.[29]

Freneau's hatred of all things British was matched by William Cobbett's "ultra and uncompromising Toryism," which ultimately damaged the Federalist cause as much as it helped it. Having left Europe behind, Cobbett established himself in America as a pamphleteer without peer, turning out ream after ream of rancor. A New Jersey newspaper noted the launching of *Porcupine's Gazette* in March 1797 with the warning: "Ye Democrats now beware, and hasten to gird on your armour and shield, that you may render yourselves invulnerable to the piercing quills of that groveling animal, the Porcupine." A student of Cobbett has written: "Cobbett needed enemies: he was happiest when he felt that the 'miscreants' of the moment were mobilizing all their forces in order to grind him into dust." Federalists as well as Republicans felt his venom, and Cobbett thought Adams had marked him for deportation. Eventually, libel suits brought against Cobbett by Benjamin Rush greatly diminished Porcupine's operating capital, and he returned to England in June of 1800. Cobbett remained a well-known literary figure and later published parliamentary debates. In the 1830s, the man of the quill realized his lifelong ambition to sit in the House of Commons.[30]

Other editors require less attention. Noah Webster demonstrated sound Federalism throughout the period, and his later works on the language went into countless editions. Among Republican editors, "James Thomson Callender was a Scotchman of whom nothing good is known." Callender was nevertheless widely read, and Jefferson aided him financially. As Donald Stewart concluded: "That Jefferson sent him money in ignorance of his scurrility defies belief."[31] Benjamin Russell of the *Columbian Centinel* imbibed his Federalism as a member of the guard which hanged the British spy, Major John André; he grew to idolize Washington and later coined the term *gerrymander*.[32]

Politicians made greater or lesser contributions to the polemic literature. Timothy Dwight, John Trumbull, Lemuel Hopkins, and Richard Alsop saw themselves as the "Hartford Wits." Hamilton wrote under numerous pseudonyms. Madison used "Helvidius" and other names, and Benjamin Austin, Jr., was "Honestus" and "Old South." Monroe was "Agricola," and John Marshall was "Gracchus" and "Aristides." John Beckley may have been "Valerius," "A Calm Observer," "Pittachus," and "Belisarius."[33]

To the same degree that they abused political figures, editors abused each other in print, and occasionally in person. A Republican newspaper complained of the Federalist editors' "base prostitution to their stepmother Britain." Callender lamented, "The newspapers printed under the presidential banner, breathe nothing but irritation, calumny, and every imaginable ingredient of civil discord." Republican editors were castigated as "those wet nurses of a French faction in the bowels of our country."[34]

The individual who received the worst treatment short of a Sedition Act jail term was Benjamin Franklin Bache. At one point he printed a pamphlet titled *Truth Will Out*, detailing some of the attacks against him. After its publication, his enemies provided material for another volume. He was called "Talleyrand Bache," "Infamous Bache," and, sarcastically, "Patriotic Bache." His paper, the *Aurora*, was seen as "a daily libel on our government," and "the pestilential retailer of sedition."[35] In an article entitled "Contempt," Bache was told that he was not considered the grandson of a philosopher (Benjamin Franklin), but rather "Ben Bache, the newsman." Wolcott wrote to Bache accusing him of a myriad of sins, and Bache was pictured in Congress as an agent of the French Directory. Porcupine, less concerned with diplomatic intrigues, wrote "Bache's Bow Wow" and dismissed his target as a fawning spaniel. Bache's veracity was also questioned: "*BACHE'S OATH* Resembles the case of a footpad, talking at the gallows of the honesty of his life and conversation, or a whore, shrieking to a bawd that her *virtue* is in danger."[36]

Becoming even more personal, Porcupine advised that Bache be treated "as we would A TURK, A JEW, A JACOBIN, OR A DOG," and Federalist ruffians answered the call. Bache was attacked by Fenno in the street, and by organized vigilantes at his office. One self-appointed censor, Abel Humphries, was fined $50 and then given a government job. Federalist newspapers could not conceal their joy when Bache succumbed to yellow fever on September 10, 1798.[37] William Duane replaced Bache as the *Aurora*'s editor and as consort to the widow Bache; Porcupine quickly labeled him "*Duane*, Mother Bache's Editor." Duane, following another Bache tradition, was attacked and beaten in the *Aurora* office on May 15, 1799, shortly after he began his editorial duties.[38]

Other editors received at least an equal amount of printed abuse. Porcupine was chastised as a "libel upon republicanism" and derided as a spaniel. Punsters mocked Cobbett as "Mr. Hedge Hog" and "The Pork Patriot," and he was more seriously attacked as an "arch-liberal and assassin of reputation."[39]

Freneau was upbraided in verse for his connection to Jefferson:

> SINBAT, the smutty link boy of the muse,
> who blacks himself to clean his master's shoes.

Fenno also noted the connection between Freneau and Jefferson and the "scurrility against the general government" that was Freneau's stock-in-trade. When Freneau began to turn the New York *Time Piece* from a literary sheet into a political organ, Noah Webster commented acidly, "The dog returns to his vomit."[40]

An anti–Callender group was formed in Richmond, with plans to treat the Scotch editor to the tar brush and feathers, but the plan evidently miscarried. A Massachusetts newspaper had good tidings for Federalists, as it noted one of Callender's many transgressions: "On the second of August, a little dirty toper, with shaved head and greasy jacket, nankeen pantaloons, and worsted stockings, was arrested at a whiskey distillery, near Leesburgh, in Virginia, under the vagrant act."[41]

Holt, the editor of the *Bee*, was mocked for the survival of one year of "his INSECT," while John Daly Burk of the New York *Time Piece* was dismissed as "this wretch, who is composed of that stuff of which the spy, the assassin, and the sycophant are formed." Fenno received little space, save Callender's statement that Fenno's yearly lie output must be "some hundreds per annum." All of these epithets help to explain why "duelling pistols were essential equipment for members of the newspaper profession."[42]

Pens, however, were the most essential equipment, and a pen in the wrong hand could be as dangerous as a dueling pistol.

Notes

1.   Morton Borden, *Parties and Politics in the Early Republic, 1789–1815* (New York: Thomas Y. Crowell, 1967), p. 28; Harry Ammon, *The Genet Mission* (New York: Norton, 1973), pp. 140–1; Frank Luther Mott, *Jefferson and the Press* (Baton Rouge: Louisiana State University Press, 1943), p. 57.

2.   GW to Edmund Pendleton, September 23, 1793, in John C. Fitzpatrick, *The Writings of George Washington*, 39 vols. (Washington, D.C.: U.S. Government Printing Office, 1939), 33:15.

3.   Jay to Pickering, August 17, 1795, in William Jay, *The Life of John Jay*, 2 vols. (New York: J. & J. Harper, 1833), 1:372; *Gazette of the United States*, March 4, 1799.

4.   *Gazette of the United States*, March 4, 1799.

5.   Allan Nevins, *American Press Opinion, Washington to Coolidge* (Boston: D.C. Heath, 1928), p. 11; John T. Morse, Jr., ed., *John Adams*, American Statesman Series (Boston: Houghton Mifflin, 1884), p. 269; Saul K. Padover, "Wave of the Past," *New Republic*, 116 (1949): 16; Page Smith, *John Adams*, 2 vols. (Garden City, N.Y.: Doubleday, 1962), 2:944.

6.   Nevins, *Press Opinion*, p. 5; Stephen G. Kurtz, *The Presidency of John Adams: The Collapse of Federalism, 1795–1800* (New York: A.S. Barnes, 1961), p. 37; James M. Banner, Jr., *To the Hartford Convention: The Federalists and the Origins of Party Politics in Massachusetts* (New York: Knopf, 1930), p. 23; Charles Warren, *Jacobin and Junto; or Early American Politics as Viewed in the Diary of Dr. Nathaniel Ames, 1758–1822* (Cambridge: Harvard University Press, 1931), p. 93; for partisanship, see Marshall Smelser, "The Federalist Period as an Age of Passion," *AQ* 10 (1958):396; Bernard A. Weisberger, *The American Newspaperman*, Chicago History of American Civilization Series (Chicago: University of Chicago Press, 1961), p. 34; Frank L. Mott, *American Journalism; A History: 1690–1960* (New York: Macmillan, 1962), p. 113; Donald H. Stewart, *The Opposition Press of the Federalist Period* (Albany: State University of New York Press, 1969), p. 12.

7.   Richard Hildreth, *The History of the United States of America*, 6 vols. (New York: Harper and Brothers, 1880), 5:228–30; Stewart, *Opposition Press*, pp. 487, 519, 543; "Party Violence, 1790–1800," *VaMHB* 29 (1921): 172; Doris A. Graber, *Public Opinion, the President, and Foreign Policy: Four Case Studies from the Formative Years* (New York: Holt, Rinehart, and Winston, 1968), p. 23; Marshall Smelser, "The Jacobin Phrenzy: Federalism and the Menace of Liberty, Equality, and Fraternity," *RP* 13 (1951): 460; Dumas Malone, *Jefferson and the Ordeal of Liberty*, vol. 3 of *Jefferson and His Time* (Boston: Little, Brown, 1962), p. 391.

8.   Graber, *Public Opinion*, p. 24; Clarence S. Brigham, *Journals and Journeymen: A Contribution to the History of Early American Newspapers* (Philadelphia: American Antiquarian Society, 1950), p. 63.

9.   Nevins, *Press Opinion*, p. 4, agrees that "the true newspaper, independent of politics, had not yet been born." McMaster, *History*, 2:58ff; *Farmer's Weekly Museum* featured "entertaining scraps" on, for example, March 7, 1797; Mott, *Journalism*, pp. 114–15, stresses commercial news.

10.   Leland D. Baldwin, *Whiskey Rebels: The Story of a Frontier Uprising* (Pittsburgh: University of Pittsburgh Press, 1939), p. 221, and Smelser, "Passion," p. 399, stress repetition; *Russell's Gazette* (Boston), June 18, 1798, and *Aurora*, October 23, 1790, admitted the lack of gossip; *Green Mt. Patriot* (Peacham, Vt.), May 14, 1800, printed the apology.

11.   Charles D. Hazen, *Contemporary American Opinion of the French Revolution*, vol. 16 of Johns Hopkins University Studies in History and Political Science, edited by Herbert Baxter Adams (Baltimore: Johns Hopkins University Press, 1897), pp. 219–20; Brigham, *Journals*, p. 88; Lewis Leary, *That Rascal Freneau: A Study in Literary Failure* (New Brunswick, N.J.: Rutgers University Press, 1941), p. 276.

12.   Stewart, *Opposition Press*, p. 19; McMaster, *History*, 2:63, cites the absence of religious papers and erroneously claims an absence of trade or literary papers. The New York *Temple of Reason* defended deism in its brief existence.

13.   Brigham, *Journals*, p. 12; Weisberger, *Newspaperman*, p. 8.

14.   Weisberger, *Newspaperman*, pp. 3, 24; Mott, *Journalism*, pp. 113, 138; Stewart, *Opposition Press*, pp. 14–15, and Weisberger, *Newspaperman*, p. 51, give the statistics for the years 1790 through 1820; Leary, *Rascal Freneau*, p. 196; Mott, *Journalism*, p. 143.

15. Mott, *Journalism*, pp. 159, 162.

16. Brigham, *Journals*, pp. 20–1, 27; Edward Channing, *A History of the United States*, 6 vols. (New York: Macmillan, 1917), 4:23 stresses medical ads.

17. Brigham, *Journals*, p. 23ff; *American* (Baltimore), *October 20, 1800*, cited in Stewart, *Opposition Press*, p. 18; Weisberger, *Newspaperman*, p. 25; Carl Bridenbaugh, "The Press and the Book in Eighteenth Century Philadelphia," *PaMHB*, 65 (1941): 7; on the value of the press to citizens, see Nevins, *Press Opinion*, pp. 5–6; Kurtz, *Presidency*, p. 137; and Graber, *Public Opinion*, p. 25.

18. Brigham, *Journals*, pp. 46–7; Philip M. Marsh, *Philip Freneau: Poet and Journalist* (Minneapolis: Dillon, 1967), p. 195.

19. Bridenbaugh, "Press," p. 13; Mott, *Journalism*, p. 114; Stewart, *Opposition Press*, p. 27; Brigham, *Journals*, pp. 71, 73, 108; Worthington Chauncey Ford, ed., "Letters of William Duane," *Massachusetts Historical Society Proceedings* 20 (1906–1907):257.

20. Mott, *Journalism*, p. 121; Stewart, *Opposition Press*, p. 386.

21. Mott, *Journalism*, p. 155; Stewart, *Opposition Press*, pp. 22–3; *Massachusetts Mercury* (Boston), March 7, 1797; Napoleon's death was noted in *Norwich Packet*, March 6, 1799; *Massachusetts Spy* (Worcester), March 6, 1799; *Middlesex Gazette*, March 8, 1799; *Courier of New Hampshire*, March 9, 1799; *Farmer's Weekly Museum*, March 11, 1799; and *New Hampshire Gazette* (Portsmouth), March 12, 1799.

22. Miller, *Crisis*, pp. 30–1; Leary, *Rascal Freneau*, p. 240; Brigham, *Journals*, pp. 56–7; *Claypoole's American Daily Advertiser* (Philadelphia), March 4 and May 17, 1797; *Courier of New Hampshire*, March 28, 1797; *Boston Gazette*, May 29, 1797.

23. Stewart, *Opposition Press*, p. 19; DeConde, *Quasi-War*, p. 35; F. Ames to Thomas Dwight, September 25, 1798, in Seth Ames, *Works of Fisher Ames, with a Selection from His Speeches and Correspondence*, 2 vols. (Boston: Little, Brown, 1854), 1:240.

24. *Green Mt. Patriot*, June 1, 1798; *New Hampshire Gazette*, March 25, 1797; *Porcupine's Gazette*, March 8, 1797; *Aurora*, May 6, 1796, for example.

25. Warren, *Jacobin*, p. 90.

26. Dr. Lemuel Hopkins to OW, August 21, 1793, and OW Sr. to OW Jr., November 23, 1795, in George Gibbs, *Memoirs of the Administration of Washington and John Adams; Edited from the Papers of Oliver Wolcott, Secretary of the Treasury*, 2 vols. (New York: William Van Norden, 1846), 1:104, 261; Gibbs adds his own comments on aliens on p. 358; John C. Miller, *Crisis in Freedom: The Alien and Sedition Acts* (Boston: Little, Brown, 1951), p. 58; Weisberger, *Newspaperman*, p. 37.

27. Edwin Emery, *The Press and America: An Interpretive History of Journalism*, 2d ed. (Englewood Cliffs, N.J.: Prentice-Hall, 1962), p. 136; *Gazette of the United States*, April 27, 1791; Margaret Woodbury, "Public Opinion in Philadelphia, 1789–1801," *Smith College Studies in History* 5 (1919–1920): 11; Claude G. Bowers, *Jefferson and Hamilton: The Struggle for Democracy in America* (Boston: Houghton Mifflin, 1966), pp. 153–4; Marsh, *Freneau*, respectively, pp. 144, 141; Robert W. Jones, *Journalism in the United States* (New York: Dutton, 1947), p. 174; JA to Rush, January 8, 1812, in John A. Schutz and Douglass Adair, eds., *The Spur of Fame: Dialogues of . . . John Adams and Benjamin Rush, 1805–1813* (San Marino, Calif.: Huntington Library, 1966), pp. 204–5; F. Ames to J.W. Fenno, February 1800, in Ames, *Fisher Ames*, 1:274.

28. Miller, *Crisis*, p. 26; Woodbury, "Public Opinion," p. 24; Bowers, *Jefferson and Hamilton*, p. 155; Mott, *Jefferson*, p. 28; Mott, *Journalism*, p. 128; Brigham, *Journals*, p. 67.

29. Alexander DeConde, *Entangling Alliance: Politics and Diplomacy Under George Washington* (Durham, N.C.: Duke University Press, 1958), p. 58; Bowers, *Jefferson and Hamilton*, p. 156ff; Ammon, *Genet*, p. 35. William Loughton Smith, *The Pretensions of Thomas Jefferson to the Presidency Examined; And the Charges Against John Adams Refuted* (Philadelphia: n.p., 1796), p. 48; Noble E. Cunningham, Jr., *The Jeffersonian-Republicans: The Formation of Party Organization, 1789–1809* (Chapel Hill: University of North Carolina Press, 1957), p. 13; and Malone, *TJ*, 2:351, cite the Jefferson-Freneau link; Mott, *Jefferson*, pp. 18, 22; Stewart, *Opposition Press*, pp. 487–8; Malone, *TJ*, 2:427–8; John C. Miller, *The Federalist Era, 1789–1801*, New American Nation Series (New York: Harper and Row, 1960), pp. 90–1, discusses Freneau's concerted efforts against AH; Marsh, *Freneau*, pp. 206, 217–28; James Morton Smith, *Freedom's Fetters: The Alien and Sedition Laws and American Civil Liberties* (Ithaca, N.Y.: Cornell University Press, 1966), pp. 204–5.

30. Hildreth, *History*, 5:121; G.D.H. Cole, ed., *Letters from William Cobbett to Edward Thornton Written in the Years 1797 to 1800* (London: Oxford University Press, 1937), p. xi and following; *Centinel of Freedom* (Newark), March 8, 1797; William Reitzen, "William Cobbett and Philadelphia Journalism," *PaMHB* 59 (1935):243; Cole, *Cobbett-Thornton*, p. xxix; Reitzen, "Cobbett," p. 229; Woodbury, "Public Opinion," p. 15.

31. McMaster, *History*, 2:338; Gibbs, *Memoirs*, 2:293; Stewart, *Opposition Press*, respectively, pp. 620, 10.

32. Jones, *Journalism*, pp. 153ff and 162.

33. Emery, *Press*, p. 142; Warren, *Jacobin*, p. 55; Ammon, *Genet*, p. 139; Philip M. Marsh, "John Beckley; Mystery Man of the Early Jeffersonians," *PaMHB* 72 (1948): 60–1.

34. *Constitutional Telegraph* (Boston), October 5, 1799; James Thomson Callender, *The Prospect Before Us*, 2 vols. (Richmond: James Thomson Callender, 1800), 1:33; David Osgood, *Some Facts Evincive of the Atheistical, Anarchical, and in Other Respects, Immoral Principles of the French Republicans, Stated in a Sermon, Delivered on the 9th of May, 1798* (Boston: Samuel Hall, 1798), p. 22.

35. *The Spectator* (New York), August 1, 1798; *Porcupine's Gazette*, June 7, 1798; *Middlesex Gazette*, June 29, 1798; *Farmer's Weekly Museum*, July 3, 1798; *Gazette of the United States*, March 7, 1797.

36. *Courier of New Hampshire*, April 18, 1797; OW to the editor of the *Aurora*, October 24, 1795, in Gibbs, *Memoirs*, 1:260; *Debates and Proceedings in the Congress of the United States*, 5th Cong., 2d sess., 1972–1973 (Washington, D.C.: Gales and Seaton, 1849); *Porcupine's Gazette*, May 18, 1797; *Farmer's Weekly Museum*, July 3, 1798.

37. Smith, *Fetters*, p. 129, cites Porcupine; Mott, *Journalism*, p. 128; DeConde, *Quasi-War*, p. 79; *Russell's Gazette* (Boston), September 21, 1798.

38. William Cobbett, *Porcupine's Works*, 12 vols. (London: Cobbett and Morgan, 1801), 10:97; John Wood, *The Suppressed History of the Administration of John Adams (from 1797–1801), As Printed and Suppressed in 1802* (Philadelphia: John H. Sherburne, 1846), p. 195.

39. John Swanwick, *A Rub from Snub* (Philadelphia: n.p., 1795), pp. 7, 16; Hazen, *Opinion*, p. 242; *Constitutional Diary* (Philadelphia), December 24, 1799.

40. *American Mercury* (Hartford), February 4, 1793; *Gazette of the United States*, September 26, 1792; *Minerva* (New York), September 21, 1797.

41. Miller, *Crisis*, pp. 214–15; *Massachusetts Spy* (Worcester), August 22, 1798.

42. *Connecticut Courant*, June 18, 1798; *Salem Gazette*, July 17, 1798; Callender, *Prospect*, 1:160; Miller, *Crisis*, p. 195.

Chapter 11

ERIC BURNS

THE END OF THE BEGINNING

THE NEW WORLD'S FIRST PERMANENT SETTLEMENT of Englishmen, and a very few women, was established on the swampy, bug-bedeviled peninsula of Jamestown, Virginia, in 1607. It did not have a newspaper. It did not even have a printing press. No one seemed to mind.

Nor were there any newspapers in Britain at the time, at least not as we know them today. Instead, as Peter Ackroyd tells us,

> there was the broadside, a sheet printed on one side which bore the latest news and the newest sensations. From the earliest years of the sixteenth century this was the language of the street—"Sir Walter Raleigh His Lamentations! . . . Strange News from Sussex. . . . No Natural Mother But a Monster . . ."[1]

These tabloid-tinted tales were the beginning of print journalism in the English-speaking world.

There was also a form of broadcast journalism, in the person of "running patterers"[2]—young men with resonant voices and muscular calves who dashed from one end of London to the other and shouted out the day's occurrences. Sometimes they would stop, collect their breath, and then "take up positions in different parts of the street and pretend to vie with each other for attention, thus heightening interest in the latest crime, murder, elopement or execution." A century later, the French would, with all disrespect intended, call these stories "public noises."[3] Those who uttered them were the predecessors of television news anchors, the "sitting patterers" of today.

People liked to hear about elopements. But then as now, crime made better copy than romance. In 1605, a London broadside told of "the 'pitilesse' Sir John Fites, 'thirstie of bloud,' who had just finished killing a man and stabbing that man's wife when he ran upon his own bloody sword." The account goes on to say that the murderer, apparently repentant, hoped for his own demise; he wanted his heart to "Split,

split, and in this onely wound die: That I thy owner may not live, to heare the honour of my credite stayned with these odious actes."[4]

Journalism was more than a century and a half old when Sir John went on his rampage, and it had not begun nobly. The world's first broadside to relate the events of the day seems to have been the work of a "Renaissance blackmailer and pornographer,"[5] the Italian Pietro Aretino, who set up shop a few years after the invention of movable type. Aretino could have done something constructive with his little publication. He could have written about Florence under the Medicis becoming the center of art and humanism in the Western world. He could have written about the founding of the University of Palermo, which would soon be a major institution for the advancement of learning. He could have written about Francesco Sforza, who had recently been named Duke of Milan and proceeded to show up at social events accompanied by a patterer of his very own, a man who would sing out poetry the duke had written himself, rhymes whose subject was not the news of the day but the virtues of the poet.

Aretino did none of this. Instead, he "produced a regular series of anticlerical obscenities, libelous stories, public accusations, and personal opinion."[6] The opinion was boldly, and often vulgarly, expressed. It was also for sale, with Aretino running a kind of protection racket on those who were the subjects of his stories: pay what he asked and he praised you; refuse and you were slathered with abuse. Either way, you were a commodity for him; he would tell the tale that suited him best and profit from you as much as he could.

But few people in Renaissance Italy read Aretino's rag, and it did not stay in business long. Few people read the British broadsides of the early seventeenth century; they, too, were ephemeral in duration and impact. It was not that Europeans disliked these nascent attempts at journalism; more fundamentally, they did not understand the reason for them, living as they did in a world in which news could not thrive as a commodity because it barely existed as a concept. How could it? The Almighty was what mattered to men and women in ages past, but they could speak to Him directly. Their families were what mattered to them, but husbands and wives and sons and daughters lived in the same room. Their livelihood was what mattered to them, but they tended their shops or worked their fields from dawn until sunset, husbands and wives and sons and daughters together by day as well as by night.

In other words, what mattered to a person in the sixteenth and early seventeenth centuries was what happened to him and to those closest to him between one sunrise and the next, on his own plot of land or in his own place of business, and in the company of his own kinfolk and perhaps hired workers. But he could see that for himself. He could interpret it for himself. No intermediary was required to give voice or meaning to the events in his life. As for the events that were not in his life, those that occurred in the lives of other people in other places, of what possible interest could they be to him? The idea that a human being could be instructed or amused by the fortunes of a stranger was as foreign to a European back then as a land across the sea. The world outside one's immediate ken was a place of mystery, not a source of enlightenment.

Occasionally there was something from afar that a person needed to know. There might be an edict from the king ordering his subjects to provide an even greater share of their harvest to the royal granaries. There might be a ruling that taxes were to be increased to help pay for a war or for yet another lordly extravagance of some sort. There might be a declaration from a religious leader that the rituals or tenets of faith had been altered, or perhaps that more money was required by the church as well as the state. Any of these would be news.

But this kind of thing did not happen often, and was so unwelcome when it did that it did not inspire an interest in the wider world. On the contrary: better ignorance than tidings that brought even more hardship to an individual than was already his lot.

But even if the news *had* been relevant to men and women of an earlier age, they would not have had time for it—which was, of course, a further reason for their indifference. They led the same kinds of lives as the first American colonists, lives of toil and repetition. They fed and milked and slaughtered their animals. They cleared and plowed their fields and dammed their streams. They spun fabric and built shelters. They prepared food and cooked meals and mended fences. They cleaned and repaired and maintained houses and barns and outbuildings. They prayed to a strict and sometimes capricious God, wanting to please, and He was ever watching, ever judging.

Which is all to say that they led the kinds of lives even a greed-besotted, hedge fund-managing workaholic of the early twenty-first century would have found punishing, every minute of every hour accounted for, every second of every minute. And journalism, which requires an appreciation of events beyond the personal, the easily observable, is to some extent a function of leisure. Not much of it existed when Aretino first inked up his press.

In the New World, leisure would not make an appearance until the eighteenth century, and then for only a few: the more successful manufacturers and shopkeepers, the wealthier men of trade, and the owners and managers of large farms and plantations. In some of their spare time, some of the hours or minutes not already allotted to Bible study or letter writing or the mastery of a musical instrument, these men and their families began to read newspapers. They were not only the first Americans to have time for journalism; they were the first to sense that knowledge might be power or profit, or that it might at least ease some of their apprehensions about the people and places they did not know.

As the century progressed and relations with Britain grew strained and argumentative and then worse, the colonists read even more and began to debate what they had read with others, sharing not only their opinions but the newspapers themselves, passing their own copies along to friends, urging them to consider this particular point, to see the fallacy of that one. What was Parliament thinking about now? How would the colonies be affected? How would the colonies respond? Who was meeting where, and when, and what steps might be taken as a result? In the buildup to war, the irrelevance of journalism became a thing of the past; urgency, even more than leisure, was driving Americans to learn the day's happenings.

Even so, the news was seldom immediate, which is another reason people did not easily warm to it. As Will Durant pointed out, this was not all bad. "Medieval man could eat his breakfast," he wrote, "without being disturbed by the industriously collected calamities of the world; or those that came to his ken were fortunately too old for remedy."[7] The same was true for the early settlers of Jamestown.

And it would remain true for decades to come. The news from Europe was a plodding traveler, a victim of distance and terrain, taking anywhere from a day to a month to make its way from its point of origin to a seaport, then another six to eight weeks to cross the Atlantic. Once it arrived in the New World, in either printed or oral form, it had to be fetched or overheard by a printer, who then returned to his shop, set the information in type for the next issue of his journal, and distributed it to subscribers, some of whom lived so far away, and were so isolated by rivers and forests and mountains, that the paper did not reach them for another week or two.

Domestic news did not cover ground any faster; it could also take six to eight weeks for reports of an event to journey from the East Coast to settlements near the Mississippi River, and then several days more for the customer to receive them from the print shop. By the time Americans learned of a proposal, it had become law; by the time they learned of a peace treaty, an unnecessary battle had been fought; by the time they learned of a death, the poor fellow had been buried and his soul had either risen or descended and his widow had remarried. Journalism would, in fact, be a dilatory matter—history more than current affairs—until the telegraph came into use in the 1840s and "threatened to overwhelm its users with information and insist on their rapid response."[8]

But we are getting ahead of our story.

For the printer who thought about publishing a newspaper in colonial times, or the man of means who thought about financing the printer, there was a further disincentive to journalism. Put simply, there were not enough customers—too few English speakers in America, too few towns and villages that were too widely scattered to allow for news to be gathered efficiently and a paper to be distributed economically. In addition, as historian of journalism Sidney Kobre points out, "[t]rade, commerce and industry were undeveloped. Settlers for a long time made their own clothes and furniture and raised their own foodstuffs. Advertising would not have been profitable, especially since money was scarce and the general income level low."[9]

But, in time, money would become less scarce, and people would begin to purchase goods as well as produce them. It would not take much time, either: the colonies, not yet a country, grew more quickly than anyone had anticipated. By 1700, it is estimated, more than 300,000 people lived along the New World's Atlantic coast, and in cities like Philadelphia, Boston, and New York the populations were increasing even more rapidly than elsewhere. Most of the immigrants were from England, where there were not only more journals than there used to be, but also more journalists of serious inclination; Pietro Aretino, it seems, had left few heirs to vulgarity. The papers were now reporting such stories as Archduke Charles's becoming king of Spain, the English conquests of Gibraltar and Barcelona, and the union between England and Scotland to form Great Britain. And they reported on Tripoli gaining its independence, Russia and Turkey going to war, and the murder of Peter the Great and his son. It was hard news, not features; substance, not filler.

Accustomed to such publications in their old home, the Europeans in America were an eager audience for them in their new one.

As the colonies increased in population, they increased as well in prosperity. More Americans could afford to go into the newspaper business now than before, and more Americans could afford to buy newspapers. More Americans needed newspapers to learn about events that might influence their livelihoods: the latest shipping regulations, the latest import policies, the latest weather conditions that might affect agriculture, the latest mechanical innovations that might affect textile production, the latest proposals for taxation or fund-raising or the expansion of government services or control, the latest decisions of the Crown on all manner of colonial enterprise. And after a few more decades had passed, a postal service, which had for so long been more a hindrance to communication than an asset, was able to relay such news dependably.

As early as 1639, Massachusetts had attempted the delivery of mail on a regular basis. It was *irr*egular at best. The main problem was roads, which either did not exist or were so rocky, rutted, and circuitous that they were as much obstacle courses as lanes of conveyance. The mail was often delayed, sometimes lost, and sometimes delivered to the wrong place. "In the early days," Kobre writes, "if one wanted to get a letter to a relative or friend in another colony, he waited for a ship captain or a traveler passing through, perhaps a merchant sending a package or a cargo of goods. Sometimes, if it were urgent, one employed a friendly Indian to deliver a letter for him."[10]

In January 1673, the Boston Post Road opened for the specific purpose of trans- porting letters, parcels, commercial goods, and newspapers from Boston to New York, a distance of 250 miles. A horse could travel it without breaking an ankle, and the rider without being thrown into a ravine as his mount stumbled. He could refresh himself by spending the night at an inn or stopping for dinner and libation at a tavern, and he could tend to his mount at any of several blacksmith shops along the way. The mail did not always arrive within two weeks, as promised, but it almost always got there eventually.

Not until the midway point of the following century, though, would postal service in the colonies become truly prompt, reliable, and inexpensive—not until Benjamin Franklin, a founding father of journalism no less than of the American republic, served in addition as parent to the post office.

There could, of course, be no news, not in the modern sense of the term, without presses on which to print it, and the first such machine did not appear in the New World until 1638, when Harvard College employed it to add to what was already the largest store of published material in the colonies. But by 1685, almost half a century later, the grand total of printing presses in the New World had risen to a mere four, and they were essentially what they had been in Gutenberg's time, which is to say cumber- some apparatuses that were as likely to break down as to grind out a story and that demanded of their operators a broad back more than sound news judgement, and manual dexterity more than a knack for layout and editing.

For the most part, they turned out Bibles, usually in English but occasionally in one of the Indian tongues. And they produced copies of sermons, laws, and official correspondence for the colonial government and the Crown, in addition to almanacs and poetry and songs.

But five years later, and more than eight decades after the first British expatriates had set foot in Jamestown, one of those presses would begin printing the first American newspaper. Its life would be short, turbulent, and unhappy.

History does not have much to say about Benjamin Harris, and when it refers to him at all, it seldom does so kindly. "He was a bigot and an opportunist," according to one historian;[11] "a rabid anti-Catholic with an eye for the sensational," in the view of another.[12] He had "mercury in his blood."[13] He was dismissed by a contemporary as "the worst man in the world."[14]

As a publisher in London, Harris had turned out a newspaper and a number of pamphlets, one of which was judged by the authorities to be seditious. He was arrested and sentenced to jail, serving a short time before being released. Then, acting as if he wanted to return to his confinement, he dashed back to the printing press and issued another pamphlet, this one called *English Liberties*—of which, in Harris's view, there were not nearly enough, and those that did exist were insufficiently promoted by the Crown. Before he could be arrested again, he came to the conclusion that his homeland was "an uneasy . . . place for an honest man," and he would dwell there no longer. He set sail for Boston, and in part because of that voyage, his new home would become the "cradle of journalism" in the future United States.

Boston was the largest urban center on the continent at the time, with a population approaching 7,000 and so much energy in the air that a person could feel a charge to the atmosphere the minute he stepped on shore. The city's shipbuilding industry had begun to thrive, as had its bankers and fishermen, its distillers and ropemakers, and its traders in rum, molasses, tobacco, and slaves. In fact, merchants had now joined Puritan clerics as community leaders, causing the latter to scramble to their pulpits and, hoping to keep up with the times, make the case as best they could for Mammon, finding a path to salvation in commerce as well as piety. The wharves were teeming, the shops overflowing with goods and buyers—Boston seemed an ideal place for a new business of any kind, and in 1690, Harris started one. He rented a small wooden shack and became the first publisher of a newspaper in North America. "[I]t is safe to say," comments John Tebbel, who has written extensively on journalism's beginnings, that "no major American institution had been launched by so unworthy a pioneer."[15]

Harris called his paper *Publick Occurrences both Foreign and Domestic*. The former he would lift from London journals brought to Boston by trading vessels; there were, after all, no copyright laws at the time. As for the latter, he would learn of them from friends, neighbors, tongue-waggers in the nearest tavern, and the occasional broadside turned out by a local publisher with an agenda of some sort. *Publick Occurrences* was four pages long, each page about six inches by ten inches. The first three pages contained two columns of news with a narrow margin between them; the fourth page was blank, so that readers could add items of their own and comment on the preceding items before sending the paper along to another reader. This made *Publick Occurrences* a source of interactive journalism a full three centuries before the Internet.

But it was also, at least to modern eyes, a jarring publication to behold. Each paragraph or two was a separate story, and there were neither breaks nor headlines between them, so that one account ran into the next without warning or context. No sooner did a reader learn that a sailor had made an escape from "*Indians* and *French*" than he discovered, in the very next line, that "The chief discourse of this month has been about the affairs of the Western Expedition against *Canada*."[16]

It made for an efficient use of paper—no wasted space, no large print, no fancy designs or insignias. For this reason, the *Publick Occurrences* style, with few modifications, would be the style of virtually all American journals during the colonial era.

Harris's first issue appeared on Thursday, September 25, 1690, the birthday of American journalism. It contained no news less than a month old, and its intentions, at least as Harris explained them, were honorable. His paper, the publisher told his readers in a front-page notice, would print "Memorable Occurrents of Divine Providence" as well as "*Circumstances of Publique Affairs . . . which may not only direct their thoughts at all times, but at some times also to assist their Businesses and Negotiations*."[17] Further, Harris wrote, *Publick Occurrences* was being offered to the residents of Boston "*[t]hat some thing may be done toward* Curing, *or at least the* Charming, *of that* Spirit of Lying *which prevails among us; wherefore, nothing shall be entered but what we have reason to believe is true, repairing to the best foundations for our information*."[18] If someone came to Harris with information that was *not* true, some "malicious Raiser of a false Report," the publisher would expose the person's dishonesty in the very next issue. "*It is Suppos'd that none will dislike this Proposal, but such as intend to be guilty of so villainous a Crime*."[19]

Harris intended to publish his journal monthly. He would do so more often, he vowed, "*if any Glut of* Occurrences *happen.*"[20]

It sounds impressive, or at least respectable, and in fact *Publick Occurrences* started out that way, with the first story ever published by the paper reading as follows:

> The Christianized *Indians* in some parts of *Plimouth*, have newly appointed a day of Thanksgiving to God for his Mercy in supplying their extream and pinching Necessities under their late want of Corn, & for His giving them now a prospect of a very *Comfortable Harvest*. Their Example might be worth Mentioning.[21]

So much for the mention. And so much for memorable occurrents of divine providence or stories that would assist the colonists in their businesses and negotiations. With story number two, *Publick Occurrences* began heading down a tawdrier trail—call it Aretino Alley—telling of "the kidnapping of two children by 'barbarous Indians lurking around Connecticut'; [and the] suicide by hanging of a citizen of 'Morose Temper.' "[22] Harris also informed his readers that some Mohawk Indians—"miserable Salvages [sic],"[23] he called them—had tortured and murdered the white men they took prisoner during a border war between the colonies and Canada. Of course, as we learn from further reading, there had been some provocation. The paper reported the testimony of "Two *English captives*" that a Captain Mason had "cut the faces, and ript the bellies of two *Indians*, and threw a third Over board in the sight of the *French*, who informing the other *Indians* of it, they have in revenge barbarously Butcher'd forty Captives of ours that were in their hands."[24]

Harris was just getting revved up. Another story in the first edition of *Publick Occurrences* revealed that a Boston man had become despondent because of "having newly buried his wife." His friends kept a close eye on him, fearing a suicide attempt. "But one evening escaping from them into the Cow-house, they there quickly followed him, found him *hanging by a Rope*, which they had used to tye their *Calves* withal, he was dead with his feet near touching the Ground."[25]

And then, most controversially, came one of the few foreign stories in the first Harris edition, a rumor, actually, about the king of France, said to be an immoral old reprobate who "used to lie with" his son's wife.[26]

Publick Occurrences seems to have been a modest success with readers. To colonial authorities, however, it was an affront. In particular, they objected to the accounts of the French monarch and the Mohawk Indian massacre; to put it mildly, the authorities "did not like [their] tone."[27] Both stories seemed to be based on hearsay as opposed to verifiable fact; the colony's leaders did not like that either. Nor did they approve of the man who had printed the stories in the first place, Benjamin Harris, who had not only demonstrated such bad taste but, perhaps even worse, had refused to get a license for his paper, as the law required, prior to publication. He had been warned about the license several times, had been told, in so many words, that it was the government's prerogative to approve or disallow any commercial enterprise anywhere in the kingdom, and that this was especially true in the colonies, where distance from the Crown tended to encourage a certain uppitiness in people. And he had been told that it was even *more* especially true when the enterprise was a newspaper, since the news, as often as not, was a record of the government's actions, or at least had an effect on people's perception of government.

Harris would have none of it. He was not the type to go through proper channels, and in fact the very notion of a proper channel struck him as an imposition, an indignity, a denial of his rights as a citizen of the New World.

He was about to be denied even more. Four days after Bostonians got their hands on *Publick Occurrences*, the colonial government, with the support of Boston's Puritan clergy, published a document of its own.

> The Governour and Council having had the perusal of the said Pamphlet, and finding that therein is contained Reflections of a very high nature: As also sundry doubtful and uncertain Reports, do hereby manifest and declare their high Resentment and Disallowance of said Pamphlet, and Order that the same be Suppressed and called in.[28]

It would not be un-suppressed. The first edition of the first American newspaper was also the last. Journalism in America was but a few days old, the ink barely dry on the pages and the printing press showing virtually no signs of wear, and already it had left readers gasping with its explicitness and politicians fuming with its impertinence.

Benjamin Harris cursed his fate and those who, in his view, had so arbitrarily brought it upon him. The historian Louis Solomon, speaking for the minority, takes his side. Harris "stands out," Solomon believes, "as the first in a long list of ornery, non-conforming, trouble-making newspapermen who have insisted on being free despite the consequences. Winners or losers, they are the pride of American journalism."[29]

But Harris was an American journalist for the briefest time, not long enough to be an influence, positive or otherwise, on those who followed. He remained in Massachusetts for a few years after *Publick Occurrences* expired, running a coffeehouse and a bookstore; then, in 1694, he returned to England, where he started another paper, this one called the *Post*. An acquaintance of his named John Dunton was not impressed. Harris, he said, "is so far from having any dealings with Truth and Honesty, that his solemn word, which he calls as good as his bond, is a studied falsehood, and he scandalizes Truth and Honesty in pretending to write for it."[30]

The *Post* lasted longer than Harris's previous venture did, but it won him no more friends and might have lost even more money. He "spent his last years as a querulous and unsuccessful editor and a vendor of 'the only Angelical Pills against all Vapours, Hysterick and Melancholy Fits' and other belauded patent medicines."[31]

It had taken the American colonies eighty-three years to get their first newspaper. Another fourteen would pass until the second, and it would be a publication of a very different kind.

Notes

1   Ackroyd, p. 174.
2   Ibid., p. 175.
3   Quoted in Darnton, p. 27.
4   Stephens, p. 2.
5   Brookhiser, *Hamilton*, p. 159.
6   Postman, *Bridge*, 59.
7   Durant, *Faith*, p. 622.

8   Simon, Linda, p. 46.
9   Kobre, *American*, p. 6.
10   Kobre, *Colonial, p. 3.*
11   Tebbel, p. 12.
12   Stephens, p. 184.
13   Quoted in Kobre, *Colonial*, p. 13.
14   Quoted in Payne, p. 14.
15   Tebbel, p. 12.
16   *Publick Occurrences*, September 25, 1690.
17   Publick Occurrences, ibid.
18   Ibid.
19   Ibid.
20   Ibid.
21   Ibid.
22   Ibid.
23   Ibid.
24   Ibid.
25   Ibid.
26   Ibid.
27   Kobre, *Colonial*, p. 16.
28   Quoted in Copeland, p. 5.
29   Solomon, p. 14.
30   Quoted in Tebbel, p. 14.
31   Mott, p. 10.

PART THREE

Age of Universal Literacy

INTRODUCTION TO PART THREE

THE 19TH CENTURY REMAINS THE CRADLE of modern communication in America when journalism became the single most important conversation in society, building on the spread of literacy, technological advancements, and the potential of large numbers of readers across the country. Only a few years earlier (1791), the First Amendment had begun to offer constitutional protection of speech and the press and with it had delivered a strong ideological basis for understanding journalism as a constitutive element of American society. The rise of an abolitionist press with the publication of the *Emancipator* (1820) and William Lloyd Garrison's *Liberator* (1831), which forced the slavery issue into the public and resulted in attacks on editors and destruction of presses, was a major test of press freedom.

The result was an unstoppable development of communication, transportation, and the dissemination of facts and fiction, which bound this vast country together politically, economically and culturally. It also raised the position of journalism to a "fourth estate," confirming its independence and defining the place of information and entertainment in a democracy. The claims of the press as a voice of the people, an upholder of the public interest, and a supporter of the public's right to know, grounded in the political and economic milieu of the 19th century, helped solidify the place of journalism, and would later mark the road of other, emerging media into the 20th century.

Population growth and the push across the West, immigration in the latter part of the century, urbanization and industrialization, as well as progress in education—especially among women, who came to represent a substantial readership of books, magazines and newspapers—provide the social and economic context for the development of the technological means of communication, which aided the press in its efforts to reach people and to further the cause of enlightenment.

Changing conceptions of space and time had become important factors in the rise of American society during the 19th century with immigration, the expansion westward and the urban pace of existence creating circumstances for change. As a personal experience, both space and time, however, found their concrete representation in the development of communication technologies, from the ever-increasing radius of railroad services by the 1840s to the advancement in printing technologies. The latter began with the introduction of the iron press, followed by the cylinder press, the use of the steam press (1810) and subsequent changes to the rotary press (1850), to help meet the growing production of print products from books and pamphlets to newspapers.

Advancements in the manufacture of paper from rags to wood pulp followed, to result in newsprint that became readily available to meet the rising demands from print media. Thus, the press became a readily-available, mediating institution whose understanding of timeliness and whose coverage of domestic news provided a sense of living in a fast-moving, expanding society.

In addition, the telegraph overcame space and increased the speed of delivering information. It was utilized by news agencies (since the 1850s) to circulate news efficiently while providing not only access to information, but also engaging in a process of cultural and political bonding across a vast country, and among multiple ethnic and religious groupings, where the reality of local independence was penetrated by the latest urban fads and fashions promoted by easily-available reading materials. In addition, the number of telephones, developed after Alexander Graham Bell had been awarded a patent in 1876, reached over 1,000,000 by 1899. Access to telephones added to the personal experience of spontaneity and became a new form of presence, which also aided the news-gathering process with its speed and efficiency. The deployment of both telegraph and telephone helped contract and control an expanding nation through the speed of communication, which facilitated the sharing of language and culture and shaped the dissemination of knowledge and information.

Also, the rising standard of living made the purchase of reading materials an affordable form of participation in information and entertainment, aided by the introduction of the penny press (*New York Sun*, 1833) at a time when even books would become much cheaper (since the 1840s). Thus, competing weeklies, such as the *New World* and *Brother Jonathan*, which were printed like newspapers to qualify for cheap postal rates, began to print serialized, frequently pirated novels, suggesting the prevalence among readers for the popular, which reflected a desire to encounter oneself or to enter into the familiar in fictional accounts. Thus, journalism flourished, combined with a natural curiosity among Americans about the outside world and their own environment.

An immigrant culture spawned a vibrant foreign-language press, dominated in the 1880s by German-language newspapers. Together, this press focused on political conditions in its respective home countries and debated adjustments to an American way of life. Recent immigrants, who had not yet learned the language, typically read these daily and weekly newspapers. Their availability in an American reality helped in the transition by legitimating through language and culture the immigrant's presence in a foreign environment. Similarly, the African-American press also began to prosper after the publication of *Freedom's Journal* (1827) and the *North Star* (1847), issued by Frederick Douglas, to serve a growing community of freed slaves. Together, these publications reflected the ethnic and racial diversity across the country.

News had become a commodity that attracted readers and the use of illustrations perfected the presentation of information. Consequently, intelligence about the battles of the Civil War (1861–65), for instance, arrived in the parlors of the North quickly, illustrated by engravings based on the work of photographers like Mathew Brady, who was the principal coordinator of these efforts in the field.

Thus imagery began to enter journalism as another way of presenting the world, by creating a visual vocabulary that helped illiterates and immigrants, in particular, to participate in society. Members of the press embraced photography after the first photograph, based on halftone technology, appeared in the New York *Daily Graphic* in 1880. But the daguerreotype had already made the family portrait an affordable middle-class product by the 1850s which was later replaced by tintypes that were cheap, and their small format was quick to produce. Tintypes became extremely popular during the Civil War, partly because they featured a robust metallic support. Later tintype technology was used for campaign buttons and even brooches and medallion cards, spreading the use of imagery even among the working class. The picture had become a familiar companion of everyday life in America during the latter part of the 19th century.

It was the penny press, however, that changed the American newspaper by introducing the idea of "news" with an abundance of information about the social and political life of its cities, regions, or the country, gathered by its own staff members and even correspondents abroad. The result was a dramatic change from a service to politicians and commercial interests to the manufacture of a product, called news, for a variety of readers, who, in turn, became a sought-after product for advertisers. Fierce competition, particularly in larger cities such as New York, led to calls for accuracy and timeliness, and created a genre of news as a reflection of everyday life with reporters hired to cover beats, like police, the courts, or commercial activities, besides sports or religion.

In the meantime, the weekly press blossomed in many rural areas of the United States to become a local institution, focusing on local news and advertising, while the struggle for readers in urban areas had resulted in fierce competition—for instance between Joseph Pulitzer (*New York World*) and William Randolph Hearst (*New York Journal*). It signaled the rise of "yellow" journalism, in which sensationalism and fictional accounts dominated the pages of newspapers. Adolph Ochs, the publisher of the *New York Times*, on the other hand, established an information style of journalism, sharply differentiating between news and entertainment.

Increasing demands for reading matter seemed to suggest that Americans had been convinced that reading was the *sine qua non* of full participation in a democratic society, coupled with the realization that knowledge was the key to understanding the world, from scientific advancements to social and political developments. The resulting overload of information in an era of enormous social, economic and political advances, for instance, led to the need felt for efficiently-packaged knowledge through abridgment and summary, or in the form of digests. People began to use print sources that offered quick relief from the flood of facts and fiction, thus publications like the *Literary Digest* (1890) became popular sources of information, which claimed to provide access to the latest intelligence regarding culture, science, economics and politics.

The rise of the press, in particular, was part of an economic development through-out most of the United States—from an aristocratic, mercantile generation of decision-makers to democratic, commercial entrepreneurs (among them publishers) who had recognized the economic potential of advertising sales, tested their power of defining tastes, and built on the potential of creating a consumer culture without yielding to any particular political persuasion. The press became an independent institution.

Weekly newspapers, as well as the substantial number of foreign-language publi-cations covering the United States, addressed a large variety of social, political and cultural interests while serving their respective communities. In fact, the existence of this type of press provided a unique experience in the relationship between the press and society; it imparted a familiarity with journalism and extended the education of individuals. Reading meant learning about a rapidly-changing American world.

It was a development that also swept through the political establishment with the rise of the professional politician in a popular and democratic milieu, in which representation became a major goal and party loyalty a mass movement. The result was a social and political climate, reinforced by the activities of the press and the interests of readers, in which the power of tantalizing expectations pushed society forward into an industrialized, urbanized and thoroughly modern future. The stage was set for the expansion of social communication, which would follow the defining ideas of news, information, education or entertainment that had been shaped and applied across America throughout the latter part of the century.

Chapter 12

H.L. MENCKEN

REFLECTIONS ON JOURNALISM
From the Baltimore *Evening Sun*, Dec. 29, 1924

T HE RAPID MULTIPLICATION OF PENNY TABLOID papers, which now spring up all over the United States, is probably not an indication that the standards of journalism are falling, as certain sour brethren appear to believe, but rather an indication that they have been rising, of late, too fast. In other words, the newspapers have gone ahead too swiftly for their readers. The latter have, as yet, but small taste for what is offered them: extensive and accurate news reports, editorials more or less sober and thoughtful, some approach to refinement in typography. What they want is cheap, trashy and senseless stuff, in bad English and with plenty of pictures. This is provided by the tabloids, or, at all events, by most of them. Their primary assumption is that the average reader of the folk is literate only in the most modest sense—that his public school education, if it has taught him to read, has still failed to teach him to read with ease. He has to spell out all "hard" words—*i.e.*, all words of more than two syllables. His vocabulary is extremely limited. He finds any reading whatever, even if there are no "hard" words, very slow work. The tabloid paper fetches him by reducing his agony to a minimum. Its news is couched in vulgar English, and brought into a small space. Whenever possible, a picture is added. Sometimes the only text is a line under this picture. Reading it thus becomes almost as simple as watching the movies.

The low average of literacy that prevails in the big American cities is kept down, not only by the incompetence and futility of the public-schools, but also by the large number of foreigners. These foreigners sometimes, though not often, read their own languages fluently, but English is difficult for them, and they thus prefer it in small doses. All of us, going abroad, are in the same boat. Like most literary gents, I have picked up some sort of crude acquaintance with most of the modern civilized languages—enough, at least, to read street signs and make out the principal contents of the newspapers. But if I am in Holland, say, I do not turn to the long editorials in the *Amsterdamsche Courant* or *Haagsche Post*. I content myself with the headlines and pictures in the lesser journals.

The general improvement in American newspapers that has been witnessed since the beginning of the present century—that is, in the larger and more serious newspapers—has not been due to any lofty moral purpose, but simply to the improvement of their financial position. They are richer than they used to be, and hence able to be more intelligent and virtuous. They got richer by first becoming poorer. In the year 1899, when I began newspaper work, two-thirds of the more eminent journals of the United States were in difficulties, or, at all events, suffering diminishing profits. What had brought them to this pass was, first, the devastating impact of yellow journalism, and secondly, an excess of competition in their own class. In most American cities there were four or five morning papers and as many evening papers, all struggling desperately for circulation and advertising. Even the paper that got both found the getting enormously expensive, and so profits diminished. In the end some of the most famous journals of the country began to lose heavily, and came upon the market. Their old owners, having, as a rule, no other resources, simply could not carry them on.

The men who bought them, in the main, were not professional journalists, but rich men who believed that it would be pleasant to play at molding public opinion. It was found to be pleasant, true enough, but it quickly turned out to be also very expensive, and the new owners accordingly began to sweat. The issue of their sweating was a series of consolidations. Two weak papers were combined to make one stronger one, and then a third and sometimes a fourth weak one was sucked in. As competition was thus reduced, prosperity began to return. Finally came the war boom in advertising, and the goose was run to the top of the pole. The principal newspapers of the United States are sounder financially today than they have ever been before. They are fewer than they used to be, but I know of none that is hard up. Some of them make annual profits that run into the millions. Money has given them dignity, as it gives dignity to individuals. They are no longer terrorized by advertisers. They show an increasing independence in politics. They are far more outspoken and untrammeled than they used to be in discussing such things as business and religion. More, they have got over their old fear of the yellow journals, and have thus abandoned all attempts to be yellow themselves. Most of them look decent, and most of them, I believe, are decent, as decency goes in this world. They are not for sale. They cannot be intimidated. They try to report the news as they understand it, and to promote the truth as they see it.

It is a curious fact, but it is nevertheless a fact, that this change, which raised newspaper salaries by at least 200 percent, and greatly augmented the dignity of the newspaper profession, was bitterly resisted by the majority of working newspaper men. That resistance, at the start, was not hard to understand. The entrance of new owners and new methods imperiled jobs, and especially it imperiled the jobs of those journalists who were most secure under the old order—the ancient, picturesque class of happy, incompetent Bohemians—the "born" newspaper men of tradition, with the intellectual and cultural equipment of City Councilmen or police lieutenants. The fact that it simultaneously benefited all men of a greater professional competence was forgotten, even by such men themselves. They all resisted the new discipline, and longed for their old irresponsible freedom.

But resistance, of course, was futile. Expensive properties, potentially worth millions a year, could not be intrusted to amiable ignoramuses. The growing salaries attracted better men, and they quickly made their way. Today the chief problem before newspaper executives is that of making these better men better still—of getting rid of the old tradition altogether and lifting journalism to genuine professional dignity. The attempts to set up schools of journalism all have that end. So far, these schools have accomplished little, but that, I believe, is chiefly because they have been manned by fifth-rate instructors—largely old-time journalists out of jobs. This, of course, is simply saying what might have been said of most medical colleges thirty years ago. The medical men have solved the problem of professional education, the lawyers are about to solve it, and soon or late the newspaper men will solve it too.

The more decorous and decent newspapers, in striving for more civilized manners, have dragged the yellows with them. They themselves have ceased to be yellow, and so there is no longer any need for the yellows to be super-yellow. More, the yellows have learned the value of outward respectability in dollars and cents. Advertisers long ago discovered that an inch of space in a newspaper read at home was worth a foot in one read only on the street cars. Thus the yellows, when the advertising boom began, found that their quieter rivals were getting all the pickings. So they began to be quieter themselves. Today most of them seem somber indeed, if one recalls their aspect twenty years ago.

This cleaning up has not altogether pleased their public. On its lower levels it longs with a great longing for the old circus-poster headlines, the old scares and hoaxes, the old sentimentalities and imbecilities. It wants thrills, not news; pictures, not text. To meet its yearning the penny tabloids have come into being. They are cheaply produced and require little capital; they invariably attain to large circulations. But I doubt that many of them are making money. The difficulty they face is the difficulty the old-time yellows faced: advertisers are doubtful, and with sound reason, about the value of their space. They are thus forced to depend largely upon their circulation revenues for existence, and in that direction, even with a half size paper, there is little hope of profit. I believe that they'd all be better off if they raised their prices to the level maintained by the other newspapers. The boobs, in all probability, would still buy them, and with careful management they might show an actual profit on circulation.

Chapter 13

ROBERT E. PARK

THE IMMIGRANT PRESS
AND ASSIMILATION

NATIONAL CONSCIOUSNESS IS INEVITABLY ACCENTUATED BY immigration. Loneliness and an unfamiliar environment turn the wanderer's thoughts and affections back upon his native land. The strangeness of the new surroundings emphasizes his kinship with those he has left.

This general effect is intensified in those whose race is still struggling for political recognition. The most able members of such an immigrant group are apt to be men exiled for their patriotic activities. In the new country they have more freedom to work for their cause than they had under a hostile government at home, and they naturally encourage their fellow immigrants to help them.

Nationalism Natural Among Immigrants

It is probably not a mere coincidence that nationalist movements have so frequently originated and been supported from abroad. In many cases national consciousness has manifested itself first of all in the exile, the refugee, and the immigrant. When schools in the native language were closed in Europe, they were opened in America. When the vernacular press was being slowly extirpated by a hostile censorship in the old country, it flourished so much the more in the new, where the government did not seem to know that it existed.

The Lithuanians refer to the United States as "the second birthplace of the nationality." But the same thing might be said by the Irish and some others.

By the middle of the last century Lithuania had been so completely Polonized that the native speech had ceased to be the language of the literate classes. It was not until 1883 that the "Young Lithuanians," as the nationalist party was called, published their first magazine, *Auzra* (Dawn). But between 1834 and 1895 no less than thirty-four Lithuanian periodicals were published in America.

The movement for the revival of the Irish language may be said to have had its origin in Boston. At any rate, the Phil-Celtic Society, organized there in 1873, had been in existence for three years before it attracted the attention of Irish scholars in Dublin, and thus led to the formation in 1876 of the Society for the Presservation of the Irish Language, since succeeded by the more popular Gaelic League.

When the Magyars closed the Slovak gymnasiums, and suppressed the Matica—a literary, linguistic, and educational society, which had been the center of the nationalist movement—schools were established in America, with the result that Slovak peasants learned in America what they were not permitted to do in Hungary—to read their mother tongue.

Efforts to Prevent Assimilation

The nationalistic tendencies of the immigrants find their natural expression and strongest stimulus in the national societies, the Church, and the foreign-language press—the institutions most closely connected with the preservation of the racial languages. In these the immigrant feels the home ties most strongly; they keep him in touch with the political struggle at home and even give him opportunities to take part in it. Both consciously and unconsciously they might be expected to center the immigrants' interests and activities in Europe and so keep him apart from American life.

> The majority of Lithuanians did not emigrate to the United States with the idea of staying there definitely. They came in order to make money and to return as soon as possible to their own country, where many of them became landowners. Thus, it has come about in recent years that considerable territory has been returned into the hands of the Lithuanians who had been dispossessed, and the money earned in America has served to increase the fortune of the mother country. The other Lithuanians are obliged to remain in America while they are waiting for change in the actual political government in Russia in order to return to their native land.
>
> Up to the present, Lithuanian emigrants to the United States have not lost their sentiment for their nationality. Thanks to their religion which unites them in their own churches, which are, in a way, their communal houses, genuine nurseries of patriotism. And thanks, also, to the numerous organizations which bring them together and establish relations between different groups, even those that are most isolated. In the great cities, where the Lithuanians form compact masses and are well organized, they are better defended against assimilation; but fortunately the patriotic societies, the number of which is constantly increasing, have extended their field of action to all the colonies and have spread among our fellow countrymen the love of the far-away homeland and the cult of the national traditions. The press, also, is a powerfully strong bond between all the Lithuanians scattered about on the American soil. The Lithuanians in America edit a score of papers. We may cite as among the most important: *Lietuva, Vienybe Lietuvnilcu, Draugas, Kathalikas* (Chicago), *Darbininku Viltis* (Shenandoah, Pennsylvania), *Tevyne*.[1]

The Church has proved an effective medium for either the assimilation of peoples or their isolation, according to the purposes of the clergy. Dominant races have used their control of a church with its missions and its schools to introduce and establish their languages and cultures among primitive and subject peoples. A people's own church, however, has always been a conservative influence. It is in the religious rituals that the ancient language forms are longest retained. The Arabic language, the sacred language of Mohammedanism, has preserved its purity more completely than other languages because in childhood the Moslems are made to learn large portions of the Koran by heart, and if a single vowel is mispronounced it is regarded as an act of infidelity. The following anecdote illustrates to what extent religion may conserve speech:

> I was one day surprised by seeing a tall, elderly black man making extracts from a theological work in the Khedivial library at Cairo. He told me he came from Sakoto (on the Kwora River), and that, although his people had a distinct language, they were all taught Arabic in their boyhood. He certainly spoke the purest and most perfect Arabic that I ever heard spoken, using all the vowels and inflexions with the utmost precision.[2]

It is an interesting fact that among the Lithuanians, at least, the Church has appeared in a double role as a nationalizing and a denationalizing influence. In Europe the Poles seem to have used their superior position in the Catholic church to Polonize the Lithuanians, and that, too, at a time when the Russian government was making efforts, rather desultory and unsuccessful, to be sure, to Russianize both the Lithuanians and Poles.

> The Polish nationalists have found powerful support in the Catholic clergy. Those of the diocese of Vilna, with the bishop at their head, have been particularly serviceable, and have been more occupied in Polonizing their parishioners than in teaching them the Christian faith and Christian morality. For this purpose all means are good. The pulpit, the confessional, are transformed by the clergy into schools of the Polish language. For a long time the Polish bishops of Vilna have employed singular tactics in the nomination of the priests. They assigned to the Lithuanian parishes priests who spoke only Polish. Instead of taking the trouble of learning the language of their parishioners, the priests forced the Polish language upon their congregations.[3]

In America, on the other hand, such of the Catholic clergy as are Lithuanian nationalists have been struggling with apparent success to win back to the Lithuanian cause those members of their race who had already become Polonized and were, apparently, not only content, but proud that they were regarded as members of a race of higher cultural status than their own.

> The most powerful bond which unites immigrants of the same nationality in a foreign country is that represented by religion and the Church. Pious people, like the Poles, Slovaks, Lithuanians, and others, carry with them to the land across the sea their own profound religious sentiment. In their churches they feel at home. The church is a little corner of the distant

fatherland. It is thus in America that religion has become the most powerful source of resistance against Americanization (assimilation).

There was a time when Lithuanians were an exception to this rule. At the time of the first emigration of Lithuanians to the United States, in 1869, the national revival had not made its appearance among the people. The Lithuanians came to America and built churches for the Poles. It is a curious thing, but the Lithuanians were Polonized in America in their own churches. Many of the new arrivals from the banks of the Niemen, instead of learning English in America and adapting themselves to the conditions of the new country, wasted their energy in learning Polish and acquiring Polish customs. Even in the parish schools, poorly conducted as they were, Lithuanian parents insisted that their children should be instructed in Polish. Nevertheless, this anomalous situation has ceased to exist. It took a good many years to persuade these ignorant people that Lithuanians are and ought to remain Lithuanians, and that it is a crime on their part to serve the purposes and plans of another nation than their own. That work of persuasion has not yet ceased. It is sufficient to mention here that in Pennsylvania there still exists a little colony, by name of Ridge, where the Lithuanians call themselves Poles. Opposed to the usage of the Lithuanian language, they steadily insist that their church shall be conducted by Polish priests who do not know a word of Lithuanian. . . .

The Lithuanians rarely have anything in common with Poles. They form distinct organizations and construct separate churches and schools. At present there are eighty Lithuanian churches in the United States and they all are strong fortresses and guardians of the nationality of the Lithuanians of America. They maintain twenty-two primary schools, in which their children learn English and at the same time their mother tongue. Five of these are directed by Polish sisters, one by French sisters, and the others by English sisters. But the teachers have learned the language of their scholars and teach the children Lithuanian. Four other schools are directed by the Sisters of St. Casimir. It is thanks to the church and the school that many hundred thousands of Lithuanians have not been absorbed in the great nation. As long as the Lithuanians construct and maintain their churches and their schools, the name and nationality of the Lithuanians will be maintained in the country of George Washington.[4]

The immigrant press serves at once to preserve the foreign languages from disintegrating into mere immigrant dialects, hyphenated English, and to maintain contact and understanding between the home countries and their scattered members in every part of the United States and America. These functions of the press naturally tend to preserve the national feeling; but beyond this there is an intrinsic connection between the desire to preserve national identity and the written mother tongue. This feeling is most defined among members of the "oppressed" races, who have identified their struggle for political recognition with their struggle for their own press. However, it has been observed that nationalism is never in effective existence without a free press. Under these circumstances it is intelligible that foreign-language newspapers in America should frequently be inspired by nationalist motives and that their editors should seek to use the press as a means of preventing assimilation.

During the past generation many thousands of Slovak peasants have emigrated to the United States, carrying with them feelings of bitterness and resentment toward the authorities of their native land. They speedily learn to profit by the free institutions of their adopted country, and to-day the 400,000 Slovaks of America possess a national culture and organization which present a striking contrast to the cramped development of their kinsmen in Hungary. There are more Slovak newspapers in America than in Hungary; but the Magyars seek to redress the balance by refusing to deliver these American journals through in Hungarian post office. Everywhere among the emigrants leagues, societies, and clubs flourish undisturbed—notably the American Slovak League (*Narodnie Slovensky Spolok*), the Catholic *Jednota* (Unity), and the women's league, *Zivena*. These societies do all in their power to awaken Slovak sentiment, and contribute materially to the support of the Slovak press in Hungary.[5]

Among the other foreign-language papers published in the United States are eight in the Arabic language. The Syrian population here, to which this press is addressed, is not large, and would hardly support such a variety of organs, except for the circulation of these papers abroad, particularly in Turkey. In his autobiography, Abraham Rihbany, now pastor of a Unitarian church in Boston, who at one time edited the *Kowkab America* (Star of America), the first Arabic newspaper in the United States, tells how this foreign circulation made the paper a force against assimilation. He had taken a lively interest in the political campaign of 1892, when Cleveland defeated Harrison for the presidency. This interest led him to urge his Syrian readers to become Americans.

It was my first great incentive to ask questions about and to idealize the possibilities of American citizenship. Again I was moved with stronger conviction than ever to renew my appeals in the *Kowkab* to my fellow Syrians to drink the nobler spirit and adopt the customs of free America.

Contrary, however, to my most confident expectations, the proprietor looked upon my policy with disfavor. He contended that my bugle calls to the Syrians to follow the path of American civilization were bound to arouse the suspicion of the Turkish authorities. The *Kowkab*, he said, was meant to be loyal to the Sultan, if for no other reason than because the majority of its subscribers were residents of Turkey. If Abdul Hamid should for any reason stop the circulation of the paper in his empire our whole enterprise must cease to be. The publisher also protested against any show of antagonism to Turkey in our columns, chiefly because his brother held office in one of the Turkish provinces, and he had written to our office that the least manifestation of disloyalty on our part might cost him not only his office, but his liberty as a citizen. That was a severe disappointment to me. The hand of the Turk was still heavy on me, even on Pearl Street, New York.[6]

The French Canadians in the Province of Quebee have maintained a long, bitter, and not always successful, struggle to preserve their language against the invasion of English idioms and English words. With the invasion of New England by French-Canadian laborers, this struggle has been transferred to American soil. In this country the French press seems to have played a leading role in the struggle. There was a time when the Canadian immigrants were "trembling," as Mr. Belisle, historian of the Franco-American press, puts it, "upon the abyss of assimilation." It was even true, according to Mr. Lacroix, editor of *Le Public Canadien*, that the younger generation seemed almost ashamed of their native language.

> The result has been that indifference, mingled with a little jealousy against the people of their own blood, has led them [Canadian French] to yield to the stranger and caused the loss of that preponderance upon those by whom they are surrounded that they should always seek to conserve. The moment they cease to speak their mother tongue they lose their rallying point and sense of association. As soon as their influence weakens they see day by day their nationality falling in ruins. The time when they were about to succumb under the weight of their indifference, certain friends of the nationality, seeing the abyss that they were digging under their feet, undertook some years ago a supreme effort in order to place them again in a position that their apathy had caused them to lose. It was for this purpose that the welfare societies, the literary and historical and mutual-aid societies were founded, the only means which remained to save from shipwreck the descendants of noble France.[7]

It was through the influence of the French newspapers that the French language and the French traditions were preserved. There was a time when it was even necessary to combat the influence of the Catholic clergy—particularly was this true during the period that Cardinal, at that time Bishop, O'Connel, was located at Portland, Maine. The Lewiston *Messenger* assailed the bishop with great violence, it appears, in its struggle to maintain the rights of the French language in the churches and in the parochial schools.

> Under the present bishop, Monseigneur Walsh, nominated 1907, the tone of the *Messenger* has somewhat moderated. But it has not surrendered, and it still continues the battle for the rights of the French language in the Church, in the schools—because it must be admitted that the acts of Monseigneur Walsh have somewhat exasperated our fellow countrymen in Maine—and even to-day it seems that religious peace in the diocese of Portland is still far from being re-established. As long as the subtle machinations of the higher Irish clergy continue, Rome will be in a state of ignorance with regard to the actual condition of the French Canadians in the United States; and as long as dioceses, where ours are in the majority or where they form a considerable part of the population, shall continue to be occupied by French-hating bishops, it seems, indeed, that the complete re-establishment of peace must be adjourned indefinitely.[8]

It was a French-Canadian paper, the *Public Canadian*, which was responsible for the first national organization, upon a Canadian-French nationalist basis, of the local mutual-aid societies, of which there was likely to be at least one in every French colony in the United States. This federation, formed in 1868, has served to bind together all the little isolated and scattered communities, particularly in New York State and

New England, and to unite them for the preservation of the language and the traditions of the French-Canadian people.

It was also in 1850, a good many years after the first Canadian families emigrated to New York, that the first society of St. Jean Baptiste was established in the more united States. These families were on the slope which leads to the gulf of assimilation. The Canadian traditions, the French language, the family names, all that had been thrown into discard by many of our good French Canadians who believed that they were obliged to go through this metamorphosis merely because of the fact of their emigration. The *Public Canadian* appeared then at an auspicious moment. We must not find too much fault with this journal for having carried to an extreme the nationalistic propaganda. Its motives were most praiseworthy. It was in order to correct mistakes that the *Public Canadian* went a little too far in the opposite direction. We may well believe to-day that this was the best thing to do at the moment in order to arrive at the desired end—namely, the safeguarding of our language and our traditions. What is certain is this— that we see in New York at that moment the organization of a magnificent movement which has since grown and developed everywhere throughout the state of New York and New England. The revival was so general and the appeals to the national sentiment made by the *Public Canadian* made such a profound impression, that a new journal appeared upon the scene. This was the *Protecteur Canadien*, founded in May, 1868, in St. Albans, Vermont, by Monsieur l'abbe Zephirin Druon, grand vicar of the diocese of Burlington, and Monsieur Antoine Moussette. M. l'abbe Druon wrote to M. Paradis proposing a fusion of the two papers. But the latter deter- mined to return to Kankakee, Illinois, whence he had come some years before, and he ceased the publication of the *Public Canadian* in October, 1868. The journal had had a short existence, but had made an immense impression upon the French Canadians. In outlining the organizations among them on the basis of nationalism and of language, M. Paradis recommended the first federation of the Canadian-French societies.[9]

Aims of Nationalism

The World War has profoundly altered the situation of most immigrant peoples in the United States. Many of the races they represent have now won the independence which was the ultimate aim of the European nationalist movements. This fact removes a strong motive, that existed before 1914, for the maintenance in America of a national organiza- tion and a nationalist press, the object of which should be to preserve the immigrant peoples against the forces that were making for assimilation and Americanization.

But foreign-language institutions and agencies, the Church and the press and the nationalist societies, have sought not merely to protect against assimilation those immigrants who were here temporarily, but to preserve among those who remained permanently in the United States the traditions and language of the home country. At least, some of the leaders among the immigrant peoples have thought of the United States as a region to be colonized by Europeans, where each language group would maintain its own language and culture, using English as a *lingua franca* and means of communication among the different nationalities.

"There is no reason for the English to usurp the name of American. They should be called Yankees if anything. That is the name of English-Americans. There is no such thing as an American nation. Poles form a nation, but the United States is a country, under one government, inhabited by representatives of different nations. As to the future, I have, for my part, no idea what it will bring. I do not think that there will be amalgamation—one race composed of many. The Poles, Bohemians, and so forth, remain such, generation after generation. Switzerland has been a republic for centuries, but never has brought her people to use one language. For myself, I do favor one language for the United States—either English or some other, to be used by everyone, but there is no reason why people should not have another language; that is an advantage, for it opens more avenues to Europe and elsewhere."[10]

From this viewpoint it is conceivable that every racial and language group should continue in this country its efforts to maintain and extend to other kindred races the influence of its language and culture. This is what the Poles have attempted to do in the case of the Lithuanians. It is what the Magyars have sought to do in the case of the Slovaks. It was to this same end that the Germans in America have striven not merely to maintain their own racial characteristics, but to make the German language and the German speech as far as possible an integral part of the cultural life of the American people.

Some years ago there appeared under the title of "The Melting Pot" a drama of which the author, a well-known Zionist leader, Israel Zangwill, announced as wisdom's last word that America has become a melting pot into which the different races and nationalities, together with everything that mark them as such—their speech, their tradition, their customs, and their rules of life—were to be thrown in order that they might there be converted into Americans.

For us German-Americans the teaching of this play is simply a mixture of insipid phrases and unhistorical thinking. It is just the contrary of that toward which we strive, and this doctrine must be so much the more sharply and decisively antagonized by us as it is enthusiastically accepted by the thoughtless rabble. For we did not come into this American nation as an expelled and persecuted race, seeking help and protection, but as a part of the nation, entitled to the same consideration as every other, and as a member of a noble race that for more than two hundred years has found here its second home and, in common with its blood-related Anglo-Saxon peoples, founded and built up this nation. Neither is it necessary for us to permit ourselves to be twisted and reformed into Americans, for we are Americans in the political sense—and only in this—as soon as we swear allegiance and unite ourselves to the common body of our German-American people. We must, however, protest in the most decided manner against the limitless assumption which would seek to force our German personality into the mold of a manufactured folk type, not only because this sort of forced uniformity would mean the destruction of all that we regard as holiest in our people and its culture, but also because such an undertaking strikes the German mind as a sacrilege. But, however praiseworthy it may seem to a shortsighted patriotism that the mixture of races and peoples of this land should be forced by every possible means into one single form, and that the God-given diversity should be permitted to be lost in an artificial mold, so much the more portentous for the future of the nation must this mistaken Roman-Gallic conception of artificial unity appear to our German minds. The illusion that it is possible to suppress or destroy the individuality of the racial type or that it is possible to force into the yoke of a single speech or a single form of government was, thanks to the German resistance, the cause of the downfall of the Roman Empire. The open or secret attempt to do away with our German cultural type—that is to say, our speech, our customs, and our views of life—in the smudge kitchen of a national melting pot has its source in a similar illusion and will likewise, even if in some other way, revenge itself.

Let us German-Americans put our trust in the secret strength of the ring which we have inherited from our fathers and "vie with one another in order to make manifest the strength of that ring." Let us believe, before all, in ourselves; our ring's strength will show itself in our children's children, in a people filled with the German ideals, in the German-American people of the future.[11]

There are only two language groups in the United States, both of them Jewish, for whom the language they speak is not associated with a movement, or at least a disposition, to preserve a nationality. These two languages are the Yiddish, the dialect of the Russian and Polish Jews, and Ladino, the language of the Oriental Jews. Most Jewish writers and editors say that they do not expect the Yiddish press in America long to outlast the stream of Jewish immigration. Abraham Cahan, editor of the Jewish Daily *Forward*, says he has no interest in Yiddish as such, though he doesn't apologize for it. He would just as lief write to Jews in English as in Yiddish.

On the other hand, with the growth of Yiddish literature in recent years, and with the realization by Yiddish writers of the value for literary purposes of a vernacular speech in which the native sentiments and character of a people find a natural and spontaneous expression, a new attitude, a more respectful attitude, toward Yiddish has made its appearance. This feeling is undoubtedly reênforced by the Zionist movement, which is the expression of the awakening of the Jewish racial and national consciousness, even though Hebrew, and not Yiddish, is the language of Zion.

Thus a recent writer in the *Day* seeks to answer the question, "Who reads the Yiddish papers?" and comes to the conclusion that the Yiddish press is no longer confined to the "greenhorns."

> . . . Superficially, at least, the world believes that the Yiddish newspapers are being read by people who have no alternative—*i.e.*, such who are not sufficiently Americanized to read English. . . . It is generally supposed that the American-Jewish youth reads no Yiddish at all, and that our

intellectual classes are ashamed of Yiddish, that our physicains, lawyers, engineers, teachers, etc., never glance at a Yiddish paper, and that, in short, it is only reading matter for the "green-horn" or un-Americanized Jew.

I am now able to refute this opinion. . . .

Our readers have, of course, noticed our new "Civil Service" department in Yiddish under the caption, "How to obtain a government position." Various positions were announced weekly, Federal and state, and I also answered questions relating to civil service.

In these Briefkasten letters, which I received from every corner of the country, there is a treasure of facts which illuminates the question as to which class the Yiddish reader in America belongs.

. . . When I first proposed this department, the project was met with derision. . . . "Those who are interested in civil service do not read Yiddish and consult the special civil-service papers in English," they said.

They argued that our readers were operators, tailors, peddlers, poor storekeepers, who do not know the meaning of civil service. . . .

First of all, we must say that most of the civil-service readers of the *Day* are versed in English. In order to pass a civil-service examination . . . it is necessary to pass in English. I have good reasons to believe that from 5 to 10 per cent of the *Day* readers are interested in civil service. . . . This, according to my statistics, shows that one out of every ten or twenty readers knows English. Moreover, these readers are American citizens. . . . They are, then, not "green" and "compelled" to read Yiddish.

The letters I receive are written in English, Yiddish, Hebrew, German, Russian, and French. The majority are, of course, in English and Yiddish, half and half. Most of the English letters are excellently written, and show that their authors are fully Americanized . . . and yet they read a Yiddish paper. . . . Some of the letters beg to be excused for not writing English. The writers include lawyers, dentists, engineers, authors, linguists, physicians, chemists, physicists, typewriters, stenographers, bookkeepers, and clerks. . . . So that many men in professions, Americanized in the fullest sense, who read English newspapers, can nevertheless not discard the Yiddish paper. . . .[12]

Another article in the *Forward* takes up the question of the Yiddish speech and reaches the conclusion from general observation that there is no longer the feverish anxiety that formerly existed among Jewish immigrants to discard the signs of their foreign descent and speak English. It is interesting, also, that this change came during the war, when immigration from Europe had practically ceased.

Do the East Side children speak more Yiddish now than they used to? Have they another feeling for it, or a different desire for its revival than heretofore?

No one has, of course, taken any census on this subject, but one may judge by general facts and general impressions. On the street, just as little Yiddish is heard to-day as in the past, and perhaps a little less. . . . About ten years ago the proportion of "green" children was higher than to-day. Then, any group of children playing around a tenement house contained always one or several who could not speak English and would speak Yiddish.

Now the proportion of "green" children is much lower, especially in the last few years since the war broke out. That is the reason why a Yiddish word is more rarely heard among the boys and girls on the street now than before. . . .

Looking into the Jewish homes, though, one sees a different picture. In thousands of homes of intelligent workingmen the parents are trying to induce their children to speak Yiddish. It is a matter of principle with them. In years past these intelligent parents would try to speak more English to their children—not for the latter's benefit, but for their own— so as to break into the English language. . . .

. . . We recall the time when there was an abyss between the parents and children. Even the more refined would be in distant contact with their parents simply because they did not understand each other and did not attempt to understand each other. Now the situation is different. It is a fact that in hundreds of Jewish homes the children, young and old, boys and girls who attend high school, who have been raised here, take an interest in Jewish newspapers, literature, and theaters.

Jewish theatrical managers declare that genuine American Jewish boys and girls are their frequent patronizers. And because of this they find it necessary to advertise their plays in the English newspapers. The chasm between the old and new generation in the Jewish quarter is far less deep to-day than of yore. The parents understand their children better, and the latter understand their parents better. They understand each other's spirit and each other's language.[13]

Perhaps the immigrant peoples have been more successful than the native born realize in preserving their language and ideals in America, in reproducing in their homes and communities the cultural atmosphere of the homeland. A proof of this success is that frequently the immigrant, who meets everywhere in this country those who speak his own language, assumes that America is populated mainly by people of his own race.

In a composite people like the American, it is inevitable that the color of the whole should appear different to those who view it from different points. The Englishman is apt to think of the United States as literally a New England, a country inhabited in the main by two classes: on the one hand, descendants of seventeenth-century English colonists, and on the other, newly arrived foreigners.

The continental European, on the contrary, is apt to suffer from the complimentary illusion, and to believe that practically all Americans are recent European emigrants, mainly, or at least largely, from his own country. Frenchmen have insisted to me that a large proportion of the United States is French, and Germans often believe that it is mainly German and that one could travel comfortably throughout the United States with a knowledge of German alone. This is very natural. A man sees his own country people flocking to America, perhaps partly depopulating great tracts of the fatherland; he receives copies of newspapers in his own language printed in America; if he travels in America he is fêted and entertained everywhere by his own countrymen, and is shown America through their eyes. "I visited two weeks in Cedar Rapids, and never spoke anything but Bohemian," said a Prague friend to me. An Italian lady in Boston said, speaking in Italian, "You know, in Boston one naturally gets so little chance to hear any English," much as Americans make the corresponding complaint in Paris and Berlin.[14]

Possibly native-born Americans are subject to a similar illusion and think that the bulk of our population is made up of descendants of the Colonial settlers. In so far as this illusion holds, native Americans are likely to think there is a much greater demand than actually exists in the United States for uniformity of language and ideas.

The fact that human nature is subject to illusions of this sort may have practical consequences. It is conceivable, for example, that if it should come to be generally regarded as a mark of disloyalty or inferiority to speak a foreign language, we should reproduce in a mild form the racial animosities and conflicts which are resulting in the breaking up of the continental imperiums, Austria-Hungary, Russia, and Germany. In all these countries the animosities appear to have been created very largely by efforts to suppress the mother tongues as literary languages.

Popularization of the Immigrant Press

So far, immigrants have found America tolerant of their languages. English is the language of the government and of public education, but except during the war, when such publications were under special surveillance, there has been no check on any use of a foreign language as such. The intellectual representative of a suppressed race is here given a free hand to do what was prohibited at home: establish a press in his mother tongue.

The foreign-language press in the United States is edited by men who have brought to this country the European conception of a press addressed exclusively to the highly educated, deliberately formal and abstruse. Naturally, at first, they seek to reproduce here the newspapers that they have known at home. To a very considerable extent they succeed; but the conditions of life in America, and particularly the conditions under which the immigrant press is published, seriously modify their effort.

It is the business manager of the paper who realizes most keenly what the paper loses by "high-brow" language. The business manager of the *Dziennik Ludowy*, the Polish Socialist paper of Chicago, said he was always begging the editors to write more simply, but they insisted on writing heavy articles that no one could understand. The business manager of the *Novy Mir* (New World), a Russian Socialist paper, said the paper was running at a deficit, but none of the editors were obliging enough to write so that they could be understood. Letters came in from the readers, who were peasants, saying: "Please send me a dictionary. I cannot read your paper"; or sending in an underlined copy of the paper with a note attached, which read: "Please tell me what this means and send the paper back to me. I paid for it and I have a right to know what it means."

The *Novy Mir* contains articles on Socialism by Lenine. One intelligent Russian, who did not have the technical vocabulary of the university, said, "I take the *Novy Mir* for

Lenine's articles, and it breaks my heart to read it." The present editor, I. Hourwich, writes editorials of four columns, and he is said to be the most difficult writer to understand of all the men who have been on the *Novy Mir*. Lecturers who have traveled among the Russians in the United States say that the peasants in their eagerness to understand what is going on in Russia puzzle over articles that no one but a philosopher could understand.

> Many of the younger men who were writers for the *Novy Mir* re-emigrated to Russia at the expense of the Kerensky government in the spring of 1917 along with two or three thousand other Russians. Detsch, the first editorial writer, became a social patriot; while Trotzky, the last editorial writer, who had belonged to no party, became a Bolshevist. Many of the journalists are now writing for the official Bolshevist newspapers—the *Isvestia* and the *Pravda*—and they are writing just as they did in New York City, for the intellectuals rather than for the people. Only Volodarsky, who was the "Question and Answer" man on the *Novy Mir*, and who became "Commissaire of the Press" for the Soviet government, discovered how to write a Socialist paper for the people.
>
> It is not only the Socialist press of the United States that writes above the heads of its readers. The big Greek dailies of New York City, the *Atlantis* and the *National Herald*, also write editorials that the readers cannot understand. While in Athens there are seven dialect papers, there is only one in the United States, the *Campana*, of New York City, which is a broadly humorous paper containing satiric verses. A plain language, similar to the spoken language, appears in the *Atlantis* and the *National Herald* only in the bitter disputes carried on between the Constantine and Venizuelos factions.[15]

The immigrant intellectual has a very poor opinion of the American newspaper and intellectual life generally, as he finds it in this country. Our newspaper, with its local news, its personal gossip, and its human-interest anecdotes, is not his conception of journalism. Its very language seems to him lamentably close to the language of the street.

> American newspapers, years ago, passed through a stage of bombast, but since the invention of yellow journalism by the elder James Gordon Bennett—that is, the invention of journalism for the frankly ignorant and vulgar—they have gone to the other extreme. . . . The great majority of our newspapers, including all those of large circulation, are chiefly written, as one observer says, "not in English, but in a strange jargon of words that would have made Addison or Milton shudder in despair."[16]

It is the American's interest in local news that justifies, perhaps, the characterization of America as a "nation of villagers." As a people, it seems we are not interested in ideas, but in gossip. That was undoubtedly the meaning of the cautious observation of a number of the Jewish *intelligentsia*, whom Hutchins Hapgood met some years ago in a Ghetto café.

"In Russia," one of them said, "a few men, really cultivated and intellectual, give the tone, and everybody follows them. In this country the public gives the tone, and the playwright and the literary man simply express the public."[17]

One ought to add, however, in order to make the statement complete, that the American public is very largely made up of the second and third generations of European peasants.

The European press was, as has been stated, addressed to the *intelligentsia*, but among immigrants, with the exception of the Jews, the Japanese, and the Letts, the *intelligentsia*, although active, is not numerous. The Ukrainians are said to have only five intellectuals in the United States. The great majority of the immigrant peoples are peasants; they speak dialects and read with difficulty. It becomes necessary, therefore, for the editor of an immigrant paper to make all sorts of concessions to the intelligence of his public.

He usually finds, with a little experience, that his own readers have the vulgar tastes of the American public in an even more primitive form, and that he must do violence to most of his journalistic ideals in order to hold their attentions.

The first concession the editor makes is in style and language. In order to get his paper read, he must write in the language his public speaks. If the literary form of his language differs widely from the vernacular, he will have to abandon it in whole or in part for the dialect spoken by the majority of his readers.

> All Croatian papers in America are written in the prevalent literary style, and the same as is used in Croatia. In some of them there appears from time to time a composition in one of the several dialects, mostly as a humoristic, entertaining fiction. We have in America a few capable fellows who do such writing. I myself do it from time to time, using the most characteristic dialect, *kajkavstina*, which was before the literary reformation the dialect of our early scholars (before 1835).[18]

The *Romanul*, of Cleveland, the only Rumanian daily of the United States, has articles in the Transylvanian vernacular, as 90 per cent of the Rumanians in this country, it is estimated, come from Transylvania. The Rumanian paper of New York City, the *Desteaptate Romane*, has fiction and verse contributed by one of the readers in the Transylvanian dialect. In general, an attempt is made to write the articles in this paper, if not completely in the dialect style, at least using words that are not the correct Rumanian of the kingdom of Rumania, but are familiar dialect words understood by any Rumanian. The word for "pocket," which is *jep* or *jepul* in the dialect, is *luzanar* in correct Rumanian. Sometimes the editor compromises by writing in the literary language on the editorial pages, discussing the conventional themes, while the rest of the paper is made up of hasty translations from the American newspapers, written in jargon, words from the vernacular interspersed with American idioms and American words with foreign endings.

The editor must make other concessions, to the interests of his readers, which take him still farther from the traditions of the European press.

The peasants are sentimental; the editor prints poetry for them in the vernacular. He fills the paper with cheap fiction and writes loud-sounding editorials, double-leaded, so that they will be easily read. The readers are very little interested in abstract discussion, so the paper is more and more devoted to the dramatic aspects of the news and those close to their own lives, the police news, labor news, and local gossip.

Sometimes the publisher is himself an ignorant man, or at least not an intellectual, who looks upon his paper as some American publishers do, as an advertising medium, which prints news merely to get circulation. These men know their public and insist on printing in the paper what their subscribers are interested in and able to read. It is said that one of the most successful Chinese editors in America cannot read the editorials in his own paper because he does not understand the literary language. Some of the most successful foreign-language papers are published by men who do not make any pretensions to education and are regarded by the writers they employ as ignoramuses. When the writers for the press despise both their employers and their public, as they sometimes do, not much can be expected from the newspaper which they succeed in producing.

The following description of an immigrant newspaper from the inside is not to be regarded as characteristic of all immigrant newspapers. It certainly would not be representative of the Socialistic and radical press. There is generally a very real sympathy and a good deal of understanding among the editors of the radical papers for the European peasant, especially after he has been transformed in this country into a laborer and proletarian. He then becomes a representative of the class for which the radical press mainly exists. But the remoteness from life of the aristocratic immigrant intellectual editor put to it for capital is reflected in this description.

> The editors of the *Szabadsag* have a curious theory which shocked me a great deal when I first joined the paper, but which I found later was working smoothly enough. It is usually summed up in the motto, "Anything is good enough for the "buddy"—buddy being the universally used term for the Hungarian immigrant worker. The word, adopted originally by the Pennsylvania and West Virginia coal miners, has been assimilated into the American Magyar idiom and is now spelled "bodi"; by the "intellectuals" it is mostly used as a term of amiable contempt. The average Magyar reader has no sense whatever for news value; in the outlying districts he gets Monday's *Szabadsag* on Wednesday, then saves it for Sunday, when the whole week's editions are carefully perused from beginning to end. The "buddy" calls any item found in a newspaper a *hirdetes*, meaning advertisement; the editorials, the news and feature stories, are all "advertisements." This does not imply—what is often the truth—that these items have been paid for; advertisement in the American Magyar idiom simply means reading matter. The big display ads. of patent-medicine druggists are perused just as religiously as the front-page war stories. In fact, they are liked better, because they are printed in bigger type and are more closely related to everyday life. And, indeed, while the editorial and news columns in most Magyar papers are written with an almost incredible carelessness, these "real" advertisements often display much ingenuity and skill—in a way, they are the most "American" items in the whole paper. It is customary for the big druggists, most of whom do mail-order business on a national scale, to employ editorial writers on the *Nepszava* and *Szabadsag* for writing advertising "copy," and there was a time when this "side line" netted more for some of the editors than their regular salaries. . . .
>
> Here I wish to say that, in the case of the Hungarian-American newspapers within the range of my personal observation, the leading consideration, as far as details of editorial routine were concerned, was

simply to get the paper out with as little effort as possible. Viewpoints of editorial and even of business policy were frequently overshadowed by the editors' unwillingness to exert themselves, by their determination to "take it easy." In other words, a more or less unconscious editorial sabotage was being practiced. The explanation lies in the conditions of the trade and the type of man engaged in editing Hungarian-American newspapers. The men working on the editorial staffs of the *Szabadsag* and *Nepszava* are not, for the most part, professional journalists at all—that is, they were not journalists in the old country; they came to the United States, not in the hopeful mood of young men determined to make good, but simply because this seemed to them the only way out of a maze of failures and mistakes. Without any particular training, without in most cases a knowledge of English, but with a strong aversion to strenuous work, they drifted into the offices of Magyar newspapers here, because they were not fitted for anything else; they considered their jobs as a sort of last refuge. In the lack of opportunity afforded by competition, real advancement is blocked to them; they are fully at the mercy of two employers—those of the *Szabadsag* and *Nepszava*. A few of them are sustained by the hope that they will ultimately be able to get out of the game; the rest, being well up in the thirties, have not even this hope left. They resign themselves to a hand-to-mouth existence, and simply cease to care.

It is not merely a matter of being overworked and underpaid; working conditions are notoriously bad in the case of the average American news-paper man, but for him there is always a chance of advancement. In the Hungarian-American press such chance does not exist; there are about a dozen jobs to go around, and no hope to come out on the top. To work on the *Nepszava* or *Szabadsag* means not only getting into a rut, but being bottled up in a cul-de-sac. From the publisher's point of view, the matter is almost equally hopeless; there is no supply of fresh talent to draw upon, but always the same crowd of twenty or thirty individuals; and in the absence of competition it hardly matters whether you turn out a good sheet or a bad one, except that it is cheaper, all told, to turn out a bad one. In trying to understand the failure of the Hungarian-American press to develop a single genuinely progressive organ of education and opinion, the psychology of the Hungarian-American editor must be taken into account.

In regard to the smaller "one-man" weeklies, the situation is not much better. For the publisher-owner-editor the chance of "making good" has hardly anything to do with the journalistic-literary quality of his sheet. As a rule, he has no local competitor, and his sources of revenue lie mostly in the way of the petty graft of parish politics and fraternal-society intrigue.

I do not hesitate to say that in the instances within my range of observation the influence exerted by the *Szabadsag* and *Nepszava* on the social life among Hungarian-Americans has been almost without excep-tion an evil one. This is to be accounted for, not by any particular personal wickedness on the part of publishers, but by the isolation of the Hungarian-American settlements and the fact that Hungarian-American newspaper power constitutes a monopoly compared to which the condition of the American press seems democratic. In a manner of speaking, these two dailies appear with the exclusion of publicity. There is no competition whatever. No movement can aspire to success without their approval and active support; their enmity means almost invariably failure for any social venture; and while their power for good is rather restricted, their power for evil is, within their own circle, practically limitless. And this power is wielded mostly to promote ends of personal vanity and ambition and revenge.

To be ignored or "teased" by these papers means, for the Hungarian business or professional man making his fortune among his people, almost certain ruin. And the worst of it is that the injured party—unless it be a matter of criminal libel—has no way at his disposal to seek redress.

Apart from a few isolated occasions I recall, it hardly ever happened that a weekly paper dared to engage in a fight against the powerful dailies; and even if it dared, its case would be hopeless; most of them command merely a local audience, and the two dailies have their ways and means of intimidation, and worse.

The *Elore*, of course, is another matter; but this labors under the handicap of being a Socialist paper. No "bourgeois" society or business or professional man would care or dare to lean upon the *Elore* against the two other dailies.

The most disgusting feature of the situation is probably the circumstance that the participants are practically always the same people, only lined up in different formations against one another. The only people who profit from this constant permutation of groups and parties within the ranks of the Hungarian intellectuals are the Socialists, one of whose chief propaganda weapons among the Hungarian workers in their permanent campaign, through the *Elore*, is the corruption of "bourgeois" fraternal societies and parish politics.[19]

The instability, lack of a policy, and general disorder exhibited by the Magyar press is likely to be characteristic of the press of all recent immigrants. It reflects the disorder that inevitably exists in every immigrant community before it has succeeded in accommodating itself to the American environment. It is not characteristic of the press of the older and more firmly established immigrant communities, like the Germans, Scandinavians, or any of those immigrants who have become permanently settled in the rural communities and small towns. This disorder means, specifically, that change and accommodation are going on.

On the whole, the significant changes that take place in the foreign-language press, under the influence of American conditions, have been in the direction of a simpler diction, closer to the despised vernacular; more attention to police news, and to personal items, matters of mere human interest; finally the substitution of nationalism and Socialism and conflicts within the immigrant community for the political discussions of the European press. This general lowering of the tones of the foreign-language papers has created a public in this country composed of peoples who, in their home country, would have read little or nothing at all. The following excerpts from the testimony of three members of the Russian Union, who were examined with reference to deportation, probably indicates the average mental caliber of the readers of *Novy Mir*:

Naum Stepanauk, of Brest-Litovsk:

Naum Stepanauk was a farm worker in Russia. He seldom read newspapers, and no philosophical or scientific books. When he came to the United States he went to New Castle, Pennsylvania, to the address of a man whom he knew. Then he spent three years in the mines at Shenandoah, Pennsylvania, and from there he went to Roderfield, West Virginia, and the Kansas farms. He also worked in a shop in Chio, and in the smelters and mines of Pueblo, Colorado. In Akron he had a job with the Goodrich Rubber Company. His average wage there was twenty-four dollars a week.

Stepanauk is a member of the Federation of Unions of Russian Workers. He said that his purpose in joining it was to educate himself further. Among a great deal of literature that he had, much of which had been left him by friends who had gone to Russia, he had actually read the following: Gorki, Tolstoi, Korylenko, *House No. 13*, L. Kralsky; *Sacrifice of War*, Kropotkin, an anticlerical pamphlet, and a song book. He was elected secretary of the Akron branch because he could write.

He explained that one of the aims of the organization was to teach men Russian as well as English, as very many members of the organization cannot read Russian. When asked why it would be of value to them to know Russian, he said, "So that they may understand life, their own lives." When asked whether he knew about the government of Russia in 1917, he replied that he knew only in a vague way. When asked, in connection with the lectures and classes of the Federation, whether he was not very little interested in forms of government, he replied, "Yes, I was only interested in Russia." When asked why he wanted to go back to Russia, he said, "Because I was born in Russia, and it is binding to that country because my ideals are there." Anarchy he understood to be love, equality, and construction.

Powell Kreczin, of Saratov, Russia:

When asked how he could tell the good from the bad, Kreczin replied: "Other people tell me what is good and what is not good. I, myself, do not understand many things." When asked who told him what was good and what was bad, he replied that those people had all gone back to Russia; and when asked whether the people who were arrested with him instructed him, he said, "They are all of the same caliber as I am; they do not know anything for themselves."

This man did not know that a republic does not have a king. All he knew was the word "republic" and the name "Wilson." When asked about the songs sung at the Union, he said, "There is one about a fellow who was sent to exile, a good, strong, husky fellow." When asked about the books he read, he said, "I was interested in works about culture and about the sea; I cannot recall what works the others were."

Nicolai Volosuk, of Grodno, Russia:

Volosuk was a member of the Federation of Russian Unions. Copies of the *Golos Truda* and the *Khlieb i Volya* were sold at their meetings. In his leisure time Volosuk attended a self-educational school, where he learned about botany, forestry, "where coal comes from, and how it is formed." When asked whether he ever read books on social subjects, he did not understand the term. Did he ever read books on government or philosophy? He replied, "I never read big books." When asked "If you were given a book like this in Russian, would you understand the language?" he said, "If the book were written very *literate*, I don't think I could understand." When asked whether he believed in Bolshevism, he said, "I only believe that if I go back to Russia I would have some land."

Here for the first time, with few exceptions, the European peasants find newspapers written about things that interest them, in the languages they speak. Here for the first time the reading habit is established among them. The newspaper brings them into contact with the current thought and the current events of their community, primarily the race group, with its interests merging on one side into the homeland and on the other into the larger American community. Gradually, and largely through the efforts of the Socialist press, the reading habit establishes the thinking habit. The net result has been to raise the intellectual level of the immigrant body.

Language and Culture Modified

The immigrant press, despised by the foreign intellectuals for its vulgarity, has power among its readers rarely equaled by more literary journals. Having created its reading public, it monopolizes it to a great extent. Nationalistic editors seek to use this monopoly to keep their readers' interest and activity focused on the home country. But under the terms of its existence the press is apt to aid rather than prevent the drift toward the American community.

This process of Americanization by contact can be seen very plainly in the changes introduced into the speech of the immigrants. Even in the rural communities, where the foreign language is preserved longer than elsewhere, it tends to become Americanized, or at least localized. This is illustrated in the case of the Pennsylvania Dutch.

> The *Morgenstern* was written for the Germans of Pennsylvania, who spoke a mixed language based on the Pfaelzer dialect and modified by the adoption of many English words and phrases.
>
> The first words that are adopted from the American are such words as "basement." Striking verbs are also introduced: Ich habe *gelcetscht* einen *Kold* (I have caught [catched] a cold). Ich bin *aufgejumpt* wie ein junger Hirsch (I jumped up like a young deer).
>
> Business transactions also serve to introduce the phrases used by Americans. An advertiser in the *Morgenstern*, after beginning his ad. in Hoch-Deutsch, finished it in Pennsylvania Dutch: Wir sind *determt Bissness zu tun* (We are determined to do business). Kommt wir wollen *einen Bargen machen* (Come, we will make a bargain). Wir *trihten* sie wie ein *Gentleman* (We will treat you like a gentleman). Sie sen *gesatisfeit* (They were satisfied).
>
> Pieces of furniture or articles of clothing that were different from those in Germany were usually referred to by their English names. The writer of a letter which was published in the paper contrasts the conditions

in an Indian (Insching) hut with the civilization of the towns: Do waren Wir net *getruvelt* mit Lichter, Schaukelstuhle, un carpets (We were not troubled with lights, rocking chairs, and carpets); im Parlor (in the parlor); Net *gebattert* von *Hupps*, oder 17 *Unterrock, Teitlacking*, un seidens *Dresses* (Not bothered with hoops, or 17 petticoats, tight lacing, or silk dresses).[20]

Yiddish has been peculiarly hospitable to new and strange words, taking up with and giving currency to every convenient locution and every striking phrase, from the languages with which it came in contact.

The changes that Yiddish has undergone in America, though rather foreign to the present inquiry, are interesting enough to be noticed. First of all, it has admitted into its vocabulary a large number of everyday substantives, among them "boy," "chair," "window," "carpet," "floor," "dress," "hat," "watch," "ceiling," "consumption," "property," "trouble," "bother," "match," "change," "party," "birthday," "picture" (only in the sense of newspaper), "gambler," "show," "hall," "kitchen," "store," "bedroom," "key," "mantelpiece," "closet," "lounge," "broom," "tablecloth," "paint," "landlord," "fellow," "tenant," "shop," "wages," "foreman," "sleeve," "collar," "cuff," "button," "cotton," "thimble," "needle," "pocket," "bargain," "sale," "remnant," "sample," "haircut," "razor," "waist," "basket," "school," "scholar," "teacher," "baby," "mustache," "butcher," "grocery," "dinner," "street," and "walk." And with them many characteristic Americanisms; for example, "bluffer," "faker," "boodler," "grafter," "gangster," "crook," "guy," "kike," "piker," "squealer," "bum," "cadet," "boom," "bunch," "pants," "vest," "loafer," "jumper," "stoop," "saleslady," "ice box," and "raise," and with their attendant verbs and adjectives. These words are used constantly; many of them have quite crowded out the corresponding Yiddish words. For example, *ingel*, meaning boy (it is Slavic loan-word in Yiddish), has been obliterated by the English word. A Jewish immigrant almost invariably refers to his "son" as his "boy," though strangely enough he calls his daughter his *meidel*. "Die boys mit die meidlach haben a good time!" is excellent American Yiddish. In the same way *fenster* has been completely displaced by window, though *tur* (door) has been left intact. *Tisch* (table) also remains, but chair is always used, probably because few of the Jews had chairs in the old country. There the *beinkel*, a bench without a back, was in use; chairs were only for the well-to-do. "Floor" has apparently prevailed because no invariable corresponding word was employed at home; in various parts of Russia and Poland a floor is a *dill*, a *poologe*, or a *bricke*. So with the ceiling. There were six different words for it.

Yiddish inflections have been fastened upon most of these loan-words. Thus, "er hat ihm abgefaked" is, "he cheated him," *zuhumt* is the American gone to the bad, *fix'n* is to fix, *usen* is to use, and so on. The feminine and diminutive suffix *ke* is often added to nouns. Thus, bluffer gives rise to *blufferke* (hypocrite), and one also notes *dresske, hatke, watchke*, and *bummerke*. "Oi! is sie a blufferke!" is good American Yiddish for "isn't she a hypocrite!" The suffix *ñick*, signifying agency, is also freely applied.

Allrightnick means an upstart, an offensive boaster, one of whom his fellows would say "he is all right" with a sneer. Similarly, *consumptionick* means a victim of tuberculosis. Other suffixes are *chick* and *ige*, the first exemplified in *boychick*, a diminutive of boy, and the second in *next-doorige*, meaning the woman next door, an important person in Ghetto social life. Some of the loan-words, of course, undergo changes on Yiddish-speaking lips. Thus, landlord becomes *lendler*, lounge becomes *lunch*, tenant becomes *tenner*, and whiskers loses its final s. "Wie gefallt dir sein whisker?" (How do you like his beard?) is good Yiddish, ironically intended. Fellow, of course, changes to the American *feller*, as in "Rosie hat schona feller" (Rosie has got a fellow—*i.e.*, a sweetheart). Show, in the sense of chance, is used constantly, as in "git him a show" (give him a chance). Bad boy is adopted bodily, as in "er is a bad boy." To shut up is inflected as one word, as in "er hat nit gewolt shutup'n" (he wouldn't shut up). To catch is used in the sense of to obtain, as in "catch'n a gmilath chesed" (to raise a loan). Here, by the way, *gmilath chesed* is excellent biblical Hebrew. "To bluff," unchanged in form, takes on the new meaning of to lie; a bluffer is a liar. Scores of American phrases are in constant use, among them, "all right," "never mind," "I bet you," "no, sir," and "I'll fix you." It is curious to note that "sure, Mike," borrowed by the American vulgate from Irish English, has gone over into American Yiddish. Finally, to make an end, here are two complete and characteristic American-Yiddish sentences: "Sie wet clean'n die rooms, scrub'n dem floor, wash'n die windows, dress'n dem boy, und gehn in butcher store und in grocery. Der noch vet sie machen dinner und gehn in street fur a walk."[21]

"Pennsylvania Dutch" is almost as distinct from the German of modern Germany as Yiddish is. What is true of German is likewise true of the Scandinavian languages, that the Scandinavian press makes no concessions to the barbarisms of the Americanized language. The effect of this is that the written and the spoken language are steadily drifting apart. So far as this is true the language of the Scandinavian press is becoming a dead language.

In the community where I was brought up Norse is spoken almost exclusively, but with a vocabulary freely mixed with English words and idioms, the words often mutilated beyond recognition by an American— and, of course, utterly unintelligible to a Norseman recently from the old country. In the case of many words the younger generation cannot tell whether they are English or Norse. I was ten or twelve years old before I found out that such words as *pa tikkele* (particular), *stæbel* (stable), *fens* (fence), were not Norse but mutilated English words. I had often wondered that *poleit, trubbel, soppereter*, were so much like the English words polite, trouble, separator. So common is this practice of borrowing that no English word is refused admittance into this vocabulary provided it can stand the treatment it is apt to get. Some words are, indeed, used without any appreciable difference in pronunciation, but more generally the root, or stem, is taken, and Norse inflections are added as required by the rules of the language.[22]

The language of the American Poles, though still etymologically Polish, contains an increasing number of American slang words which are treated as roots and used with Polish inflections and prefixes, but their syntax and literary application (the latter more easily influenced than etymology by changes in the form of thought) are growing more and more specifically local, and neither Polish nor American.[23]

The culture of the immigrants is also influenced by American life and tends to become, like their speech, neither American nor foreign, but a combination of both.

I might sum up my general impression of Polish-American life in the following way:

The fact that the social atmosphere here struck me at once as non-Polish cannot be attributed to the mere addition of American elements to the stock of Polish culture which the immigrants possessed, for after a closer acquaintance with American life I could not recognize the essential features of American culture in those non-Polish characters of Polish-American society, and at this moment the latter seems more unfamiliar to me than any of the American social circles I know, which range from Middle West university professors to New England fishermen.

Of course, the contents of this new "Polish-American" culture are drawn chiefly from Polish, but partly from American life. For instance, the roots of the language are 95 per cent Polish, 5 per cent American slang. But not only are those contents mixed and melted, but they have received a form which is essentially original. Thus, not only do English words receive Polish inflexions, prefixes, and suffixes, and vice versa—the etymology of Polish words is sometimes simplified according to English models—but the construction of the phrase is entirely peculiar; not Polish, but not imitated from English either. Similarly, the social ceremonial includes some fragments of the Polish peasant ceremonial, a few notions imperfectly borrowed from the Polish upper classes, a few American customs, all this still very roughly combined but already showing a tendency to simplification and organization.

These original features of the Polish-American culture which at this moment, in view of the low level of this culture and of its recent beginnings, are difficult to characterize in exact terms, have probably their source in the fact that the immigrants are mostly recruited from the peasant class and have here to adapt themselves to conditions entirely different from the traditional ones. The peasant class has not participated much in the higher Polish culture which has been, and still is, chiefly the product of the upper and middle classes, and those peasants who actually do participate in it seldom emigrate. Thus the peasant brings with him here only his own particular class culture, fully adapted to the specific conditions of agricultural communities; and he is forced to drop much of it in the new industrial environment and to substitute something else instead. The higher Polish culture, which a few of the Polish intellectual leaders try to impose upon him, contains some elements which he accepts and adapts to his own use; but most of it has no vital significance for him, and grows more and more distant with the progressive adaptation to the new circumstances. Thus, for instance, the official language in which formal speeches are made, and reports of institutions written, is hollow and bombastic; the professed acceptance of the Polish national ideal is with the great majority purely superficial, like a Sunday dress, etc. Art, particularly music, is perhaps the only field in which Polish cultural values really mean something to the immigrant colonies. On the other hand, of the American values only a few are really felt as important by the immigrant community, particularly in the first generation, and these are selected and reinterpreted in a way which often makes them entirely unrecognizable. In this case, the selection being made freely, not under the pressure of leaders, whatever American elements enter into the current of Polish-American life are vital at once, and the second generation acquires more, and understands and assimilates better, so that there is a gradual drifting of the whole Polish-American society toward American culture.

But at the same time this society continues to evolve in its own specific line and—like every living society—produced in addition to the Polish and American values it assimilates new and original customs, beliefs, ways of thinking, institutions; this original productivity prevents its complete absorption in the American *milieu* probably as much as the Polish traditions. However, the fact that this Polish-American society is enveloped by a higher cultural *milieu* must keep its own specific culture always on a low level, since with a few exceptions all the individuals who grow able to appreciate and produce higher values naturally tend to participate in American life; they do not lose contact with their original *milieu*, but this contact becomes limited to primary-group relations, whereas the result of their productive activity, performed with the help of American secondary institutions, goes to American society.[24]

It is a question whether the foreign-language press is a brake or an accelerator in this process of assimilation. The editor of the Lithuanian paper *Draugas* has asserted that it is, on the whole, a means of segregating and isolating the foreign-language communities and so preventing assimilation. Other editors have asserted that it assists the immigrants, particularly the first generation, to orient themselves in the American environment and share in the intellectual, political, and social life of the community.

In the Swedish and Norwegian wards of such cities as Chicago, Minneapolis, St Paul, and Rockford, and in a county like Goodhue in Minnesota, where the presence of large numbers of the foreign born makes the use of the foreign tongue imperative in the homes, streets, markets, and places of business, and where the news is read in a Scandinavian daily or weekly, the tendency to keep the speech of their ancestors is strong. The preacher and the politician alike understand this, and the literature, speeches, and even the music, in the campaigns for personal and civic righteousness are presented in no unknown tongue, as the theological seminaries and Scandinavian departments in other institutions, and the Swedish and Norwegian political orators in critical years, bear abundant witness.[25]

The mere facts of residence and employment give the immigrant an interest in American events, customs, ideas. He needs some familiarity with these in order to "get along." The foreign-language press must print American news to fill this need of its readers, and by so doing it hastens the development of this personal necessity into a general interest in America.

Editors of the foreign-language papers have claimed that their press is not merely a medium for the communication of news, thus initiating the immigrant into American environment, but is likewise a means of translating and transmitting to him American ways and American ideals.[26]

It is in accordance with this conception of the role of the foreign-language press that the Interracial Council purposes to Americanize the immigrant by encouraging American manufacturers to advertise in foreign-language papers. "Practical Americanization is the use of American things, and by using them getting our foreign people to like them and prefer them to other things."[27]

It seems fairly clear that what the foreign-language press actually does, whether or not the editors desire it, is to facilitate the adjustment of the foreign born to the American environment, an adjustment that results in something that is not American, at least according to the standards of an earlier period, but that is not foreign either, according to existing European standards.

How far the foreign-language press enables the immigrant to *participate* in the national life is the question raised by a study of Americanization methods. For it is participation rather than submission or conformity that makes Americans of foreign-born peoples.

Notes

1. J. G., "Les Colonies Lituaniennes aux Etats-Unis," in *Annales des Nationalites*, 1913, vol. ii, pp. 231–2.
2. E. T. Rogers, "Dialects of Colloquial Arabic," in *Journal of the Royal Asiatic Society*, 1879, p. 366.
3. A. Jakstas, "Lituaniens et Polonais," in *Annales des Nationalites*, 1915, vol. iii, p. 214.
4. A. Kaupas, "L'Église et les Lituaniens aux États-Unis d'Amérique," in *Annales des Nationalites*, 1913, vol. ii, pp. 233–4.
5. Seton-Watson, *Racial Problems in Hungary*, 1908, pp. 202–3.
6. Abraham Mitrie Rihbany. *A Far Journey*, 1914, pp. 239–40.
7. A. Belisle, *Histoire de la Presse Franco-Américain*, 1911, pp. 40–1.
8. A. Belisle, *Histoire de la Presse Franco-Américain*, 1911, p. 206.
9. A. Belisle, *Histoire de la Presse Franco-Américain*, 1911, 44–6.
10. Emily G. Balch, *Our Slavic Fellow Citizens*, 1910, pp. 398–9. (Conversation with a Polish-American priest.)
11. J. Goebel, *Kampf um deutsche Kultur in Amerika*, 1914, pp. 11–13.
12. R. Fink, *Day*, July 14, 1915.
13. Jewish Daily *Forward*, March 9, 1917.
14. Emily G. Balch, *Our Slavic Fellow Citizens*, pp. 399–400.
15. Winifred Rauschenbush, *Notes on the Foreign-language Press*, New York (manuscript).
16. H. L. Mencken, *The American Language*, 1919, p. 313.
17. Hutchins Hapgood, *The Spirit of the Ghetto*, 1902 and 1909, p. 282.
18. Francis K. Kolander, editor of *Zajednicar*, organ of Narodna Hrvatska Zajednica Society, Pittsburgh, Pennsylvania. (Correspondence, October 27, 1919.)
19. Eugene S. Bagger, *The Hungarian Press in America* (manuscript).
20. *Der Morgenstern und Bucks und Montgomery Counties Berichter.*

21.   H. L. Mencken, *The American Language*, 1919, pp. 155–7. (A footnote to this passage credits Abraham Cahan for the information in this passage.)

22.   Nils Flaten, *Notes on American Norwegian, with a Vocabulary, Dialect Notes*, vol. ii, Part ii, 1900, p. 115.

23.   Thomas and Znaniecki, *The Polish Peasant*, vol. v.

24.   From a personal letter of Florian Znaniecki, Professor of Philosophy, University of Posen.

25.   C. H. Babcock, "Religious and Intellectual Standpoint," in *The Scandinavian Element in the United States*, pp. 123–4.

26.   Frank Zotti, "Croatians: Who They Are, and How to Reach Them," in *Advertising and Selling*, July 5, 1919, 29, no. 5, p. 19.

27.   Coleman T. Du Pont, "The Interracial Council: What It Is and Hopes to Do," in *Advertising and Selling*, July 5, 1919, 29, no. 5, pp. 1–2.

Chapter 14

ISHBEL ROSS

FRONT-PAGE GIRL

FIVE YEARS AFTER THE CIVIL WAR an eighteen-year-old girl named Sally Joy left the plush security of her home in Vermont and talked herself into a job on the Boston *Post*. It was only a matter of weeks until the men in the office were lining the floor with papers to keep her white satin ball gown from picking up the dust.

Sally did not need this newsprint carpet laid for her ambitious feet. It merely set the key for the befuddled dismay with which the normal newspaper man regards the unwelcome sight of a woman in the city room. Things have changed in the newspaper world since Sally's time. The typewriter has taken the place of the pen; the linotype has supplanted hand composition; there is little dust on the floor of the metropolitan city room; and the girl reporter rarely shows up during working hours in a white satin gown.

She must be free to leap nimbly through fire lines, dodge missiles at a strike, board a liner from a swaying ladder, write copy calmly in the heat of a Senate debate, or count the dead in a catastrophe. She never takes time to wonder why someone does not find her a chair, change the ribbon of her typewriter or hold smelling salts to her nose as she views a scene of horror.

"I want to be treated like a man," said Sally, who was a little ahead of her time. But she could not persuade her colleagues that she was anything but a helpless female. At first there was indignation about having "a woman on the sheet" and the youth assigned to escort her to all functions beginning after seven o'clock was the butt of the staff.

But the girl reporter hung on and got her reward. She was sent without masculine aid to cover a suffrage convention in Vermont, traveling with Lucy Stone and Julia Ward Howe. As the only woman at the press table, an admiring colleague chronicled her presence:

> Miss Sally Joy of Boston has a portfolio at the Reporters' table in the Convention for the *Post* of her native city. She is pretty, piquante, and dresses charmingly. She has a high regard for Mrs. Bloomer, although she

diverges from that good lady on the science of clothes. Miss Joy has made a reputation as a newspaper correspondent and reporter of which any man might well be proud. And this is saying a good deal for a woman. Miss Joy is as independent as she is self-supporting and she votes for Woman's Suffrage.

Sally was neither the first nor the best of the early women reporters. She was merely the symbol of a point of view that has changed surprisingly little in the last half century. She went from the Boston *Post* to the *Herald* to do a society column. She called herself Penelope Penfeather and sometimes wrote about fashions and the home. In due time she married and faded into the mists, but not until she had helped to found the General Federation of Women's Clubs and had served as the first president of the New England Women's Press Association.

Her demand to be treated as a man has echoed innumerable times in city rooms throughout the country. And all that she stood for is still regarded as a threat to the peace, honor and coziness of that sound haunt of masculinity—the city room, practically as sacred to men as a stag club or the pre-Volstead saloon.

To-day there are nearly twelve thousand women editors, feature writers and reporters in the country. They have found their way into all of the large newspaper offices and most of the small ones. They have invaded every branch of the business, but have not made much impression in the front-page field.

This does not mean that they have failed to make themselves felt in newspaper work; on the contrary, their success has been substantial. They hold executive posts. Two have dominant voices in important papers on the Eastern seaboard. Many of them edit small papers of their own. They run Sunday magazines and book supplements, write editorials, do politics, foreign correspondence, features, straight news, criticism, copy reading and sports writing, as well as the old standbys—the woman's page, clubs and social news.

They excel in the feature field and dominate the syndicates. They stop only at the political cartoon. They function in the advertising, business, art, promotion and mechanical departments, as well as in the editorial rooms. They have arrived, in a convincing way. But the fact remains that they have made surprisingly little progress on the front page, which is still the critical test. Not even a score of women take orders direct from the city desks in New York. The proportion is even less in other cities. They come singly or in pairs on a paper, rarely more. There are just as few on the general staff as there were at the turn of the century.

Whenever possible, they are steered into the quieter by-waters of the newspaper plant, away from the main current of life, news, excitement, curses and ticker machines. They are segregated where their voices will not be heard too audibly in the clatter. They get tucked away on the upper floors where the departments flourish. They lurk in the library, diligent girls wedded to the files.

Most of them would rather be where they are. The specialists increase in number and usefulness each year. They have better hours, fair pay, a more leisured existence. They get their own following. They don't have to beat the drums every day they live. They can make dinner engagements and keep them. They have time to buy their hats.

But out in the city room—where high-powered lights blaze on rows of desks, where copy readers bend like restless caterpillars over the reporter's work, where the city editor usually resembles a sedate professor rather than the Mad Hatter of the films, where phones jangle and tickers click—only two or three women can be found, working quietly at their typewriters in a fog of abstraction.

They are the front-page girls who somehow have weathered storms of prejudice—the odd creatures who have been pictured as doing things only slightly more impossible than they all have attempted at one time or another. They are on the inner newspaper track. They are there because they have felt the bewitchment of a compelling profession. There is little else they can do once they have tasted its elixir. Strange music sings in their ears. Visions haunt them as they walk the streets. They fall asleep with the sound of rumbling presses in their heads. They have seen too much and it hasn't been good for their health.

For the woman reporter goes beyond the news into the raw material from which it springs. She catches the rapt look of the genius and the furtive glance of the criminal. She detects the lies, the debauchery and the nobility of her fellow men. She watches the meek grow proud and the proud turn humble. She marvels only when people who have feared publicity get drunk with it, and strain for a place on the front page.

She walks unscathed through street riots, strikes, fires, catastrophes and revolution, her press card opening the way for her. She watches government in the making, sees Presidents inaugurated, Kings crowned, heroes acclaimed, champions launched on the world. She has a banquet seat with the mighty. She travels far and wide in search of news, and uses every vehicle known to man. She sees a murderer condemned to death and watches the raw agony of his wife while he dies.

Nine times out of ten her day's work takes her to the fringes of tragedy. News visits a home most often to annihilate it. The shadow of a reporter falling across the doorstep may presage the collapse of a lifetime of work. The woman reporter must face harsh facts without any qualms about her business. She must be ready for such hazards as may befall her. She must be calm and full of stamina. For she will savor strange bitters as well as alluring sweets; endure fatigue and disappointment beyond reason; withstand rebuffs that wither or exhilarate in turn; meet abuse with the equanimity born of self-control; and function with complete belief in what she is doing and loyalty to her paper.

She must have a sound sense of the values of life and great capacity to withstand the shocks of human emotion. She must see with clairvoyance, judgment or experience the salient points of any situation; be resourceful and good-natured; have initiative and enough perception to avoid being taken in. She must know how to get her facts, to weigh them with sagacity and, above all, how to write.

Where is this paragon to be found? No editor believes that she exists. She probably doesn't. And if she did, she would not have much chance to prove it, for although women have hit the sky in feature writing, they still have a long way to go to establish themselves as first-string news reporters. There have been no great women war correspondents. Few have written well on politics or economics, although Anne O'Hare McCormick, Dorothy Thompson and Ruth Finney are striking exceptions. But in the feature field they are hard to beat. They cover the town. They write with an interpretative touch. They put more emotion, more color, more animation into their work than the first-string girls. This is the special field for women. They get opportunities and they do it well. There were four at the Thaw trial in 1907. Dozens crowded the press rows at the Hauptmann trial twenty-eight years later. They have the excitement of going out on the big stories without the strain and responsibility of writing the news leads. They rarely have to bother with trivial events, but go from one major assignment to another. They are valued for their capacity to write.

With a smooth touch and a dramatic sense they often make names for themselves. Their salaries go up in proportion. The brightest and the most original step into the syndicate field. But the front-page girl is essentially an anonymous creature, a hard-working wretch who does not lightly exchange her job for the softer road.

She is in love with her work. She has the fantastic notion, shared by no one else, that an unsigned front-page story that passes through several thousand hands and soon lands in the gutter, most likely unread, is its own reward. The results are visible, immediate, alive—at least to her. A few hours earlier she watched the scene, talked to the people about whom she writes. There is speed and flavor to this rapid transfer of thought. In another twenty-four hours she will scarcely find the story readable, so soon does newsprint grow cold. But for the moment it possesses her imagination.

She cares little if she eats or sleeps until it is finished and the last fact is carefully checked and fitted into its niche. She moves in a trance. She forgets that she has a home, a husband, a child, a family. She hangs on by day and night, so physically exhausted that her head sings, waiting to get what she is after. In some respects she is almost as spectacular as the movies have made her; in others, she is a weary drudge, coping with minor obstacles.

But when things are running high, and her assignment is first rank, nothing stops her—neither storm, fire, frost, broken-down telegraph wires nor the rudeness of man. She is an implacable creature, bent on gaining her ends. When the story is in the paper, she rarely remembers what she has suffered in the pursuit of news. The excitement is its own anesthesia. Nothing is left but the afterglow.

So it never surprises her to hear an eager girl say, "How thrilling! I should love to do newspaper work." The girl is right. It is. The picture is not overdrawn. But good candidates for the job are rare. They are usually freaks who have landed head first at their goal, either by opportunity, hard work or luck—most often luck. Few women have what Mrs. Eleanor Medill Patterson, of the Washington *Herald*, calls flash in the handling of news. It's a gift that no school of journalism, no city editor, can impart.

The front-page girl has everything against her at the start. She may write quite well. She often does. But the most delicate test a reporter meets is in marshaling facts and assembling a big news story in perfect proportion, under pressure. This calls for lucid thinking, good judgment, and absolute clarity of style. The pace is like lightning. The most experienced men sometimes fumble among the countless intricate threads when hell is let loose too close to the deadline.

The woman reporter rarely gets the chance to try it. This is where she falls down flat in her editor's estimation, for it is the job that the star reporter is paid to do. It is his chief function for the paper. On the big story her vision is apt to be close and her factual grasp inadequate. The broad view is needed for a sound round-up. There is little time on a newspaper to cover up major mistakes in the construction of an important story.

The afternoon papers, which play their women feature writers to the limit, rarely trust them with the lead on a big running story. It has been done, but not often in metropolitan centers. Here the time element is of the utmost importance. If they fail, the paper is the loser. On the morning paper there is usually more time to pick up the stray ends when a woman has muffed her job. A crack rewrite desk is always waiting to iron out the imperfections of the reporters who go out on the street.

But city editors rarely take chances. They want complete reliability. They can't depend on the variable feminine mechanism. They might get a superb job. They might get a dud. No allowances are made for the failure of the woman reporter. She must stand on her own feet and prove her worth every day. When she draws a big story she is definitely on the spot. Nothing anywhere is going to help her, except her own intelligence and quick-trigger thinking. When a train has been wrecked, three hundred are dead, contradictory facts are pouring in on her and it is right on the deadline, all the copy-book rules melt away and she simply has to use her head.

There is no covering up as she sits before her typewriter with the lead story of the day at her mercy. The words must rip from her fingers in orderly procession. The facts behind them must be sharp and clear and the balance perfect. There are no excuses when the paper comes up and the lead story is feeble. The front page is exacting. The front-page girl had better know her stuff if she wants to function under the garish lights that burn down on the city room, revealing the flaws in her equipment with shocking candor.

This, definitely, is where women have made little headway and probably never will. It is the inadequacy that keeps them from ranking with the men stars. It has no bearing on their success in other newspaper departments, but it is the real reason why there is such a small percentage of women reporters on any large paper, in any part of the country.

Their second big hazard is in handling groups of men, which they must inevitably do on a first-string assignment. This is always a ticklish matter, although it has been done repeatedly with success. The best-natured newspaperman in the world—and they are an amiable and generous lot—is not apt to relish taking orders from a woman reporter. Yet back in the nineties Mabel Craft, of the San Francisco *Chronicle*, led a squad of men in a leaky launch through the Golden Gate to meet the ships returning from the Spanish-American War. The *Examiner* crew was already under way in a fine large tug. A storm was raging, they were warned that their launch would sink, but Miss Craft insisted on going ahead. She knew that her competitors were far out to sea and she feared that her paper might be beaten.

The men called a council and overruled her. Miss Craft took it with grace, conducted her expedition ashore, and hastily chartered a sea-worthy tug. They started off again and met the ships. They wrote their stories on the way in, with the tug lurching under them. Their editors were frantic by the time they showed up, waving their copy in their hands. It was the story of the year and they made it by a margin of minutes. They were not scooped by the *Examiner*. This was remarkable in the nineties. It would be remarkable to-day.

But here and there throughout the country there have always been girls who could meet the front-page test. Within recent years they have had more opportunity. The press services have given them golden chances. So have some of the conservative papers.

Lorena Hickok repeatedly wrote the news leads on stories of national importance for the Associated Press, which has gone in heavily for women after years of indifference to their merits. Genevieve Forbes Herrick brought distinction to her craft by her work for the Chicago *Tribune*. She outmatched her competitors time and again, doing the major stories of the day with grace, speed and accuracy. Marjorie Driscoll, of the Los Angeles *Examiner*, is another example of the finest type of news writer.

Grace Robinson has starred so often in the rôle of front-page girl that she has no competitor in the number of big stories she has covered within a given period of time. She did the Hall-Mills and the Snyder-Gray trials for the New York *Daily News*, and scores of other assignments that any man might envy. Elenore Kellogg, who died in the summer of 1935, led the *World* repeatedly with brilliantly handled news stories, and had the satisfaction of seeing her work under banner heads. Ruth Finney, a Scripps-Howard star, tops the field for Washington. She has achieved spectacular success in the political field and ranks with the best men in the Press Gallery.

These six are perfect examples of the successful front-page girl. They represent press services, conservative papers and tabloid journalism. They could handle any story from any given angle and walk away with the honors. They are the best refutation of all the criticism that has been leveled at the woman reporter. They have proved that a woman can cover a news story of prime importance as well as a man.

They have starred in the metropolitan field—the most severe test of all. Women get better front-page opportunities in smaller cities. A number throughout the country can point to front-page streamers, stories leading the paper, a heavy play on the big assignments of the day. But there are not enough of them to make much difference to the profession as a whole. They have merely established the fact, not revolutionized the status of their colleagues. They are remarkable only because they are the exceptions.

A newspaper woman's capacity, of course, should always be measured by her opportunity. It is the conviction of every woman reporter of wide experience that she could match the best of the men if she had half a chance. The point is debatable. The city editor—chivalrous soul—keeps her down for two reasons: he doubts her capacity, and he hates to throw her to the wolves in the rough and tumble of big news events. He handles her with kid gloves when she wouldn't object to brass knuckles. He would rather she went home and never bothered him again.

However, if she has failed to make much headway with the city editor, she has attained some solid standing with her fellow workers in the city room. She can sit at adjoining desks with the reigning stars and neither be scorned nor pampered. No man needs to lay newsprint for her capable feet, or even spell a word for her. All that she ever asks him for is a match.

It is much more likely that the front-page girl will help her colleague with his story when he has been wooing the bottle, console him the night his sixth child is born, admire its picture a few weeks later, spur his ambition to write a great novel, or help him to buy a birthday present for his wife. She clucks over him like a mother hen. She nearly always likes him. It never occurs to her that he stands in her way and keeps her from the best assignments.

One of the more benign aspects of her job is the good fellowship of the men on the paper. They accept her as part of the newspaper picture. She sits with them through the mad hours of a political convention, writing quite sensible copy; she appears at the prize ring, unmoved by the noise and gore; she bobs up at a disaster and never lets her feelings get in her way. She isn't insensitive. Good reporters rarely are dead to what they see. They are objective first; but they must interpret the passions of their fellow men with some degree of insight. The apathetic man or woman does not make a fine reporter. The harp should twang a bit.

The woman reporter may be a paradoxical person, gentle in her private life, ruthless at her work. She may be of any age, type or race. She may be blonde, red-haired or brunette—a scholar who labors over polished phrases, or a rough and tumble slang expert who jollies the bailiff. Sometimes she is small, demure and savage; sometimes big, brassy and soft-hearted. One never can tell. She may wear pearls and orchids, be a débutante and sport a title, or shuffle along, a weary beldame with faded hair.

The outer shell has little to do with the value of a good reporter. The shrinking ones are often the lion-hearted; a feather may rock the Amazon. The best women reporters were once on the frowsy side. This is no longer true, although here and there a brainy girl may scorn the details of her costume. But the effect created by a group of women reporters to-day is one of good grooming, personality and poise. They have lost their distraught look somewhere along the years.

Forty years ago a few glamour girls got loose among the stringy-looking spinsters whose hair was always ruffled and whose shirt-waists bulged. But they were the exceptions. In the late nineties there was the general feeling that only a homely woman would barge out of the home and neglect her social life in order to write for the papers. But William Randolph Hearst took the stuffing out of this tradition by employing handsome girls with Lillian Russell figures and Harrison Fisher profiles; and Elizabeth Jordan, working for Joseph Pulitzer, so overawed Benjamin Harrison's butler with her elegant costume and ostrich feathers that she marched in and got a presidential interview at Cape May, when the door was closed to all other reporters.

To-day, the more smoothly they fit into the social scene the better their editors like it. If they must be eccentric and wear odd hats, their work should be good enough to justify it. An untidy woman is as out of date in the metropolitan newspaper office as papers on the floor, cigarette butts burning holes in the desks, or hats tossed blithely in the waste-paper baskets.

On the other hand, the girl reporter should not be too beguiling. When she dazzles the cubs and starts the copy boys writing poems, her stock begins to go down. Trouble, beauty and sex are threats in any city room, and the three can telescope remarkably quickly into one. Some gorgeous peonies have bloomed among the typewriters and ticker machines. The tabloids welcome them and encourage the ornamental touches. They argue that face, figure and clothes help to make the good woman reporter. They have proved the point repeatedly, but the rule is not infallible.

The most sensible usually make the best reporters. The women who have gone farthest in journalism are not those who have yipped most loudly about their rights. Unless aggressiveness is backed by real ability, as in Rheta Childe Dorr's case, it is only a boomerang. Nothing has done more to keep women reporters in the shade. Peace at any price is the city room philosophy.

It is absurd to maintain that a woman can do everything a man can do on a paper. She can't get into the Lotus Club in New York, or cross the Harvard Club threshold. She is denied the chummy barroom confidences of the politician, and cannot very well invade a Senator's room in Washington when he has no time to answer her questions except as he changes for dinner.

The rule does not work so conclusively the other way. The only obstacle the gentlemen of the press have encountered is Mrs. Roosevelt's Monday morning conferences. The youths who are picked for the pink tea assignments are welcomed with joy at the woman's meeting. It is a sad reflection for the woman reporter who swears by her sex that the most pampered scribe at feminine gatherings is usually a man—and a man who would rather not be there.

But admitting that there are a few places from which women reporters are debarred, this is scarcely an important argument against their usefulness. It has no more significance than the inability of a man to write a good fashion story without expert aid. The functions of the city staff are always interchangeable. A woman may cover a subway wreck and a man do a fashion show on the same afternoon, with excellent results in both cases. A good reporter can do telling work with almost any set of facts, short of relativity. He need not be a specialist. He need not even be initiated.

But the feeling is there and the seasoned newspaper woman has to recognize it. If she is wise she will go on her way, taking things in her stride. She will not fuss over periods of quiet. She will mind her own business, take the assignments handed out to her and never grouse unduly. She cannot always live in the news writer's seventh heaven. There are dull days with nothing but obits to write. But as sure as she lives, news will stir again. She will watch it rustle through the office. The city editor will come over to her, hand her a bulletin, and from this cryptic note may spring the story of the decade.

For news breaks with astonishing speed. It strikes a newspaper office like lightning. The front-page girl feels its impact from day to day. She never quite gets hardened to the sudden jolt when she sees a well-known name obviously bound for the gutter in a four-line bulletin, or hears a voice giving her the incredible news over the telephone: "Wall Street has just been bombed. Will you hurry down and see what's doing."

Not until a story is focused in black type does it have much reality for her, so absorbed is she in the mechanics of what she is doing. Yet this is the eternal fascination of her profession—to be in the thick of things; to move always where life is stirring; to have a grand-stand seat at the world events of the day, yet without responsibility for anything that may happen, beyond the task of turning out a good story on what she has seen and heard. She writes before the fever of the moment passes. Her best work is torn from her, take by take, under pressure. She lives herself through the news. If she is skilled at her job, she manages to convey the excitement to her readers.

For she must know how to write. There is practically no place in the modern newspaper office for the woman who is merely a news gatherer. There are men who work year after year for their papers and never actually write a line of copy. But the front-page girl must have a facile touch. The only way in which she can hope to prove her superiority is by the excellence of her style. She is rarely a wizard at getting facts.

The doubts raised by editors about her are legion. Can she write? Usually. Can she spell? At least as well as her masculine colleagues, often better. Is she lacking in a sense of humor? Probably, but only to the same degree as the rest of her sex. It doesn't make much difference to her paper. Is she emotional in her work? Rarely. Reporting now is largely realistic, except for the occasional word orgies at a sensational trial, and then it is an assumed frenzy, done with the tongue in the cheek. News writers have too much sense to beat their breasts in public now. Their editors no longer expect it. The public would laugh.

But the most serious charge brought against the newspaper woman is inaccuracy. This is the one real chink in her armor. Precision of thought is the first requisite of good reporting. As far back as 1898 Arnold Bennett seized on this weakness in the woman reporter. His criticism is much the same as the city editor's to-day. No amount of careful work has served to uproot it. Even the most unprejudiced editor shudders a little when a new woman walks through the city room. Will her sentences parse? Will she get the paper in a libel suit? Will she verify every fact? Will she know how to round up a story? Will she cause trouble in the office? He values the women who happen to have succeeded in his own organization, but he thinks of them always as the exceptions. He has not yet been able to accept the species without reservation.

Therefore, the newspaper woman has to be twice as careful as the newspaper man in order to make headway at all. The tradition of sloppy work dies hard. She has every reason to worry when the copy boy brings the wet paper fresh from the presses and lays it on her desk. There is something particularly appalling about the error in print. Her eye rushes to the head the copy reader has given her story. It isn't vanity that makes her read every line with care. She is desperately anxious to know if everything is right.

The layman who cherishes the foolish belief that only half of what he reads in a newspaper is true, never dreams of the conscientious work that lies behind the columns he hastily scans. No human being but a well-trained reporter would hunt through five books of reference to get a middle initial correct. No one else would find so many ways of checking a circumstance that the average person accepts at face value.

The reporter scourges himself to perfection. Yet the public still believes that he is slipshod, inaccurate, a deliberate falsifier. In actual fact, the conscientious news writer on a responsible paper is the most slavishly exact person in the world. He splits hairs and swears by books of reference. He has a passion for verification, an honest love for facts. The good woman reporter has the same exacting code. The crispness of her style, the keen viewpoint, the explicit phrase, the potent paragraph, are all nullified if she does not have the essential newspaper virtue of absolute accuracy.

Often her early training has a bearing on the exactitude of her mental processes. The newspaper women have arrived at their various goals by odd routes. They have taught and nursed and been stenographers. They have scrubbed floors and sold in shops and danced in the chorus. The present tendency is for them to break in fresh from college. Some have wandered into the profession by accident; others have battered their way in; a few have simply walked in the front door without knocking. But the same spirit of enterprise has propelled most of them into the exciting newspaper game.

In their off-moments they have unexpected tastes. There is no consistency in them. The girl who is most at home inside fire lines, checking up on casualties, is apt to spend her days off weeding her garden or reading Pater. She may worm her way into jail or sit without blinking as a jury condemns a man to death, but when she gets home she is likely to turn thoroughly feminine. She wants a quiet evening with her husband, an hour's play with her baby, a chance to mix a salad or knit a sweater.

She is often a little sharp of tongue, because she has listened to so much rot. She has seen strange things of which most women never dream. She is neither the terrible hard-boiled reporter who beats the town nor the angel-faced cutie who wins her way by guile. As a rule she is matter-of-fact. The code of her profession is an intangible one, not generally understood. She must be resourceful with honor, searching without being rude; she must not be put off easily by the lies constantly flung in her face; she must sense the important, discard the trivial, have a sense of proportion and the ability to make subtle decisions between right and wrong. She must build her own code as she moves, for the copy-book standards scarcely cover her profession.

On the whole, newspaper women make few demands on their city editors. They would gladly work for nothing, rather than be denied the city room. They scarcely ever fuss about their salaries, which range from $35 to $150 a week in the large cities, and from $7 to $50 in the smaller ones. They rarely ask for increases, or complain about their fate. They work hard and have a somewhat touching faith in what they are doing. They are seldom lazy. But the highest compliment to which the deluded creatures respond is the city editor's acknowledgment that their work is just like a man's. This automatically gives them a complacent glow, for they are all aware that no right-minded editor wants the so-called woman's touch in the news.

The fact remains that they never were thoroughly welcome in the city room and they are not quite welcome now. They are there on sufferance, although the departments could scarcely get along without them. But if the front-page girls were all to disappear tomorrow no searching party would go out looking for more, since it is the fixed conviction of nearly every newspaper executive that a man in the same spot would be exactly twice as good.

They may listen to smooth words and chivalrous sentiments, but what every city editor thinks in his black but honest heart is: "Girls, we like you well enough but we don't altogether trust you."

Chapter 15

ALFRED McCLUNG LEE

THE EDITORIAL STAFF

MORE DRIVEL HAS POURED FROM TYPEWRITERS regarding the life and times of newspaper editorial employees than of workers for any other commercial organization. Writers—newspapermen as well as others—melodramatize reporters as romantic sleuths, drunken cynics, dapper youths who marry debutantes, hardened allies of gangsters, destroyers of wicked politicians, happy men-about-town, courageous prodders behind the walls of social sham, etc. Many reporters join the public in accepting such a fictional character. Publishers and Hollywood hacks, more practical, capitalize upon it.

While reporters "share the exciting adventures and power of the people they write about, their spirits are high," notes a reporters' journal[1] in commenting upon the suicide of a foreign correspondent. "But when the shot in the arm ends, too often they have no other resources or satisfactions left and life seems unbearably flat." Proximity to "great personages," the illusion of an active rôle in affairs of moment, and the glamor of being pointed out as a reporter combine to furnish this intoxicating "shot in the arm."

How did this "romantic profession" arise? How do reporters and the balance of editorial staffs function, parts as they are of the industrial and social situation portrayed in the preceding chapters? How does this crucial department influence the nature of this daily communications instrument? The following facts indicate general but tentative answers to such questions.

The Staff, Editorials, and News Evolve

Early "conductors" of dailies paid little attention to local happenings. They printed official municipal documents usually because they were paid for doing so. Serving a limited class of readers, the commercial, industrial, and political leaders, they supplied routine shipping news, prices current, and similar records available at the taverns and merchant exchanges. They restricted court news to reports on trials relating to commercial or political matters or to a few lines regarding a murder. The bulk of their offerings until well into the nineteenth century was gleaned from coffee-house books and newspapers or from their own exchanges.

With the growth of dailies' budgets, printer-publishers improved their paper's contents by hiring an editor. George Bunce & Co., publishers of the New York *American Minerva*, started in 1793, obtained the services of Noah Webster. A graduate of Yale, member of the Hartford bar, school teacher, and author of a combination speller, grammar, and reader, Webster had attracted attention with articles in the Hartford *Connecticut Courant* and with a pamphlet arguing for a strong federal constitution. Under the guidance of such men, many of them foreigners, the "editorial, heretofore practically unknown, now gradually made its appearance, at first in the shape of a modest paragraph, suggesting some course of action, or criticising what had been already done or proposed. Toward the close of Washington's second administration we find the newspapers taking opposing sides in politics, indicating a positive and distinct cleavage in party lines."[2]

Long pamphlets and other essays, sliced into daily installments for the editorial page, had begun to tire both party leaders and business men. While the editors continued these series "as heavy artillery, small guns and rifle fire were needed. After 1795, the dashing franc-tireurs of journalism, such as William Duane of the *Aurora*, showed a marked preference for the brief editorial, peppered with denunciatory epithets and harsh accusations, and casting to the winds the dignity of the chief Federalist penmen." The Federalists, numbering such capable writers as Webster and William Coleman of the *New-York Evening Post*, also "began to intersperse the pamphlet-style articles by Hamilton, Rufus King, Oliver Wolcott, and other leaders with shorter, livelier comments of their own."[3]

Little wonder, in view of their contents, that J. W. Fenno of the Philadelphia *Gazette of the United States* labeled contemporary organs on March 4, 1799, "the most base, false, servile and venal publications, that ever polluted the fountains of society—their editors the most ignorant, mercenary, and vulgar automatons that ever were moved by the continually rusting wires of sordid mercantile avarice." For party shibboleths and the thobbings of their passionate minds, editors fought duels with weapons as well as words and had frequently to face injured citizens in court.

Conditions change, but the paternity of modern editorialists—the Brisbanes, Lawrences, et al.—is clear. Thobbery, "*the confident reasoning of a person who is not curious about verifying his result,*"[4] characterizes much published in both the eighteenth and twentieth centuries as unsigned editorials and signed editorial articles, not to mention other utterances for popular consumption. Generalizations well founded on fact are not nearly so acceptable as are catchwords and "logical cases" built on traditional premises, especially when the former run counter to the latter. Readers value a display of selected statistics or descriptive instances the interpretation of which only an expert could check. Lacking this sure-fire evidence, an assurance that unmentioned "facts" or "experience" sustain an enticing notion frequently does just as well. When a fair sampling of facts on a given subject yields a tentative conclusion, few informed persons would vehemently spring to its defense.

Efforts to increase advertiser support led publishers to strengthen their financial reports. Enos Bronson of the Philadelphia *United States Gazette*, upon expanding his local coverage in 1805, began to devote as much as a full page to prices current. Of the New York *Commercial Advertiser*, some said that its editor treasured a single ship arrival above the fall of a dynasty or the ravages of a plague. In most urban sheets, a small but increasing amount of news was injected to add spice, but it remained modest until after 1825. Some "crying local needs," however, got editorial attention. The vast number of hogs running throughout New York, the filthy streets, and the recurrent yellow fever epidemics irritated editors.

The second war with England gave new zest to news reporting, but limited finances hampered coverage. The Baltimore *Weekly Register* on May 8, 1813, observed that "a person may easily fall into an opinion that the *manufacture of news* has nearly become a *regular business*." It admitted that there are "a few beings, possessed of types and presses, of whom we reasonably expect all sorts of reports that may depress the spirit of the people; or, if possible, embarrass the government—but there are others, of whom we hoped better things, that fall into the same error, from a too ardent thirst for news—*for the honor of first giving some strange report to the public*." War excitement had temporarily given the press something of the anxiety for novelty that stamped it more markedly from the late 1820s. Striking headlines, small but graphic, signaled this change. "A new conception, that of news, which would cease to be of value when it ceased to be news, as opposed to mere communication which could be carried on at one time as well as another, had [again temporarily] emerged,"[5] as it had during previous excitements. Upon becoming editor of the *Boston Daily Advertiser*, Nathan Hale called this "insatiable appetite" for news, in an editorial on April 7, 1814, an indication of a "diseased state of the public taste." While an "editor is waiting for the arrival of a true statement of any affair, his readers are satisfied with the distorted representation that had gone forward." With his scholarly editorials, which he insisted upon writing himself, Hale contrasted sharply with many of his contemporaries, "printers whose expectations were that their pages would be filled with advertisements, tales, news extracts, and gratuitous contributions from politicians and a few public spirited writers."[6]

One historian[7] calls the years after the War of 1812 the "darkest period in the history of American journalism." His examination of the papers revealed "that all of the customary courtesies of life were put aside; . . . that the newspapers . . . even so forgot themselves as to attack wives and sisters in their disgraceful accounts of the personal activities of office-holders." The papers reflected their times. During the first quarter of the nineteenth century, mobs attended public hangings that many sheets described in fair detail. Even in those days preceding the full flowering of "trial by newspaper," popular disappointment ran high in June, 1819, when Rose Butler, a Negress, was given a respite just as she was to be hanged in Potter's Field, New York, on the site of Washington Square. An early writer[8] noted that in about 1820 New York papers' "contents usually were advertisements, a little badly arranged ship news, gathered from the reading-rooms of the principal ports and from newspapers, a narrow column or more of news, a few lines of editorial."

During these years, J. G. Bennett learned the rudiments of the art he practiced so profitably a decade later. Working for J. T. Buckingham of the weekly Boston *New-England Galaxy* in the middle 1820s, he discovered that "no editor could break the mental and monied monopoly held by the old newspapers, except by adopting an extravagant and severe style. . . . People scolded and fretted, . . . but they would read, and with most zest devoured those articles which were most declamatory and personal, and least instructive and valuable." This significant "condition of the public mind and of Journalism"[9] deeply impressed Bennett.

During the 1820s, more numerous competitors and sheets specializing in price quotations led some dailies, with space restricted by advertisements and their four-page format, to concentrate more upon other bids for support. Bennett in 1826, for instance, as a reporter for the New York *National Advocate*, had a knowledge of shorthand, rare then as now among reporters, that enabled him to record more than one "important charge" of a judge to a jury, "taken down *verbatim* as it was delivered."[10] By the late 1820s, the "editorial force of an office . . . consisted of two or three political writers and one news editor, who was at the same time general reporter, 'paste and scissors,' and money editor."[11] In the case of such a prominent journal as the Philadelphia *United States Gazette* in 1829, however, J. R. Chandler performed all the editorial work, "including the letters from 'Our Special Correspondent' at London, Paris, New York, Constantinople, Boston, or Pekin."[12]

Established dailies, on the whole, pleaded with their wayward contemporaries not to indulge in printing police and sensational court reports. Bennett,[13] however, reporting in 1830 a trial in Salem, Massachusetts, revealed thus the extent to which the rising profession of sensation mongers had rationalized "trial by newspaper":

"Is it possible that the publication of facts, or even rumors, can have any tendency to defeat the general operations of justice? If this were true, the more utterly ignorant a man is, the fitter he is to sit as a juror. . . .

"The honesty, the purity, the integrity of legal practice and decisions throughout this country, are more indebted to the American Press, than to the whole tribe of lawyers and judges, who issue their decrees. *The Press is the living Jury of the Nation.*"

In bidding for purchasers among the expanding class of literates, the one-cent press gave new status to local news. G. W. Wisner, editor of the New York *Sun* from 1833, "relied largely on police reports and the coarse humor of the police courts for interesting matter for his columns."[14] Such an editor's news beat, however, was not extensive. William Durant,[15] an early editor of the Boston *Evening Transcript*, recalled that in 1834 a Boston editor "made a daily call at Topliff's reading room, the insurance offices and public places, all conveniently located on or around State street; spending most of the day in the chair editorial, poring over the exchanges that came in the mail with more or less regularity." In Philadelphia, even after the start of the *Public Ledger* in 1836, the "reporter was not considered essential to the success of the journal giving him employment, but was rather looked upon as a hunter-up of 'unconsidered trifles' of no great value, but still well enough to have." Even the one-cent *Ledger*, begun "upon purely a local basis, did not," according to a Philadelphia writer,[16] "see the importance of having prompt and reliable local intelligence, as its files show that subjects of importance were often barely mentioned. Ordinarily affairs did not receive attention until two or three days after their occurrence." This journalist then describes as follows adjustments in local coverage in Philadelphia until the 1850s:

"At that time, each paper generally employed only one reporter, who was expected to furnish information of all important local events, unaided by telegraph or passenger railroads. In consequence of this fact, a system of exchange was inaugurated by these knights of the quill, among whom the city was divided into districts. After each had traversed the portion allotted to him, they all met in the evening and compared notes, each giving and receiving. The *Ledger*, however, soon employed a sufficient number of men to render that paper, it was thought, independent of this exchange of news. . . .

"The district system . . . was still continued on the *Ledger*, there being no particular head to the department, thus leaving the reporters to divide the city among themselves. This arrangement often worked badly for the paper. . . . Items were sometimes missed, because occurrences took place outside of the reporter's district, which were not heard of by the one who had charge of that particular locality. But the other papers frequently contained the missing articles because their reporters continued the combination plan."

Here are the rudiments of both individual city staffs and city newsgathering agencies. Before the day of police and fire-alarm telegraph systems, long before telephones, and with inadequate transportation, reporters trudged many a mile in search of news.

The New York *Sun* sprang into prominence in 1833 through its one-cent price and its specialization in police-court items and especially in humorous remarks allegedly originating at the magistrate's bench. W. H. Attree, typical of many, graduated from being a printer in a type foundry to the job of police reporter for the one-cent *New-York Transcript*, started in 1834. His merits consisted in "being facile with his pen, and sufficiently indifferent (after the fashion of the press generally, of that day) to the feelings of the poor creatures left to its mercy."[17] Bennett's *Herald*, guided by the sort of viewpoint that later brought Pulitzer, Hearst, and others to fame and wealth, covered the news sources of the *Sun* and *Transcript* and added new ones. Bennett at first reported all his police, city, and money news himself. His keen observations on Wall Street, widely reprinted in one-cent sheets, irritated financiers and delighted the populace. He[18] had determined that "*One journal shall tell what Wall Street really is and what is done there.*" To further excite interest, he twitted the public with fairly palpable fakes. As that prototype of the "yellow" journalist once said, "I am hard at work—mean to make a commercial newspaper for the million, and not for Wall Street—am always serious in my aims, but full of frolic in my means."[19]

The *Sun*, *Transcript*, and *Herald* and other cities' one-cent sheets revelled in cases involving illicit sex relations, locally or clipped and pointed up from the exchanges, and gave extensive space to prize fights, foot and horse races, and other sports. The *New-York Transcript* on February 4, 1835, had two columns on a prize fight that went forty-six rounds. The *Sun*[20] liked to condemn prize-fighting as "a European practice, better fitted for the morally and physically oppressed classes of London than the enlightened republican citizens of New York," but it covered in 1835 such bouts as the Williamson-Phelan fight at Hoboken.

These sheets pandered to the masses by sensationalizing the trivial and easily understood at the expense of the economically and politically significant. The *Sun* created a furore in 1835 with R. A. Locke's moon hoax, allegedly taken from a "Supplement of the *Edinburgh Philosophical Journal*." Locke told of fabulous discoveries on the moon by J. F. W. Herschel through a new telescope. He followed this success with a series on the "Life and Adventures of Manual Fernandez, otherwise Richard C. Jackson, convicted of the murder of John Roberts, and to be executed at the Bellevue Prison, New York on Thursday next," November 19, 1835. The murder of Helen

Jewett on April 10, 1836, inmate of a New York brothel, by R. P. Robinson gave the cheap papers the sort of crime that has filled popular journals ever since. "The exploit-ation of this crime and trial by the first penny papers, not only in New York but in Boston and Philadelphia," notes an historian of journalism,[21] "marked the culmination of their effort to attract readers by a degree of sensationalism hitherto unknown in American journalism." Reports of this trial also illustrate the first widespread "trial by newspaper," the first widespread submission of columns upon columns of evidence, testimony, and editorials to what Bennett had called in 1830 *the living Jury of the Nation.*" After Robinson's acquittal, the Philadelphia *Public Ledger* published a series of six editorials condemning witnesses, counsels, judges, and jury, and strenuously arguing that the verdict did not accord with the facts.

Bennett, with his blatant "poor taste," even according to contemporary mores, his Rabelaisian humor, and his Machiavellian expediency, epitomized in his paper the popular fancies of his day. He knew what would sell during a "consumers' market" in newspaper circulation, and he produced it. To him "must go the distinction—some would say infamy—of having invented news as we know it today. . . . None of the existing taboos or sacred cows were respected by this irrepressible reporter."[22]

With growing incomes, the popular sheets added both to their staffs and their fields of news coverage. Bennett freed himself of much of his routine by hiring in 1835 a police reporter and in 1837 Frederic Hudson, long his "right hand" on the *Herald.* Hudson organized news-slip exchanges with out-of-town papers, and gradually made for himself the post of managing editor, director of the paper's general newsgathering and news-editing activities. Thus strengthened, the *Herald* broke precedent and in 1839 "undertook to report the proceedings of . . . religious anniversary meetings. . . . These large religious societies had met in that city for years, but their doings, so far as the public were concerned, were only to be found in their annual reports, printed by the societies, of limited circulation, and which gave the public only the financial exhibit of each." The *Herald* decided to tell "of the spirit of the meetings" and of "what good the money had accomplished."[23] The "blanket sheets" shrieked; the clergy objected; the religious press condemned Bennett's "atheism." Later, Hudson recalls, the same bodies objected if the *Herald* did not send reporters. By 1844, Bennett also took up the reporting of leading sermons, but he could not print them until Tuesday morning.

The staffs did not grow rapidly. By 1840, the "Chief Editor of a newspaper in New York rarely employed more than two or three assistants. Limited capital, small circula-tion, cheap advertising, all forbade great outlay. Editors were reporters and editors alternately; and their emoluments were not commensurate with the labors required of them."[24] The Philadelphia *Public Ledger* dignified its ordinary local items in 1840 with a *title,* "City Gleanings," gathered by one man, Charles Ritter. It also began to imitate the *Herald's* "money articles" on July 1, 1840, with contributions by Joseph Sailer. The *New-York Evening Post,* typical of the "blankets," did not give its locals a heading, "City Intelligence," and much attention until 1845. On May 13, of the same year, however, the *Herald* covered a race between horses representing the north and south with "eight competent reporters and writers" and issued an extra after each heat. By then, the *Herald's* editorial staff included twelve editors and reporters in addition to Bennett himself. The Philadelphia *North American and United States Gazette* at the time of its merger in 1847 employed only one "political editor," one associate editor, a city reporter, a "miscellaneous" writer, and two general contributors and reporters, a total of six. The pigeon expresses established in the late 1830s and the 1840s by papers at

Baltimore, Philadelphia, New York, and Boston occasionally aided in local as well as long distance newsgathering, but they had the weaknesses inherent in one-way communication.

Horace Greeley, who started the *New-York Tribune* in 1841, gave an impetus to two tendencies in the industry. His example aided in making the editor a more independent functionary and helped increase for a time through the identification of editor with paper the popular following of the editorial page.

Greeley assumed a prominent position in the enlarging group of editorialists who during the 1840s began successfully to compete with politicians as well as ministers for the political leadership of the "rising" common man. Other than business men, politicians alone, when Bennett started his *Herald* in 1835, "consulted public journals on questions of commerce, peace, and war, or on the probable effect of any measures adopted by the government. The mass of the people were contented to be ruled by those, who, through interest or ambition, were aiming to obtain place and power. . . . It would have been folly, therefore, to have attempted to make a daily offering to the public of a newspaper" such as appeared during the 1840s.[25]

Greeley expressed himself frequently and fully on economic, political, and social problems with all the vehemence of a thobber's enthusiasm for the ideals and ideas he holds. He sought, as he stated in his announcement, "to advance the interests of the People, and to promote their Moral, Social, and Political well-being." He wanted his paper to be "worthy of the hearty approval of the virtuous and refined, and a welcome visitant at the family fireside." To crown the blurb, he attributed the election of W. H. Harrison to "a triumph of Right, Reason, and Public Good over Error and Sinister Ambition." A partnership with Thomas McElrath at the end of four months operation left Greeley to play with his catchwords. McElrath cared little for what Greeley did so long as he did not hurt the "box office." Business considerations led the McElraths after the Civil War again to restore editors gradually to the status of dependent employees.

Greeley's predecessors dealt mostly in sensations and local crusades. Greeley liked "isms." Albert Brisbane imported Fourier socialism, a "subversive foreign doctrine"—as his son, Hearst's faithful Red-baiter, Arthur Brisbane, would have called it—and sold it to Greeley in the fall of 1841. Greeley also wanted a national circulating medium, protection for American industries, land distribution, "justice" in the Kansas question, women's rights, etc. "It is fair to suppose that the editor of the *Tribune* was sincere," granted a competitor.[26] "But novelty was attractive to him, and this was his idea of progress, and success and progress were necessary to the happiness of the world." Greeley answered such disparagements in an editorial on April 24, 1859, thus:

> "Doubtless many of our readers have heard of the *Isms* of *The Tribune*, its disorganizing doctrines, its numerous hobbies, and its frequent changes from one of these to another. And yet, as one mind has presided over its issues from the outset, so one golden thread of purpose may be traced through them all, under every variety of circumstance and condition. That purpose is the elevation of the masses through the diffusion and inculcation of intelligence, freedom, industry, skill, virtue, and the consequent abolition or limitation of ignorance, slavery, idleness, pauperism, and vice."

He used a common device. Directing attention to what society was ready to call a maladjustment, he then asserted that his solution—always novel and "reasonable"—*must* be adopted.

While smart business managers were allowing their editors to capitalize upon the public's love of a "great man," editors did not neglect their newsgathering arrangements. Greeley, for one, "quickly collected about him the ablest staff yet known in the history of American journalism."[27] He hired C. A. Dana in 1847 to organize local newsgathering as city editor. By 1850, the *Tribune* employed twelve editors and reporters and bought material from seventeen correspondents. In addition to Greeley and Dana, his managing editor by then, the *Tribune* in 1854 had ten so-called associate editors, fourteen reporters, and thirty-eight correspondents. One of Greeley's biographers[28] described the activities of the assistants to his city editor thus:

> "One of these keeps an eye on the Police, chronicles arrests, walks the hospitals in search of dreadful accidents, and keeps the public advised of the state of its health. Three report lectures and speeches. Another gathers items of intelligence in Jersey City, Newark, and parts adjacent. Others do the same in Brooklyn and Williamsburgh. One gentleman devotes himself to the reporting of fires, and the movements of the military. Two examine and translate from the New York papers which are published in the German, French, Italian and Spanish languages. Then, there is a Law Reporter, a Police Court Reporter, and a Collector of Marine Intelligence."

The managing editor on most sheets handled most of the administrative routine; he could not yet be facetiously described as the "guy who gets out the paper when the city editor is sick, unless he can induce one of the copy boys to do it."[29] Frederic Hudson, as "m. e." of the *Herald*, answered in 1855 a "voluminous correspondence" and "entered the duties of each reporter in the daily journal kept for their inspection and guidance" in addition to editing copy.[30]

The *Tribune's* three lecture and speech men reflected a marked change that had taken place in reporting, particularly during the late 1840s. "When the public Press did not report the speeches of citizens," noted a contemporary,[31] "there was little incitement to address audiences." The "rapid improvements introduced into newspapers," however, "brought into the field of oral literature thousands of speakers, including many females, who have had a great influence upon the public mind. This fact has proved very troublesome to the old political parties." Many factors other than the journalistic contributed, but "phonographic reporting" of speeches and later interviewing helped to entice into prominence many new "intellectual guides" for the populace, competitors of editors as well as of the older kinds of leader.

The extensive strides of the industry during the 1850s toward financial stability prompted organizing editorial departments along more efficient lines. "The time will soon arrive, if it has not arrived already," an historian[32] commented in 1850, "when the chief editor of a daily paper, which aspires to circulation and influence, will not presume to treat every topic that may arise, or to venture into every region of thought and science, but will confine himself to a comparatively limited sphere of writing, and leave the rest to the labors of the most numerous and able corps of assistants at his command." As editors thus sheared themselves of part of their assumed intellectual catholicity, news coverage expanded. T. M. Coleman,[33] first head of the city department of the Philadelphia *Public Ledger*, told of his elevation to that post in 1857 as follows:

> "About that time, the writer . . . proposed to the proprietors of the Ledger to take charge of the local department, agreeing for a certain sum to furnish the news, the proprietors giving him the right to employ such a force as he might think best. The proposition was accepted, and the new experiment at once commenced. The rule of obtaining news exclusively for the paper was strictly enforced, and was found to work so well that the other papers of this city soon saw the necessity of increasing their force, and making the 'Local' a regular department, having a distinctive head, holding the chief reporter, or, what is more popular now, the city editor, responsible for the correctness of the reports."

Such "chief reporters," whether on an exclusive contract or on a salary, usually paid their subordinates by the line, making the "penny-a-liner" appellation famous.

Papers in smaller cities got to this stage much later. *The Charleston* (South Carolina) *Daily News* hired a "City Editor" in 1865; it gave that title to a paragraphist and humorist who was the whole city staff. Its competitor, the *Courier*, had a "Phonographic Reporter" in 1857 but did not add a "City Reporter" until 1865. The New York *Sun* hired its first managing editor in 1868, a post such papers as the *St. Louis Republic* had established as early as 1864. In addition, the *Republic* and others then had a "leader writer," a contributor of leading articles, in the manner of English sheets then and now.

These developing staffs reflected the broadening use of news. The Mexican War and the introduction of the telegraph in the late 1840s popularized placing some news on front pages, surmounted by one-column headlines with numerous "decks" in a variety of type sizes. Most news, however, continued to appear inside. The front pages of the 1850s, in addition to advertisements, usually carried telegraphic reports on Congress and the administration and on European affairs. A much larger amount of the latter was printed in proportion to the size of the paper than subsequently until the World War.

These changes affected chiefly the cheap papers. The "blankets" of the 1850's as "relics of the old times" were the "chosen medium of such wholesale merchants as require but little publicity for their announcements. Devoting comparatively little space to news and editorial matter, and charging high prices to their subscribers, they are able to fill up their big sheets with standing advertisements" at low rates.[34] Among the cheap papers in New York as in other large cities, readers could choose between such a paper as the *Tribune*, feared by the "respectable" because "its teachings were the apotheosis of vice," and such sheets as the *Herald*, from which one gleaned the news "only at the cost of wading through heaps of rubbish."[35] *The New-York Daily Times*, established in 1851 by H. J. Raymond, spurred by its example the development of newsy but conservative sheets for the "middle class."

In his introductory number on September 18, 1851, Raymond asserted, "We shall be *conservative*. . . . We do not believe that *every thing* in society is either exactly right or exactly wrong. . . . *We do not mean to write as if we were in a passion* unless that shall really be the case, and we shall *make it a point to get into a passion as rarely as possible*." In addition to the usual label headings, "The News From Europe," "Brooklyn," "New York," and "Latest Intelligence, By Telegraph," the *Times* gave bulletin headlines to unusual incidents, such as a panic in September, 1851, in a New York schoolhouse that resulted in the death of forty-four children and several teachers. The rising regard for news in the 1850s led James Parton[36] to assert, "An editorial is a man speaking to men, but the news is Providence speaking to men." Parton did not mention that "Providence" thus spoke to men through a very human medium.

Sports attained more prominence before the Civil War. "In the early fifties," recalled Henry Chadwick,[37] an early sports writer, "the only member of the newspaper staff who in any way resembled the modern sporting editor was the 'turf man.' . . . Cricket was at that time the only popular sport outside of racing." Only the New York *Anglo-American* and *Albion*, "English" weeklies, however, covered cricket matches regularly. Chadwick started to report games between United States and Canadian teams in the 1850s for the *Times, Tribune*, and other papers, "but nothing was paid me for the copy, as the New York dailies had been giving no attention to athletics, and I was merely endeavoring to interest them." The visit of a British cricket eleven in 1859 helped to modify editors' attitudes, and the *New York Herald* finally hired Chadwick to cover baseball games regularly in 1862. Such prize fights as one between John Morrissey and Bill Poole in 1855 attracted more attention but in this case for a special reason. Morrissey championed the Irish-American faction; Poole, the anti-Catholic "Know Nothing" party.

The expanding profession of reporters apparently invented the interview in 1859 or thereabouts. Horace Greeley, upon visiting Brigham Young at Salt Lake City in 1859, wrote up his interview in dialogue form under date of July 13 and dispatched it to his and other papers. The following quotation from the Portland *Weekly Oregonian*[38] suggests the style:

"H. G.—Am I to regard Mormonism (so-called) as a new religion? . . .
"B. Y.—We hold that there can be no true Christian church without a priesthood directly commissioned."

Three months later, after John Brown's famous raid at Harpers Ferry on October 16, the *New York Herald* sent a staff writer to visit Gerrit Smith, who had been implicated in the affair. The reporter "had a long interview with that distinguished philanthropist. This was published in full, in conversational style, and produced a sensation." The *Herald* also obtained such dialogues "on the eve of the rebellion . . . with leading rebels at their homes. . . . After the war they were continued with leading statesmen, army and navy officers, and politicians, giving these prominent men an excellent opportunity to communicate with the people. . . . Every body of any note, or who had been guilty of any crime or extraordinary act, was immediately called upon by a reporter. . . . Interviewing, indeed, became a journalistic mania."[39] The interview aided in augmenting the roll of expounders of what The People *should* "think," no aid to the popular status of the "great editor."

Bennett[40] gave a notion of the peak reached in the pomposity of "great editors" during the 1850s, probably the flood stage of editorial power, in the following statement:

"My ambition is to make the newspaper Press the great organ and pivot of government, society, commerce, finance, religion, and all human civilization. I want to leave behind me no castles, no granite hotels, no monuments of marble, no statues of bronze, no pyramids of brick—simply a name. The name of JAMES GORDON BENNETT, as one of the benefactors of the human race, will satisfy every desire and every hope."

Such arrogance and the actual influence of editors and editor-publishers worried many an observer. "I charge the American newspaper press," one bitter critic[41] declared, "with the tyrannical exercise of power and authority to which it has no just pretentions; and I assert that its usurpation of such power and authority is a daring infringement on the rights and liberties of the American people." This was just the first of fourteen "*serious charges.*" Another writer,[42] concluded in 1856 that the "PRESS has gradually sapped the influence—literary, political, and secular—of the priest." He lamented that the press "is not immaculate" but resembles "all other half omnipotent human fabrics." As the publisher or publisher-editor superseded the editor as the dominant factor in newspaper organizations, the abuses complained of did not disappear.

The Civil War effected many changes in journalism. Its stirring events made for even greater sensationalism. W. F. Storey, for example, upon purchasing the *Chicago Times* in 1861, decided to "Raise Hell and Sell Newspapers!" One of his staff writers is credited with originating that famous headline for hangings, "JERKED TO JESUS." The "copperhead" vigor of this sheet occasioned its temporary suppression in 1863. In treating the Civil War as much as possible like a circulation promotion venture, editors inflamed their headings to the extent practicable between rigid column rules. Such top-column bulletins as follows commonly introduced war dispatches: "CIVIL WAR—BOMBARDMENT OF FORT SUMTER—A DAY'S FIGHTING" "RETROGRADE MOVEMENT OF OUR ARMY!—GEN. MCDOWELL FALLING BACK ON WASHINGTON—OUR LOSS 2,500 TO 3,000." Other decks continued the summary. War news definitely eclipsed the editorial.

In view of the increasingly complicated nature of editorial organization roughly from Civil War times, the discussion from this point is separated into more specialized fields. These are: the newspaper's "memory," city news bureaus, staff organization, journalistic education, and press clubs and unions.

The Newspaper's "Memory"

An indexed file of *Niles' Weekly Register* and an unindexed file of the newspaper itself constituted the information file—other than occasional published reference works and some ready-made obituaries—of the average pre-Civil-War newspaper. The *New-York Evening Post* used its *Register* file on May 21, 1850, for a noteworthy hoax. Since Daniel Webster had modified his stand on compromising the admission of free and slave states, the *Post* lifted from the *Register* of December 11, 1819, a talk he had given in Boston. Webster had then claimed that Congress had a constitutional duty to prohibit slavery in all territory other than the original thirteen states. The "copperhead" press ranted.

The Philadelphia *Evening Telegraph* organized one of the earliest extensive morgues in this country. Started with the paper in 1864, the *Telegraph's* information index by 1871 "contains between three and four thousand references, many of which refer to matter sufficient for one or two pages of the paper. . . . Large portions of this material are kept constantly in the most available shape—already in type—awaiting the opportunity for use. This was the case with the obituaries of the late Admiral Farragut and Thaddeus Stevens, elaborate and detailed sketches of whom, exceeding a full page each, had been in type for some months previous to their deaths."[43] Hudson[44] of the *New York Herald* noted in 1873 that "All well-arranged newspaper offices have such matters [as obituaries] carefully prepared."

From files of pre-written obituaries, morgues branched out more and more into general information. A writer[45] in 1892 said that one complete reference system included the following:

"1.   Newspaper clippings, in envelopes, scrapbooks, and boxes.
"2.   Files of the publication issued by the house.
"3.   A well-selected working library of about one thousand volumes.
"4.   The cuts that have appeared from time to time in the publications of the house.
"5.   Photographs and prints of persons, horses, dogs, buildings, ships, etc.
"6.   A card index of the clippings, files, books, and cuts."

The morgue took on new dignity after the World War as the newspaper's "reference laboratory." The demand for data to enrich stories or check facts, stimulated by the increasingly complex problems of journalism, made the management of such departments a highly specialized task. "Newspapers are following the example of the great manufacturing plants," F. J. Miller,[46] director of the *Detroit News* reference department, said in 1920, "in setting up this laboratory, where the research for truth may be carried on side by side with the getting out of a many-editioned daily." Even smaller papers joined in the movement. The *Sheboygan* (Wisconsin) *Press* by 1927 had a library of 1,068 cuts and photographs of local men and women, 2,785 mats, casts, and photographs of other people, and some 100,000 clippings, all filed and cross-referenced under 15,232 subjects.

Large dailies accumulated massive files. The combination of the New York *World* and *Telegram* morgues in 1931 yielded a total of 10,000,000 clippings, required three linear miles of drawer space. In addition, the paper had 30,000 volumes of bound papers, governmental reports, and reference works. The *New York Daily News* by 1935 filed daily upwards of 400 pictures, used and unused. Its library comprised 3,000,000 pictures, 6,000,000 clippings, more than 200,000 cuts, 400,000 negatives, and 2,000 up-to-date reference books.

Newspaper librarians spend a lot of time worrying about the quality of their material. Irving Brant,[47] editor of the *St. Louis Star's* editorial page, characterized the situation thus:

> " 'Boy,' calls the editor of the Times-News, 'go into the morgue and get me the clips on the shopmen's strike.'
> "As the Times-News is a conservative newspaper, the editor soon finds himself taking all of his 'facts' and most of his arguments from the copious propaganda furnished by W. W. Atterbury, of the Pennsylvania Railroad.
> "While this is going on, his more liberal rival, the editor of the New Times, is absorbing 'facts' and arguments furnished with equal copiousness from the cranial laboratory of W. Jett Lauck, statistician for the railroad brotherhoods."

A group of such "Authentic News and Reference Sources" began advising editors in 1935 of their willingness to furnish "accurate and recent information on industry and its relationships to society" for reference purposes. As W. C. Conrad,[48] editorial writer for the *Milwaukee Journal* and one-time newspaper librarian, told the Newspaper Group of the Special Libraries Association in 1933,

> "We can no longer trust many of the apparently reliable sources. The propagandists have reached into them. . . . We need a testing machine for the knowledge for which we take responsibility when we put it before our readers. My answer is the library of creative research."

Few papers could or would afford "creative research."

The Newspaper Group of the Special Libraries Association undertook a number of studies with which to improve the quality and to establish the value of their services. J. F. Kwapil, librarian of the Philadelphia *Public Ledger* and chairman of the Group's committee on standardization, got an analysis under way in 1928 of the eighty-seven affiliated libraries in order to simplify filing methods. This committee worked out a standard list of categories. Kwapil also published in 1930 a summary of the services of his library to the *Ledgers*, morning, evening, and Sunday. With a personnel of fourteen and operating on a 24-hour day and 365-day year, his library averaged 531 requests daily. The calls for cuts and photographs resulted in the publication of 30,000 pictures. "Our reference department," said D. G. Rogers,[49] reference director of the *New York Herald Tribune*, in telling of his organization's services, "effects a large annual saving in telegraph and cable tolls, by providing the background and facts inadequately dealt with in telegraph and cable copy reaching the editors' desks."

Small dailies usually file cuts that may have additional utility, obituaries furnished by A. P. and others, and some local matter, but they depend largely upon memories, feature and wire services, and a few reference books for the verification and elaboration of stories. *The World Almanac and Book of Facts*, started by Pulitzer's New York *World* with an issue for 1886, is a reference work almost every news and editorial writer thumbs. It is one of several published by large dailies. Many an editorial and short feature article, suggested by some news event, flourished upon information from *The World Almanac's* pages.

At the least excuse, it belches forth accounts of long-forgotten murder and divorce trials. Newspapermen are proud of their melodramatizations of another day. How often in the future will readers of Sunday magazines stare at rehashes of the Thaw case, the exploits of "Peaches", Heenan and "Daddy" Browning, the Lindbergh saga, and the romance between Edward VIII and Mrs. Wallis W. Simpson?

City News Bureaus

The drain of reporters to the battle fronts during the Civil War together with the general shortage of men not only opened newspaper offices to many women but also prompted smart organizers to systematize the joint coverage of local events. Thomas Stout, among others, recognized the need, established "Stout's Agency" in New York, and employed ten reporters to cover assignments ordered by short-handed city editors. This soon evolved into "a more systematic scheme of reporting routine news, charging so much a week for the same."[50] C. A. O'Rourke's bureau, launched in 1869, combined advertising selling with news getting and later introduced the first local telegraph ticker service for newspapers in the city. Newton Bigony, a former O'Rourke man, precipitated price-cutting by starting still another agency; the service, in consequence, deteriorated. The old United Press eventually took over the Bigony bureau and placed it on a more substantial basis.

The A. P. bureau at New York handled some local news for New York papers, but the first extensive coperative agency was formed in 1894 under A. P. auspices as the New York City News Association. With the fall of the old U. P. in 1897, the other papers transferred their business to City News. This bureau by 1912 employed 150 people through three branch offices. It tipped the regular paper staffs to big news "breaks" by ticker and, until the introduction of the teletypewriter, manifolded and delivered by messenger its full reports. "Its province," said a long-time manager[51] of City News, "is to report news events in accordance with their news value to the whole and not to the individual newspaper." Membership in the association reached a peak of twenty-two papers in addition to A. P. during the World War, but consolidations and eliminations reduced the roll to eight. Manhattan papers, the *Brooklyn Eagle*, and A. P. from 1931. Leaving drama, sports, and society news to individual staffs, its sixty "leg men" keep 24-hour watch over police stations, courts, jails, hospitals, morgues, and governmental administrative offices in Manhattan and The Bronx. Their reports send some 75,000 words a day over a quadruple teletypewriter circuit and by messenger to subscribers, including ten to twenty complete general-assignment "big" stories as well as routine developments. Standard News similarly covers Brooklyn and its suburbs and transmits its output over a double teletypewriter service. Only for elections does City News take over the whole city. This usually requires 250 extra workers and is called by some the "biggest single piece of reporting in the country."[52]

One practice of City News attracted wide attention within the craft. It places "SXI" at the beginning of material furnished by a press agent or other interested person. "The symbol was created years ago from the first . . . letters of 'sent in,' with X inserted to make a familiar three-letter combination."[53] The *Westchester* (New York) *County Times* in 1931 went a step further. It began inserting this symbol as a protection to readers at the start of handouts it printed. The practice, however, has not been widely copied.

Similar agencies took shape in Chicago, Boston, Los Angeles, Pittsburgh, and elsewhere to minimize unnecessary local competition in newsgathering. Consolidations reduced the number drastically during the 1920s. Pittsburgh's Tri-State News Bureau, for example, lost the support of the local dailies in 1927 with the reduction of the city's papers from five to three.

City News Bureau of Chicago, familiarly called "city press," as well as the others, achieved some fame as a training school for metropolitan newspapermen. Started in 1892, it functions cooperatively under A. P. auspices like New York's City News. Not so extensive as the latter, its "purposes are to prevent scoops, to break in new reporters and to check up on details that the big sheets sometimes haven't time to bother with. The city-press reporters duplicate many of the tasks of the regular staff members of the big dailies. Therein lies the value of their training."[54] Its twenty-two reporters in 1935 covered Chicago's city, county, and federal buildings. Large cities with more than one local newspaper organization but too few for a regular bureau frequently work out an arrangement like one in Philadelphia to handle election returns. The Philadelphia City Editors' Association was organized before the World War for this specific purpose.

United Press Associations controlled two city news bureaus by 1934, Los Angeles City News Service and Washington News Service. The Washington agency, started that year, quickly built a list of thirty subscribers that included the White House, U. S. Treasury, and National Recovery Administration as well as "many Washington correspondents who have found it a physical impossibility adequately to cover the scores of government bureaus and important sources of news with their limited staffs." Over a teletypewriter circuit, the bureau transmitted "the bulletins of approximately two score news men stationed at strategic points throughout the city." The copy is not for publication but "is to 'tip off' clients as to the time and place of press conferences, released and expected statements, developments in Congressional committees, registrations at important hotels, general news happenings, local, national and international."[55]

Staff Organization and the News

The expanding size of morning journals, facilitated by mechanical devices mentioned in Chapter V, increased the volume of local and wire news as well as of features and paid insertions. By 1870, the *New York Herald* and the *Times* devoted as much as two full pages to wire and cable dispatches and had as many as twenty-three reporters on their local staff. By that time, metropolitan morning papers had adopted an organizational setup resembling twentieth century practice. The chief editor of a New York morning daily in 1870, according to a contemporary,[56] "controls all the details of the Editorial department; his decrees being final in all matters concerning the tone of the Journal, the engagement of assistants, and the preparation of the contents of each sheet. His partners are charged with the affairs of business, and he meets them in consultation; but in his own department he is supreme." His assistants comprised a night editor, "placed in charge of the news"; a city editor, to direct local reporters; a financial editor; a literary editor; a critic of the drama and opera; and editorial writers. The latter "are in direct daily communication with the Chief, receiving his suggestions and writing articles upon topics indicated by him, or upon others of their own selection, to which he gives his approval." This division of labor "is now generally adopted."

Other papers interposed a managing editor between the chief editor and news department heads, a somewhat larger job than that given the night editor above. Many, too, had a special telegraph editor, and some, a ship news editor. Several technological changes, notably photo-engraving, the typewriter, and the telephone, brought further refinements in staff setup by the 1890s.

A city editor of 1870 had developed into more than a mere chief reporter. He had "to cut down such reports as are sent in to him, and are deemed worth a certain amount of space—to reject those which are considered devoid of interest,—and to put into proper order the whole of the civic matter to be used." The city editor, an English journalist[57] observed, "is, on the whole, the most important functionary on the establishments of the New York daily journals." This writer also marveled at the ship news editor. Under " 'Ship News,' the New York daily journals, give accounts of shipwrecks, or disasters, or anything in the shape of exciting accidents at sea . . . worked up in the most sensational manner." This department "is unknown in the daily press of London and Paris." Our reporters, too, were much more numerous than the English. The *New York Herald* hired twenty-three to the London *Times's* nineteen; New York City had some 100 "professional reporters" for the press. British writers, however, averaged $25 a week to the Americans' $15. "The manner of reporting in America," said the Englishman, "wherever the reporter mixes up some of his own observations with those of the speaker, which is quite common, is very different from what, in that respect, it is with us." He did not refer here to interviewing; that novelty also impressed him.

Sensationalism in the selection and writing of news reached into all fields but two. Newspapers, on the whole, sought to preserve the sanctity of the "American system" of individualism in business, and "the conductors of the New York journals rarely allow anything to appear in their columns by which readers of a religious turn of mind could feel offended."[58] The *New York Herald* reported with equal care a Jewish Rabbinical Convention at Philadelphia, a Protestant Convention at Worms, and a meeting of the Œcumenical Council at Rome. On Mondays, it devoted one or two full pages to sermons preached the day before in the principal pulpits of New York, Boston, Philadelphia, and Washington, and to cabled résumés from Rome, Paris, Dublin, and London. Sermons then got news space largely for religious reasons. As journalism became more and more "yellow," however, ministers found that their offerings had to have progressively stronger "news value," preferably a sensational angle, to get attention.

With the disappearance of the battles of the Civil War and blunders afterwards as dependable sources for paper-selling news, journalists again turned to murders, divorces, and other crimes and scandals. "Many writers for the press are employed to do nothing else but get up sensational articles, and they are all constantly tempted to expand simple facts into the most romantic and fantastic combinations. This weakness . . . reaches a climax in the headings."[59] These were graphic and sometimes alliterative. *The New York Times* topped at 17-bank heading on October 9, 1872, with "EXIT GREELEY!" The *Chicago Times* told on December 7, 1876, of the Brooklyn Theater fire of December 5 in which 289 died under "BROOKLYN'S BAKE." "HELL'S HALO" headed an account of an Indian massacre in California in the same journal on July 12, 1877.

C. D. Clark,[60] who has made an extensive study of news, comments thus on this rising sensationalism:

> "Yellow journalism was a phenomenon brought about by the new and peculiar social situation created by the modern city. The character of news . . . and the evolution of the concept of news have been closely tied up with the development of urban modes of existence, for it is the city which has forced the substitution of secondary for primary forms of association. . . .
>
> "The yellow journalists vied with the hosts of a commercialized recreation in the effort to supply the much craved substitutes for activities interesting in their own right and warm in human feelings. . . . The inhabitants of the fashionable districts were made to feel their flesh creep at the accounts of vice and crime in the slums, while the denizens of the tenements were regaled with the scandals of the idle rich, or the romance and glamour of life in 'high society.' "

Reporters had taken on by the early 1870's the reputation for Bohemianism that continues to characterize them. "The vicissitudes of a reporter's life are very great, and they tend to make him reckless, improvident, and dissipated," remarked a writer[61] in 1871. He continued,

> "No occupation, excepting perhaps politics, attracts so many persons to it for a short time, or is subject to such fluctuations. . . .

"The pay of an ordinary reporter varies from $15 to $30 per week; the average being $20. A 'Free Lance' will earn as high as $60 per week. . . .

"One could hardly lead a more unsettled existence. His hours of sleep and meals vary almost daily, and unless a man has strong self-command, these irregular habits . . . will have a bad effect on him. . . . On the average, . . . a reporter is occupied twelve hours per day, and he is expected to write half a column of reports. . . . Short-hand reporters have the double labor of taking down their notes and then copying them out. . . . Short-hand reporters get the highest pay usually, but they can do so much better at law reporting and other work that they do not as a rule stay long upon the press."

Difficult hours, inadequate pay, the consequent rapid turnover of men, the ever-present fringe of floaters, the romantic allure of interviewing murderers and "big shots," and the favors extended the "gentlemen of the press" were all characterizing the "profession." Chapter VII reveals how outlays for materials, wages of unionized craftsmen, salaries for executives and advertising employees, investments, taxes, and profits squeezed allotments for editorial workers.

Post-Civil-War sensationalism concentrated upon crusades as well as crime and sex. Some papers, even *The New York Times*, albeit a Republican journal, refused to hold their noses at "the scandals which flourished in Washington, invisible to the somewhat too long-sighted eye of President Grant."[62] Joseph Pulitzer served in the Missouri legislature in 1870 and reported its affairs for the St. Louis *Westliche Post*. "The halls were filled with adventurers and the lobby with agents of corruption. These he assailed in print and on the floor with all the zeal of his fiery soul."[63] *The New York Times* published on its first page on July 22, 1871, its first three-column heading over figures illustrating some of "Boss" Tweed's thefts from the city's treasury. In spite of threats, the *Times* had been attacking this "Tammany Ring" since December, 1870. The transfer of control of the paper July 19, 1871, to E. B. Morgan and George Jones gave its staff the freedom needed to attract national attention with these disclosures. On July 28, the *Times* issued a supplement demonstrating the ring's frauds; repairs and furnishings for the new Court House and so forth had cost almost $10,000,000, of which some ninety per cent was graft. The St. Louis *Missouri Democrat*, soon aided by other sheets locally and in other cities, made a similar crusade against a notorious "Whiskey Ring."

The larger papers also turned to "making news." The *New York Herald* sent H. M. Stanley to find David Livingstone, an English missionary, "somewhere in Africa." On July 2, 1872, it made a sensation by reporting that Stanley had reached Livingstone at Ujiji. "Newspapers," said *The Proof-Sheet* in May, 1873, "are getting to be much more than mere transcripts of the news and gossip of the day. They are pioneers in learned exploration; they are foremost in geographical and historical discovery; they are the teachers of social science. . . . The reporter of to-day is the adventurer who penetrates the desert and the jungle; the scholar who searches for relics of the forgotten past; the courier who bears the news of victory to courts and congresses across a wilderness and through hostile armies; the detective who pries into public abuses; and discovers hidden wrongs; the pioneer who throws new countries open to the world; the philanthropist who unbars the door of the torture chamber; the chemist who detects adulteration in the spice-box; the inspector who seizes false weights and measures; the auditor who exposes a public theft in the public treasury. . . . Year by year its ambition becomes larger." Such stunts helped boost circulation and give the press a reputation for public-spiritedness. Many readers assumed, then as always, that a paper which attacked one flagrant abuse served their interests in all things, a profitable *non sequitur*.

Typewriters and telephones, introduced into newspaper offices from the late 1870s, further differentiated staff organization. C. L. Sholes, editor of the *Milwaukee Daily Sentinel* in 1861–63, developed the first practical typewriter in 1866–67, patented it in 1868, and continued improving it until it reached salable form. S. N. D. North, author of *The Newspaper and Periodical Press,* is said to have first made business use of a typewriter in 1872 at Utica, New York. While typewriters were placed on the market in 1874, they did not attain any great popularity until 1878 when Remington equipped them to print both small and large letters. By 1881, the Remington company, chief manufacturers of the machine, had built 1,200, many of which went to improve the legibility of newspaper copy.

The telephone, invented by A. G. Bell in 1875, was first used to send a dispatch to a newspaper on February 12, 1877, at a popular lecture and demonstration Bell gave at Salem, Massachusetts. The first commercial contract for telephone service was made three months later at Charlestown, Massachusetts. With 54,000 telephones by 1880, the separation of routine reporting between "leg men" and writers who did not leave the office began to become marked in news bureaus and on the larger sheets. Deskmen learned to speed their headline and story production with the type-writer—manipulated usually with but two fingers then as now—before special assignment men mastered its mysteries. Only special assignment reporters, handling "important" interviews and eye-witness accounts, continued to write their own yarns. This specialization, together with increasing attention to staff efficiency, eventually made payment by the line or inch for copy impractical, except in the case of special correspondents. "Much of the editorial work of the modern newspaper," a writer[64] stated in 1884, "is paid for by the piece, even when done by editors regularly employed, and this is more frequently the case with those engaged in the purely reportorial duties of the newspaper." By that time, however, a special department condensed and prepared news and wrote headings, distinct from one that edited telegraphic reports and correspondence. The *New York World*, too, had made the "Sporting Editor" by 1883 head of a special staff division.

The systematization occasioned by these mechanical devices and by business office demands for efficiency made "old time" reporters bemoan the passing of "rugged individualism." *The Journalist* on April 5, 1884, asserted that it "is no longer easy for a capable man to distinguish himself by any feat in reporting, because opportunities are not common." Personal contacts still counted, however, and placed progressively greater emphasis upon "reporters' confidences." The growing rarity of "scoops" on ordinary events also attached greater significance to examples of news enterprise that were largely produced under special assignment or as a staff project.

Where once editors prided themselves on their carefully "thought out" editorials, by the 1870s news held the center of the stage. Asked for his ideas on the newspaper, Whitelaw Reid,[65] editor of the *New York Tribune*, declared in 1875, "I should say what its name expresses; a *news*paper, with the promptest and best obtainable elucidation . . . of the news to attend it. I know there is another idea urged by men who are anxious to become propagandists; but whenever such men have obtained exclusive control of a daily newspaper they have ruined it. The essence, the life-blood of the daily paper of to-day, is the *news*." Reid also had ideas on the relation of editors to readers, frequently used since by editor-publishers. "Each newspaper," he continued, "caters to its own constituency, and its success depends on reading with the utmost promptness every indication of what that constituency wants, and looking out for fresh subjects which are likely, while retaining the old set, to attract recruits." Reid stated a viewpoint that, generally speaking, fits the facts, but it over-simplifies a highly complex relationship.

Impersonal journalism was displacing personal journalism. "That appears to mean a sort of journalism in which nobody will ask who is the editor of a paper or the writer of any class of article, and nobody will care."[66] But, as the New York *Sun* commented editorially on December 6, 1872, "Whenever, in the newspaper profession, a man rises up who is original, strong, and bold enough to make his opinions a matter of consequence to the public, there will be personal journalism; and whenever newspapers are conducted only by commonplace individuals whose views are of no consequence to anybody, there will be nothing but impersonal journalism." Journalism merely follows other professions of its sort in this regard. Such outstanding editor-publishers as Joseph Pulitzer, W. R. Hearst, W. A. White, and, more recently, J. M. Patterson and J. D. Stern, joined by such writers of editorial columns as Arthur Brisbane, Walter Lippmann, and Heywood Broun, cast thousands of other editorial writers into the obscurity of their shadows.

Journalism on the whole during 1880–1900 thus began to present "the apparent paradox of an editorial policy tending to become spineless or conservative while the treatment of day-by-day news became increasingly sensational. No generalization, however, could fit so diversified a world." The *Boston Evening Transcript* and New York *Evening Post* "made few concessions to the moronic mentality of the enlarged reading public" and contented themselves with small circulations. The *Chicago Daily News* and *Kansas City Evening Star* "battled for the common weal."[67]

The growing evening sheets and particularly the Scripps chain and W. R. Nelson's *Kansas City* (Missouri) *Evening Star*, begun in 1880, pointed the way toward more local and newsy sheets with their cheap, four-page editions. Lacking funds, time, and space, they did not let sensationalism steal their shows. During Nelson's life, the *Star* carried no large headlines, halftone illustrations, colored "comics," or sensational Sunday articles. In a greatly changed world, the *Star* and its morning edition, the *Times*, kept up much of this tradition in the 1930s for Kansas and Missouri farmers. They added colored "comics" and half-tones, but only "world-shaking" events rate as much as three- or four-column headlines. As for E. W. Scripps's papers, Lincoln Steffens[68] characterized them in describing their owner thus:

> "He is onto himself and the world, plays the game and despises it. He is sincere and not cynical . . . he avoided other rich men, so as to escape being one; he knew the danger his riches carried for himself, for his papers and for his seeing.
>
> "Rough, almost ruthless force, but restrained by clear, even shrewd insight; an executive capable of fierce action, restrained by the observation that a doer must not do too many things himself, but use his will to make others do them."

Nelson fought the granting of public utility franchises that did not protect Kansas Citians, promoted parkways, boulevards, parks, and other projects with which to transform a frontier settlement into a modern city. Scripps also agitated local improvements, but he gave as much attention to the predicaments of union labor and of other workers. In 1889, the five Scripps League papers sent "a company of workingmen, selected from various Western cities and representing different crafts, to the Paris Exposition and Great Britain." Each worker wrote out his observations, and the five sheets printed them "for the benefit of the crafts and the public generally."[69] Such Scripps papers as the *Cincinnati Post* even raised funds to buy food and clothing for strikers.

The *Chicago Times* of "JERKED TO JESUS" fame exceeded many contemporary limits of sensationalism in 1861–78 during W. F. Storey's editorship. The *New York Herald* continued to startle, excite, and, above all, attract new readers. The evening *New York Daily News* was building a huge circulation in that relatively new field with fast and sensational news coverage. With new droves of immigrants and other illiterates and semi-literates waiting to be blessed with papers they would *have* to learn to read, Joseph Pulitzer brought his sensational reforming vigor to flower in the 1880s at St. Louis and New York, and then came Hearst.

Circulation figures for the *New York Daily News* in the early 1880s illustrate popular reactions then to various types of sensational news. On the assassination of President J. A. Garfield, July 2, 1881, the *News* sold 167,000 copies, but the execution of Guiteau on the following June 30 sold 305,570, a tribute to the build-up of a running story. The Presidential election of 1884 made the demand reach 265,510 on November 5 and during the next three days 274,440, 273,080, and 232,970. The execution of McGloin and Magone on March 9, 1883, however, had disposed of 296,360 copies, a figure surpassed in 1881–86 only by the Guiteau execution. Such figures and others make the newspaper formula in its broad outlines obvious. Sensationalism, however, could be used as an entertaining bait with which to merchandise a *news*paper or as the whole show, a means of obscuring significant issues. Pulitzer made the former profitable; Hearst, the latter.

Pulitzer, brought to this country to fight for the Union army, drifted into German- and then English-language journalism in St. Louis. Carl Schurz gave him a chance to experiment with crusading journalism on the St. Louis *Westliche Post*, a paper in which Pulitzer owned an interest for several years. In 1878, several years after selling this interest, "J. P." bought and merged the St. Louis *Post* and *Dispatch* and then in 1883 took over the *New York World*. The doctrines he announced in the *World* on May 17, 1883, indicate his views on the rôle of journalism. They were:

"1. Tax Luxuries.
"2. Tax Inheritances.
"3. Tax Large Incomes.
"4. Tax Monopolies.
"5. Tax the Privileged Corporation.
"6. A Tariff for Revenue.
"7. Reform the Civil Service.
"8. Punish Corrupt Officers.
"9. Punish Vote Buying.
"10. Punish Employers who Coerce their Employees in Elections."

This "popular platform of ten lines" Pulitzer recommended "to the politicians in place of long-winded resolutions." His sincerity as well as his pretensions amazed the rulers of both cities and even the populace.

Pulitzer battled to limit the ravages of the largely unrestrained capitalists, forced the federal government through exposures to cease making secret bond issues, "fought nobly against special privilege in the form of tariffs, subsidies, grabs, bonuses, and all sorts of raids upon the Treasury," and usually opposed imperialism. But, as O. G. Villard,[70] a scathing critic of most papers, asserts, "the *World* has not escaped the wide criticism of New York's dailies that they are of the 'kept press,' and that they reflect primarily the views of the great capitalists. . . . Nobody forgets like the American public and it forgets nothing so rapidly as a newspaper's good deeds." Both Scripps and Pulitzer resembled Greeley in their general purposes, but both had a respect for *possibilities* that escaped Greeley's "thinking."

Such editor-publishers as Pulitzer and V. F. Lawson of the *Chicago Daily News* led the way toward making newspapers participate in public welfare projects actually as well as verbally. The *Evening World* commissioned a physician in 1888 to treat slum children, and Lawson established a Fresh-Air Sanitarium the same year. Others joined the movement; it convinced readers emotionally that a paper represented them even when adequate evidence was lacking. The *New York Herald's* "ice charity," continued for many years, was started in 1892 with a popular subscription of over $10,000, used to open thirteen depots in the slums and to distribute twenty tons of ice daily to the poor. Two years later, it gave $1,000 to start a fund to make the newly discovered diphtheria antitoxin available to American physicians. W. R. Hearst's *San Francisco Examiner* started in 1889 to do something concrete about the "Yellow Menace" to white labor by setting up free employment bureaus for whites and even sending out special labor trains to collect them.

"Trial by newspaper," called by *The Journalist* on July 5, 1884, "BLOODTHIRSTY JOURNALISM," continued to grow in intensity and flagrance during the 1880s. "The criticism of judicial and legal performances while in process of settlement," said *The Journalist*, "is one of the unjustifiable prerogatives which the American Press often arrogates itself." The "liberty of the press," it warned, "may very frequently degenerate into license." On April 5, the same trade journal had pointed to another aspect of the situation. It claimed that crime publicity "is dreaded by loose characters more than any other punishment," and asked, "How are the people of one community to know the criminals of another, if there is no means such as the press presents of conveying information?" The trade paper thus suggested the "horns" of the crime dilemma. A ban on crime and trial publicity would multiply the instances of collusion between criminals and "public servants." Unrestricted trial publicity, on the other hand, leads straightway to trial by newspaper.

This anxiety for the bizarre and horrible also led to what *The Journalist* on March 28, 1885, labeled, "KEYHOLE JOURNALISM." For this, it said, the "reporter is not to blame. . . . He is sent for certain news, and he must get that news or he loses his position." The "average reporter is a gentleman, and it affords him no pleasure to pry into private affairs and ask impertinent questions. . . . There is no doubt that it is all wrong, . . . but it sells the paper." To get such material, reporters then as always got themselves into the confidence of persons whose identity they were obliged to conceal. This practice contradicted the general impression, *The Journalist* asserted on July 5, 1884, "that the average newspaper man will go to any length for news, that no confidences are sacred, that nothing delights him so much as spicy scandal, the details of which may injure many who are innocent of active participation in the affair. . . . Workers in journalism, especially space men, lose hundreds of dollars every year by suppressing facts which are legitimate news, but which tend to injure innocent parties." As certain papers tended more towards sensationalism, this solicitude for the innocent diminished. Others continued to avoid pillorying any and all merely to elaborate a story. C. A. Dana,[71] sage editor of the New York *Sun*, advised young reporters in 1888, "Get the news, get all the news, and nothing but the news. . . . Never print an interview without the knowledge and consent of the party interviewed." His paper, frequently called "the newspaperman's newspaper" because of its spriteliness, terseness, accuracy, and "ethical standards," reflected such policies.

The growth of newspaper organizations, the integration of staff activities, and the increasing complexity of urban life continued to modify staff organization. The *World* by 1885 was sending reporters in carload lots to cover "big" stories. The special interests of sections in big cities led certain papers in the 1880s to publish daily pages of their affairs and even special editions for them. Engraving developments, too, were starting to bring new specialists into newspaper offices. In addition to cartoonists, evident for many years, more and more illustrators and even some photo-engravers were being hired. In the 1890s, then, photographers gradually worked themselves into "steady" berths.

During his exciting stay at Harvard in 1883–85, Hearst studied the Boston sheets, but Pulitzer's successes particularly fascinated him. In Pulitzer's digging into unsuspected or neglected public scandals, "news creation," this inveterate practical jokester saw a device with which to amuse himself and obtain power. Tricking Harvard professors could never compare with playing jests upon whole cities and even the entire country. The *San Francisco Examiner* became his laboratory.

A fisherman was marooned on a rock outside the Golden Gate. Finding that the federal life-savers had not launched their boat, Hearst's men chartered a tug and rescued the stranded man. While other morning papers still had the unfortunate on his rock, the *Examiner* gloated over its "daring" rescue. H. R. Haxton, Sunday supplement editor and a skilled swimmer, then jumped from a ferryboat and timed his rescuers. These feats precipitated reorganizations of life-saving provisions in San Francisco waters.

Pulitzer viewed imperialism "with alarm," but Hearst revived in 1891 the Panama Canal project and persistently demanded its completion under American control. In those days, too, Hearst did not regard it "un-American" to attack business corruption. He reveled, for example, in a battle with the Southern Pacific Railroad and talked of "Public Plunder by Pirate Privilege." Hearst did not match, nevertheless, the *World's* efforts in connection with the Homestead riots of 1892 and the Venezuela-British-Guiana boundary crisis of 1895. In the former, Pulitzer condemned H. C. Frick for having Pinkerton detectives and Coal and Iron Police slaughter the workers. In the latter, with the United States coasting towards another war with Great Britain, the *World* led in halting the press's general jingoism by printing numerous statements obtained from leaders in England and this country. Pulitzer, Hearst, Scripps, and others seeking purchasers among the near-literate tried on the whole to convince the masses, especially the urban laborers, that they had popular causes at heart. Scripps and Pulitzer continued to do so even after they had stabilized their properties. Hearst and many others passed on to another stage as their sheets and the industry generally attained "firmer ground." They still sought to "stand" for the "best interests" of the masses, but their ways of serving those "best interests" were no longer necessarily the popular ones.

Hearstism spread to New York in 1895 when W. R. bought the *Morning Journal* and then gradually seeped into other cities by emulation, the expansion of his chain, and the sale of his features and news. The next year, A. S. Ochs, publisher of the *Chattanooga* (Tennessee) *Times*, also invaded the New York field. He bought the *Times* and started to prove that people would buy a daily encyclopedia of "All the News That's Fit to Print." On August 15, 1896, too, W. A. White published an editorial on "What's the Matter With Kansas" that brought that 28-year-old editor-publisher of the *Emporia* (Kansas) *Gazette* within the next two weeks national prominence. The wide publication of his common-sense editorials and articles, flavored with a "folksy" type of humor, impressed his sane liberalism upon some newspaper writers and gave the small-town middle-western press a model to imitate. Hearst, of these three, drew the most imitators; Ochs and White, the most admirers.

Hearst and White both operated "schools of journalism." Hearst trained sensation-mongers and jugglers of catchwords for big-city dailies. The "Sage of Emporia" inspired many a reporter and editor, later "graduated" to responsible posts on other sheets and on agencies and syndicates, with such homely maxims as:

> "Boil your story down. Never use two words when one will do."
> "Laugh *with* and not *at* people, and you will never get into trouble."
> "Dip your pen into your arteries and write."[72]

White wanted his 'students" to be sane, human, and representative. He treated his staff as part of his family. Hearst wanted Bohemians, "romantic figures," to whom a drowned child's mother would merely be a character in a yarn, not a fellow human being in distress. Sentimentality, unless carefully manipulated as a stage property, would "spoil" a story calling for the flagrant invasion of privacy.

The battles between Hearst and Pulitzer, beginning in 1895 and reflected by many papers throughout the country, gave the press new pretentiousness and the country the Spanish-American War. To facilitate his creation of news, Hearst organized a mobile "murder squad," charged with solving crime mysteries in advance of the police. "Time has been," asserted W. R.,[73] "when the utmost art of the literary man or the journalist had been employed in making a criminal a heroic figure in an engrossing romance. That was in the era of the old journalism. The new journalism strives to apprehend the criminal, to bring him to the bar of justice and thereafter not to convict him but to show him as he is." Typical Hearst rationalizing: not to convict him, just to show how guilty he is. Contrary to this statement, Hearst did not discard the exploitation of criminals' heroics, granted they fit his purposes. Not satisfied with trial by newspaper *alone*, he had decided to tamper with the whole course of crime detection and adjudication to an extent never before witnessed. In the summer of 1897, the *New York Morning Journal* seized upon the discovery of a dismembered body, wrapped in oil-cloth. It reproduced the oil-cloth in colors, sent thirty "leg men" to find its purchaser, and occasioned the arrest of an east side midwife and her male aid in the killing of her husband.

A number of books have been written on the Hearst-Pulitzer circulation campaign that precipitated American interference in Cuba.[74] "From March, 1895, to April, 1898," concluded one of these writers, J. E. Wisan, "there were fewer than a score of days in which Cuba did not appear in the day's news. . . . The effect was cumulative. . . . Little wonder that the 'average reader,' indoctrinated with these opinions, called on his Government for War." The *New York Journal's* owner had the gall to run in the "ears"—the little boxes in the upper corners—of the paper's front page the question, "HOW DO YOU LIKE THE JOURNAL'S WAR?" By the time that Cervera's fleet was destroyed on July 3, 1898, Pulitzer had had enough. Fleets of tugs and voluminous cable charges were wiping out *World* profits. He turned to demanding peace.

The Spanish War firmly established the "banner" head on the front page of the more sensational dailies. The war's "chief effect, however, was the more vitally significant one of making the headline 'the thing,' the supremely important feature in news-presentation. In this capacity it has since constantly increased in significance."[75] G. C. Bastian, a newspaperman, in writing more recently (1923) a journalism text, *Editing the Day's News*, characterizes thus the rôle of the headline:

> "A good headline is a work of art, a picture of an event, . . . done in bold, swift, telling word-strokes, the omission of even a single one of which would blur the effect. It does not transcend the bounds of the story it announces and summarizes; it is sympathetic; its economy of words creates a compelling dynamic force."

He exaggerates somewhat. He speaks of "good" practice. All headlines do not stick to the literal "bounds of the story."

Pulitzer tired of competing directly with Hearst. He returned to the sort of crusading and liberal news presentation in 1901 that characterized his sheet in 1883–95. But "yellowism" forged on. It had to concoct stories that created the "emotional equivalent of war." Arthur Brisbane, hired by Hearst away from Pulitzer's *World* in 1897, became Hearst's "right-hand man," the high priest of "yellow" journalism. "No man," once asserted Will Irwin,[76] "can be so sincere or so plausibly insincere as Brisbane. To analyze his best flights, to show how artfully he conceals the one necessary flaw in an otherwise perfect chain of logic, is an exercise which I recommend to our university classes in forensics." Brisbane's[77] own statement of his journalistic philosophy illustrates Irwin's contention:

> "The papers pander to a depraved appetite because the people demand it. They do not, however, create this appetite, and when there is an improvement in the people it will be accompanied by an improvement in the papers, because the newspaper will always be on the watch for such change. . . .
>
> "I am the yellowist journalist in the world. If I am not, I want to be. . . .
>
> "I addressed a meeting of 100 Presbyterian ministers once, and when they criticized this method of journalism, I told them that when God gets ready to send a storm he creates ugly black clouds which are typified in the paper in black type; the lightning is the red type that they frequently use and the colored supplement on Sunday is the rainbow."

Hearst layouts, news, and editorials reflected this Hearst-Brisbane viewpoint.

The celebration on the occasion of Hearst's launching of his *Los Angeles Examiner* on December 12, 1903, demonstrates the extent to which workers thought he represented them. "Representatives of union labor from all over Southern California, to the number of 20,000, marched in procession through the principal streets of Los Angeles"[78] to welcome this competitor to the anti-union-labor *Los Angeles Times*.

References

1. Editorial, *The Guild Reporter*, *2:* 23, December 1, 1935, p. 4.
2. W. Nelson in *Annual Report of the American Historical Association for the Year 1908*, 1909, pp. 221–2.
3. A. Nevins, *American Press Opinion*, 1928, p. 5. By permission of the author.
4. H. Ward, *Builders of Delusion*, 1931, p. 131.
5. H. O. Mahin, *The Development and Significance of the Newspaper Headline*, 1924, p. 47.
6. F. Hudson, *Journalism in the United States*, 1873, p. 380.
7. J. M. Lee, *History of American Journalism*, rev. ed., 1923, p. 143. By permission of Houghton Mifflin Co., publishers.
8. [I. C. Pray,] *James Gordon Bennett*, 1855, p. 45.
9. *Ibid.*, p. 44.
10. *Ibid.*, p. 75.
11. W. F. G. Shanks in *Harper's New Monthly Magazine*, *34* (1867): 512.
12. E. H. Munday in *The Proof-Sheet*, *3:* 17, March, 1870, p. 68.
13. [I. C. Pray,] *James Gordon Bennett*, 1855, p. 119.
14. F. Hudson, *Journalism in the United States*, 1873, p. 418.
15. *Fifty Years of Service, 1834–1884*, 1884, p. 14.
16. T. M. Coleman in *The Proof-Sheet*, *5:* 27, November, 1871, p. 38.
17. [I. C. Pray,] *James Gordon Bennett*, 1855, p. 183.
18. F. Hudson, *Journalism in the United States*, 1873, p. 437.
19. [I. C. Pray,] *James Gordon Bennett*, 1855, p. 194.
20. F. M. O'Brien, *The Story of the Sun*, 1918, p. 59.
21. W. G. Bleyer, *Main Currents in the History of American Journalism*, 1927, p. 183.
22. C. D. Clark, *News: A Sociological Study*, doctoral dissertation deposited in the University of Chicago Library, 1931, MS., p. 255.
23. F. Hudson, *Journalism in the United States*, 1873, p. 453.
24. A. Maverick, *Henry J. Raymond*, 1870, p. 324.
25. [I. C. Pray,] *James Gordon Bennett*, 1855, p. 202.
26. F. Hudson, *Journalism in the United States*, 1873, p. 525.
27. A. Nevins, *American Press Opinion*, 1928, p. 113. By permission of the author.
28. J. Parton, *The Life of Horace Greeley*, 1855, p. 396.
29. "The Old Crab" in *The American Press*, *54:* 7, May, 1936, p. 10.
30. [I. C. Pray,] *James Gordon Bennett*, 1855, p. 463.
31. *Ibid.*, pp. 417–18.
32. J. Munsell, *The Typographical Miscellany*, 1850, p. 202.
33. *The Proof-Sheet*, *5:* 27, November, 1871, p. 39.
34. J. Munsell, *The Typographical Miscellany*, 1850, p. 204.
35. A. Maverick, *Henry J. Raymond*, 1870, p. 53.
36. Quoted by F. Hudson, *Journalism in the United States*, 1873, p. 548.
37. *The Editor and Publisher*, *6:* 30, January 12, 1907, p. 3.
38. Quoted by G. Turnbull in *The Publishers' Auxiliary*, *68:* 47, November 24, 1934, p. 5.
39. *Journalism in the United States*, 1873, pp. 563–4.
40. [I. C. Pray,] *James Gordon Bennett*, 1855, p. 465.
41. L. A. Wilmer, *Our Press Gang*, 1859, p. 51.
42. T. W. M. in *American Publishers' Circular and Literary Gazette*, *2:* 1, January 5, 1856, p. 1.
43. E. H. Munday in *The Proof-Sheet*, *5:* 26, September, 1871, p. 22.
44. *Journalism in the United States*, 1873, p. 481.
45. I. D. Marshall in *Newspaperdom*, *1:* 1, March, 1892, p. 8.
46. *Editor & Publisher*, *52:* 35, January 29, 1920, p. 7.
47. *Ibid.*, *55:* 28, December 9, 1922, p. 5.
48. *Ibid.*, *66:* 23, October 21, 1933, p. 24.
49. *Ibid.*, *63:* 43, March 14, 1931, p. 9.
50. J. E. Hardenburgh, quoted in *The Editor and Publisher and Journalist*, *12:* 19, October 26, 1912, p. 5.

51. *Ibid.*
52. D. Resnick in *Editor & Publisher, 62:* 15, August 17, 1929, p. 26.
53. Editorial, *Editor & Publisher, 64:* 31, December 19, 1931, p. 28.
54. D. Boyd in *The Quill, 19:* 12, December, 1931, p. 5.
55. *Editor & Publisher, 66:* 48, I, April 14, 1934, p. 34.
56. A. Maverick, *Henry J. Raymond,* 1870, pp. 325–6.
57. J. Grant, *The Newspaper Press,* 1871, II, pp. 423, 421, 425.
58. *Ibid.,* p. 424.
59. "Felix" in *American Newspaper Reporter and Advertisers Gazette,* 5 (1871): 218.
60. *News: A Sociological Study,* doctoral dissertation deposited in the University of Chicago Library, 1931, MS., pp. 307, 312–13.
61. "Felix" in *American Newspaper Reporter and Advertisers Gazette,* 5 (1871): 217.
62. E. Davis, *History of The New York Times,* 1921, p. 120.
63. D. C. Seitz, *Joseph Pulitzer,* 1924, p. 63. By permission of Simon and Schuster, Inc., publishers.
64. S. N. D. North, *The Newspaper and Periodical Press,* 1884, p. 83.
65. C. F. Wingate, *Views and Interviews on Journalism,* 1875, pp. 25, 27.
66. G. H. Payne, *History of Journalism,* 1920, p. 340.
67. A. M. Schlesinger, *The Rise of the City: 1878–1898,* 1933, p. 187.
68. *Scripps-Howard News,* September, 1929, p. 2.
69. M. A. McRae, *Forty Years in Newspaperdom,* 1924, p. 88. By permission of Coward McCann, Inc., publishers.
70. *Some Newspapers and Newspaper-Men,* 1923, pp. 51–2. By permission of Alfred A. Knopf, Inc., publishers.
71. *The Art of Newspaper Making,* 1895, p. 19.
72. Quoted by Jennie S. Owen in *Editor & Publisher, 69:* 39, August 15, 1936, p. 31.
73. J. K. Winkler, *W. R. Hearst,* 1928, pp. 132–3.
74. See W. Millis, *The Martial Spirit,* 1931; M. M. Wilkerson, *Public Opinion and the Spanish-American War,* 1932; and J. E. Wisan, *The Cuban Crisis as Reflected in the New York Press,* 1934.
75. H. O. Mahin, *The Development and Significance of the Newspaper Headline,* 1924, p. 113.
76. *Collier's, 46:* 22, February 18, 1911, p. 24.
77. *The Editor and Publisher and Journalist, 11:* 24, December 9, 1911, p. 5.
78. *The Editor and Publisher, 3:* 26, December 19, 1903, p. 5.

Chapter 16

JAMES W. CAREY

TECHNOLOGY AND IDEOLOGY
The Case of the Telegraph

IN ONE OF THE MOST FAMOUS PARAGRAPHS of our most famous auto-biography, Henry Adams located the precise moment when "eighteenth-century troglodytic Boston" joined industrial America: "the opening of the Boston and Albany Railroad; the appearance of the first Cunard Steamers in the bay; and the telegraphic messages which carried from Baltimore to Washington the news that Henry Clay and James K. Polk were nominated for the presidency. This was May, 1844" (Adams, 1931: 5).

Adams signaled the absorption of genteel New England into industrial America by three improvements in transportation and communication. Yet for all the significance attached to the telegraph in that famous passage, it remains a product of one of the least studied technologies, certainly the least studied communications technology. The effect of the telegraph on modern life and its role as a model for future developments in communications have scarcely been explored. The first twenty-three volumes of *Technology and Culture* are virtually without reference to the telegraph. Robert L. Thompson's *Wiring a Continent*, the principal history of the telegraph, is now more than forty years old, takes the story only to 1866, and focuses almost exclusively on the formation of Western Union (Thompson, 1947).

I take the neglect of the telegraph to be unfortunate for a number of reasons. First, the telegraph was dominated by the first great industrial monopoly—Western Union, the first communications empire and the prototype of the many industrial empires that were to follow. The telegraph, in conjunction with the railroad, provided the setting in which modern techniques for the management of complex enterprises were first worked out, though for the telegraph in what was eventually monopolistic circumstances.[1] Although the telegraph did not provide the site for the first of the titanic nineteenth-century patent struggles (that prize probably goes to Elias Howe's sewing machine) it led to one of the most significant of them in the rewriting of American law, particularly in the great "telegraph war" between Jay Gould and the Vanderbilt interests for control of the Edison patents for the quadraplex telegraph system, the innovation that Gould rightly prized as the "nerve of industry."[2]

Second, the telegraph was the first product—really the foundation—of the electrical goods industry and thus the first of the science- and engineering-based industries. David Noble's *American Design: Science, Technology and the Rise of Corporate Capitalism* (1977) implies throughout a sharp distinction between forms of engineering, such as civil engineering, grounded in a handicraft and guild tradition, and chemical engineering and electrical engineering, which were science-based from the outset. Much that is distinctive about the telegraph, from the organization of the industry to the rhetoric that rationalized it, derives from the particular nature of the engineering it brought into being. More to the point, the telegraph was the first electrical engineering technology and therefore the first to focus on the central problem in modern engineering: the economy of a signal.[3]

Third, the telegraph brought about changes in the nature of language, of ordinary knowledge, of the very structures of awareness. Although in its early days the telegraph was used as a toy—as was the computer, which it prefigured—for playing long-distance chess, its implications for human knowledge were the subject of extended, often euphoric, and often pessimistic debate. Adams saw the telegraph as a demonic device dissipating the energy of history and displacing the Virgin with the Dynamo, whereas Thoreau saw it as an agent of trivialization. An even larger group saw the telegraph as an agency of benign improvement—spiritual, moral, economic, and political. Now that thought could travel by "the singing wire," a new form of reporting and a new form of knowledge were envisioned that would replace traditional literature with a new and active form of scientific knowledge.

Fourth, and partly for the foregoing reasons, the telegraph was a watershed in communication, as I hope to show later. Now, it is easy to overemphasize the revolutionary consequences of the telegraph. It is not an infrequent experience to be driving along an interstate highway and to become aware that the highway is paralleled by a river, a canal, a railroad track, or telegraph and telephone wires. In that instant one may realize that each of these improvements in transportation and communications merely worked a modification on what preceded it. The telegraph twisted and altered but did not displace patterns of connection formed by natural geography: by the river and primitive foot and horse paths and later by the wooden turnpike and canal.

But the innovation of the telegraph can stand metaphorically for all the innovations that ushered in the modern phase of history and determined, even to this day, the major lines of development of American communications. The most important fact about the telegraph is at once the most obvious and innocent: It permitted for the first time the effective separation of communication from transportation. This fact was immediately recognized, but its significance has been rarely investigated. The telegraph not only allowed messages to be separated from the physical movement of objects; it also allowed communication to control physical processes actively. The early use of the telegraph in railroad signaling is an example: telegraph messages could control the physical switching of rolling stock, thereby multiplying the purposes and effectiveness of communication. The separation of communication from transportation has been exploited in most subsequent developments in communication down to computer control systems.

When the telegraph reached the West Coast eight years in advance of a transcontinental railroad, the identity of communication and transportation was ended in both fact and symbol. Before the telegraph, "communication" was used to describe transportation as well as message transmittal for the simple reason that the movement of messages was dependent on their being carried on foot or horseback or by rail. The telegraph, by ending the identity, allowed symbols to move independently of and faster than transportation. To put it in a slightly different way, the telegraph freed communication from the constraints of geography. The telegraph, then, not only altered the relation between communication and transportation; it also changed the fundamental ways in which communication was thought about. It provided a model for thinking about communication—a model I have called a transmission model—and displaced older religious views of communication even as the new technology was mediated through religious language. And it opened up new ways of thinking about communication within both the formal practice of theory and the practical consciousness of everyday life. In this sense the telegraph was not only a new tool of commerce but also a thing to think with, an agency for the alteration of ideas.

II

A thorough treatment of the consequences of the telegraph would attempt to demonstrate how this instrument altered the spatial and temporal boundaries of human interaction, brought into existence new forms of language as well as new conceptual systems, and brought about new structures of social relations, particularly by fostering a national commercial middle class. These consequences were also displacements: older forms of language and writing declined, traditional social interactions waned, and the pattern of city-state capitalism that dominated the first half of the nineteenth century was broken up (Carey and Sims, 1976: 219–41). I intend now to concentrate on the relationship between the telegraph and ideas, between, broadly, the telegraph and ideology. I hope also to insinuate throughout some observations on the broader matters noted earlier.

There are three relationships between the telegraph and ideology. Two of them have received some attention, and I will mention them only in passing in order to concentrate on a relationship that has not as yet been investigated.

The first is the relationship between the telegraph and monopoly capitalism, the principal subject of Thompson's *Wiring a Continent*. That is, the telegraph was a new and distinctively different force of production that demanded a new body of law, economic theory, political arrangements, management techniques, organizational structures, and scientific rationales with which to justify and make effective the development of a privately owned and controlled monopolistic corporation. This problem can be looked at as one of the relationships among a force of production, the organizational forms and administrative techniques that realize it, and the explanatory and justifying ideology that guides and legitimates its institutionalization. Unfortunately, even in this context the telegraph has not been investigated adequately, partly because of the tendency to eschew historical investigations and to treat forces of production, *tout court*, as all-encompassing rather than to investigate the particular consequences and ideological implications of particular technologies. Technology as such is too abstract a category to support any precise analysis; therefore, changes in technology go unanalyzed except for classifying them within various stages of capitalist development.

Before the telegraph, business relations were personal; that is, they were mediated through face-to-face relations, by personal correspondence, by contacts among people who, by and large, knew one another as actual persons. The overall coordination of these atomic relations and transactions was provided by the "invisible hand" of the market.

With the telegraph and, of course, the railroads and improvements in other techniques of transport and communication, the volume and speed of transactions demanded a new form of organization of essentially impersonal relations—that is, relations not among known persons but among buyers and sellers whose only relation was mediated through an organization and a structure of management. "The visible hand of management replaced the invisible hand of market forces where and when new technology and expanded markets permitted a historically unprecedented high volume and speed of materials through the process of production and distribution" (Chandler, 1977: 9). Through the telegraph and railroad the social relations among large numbers of anonymous buyers and sellers were coordinated. But these new and unprecedented relations of communication and contact had themselves to be explained, justified, and made effective. What we innocently describe as theory, law, common sense, religion were means by which these new relations were carried through to explicit consciousness and "naturalized"—made to seem merely of the order of things.

The second connection between ideology and the telegraph resides in the popular imagery, largely religious, that accompanied the latter's introduction. This aspect of the problem has been rather more thoroughly investigated, at least in a general way, within American studies and particularly within what is called the "myth and symbol" school. The telegraph, widely hailed at the time of its introduction as the "noiseless tenant of the wilderness," was clothed in the language of religious aspiration and secular millenarianism, a language Leo Marx names the "rhetoric of the technological sublime." John Quirk and I, thinking more directly of the telegraph and subsequent developments, have called this same language the "rhetoric of the electrical sublime."

There were other technological marvels of the mid-nineteenth century, but the inscrutable nature of the telegraph made it seem more extraordinary than, and qualitatively different from, other inventions. The key to the mystery was, of course, electricity—a force of great potency and yet invisible. It was this invisibility that made electricity and the telegraph powerful impetuses to idealist thought both in religious and philosophical terms. It presented the mystery of the mind-body dualism and located vital energy in the realm of the mind, in the nonmaterial world. Electricity was, in standard terms of the day, "shadowy, mysterious, impalpable. It lives in the skies and seems to connect the spiritual and material" (Czitrom, 1982: 9).[4]

Electricity, the Reverend Ezra S. Gannett told his Boston congregation, was both the "swift winged messenger of destruction" and the "vital energy of material creation. The invisible, imponderable substance, force, whatever it be—we do not even certainly know what it is which we are dealing with . . . is brought under our control, to do our errands, nay, like a very slave" (Czitrom, 1982: 19). Another preacher of the era, Gardner Spring, exclaimed that we were on the "border of a spiritual harvest because thought now travels by steam and magnetic wires" (Miller, 1965: 48). This new technology enters American discussions not as mundane fact but as divinely inspired for the purposes of spreading the Christian message farther and faster, eclipsing time and transcending space, saving the heathen, bringing closer and making more probable the day of salvation.

There were dissenters, of course, but the general uniformity of reaction to the telegraph demonstrated how it was able to fuse the opposite poles of the electrical sublime: the desire for peace, harmony, and self-sufficiency with the wish for power, profit, and productivity. The presumed "annihilation of time and space" heralded by the telegraph promised to bind the country together just as the portents of the Civil War were threatening to tear it apart. Here the organic metaphors, so easily attributed to German philosophy, floated into American thought as means to describe how the telegraph would change life. As early as 1838, Morse anticipated twentieth-century notions of the "global village." It would not be long, he wrote, "ere the whole surface of this country would be channeled for those nerves which are to diffuse with the speed of thought, a knowledge of all that is occurring throughout the land; making in fact one neighborhood of the whole country" (Czitrom, 1982: 11–12).

And finally, a piece of doggerel typical of the era, entitled "To Professor Morse, In Pleasant Memory of Oct. 9, 1856, at the Albion," expresses the mixture of science, commerce, politics, and pious religious unity that surfaced in popular consciousness with the telegraph:

> A good and generous spirit ruled the hour;
>   Old jealousies were drowned in brotherhood;
> Philanthropy rejoiced that Skill and Power,
>   Servants to Science, compass all men's good;
>   And over all Religion's banner stood,
> Upheld by thee, true patriarch of the plan
> Which in two hemispheres was schemed to shower
> Mercies from God on universal man.
>   Yes, this electric chain from East to West
> More than mere metal, more than mammon can,
>   Binds us together—kinsmen, in the best,
> As most affectionate and frankest bond;
> Brethren as one; and looking far beyond
>   The world in an Electric Union blest!
>
>   (Martin F. Typper, in *Prime*, 1875: 648).

One finds in this rhetoric of the electrical sublime a central tenet of middle-class ideology: that "communication, exchange, motion brings humanity, enlightenment, progress and that isolation and disconnection are evidence of barbarism and merely obstacles to be overcome" (Schivelbusch, 1978: 40). The eighteenth-century ideal of universalism—the Kingdom of God and the Brotherhood of Man—included a belief in a universal Human Nature. People were people—everywhere the same. Communication was the engine that powered this ideal. Each improvement in communication, by ending isolation, by linking people everywhere, was heralded as realizing the Universal Brotherhood of Universal Man.

The argument is not an abstract one. Charles F. Briggs and Augustus Maverick, writing in 1858, made the equation precise:

> It has been the result of the great discoveries of the past century, to effect a revolution in political and social life, by establishing a more intimate connexion between nations, with race and race. It has been found that the old system of exclusion and insulation are stagnation and death. National health can only be maintained by the free and unobstructed interchange of each with all. How potent a power, then, is the telegraph destined to

become in the civilization of the world! This binds together by a vital cord all the nations of the earth. It is impossible that old prejudices and hostilities should longer exist, while such an instrument has been created for an exchange of thought between all the nations of the earth (Briggs and Maverick, 1858: 21–22).

In another work of the era, Sir William P. Andrews, justifying the Euphrates Valley Railroad connecting India to Africa, quotes an anonymous writer who got the whole matter rather more correctly:

Nor can it for a moment be doubted that a line of electric telegraphs between Europe and India must be a successful commercial enterprise, putting altogether out of sight the important moral effects which such a means of rapid communication must of necessity bring about. It may, on the contrary, be doubted whether any more efficient means could be adopted to develop the resources of India, and to consolidate British power and strengthen British rule in that country, than by the formation of the proposed system of railways in central Asia and the carrying out of the proposed telegraph communication with Europe (Andrews, 1857: 141).

An essentially religious view of communication—or one cloaked, at least, in religious metaphors—is as a mediator—a progressively vanishing mediator—between middle-class aspiration and capitalist and, increasingly, imperial development.[5] Max Weber's tour de force retains its original significance in this context; for Weber's archetype of the formation of the Protestant ethic, Benjamin Franklin, reappears in the mid-nineteenth century as the first electrician, the first to release this new force of moral and social progress. But what needs to be more closely investigated is the relationship between a later stage of economic development, new forms of electrical technology, and a transposed body of religious belief. This is particularly true because, from the telegraph forward, technological development came to be housed in professional engineering societies, universities, and research laboratories. As technological development became more systematic, so did the development of justifying ideologies become more consciously planned and directed by these same groups.

III

In the balance of this chapter I wish to concentrate on the effect of the telegraph on ordinary ideas: the coordinates of thought, the natural attitude, practical consciousness, or, less grandly, common sense. As I have intimated, I think the best way to grasp the effects of the telegraph or any other technology is not through a frontal assault but, rather, through the detailed investigation in a couple of sites where those effects can be most clearly observed.

Let me suggest some of the sites for those investigations—investigations to be later integrated and referred for elucidation to some general theoretical notions. First, much additional work needs to be done on the effects of the telegraph on language and journalism. The telegraph reworked the nature of written language and finally the nature of awareness itself. There is an old saw, one I have repeated myself, that the telegraph, by creating the wire services, led to a fundamental change in news. It snapped the tradition of partisan journalism by forcing the wire services to generate "objective" news, news that could be used by papers of any political stripe (Carey, 1969: 23–38). Yet the issue is deeper than that. The wire services demanded a form of language stripped of the local, the regional; and colloquial. They demanded something closer to a "scientific" language, a language of strict denotation in which the connotative features of utterance were under rigid control. If the same story were to be understood in the same way from Maine to California, language had to be flattened out and standardized. The telegraph, therefore, led to the disappearance of forms of speech and styles of journalism and story telling—the tall story, the hoax, much humor, irony, and satire—that depended on a more traditional use of the symbolic, a use I earlier called the fiduciary.[6] The origins of objectivity may be sought, therefore, in the necessity of stretching language in space over the long lines of Western Union. That is, the telegraph changed the forms of social relations mediated by language. Just as the long lines displaced a personal relation mediated by speech and correspondence in the conduct of trade and substituted the mechanical coordination of buyer and seller, so the language of the telegraph displaced a fiduciary relationship between writer and reader with a coordinated one.

Similarly, the telegraph eliminated the correspondent who provided letters that announced an event, described it in detail, and analyzed its substance, and replaced him with the stringer who supplied the bare facts. As words were expensive on the telegraph, it separated the observer from the writer. Not only did writing for the telegraph have to be condensed to save money—telegraphic, in other words—but also from the marginal notes and anecdotes of the stringer the story had to be reconstituted at the end of the telegraphic line, a process that reaches high art with the news magazines, the story divorced from the story teller.

But as every constraint is also an opportunity, the telegraph altered literary style. In a well-known story, "cablese" influenced Hemingway's style, helping him to pare his prose to the bone, dispossessed of every adornment. Most correspondents chafed under its restrictiveness, but not Hemingway. "I had to quit being a correspondent," he told Lincoln Steffens later. "I was getting too fascinated by the lingo of the cable."[7] But the lingo of the cable provided the underlying structure for one of the most influential literary styles of the twentieth century.

There were other effects—some obvious, some subtle. If the telegraph made prose lean and unadorned and led to a journalism without the luxury of detail and analysis, it also brought an overwhelming crush of such prose to the newsroom. In the face of what was a real glut of occurrences, news judgment had to be routinized and the organization of the newsroom made factory-like. The reporter who produced the new prose moved into prominence in journalism by displacing the editor as the archetype of the journalist. The spareness of the prose and the sheer volume of it allowed news—indeed, forced news—to be treated like a commodity: something that could be transported, measured, reduced, and timed. In the wake of the telegraph, news was subject to all the procedures developed for handling agricultural commodities. It was subject to "rates, contracts, franchising, discounts and thefts."[8]

A second site for the investigation of the telegraph is the domain of empire. Again, it is best not to assault the problem as an overarching theory of imperialism but, rather, to examine specific cases and specific connections: the role of the telegraph in coordinating military, particularly naval, operations; the transition from colonialism, where power and authority rested with the domestic governor, to imperialism, where power and authority were reabsorbed by the imperial capital; the new forms of political correspondence that came about when the war correspondent was obliged to use the telegraph; and the rise of the first forms of international business that could be called multinational.

While the growth of empire and imperialism have been explained by virtually every possible factor, little attention has been paid to telegraphy in generating the ground conditions for the urban imperialism of the mid-nineteenth century and the international imperialism later in the century.[9] It is probably no accident that the words "empire" and "imperialism" entered the language in 1870, soon after the laying of the transatlantic cable. Although colonies could be held together with printing, correspondence, and sail, the hold, as the American experience shows, was always tenuous over great distance. Moreover, in colonial arrangements the margin had as much power as the center. Until the transatlantic cable, it was difficult to determine whether British colonial policy was being set in London or by colonial governors in the field—out of contact and out of control. It was the cable and telegraph, backed, of course, by sea power, that turned colonialism into imperialism: a system in which the center of an empire could dictate rather than merely respond to the margin.[10]

The critical change lay in the ability to secure investments. There was no heavy overseas investment until the control made possible by the cable. The innovation of the telegraph created, if not the absolute impetus for imperial expansion, then at least the wherewithal to make the expansion theoretically tenable. But it also created a tension between the capability to expand and the capacity to rule.

With the development of the railroad, steam power, the telegraph and cable, a coherent empire emerged based on a coherent system of communication. In that system the railroad may be taken as the overland extension of the steamer or vice versa, and the telegraph and cable stood as the coordinating, regulating device governing both.[11]

Although the newspaper and imperial offices are among the best sites at which to look for the effects of the telegraph, there are humbler locations of equal interest. It surely is more than an accident that many of the great nineteenth-century commercial empires were founded in the humble circumstances of the telegraph operator's shack. The case of Richard B. Sears of North Redwood, Minnesota, is instructive. One must not forget that Edison and Carnegie began the same way and that the genius of Jay Gould lay in his integration of the telegraph with the railroad. The significance of the telegraph in this regard is that it led to the selective control and transmission of information. The telegraph operator was able to monopolize knowledge, if only for a few moments, along a route; and this brought a selective advantage in trading and speculation. But it was this same control of information that gave the telegraph a central importance in the development of modern gambling and of the business of credit. Finally, it was central to the late nineteenth-century explosion in forms of merchandising, such as the mail-order house.[12]

In the balance of this essay I want to cut across some of these developments and describe how the telegraph altered the ways in which time and space were understood in ordinary human affairs and, in particular, to examine a changed form in which time entered practical consciousness. To demonstrate these changes I wish to concentrate on the developments of commodity markets and on the institutionalization of standard time. But first let me reiterate the basic argument.

The simplest and most important point about the telegraph is that it marked the decisive separation of "transportation" and "communication." Until the telegraph these words were synonymous. The telegraph ended that identity and allowed symbols to move independently of geography and independently of and faster than transport. I say decisive separation because there were premonitions earlier of what was to come, and there was, after all, pre-electric telegraphy—line-of-sight signaling devices.

Virtually any American city of any vintage has a telegraph hill or a beacon hill reminding us of such devices. They relied on shutters, flaps, disks, or arms operating as for semaphoric signaling at sea. They were optical rather than "writing at a distance" systems and the forerunners of microwave networks, which rely on relay stations on geographic high points for aerial transmissions.

Line-of-sight telegraphy came into practical use at the end of the eighteenth century. Its principal architect was a Frenchman, Claud Chappe, who persuaded the Committee of Public Instruction in post-Revolutionary France to approve a trial. Joseph Lakanal, one of its members, reported back to the committee on the outcome: "What brilliant destiny do science and the arts not reserve for a republic which by its immense population and the genius of its inhabitants, is called to become the nation to instruct Europe" (Wilson, 1976: 122).

The National Convention approved the adoption of the telegraph as a national utility and instructed the Committee of Public Safety to map routes. The major impetus to its development in France was the same as the one that led to the wave of canal and railroad building in America. The pre-electric telegraph would provide an answer to Montesquieu and other political theorists who thought France or the United States too big to be a republic. But even more, it provided a means whereby the departments that had replaced the provinces after the Revolution could be tied to and coordinated with the central authority (Wilson, 1976: 123).

The pre-electric telegraph was also a subject of experimentation in America. In 1800, a line-of-sight system was opened between Martha's Vineyard and Boston (Wilson, 1976: 210). Between 1807 and 1812, plans were laid for a telegraph to stretch from Maine to New Orleans. The first practical use of line-of-sight telegraphy was for the transmission of news of arriving ships, a practice begun long before 1837 (Thompson, 1947: 11). But even before line-of-sight devices had been developed, alterations in shipping patterns had led to the separation of information from cargo, and that had important consequences for international trade. I shall say more on this later.

Despite these reservations and qualifications, the telegraph provided the decisive and cumulative break of the identity of communication and transportation. The great theoretical significance of the technology lay not merely in the separation but also in the use of the telegraph as both a model of and a mechanism for control of the physical movement of things, specifically for the railroad. That is the fundamental discovery: not only can information move independently of and faster than physical entities, but it also can be a simulation of and control mechanism for what has been left behind. The discovery was first exploited in railroad dispatching in England in 1844 and in the United States in 1849. It was of particular use on the long stretches of single-track road in the American West, where accidents were a serious problem. Before the use of the telegraph to control switching, the Boston and Worcester Railroad, for one example, kept horses every five miles along the line, and they raced up and down the track so that their riders could warn engineers of impending collisions (Thompson, 1947: 205–206). By moving information faster than the rolling stock, the telegraph allowed for centralized control along many miles of track. Indeed, the operation of the telegraph in conjunction with the railroad allowed for an integrated system of transport and communication. The same principle realized in these mundane circumstances governs the development of all modern processes in electrical transmission and control from guided gun sights to simple servo mechanisms that open doors. The relationship of the telegraph and the railroad illustrates the basic notion of systems theory and the catch phrase that the "system is the solution," in that the integrated switched system is more important than any of its components.

The telegraph permitted the development, in the favorite metaphor of the day, of a thoroughly encephalated social nervous system in which signaling was divorced from musculature. It was the telegraph and the railroad—the actual, painful construction of an integrated system—that provided the entrance gate for the organic metaphors that dominated nineteenth-century thought. Although German romanticism and idealism had their place, it is less to the world of ideas and more to the world of actual practice that we need to look when trying to figure out why the nineteenth century was obsessed with organicism.

The effect of the telegraph on ideology, on ordinary ideas, can be shown more graphically with two other examples drawn from the commodities markets and the development of standard time. The telegraph, like most innovations in communication down through the computer, had its first and most profound impact on the conduct of commerce, government, and the military. It was, in short, a producer good before it was a consumer good. The telegraph, as I said earlier, was used in its early months for the long-distance playing of chess. Its commercial significance was slow to be realized. But once that significance was determined, it was used to reorganize commerce; and from the patterns of usage in commerce came many of the telegraph's most profound consequences for ordinary thought. Among its first effects was the reorganization of commodity markets.

It was the normal expectation of early nineteenth century Americans that the price of a commodity would diverge from city to city so that the cost of wheat, corn, or whatever would be radically different in, say, Pittsburgh, Cincinnati, and St. Louis. This belief reflected the fact that before the telegraph, markets were independent of one another, or, more accurately, that the effect of one market on another was so gradually manifested as to be virtually unnoticed. In short, the prices of commodities were largely determined by local conditions of supply and demand. One of the leading historians of the markets has commented, "To be sure in all articles of trade the conditions at all sources of supply had their ultimate effect on distant values and yet even in these the communication was so slow that the conditions might change entirely before their effect could be felt" (Emery, 1896: 106).

Under such circumstances, the principal method of trading is called arbitrage: buying cheap and selling dear by moving goods around in space. That is, if prices are higher in St. Louis than in Cincinnati, it makes sense to buy in Cincinnati and resell in St. Louis, as long as the price differential is greater than the cost of transportation between the two cities. If arbitrage is widely practiced between cities, prices should settle into an equilibrium whereby the difference in price is held to the difference in transportation cost. This result is, in turn, based on the assumption of classical economics of perfect information—that all buyers and sellers are aware of the options available in all relevant markets—a situation rarely approached in practice before the telegraph.

Throughout the United States, price divergence between markets declined during the nineteenth century. Arthur H. Cole computed the average annual and monthly price disparity for uniform groups of commodities during the period 1816–1842, that is, up to the eve of the telegraph. Over that period the average annual price disparity fell from 9.3 to 4.8; and the average monthly disparity, from 15.4 to 4.8 (Cole, 1938: 94–96, 103). The decline itself is testimony to improvements in communication brought about by canal and turnpike building. The steepness of the decline is probably masked somewhat because Cole grouped the prices for the periods 1816–1830 and 1830–1842, whereas it was late in the canal era and the beginnings of large-scale railroad building that the sharpest declines were felt.

Looked at from one side, the decline represents the gradual increase in the effective size of the market. Looked at from the other side, it represents a decline in spatially based speculative opportunities—opportunities, that is, to turn trade into profit by moving goods between distinct markets. In a sense the railroad and canal regionalized markets; the telegraph nationalized them.

The effect of the telegraph is a simple one: it evens out markets in space. The telegraph puts everyone in the same place for purposes of trade; it makes geography irrelevant. The telegraph brings the conditions of supply and demand in all markets to bear on the determination of a price. Except for the marginal exception here and there, it eliminates opportunities for arbitrage by realizing the classical assumption of perfect information.

But the significance of the telegraph does not lie solely in the decline of arbitrage; rather, the telegraph shifts speculation into another dimension. It shifts speculation from space to time, from arbitrage to futures. After the telegraph, commodity trading moved from trading between places to trading between times. The arbitrager trades Cincinnati for St. Louis; the futures trader sells August against October, this year against next. To put the matter somewhat differently, as the telegraph closed down spatial uncertainty in prices it opened up, because of improvements in communication, the uncertainty of time. It was not, then, mere historic accident that the Chicago Commodity Exchange, to this day the principal American futures market, opened in 1848, the same year the telegraph reached that city. In a certain sense the telegraph invented the future as a new zone of uncertainty and a new region of practical action.

Let me make a retreat from that conclusion about the effects of the telegraph on time because I have overdrawn the case. First, the opportunities for arbitrage are never completely eliminated. There are always imperfections in market information, even on the floor of a stock exchange: buyers and sellers who do not know of one another and the prices at which the others are willing to trade. We know this as well from ordinary experience at auctions, where someone always knows a buyer who will pay more than the auctioned price. Second, there was a hiatus between arbitrage and the futures market when time contracts dominated, and this was a development of some importance. An approximation of futures trading occurred as early as 1733, when the East India Company initiated the practice of trading warrants. The function of a warrant was to transfer ownership of goods without consummating their physical transfer. The warrant did not represent, as such, particular warehoused goods; they were merely endorsed from person to person. The use of warrants or time contracts evolved rapidly in the United States in the trading of agricultural staples. They evolved to meet new conditions of effective market size and, as importantly, their evolution was unrestrained by historic practice.

The critical condition governing the development of time contracts was also the separation of communication from transport. Increasingly, news of crop conditions reached the market before the commodity itself. For example, warrant trading advanced when cotton was shipped to England by sail while passengers and information moved by steamer. Based on news of the crop and on samples of the commodity, time contracts or "to-arrive" contracts were executed. These were used principally for transatlantic sales, but after the Mississippi Valley opened up to agricultural trade, they were widely used in Chicago in the 1840s (Baer and Woodruff, 1935: 3–5).

The telegraph started to change the use of time contracts, as well as arbitrage. By widely transmitting knowledge of prices and crop conditions, it drew markets and prices together. We do not have good before-and-after measures, but we do have evidence, cited earlier, for the long-run decline in price disparities among markets. Moreover, we have measures from Cincinnati in particular. In the 1820s Cincinnati lagged two years behind Eastern markets. That meant that it took two years for disturbances in the Eastern market structure to affect Cincinnati prices. By 1840 the lag was down to four months; and by 1857—and probably much earlier—the effect of Eastern markets on Cincinnati was instantaneous. But once space was, in the phrase of the day, annihilated, once everyone was in the same place for purposes of trade, time as a new region of experience, uncertainty, speculation, and exploration was opened up to the forces of commerce.

A back-door example of this inversion of space and time can be drawn from a later episode involving the effect of the telephone on the New York Stock Exchange. By 1894 the telephone had made information time identical in major cities. Buyers and sellers, wherever they were, knew current prices as quickly as traders did on the floor of the exchange. The information gap, then, between New York and Boston had been eliminated and business gravitated from New York to Boston brokerage firms. The New York exchange countered this movement by creating a thirty-second time advantage that ensured New York's superiority to Boston. The exchange ruled that telephones would not be allowed on the floor. Price information had to be relayed by messenger to an area off the floor of the exchange that had been set aside for telephones. This move destroyed the temporal identity of markets, and a thirty-second monopoly of knowledge was created that drew business back to New York (Emery, 1896: 139).

This movement of commodities out of space and into time had three other consequences of great importance in examining the effect of the telegraph. First, futures trading required the decontexualization of markets; or, to put it in a slightly different way, markets were made relatively unresponsive to local conditions of supply and demand. The telegraph removed markets from the particular context in which they were historically located and concentrated on them forces emanating from any place and any time. This was a redefinition from physical or geographic markets to spiritual ones. In a sense they were made more mysterious; they became everywhere markets and everytime markets and thus less apprehensible at the very moment they became more powerful.

Second, not only were distant and amorphous forces brought to bear on markets, but the commodity was sundered from its representations; that is, the development of futures trading depended on the ability to trade or circulate negotiable instruments independently of the actual physical movement of goods. The representation of the commodity became the warehouse receipts from grain elevators along the railroad line. These instruments were then traded independently of any movement of the actual goods. The buyer of such receipts never expected to take delivery; the seller of such receipts never expected to make delivery. There is the old joke, which is also a cautionary tale, of the futures trader who forgot what he was up to and ended up with forty tons of wheat on his suburban lawn; but it is merely a joke and a tale. The futures trader often sells before he buys, or buys and sells simultaneously. But the buying and selling is not of goods but of receipts. What is being traded is not money for commodities but time against price. In short, the warehouse receipt, which stands as a representation of the product, has no intrinsic relation to the real product.

But in order to trade receipts rather than goods, a third change was necessary. In futures trading products are not bought or sold by inspection of the actual product or a sample thereof. Rather, they are sold through a grading system. In order to lend itself to futures trading, a product has to be mixed, standardized, diluted in order to be reduced to a specific, though abstract, grade. With the coming of the telegraph, products could no longer be shipped in separate units as numerous as there were owners of grain. "The high volume sales required impersonalized standards. Buyers were no longer able personally to check every lot" (Chandler, 1977: 211). Consequently, not all products are traded on the futures market because some resist the attempt to reduce them to standardized categories of quality.

The development of the futures markets, in summary, depended on a number of specific changes in markets and the commodity system. It required that information move independently of and faster than products. It required that prices be made uniform in space and that markets be decontextualized. It required, as well, that commodities be separated from the receipts that represent them and that commodities be reduced to uniform grades.

These were, it should be quickly added, the conditions that underlay Marx's analysis of the commodity fetish. That concept, now used widely and often indiscriminately, was developed in the *Grundrisse* and *Das Kapital* during the late 1850s, when futures trading became the dominant arena for the establishment of agricultural values. In particular, Marx made the key elements in the commodity fetish the decontextualization of markets, the separation of use value from exchange value brought about by the decline in the representative function of the warehouse receipt, and the abstraction of the product out of real conditions of production by a grading system. In the *Grundrisse* he comments, "This locational movement—the bringing of the product to market which is a necessary condition of its circulation, except when the point of production is itself a market—could more precisely be regarded as the transformation of the product into a commodity" (Marx, 1973: 534).

Marx's reference is to what Walter Benjamin (1968) would later call the "loss of aura" in his parallel analysis of the effect of mechanical reproduction on the work of art. After the object is abstracted out of the real conditions of its production and use and is transported to distant markets, standardized and graded, and represented by fully contingent symbols, it is made available as a commodity. Its status as a commodity represents the sundering of a real, direct relationship between buyer and seller, separates use value from exchange value, deprives objects of any uniqueness (which must then be returned to the object via advertising), and, most important, masks to the buyer the real conditions of production. Further, the process of divorcing the receipt from the product can be thought of as part of a general social process initiated by the use of money and widely written about in contemporary semiotics; the progressive divorce of the signifier from the signified, a process in which the world of signifiers progressively overwhelms and moves independently of real material objects.

To summarize, the growth of communications in the nineteenth century had the practical effect of diminishing space as a differentiating criterion in human affairs. What Harold Innis called the "penetrative powers of the price system" was, in effect, the spread of a uniform price system throughout space so that for purposes of trade everyone was in the same place. The telegraph was the critical instrument in this spread. In commerce this meant the decontextualization of markets so that prices no longer depended on local factors of supply and demand but responded to national and international forces. The spread of the price system was part of the attempt to colonize space. The correlative to the penetration of the price system was what the composer Igor Stravinsky called the "statisticalization of mind": the transformation of the entire mental world into quantity, and the distribution of quantities in space so that the relationship between things and people becomes solely one of numbers. Statistics widens the market for everything and makes it more uniform and interdependent. The telegraph worked this same effect on the practical consciousness of time through the construction of standard time zones.

IV

Our sense of time and our activities in time are coordinated through a grid of time zones, a grid so fixed in our consciousness that it seems to be the natural form of time, at least until we change back and forth between standard and daylight saving time. But standard time in the United States is a relatively recent invention. It was introduced on November 18, 1883.

Until that date virtually every American community established its own time by marking that point when the sun reached its zenith as noon. It could be determined astronomically with exactitude; but any village could do it, for all practical purposes, by observing the shortest shadow on a sundial. Official local time in a community could be fixed, as since time immemorial, by a church or later by a courthouse, a jeweler, or later still the railroad stationmaster; and a bell or whistle could be rung or set off so that the local burghers could set their timepieces. In Kansas City a ball was dropped from the highest building at noon and was visible for miles around, a practice still carried out at the annual New Year's Eve festivities in New York City's Times Square (Corliss, 1952).

Not every town kept its own time; many set their clocks in accord with the county seat or some other nearby town of commercial or political importance. When the vast proportion of American habitats were, in Robert Wiebe's (1967) phrase, "island communities" with little intercourse with one another, the distinctiveness of local time caused little confusion and worry. But as the tentacles of commerce and politics spread out from the capitals, temporal chaos came with them. The chaos was sheerly physical. With every degree of longitude one moved westward, the sun reached its zenith four minutes later. That meant that when it was noon in Boston it was 11:48 a.m. in Albany; when it was noon in Atlanta it was 11:36 a.m. in New Orleans. Put differently, noon came a minute later for every quarter degree of longitude one moved westward, and this was a shorter distance as one moved north: in general thirteen miles equaled one minute of time.

The setting of clocks to astronomically local time or, at best, to county seat time led to a proliferation of time zones. Before standard time Michigan had twenty-seven time zones; Indiana, twenty-three; Wisconsin, thirty-nine; Illinois, twenty-seven. The clocks in New York, Boston, and Philadelphia, cities today on identical time, were several minutes apart (Corliss, 1952: 3). When it was 12:00 in Washington, D.C., it was 11:30 in Atlanta, 12:09 in Philadelphia, 12:12 in New York, 12:24 in Boston, and 12:41 in Eastport, Maine.

As the railroads spread across the continent, the variety of local times caused enormous confusion with scheduling, brought accidents as trains on different clocks collided, and led to much passenger irritation, as no one could easily figure when a train would arrive at another town. The railroads used fifty-eight local times keyed to the largest cities. Moreover, each railroad keyed its clocks to the time of a different city. The Pennsylvania Railroad keyed its time to that of Philadelphia, but Philadelphia's clocks were twelve minutes behind New York's and five minutes ahead of Baltimore's. The New York Central stuck to New York City time. The Baltimore and Ohio keyed its time to three cities: Baltimore; Columbus, Ohio; and Vincennes, Indiana (Bartky and Harrison, 1979: 46–53).

The solution, which was to establish standard time zones, had long attracted the interest of scholars. The pressure to establish such zones was felt more strongly in North America, which averaged eight hours of daylight from Newfoundland to western Alaska. Although standard time was established earlier in Europe, the practical pressure there was less. There is only a half-hour variance in sun time across England; and France, while larger, could be run on Paris time. But England, for purposes of empire, had long been interested in standard time. The control of time allows for the coordination of activity and, therefore, effective social control. In navigation, time was early fixed on English ships according to the clock of the Greenwich observatory; and no matter where a ship might be in the Atlantic, its chronometer always registered Greenwich time. Similarly, Irish time was regulated by a clock set each morning at Big Ben, carried by rail to Holyhead, ferried across the Irish sea to Kingstown (now Dun Laoghaire), and then carried again by rail to Dublin, where Irish clocks were coordinated with English time (Schivelbusch, 1978: 39).

And so it was no surprise when in 1870 a New Yorker, Charles Dowd, proposed a system of standard time zones that fixed Greenwich as zero degrees longitude and laid out the zones around the world with centers 15 degrees east and west from Greenwich. As 15 degrees equals one hour, the world was laid out in twenty-four zones one hour apart.

Dowd's plan was a wonderful example of crackpot realism. The lines were laid out with geometric exactness and ignored geography, topography, region, trade, or natural affinity. Maine and Florida were put in separate time zones. It is a wonderful example of the maxim that the grid is the geometry of empire. Dowd recommended the plan to the railroads, which adopted it provisionally and created an index out of it so that the traveler could convert railroad time to local time by adding or subtracting so many minutes to or from the railroad schedule.

For thirteen years the Dowd system was debated but never officially adopted by the General Time Convention. The railroads tried during that period to get Congress to adopt it as a uniform time system, but Congress would not and for an obvious reason: standard time offended people with deeply held religious sentiments. It violated the actual physical working of the natural order and denied the presence of a divinely ordained nature. But even here religious language was a vanishing mediator for political sentiments; standard time was widely known as Vanderbilt's time, and protest against it was part of the populist protest against the banks, the telegraph, and the railroad.

In 1881, the Philadelphia General Time Convention turned the problem over to William Frederick Allen, a young civil engineer; two years later he returned a plan. It was based on Dowd's scheme but with a crucial difference: it allowed for the adjustment of time zones for purposes of economy and ecology. In his scheme time boundaries could be shifted up to 100 miles away from the geometric lines in order to minimize disruption. Most important, he recommended that the railroads abandon the practice of providing a minute index and that they simply adopt standard time for regulating their schedules and allow communities and institutions to adjust to the new time in any manner they chose.

In the Allen plan the United States was divided into four time zones, with centers on the 75th, 90th, 105th, and 120th meridians: Philadelphia, St. Louis, Denver, and Reno were the approximate centers. The zones extended seven and a half degrees to either side of the center line. November 18, 1883, was selected as the date for the changeover from local to standard time, and an ambitious "educational" campaign was mounted to help citizens adjust to the new system. On that date Chicago, the railroad hub, was tied by telegraph to an observatory in Allegheny, Pennsylvania. When it reached one o'clock over the center of the Eastern time zone, the clocks were stopped at noon in Chicago and held for nine minutes and thirty-two seconds until the sun centered on the 90th meridian. Then they were started again, with the railroad system now integrated and coordinated through time.

The changeover was greeted by mass meetings, anger, and religious protest but to no avail. Railroad time had become standard time. It was not made official U.S. time until the emergency of World War I. But within a few months after the establishment of railroad time, the avalanche of switches to it by local communities was well under way. Strangely enough, the United States never did go to 24-hour time and thus retained some connection between the diurnal cycle of human activity and the cycle of the planets.

The boundaries of the time zones have been repeatedly adjusted since that time. In general they have been made to follow state borders, but there are a number of exceptions. The western edge of the Eastern time zone was once in eastern Ohio, but now it forms a jagged line along the Illinois-Indiana border. Boise, Idaho, was moved from Pacific to Mountain time, and recently twelve thousand square miles of Arizona was similarly moved. The reasons for such changes tell us much about America's purposes. One gets the distinct feeling, for example, that the television networks would prefer a country with three time zones: east, central, and west.

Standard time zones were established because in the eyes of some they were necessary. They were established, to return to the point of this chapter, because of the technological power of the telegraph. Time was sent via the telegraph wire; but today, thanks to technical improvements, it is sent via radio waves from the Naval observatory in Maryland. The telegraph could send time faster than a railroad car could move; and therefore it facilitated the temporal coordination and integration of the entire system. Once that was possible, the new definitions of time could be used by industry and government to control and coordinate activity across the country, infiltrate into the practical consciousness of ordinary men and women, and uproot older notions of rhythm and temporality.

The development of standard time zones served to overlay the world with a grid of time in the same way the surveyor's map laid a grid of space on old cities, the new territories of the West, or the seas. The time grid could then be used to control and coordinate activities within the grid of space.

V

When the ecological niche of space was filled, filled as an arena of commerce and control, attention was shifted to filling time, now defined as an aspect of space, a continuation of space in another dimension. As the spatial frontier was closed, time became the new frontier. Let me mention, in closing, two other dimensions of the temporal frontier.

An additional time zone to be penetrated once space was exhausted was sacred time, in particular the sabbath. The greatest invention of the ancient Hebrews was the idea of the sabbath, though I am using this word in a fully secular sense: the invention of a region free from control of the state and commerce where another dimension of life could be experienced and where altered forms of social relationship could occur. As such, the sabbath has always been a major resistance to state and market power. For purposes of communication, the effective penetration of the sabbath came in the 1880s with the invention of the Sunday newspaper. It was Hearst with his New York Sunday *World* who popularized the idea of Sunday newspaper reading and created, in fact, a market where none had existed before—a sabbath market. Since then the penetration of the sabbath has been one of the "frontiers" of commercial activity. Finally, when the frontier in space was officially closed in 1890, the "new frontier" became the night, and since then there has been a continuous spreading upward of commercial activity. Murray Melbin (1987) has attempted to characterize "night as a frontier." In terms of communication the steady expansion of commercial broadcasting into the night is one of the best examples. There were no 24-hour radio stations in Boston, for example, from 1918 through 1954; now half of the stations in Boston operate all night. Television has slowly expanded into the night at one end and at the other initiated operations earlier and earlier. Now, indeed, there are 24-hour television stations in major markets.

The notion of night as frontier, a new frontier of time that opens once space is filled, is a metaphor, but it is more than that. Melbin details some of the features common to the spatial and temporal frontiers: they both advance in stages; the population is more sparsely settled and homogeneous; there is solitude, an absence of social constraints, and less persecution; settlements are isolated; government is decentralized; lawlessness and violence as well as friendliness and helpfulness increase; new behavioral styles emerge. That is, the same dialectic between centralization and decentralization occurs on the temporal frontier as on the spatial frontier. On the one hand, communication is even more privatized at night. On the other hand, social constraints on communication are relaxed because the invasive hand of authority loosened.

The penetration of time, the use of time as a mechanism of control, the opening of time to commerce and politics has been radically extended by advances in computer technology. Time has been redefined as an ecological niche to be filled down to the microsecond, nannosecond, and picosecond—down to a level at which time can be pictured but not experienced. This process and the parallel reconstruction of practical consciousness and practical activity begins in those capacities of the telegraph which prefigure the computer. The telegraph constructed a simulacrum of complex systems, provided an analogue model of the railroad and a digital model of language. It coordinated and controlled activity in space, often behind the backs of those subject to it.

E. P. Thompson finds it ominous that the young Henry Ford should have created a watch with two dials: one for local time and another for railroad time. "Attention to

time in labour depends in large degree upon the need for the synchronization of labour"
(Thompson, 1967: 70). Modern conceptions of time have rooted into our consciousness
so deeply that the scene of the worker receiving a watch at his retirement is grotesque
and comic. He receives a watch when the need to tell time is ended. He receives a watch
as a tribute to his learning the hardest lesson of the working man—to tell time.

As the watch coordinated the industrial factory; the telegraph via the grid of time
coordinated the industrial nation. Today, computer time, computer space, and computer
memory, notions we dimly understand, are reworking practical consciousness coordinating and controlling life in what we glibly call the postindustrial society. Indeed, the micro-
computer is replacing the watch as the favored gift for the middle class retiree. In that new
but unchanging custom we see the deeper relationship between technology and ideology.

Notes

1.   See Chandler (1977), esp. Part II.
2.   Among the most readable, accessible sources on the patent struggles is Josephson (1959).
3.   See Wiener (1948: 38–44).
4.   Whereas I have commented on the essentially religious metaphors that greeted the tele-
     graph in the essays cited, Czitrom (1982) brings this material together in a systematic way.
5.   By a vanishing mediator—a concept borrowed from Fredric Jameson—I mean a notion
     that serves as a bearer of change but that can disappear once that change is ratified in the
     reality of institutions. See Jameson (1974: 111–49).
6.   See chapter 1. On changes in styles of journalism, see Sims (1979).
7.   Steffens (1958: 834). For a memoir that discusses the art and adversity of writing for
     the cable, see Shirer (1976: 282 ff.).
8.   The quotation is from an as yet unpublished manuscript by Douglas Birkhead of the
     University of Utah. Birkhead develops these themes in some detail.
9.   On urban imperialism, see Schlesinger (1933) and Pred (1973).
10. Among the few studies on the telegraph and empire, the most distinguished is Fortner
     (1978); see also Field (1978: 644–68).
11. In making these remarks I am much indebted to the work of Fortner and Field.
12. On these matters there are useful suggestions in Boorstin (1973).

Works Cited

Adams, Henry (1931). *The Education of Henry Adams*. (Original edition, Massachusetts Historical Society, 1918). New
     York: Modern Library.
Andrews, William P. (1857). *Memoirs on the Euphrates Valley Route to India*. London: William Allen.
Arnold, Matthew (1954). "On the Modern Element in Literature" (1857). In John Bryson, ed., *The Poetry and Prose of
     Matthew Arnold* (pp. 269–283). Cambridge: Harvard University Press.
Axtell, James (1985). *The Invasion Within: The Contest of Cultures in Colonial North America*. New York: Oxford University
     Press.
Baer, Julius B., and George P. Woodruff (1935). *Commodity Exchanges*. New York: Harper and Bros.
Bailyn, Bernard (1986). *The Peopling of British North America: An Introduction*. New York: Alfred A. Knopf.
Bartky, Ian R., and Elizabeth Harrison (1979). "Standard and Day-light Saving Time." *Scientific American*, 240 (5), 46-53.
Barnes, Harry Elmer, ed. (1966). *An Introduction to the History of Sociology* (abridged ed.). Chicago: University of Chicago
     Press.
Beard, Charles A. (1914). *Contemporary American History*. New York: Macmillan.
Beard, Charles A., and Mary Beard (1940). *The Rise of American Civilisation*. New York: Macmillan.
Bendix, Reinhard, and Guenther Roth (1971). "Sociology and the Distrust of Reason." In *Scholarship and Partisanship: Essays
     on Max Weber* (pp. 84–105). Berkeley: University of California Press.
Benjamin, Walter (1968). *Illuminations*. New York: Harcourt, Brace and World.
Benson, Lee (1951). "The Historical Background of Turner's Frontier Essay." *Agricultural History*, 25, 59–82.
Berger, Peter L. (1967). *The Sacred Canopy*. Garden City, NY: Doubleday.
Berger, Peter, and Thomas Luckmann (1966). *The Social Construction of Reality*. Garden City: NY: Doubleday.
Birkenhead, Earl of (1930). *The World in 2030 A. D.* New York: Brewer and Warren.
Boorstin, Daniel J. (1973). *The Americans: The Democratic Experience*. New York: Random House.
—— (1974). *Democracy and Its Discontents*. New York: Random House.
Bourdieu, Pierre (1984). *Distinction: A Social Critique of the Judgment of Taste*. Cambridge, MA: Harvard University Press.

Chapter 17

HAZEL DICKEN-GARCIA

CHANGES IN NEWS DURING THE NINETEENTH CENTURY

The transfer of our newspapers from personal to corporate ownership and control was not a matter of preference, but a practical necessity. . . .

These newcomers . . . naturally looked at everything through the medium of the balance-sheet. Here was a paper with a fine reputation, but uncertain or disappearing profits; it must be strengthened, enlarged, and made to pay. Principles? Yes, principles were good things, but we must not ride even good things to death. The circulation must be pushed, and the advertising patronage increased. More circulation can be secured only by keeping the public stirred up. Employ private detectives to pursue the runaway husband, and bring him back to his wife; organize a marine expedition to find the missing ship; send a reporter into the Soudan to interview the beleaguered general whose own government is powerless to reach him with an army. . . . If nothing new is to be had, refurbish something so old that people have forgotten it. . . .

. . . A craving for excitement was first aroused in the public and then satisfied by the same hand that had aroused it. . . . In such a race for business success . . . can we marvel at the subsidence of ideals? . . . is not the wonder rather that the moral quality of our press has not fallen below its present standard?

Francis E. Leupp, *"The Waning Power of the Press,"* The Atlantic Monthly *(1910)*

NEWSPAPER CONTENT DURING THE THREE ERAS we have identified in nineteenth-century journalism reveals dramatic shifts in "news" across the century, confirming major changes in the role of the press in American society. Content in the earliest decades was idea-centered; by mid-century, it was event-centered; and by the 1890s, it represented an amalgam of event, idea, and "story" or drama. Although these marked changes occurred, content across the century also shows continuities. Furthermore, it shows what press critics were discussing, as we might expect when we view criticism as an intersection of press and society. Finally, content shows the relation of journalistic standards to the press's role in each era. This chapter considers press content in the three eras of the nineteenth century.

Regarding press role changes and criticisms throughout the century, the earliest critics emphasized partisanism and the press's great power over ideas in the polity, as Chapter 5 will show. Newspaper content reveals that partisanism and ideas did indeed dominate the press in the first decade of the century. As we shall see in Chapter 6, critics at mid-century emphasized a trivialization of news and had begun to consider journalistic taste and the press's intrusions into individuals' lives. Content during this era emphasized individuals and detailed descriptions of events. Post–Civil War critics focused on several excesses: profit seeking, invasion of privacy, sensationalism, and reporting that jeopardized the accused's right to a fair trial. Content of the 1890s shows journalists driven to get every detail that might satisfy curiosity, heighten thrill, and sell newspapers. Newspapers in the last decade of the century reveal several changes, all of which seemed dictated by the era's emphasis on business and the press itself as a business. Among these changes was the development of a clear story model that significantly affected news reporting.

Several elements of continuity emerge from a long-term view of newspaper content. From 1800 through the 1850s, for example, partisanism continued to characterize the press, while at the same time content emphasis shifted from ideas to events. From 1850 to 1890, partisanism diminished, especially after the Civil War, and reporting of events was increasingly stressed—at the expense of airing ideas—until it dominated newspapers in the 1890s. Interest in individuals represents a kind of continuity, although subtle shifts occurred in the nature of that interest. In the earliest decade, the interest was in important personages; by mid-century, the "ordinary" individual figured prominently. In the 1890s, the important personage (what today would be called the celebrity more than the statesman emphasized in newspapers of the first decade) again received much news space, but the ordinary person continued to draw a great deal of attention—although by that time it seemed that, to merit news space, such individuals must be part of an event that yielded significant drama. Also, the importance of ideas in news represents continuity. In the earliest decade, discussion of ideas dominated virtually all content, but by 1850, its place had diminished and it was beginning to be relegated to editorial commentary. By the 1890s, the idea—as *the* reason for a newspaper item—almost never appeared outside the editorial page except as the basis of fictional pieces.

Content also correlated with issues of journalistic conduct raised by critics in each era. Content in turn flowed from the press's role as perceived by contemporaries and as defined by the press's place in society's overall structure. This means, in effect, that drama (or the "story") as a journalistic goal was to late-nineteenth-century American journalism what partisanism was to the press of the first decades, and what trivialization was to mid-century journalism. When considered as part of journalistic goals dictated by the press's role, excesses such as the sensationalism of the 1880s are more understandable. That is to say, although this perspective makes excesses no more acceptable, it does make sense of them. Viewed as part of a larger framework of forces rather than as simple, individual instances of base conduct (although, as is always true, some journalists upheld, higher—or lower—standards than others), excesses are revealed as by-products of the press's role as it was interpreted and understood at different times. Such a perspective may help in interpreting excesses, and therefore in arriving at decisions about changing them.

Samples of newspapers across the century were studied with attention to what journalists intended newspapers to do. In other words, what role did newspaper content itself suggest the press served? Did that role change with time? And if so, how did it change? In this work, evidence about the press's role was gathered through examining whatever purposes journalists seemed to intend newspapers to serve, and through analyzing newspapers' content and form. Changes in these purposes and in content and form over time would indicate a changing press role. But equally important, newspapers were studied to determine what kind of journalistic standards might have governed their production; to collect and analyze any discussions of the press, news, or journalism that appeared; and to determine the dominant message, in the largest sense, the press conveyed in each era. Finally, content was examined to see what critics were discussing and to gain perspective on press criticism across the century.

Newspapers from the first, middle, and last decades (1800–1810, 1850–1860, and 1890–1900) of the century were read because they marked significant points in the eras studied. The first decade coincided with early efforts to determine the course of a new government and nation; the middle decade was a period when significant changes affecting the press and the nation were under way—and it was chosen also to avoid the unique decade of civil war; the final decade represented a time after the nation's economic base had shifted, technological developments had spiraled, and the press had moved toward a corporate structure. Although press criticism was studied only up to 1890, newspapers of the 1890s were examined because the decade marked the near-culmination of post–Civil War changes in society and the press. Furthermore, it was assumed that content in the 1890s was of the same genre as that addressed by critics through the 1880s. The study thus presupposes that newspaper content for the three eras would reflect trends and values across the century, and that shifts in the press's role and standards resulting from changed trends would be visible. The study also assumes that examining the press in decades at wide intervals would make changes more readily discernible.

Sample titles were drawn from lists of newspapers published throughout each of the three decades.[1] Newspapers that had published for at least ten years were judged as more indicative of prevailing conduct than short-lived papers or those that began or ended during the decade. For the first decade, all newspapers were included. For the other two decades, only those with the highest circulations were selected; here it was assumed that because these papers reached more people they had more influence and are thus a better index to what others either did or strived to do. Although not tested in this research, evidence suggests that today's "umbrella" hypothesis, that other newspapers tend to imitate those in high-circulation markets, holds true for the nineteenth century. The sample weighs heavily toward the eastern United States because fewer newspapers were published in other parts of the country, because high-circulation newspapers were concentrated there, and because of availability. To diversify geographical representation, noneastern newspapers were substituted for those unavailable in the sample, but this did not significantly alter the predominance of eastern papers among those read.

Samples were selected from two years in each decade—one near the beginning and one near the end to avoid distortion by any phenomena that might be passing fads. After sample newspaper titles were randomly selected, sample issues of each were drawn, and all were then read thoroughly.

The first-decade sample constituted approximately one-fifth of the newspapers published throughout the ten years, and every issue of each was read for three months—January, June, and December—in each of two years (1801 and 1809). Some were dailies and others biweeklies, but most were weeklies. For the other two decades, six titles were selected and three issues a year of each was drawn randomly and read for the years 1852 and 1858; for 1891, the sample was three issues of four titles; for 1899, three issues of two titles.[2] The results are preliminary, since the number is insufficient to support statistically valid conclusions. Nevertheless, the findings, although tentative, are important. First, nothing so far suggests that additional research will significantly alter them. Second, the patterns discovered correlate to what critics discussed in each era. Third, they support the thesis of this work, that press role is dictated by culture and that standards are by-products of that role and, in turn, of culture.

Before proceeding, some comment regarding standards is necessary. Reading the papers in the sample to deduce standards governing news presentation and to collect discussions of journalism presented immediate problems. First, the sample issues contained little discussion of the press, news, or journalism—even though journalists frequently berated each other through newspaper columns in the early years. Journalists did often discuss the press, news, and journalism in newspapers throughout the century; the sample selected for this research, however, simply turned up little of that discussion. Additional newspapers selected at random—as well as secondary sources—yielded many such discussions. A second problem is that standards cannot be realistically assessed on the basis of what appeared in newspapers so long ago. Accuracy, for example, is elusive. We simply do not know today what was precisely true about an event reported in 1850.

News items did not identify sources, or did so so rarely—even as late as the 1890s—that it is impossible to search out whatever sources might still exist. News items did not specify how information was gathered; this in itself says something about standards and values at the time, but it leaves little basis for studying what standards might have governed news collection, preparation, and presentation. The absence of indications of how information was gathered suggests a definition of news that would also have affected views about its presentation. As this definition evolved away from partisanism, the validation of information through explication of sources, for example, became more important. Although by the 1890s some indications point toward such explication, the shift from partisanism was not yet so complete as to change underlying assumptions about presentation dramatically. Lack of explanations of sources may also have related to journalists' "protected" status. An embedded American tradition, for example, had operated against the use of journalists' bylines until the Civil War. Although this practice may have protected them, it also absolved them of accountability. It is easy to see how such a long-engrained habit of nonaccountability might lead to proceeding as if accountability on other counts—such as source identification—was superfluous. In short, it seems most likely that sources were not identified simply because the significance of doing so had not yet become clear.

The lack of information about sources and how material was gathered nevertheless leaves the historian without a basis for assessing standards governing procedures. A further difficulty is that distortions can hardly be judged without perspective—which is perhaps even more elusive than accuracy. To determine what might have been a balanced perspective (an undistorted account) virtually requires being there.

Sources used by journalists, then, are, except for government proceedings, generally unknown and unavailable. In rare instances in which multiple accounts of an event exist, newspaper stories of the event might be compared with the various accounts, but even multiple accounts may have come from the same general sources.[3] In any event, the researcher is left with rare, isolated news content that may not have appeared in all—or even a few—of the newspapers at the time. Hence, one cannot generalize regarding accuracy, either about one newspaper's entire contents from one story, or about several newspapers from multiple reports of the same event.[4]

Focusing on the press as a product of cultural context therefore quickly made specific late-twentieth-century standards inappropriate measures for newspapers in the 1800s, 1830s, or even 1890s. There is no way of knowing what was unreported; and accuracy, for example, is in any case irrelevant as a measure of content that was intended to argue political points of view—as was true of most content up to the Civil War. These circumstances confirm the importance of examining social developments, journalistic purpose, and press role to understand nineteenth-century standards. Some judgments can be made, of course; to illustrate, whether the reporter was at the scene or not can often be ascertained by looking at details in a story. And general judgments can be made about bias and taste based on what appeared. One can examine content for tone, substance, and excesses in emphasis and speculate about the extent to which these may have offended taste or opposed values of the time. And, of course, one can look for manifestations of what critics emphasized, such as partisanism, crime reporting, or sensationalism.

Another important area of interest in reading the sample newspapers was to examine how content changed over time, and how any changes related broadly to the press's role and journalistic standards. In other words, what was the medium's dominant message form in any era? As a medium, or vehicle, did it predominantly emphasize ideas? events? life's substance? individuals? And what interests does newspaper content emphasize that might reveal the press's institutional role in society?

Newspaper content for the three decades was studied for topic, tone, form, and some indication of the intended audience. *Content topic* involves categories—political, business, social—and whether reports were local, national, or international. *Tone* is defined as the overall impression conveyed: that is, whether content is personal or impersonal, and what the emotional impact is, whether factually straightforward or dramatic (accusatory, derogatory, titillating, suspenseful). *Personal* items address specific individuals directly or focus primarily on one or more individuals, with attention to character. Personal items include, for example, the invective hurled by one editor against a rival (quoted below), in which he addressed the other with "Halloo, Billy Brown" and accused him of lying as well as having other character flaws, and the story of Brackenridge's drunken spree in which he repeatedly removed all his clothes. Impersonal items report simply that something occurred or discuss ideas as to their soundness, basis, or implications. Such discussions of ideas, if they called into question another's views (or the views of a group) without aspersing character (such as calling people deluded), were straightforward. If they did asperse character in any way, they were classified as personal. The excerpts below, claiming that property is essential to government, and that Americans had erred in assuming they could successfully establish a republic, are straightforward items.

Definition of *form* involved two dimensions: whether the item was idea-or event-centered, and whether it presented a "story" or simple information. Idea-centered means the reason for the item's being in the newspaper was an idea or ideas, whereas event-centered means that the reason for the item being in the newspaper was a specific occurrence at an identifiable time and place. "Story" was defined as any news item emphasizing what might generally be called fictional techniques—suspense, conflict, plot, central character, dialogue. These elements were defined as "drama." In some cases, these were event-centered—that is, an event (or events) was the reason for the news item—but dramatic elements dominated the reporting; in other cases, items would not have been reported if the occasion for them had lacked dramatic elements. In other words, in the latter, an item's dramatic quality was the reason for its inclusion in the news. Finally, items with simple, factual information were defined as straightforward accounts of events, ideas, or processes—without any effort to provoke or involve the reader's emotions. The example below about the woman committed to an insane asylum by her sister is a "story"; an example of simple information reported in a straightforward manner is the account under the headline ARCHBISHOP IRELAND TO BE HONORED that tells that Ireland would be asked to preside over French festivities honoring Joan of Arc.

Intended audience was deduced from the categories and kinds of items published. What sector or sectors of society did the newspaper address—government, institutions, individuals? And what composition of society did the content reflect—were ethnic groups, minorities, and women recognized as newspaper consumers? Obviously, this dimension calls for speculation that is risky, although it was clear by the 1890s that journalists recognized women as newspaper readers. Minorities and ethnic groups, however, were rarely reported on, which might suggest that these groups were not viewed as intended audiences; nevertheless, there is evidence that some editors did aim content to minority groups, especially to immigrants.

In broad outline, the characteristics of press content paralleled those of American culture in the nineteenth century. For two reasons, it was assumed that the early American newspaper press would be idea-centered. First, journalists had been active in the Revolution and increasingly involved with issues afterward, and such activities heightened their emphasis on ideas involved with issues. Second, the fact that the new government was itself a new idea, and that debates about its—and the nation's—future shape were dominated by competing ideas, made press content idea-centered. If this was true for the first era under study, how did press content change in the other eras?

After 1830, the press increasingly emphasized events and individuals over ideas. By the middle decades of the nineteenth century, the succession of events in the nation's own history shaped its course of development. Very conscious of many of these events and their implications, Americans were increasingly drawn to consider them.

Because the press by the last decade of the century was driven by a compulsion to "market" news, diversity came to characterize content. By the 1890s, press content reflected an amalgamation of ideas, events, individuals, and groups.

Newspapers, 1800–1810

The sample newspapers confirm that the early press was, indeed, idea-centered. Excluding foreign items, virtually every page—except of course those given over to advertising—of every newspaper read contained political content in which ideas were presented or exchanged and debated: Concepts of democracy, federalism, republicanism, office seeking, parties, factions, policies, "monarchical" and "aristocratic" tendencies, qualities needed for leadership, law and order, equality. The debate almost always spilled over into aspersions on persons advancing opposing ideas, but the content remained idea-centered.

Although the discussions were often tasteless, the participants could not have been more serious about the underlying purpose. They were, however, inexperienced in this kind of debate. They were having to learn several momentous lessons in the process of doing: how to debate political issues, how to function in a new kind of government, how to use the press in a new kind of political milieu, and how to ensure that public opinion would serve as a check on government, as the new order decreed. Therefore, what they said and how they said it might be better judged on the basis of their inexperience rather than how distasteful the exchanges were. In fact, some evidence suggests that what would now be considered distasteful was not then viewed by the majority as beyond acceptable limits in such debates.

To journalists of the early nineteenth century, the best journalistic conduct was whatever succeeded in making points for their party and advancing its views. As one historian has noted, to have failed their party would have been, in their minds, tantamount to treason.[5] Passion for their convictions often outdistanced reason, but every generation since has been a beneficiary of their tenacity and assiduity in earnestly debating issues of paramount importance to the nation's future.

It is difficult to arrive at a description of the "typical" newspaper of this period because papers varied so much in news placement and format. Some included editors' comments, for example, but in different locations, and they differed also in treatment of news from other states; some contained clearly identifiable entertainment sections; most faithfully reported congressional and state legislative news, but treated these items differently; most included ship news, and all emphasized foreign news. Furthermore, numerous items duplicated material from other papers.

Newspaper issues selected randomly from those read show five to twenty items in a four-page newspaper (excluding advertising items and foreign news). (Foreign news items are not enumerated for the early papers because the focus of interest is on how the papers reported on or reflected *American* society.) The low number of items in a paper is indicative of length of items published. Political essays especially often ran more than a page and frequently continued from issue to issue. One issue, for example, contained ten items, of which four and a half columns (excluding two columns devoted to Congress) contained idea-centered items. (According to the categories set forth above, reports of Congress are technically idea-centered, but they are here identified as event-centered since the session—occurring at a specifiable time and place—led to the report.) The idea items included an essay on the change in government, comment about opposition to the newspaper's views, an article by Thomas Cooper examining the logic behind the Alien and Sedition Acts, and a letter from Aaron Burr explaining why his views were not Federalist. Five columns were filled with advertisements, two were devoted to Congress, and one contained entertaining items—a poem and anecdotes. One other item was event-centered—reporting an unfavorable response to Samuel H. Smith's request for permission to report on proceedings of the House of Representatives from inside the bar. Another issue contained twelve items, five of which were idea-centered and occupied more than three columns. Two columns were devoted to foreign news, one reported on Congress, two reported news from "the Mails," and one entertainment column contained anecdotes and short essays. The remainder of the newspaper was advertising. Another newspaper issue selected at random from 1809 yielded five items, with three devoted to ideas and two to events (one was the printer's announcement that Bonaparte was at Madrid; the other gave ship news). Twelve and three-fourths columns were devoted to advertising; three-fourths of one column reported news of Congress; five and a half columns gave foreign news.

The examples included below convey the passion and sense of responsibility for the new nation (if not for the press) of early American journalists, competing values, exultation in freedom to debate (as rawly as they might), and the often very personal desire to triumph in debate.

A printer in 1801 succinctly stated what seemed to typify views of the press's function during this era. In a long article, he wrote that presses had "been multiplied on the American continent from the Delaware to the Ohio . . . not to print books and diffuse a love of literature, but to publish newspapers and disseminate intelligence." His definition of intelligence (used synonymously with "news") revolved on party principles, for he continued, "It is from newspapers that the mass of the people derive their knowledge; and the principles of many thousands have been determined in support or opposition of federal measures, by the accidental perusal in youth, of a federal or antifederal paper." In concluding, he took a swipe at those who sneered at newspaper content, saying, "Indeed many persons of wealth and reputation . . . have gotten their knowledge from no other source than . . . a newspaper, tho' by some silly shame none will confess it."[6]

Newspaper content also, of course, reveals competing values. And a personal tone permeated content as individuals tried to outwit opposition spokesmen and undermine those advocating rival views and values. Federalists and Anti-Federalists denounced each other, and the intense competition continued throughout the decade. The examples are mostly taken from newspapers published in 1801, in part because competing values were clearer then than later, but as the few excerpts from later in the decade show, tone and substance did not change much by 1809.

Discussion of the changed administration dominated newspapers in 1801. Federalist printers bewailed Thomas Jefferson's election as president and then seized every opportunity to berate his administration. Using his inaugural speech as a basis for ridiculing him and all he stood for, they lifted phrases from it to illustrate just how "dangerous" the new administration would be. A Boston newspaper item that also appeared in several other Federalist papers shows the consternation over the incoming administration and suggests the era's underlying competing values and notions of government. In part, the item said:

> To the Public
> The time has at length arrived, when the administration of our government is about to pass out of the hands of those, who have been in the councils, and confidence of our departed *Washington*! Men who are principally known, only as the leaders and favourites of a *faction*, composed in a great measure of *discontented, fortune-hunting*, foreigners, are now to succeed. This is a serious and portentious moment. . . .
> We have all observed . . . that this country has been tranquil, prosperous and happy, in proportion as the faction now about to predominate, has been restrained. . . .
> Men of uneasy and turbulent tempers have existed in the country from the first . . . ; but they have been . . . men of little personal character, and deserving of little consideration. At length, however, from the alliances of numerous men of *desperate fortunes*, of *corrupted morals, aliens, desperados, expatriated [patricians?], refugees* from European justice, together with many well meaning but mistaken and deluded persons, they have increased to a formidable, and regularly organized phalanx. . . .

Such is the faction, against which the good and the wise have now to contend:—a noxious, poisonous weed, which . . . has sprung up and gained its maturity during the night of neglect . . . till its spreading branches have become co-extensive with the nation, threatening to smother the growth of our morals, religion, liberty and national dignity. . . .

In a land of universal suffrage, like ours, it is not the conduct of one or two individuals that we have most to dread. It is the general ascendency of the worthless, the dishonest, the rapacious, the vile, the merciless and the ungodly, which forms the principal ground of alarm. These are the men who have incessantly maligned the officers of our government, collectively and individually, our courts of justice, our laws, our clergy, and our seminaries of learning. These are the men who called Washington a *murderer*, and these are the men to whom Mr. *Jefferson* and Mr. *Burr* are indebted for the two highest offices in the nation. . . .

It is a consideration sufficiently deplorable in a Christian country, that a reputed infidel, an open scoffer at the person and character of the Saviour, and a reputed sharper, speculator and libertine, should be elevated to the highest stations in the government. . . . their administration will certainly be dangerous to the peace and constitution of this country. . . .[7]

Several Federalist printers published an article calling Jefferson's inaugural speech a "net to snare popularity" that adumbrates sentiments in 1830s criticism. One printer lamented, "It is with reluctance, with painful reluctance, that we are compelled to declare the sincerity of our belief that 'a political intolerance as despotic as wicked,' is about to become the disgraceful and contradictory comment of an amiable text of the President's fallacious speech. . . ."[8]

Ideas about government and who should control it were frequent themes of articles, and the views expressed do not differ substantially from those in British and American press criticism into the 1830s. An article in a Maine newspaper, calling on society's propertied sector to bring the disintegrating polity under control, asserted that the "daring [persons] must be over-awed by an union of the wise; and, above all, the ignorant and misguided must be instructed and set right, by industry unremitted and extensive as that which has been used for their delusion." The author warned, "If men of property and integrity will not stoop to these means, they will be bowed under [by] the consequences."[9] An article in another issue declared, "The ruling part of any state must always have considerable property" because "property has such an invariable influence, that whoever possesses property must have power." Furthermore, "Property in a state, is also some security for fidelity, because interest then is concerned in the public welfare."[10] In a later issue of the same newspaper, another writer called it "the strangest doctrine ever promulgated by a statesman and philosopher [i.e., Jefferson], that *the offices of government are created for the benefit of individuals*." He also rejected the idea that "minorities have equal rights," arguing that "by the very construction and nature of our government, a *majority* constitutes, or is, in legal understanding, the *whole* [word illegible] *or body politic*." This body's "will" and "rights" were "indivisible" and "cannot be separated even in idea," the writer contended, arguing: "A will of the majority is a will of the whole. There is no such thing as will, or rights attached to a minority as such. The individuals who compose a minority have the same personal and political rights of a majority."[11] And a New York newspaper article said in part:

> One fundamental error, in the opinions of Americans . . . on which has been reposed an undue . . . confidence in the practicability of a free elective government, is the belief that the citizens . . . enjoy . . . the *fairest* opportunity, of founding and rendering durable a republican form of government. This error is of the more consequence, as it has led the legislators . . . to neglect to raise those barriers against popular violence and corruption. . . .[12]

Renewal of the Alien and Sedition Acts of 1798, or institution of similar laws, received much debate during the decade and was always an occasion for arguing the merits and demerits of self-government. A Maine newspaper reported John Randolph as stating during the "late debates of Congress upon the Sedition Law" that "how strongly soever the gentleman supposed that question to have been decided by the Congress who passed the law; the judges who gave their opinion upon it, or the juries who had settled cases exhibited to them, he would tell that gentleman and all his adherents, that he had a still higher tribunal to appeal to, and higher than than [sic] they could produce." The printer, to emphasize the important implications to his readers, told them that "he meant the *American People*," saying Randolph was arguing that "their voice was more powerful than those courts, these two branches of the legislature, these judges, and this president, to whom the gentleman referred." The printer scoffed, "This sounds like revolutionary language, and comes with a bad grace from a legislator," continuing:

> When a law has passed both houses of Congress, been approved by the President and declared to be constitutional by the judges, is there still an appeal to the people? Does our constitution recognize the people, as a forum competent to decide upon the constitutionality of a law?—Should this new doctrine of Mr. Randolph's come into operation, the constitution would be annihilated, the people erected into a *revolutionary tribunal*, and a new order of things begin.[13]

Anti-Federalists were equally adamant in condemning Federalists. A New Jersey printer exclaimed, "The many pretensions of the *federalists* to the title of *exclusive friends to order*, is as hypocritical as it is false and deceptious."[14] And a Maryland printer complained in 1809, "The Federalists will exert every nerve to divide," saying, "They pursue this course in their endeavors to shew a change of conduct in the present administration. . . ."[15] A long article addressed to "Americans" said, in part, "I appeal to my fellow citizens, if men who possess such opinions as these [Federalists], are fit to represent you in any office of trust? No, they now begin to receive the just detestation of all true Americans."[16]

The Anti-Federalists especially denounced the Alien and Sedition Acts and efforts to revive them or establish similar laws. A New York paper reported resolutions in the Virginia House of Delegates against any such laws—resolutions that emphatically declared English common law had no force in the United States:

> And whereas the said . . . General Assembly by their resolution passed on the 12th day of Januaray last, instructed the Senators from the state in the Congress of the United States to oppose the passing of any law founded on or recognizing the doctrine lately advanced that the common law of England is in force under the government of the United States, a doctrine which they truly declare to be novel in its principle and tremendous in its consequences. . . .[17]

The remainder of the item can't be completely deciphered, but a final resolution urged senators and representatives in Congress to take "every opportunity" to oppose the law and any resolution containing a recognition of "the said doctrine."[18]

Personal invective and aspersions on individual character permeated most of the writing in both Federalist and Anti-Federalist papers, and it seems that nothing was too gross for publication. A Federalist paper in Connecticut, for example, reported an event-centered item on the return of an American diplomat from France that was the context for ridiculing the incumbent administration's efforts, policies, and personnel. The item noted that "Col. Swift, the late Secretary of the Legation to France has (we are sorry to say it) returned," and continued:

> We have it from Federal authority that the Col. peremptorily asserts [that] every woman in France is without exception, a prostitute. Does the Col. *Know* this to be true? If he does not, it will be agreed that he ought not to say it.—And if he does, Lord bless us, what a hero he must be! . . . What, every woman in France! Why there must be seven or eight million of them! No, no, the Col. does not know quite so much. But if we will give the Col.'s assertion that construction which reason and charity demand—that is to say—that his acquaintance was confined to Ladies of that description, it will appear by no means improbable. . . .[19]

An example from the *Maryland Herald and Hagers-town Weekly Advertiser* for 1809 is quoted at length below because it exemplifies the personal tone in addition to the very common taunting among printers through the first half of the century. However, this exchange is more good-natured and less malicious than most. William Brown, the printer of a new Hagers-town paper, the *Gazette*, used its prospectus and first issue to lambast the Anti-Federalists, or Republicans. Thomas Grieves, an established Hagers-town printer, responded by trying to goad the rival printer into a debate of Anti-Federalist versus Federalist views, and kept it up in every issue in the sample for June of 1809.

> The editor of the Hagers-Town Gazette takes a long time to "arrange the business of his office." When we noticed the shameful and barefaced falsehoods and assertions . . . in his paper three weeks ago, we thought he would have made some justification. But lo! he is contented to stand forth convicted before the citizens of this country, of having asserted the most palpable falsehoods.[20]

Continuing, apparently playing on a statement Brown had made, Grieves asked Brown if he believed his actions would please "*us poor ignorant people*," and asked what confidence people could have "in a paper, which in its very first publication makes the most false charges against a virtuous administration, without the least shadow of a justification." Writing that he had "promised to jog" Brown's memory about promising to prove his assertions *"as soon as he had arranged the business of his office,"* Grieves noted that two weeks had passed without a word from Brown; so, he wrote, he was keeping his own promise and reminding him. He added:

> Halloo, Mr. Brown, have you forgotten your promise?—Do keep up appearance, by a sort of defence if no more. We are anxious to hear from you.—For these two last weeks we have been much disappointed. We promised ourselves much amusement from your great talent at *punning.* Your witticisms must always divert and amuse the public. As we are an *ignorant set of people* in this county, suppose you give us further specimens of your *punnings* and *witticisms*[;] perhaps we may profit by them and in time become as *witty* as yourself.[21]

The following week, Grieves, still awaiting a response, goaded Brown further:

> Halloo, Billy Brown, halloo! Awake from your sleep.—Do not forget your promise.—Remember that truth is a virtuous guide.—Although we do not agree with you in your political creed, still as a brother editor, we will remind you of your promise and endeavor to save you from ruin.[22]

Grieves asked what people would think if Brown did not honor his promise, and answered his own question: "Why . . . as they ought," that Brown was "a base asserter of falsehoods" and his "paper is the vehicle of pestilential doctrines." Grieves reminded Brown of his charges against the administration, of his own denial of them, and of Brown's promise to respond. But, Grieves surmised, Brown's silence must mean he could not substantiate the charges and feared Grieves would show the public the *Gazette's* "true colors—the channel of falsehood and party-lies." And he would, Grieves asserted, adding that he would "never fail to expose" Brown's party and the "sentiments" he advocated. However, Grieves concluded, perhaps Brown's silence meant that he had "repented of . . . error," so "why not confess . . . ?"[23]

And still the following week, Grieves again taunted:

> Halloo Billy Brown!! They have started you again Billy, have they? Well done Billy, your correspondent has a turn for blackguarding—for you did not write the paragraph in your paper of yesterday afternoon Billy—although it seems on perusal, to be one which might come from a man of about your size and understanding.[24]

Saying he was pressed for time to "set up" for his morning paper, Grieves wrote that, "still, however, we must find time and room to insert a few lines, by way of congratulating the Hagers-town Gazette's correspondent, on his *sobriety*—his *great wealth* and talent for writing." He continued that he saw "by the paper" that "Mr. Bourne of Baltimore" was writing a history of the United States, and if he might "be permitted to give advice," he recommended Brown's correspondent as co-author. Saying that "a small difference" might occur in that neither Brown nor his correspondent knew anything of the civil, political, or religious state of the country then or before, he added that they did have "great talents of a certain kind"—as "yesterday's *Gazette*" showed. But he asserted that when he had asked for proof of Brown's charges, he wanted an answer based on reason instead of invective. He asked Brown not to allow himself to be misled, saying he knew Brown's party formerly "pretended to all of the piety, wealth and wisdom in the country," but "those days are gone"; so, Grieves warned, "be careful . . . how you indulge warm-headed, misguided and uninformed young men with a place for invective in your columns." He added that "none but frothy minds actuated by malice, could either have originated or given currency to the remarks, stamped with the sanction of editorial insertion [in] yesterday's Gazette." Grieves continued:

> Take warning, Sir, and do not begin too soon to throw your fire-brands among neighbors.—If it be *reasoning* you want, republicans, having truth with them, are *at all times prepared*; if it be scurrility, they will yield the palm of victory, and hail you with the "ID TRIUMPHO!" but if true *wit* and *genuine humor*, be your object, we'll meet you on your own or middle ground. However, for your own sake Mr. B. beware both of ill nature and *sarcasm*, for, in either case, both you and your correspondent might enter into a very unequal contest.[25]

Grieves concluded he was disinclined to "take further notice" of Brown's paper, but the following week, he again addressed Brown, who had apparently threatened "vengeance" if he did not print a certain *Gazette* item. The *Gazette* editor, Grieves wrote, was further revealing himself, acting "the part of a little dictator" who "prescribes . . . our conduct . . . tells us what to print and . . . when," continuing:

> This order of Billy the 1st by the Grace of God not *yet* Emperor of the West, puts us in mind of an anecdote, told by . . . *Peter Porcupine* of himself. When the federalists were in the saddle, Peter always riding before, and long John Fenno, of the United States Gazette behind, (for in those days they rode double) one of the leaders . . . thinking Peter galloped too fast, and dreading lest the whole batch might get a tumble— wrote him a severe letter of reprimand—this raised the mettle of Peter, and only served to make him whip and spur the harder, till at last, sure enough, the whole cavalcade were "unhorsed"—and have not remounted even until this day.[26]

After much more of the same, Grieves wrote that he was wary of copying public documents from "Billy's" paper, "not having implicit faith in the truth of all he says," and concluded with what he called a "jog": "William why does thou not endeavor to substantiate the calumnies . . . in thy prospectus, against republicans?"[27]

Such goading may well have continued uninterrupted through succeeding weeks. The sample omitted subsequent issues, but sure enough, Grieves was still taunting in the December 13 issue: "Billy Brown has again let fly at us in his last week's Gazette, but in a manner so vile, low and ungentlemanly, as renders it scarcely worthy of notice." Brown had apparently written that Grieves had no genius, for the latter continued that he was "led to reply to the very wise question—'Does he pretend to deny our assertion that he has no genius?' " In response, Grieves said he had received what talents he had from God, and he trusted that they, "such as they are," had "never been devoted to or sullied by the invention and propagation of calumny." Brown had gone beyond "vague and indefinite abuse," Grieves wrote, and had directly charged "fraudulent stuffing the Herald upon our subscribers." Brown had apparently asked if Grieves wished "to assert" that he had "either honor or honesty," for Grieves retorted, "Dare you, Billy, assert the contrary?" and added, "There is a measure of subtlety and coward-ice in the dark insinuation, which must have proceeded from the basest malice, and to give it vent, we challenge Billy and the world to point out the smallest deviation from the paths of honor or honesty."[28]

Although ideas dominated these early papers, printers did report events. Generally, however, they simply told that an event had occurred, without elaboration or des-cription. Vivid descriptions were the exception. If the information's source was a letter, the letter writer's description appeared; but such descriptions were terse because of the editor's haste and lack of space. Aside from reports on congressional proceedings, eyewitness news accounts were extremely rare. Furthermore, reports were fairly anonymous and impersonal—that is, neither the person publishing the account nor those reading it had actually seen the event. Event reports were generally created out of secondhand knowledge, assembled from accounts of one person—who may have been reporting hearsay from several sources—or from several persons, who also may have been reporting from second or third hand. Generally, the rare accounts that did feature individuals and events did so in the context of a political argument or idea (exceptions were tributes to "great" figures, such as George Washington). The tone was very personal, often ridiculing the individuals involved, and one suspects that details (or even whole stories) were frequently fabricated. The following, from a newspaper in 1801, illustrates:

> In July last Mr. Brackenridge, desirous of displaying his new dignity of Judge among his old acquaintances, came over to Washington dressed with unusual neatness. Finding . . . no decent person of the place called to see him, he walked through the town, accosted the people with studied courtesy as he passed the streets in some instances advanced to the door of his former friends but was received with marked coolness, and although not directly insulted, yet he found himself so much detested, that with all his insinuating civilities no person invited him into his house. Mortified beyond measure at this treatment, he returned to his tavern, called for brandy to cure his vexation, and after drinking hastily and usual portions of that [word illegible] liquor he rode away to Canonsburg.
>
> Although evidently intoxicated when he alighted there, yet he went on drinking whiskey to great excess and abusing the gentlemen of Washington. Sometimes he pretended to be asleep in his chair, suddenly would start up with some incoherent exclamation, and take another drink. After a while he said he had a fever, proceeding to strip himself naked, took a sheet and hung it over his shoulders, and walked before the door thus exposed. This soon collected a multitude of boys, to whom he addressed many pleasant things affecting to talk and act like one of themselves.—Presently he ordered water to be carried to the stable, and compelled a black smith's boy to throw several buckets of cold water on him. The other boys, and even men, gathered round the stable and

diverted themselves with this whimsical figure of a naked judge upon all fours among the horses . . . washing and rubbing. One lad said he should be drenched also.—Others said he was already drenched with whiskey.[29]

The report continued that the judge, offended by "these fellows' " laughter, ordered them away, threatening to "commit them." Telling them he was a judge, he promised the blacksmith's boy something for staying with him and sent the others home. Leaving the stable, wrapped in a sheet, he drank more whiskey at the tavern, then dressed and started for Pittsburgh, although he was "altogether unfit for travelling" and almost unable to mount his horse. By then having heard he was either drunk or mad, the townspeople laughed as he passed. The report continued, "Near the end of the Village he saw several men . . . with sickles. . . . Fancying them to be enemies, he damned them to clear the road for a Judge of the Supreme Court; then clapping spurs to his horse he raised a frightful warshoop, and dashing through the midst of them, went off at full speed yelling wildly. . . ." According to the report, Brackinridge repeated the drinking, disrobing, and drenching when he arrived at a Mr. Agga's and again at a Mr. Hamilton's taverns. The printer concluded that, with such actions by officials, "we can't expect reformation of the dissolute among us," and wrote that "office is degraded, religion dishonored" and "good men everywhere will lament the misfortune to society when such men are appointed."[30]

In summary, newspaper content in the first decade of the nineteenth century was primarily idea-centered and permeated with personal invective; when printers emphasized individuals, they reported on "important" people—most often officeholders. Event-centered items did appear, but they were often prompted by or used as a basis for discussing ideas. These news traits shifted significantly by 1850.

Newspapers, 1850–1860

By the middle decade of the century, content of papers reflected the changed role of the press—the information model oriented to the individual and the community—and the movement toward democratization that emphasized the individual's role in society and government. No longer idea-centered, most items were local and event-oriented. The newspaper press informed individuals about the society they were part of to increase their knowledge of their surroundings, institutions, and government, providing what they needed to participate as citizens. At the same time, the newspaper press emphasized the individual and individual perspectives in content.

Criticisms during this era that the press was destroying values, creating an injurious current in society, and encroaching on firesides indicate the attention attracted by changed reporting procedures resulting from the press's changed role. Charges of distortion, damage to individuals' reputations especially, and invasion of privacy emerged as a natural consequence of the changed press role. To inform individuals about their environment required a journalistic procedure of description. Any description of an event would naturally lead to charges of distorted reporting, for no two persons ever see an event exactly alike, and those who saw and also read a report of an event were likely to believe that the journalist had distorted the news. But reading descriptions of unfolding events that one had witnessed in person was a new experience. Furthermore, describing events to inform individuals of the kind of society they lived in naturally raised charges of immoral reporting, for the press had begun to describe matters traditionally reserved only for conversation—and even then not for "polite" conversation —views that were not intended to circulate. Describing events meant portraying both the good and the bad of society, and the latter was presumed by those attached to traditional values as unfit to be published. Many believed that such material was injurious even if published as part of novels. Humankind's baser instincts were not to be dignified by being committed to print and commonly circulated. This kind of reading matter did not elevate or ennoble, nor did it provide the most meritorious record to pass on to future generations or the rest of the world. Some saw such news not only as poor reading material that lowered general erudition but also as tending to corrupt those who read it. Second, the focus on individuals, their milieu and who they were, naturally led to charges of invasion of privacy, for to describe individuals' behavior more closely than would be offered in the barest sketch meant intruding into their lives further than the values of many at the time condoned.

The typical high-circulation newspaper of the 1850s was four to eight pages long, with half or more devoted to advertising.[31] By the 1850s, the press had become centered on the event—that is, an occurrence at some specific time and place occasioned most reports. A typical four-page paper contained thirty-five to forty items about events, whereas items dealing purely with ideas per se were few. In one issue, only two items—one having to do with women's role in society, and the other with the institution of slavery—were identified as idea-centered. Through a generous interpretation, one could classify some of the political pieces as idea-centered when, for example, they focused on political platforms; however, these articles primarily aimed to report an event, such as a convention or meeting.[32]

The newspapers of the 1850s were published to serve the individual, and they emphasized local news—events in the city where the paper was published. Thirty-five to forty items reported local news as opposed to twenty to twenty-five non-local items. Foreign or international news was rare; in one issue only four international items appeared. Twenty-five to thirty items were political.[33] The emphasis on individuals and local news no doubt also flowed from newspapers' need to interest people and to achieve greater circulation. Changes in the press made higher circulation possible; the use of new equipment, however, made publishing more expensive, so the need to increase circulation led to studied attempts to reach the greatest number. Whatever content sold papers was emphasized. The event orientation probably had to do with such changes; as journalists tried to achieve greater circulation, they published dailies and even separate weekly editions. This and the editor's expanded role as policymaker did not leave time for the contemplation necessary to write idea-centered articles. A daily demanded quick production. Finally, the development of news gathering took journalists outside the office and kept them on the go more than ever before, and the new reporting practices left little time for preparing idea pieces. It must be noted here, however, that many of the first decade's idea articles may have been contributed to the newspaper and not actually prepared by the editor. Contributed articles were scarce in papers in the 1850s, probably because of the drive for circulation and its consequent emphasis on events, which crowded out "think" pieces except for the editor's own commentaries.

Trying to convey what was happening in the world for the individual's edification meant creating as complete a picture of any event as possible. Hence, new writing techniques emerged in news reports, influenced to a great extent by the employment of literary figures as journalists. Linda Patterson Miller notes that Edgar Allen Poe, for example, working in New York as one of the first urban journalists, brought literary elegance to descriptions of the city, including street noise and social inequalities, in a series called "Doings of Gotham," which appeared in the *Columbia Spy* between May 28 and July 6, 1844; soon after, a series called "Slices of New York," by a reporter for the *New York Tribune*, followed "almost exactly, the plan . . . Poe had established." A series published in the 1850s, "Hot Corn Sketches," imitated the pattern in trying to describe "city life and its effect on people."[34]

Politics remained important, as indicated by the large number of items devoted to it—even if the pieces were more event- than idea-centered—but journalists in the 1850s in effect attempted to describe what occurred on a daily basis, and aimed as often as possible to describe the process. Reports of social context—that is, descriptions of city life and physical surroundings—were common, and more substance of events in process began to appear. A New York newspaper's report of a riot illustrates the emphasis on event, the eyewitness account, and the description of process. Inclusion of the color of people's shirts and other minutiae suggests that the writer saw the event in person. Under headlines, in the following order, the editor reported "CITY INTELLIGENCE/Riot Among the Firemen—Paving Stones and/Politics—Engines Taken From the Bellige/rants by order of the Chief Engineer":

> Yesterday morning, at about half-past eleven o'clock, the fire bells rang out an alarm for the Fifth district, and the Bowery was soon filled with engines and hose carts, making their way up town. Engine 41, which lies at the corner of Delancey and Attorney streets, was going up under full headway, when, at the junction of the Bowery, Third avenue and Sixth street, engine No. 6 came up with a very strong force, and ran into No. 41, taking off one of the forward wheels of the vehicle, thus crippling the apparatus so as to bring it to a stand still. . . . it was at once understood that a fight was to ensue, and so the members of No. 6 followed up the attack upon the engine by an attack upon the men, who had it in charge. At this time the company of No. 6 far outnumbered their adversaries, and the members of 41 were obliged to give way. Presently, however, other engines and hose companies came up, and were soon engaged, taking different sides, according to their predilections. As the alarm spread, the friends of both sides came up, and the war became general. Conspicuous among those who were actively engaged were, besides the members of 6 and 41, many . . . whose caps bore the numbers 4, 16, 26, 15 and 44. The battle ground was in the open space at the head of Sixth street, known as the Hay Market. A few rods down Sixth street was a large pile of bricks, placed there for building purposes. The party of No. 6 took possession of this lot of ammunition, and commenced to pour in a lively shower of brickbats upon their opponents. No regard was had for passing vehicles. The stages, railroad cars, and wagons, were obliged to take the chances of getting hit, and considerable damage was thus done by the flying missiles. Many persons were injured who had nothing to do with the fight. A man standing quietly in the corner of the Bowery and Sixth street, received a blow from a brick which knocked him down. . . . Some . . . bystanders took him up, and conveyed him out of the reach of danger. . . . Very

conspicuous among the rioters were a set of rowdies dressed in red shirts, and armed with axes, cleavers, iron bars, and clubs. . . .

While the fight was going on, and when it was at its height, a detachment of police officers . . . made their appearance, and went boldly into the midst of the rioters, and behaved with such coolness, and courage that a check was soon put to firing of missiles.[35]

The journalist of the mid-nineteenth century emphasized individuals in reporting, often describing their appearance, activities, feelings, thoughts, and conversation. An element of continuity, however, was the interest in "important" persons, which coincided with the increasing emphasis on "ordinary" people. Another new element was that of quoting individuals directly.

Reports of Daniel Webster's death illustrate these points, especially in their emphasis on individuals—in this case, an important personage. The article that follows, excerpted from the *New York Herald*, also illustrates careful explication of the details of Webster's last days, along with exposure of what some surely at the time considered trivial—as well as overly intimate, private, and personal. The story is quoted at length because it is in many ways characteristic of 1850s reporting. Pages and pages of an issue of the *New York Herald* were devoted to Webster's last days and hours.

ANOTHER NATIONAL CALAMITY

DEATH OF

DANIEL WEBSTER,

the

GREAT NEW ENGLAND STATESMAN.

THE expounder of the constitution NO MORE

HIS SICKNESS, AND LAST MOMENTS.

SAD AND TOUCHING DEATH SCENE

Biographical Sketch of the Great Man

The Effect of his Death Here and Elsewhere

&c., &c., &c.

When news reached here on Friday morning that Mr. Webster's indisposition, by which he had been affected for some ten days previously, had suddenly assumed a dangerous and alarming phase the deepest solicitude and anxiety was manifested by all classes of citizens, and the most intense excitement existed to learn, from time to time the contents of each succeeding despatch.

The melancholy tidings were first communicated by . . . a special messenger . . . from Mr. Webster's residence at Marshfield, carrying the sad intelligence that the distinguished statesman could not survive the day. On the previous Tuesday not the slightest danger had been apprehended from Mr. Webster's illness which was disease of the bowels, accompanied by dropsical affection of the stomach, and his physicians anticipated that he would be able to resume the duties of his office in a few days; but on that afternoon the disorder unexpectedly assumed a more menacing aspect, and he gradually grew worse and worse, until Thursday, when Dr. Jeffries, the physician in attendance, began to feel alarmed. . . .

On Thursday night Mr. Webster had a very severe attack of vomiting, but at five o'clock on Friday morning, when the special messenger left Marshfield, he had sunk into a sleep.

The Hon. George T. Curtis, who had been in attendance on the dying statesman, returned to Boston on Friday morning, and confirmed the sad intelligence of the hopelessness of Mr. Webster's recovery; and on the same morning a letter was received from his private secretary, by the Hon. Edward Everett stating that he was not expected to survive many hours. . . .

Mr. Webster, fully sensible of his approaching end, but looked forward to it with magnanimous resignation. . . . His intellectual faculties were as bright and powerful as in their most halcyon days, and among all the sorrow-stricken friends, relatives and admirers, who surrounded his couch, and with whom he conversed freely, he was of all the most placid, serene, and unaffected.

Nor in this last scene and preparation for eternity was the great man unmindful of his duties to his family, his household, and his country. On Thursday forenoon he received his mail as usual and gave the directions for answers to his letters. . . . To the workmen on his farm he also gave directions . . . and . . . proceeded to complete various matters of business.

On Thursday evening he executed his last will and testament. . . .

During Friday, the dying statesman had three attacks of vomiting— one at two o'clock in the morning, one at eight . . . and one at four o'clock in the afternoon. From that time up till seven o'clock he lay in a placid state apparently free from pain, and conversing a little. . . . His physician . . . forbade general conversation, as talking produced nausea. . . .

. . . At eleven o'clock on Friday night he was again seized with vomitings, though they were not very severe; but between one and two o'clock on Saturday morning, vomiting recurred and continued for three quarters of an hour, during which time he suffered terribly. . . .

About half past five o'clock [on Saturday afternoon], Mr. Webster was again seized with violent nausea and raised considerable dark matter tinged with blood. Exhaustion now increased rapidly, and his physicians held another consultation which resulted in a conclusion that his last hour was fast approaching.

He received the announcement, and requested that the female members of his family might be called in. . . .

Next he had called in the male members . . . and the personal friends. . . .

He now had Mr. Peter Harvey called in again, and said to him:—

"Harvey, I am not so sick but that I know you. . . . I am well enough to love you . . . don't leave me till I am dead. . . ."

Then as if speaking to himself, he said—

"On the 24th of October, all that is mortal of Daniel Webster will be no more." . . .

At half-past seven o'clock, Dr. J. M. Warren arrived from Boston. . . .

Shortly after he conversed with Dr. Jeffries, who said he could do nothing more for him than to administer occasionally a sedative potion. "Then," said Mr. Webster, "I am to be here patiently till the end; if it be so, may it come soon."

At ten o'clock he was still lower, but perfectly conscious . . . and at twenty-two minutes before three o'clock yesterday morning, "the 24th of October, all that was mortal of Daniel Webster was no more."[36]

Historians would expect James Gordon Bennett to report such details, but might be surprised that other editors of the mid-nineteenth century would. Comparison with another newspaper on the same day, however, showed that such reporting was not unique. The Boston *Daily Evening Transcript*; the most staid paper in the sample, published a report so similar to the *Herald*'s as to suggest that the news came via the telegraph in both cases. But neither account appeared under the telegraph headline. Webster had called for "poetry—Gray—Gray," and both stories reported this and that the "Elegy in a Country Churchyard" was read to him; both also reported, "The last words of Webster are said to have been the remarkable ones, 'I STILL LIVE' "[37]

Although newspaper content was no longer dominated by politics and no longer idea-centered, the degree of partisan bias hardly differed from that of the early newspapers. An item selected at random from the *New York Times* illustrates:

Our fastidious neighbors of the *Evening Post* are not pleased with the Whig City nominations. We are very sorry, but the thing cannot be helped now. Two of the leading nominations are from the working classes. This loses the party the countenance of the philosophers and poets of the *Post*. Their ideas run upon the ideal—not the practical. Alderman (Sheriff, that is to be) Kelly is "a *baker* in Beekman-street!" "generally liked by those who know him," but only a bread-baker, and no one knows him in the *Post*'s "set." He drives an honest trade in Beekman-street, not a turn-out above Bleecker!

And the *Post* is not pleased with Morgan Morgans either. This surprises us. Mr. M. is an older worker in *brass*. Respect for a metal constituting no mean ingredient in their own composition, should otherwise incline our neighbors—it should.[38]

But even though editors' public animosities toward each other had lessened, many items showed that exchanges of insults remained common. Under the headline FUNNY NEWSPAPER WAR, for example, an editor noted in 1852:

The Pick and the Picayune, two flashy weekly journals, are at war, both in their columns and in the police office. The Pick is the new one started by Joe Scoville—the Picayune is the old one, owned by two or three nobodies. The Pick began with a circulation of 25,000 at the first step. This frightened the old boys, and they retaliated by two or three arrests of the Pick man for libel. This is a mean mode of putting down a new rival, and will hardly succeed. Let master Pick keep cool, stick to his text, say nothing of his rivals, make a good paper, amuse all the pretty girls with funny stories, and he is in no danger of damnation.[39]

Common in the first decade, such editorial insults had decreased by the century's middle decade and virtually disappeared by the last decade.

Newspapers, 1890–1899

By the 1890s, the definition of news had changed even more, emphasizing events, dwelling on individual personalities, and using drama to lure readers. In other words, the stress on events, the individual perspective, and the use of drama as a lure had merged into the "story," a product that was marketed and sold. However, the merging blurred the significance of each element, obscuring distinctions and the purity of focus of any one strand. The event was, at one level, the hard news story—the accurate, factual information; at another level, it was the "plot" or part of a plot around which drama was woven to create the thrill that would make people want to read and therefore buy the newspaper. The role of ideas in newspapers was relegated principally to the editorial page, which developed after the 1850s; but even so, ideas were less identifiable in papers at the end of the century. Editorials most often departed from actions—which ideas underlay, to be sure, but the ideas were, if only ever so slightly, out of focus.

Press content of the 1890s reflected a further changed role. The news "packaging," the tightly crowded pages of variety and diversity, and the story model are only three broad traits that signify a press engaged in selling and marketing news. The evidence of drama—what most at the time called sensationalism—to lure readers and sell papers is overwhelming; this, however, did not suddenly burst upon the scene.

In a sense, although the story model preceded the Civil War, the post-war infusion of drama in news may be attributed to the war. The events journalists conveyed to the public during those four years of crisis and during the preceding decade had been constantly thrilling—not pleasant, but thrilling nevertheless. Regardless of how bad or good it was, the news was always exciting; and readers became habituated to looking to newspapers for excitement as well as information. The effect was no doubt similar to the much shorter American media experience during the Watergate hearings in 1974. In that case, a story built over months about whether the president had possibly violated the public's good faith, at the very least, and at the worst, his oath of office, the nation's Constitution, and federal laws. The revelations increasingly cast suspicion, culminating in the hearings that kept the nation riveted to the news media to learn the truth and whether the president might be impeached. The president's resignation and the swearing in of a new president, who then pardoned his predecessor, ended a series of electrifying events. The news had thrilled and excited Americans, keeping the public rapt through a national crisis. But when the crisis was over. . . . A certain sense of letdown followed because the news no longer excited on a daily basis; journalists recognized this anticlimax and the pressure it signified to find a way to keep the public's attention when such absorbing events no longer occurred daily.

Surely, such was the situation of journalism after the Civil War, although no one may have recognized it then as representing a media problem. But surely, too, journalists who had "grown up" during the war and whose experience had necessarily taught them how to thrill readers continued to try to do so as they aimed to fulfill the public's desire for excitement that the war had so elevated. "Sensational" postwar stories about corruption and reforms provided a way to continue to thrill. Journalists simply adapted wartime lessons to a time of peace. And as they adapted news-gathering and other techniques learned during the war—such as using multiple sources, interviewing, ferreting out stories against all objections and odds, disguising themselves for safety in order to pursue the Southern story, and describing events so that readers might almost feel that they were there—they increasingly went beyond what some at the time believed were the appropriate bounds of journalistic conduct; hence the shrill denunciations of the press during the 1880s.

Criticisms focused on these several excesses: invasions of privacy as journalists tried to get every detail that might satisfy what many saw as the most tasteless curiosity; sensationalism that heightened thrill at the expense of perspective and facts; and jeopardizing the accused's right to a fair trial by publishing details that seemed virtually to convict outside the justice system. But considering news drama of the late nineteenth century as part of journalists' efforts to package news for marketing, we can understand it better than by simply excoriating it as sensationalism. It was journalistic conduct dictated by press role.

Newspapers in the 1890s were eight to sixteen pages long, page size was larger than earlier, and up to three pages of an eight-page paper were devoted to advertising. Several new elements were apparent in the papers, each confirming the late-nineteenth-century business model of journalism, which was dedicated to selling news as a commodity:

1. Drama in the reporting was intended to excite and entice readers to buy papers.
2. Personals columns and vital statistics were intended to meet specific interests and attempt to offer something for virtually everyone. This effort to please all readers was a holdover from the mid-century emphasis on the individual. It may be that journalists had tried to meet the charges of trivialization by reducing the space allotted to each story of this type; still, they saw such news as important because it appealed to many readers. It seems worth noting, however, that these short items seemed a far greater trivialization of news than had earlier articles that unabashedly celebrated individuals—ordinary or not-so-ordinary. In the 1890s, however, "personals" attracted those interested in tidbits about the "rich and famous," flattered readers who found themselves mentioned, and injected a personal element in what had become an increasingly impersonal journalism.
3. Reporting on business indicated the press's role in supporting and promoting that trend in American society. Significant designated space devoted to financial news was a new element; in fact, a well-defined financial page appeared in most newspapers of the 1890s. The amount of attention given to business should not have been surprising since national interests were preoccupied with the subject at the time, but it was. A close study of business stories would likely reveal a great deal about competing values during the latter part of the century. It is interesting, for example, that the tone of some articles on American business was mocking whereas that of others was laudatory.
4. Significant space devoted to international news, especially compared to papers of the 1850s, confirmed the "internationalization" of the press following the Civil War.

5. Fashion pages, well defined in some newspapers, showed that journalists were consciously trying to appeal to women.
6. Well-defined sports pages also appeared—another signal of the intent to meet diverse interests.
7. Advertising was interspersed with news columns throughout the newspaper, indicating clear intentions to ensure that readers would not overlook ads or read only the news and throw away pages given over entirely to advertising. Single ads were also larger—often multiple-column—and contained display type, illustrations, and copy that appealed to the emotions more than any previous ads had. Fewer ads ran on front pages, although some newspapers devoted as many as two of seven front-page columns to advertising.
8. Well-defined editorial pages kept alive a function of dealing with ideas. However, the original idea-centered emphasis of the early national press was gone. Although editorial pages of course involved ideas, editorials themselves most often focused on particular actions of groups, organizations, or companies rather than underlying ideas. Thus the activity or the group—not the idea—was the reason for an editorial's having been written.
9. Inclusion of fiction—that is, short stories—reflected the effort to entertain and provide yet another reason for readers to buy papers. This element capitalized on what journalists had learned about readers' interest in "stories"—demonstrated by journalists in the 1830s who reported the "moan hoax" and coopted literary figures such as Edgar Allan Poe. Fiction also complemented and paralleled the use of drama in news. Both were part of 1890s trends.

The three most striking new elements, in larger terms; were the abundant number of items crowded onto a page, the degree of often contrived drama interwoven in reports of every kind, and the packaging of the news.

The abundance of items is overwhelming. Newspapers commonly fit twenty-five to sixty-five items on the front page, which seemed intended to offer something for everyone—although society's ethnic diversity was hardly recognized. An average number of front-page items calculated from eleven issues of different newspapers was 40.5—and some of those papers gave two front-page columns to advertising. One particular issue had thirty-seven items on the front page, of which nine were local, eleven national (most dealt with events in other states, with two about general national affairs) and seventeen international. Three were political, and four were about business. Thirty were event-centered; none was idea-centered. Twelve of the total front-page items were infused with drama and told as suspenseful stories. The lead story, under the headline AWAITING THE SHOCK, told of crowds waiting for the electrocution of prisoners at Sing Sing.[40] Another entire issue contained thirty dramatized items. Twenty-six items were business news and twenty were political. The breakdown according to locality was twenty-six local, fifty-eight national, and twenty-five international items.[41]

Obviously, most items were short; however, the most dramatic stories got most space. Front pages commonly had one or two long stories (filling a column or more and continuing on the inside), so additional items crowded into remaining space were short and numerous, indeed.

Regarding form, one may cautiously say that the story dominated—more because of its stronger impact, perhaps, than because it outnumbered straightforward items.

Certainly, journalists seized every opportunity to inject drama into their reports; although they did not dramatize every account, they dramatized every kind at one time or another—from political to business to international. News items in the 1890s were, indeed, *stories*. Their headlines were crafted to draw attention to their inherent drama, and those without strong emotional overtones were nevertheless often infused with drama. The headlines for a Philadelphia newspaper's leading front-page story illustrate:

ANNA DICKINSON
She Has Been Declared Sane and a Victim of a Plot.
Taken Away by Force.
She Tells a Startling Story of Alleged Cruel Persecution.
Cut Off from the World—The Horrors of a Mad House—Charges
Against Her Sister.[42]

The story, which filled two columns and continued on page 2, told about an apparently wealthy woman committed to an asylum by a sister who she said was insane.

Other headlines on the same page included

THEY ARE PIRATES
So Ex-leader Barry Called the Knights of Labor Whitty's Unpaid Bill
Evidence Produced to Show that He Has a Just Claim—
How the Organization Expends Its Money.

The story was about the trial in William Whitty's suit against the executive board of the Knights of Labor.

FIRED THE BUILDING
Terrible Charge Against the Proprietor of a Burned Hotel

THE DEED OF A BRUTAL PARENT

TURNED THE HOSE ON HIM
Then There Was a Riot, in Which Men, Irrespective of Station,
Participated

LYNCHED BY A MASKED MOB
A Hundred Men Take Murderer Bales from Jail and Hang Him to a Tree.[43]

The lead story in an Ohio newspaper, about a meeting of Methodist ministers, ran under the headlines

GRAVE SUBJECT
How Shall the Dead Be Buried?
M. E. Ministers Discuss It
Undertakers Again Hauled Over the Coals
The Brethren Start the Jury Wheel A-rolling[44]

Some other headlines were

DISAGREEING DOCTORS
An Asylum Superintendent Defiantly Trails the Tail of His Coat.[45]

BOY BRAINS A MAN[46]

AN INHUMAN MOTHER?
She Sells Her Daughter's Virtue and
Then Pleads for Mercy[47]

MURDERED BEFORE THE ALTAR[48]

HACKED TO PIECES[49]

Headlines in 1899 reached for even more drama, as these examples illustrate:

GROUND TO PIECES IN REVOLVING SHAFT[50]

—a particularly gruesome story about a twelve-year-old boy's death in an elevator;

Complaints of Gardiner
Newburger Adjourns Court, De-
Clining to Try Dead Men
Judges Besought by the Dry Goods District
To see that Bachrach and Wereter Are
Tried. Merchants Declare There is Some
Hidden Influence Behind the Thieves[51]

Pronounced a Leper By the Man She Loved[52]

Was "Excited" When He Stole Trousers, Three Months a Pair[53]

A Woman Burned by a Bonfire[54]

Cabin Boy M'Kinley Was a Girl[55]

Not all headlines or stories in this era were "sensational" or contained the drama reflected in these. Many newspapers, in fact, had little excessive drama, but most—if not all—included drama. Even headlines that were mere labels—as many were—included some element of drama (suspense, humor, or punning) intended to hook readers. These headlines illustrate: A CHEEKY REQUEST; A FIRM OLD FIRM; BOTH EYES OPEN; FATAL KICK; AWFUL FATE; THIS IS AWFUL; STOLE A SECRET; NO LONGER A SECRET; CAME TO BLOWS? BOUNCED BY DOCTORS? SMASHED WITH A SANDBAG.[56]

Drama was, of course, a part of packaging the news. But packaging included several other elements, the most important of which was confining particular kinds of content to special pages. Journalists in the Civil War era began the packaging of selected *items* with multi-deck headlines and leads; by the 1890s they had expanded this practice to the entire newspaper. Dividing news according to broad categories and interests, they designated places for each—sports, financial reports, editorials, fashion—packaging and labeling it to create systematized order and facilitate readers' ease in finding what interested them most. Lincoln Steffens' description of newspapers in the 1890s was apt: the pattern did indeed imitate a department store, where commodities were separated into different areas. Other packaging elements included illustrations to "dress up" a story, multiple headlines to provide the gist of a story quickly, and the many short items that enabled one to read "complete items" in quick takes. All these techniques helped to sell the news.

Newspaper content over the course of the nineteenth century confirms changes in the press's role in each era. Constants throughout were the relationship of press role to journalism's expansion as a social institution and to values. As values changed, role changed, and journalistic standards changed in turn. When journalistic standards are viewed as part of a larger framework of forces—against a background of social developments, changing values, press criticism, and newspaper content, they come into focus. From partisanism to trivialization to sensationalism, journalistic excesses were by-products of how the press fulfilled particular roles as these were interpreted at different times. Since the press's role has implications for standards, discussion now turns to that issue, beginning with a consideration of journalists' views.

Notes

1.   An exception is the *New York Times*, which began in 1851.
2.   The number of newspapers publishing continuously in the earliest years of the nation is difficult to calculate because of numerous name changes. Seventy-nine were counted, based on Clarence S. Brigham, *History and Bibliography of American Newspapers, 1690–1820* (Worcester, Mass.: American Antiquarian Society, 1947). The highest-circulation newspapers in 1890, according to Ayer's *Newspaper Annual*, were as follows:

     1.   *Chicago News*, 262,000
     2.   *Philadelphia Evening Item*, 207, 460
     3.   *Philadelphia Record*, 186,387
     4.   *New York News*, 178,560
     5.   *Cincinnati Post*, 176,805
     6.   *Philadelphia Inquirer*, 157,552
     7.   *New York Sun*, 120,000
     8.   *Philadelphia Bulletin*, 117,281
     9.   *Chicago Tribune*, 110,000
     10. *Boston Evening Record*, 109,516
     11. *Cleveland Press*, 107,788
     12. *Cincinnati Times-Star*, 103,405

     Some newspapers were unavailable, so any six on the list were acceptable, but some substitutions were still necessary.
3.   John Martin and Harold Nelson have developed a standard for measuring the accuracy of reports of one event (or series of events), but they concede that the problem of determining accuracy is difficult. L. John Martin and Harold L. Nelson, "The Historical Standard in Analyzing Press Performance," *Journalism Quarterly* 33 (Fall 1956): 456–66.
4.   A very narrow study, focusing on a few or on just one category of stories, could perhaps accomplish what was not possible through this broader perspective.
5.   Shilen, "The Concept of Objectivity," 38, quotes Mott's testimony before the Federal Communications Commission, January 22, 1942, that "indeed, one of these newspapers would be considered a traitor to its party and to its cause if it" printed news of the opposing party. See *Freedom of the Press* (New York: Newspaper-radio Committee, 1942): 24.
6.   *New Hampshire Gazette*, June 2, 1801; published on Tuesdays by John Melcher, printer

to the state of New Hampshire. Columns 1 and 2 of page 1 and all of page 4 were filled with advertisements.

7. *Boston Gazette*, January 22, 1801; published Mondays and Thursdays by John Russell and James Cutler.

8. *Hampshire Gazette*, June 24, 1801; published in Northampton, Massachusetts, on Wednesdays by William Butler; all of page 4 was advertising.

9. *Jenks' Portland Gazette*, February 2, 1801; published Mondays by Eleazer Alley Jenks, printer of the laws of the United States for the District of Maine. This issue was not in the sample, but was studied for reports of debates on renewing the Alien and Sedition Acts.

10. Ibid., June 22, 1801.

11. Ibid., December 14, 1801.

12. *The Spectator*, January 3, 1801; published in New York City on Wednesdays and Saturdays by E. Belden & Co., printers of the laws of the United States for the District of New York. Column 5 of page 3 and all of page 4 were typically all advertising in this newspaper.

13. *Jenks' Portland Gazette*, February 16, 1801.

14. *Centinel of Freedom*, June 30, 1801; published in Newark, New Jersey, on Tuesdays by Samuel Pennington and Stephen Gould. Typically, the paper had ads filling three columns on the front page, the fourth column of both inside pages, and all of page 4.

15. *Republican Star or Eastern Shore General Advertiser*, June 13, 1809; published in Easton, Maryland, on Tuesdays by Thomas Perrin Smith, printer of the laws of the United States.

16. Ibid., January 3, 1809.

17. *Mercantile Advertiser*, January 2, 1801; printed in New York City daily (except Sundays) by John Crookes "for the proprietor." Page 1, columns 1–2 of page 2, and pages 3 and 4 were all advertising; the paper sold for $8 a year.

18. Ibid.

19. *American Mercury*, January 15, 1801; published in Hartford, Connecticut, on Thursdays by Elisha Babcock.

20. *Maryland Herald and Hagers-town Weekly Advertiser*, June 7, 1809; published in Hagerstown, Maryland, by Thomas Grieves.

21. Ibid.

22. Ibid., June 14, 1809.

23. Ibid.

24. Ibid., June 21, 1809.

25. Ibid.

26. Ibid., June 28, 1809.

27. Ibid.

28. Ibid., December 13, 1809.

29. *Hampshire Gazette*, January 7, 1801; reprinted from the *Pittsburgh Gazette*.

30. Ibid.

31. Advertising generally filled two and one-fourth pages in a four-page paper and four pages in an eight-page paper.

32. For example, one issue's editorials discussed the national political conventions (of the Whig party in Baltimore, the Free Soil party in Cleveland, and the Liberty party in Buffalo), considered Franklin Pierce's candidacy, and summarized Pierce's voting record in Congress; *Springfield* (Massachusetts) *Republican*, June 8, 1852. Editorials in an issue of another paper commented on a new book by Genet, the approaching national elections, and the contributions of science to civilization; *Boston Transcript*, February 2, 1858. Still another newspaper editorialized on a specific court case, taking occasion to evaluate critically a rival paper's coverage, and assessed the agenda of the impending congressional session; *New York Daily News*, November 19, 1852.

33. *Springfield Republican*, August 31, 1852; the *Boston Transcript*, April 8, 1858, had only four international items, only one of which (about revolution in Venezuela) constituted significant news; another consisted of two lines datelined Halifax, Nova Scotia; another, headed "Siberia," was commentary prompted by publication of a journal of seven years' travel abroad; the fourth announced a local exhibit of British art.

34. Linda Patterson Miller, "Poe on the Beat: 'Doings of Gotham' as Urban, Penny Press Journalism," *Journal of the Early Republic* 7 (Summer 1987), 164.

35. *New York Herald*, August 30, 1852, p. 1, col. 4.
36. Ibid., October 25, 1852, p. 1, col. 3.
37. *Boston Transcript*, October 25, 1852.
38. *New York Times*, September 30, 1852.
39. *New York Herald*, February 26, 1852.
40. *Philadelphia Evening Bulletin*, July 6, 1891.
41. Ibid., April 10, 1891.
42. Ibid.
43. Ibid.
44. *Cincinnati Post*, January 5, 1891.
45. Ibid.
46. Ibid., March 10, 1891.
47. St. Paul, Minnesota, *Daily Pioneer Press*, April 18, 1891.
48. Ibid.
49. Ibid., June 19, 1891.
50. *Philadelphia Evening Bulletin*, January 23, 1899.
51. *New York Sun*, April 20, 1899.
52. *Philadelphia Evening Bulletin*, January 23, 1899.
53. Ibid.
54. Ibid., April 14, 1899.
55. Ibid., January 23, 1899.
56. *Cincinnati Post*, January 5, March 10, July 16, 1891; *Daily Pioneer Press*, January 16, April 18, June 19, 1891; *New York Sun*, January 3, 1891.

Chapter 18

MICHAEL L. CARLEBACH

PAPER PRINTS FOR THE MASSES

The ability to publish and disseminate photographic views was both necessary and desired; it had to wait for the practical advent of paper photographs, printed from negatives, to allow for such dissemination.

ROBERT A. SOBIESZAK, *San Francisco in the 1850s*

THE PUBLICATION AND DISSEMINATION OF PHOTOGRAPHS was a goal of the men who invented and worked with the first processes, but in America the mass production of the camera's images was stalled by the early hegemony of the daguerreotype. "I have proposed to myself an important problem for the arts of design and engraving," Joseph Niepce, Daguerre's partner and inventor of the heliotype, wrote in a letter to the Royal Society in 1827.[1] His experiments were intended not just to find a method of preserving the images produced by the camera but also, and more important, to find a mechanical means of reproducing those images on the printed page.

In 1826, Niepce succeeded in producing a copy of an engraving of Georges d'Amboise, archbishop of Rouen whom Pope Alexander VI made a cardinal in 1499. For Beaumont Newhall, Niepce's heliograph of the good cardinal was momentous. "It was the first of those photomechanical techniques that was soon to revolutionize the graphic arts by eliminating the hand of man in the reproduction of pictures of all kinds." Niepce demonstrated the crucial link between photography and the mass production of the camera's images. It was his most important contribution, according to Newhall, "for it involved a principle that became basic to future techniques: the differential hardening by light of a ground that would control the etching in exact counterpart of the image."[2]

Daguerreotypes could be published, as we have seen, but it was never easy. They had first to be transformed by hand into engravings, etchings, or woodcuts. What photographers and publishers wanted was a method of mass producing and disseminating the camera's images that yielded a final product that looked photographic, a paper print that retained the original's details and delicate halftones. Talbot had invented such a process, but outside of England, calotypes were little used, since they could not effectively compete with daguerreotypes in terms of cost or delineation of detail. Throughout the history of printmaking, as historian William Crawford notes, the most successful processes have been those that present the most visual information at competitive prices. In the early days of photography the daguerreotype prevailed on both counts. The principle underlying Talbot's process, the unlimited production of identical positives from a single negative, however, was recognized as sound. What was needed in order to mass produce and disseminate photographs was a "process that combined the optical precision of the daguerreotype with the reproducibility of the calotype."[3]

By the late 1840s, dissatisfaction with Talbot's paper-negative process and with the continuing difficulty of copying daguerreotypes was widespread. The solution adopted by photographers was the use of glass as a base for the negative. As with the invention of photography itself, there is some dispute as to whose process takes precedence. Apparently, several inventors arrived at the solution at roughly the same time. The first to publish an alternative method was the nephew of Joseph Niepce, Claude-Félix-Abel Niepce de Saint-Victor. In 1848, he announced that glass plates coated with albumen and sensitized with salts of silver produced fine negatives that yielded clear and detailed prints.

John Adams Whipple, one of Boston's most prominent and successful photographers, was taken aback by Niepce de Saint-Victor's announcement, for he, too, had been experimenting with glass plate negatives and sensitized albumen emulsion. Whipple's process differed in several crucial aspects from that of his French counterpart, however, and in 1850 he was awarded a patent for the production of what he called crystalotypes. Whipple coated his glass plates with a mixture of albumen and pure, crystalline honey (thus the name). The plates were then sensitized in a solution of silver bromide. They could be used when either slightly damp or dry, though the exposure times increased significantly when the plates were completely dry.[4]

Whipple marketed his process aggressively, and by 1852 it was receiving rave reviews from American photographic publications. Samuel Humphrey complimented the inventor for three "very fine specimens of Photography on paper": a large view of Boston's new atheneum and two portraits. "We have seen many of the paper pictures taken on the other side of the Atlantic," Humphrey wrote, but "for richness in tone and . . . delineation we never have seen anything superior to these specimens before us."[5]

As increasing numbers of American photographers purchased the rights to Whipple's process (the price for a license was a relatively inexpensive fifty dollars, with another fifty thrown in for instructions, if desired), the usefulness of paper photography began to be appreciated. Suddenly, photographers were able to produce perfect copies of their work with little fuss and at low cost. "Hitherto the photographists of this country have confined themselves exclusively to the practice of their art upon the silvered plate," wrote an observer in 1852, "but, if we are to judge from the constantly increasing demand for photogenic paper and paper chemicals—it will not be long before photography on paper will be as extensively practiced as the daguerreian art."[6] This prediction appeared in Henry Hunt Snelling's *Photographic Art-Journal*, an early advocate of the new process. In December 1852, Snelling praised Marcus Root's crystalotypes of New York City. The new paper prints, he wrote, combined the "beauty of an actual painting with the unerring accuracy of the daguerreotype." Most important for Snelling was the production of a negative from which "hundreds of copies may be taken—thus in a measure rivalling the steel plate press."[7]

Horace Greeley's *New York Daily Tribune* was also enthusiastic about Whipple's process, though the editors had some reservations. The fact that a single negative could now be used to produce thousands of identical copies and the "rapidity and cheapness" of the process promised to "make it a popular method of illustration for books." But the actual prints still left something to be desired. In comparison to the crisp highlights and deep shadows of daguerreotypes, crystalotype portraits seemed curiously lacking in contrast, and landscapes were "without an atmosphere."[8] Within a year, this criticism of paper prints was obviated as photographers learned how to deepen the contrast, gloss, and brilliance of their prints.

The first paper prints were made by sensitizing ordinary writing paper in baths of silver nitrate. Since this process permitted the solution to be absorbed into the fibers of the paper, the final product was often flat and dull-looking. As a remedy, photographers and photographic suppliers began coating photographic paper before it was sensitized. The image thus remained more on the surface of the paper, enhancing both the contrast and luster of the final print.

The various albumen processes for making glass-plate negatives and prints were messy and required extremely delicate handling. The English photographer John Mayall noted the necessity of exercising "every precaution . . . to avoid dust." He also argued that the albumen collected from ducks' eggs was more suited to use in photography than that of hens, and that goose egg albumen was probably the best of all.[9] Problems of dust and albumen sensitivity notwithstanding, the switch to a negative-positive process revolutionized photography.

As if to demonstrate the applicability of his process to the world of publishing, Whipple supplied the prints used in *The Crystalotype World of Art*, published in a limited edition by George Putnam in 1854. The book was designed as a catalogue of several of the most impressive works of art at the New York world's fair of 1853, housed in an American version of London's spectacular Crystal Palace. Whipple's crystalotypes of sculptures, each carefully pasted onto a page, constitute the first significant use of photographs (as opposed to engravings or woodcuts of photographs) in a published book in America.

It was not, however, Putnam's original intention to use actual photographs in his book on the New York exhibition. Early in 1854, Putnam published his first guide to the wonders of the New York fair, entitled *The World of Science, Art, and Industry*, which was edited by Professor Benjamin Silliman and Charles Rush Goodrich. It included a great many engravings made under the supervision of C. E. Dopler from daguerreotypes made by H. Whittemore of the various exhibitions.[10] Later in the year Putnam saw Whipple's paper prints of the moon (they received a first-place award) and was clearly impressed with their potential to be used in the publishing industry. He reissued his original book on the Crystal Palace show with the addition of several of Whipple's crystalotypes.[11]

While Whipple was experimenting with albumen coatings on glass, others were working with a substance called collodion, a clear, viscous solution made by dissolving an explosive substance called guncotton in a solution of alcohol and ether. Collodion was destined to transform photography. By 1855, it had replaced all the albumen processes. Known familiarly as the "wet-plate process," collodion photography was used for some three decades to produce millions of negatives on glass or metal. Though volatile and extremely flammable, collodion poured onto glass plates formed an ideal base for light-sensitive silver salts.

Guncotton, or cellulose nitrate, is made by soaking natural cotton in a hot mixture of nitric and sulphuric acids. It was discovered in 1846 by Swiss and German chemists and was initially intended to be used in the military. Its extreme volatility made it far too dangerous and unmanageable, however. The British Board of Ordinance actually considered using guncotton in artillery shells, but because of its tendency to explode at lower temperatures than gunpowder, they abandoned the idea in 1847.[12] Later the same year, Flores Domonte and Louis Menard, a brilliant and eccentric chemist, painter, and philosopher, discovered the use of guncotton to make collodion.[13] For several years its main use was in medicine; applied to burns and abrasions, collodion forms a tough, leathery second skin.

In 1851, an English sculptor, Frederick Scott Archer, suggested in an article in the *Chemist* that collodion was far superior to albumen as a base for light-sensitive silver. To maximize the speed of exposure, both collodion and albumen were best used while slightly damp. But according to Archer, albumen-coated plates were virtually impossible to handle except when completely dry, whereas collodion "is admirably adapted for photographic purposes. . . . It presents a perfectly transparent and even surface when poured on glass, and being in some measure tough and elastic, will, when damp, bear handling in several stages of the operation."[14]

John Towler, author of *The Silver Sunbeam*, one of the first studies of photography published in America, wrote in 1864 that he found it "impossible to calculate the impetus given to photography by this discovery, or its value to society."[15] Archer refused to patent the wet-plate process, and photographers eagerly adopted his method of making glass-plate negatives. After the process was introduced in America in 1853, great strides were made "in many parts of [the] country in the making of guncotton for use in collodion," recalled S. Rush Seibert, a portrait photographer who worked for many years in Washington, D.C. The pristine daguerreotype was doomed. The wet-plate process "was immediately made a success," Seibert wrote, "and Daguerreotypes were laid aside in many establishments, although I continued to make them at intervals between 1840 and 1874."[16]

Gustave Le Gray, who pioneered the use of albumen plates in France, saw the proliferation of paper prints as a boon to education and a further argument for realism in art. "The popularity that daguerreotypes have obtained," he wrote in 1852, "will soon be surpassed by that of photographs on paper, and their great number scattered among the masses, will form an artistic taste and education, while art itself will no longer be permitted to deviate from the only true path, that of nature."[17] Le Gray's countryman, Gaston Tissandier, was just as enthusiastic. He saw the paper print as a means to broaden the distribution of photographs. "The printing processes of photography are destined to follow an ever-widening sphere," he predicted. "The permanent sun-print must be regarded as one of the greatest discoveries of modern science, fitted as it is to supply faithful impressions of almost anything that may be brought within the field of the astronomical telescope, the microscope, or the camera."[18]

Photographers used collodion almost exclusively from 1855 to the early 1880s, when the commercial production of dry plates again transformed the market. Collodion enabled photographers to make countless copies of their most important and sought-after pictures. Moreover, it made possible several new kinds of photographs: ambrotype, tintype (ferrotype), carte de visite, and stereograph. Sensitized and applied directly to the blocks of end-grain boxwood used in engraving, collodion was also discovered to be a boon to draftsmen. Photographs could be printed directly onto the wood blocks, forming perfect templates for engravers. Finally, collodion was portable. Photographers thought little of traveling long distances with their entire darkrooms packed into rugged backpacks or horse-drawn buggies.

Their methods now may seem hopelessly complicated and arcane, but the necessity of preparing, sensitizing, exposing, and developing each plate while the collodion base was still moist was actually considered an improvement over the baths of hot mercury used in the daguerreotype process. Collodion could be used on a variety of surfaces (wood, glass, and metal) and was easily adapted for use outside the studio or darkroom. Its tough, pliable nature made it possible for the photographer to peel the finished collodion negative from its glass support; it could then be rolled in blotter paper for easy storage and the glass plate used to make another negative. Thus, the photographer did not have to carry large numbers of heavy and fragile glass plates when working outside the studio.

George Mary Searle, an astronomer, Paulist priest, and "photographer of considerable skill,"[19] reminisced about the wet-plate process in an article published in *Anthony's Photographic Bulletin* in 1882. He did not recall the process with particular fondness, though it is clear that the collodion scenario he described was typical. What is important about his account is the emphasis on the portability of wet-plate photography. It may not have been easy to move about the countryside lugging one's entire darkroom, but it was commonly, even routinely done. "Perhaps a few years ago you may have met . . . an adherent of the old school, a wet-plate man," wrote Searle, "wheeling about or laboriously carrying on his back, besides his camera and plates, a small cart-load of fixtures of various kinds."

> When he arrives at a suitable spot for his view he has to set up his tent, and in the orange colored light which it gives prepare his plate and set it all dripping in the shield; then put it in the camera, which also he had to unpack and set up. If meanwhile the circumstances of light, etc., have not changed so much as to make the view of comparatively little value, he secures it; but then again he has to repair to his tent and develop his picture on the spot. Then carefully putting up his baths and bottles and replacing his heavy load, he has to trudge along again with it on his back, and so on through the day.[20]

Backpacking one's darkroom was not the only obstacle associated with collodion photography. From 1853 to 1855, before the photographic supply houses began marketing ready-to-use collodion, photographers had to make their own. Getting the guncotton just right without having it explode was never easy. "The making of soluble cotton . . . was attended with much difficulty and uncertainty," wrote photographer I. B. Webster in 1873, "and became a great stumbling block to the progress of the art. For three long years it was a sore trial and vexatious job." After 1855, though, firms in New York and Boston began stocking enough collodion to keep American photographers amply supplied.[21]

A more serious obstacle to the free use of the wet-plate process arose in 1854, when James Ambrose Cutting, a Boston-based photographer, inventor, and entrepreneur, applied for and was granted three patents relating to the use of collodion. One of them concerned a particular method of producing ambrotypes; the others, the process of sensitizing the coated plate. Cutting's patents nearly did to wet-plate photography in America what Talbot's patents did to calotypes.

Introduced in America in 1854, the ambrotype was described by some as a daguerreotype on glass. A slightly underexposed negative was made on glass plate by the collodion process. When the glass was coated with dark varnish or backed with black felt, cardboard, or even another plate of dark glass (called "ruby glass"), the negative appeared as a positive. Ambrotypes, like daguerreotypes, were unique, one-of-a-kind items, and were usually presented in filigreed gutta-percha or pressed-leather cases. They were almost always portraits, intended to be kept as personal mementoes, though some, of celebrities, were copied and printed as engravings in the illustrated journals. Cutting's ambrotype patent dealt with a particular method of cementing the glass plates together (he used balsam of fir). He was vigorous in protecting the patent and charged high fees for its use (one hundred dollars in towns of five thousand inhabitants), but other photographers easily circumvented the patent by using alternative methods of backing the glass negative.

Cutting's other patents were more problematic. On both sides of the Atlantic, photographers routinely mixed collodion with potassium bromide, which reacted with silver to form light-sensitive silver bromide. The process was widely used and unprotected by patent, at least until Cutting came along. There was nothing new or unusual in Cutting's request for a patent on the bromide process, but because of a dearth of documentary evidence of previous usage or invention, he was awarded all rights. Many photographers in America simply ignored it; others switched to potassium chloride as the sensitizing agent.[22] When Cutting began prosecuting those he suspected of infringing upon his patents, however, American photographers howled in protest. Charles A. Seeley, editor of the *American Journal of Photography*, spoke for many when he said that he was "adamantly opposed to patents restricting the freedom of photographers to ply their trade. . . . Nine tenths of the letters received by the *Journal* support the anti-patent stand." Both Seeley and Henry Hunt Snelling of the *Photographic and Fine Art Journal* encouraged their readers to ignore the ambrotype patent and stand united against the bromide patent.[23]

Encouraged by the photographic press, photographers fought Cutting's patents in the courts, and many, especially those far from the cities of the East, ignored it altogether. "That the so-called 'Cutting Patents' are a fraud upon the community throughout the United States, no one can doubt," commented Samuel Humphrey in April 1860. He went on to enumerate the various methods used by American photographers to resist the patents.[24] The bromide patent was finally voided in 1868, though by that time few photographers in America paid any attention to it. Cutting had died, quite mad, a year earlier in an asylum in Worcester, Massachusetts.

One other patent was associated with the collodion process, but it had none of the stultifying effects of those of Cutting. In early 1856, Hamilton Lamphere Smith, a Yale-educated professor of natural philosophy and astronomy at Kenyon College in Gambier, Ohio, patented the ferrotype method of making pictures. Like the daguerreotype and ambrotype, the ferrotype, or tintype as it was commonly called, was a one-of-a-kind process in which a positive image was produced with no intervening negative. In Smith's process, a thin sheet of blackened, japanned iron was coated with collodion, sensitized, exposed, and developed. As in the ambrotype, the light areas of the subject contained the most silver on the plate and thus appeared light, while the dark and shadow areas were virtually transparent and thus revealed the blackened metal underneath the collodion.

Smith assigned his patent to his friend and colleague at Kenyon, Peter Neff, and his father, William Neff, in return for their assistance in his early experiments.[25] The charge for using the tintype process was only twenty dollars. Since the materials were inexpensive and easy to use, tintypes became enormously popular and were still being produced long after dry plates were introduced in the 1880s.[26]

The impact of tintypes and ambrotypes upon the press was slight. They were the staple of small town and village studios that specialized in recording the faces of the citizenry. Photographers interested in making pictures for wider distribution turned to one of the negative-positive processes that used collodion. Now for the first time it was possible for photographers to build libraries of negatives that could be used to produce countless positive copies. They could vary print size and style according to the wishes and budgets of clients, and they could supply newspapers, magazines, and book publishers with low-cost paper prints. "That the delicate and fading images of the camera obscura should be permanently secured upon plates and metal and glass, and on paper, was, at one time beyond the dreams of science," wrote an enthusiast in 1855. "What, then, may we not expect from photography with the advent of science?"[27]

Developed by Sir David Brewster and Charles Wheatstone in England in the late 1830s, the stereograph added the illusion of a third dimension to the photograph. Two views of the same object, taken with a camera with lenses separated by a few inches, were mounted side-by-side on rectangular cardboard measuring approximately 3½ by 7 inches and were viewed in a device called a stereoscope that allowed the left eye to see only the left-hand image, and the right eye to see only the one on the right. As in normal binocular vision, the effect was to create the feeling of depth. The added third dimension, although illusory, enhanced the realism of the picture.

The principle of stereoscopy was known but little practiced during the daguerreian period, from 1839 to 1849, primarily because the highly polished, mirrored surface of daguerreotypes was difficult enough to see singly, let alone doubled up and placed in a viewing device.[28] The Langenheim brothers in Philadelphia, who always seemed to be at the forefront of photographic technology, did produce stereographs from daguerreotypes, mostly of travel scenes, and they were well received by the press. "When they are looked at in a couple of reflectors properly arranged," wrote an observer in 1852, "the scene itself seems visible in bold relief." The stereo effect was especially noteworthy in a view by Frederick Langenheim made on the banks of the river Volga. In the twin images, one could see and "inspect the piles and works of a great unfinished bridge, forming a track partly across the tide from bank to bank, every post as round and real as though the river . . . and the great work there in progress had been modelled by the fairies."[29]

In 1850, Brewster took his stereo instruments with him to London, where they were exhibited at the Crystal Palace exhibition. They attracted the attention of the public and also of Queen Victoria, who enthusiastically approved of the new process. When Archer introduced his collodion negatives in 1851, the success of stereos was assured. Paper prints, mounted side by side on cardboard, were easy and inexpensive to produce and could be viewed without straining to find just the right angle of light. Most important, they could be multiplied at will and mass marketed by either individual photographers or publishers. By 1860, they were the most popular and widely used method of transmitting visual information. More than two hundred photographers in America were producing stereos on the eve of the Civil War, and the Anthony brothers in New York City reported that during 1861 they sold several hundred thousand cards.[30]

Prior to 1861, stereo viewers were ornate and bulky affairs in the form of consoles or large boxes with eyepieces attached to one side and a slot for stereo cards on the opposite. Oliver Wendell Holmes changed all that, however. In 1861, he introduced a new, compact, and easily operated viewer. Holmes was an avid admirer of photography in general and stereoscopy in particular; his viewer, known everywhere as the American, or Holmes, stereoscope, was lightweight and completely portable. "I believed that it would add much to the comfort and pleasure of the lover of stereoscopic pictures," he wrote. "I believed also that money could be made of it. But considering it was a quasi scientific improvement, I wished no pecuniary profit from it, and refused to make any arrangement by which I should be a gainer."[31]

The development of small, lightweight stereo cameras, with lenses placed two and one-half inches apart, soon obviated the tiresome necessity of making two separate exposures with a camera that was carefully moved to the right or left after the initial exposure. Now both exposures were made at once and on a single glass plate that when developed and dried could be used to produce thousands of paper positives. The twin-lensed stereo camera was designed to produce a picture that could be mass produced and distributed to the public. In the latter half of the nineteenth century, when a photographer intended to make pictures to sell to the public—pictures of events or scenes or persons in the news—the instrument of choice was usually the stereo camera.

For those already impressed with the descriptive detail contained in daguerreotypes, the added third dimension of stereographs seemed almost miraculous. The stereo photographer possessed a power "mightier than kings," wrote Edward L. Wilson, editor of the *Philadelphia Photographer*, who was not, admittedly, an entirely objective source. Still, his enthusiasm for stereo cards was hardly atypical; they seemed to many Americans to be the ultimate in realistic art and reporting. Apparently nothing could compete with the accuracy of stereos, not "the countless published pages of the naturalists of the world, the numberless books of travel, nor the eloquence of Agassiz."[32] Holmes spoke of the beginning of a "new epoch in the history of human progress," opened by a product that possessed "an appearance of reality which cheats the senses with its seeming truth."[33]

For fully half a century, the stereograph was the most popular and common form of photograph. Scarcely a middle-class parlor existed in America that did not contain at least one stereoscope and a collection of views, purchased at a local bookseller's or at one of the many stereo emporiums that catered to the growing audience for photographs. "It is wonderful what becomes of countless stereoscopes that are made during a year," wrote the Anthonys in 1870. "Pile upon pile, dozen after dozen, gross after gross" were supplied, yet still the demand was unsatisfied. No matter how fast they were turned out, stereoscopes and stereo cards were "swallowed up in the vortex of popular consumption."[34]

A companion to the stereo view was the carte de visite, a small print on paper measuring roughly 2½ by 4 inches, the approximate size of a visiting card. André Adolphe Eugène Disdéri, the official court photographer of Napoléon III, introduced cartes de visite in Paris in November 1854, and they spread quickly to England and America. By 1860, cartes were by far the most popular format for the portrait photograph, far eclipsing the ambrotype and daguerreotype.

Their cheapness and the ease with which they were produced (four, six, or even eight separate views were made on a single glass negative that was then contact printed onto paper) made them, according to John Werge, "a more republican form of photography," a fact he found ironic considering their origin in an "empire not remarkable for freedom of thought." Since cartes de visite were inexpensive, and because of "their convenient size and prettiness of form," they were an immediate sensation.[35] Some referred to the public's response as "cardomania."

"The kind of pictures mostly in demand at the large galleries," reported Samuel Humphrey in 1861, "is the Carte de Visite." He reported that in New York City many galleries had begun copying the painted and engraved likenesses of deceased persons into photographs, "as the times [had] not yet had any tendency to take away that deep affection which holds the memory of one friend to another."[36] One could purchase, for instance, card photographs of George Washington, Ben Franklin, and other heroes of the Republic.

Because they were made from glass negatives, card photographs of celebrities and other persons in the news were printed by the thousands and sold to a public eager to see and own likenesses of the rich and famous. "No picture," wrote John Towler in 1864, "has ever had so wide a sphere of action, has gratified taste so long, or has been as productive of gain to the photographer as the card picture. It is the picture of the day," he added, "and has tended considerably to simplify the photographic establishment."[37] Cards were often collected and displayed in special albums that held from fifty to one hundred images. Most often, as historian William Culp Darrah notes, card photographs were grouped in albums according to subject matter. Family albums were the most common, as one would expect, but others contained portraits of celebrities, of scenics and travel scenes, and of news events. In 1862, for example, the Anthony brothers began marketing albums of cartes de visite of Civil War scenes produced by Brady's teams of photographers.[38]

In his manual on card pictures and stereographs, published in 1862, Nathan Burgess suggested that the carte de visite was a natural outgrowth of the stereo phenomenon. Approximately the size of half a stereo picture, cartes "are in reality stereographs, only not viewed in pairs," he wrote.[39] Indeed, photographers began to print their photographs in various formats, depending on the wishes of their clientele. Stereo negatives could be made into card photographs or enlarged into display prints. The various collodion processes gave photographers the option to make a variety of print types from the same negative without losing any of the sharpness or brilliance of the original. The same negative might create a stereo card, a carte de visite, an "imperial" enlargement, and the positive template for an engraving in one of the weekly illustrated magazines.

Late in 1866, a larger version of the carte de visite, the cabinet card, was introduced in America. Measuring approximately 4½ by 6½ inches, the new print size gradually supplanted the carte de visite, the public no doubt responding to the cabinet's larger picture area and more substantial mount-board backing. Still, it was not until the late 1870s that cabinet cards began to predominate; today, it is rare to find cabinets made prior to 1876.[40]

Photographs made of Abraham Lincoln during his campaign for the presidency in 1859 and 1860 were produced in a wide variety of sizes and styles and disseminated by the Republican party as well as by individual photographers and publishers. The now famous Cooper Union portrait of Lincoln, made on February 27, 1859, by Mathew Brady on a single large glass plate, was copied and printed in carte-de-visite size and sold to the public by the thousands. Brady also supplied prints to *Harper's Illustrated Weekly* and *Frank Leslie's Illustrated Newspaper,* both of which published the print as a wood engraving. In each case the engraver made significant changes in Brady's original, though each image was captioned as a photograph.[41] Clearly, once a photograph was in the hands of an engraver or draftsman, there was no guarantee that the finished product would be a perfect match of the original. The only way to assure accuracy was to make paper copies from the original negative.

The Chicago photographer Alexander Hesler did precisely that in June 1860. He journeyed to Springfield, Illinois, where he made four separate views of the Republican nominee, over a hundred thousand copies of which were distributed during the course of the campaign, many in the form of campaign badges.[42] Hesler had photographed Lincoln once before, in February 1857. That first sitting produced a side-view portrait of Lincoln, beardless and tousle-haired, that delighted editorial cartoonists in the East. The new portraits, especially Brady's Cooper Union image, depicted Lincoln as thoughtful, serious, perhaps even presidential. It was the new set of pictures that was used by the Republicans in 1860, the first time photographs were extensively used in a campaign for the White House.[43]

Lincoln pictures were everywhere. Silas Hawley, an agent for an original crayon portrait of the Republican nominee, wrote to a friend that "the country is flooded with the pictures of Lincoln, in all conceivable shapes and sizes, and *cheap*. The newspapers have his likeness; it is in the medal form; it is on envelopes; it is on badges; it is on cards; it is, indeed, on everything, and everywhere. And all for a *few cents!*"[44] It was becoming much harder for artists to compete with photographers who could now mass produce accurate pictures on paper cheaply and quickly. Photography was fast becoming the dominant graphic art.

By 1860, photographic coverage of major news events was becoming common-place. City fires and train wrecks often attracted the attention of photographers who produced pictures in stereo and carte-de-visite size for mass distribution and enlarged prints from which engravings could be made. It was still rare for ongoing events to be captured on glass plate, but increasingly, photographers made and distributed pictures that showed the blackened husks of buildings after fires or the smashed and twisted remains of train wrecks. And photographers regarded people in the news for whatever reason as fair game; celebrity portraits were always best-sellers.

"Photography is now the historian of earth and animated nature, the biographer of man," wrote British historian John Werge in 1890. The proliferation of photographs on paper had seen to that.[45] Albert Southworth, the partner of Josiah Hawes in Boston and one of the most highly regarded photographers in America, spoke of the early history of photography in America in an address delivered to the National Photographic Association in 1871. "In thirty years," he said, "from a few crude experiments in the laboratory of a private chemist and artist, [photography] has extended its various applications and uses throughout the length and breadth of . . . our globe."[46]

When in 1860 the Prince of Wales came to America, photographers recorded the entire grand tour. Stereos and card pictures of the prince flooded the market; Americans in 1860 seemed every bit as enthralled by England's royal family as they are today. The nation temporarily put aside talk of disunion and war, and united in a collective spasm of royalty worship. Photographs of Victoria's son and heir making his way with appropriate pomp and circumstance about the former colonies were a lovely little diversion from the looming storm clouds of war. It was a news event with enormous popular appeal, and American photographers took every advantage of it, armed as they were with the new paper processes. None was more alert to the possibilities than Mathew Brady.

On the morning of the thirteenth of October 1860, the prince summoned Brady to his rooms at the Fifth Avenue Hotel and conferred upon him the high honor of making his semiofficial American portrait. When Brady asked why the prince had chosen him above all the others, he is said to have replied, "Are you not *the* Mr. Brady, who earned the prize nine years ago in London? You owe it to yourself. We had your place of business down in our notebooks before we started."[47] Edward's gracious response may be apocryphal; Brady did occasionally embellish the truth. Yet the fact is that the prince and his retinue did visit the Brady studio and sit for several portraits and group shots. Even more important, Brady made the pictures available to the public in a variety of sizes and styles, and sold copies to the illustrated journals. He may not have been the best photographer of his day, but more than any of his peers he understood how photographs could be mass marketed. "I think Brady stands at the head as to prominence," said Ohio photographer James Ryder to his assistant. "He has taken portraits of more public and prominent people than any of his rivals. Presidents, senators, governors, congressmen, ambassadors, statesmen of all degrees, notables of all countries have sat [for] him."[48]

It is the public dimension of photography that seems to have motivated Mathew Brady, making him the first photographer in America to take full and complete advantage of the journalistic uses of photographs. It is not surprising that when war finally came in the spring of 1861, he was the first to see it as an opportunity to make and sell pictures on a vast scale.

Notes

1. Joseph-Nicéphore Niepce to the Royal Society, London, December 8, 1827, reprinted in the *Literary Gazette*, no. 1154 (March 2, 1839), 138.
2. Newhall, *Photography and the Book*, 111–15.
3. William Crawford, *The Keepers of Light: A History and Working Guide to Early Photographic Processes* (Dobbs Ferry, N.Y.: Morgan and Morgan, 1979), 41.
4. Charles Ehrmann, "Whipple's Crystallotypes," paper presented to the Photographic Section of the American Institute, April 7, 1885, printed in *Anthony's Photographic Bulletin* 16, no. 8 (April 25, 1885): 247–8.
5. "Crystolotype," *Humphrey's Journal* 4, no. 5 (June 15, 1852): 75. Humphrey, like many others, had trouble with the spelling of Whipple's process. In December 1852, Humphrey again praised Whipple's crystalotypes, this time correctly. *Humphrey's Journal* 4, no. 17 (December 15, 1852): 269.
6. *Photographic Art-Journal* 4, no. 5 (November 1852): 317.
7. "A New and Important Invention," *Photographic Art-Journal* 4, no. 6 (December 1852): 380.
8. "Photography in the United States," *New York Daily Graphic*, April 29, 1853, 7.
9. Cited by Robert Hunt, *Photography: A Treatise on the Chemical Changes . . . and Other Photographic Processes* (New York: S. D. Humphrey, 1852), 98.
10. B. Silliman, Jr., and C. R. Goodrich, eds., *The World of Science, Art, and Industry Illustrated from Examples in the New York Exhibition, 1853–1854* (New York: G. P. Putnam, 1854). Whittemore was well-known for his daguerreotype views of South America and the Caribbean. Shortly after producing the images for this book, he sold his New York City gallery. Nothing is known of his subsequent activities.
11. "The Crystalotype," *Putnam's Monthly* 5, no. 27 (March 1855): 335.
12. "Gun Cotton," *Dwight's American Magazine* 3, no. 7 (February 1847): 109. Many Americans, among them Fitzhugh Lee, the ambassador to Cuba, were convinced that the battleship *Maine* was blown up in 1898 by a crude mine consisting of a barrel of some sort stuffed with guncotton. See Joyce Milton, *The Yellow Kids* (New York: Harper Perennial, 1990), 231.

13.   Josef Maria Eder, *History of Photography*, 4th ed., trans. Edward Epstean (New York: Columbia University Press, 1945; Dover Publications, 1972), 342–3. See also C. F. Chandler, "Photography: A History of Its Origins and Progress," *Anthony's Photographic Bulletin 15*, no. 3 (February 14, 1885): 65.

14.   Frederick Scott Archer, "On the Use of Collodion in Photography," *Chemist* 2 (March 1851): 257.

15.   John Towler, *The Silver Sunbeam* (New York: J. H. Ladd, 1864), 17.

16.   S. Rush Seibert to Samuel C. Busey, October 19, 1896, cited in Samuel C. Busey, "Early History of Photography in the City of Washington," *Columbia Historical Society Records*, 3 (1900): 93.

17.   Gustave Le Gray, "Photography on Paper and Glass," *Humphrey's Journal* 4, no. 3 (May 15, 1852): 33.

18.   Tissandier, *History and Handbook of Photography*, 22.

19.   *Appleton's Cyclopaedia of American Biography* (New York: D. Appleton, 1888), 5: 447.

20.   Rev. George Mary Searle, "Every Man His Own Photographer; or, the Recent Invention of Gelatin Dry Plates," *Anthony's Photographic Bulletin* 13 (April 1882): 114.

21.   I. B. Webster, "Photographic Mincemeat," *Philadelphia Photographer* 10, no. 3 (March 1873): 73.

22.   New York photographer J. J. Clark's method of substituting chlorine for bromide in collodion was described in the *American Journal of Photography and the Allied Arts and Sciences* 8, no. 13 (January 1, 1866): 312.

23.   "Letters on the Bromide Patents," *American Journal of Photography and the Allied Arts and Sciences* 1, no. 19 (March 1, 1859): 298; *Photographic and Fine Art Journal* 8 (August 1855): 255–56.

24.   [Samuel Humphrey], "Resistance to Cutting Patents," *Humphrey's Journal* 11, no. 23 (April 1, 1860): 356.

25.   "List of Patent Claims," *Scientific American* 11, no. 25 (March 1, 1856): 194.

26.   Peter E. Palmquist, "A Portfolio: The Ubiquitous Western Tintype," *Journal of the West* 28, no. 1 (January 1989): 89–108.

27.   "The Chemical Power of the Sunbeam," 237.

28.   "3-D Daguerreotypes in America," *Image 3*, no. 1 (January 1954): 2–3.

29.   "The Stereoscope," *Graham's Magazine* 43, no. 5 (November 1853): 538.

30.   Peter Palmquist, *Lawrence and Houseworth/Thomas Houseworth and Co.: A Unique View of the West, 1860–1886* (Columbus, Ohio: National Stereographic Association, 1980), 6–7.

31.   Oliver Wendell Holmes, "History of the 'American Stereoscope,' " *Philadelphia Photographer* 6, no. 61 (January 1869): 2.

32.   "Kohl's Regulation Stereoscope," *Philadelphia Photographer 3* (November 1866): 370.

33.   Holmes, "The Stereoscope and the Stereograph," 748, 742.

34.   *Anthony's Photographic Bulletin* 1 (November 1870): 208.

35.   Werge, *Evolution of Photography*, 193.

36.   "The State of the Art in the City of New York," *Humphrey's Journal* 12, no. 21 (March 1, 1861): 324.

37.   Towler, *Silver Sunbeam*, 218.

38.   William Culp Darrah, *Cartes de Visite in Nineteenth-Century Photography* (Gettysburg, Penn.: W. C. Darrah, 1981), 9, 81.

39.   N.G. Burgess, *The Photograph Manual*, 19.

40.   Darrah, *Cartes de Visite*, 10.

41.   The Cooper Union portrait was published again in E. G. Squier, ed., *Frank Leslie's Pictorial History of the Civil War* (New York: Frank Leslie, 1862), i:ix. In the book version, the background of the original is completely altered. The scene was transposed to an interior room of the White House and the caption reads, "Abraham Lincoln, President of the United States." No credit is given to the engraver or, for that matter, to Brady.

42.   William Welling, *Photography in America: The Formative Years, 1839–1900* (New York: Thomas Y. Crowell, 1978), 143.

43.   W. Fletcher Thompson, *The Image of War: The Political Reporting of the American Civil War* (New York: Thomas Yoseloff, 1960), 166. See also Frederick Hill Meserve and Carl Sandberg, *The Photographs of Abraham Lincoln* (New York: Harcourt, Brace and Co., 1944), 30–45.

44. Silas Hawley to George W. Nichols, October 30, 1860, cited by Harold Holzer, Gabor S. Boritt and Mark E. Neely, Jr., *The Lincoln Image: Abraham Lincoln and the Popular Print* (New York: Charles Scribner's Sons, 1984), 67. See also Earl Schenck Miers, ed., *Lincoln Day by Day: A Chronology, 1809–1865* (Washington, D.C.: Lincoln Sesquicentennial Commission, 1960), 2:283.
45. Werge, *Evolution of Photography*, 192.
46. Southworth, "Early History of Photography in the United States," 532.
47. Cited by Roy Meredith, *Mr. Lincoln's Camera Man: Mathew B. Brady*, 2d rev. ed. (New York: Dover Publications, 1974), 62.
48. Ryder, *Voightländer and I*, 112, 114.

Chapter 19

GERALD J. BALDASTY

AMERICAN POLITICAL PARTIES
AND THE PRESS

IN THE EARLY 1830s, MEMBERS OF THE Antimasonic party in Plymouth, Massachusetts, spent nearly two years trying to start a newspaper to promote their party and candidates. Few in number and lacking major financial resources, they struggled to raise enough money to buy a press and type, ensure 200 subscribers, and find a competent printer-editor who shared their views. Several times, they almost gave up. They persevered because a newspaper was the key to reaching voters and ultimately to winning elections. The appearance of *We The People and Old Colony Gazette*, just two weeks before the 1832 election, was a major organizational victory for the Antimasons. It enabled them to compete with other parties for voters.[1]

Such an ordeal in starting a newspaper was perhaps unusual in the Jacksonian era, when newspapers often seemed to spring up overnight to espouse political causes. Nonetheless, the Plymouth experience demonstrates the intimate relationship between party and press in the late 1820s and 1830s. American political parties saw the press as a vehicle to inform, propagandize, and exhort voters. William Henry Seward, one of the organizers of the Antimasonic party in the late 1820s, said that the press was the *only* channel to the people; without it, a party "never can gain the public favor."[2]

Jacksonian Era Politics and Press

The close relationship between party and press wasn't new in the 1820s. The two had supported one another since the early days of the American Revolution. The relationship became more emphatic and extensive, however, in the 1820s and 1830s, when growing interest in presidential elections and changes in the political process dramatically increased voter participation.

After 1800, presidential politics had lapsed into somnolence, because presidents chose their successors and the congressional caucus rubber-stamped that choice. In 1824, however, the incumbent James Monroe refused to anoint a successor, and the ensuing factionalism discredited the caucus. In the first major battle for the presidency in a generation, no one obtained a majority of the electoral college votes, pushing the election into the House of Representatives. Amid charges, countercharges, and histrionics, the House elected John Quincy Adams, the runner-up in the popular vote, prompting charges of corruption by the supporters of Andrew Jackson, who led the popular vote.[3]

The result, other than mutual recrimination, was the formation of national political organizations to contest the *next* presidential election. No sooner had the House voted than the next campaign began. The Jacksonians pioneered in this organizational work.

The growth of national political activity paralleled several changes in politics at the state level. The number of statewide (as opposed to county) elections dramatically increased. Earlier in the century, voters elected only state legislators, who in turn elected governors and other state officials. In 1800, presidential electors were subject to statewide popular vote in just two states; by 1832, all but South Carolina had adopted the popular vote for the position of presidential elector.[4] Consequently, state political party organizations came into being in the late 1820s and early 1830s to nominate candidates and organize campaigns in statewide elections.[5]

More candidates were elected, rather than appointed, to office by the 1820s and 1830s. State constitutional revisions in the 1820s and the 1830s made many county-level positions, such as sheriff and clerk, subject to popular vote. Thus the populace elected more officials, while parties faced a greater task of recruiting, nominating, and supporting candidates.[6]

There were more people voting in the Jacksonian era. The population grew rapidly, doubling every 20 years. Suffrage requirements loosened by the 1820s, so that all adult white males could vote.[7] By 1826, 21 of the 24 states had adult white male suffrage or small poll taxes that were tantamount to adult white suffrage. Voter participation grew nationwide throughout the 1820s, rising from 9 percent of adult white males in 1820 to 57 percent by 1828.[8]

A ban on self-promotion by candidates made political organization all the more difficult. The era of stump speeches, press conferences, and public debates among candidates had not yet arrived. Tradition dictated a disinterested approach. As Robert V. Remini notes, the "accepted decorum of presidential candidates" was to keep "aloof from the campaign." When Andrew Jackson attended a party barbecue in Lexington, Kentucky, the Washington, D.C., *National Intelligencer* commented, "We do not recollect before to have heard of the President of the United States descending into the political arena."[9] One newspaper writer said that presidential candidates ". . . ought not to say one word on the subject of the election. Washington, Jefferson and Madison were as silent as the grave when they were before the American people for this office."[10] Even on the state and county level, candidates generally were expected to refrain from self-promotion.

Americans simply distrusted the man who grasped for office. The ideal official was one who answered the call to office by those who knew him best—his neighbors. Self-promotion meant that a candidate lacked the fame or support that came from his own qualifications. One Jacksonian condemned the "lust for office," calling it "a crying evil." He argued that "place should be sought by no man, and it is tolerable and honorable only when we are called to it by the unsolicited suffrages and spontaneous preferences of the people and their representatives."[11]

Voters at political rallies in Nash and Beaufort counties, North Carolina, vowed that they would not support any candidate who stooped to electioneering.[12] When one congressional candidate in Massachusetts wrote an anonymous essay on his own behalf, self-promotion became a major campaign issue once his authorship was disclosed. Opponents dredged up that indiscretion for at least a decade.[13] One of his critics noted that "New Englanders hold no fellowship with 'stump orators' and do not like to hear a man sound his own Trumpet or sing his own praise."[14] A Pennsylvania editor sought biographical information from a gubernatorial candidate in the early 1820s but promised he would never divulge the source lest the candidate appear to be campaigning for himself.[15]

This style of electioneering worked only when electoral units were small (e.g., township or county) and voters knew the candidates personally. But the structural changes in politics in the 1820s upended this quaint local system. The ban on self-promotion quieted candidates, but it left all organizational tasks—recruitment, nomination, and campaigning—to the parties.

In most states, a state central committee and a network of county committees carried on this organizational work. These committees wooed voters with conventions, campaign songs, parades, and barbecues. The 1840 William Henry Harrison Log Cabin campaign is the most vivid example of such spectacles.[16]

The single most important link between party and electorate, however, was the partisan newspaper.[17] Newspapers *alone* were not sufficient; even the best newspaper could not sell a poor candidate. But political newspapers, as a link between party and electorate, were vital. They helped the party mobilize voters and were an extremely efficient way to reach a dispersed rural population. Political parties did not have a paid staff to send out to court voters, and even if they had, travel was difficult and slow. Farmers, laborers, merchants, and other voters simply could not attend many party meetings or rallies. But the newspaper took the party's views, arguments, and candidates to them. Newspapers circulated widely not just to individual subscribers but also to taverns and crossroads stores, so they were accessible to non-subscribers, too.[18] Some newspapers and towns established reading rooms so that the public could peruse papers from around the country.[19]

Parties also valued newspapers because they weren't as ephemeral as rallies and speeches. Newspaper essays could be read, discussed, and debated a week, a month, or more after publication. And people read these papers. Tocqueville noted Americans' near-addiction to newspapers. Russel B. Nye wrote of the "compulsive reading habits" of nineteenth-century citizens. "Addicted" to print, Americans had a higher literacy rate (90 percent among whites) than England or the Continent.[20]

The regular publication schedule of most newspapers—daily in metropolitan areas and many state capitals, weekly elsewhere—meant that a party could constantly reiterate its views and support its candidates. Newspapers also provided the foundation for a national political network particularly as the number of newspapers grew (to 1,200 in 1833)[21] and as postal laws encouraged the free exchange of newspapers among editors throughout the country. This free-exchange system facilitated the circulation of newspapers throughout the nation, providing knowledge about partisan allies and an infusion of propaganda and enthusiasm.[22] The most widely circulated newspapers of the 1820s and 1830s were those in Washington, D.C., but other newspapers, such as the *Albany Argus* (New York), circulated throughout the country.[23]

For readers, the political newspaper served as a reliable source of party news and views. Editors frequently were part of a party's hierarchy (e.g., a member of a county central committee) and could speak for the party. Francis Preston Blair and the Washington, D.C., *Globe* represented the national Jacksonians in the early 1830s. The *Albany Argus* was the voice of Martin Van Buren's political machine (the Regency), while the *Albany Evening Journal* represented Thurlow Weed and the New York Antimasonic party. In metropolitan areas, editors such as Henry Laurens Pinckney of the *Charleston Mercury* and Charles Gordon Greene of the *Boston Morning Post* served as spokesmen for their parties.[24] This pattern is repeated again and again, both in capital cities and in smaller towns.

Newspapers were ideal for organizing grass-roots political support, particularly for new political parties or groups supporting a certain candidate or program. The Antimasons, a third-party movement in the late 1820s and early 1830s, relied extensively on the press simply because they had few other means of reaching the public. The first New York State Antimasonic convention, in 1829, concluded with a report that stressed: "Free presses constitute the means upon which the country must rely to uproot and overthrow Free Masonry. They enlighten and stimulate public opinion."[25]

Many believed that newspapers really could sway voters. One Antimasonic editor in upstate New York refused to give up the fight in the early 1830s, even after his party had lost several key elections. "Constant dropping will wear away stones," he told his brother. "A perpetual exhibition before the public eye" and "the constantly repeated exposition" of Antimasonry's goals and policies "will eventually succeed in winning over the people."[26] Others believed in the efficacy of political newspapers. James Gordon Bennett wrote in his diary, "It only requires a circulation of newspapers in the West to kill anti-masonry . . ."[27] When John C. Calhoun broke with President Jackson, he believed he would be publicly vindicated through the press. "Let the press direct the public indignation against the continuance of this profligate intrigue," he told one ally.[28] When President Jackson opposed the rechartering of the Second Bank of the United States, the bank's president, Nicholas Biddle, turned to a press propaganda campaign to win public support for his bank. Biddle believed that a "direct appeal to the reason of the country" could "resist the pressure of the authority of great names and the force of party discipline" and thus restore public confidence in the bank.[29] That appeal would be through the press—"the channel of communication between the Bank and the country."[30]

The political profile of the press varied from place to place and from newspaper to newspaper. Politics was most clearly the mission of the press in Washington, D.C., and in state capitals, where newspapers served as the flagships for their state party organizations. In the small cities and towns, partisan newspapers flourished as part of county-wide political organizations.

In metropolitan areas, however, papers were concerned with both politics, which accounted for about half of their content,[31] and business, which accounted for about a quarter of their content.[32] They also had substantially more advertising than did their non-metropolitan counterparts.[33]

Even with this relative emphasis on business, many metropolitan newspapers were still highly partisan.[34] The *Boston Morning Post*, the *Boston Daily Advertiser*, and the *Charleston Mercury*, were clearly recognized as party organs. Other newspapers, such as the New York *Courier and Enquirer* or the *Charleston Courier*, had close ties to political parties but were relatively independent of party control.[35] And still others were less partisan. The *Savannah Republican* or the *New York Journal of Commerce* regularly took political positions but devoted themselves primarily to business.

(Metropolitan newspapers represented only a small portion of United States journalism in the 1820s and 1830s. According to the 1830 census, only 8.8 percent of the nation's population lived in "urban" areas [i.e., with a population of 2,500 or more].[36] Only 4.1 percent of the population lived in cities with a population of 25,000 or more.[37] Most of the population—and most of the political newspapers—were outside metropolitan areas.)

Establishing and Maintaining Party Presses

Because newspapers were so vital to party success in the Jacksonian era, politicians worked hard to establish and maintain, primarily through subsidies, reliable party organs in every hamlet, town, or city of the nation.

Establishing Newspapers

Party organization in the Jacksonian era usually began with the formation of a central committee to coordinate party activities. The next task was to establish political newspapers.

The Jacksonian coalition provided the model in newspaper establishment. Shut out of the presidency in 1824–25, the Jacksonians turned to establishing newspapers to contest the 1828 election. Robert Remini contends that "perhaps the single most important accomplishment" of Jackson's allies in Congress in the middle 1820s was the "creation of a vast, nationwide newspaper system."[38]

The most important newspaper for the Jackson campaign was the *U.S. Telegraph* in Washington, D.C., established in 1826 to lead the fight against the administration.[39] Jackson's friends arranged for a loan for Duff Green, the editor who took over the paper in 1826.[40] During the 1828 campaign, Green issued a special paper (an extra), circulating 40,000 issues weekly throughout the country in the months before the election.

Even after Jackson's victory in 1828, party activists established newspapers while new party battles emerged and party lines were redrawn. In 1832, Jacksonians established the *Carolina Watchman* in Salisbury, North Carolina, to counteract the shift of the other Salisbury newspaper from supporting Jackson to supporting John C. Calhoun.[41] In the early 1830s, new Jackson papers appeared in Milton, Roanoke, and Elizabeth City, North Carolina; Peterson and Trenton, New Jersey; Logansport, Indiana; Springfield, Illinois; Lebanon, Ohio; Worcester, Massachusetts; Norfolk, Virginia; and Juniata, Harrisburg, Pittsburgh, Philadelphia, and Lancaster, Pennsylvania.[42]

Among Jackson's opponents, the Antimasons were the most active in the establishment of political newspapers in the late 1820s and early 1830s. The Antimasons had no choice but to establish newspapers. Most older party papers spurned the Antimasons. The older party organizations included many Masons; consequently their newspapers refused to deal sympathetically with Antimasonic principles or policies. In 1826, only two or three newspapers in New York State championed the Antimasonic cause. By the end of 1827, the Antimasonic party had 22 papers in New York; by 1832 they had 70.[43] By 1832, Antimasons had established 32 newspapers in Pennsylvania, 5 in Massachusetts, and 1 each in Vermont and New Hampshire.[44] The party also tried to establish a newspaper in Washington, D.C., that year to support its first (and last) presidential candidate, William Wirt. Both the candidate and the project failed.[45]

In the South, particularly in South Carolina, political activists established newspapers as part of the fight over state rights in the 1820s and 1830s. Extreme state rightists established the Charleston *State Rights and Free Trade Evening Post* in 1829 to counteract the more moderate political agenda of the older, established Charleston papers.[46] Outside Charleston, extreme state rightists helped establish newspapers in Greenville (the *Sentinel*), Abbeville (the *Whig*), Georgetown (the *Winyaw Intelligencer*), Yorkville (the *Banner*), and Camden (the *Camden and Lancaster Journal*).[47]

When retiring editors sold their newspapers, they and the politicians allied with them tried to keep these papers in the party fold. When Charles McDowell announced his plan to sell the *Bedford Gazette* (Pennsylvania), he promised to sell to a loyal Democrat. When S. C. Stambaugh left the Harrisburg *Pennsylvania Reporter*, he assured his readers the paper was in "safe hands."[48] When John Brazer Davis wanted to sell the *Boston Patriot*, the National Republican party helped find a new editor.[49]

Politicians and parties discarded disloyal or unreliable editors. In South Carolina, when the Jacksonian coalition divided in the late 1820s over the tariff and state rights philosophy, moderates such as Charles F. Daniels, editor of the *Camden Journal* (South Carolina) found that some of his old supporters (including U.S. senator S. D. Miller) deserted him.[50] The Jacksonians broke ties to the New York *Courier and Enquirer* in 1832 when the paper endorsed the rechartering of the Second Bank of the United States, despite Jackson's hatred of that institution. Jacksonians had long been fairly tolerant of the maverick nature of *Courier and Enquirer*, but its support for the bank cut its ties to Jackson. Jacksonians dropped their subscriptions and withdrew patronage.[51]

Similarly, the Jacksonians broke with southern political newspapers (and ended financial subsidies) that opposed the president in the nullification controversy in late 1832 and early 1833. Jacksonians dropped the *Augusta Chronicle* (Georgia) and the Milledgeville *Georgia Journal*.[52]

At times, parties had such direct and powerful control over newspapers that they could replace recalcitrant editors. When the editor of the *Albany Argus*, Isaac Q. Leake, refused to support the Regency's presidential candidate in 1824, he was hurried into retirement and replaced by Edwin Croswell.[53] When Luther Tucker of the *Rochester Daily Advertiser* wanted to support Andrew Jackson in 1828, his co-editor balked. The Regency helped Tucker buy out his partner.[54] In Lynn, Massachusetts, Jonathan Buffum, owner of the Antimasonic *Lynn Record*, fired his half-hearted Antimasonic editor.[55] In Albany, New York, the Antimasons forced Solomon Southwick out as editor of the *Albany Observer*, because he was simply unwilling to work within the party.[56]

When editors owned their own printing establishments, they could not be dislodged easily if they proved unreliable or disloyal. In these cases, political parties usually started a new newspaper to compete with the older one. When Jacksonians decided that Duff Green's *U.S. Telegraph* was disloyal, they helped establish the Washington *Globe*, edited by Francis Preston Blair.[57]

Financial Subsidies

Financial subsidies to the partisan press were common and vital. For editors, the subsidies often provided financial stability in a notoriously unstable business. One historian has noted that approximately two-thirds of all newspapers established in North Carolina between 1815 and 1836 failed within a few years of their establishment.[58] The *Fayetteville Observer* (North Carolina), in 1834, reported that seven newspapers had failed during the preceding 12 months.[59] Many subscribers simply did not pay for their newspapers. In 1832, one North Carolina editor estimated that only 10 percent of his 600 subscribers had paid for the paper.[60] In 1844, the *Carolina Watchman* had about 800 subscribers, but a tenth were eventually dropped for delinquency.[61] Editors frequently had to beg their readers for payment.[62]

Outside the metropolitan areas, when newspaper subscribers paid, they usually bartered farm products or other goods.[63] Although editors were happy to be paid at all, bartered goods didn't provide the cash to pay for paper, ink, presses, and types.[64]

The importance of financial subsidies varied from paper to paper. Carolyn Stewart Dyer's pioneer work indicates that patronage could constitute half or more of a newspaper's income. Dyer deals only with Wisconsin, but there is evidence elsewhere that patronage was important to most newspapers. Editors vied with one another for contracts, and when they lost them they faced hardship or failure. For small rural papers, these subsidies provided *cash*. Even small amounts of cash were valuable. One weekly editor in upstate New York highly prized a patronage contract that paid only $3.50 per year.[65] Thurlow Weed found that the income of two or three dollars a week from a patronage job was a great help in supporting his family in the early 1820s.[66]

Partisan subsidies were important for larger papers, too. Donations by wealthy members of the National Republican party in Massachusetts provided the financial underpinning for the *Boston Daily Advertiser* in the early 1830s.[67]

Federal Patronage of the Press

Government printing contracts were the major source of patronage in the Jacksonian era. The federal government—the executive branch, both houses of Congress, and the Supreme Court—used printers for a variety of jobs, such as printing the proceedings of Congress or producing stationery for executive departments. Partisan editors were the key beneficiaries of these contracts. From 1819 to 1846, each house of Congress elected a printer to publish its proceedings, debates, and laws. These lucrative contracts ran for two years with profit margins running from 20 to 55 percent.[68] Editors used the profits to maintain their political papers and to undertake other partisan activities, such as publishing campaign newspapers.

The other key congressional subsidy to political newspapers was the extensive use of the franking privilege in the late 1820s and 1830s. Senators and representatives could send newspapers or pamphlets free of charge through the postal system if they signed their names to these items. During campaigns, franking was an important subsidy to political newspapers, because it allowed them to circulate through the postal system at no cost. Remini wrote that franked newspapers cost the federal government about $40,000 a year and that "hundreds of newspapers circulated freely throughout the country."[69]

Other federal subsidies nurtured the partisan press, too. Throughout the 1830s, executive branch expenditures on printing increased steadily, rising from $110,004.24 during the Twenty-second Congress (1831–33) to $174,244.00 during the Twenty-sixth Congress (1839–41).[70] Under Jackson, the preponderance of the executive patronage went to Jacksonian newspapers in Washington, D.C. (primarily the Washington *Globe*), in metropolitan areas (Louisville, Boston, and Philadelphia), and in state capitals (Boston, Concord, and Columbus).[71]

Jackson also appointed editors to a relatively large number of salaried political posts. Some of Jackson's closest advisers were either editors or former editors. The Kitchen Cabinet included Blair, Amos Kendall, former editor of the *Argus of Western America* (Frankfort, Kentucky), and Isaac Hill, former editor of the Concord *New Hampshire Patriot*. The most common patronage job for editors was postmaster. Milton Hamilton notes that 22 editors served as postmasters in New York State in 1830.[72] In all, about 50–60 editors around the country actually received patronage jobs.[73]

State Patronage of the Press

State governments and party organizations also subsidized Jacksonian era newspaper editors. Dyer found four major sources of state patronage: printing contracts, publishing official notices and laws, providing newspapers to members of the legislature, and appointive patronage jobs (such as clerks or watchmen).[74] These subsidies varied from state to state. Some legislatures provided rather healthy profits to printers, while others were more frugal. The experiences of three states—New York, Pennsylvania, and Georgia—illustrate the state patronage system.

In New York, state printing contracts were the centerpiece of press patronage into the 1840s. Throughout the 1820s and for most of the 1830s, Martin Van Buren's political machine controlled this patronage. The Regency's editor, Edwin Croswell of the *Albany Argus*, received much of the funding. From 1827 to 1832, Croswell averaged $15,700 in state printing contracts annually.[75] Regency patronage also went to loyal party newspapers throughout the state. In all, about 40 newspapers received patronage, usually for printing state notices and laws. The sums paid to country printers in New York State were not big. Most ranged from $20 to $50 a year; the largest was about $150.[76] The state also paid for two or three newspaper subscriptions for each legislator.[77]

In Pennsylvania, the state printing contracts amounted to about $15,000 a year in the 1830s. They were divided among three printers: one printed the *Journal of Proceedings* in English; another, the *Journal of Proceedings* in German; and a third, a compendium of laws passed. These contracts generally went to editors in Harrisburg, the capital.[78] Pennsylvania legislators also received two or three daily newspapers (the number varied during the 1820s and 1830s).[79] And the governor frequently gave patronage appointments to editors. The stipends for these positions varied, but some were quite lucrative.[80]

As in other states, the Georgia legislative printing contracts were the most important aspect of state subsidies to the press. Throughout the late 1820s and early 1830s, the Troup party controlled the state legislature and awarded printing contracts to the Milledgeville *Georgia Journal*, the party's chief paper in the capital.[81] Georgia editors—especially those associated with the leading newspapers in the state capital—also benefited from patronage appointments, serving as secretary to the governor or in various paid advisory posts.[82]

The patronage practices in these three states appear common elsewhere. Most states awarded legislative printing contracts to subsidize editors. In Virginia, for example, Thomas Ritchie of the *Richmond Enquirer* held the state printing contracts throughout the 1820s and 1830s, earning an annual stipend of $2,600. Additional printing orders (for an extra session of the legislature, for example) could double the amount he was paid.[83] North Carolina's legislature was not as generous as other states, paying only $900 a year for printing session laws, journals, and bills. Nonetheless, editors still vied for the patronage.[84]

Patronage of the Press on the Local Level

In New York, Georgia, and Pennsylvania, newspapers in the state capitals were the major recipients of state financial subsidies. Other editors received funds from the state, but those amounts were generally not large. Dyer's study of the Wisconsin press indicates that state patronage provided major support for newspapers in Madison, the state capital, and for the financially troubled newspapers on the sparsely settled frontier counties (where local subsidies would have been scarce). Many local newspapers received patronage from city or county governments. Printing contracts from the sheriff, for instance, were important, for they could constitute half of a weekly newspaper's annual income.[85] Other local governmental units also supported the press with printing and advertising contracts. The advertising alone for Dauphin County (Harrisburg), Pennsylvania, in 1830 amounted to $118.[86] And the printing and advertising for Philadelphia County totaled $340.50 in 1828.[87]

Some local newspapers drew support from government at all levels. The *St. Lawrence Republican* in upstate New York received patronage from the federal government (from the customs house and post office), from the state government (for advertising), and from the county government.[88]

Other Patronage

Although the largest subsidies came through government contracts, control over those contracts rested with political parties. When parties controlled the contracts, their editors benefited through patronage. But even when parties lacked such political control, their editors often received financial aid from the party faithful. Funds might be less ample, but they existed. Throughout the country, political parties and interest groups used gifts, donations, loans, and sometimes even outright ownership of newspapers to assure that the party's views were advanced.[89]

Partisan Content: Wooing and Mobilizing the Voters

Newspapers of the Jacksonian era were opinionated, politically biased, one-sided, argumentative, and frequently strident. As table 19.1 shows, content was primarily political in nature—a mix of reports on political events, political essays, and other political exhortations or propaganda. Editors debated with one another over the political issues and candidates as if the fate of democracy and of the nation itself was at stake.

The partisanship of the non-metropolitan newspapers is clearest. Those newspapers devoted more than two-thirds of all content to politics. Politics dominated the

Table 19.1 Percentage distribution of contents, by category, among nine antebellum newspapers, 1831–32

	Five metropolitan newspapers	Four non-metropolitan newspapers
Politics	50.5	69.6
Crime and courts	2.5	2.3
Accidents	3.6	4.8
Society and women	2.5	1.4
Leisure	2.8	5.0
Business and labor	22.9	2.3
Religion	0.6	4.2
Science and education	1.7	1.2
History	0.3	0.0
Weather	0.5	0.6
Other	0.8	1.7

Note: Figures are median percentages of column inches for each content category.

metropolitan press as well, constituting half of all content. Three of the metropolitan newspapers studied here—the *Boston Daily Advertiser*, the *Charleston Mercury*, and the New York *Courier and Enquirer*—were leading political organs in their respective cities and states.[90]

Newspapers became the symbol of party strength, and the leading cities and towns of the nation all had rival political newspapers in the late 1820s and 1830s. In the early 1830s, Charleston, South Carolina, had five major political newspapers—three supporting the Unionist party and two supporting the nullifiers. Columbus, Ohio, had newspapers representing the Jacksonians, National Republicans, and Antimasons. This kind of competition existed in cities and towns across the country. Even Boston, where voters overwhelmingly favored the National Republican party in the early 1830s, had both Jacksonian and Antimasonic daily newspapers, in addition to three National Republican dailies. In New York State, 65 percent of county seats had rival newspapers in 1830. Editors without competition at home usually found a rival nearby. When the *Lyons Countryman* (New York), an Antimasonic newspaper, failed in late 1831, the editor of its cross-town Jacksonian rival, the *Lyons Western Argus*, turned to fighting the Antimasonic editor of the *Penn Yan Enquirer*. The Jacksonian editor in Cortland, New York, debated not only his home-town rival but also two anti-Jackson newspapers in a town four miles away.[91]

Such competition probably was inevitable, given the belief that newspapers were necessary for the success of any political party. The presence of one party's paper in a town dictated that opposing partisans maintain a newspaper if those partisans wanted an active political presence. In Greenville, South Carolina, the popularity of the moderate, pro-Union *Greenville Mountaineer* propelled the establishment of a nullification newspaper in the early 1830s. Similarly, unionists contemplated establishing a newspaper at Beaufort, South Carolina, primarily because nullifiers had just done so.[92]

The patronage system served to *guarantee* this competition and diversity in the press. With three major sources of funding in most states and on the national level (the two houses of the legislature and the executive branch), competing newspapers all could receive subsidies simultaneously. During the last two years of the John Quincy

Adams administration, federal patronage went to the three major political newspapers in the nation's capital: the executive patronage went to the *National Journal*, Adams' official organ; the House printing contracts went to Joseph Gales and William Seaton of the *National Intelligencer*, and the Senate printing contract to Duff Green of the *U.S. Telegraph*. Consequently, during the 1828 presidential campaign, federal patronage funds were supporting two papers that advocated the reelection of Adams and one newspaper that advocated the election of Andrew Jackson.[93]

Patronage also nurtured competition and diversity on the state level. In Boston, subsidies went to all the leading newspapers. Federal funds sustained the *Boston Morning Post*, the Jacksonian newspaper. The editors of the Boston *Columbian Centinel*, a National Republican journal, held the state printing contracts. Funds from the party faithful went to the other three major political papers in the city: the *Boston Daily Courier* (representing the old Federalist wing of the National Republican party), the Antimasonic *Boston Daily Advocate*, and the National Republicans' *Boston Daily Advertiser*.[94]

Editors saw their readers as *voters* and provided content that would woo them to a particular party and then mobilize them to vote. There was no room for indecision or neutrality in the press. The *Louisville Public Advertiser* condemned a purportedly neutral Indiana paper: "We do not know how it is in Indiana, but, in this State, people have more respect for an open, independent adversary than for dumb partisans or shuttlecock politicians, who are considered too imbecile to form an opinion, or too servile to express an opinion when formed."[95] The Washington, D.C., *U.S. Telegraph* condemned a purportedly neutral Baltimore paper, noting that the neutrality was probably indicative of a complete lack of principle and an abundance of opportunism.[96]

In a comment quite typical of the age, a Jacksonian editor in upstate New York commented on a newspaper he had received through the mail, noting that it was

> . . . precisely what we most of all things abhor and detest, to wit, a neutral paper. It pretends to be all things to all men. Now we would wish to be civil to the editor, but we can never consent to an exchange with any such paper, for we verily think they should all, one and all, be thrown out of the pale of the press. If we are asked why, we answer that the Editor must be doing violence to his opinions, or else he had none to abuse; and in either case, he is hardly entitled to the common civilities of his typographical brethren.[97]

It wasn't just the love of a good fight that led editors to advocacy; they also saw themselves as having a *duty* to debate. The editor of the *Greensborough Patriot* (North Carolina) noted that editors had a responsibility to the public "because PUBLIC OPINION is measurably formed from the TONE OF THE PRESS."[98] A. W. Thayer, editor of the *Essex Gazette* in Haverhill, Massachusetts, maintained that an editor was a "political preacher" and "a sentinel placed in his country's watch tower."[99]

Editors proudly announced their political affiliation. Indeed, that political affiliation was part of their appeal for subscribers, because editors who intended to establish a paper first issued a prospectus to obtain subscribers. The prospectus for the *Carolina Watchman* in Salisbury, North Carolina, promised to support the Jackson administration and to oppose internal improvements, the tariff, and extreme state rights agitation. Such declarations clearly defined that newspaper in terms of both national and state politics.[100] In his prospectus for the *Boston Morning Post*, Charles G. Green promised that he would urge that the tariff be modified, would call for the abolition of imprisonment for debt, and would give "a candid and temperate support to the National Administration."[101]

The mainstay of the newspaper advocacy was the partisan essay, with often sharp and vituperative commentary. Marmaduke Slade, editor of the *Macon Advertiser* (Georgia), attacked northerners who supported the protective tariff, saying, "They have mistaken our moderation for pusilanity and our devotion to the Union for a craven dependence upon their physical strength."[102] He criticized southerners who were willing to compromise on the tariff issue as "submissionists."[103] The Columbus, Georgia, *Democrat* expressed the hope that Georgians would "not be gulled on the present occasion" by the "nullification demagogues" who try to lure Georgians into "schemes of violence and revolution."[104] The editor of the *Macon Telegraph* urged Georgians to reject the "nullification kisses" of the "South Carolina python."[105]

The era's political essays could be lengthy. After Andrew Jackson vetoed the recharter of the Second Bank of the United States in 1832, Francis Preston Blair's Washington, D.C., *Globe* presented a multi-part series of essays defending the veto. Before the 1832 election, Gales and Seaton of the Washington *National Intelligencer* presented nine essays ("The Ancient Mariner" series) detailing the heinousness of Jackson's first term as president.[106]

The object of these essays was to convince the reader-as-voter. Consequently, it was the argument presented rather than its timeliness that was of crucial importance. When President Jackson vetoed the bill to recharter the Second Bank of the United States, the editors of the *National Intelligencer* at first provided only a brief notice of the veto. Ten days later, after a good deal of thought, the editors finally analyzed and condemned the veto message itself. In such essays, the motive was to present a compelling and convincing argument to the voters, not to recount events quickly.

The give and take of political debate and competition was a central ingredient of the press. As one Pennsylvania editor noted:

> When an editor firmly supports his principles in politics, and his preference as to men, he meets with rubs, as a matter of course, from those who espouse different principles and prefer other men; but whether he wins or loses in the contest, no reasonable man quarrels with him for the part he has taken. Those who take an active part in the strife of politics, generally consider that they give back to their adversaries as good as their adversaries sent them—and at the close of the contest, the account is about square between them.[107]

These "rubs" dealt with the key issues of the day, ranging from national economic and trade policy to local political issues and candidates. In the late 1820s and early 1830s, Essex County, Massachusetts, had newspapers that represented two factions of the National Republican party and the Jacksonian Democrats. These papers were engaged in a constant debate with each other over local and national issues, including the tariff, Andrew Jackson, and the Second Bank of the United States, as well as national and local elections.[108] Newspapers throughout the country—and particularly in the South—divided and fought over tariff policy and the novel constitutional theory that individual states could nullify laws deemed unwise.[109] A good deal of debate and discussion naturally surrounded the political campaigns of the era[110] and the protracted debate over the Second Bank of the United States.[111]

Although national issues were important considerations throughout the era, many newspapers were concerned primarily with local issues. American political parties in the age of Jackson were essentially not *national* parties but a coalition of local and state political interests. So local issues often dominated, both in politics and in the political press. In North Carolina, debates centered on legislative representation;[112] in Virginia, on the state constitutional convention in 1830–31;[113] in Massachusetts, on licensing laws and separation of church and state;[114] in Georgia, on the local parties (Troupites versus Clarkites) and on national Indian policy;[115] in South Carolina, on nullification, the state's own nullification convention and ordinance;[116] and in New York, on the state's banking system, its canal system, local competition between parties, and the potential for an amalgamation between the National Republicans and the Antimasons.[117]

All these debates, whether national or local in nature, eventually came to fruition on election day. Above all else, Jacksonian-era newspapers were devoted to winning elections. Editors tried to involve their (male) readers in the party itself. Newspapers carried announcements of forthcoming conventions and meetings from the local to the state level. In 1828, the *Louisville Public Advertiser* urged attendance at a political barbecue "at which the principles involved in the present struggle will be freely discussed."[118]

Newspapers routinely informed readers about party meetings and conventions and urged attendance. The Springfield, Massachusetts, *Hampden Intelligencer* announced one party meeting and added, "We trust it will not be necessary to again urge the necessity of a punctual attendance on this occasion."[119] In September 1832, the Boston *Columbian Centinel* urged National Republicans "in every county and town throughout the state" to prepare for the forthcoming election. "All must get going." The paper urged voters to hold organizational meetings to support the party ticket and to encourage voting.[120] Newspapers also printed party tickets, identifying and endorsing various candidates.[121]

Obviously, not all readers attended such meetings, and consequently newspapers devoted a lot of space to the proceedings and discussions of party meetings, reporting speeches and resolutions. Papers often printed the formal addresses to the electorate that were produced by the end of the conventions. Papers produced column upon column of reports on these political happenings, ranging from the county level to the national conventions first held in 1831 and 1832. The *Albany Argus* printed proceedings of county party meetings and of a Young Men's Democratic-Republican meeting in late 1831.[122] The *Charleston Mercury* printed proceedings of various nullification meetings throughout South Carolina in 1831 and 1832,[123] while the Milledgeville *Federal Union* reported antinullification meetings throughout Georgia.[124]

The key to success, of course, was voter turnout, and Jacksonian-era editors worked hard to exhort their readers to vote for the party. In early 1831, just before the New Hampshire state elections, the editor of Concord's Jacksonian *New Hampshire Patriot* reminded his readers that "one week from tomorrow, you will again be called on to exercise one of the most valuable privileges and dearest rights, sacred to us by our republican institutions—that of electing our rulers." The editor warned his readers that only "eternal vigilance" would win the day.[125] In 1832, the Worcester *Massachusetts Spy* told its readers: "Go to the polls and see that your neighbor goes, and there vote for the men who have always been faithful to you and your interests—who have stood by you, through good report and through evil report, and will not abandon you in the hour of peril. Go to the polls . . . Hearken not to those who would create divisions among you."[126]

The Limits of the Partisan Press

Such advocacy precluded an objective discussion of other parties or other issues. Newspapers did not try to be all things to all people, and they did not seek to cater to every interest. In the 1820s, the nascent Antimasonic party found that the existing partisan newspapers would not publicize its views. Antimasons complained bitterly about what they saw as hostility to their views on the part of the established partisan press.

Within the context of an advocacy press system, however, such exclusion made sense. The intent of an editor was to woo and to mobilize the voters, and neutrality or evenhandedness (admitting that the opposition might be right, for instance) certainly did not constitute effective campaigning. Evenhandedness or objectivity was not so much bad as inappropriate.

Other limits to press content existed, too. The political system itself, circa 1830, included only a third or so of the nation (the vote was denied to all but adult white males), and partisan newspapers thus dealt with a world of relatively elite men. These partisan newspapers seemed dedicated to upholding the political world as they knew it. They did not accept challenges to that status quo without reluctance if not actual hostility. They were, as a Pennsylvania editor noted, ready to meet "with rubs" during the course of political debate and battle and to give as good as they received,[127] but primarily with others who were part of that two-party electoral system. Little sympathy existed for those, such as abolitionists, who sought to disrupt the political status quo. When an angry mob in Alton, Illinois, killed abolitionist editor Elijah P. Lovejoy in 1837, newspapers from *both* major American political parties quickly blamed Lovejoy for his own death. Jacksonian and Whig newspapers in Missouri and in Washington, D.C., all condemned the "dislocating doctrines" of abolitionism and argued that Lovejoy, by insisting upon the right to publish whatever he chose, had caused his own death.[128]

Editors as Political Activists

The precise nature of political roles varied from editor to editor, from state to state, depending on factors such as the editor's personality or ambition. No single model for political activism existed. Some editors were de facto county or state directors of their parties, while others were political lieutenants rather than party leaders. Whatever the position, a common pattern existed: editors did much more than edit newspapers. They were extensively involved in politics outside of their newspaper offices. They served as central committee members, public speakers, and organizers of meetings and conventions.

The central committee (national, state, county, or even township) was the key organizational structure in Jacksonian-era political parties. These committees coordinated the day-to-day operation of the party, organized meetings and conventions, drew up lists of nominees, and promoted voter turnout. Thomas J. Lemay and Alexander J.

Lawrence, editors of the Raleigh, North Carolina, *Star*, both belonged to the state central committee supporting the Jackson-Barbour ticket in 1832.[129] Three of the eight members of the Pennsylvania Antimasonic State Central Committee were editors.[130] David C. Miller, editor of the Batavia, New York, *Republican Advocate*, was a member of the first Genesee County Antimasonic Central Committee. James Percival, editor of the *Livingston Register* in Geneseo, New York, helped organize the town's first Antimasonic meeting in early 1827 and served on the county central committee for three years. E. J. Fowle, editor of the *Yates Republican* in Penn Yan, was a founder of the local Antimasonic party and served for five years on his county's central committee.[131] J. A. Hadley, editor of the *Lyons Countryman* (New York), was on the three-member Wayne County Central Committee and also served on the Wayne County Young Men's Central Committee.[132] In early 1831, another member of the Wayne County Central Committee, Myron Holley, became joint proprietor of the *Lyons Countryman* with Hadley. Holley continued to publish the paper and serve on the county central committee after Hadley retired.[133] Beriah B. Hotchkin, who served as editor of several Antimasonic newspapers in New York,[134] was a member of the New York Antimasonic Young Men's State Central Committee.[135] In Virginia, Thomas Ritchie, editor of the *Richmond Enquirer*, was on each of the six state central committees between 1824 and 1844; many considered him to be the key political leader in Virginia.[136] Elsewhere in the country—in New Hampshire, Massachusetts, Pennsylvania, New Jersey, and South Carolina—editors were members of party central committees.[137]

At times, editors were members of other party committees. They served as poll watchers (called committees of vigilance). Others served on committees of correspondence, writing letters to other partisans in efforts to coordinate political activity.[138]

Editors also performed some of the campaign tasks that candidates, by tradition, avoided. Benjamin Hallett, editor of the Antimasonic *Boston Daily Advocate*, spoke throughout Massachusetts in the early 1830s, urging party unity and promoting candidates.[139] Samuel A. Towne, editor of the Abbeville, South Carolina, *Whig*, delivered a partisan oration for Abbeville's Fourth of July celebration in 1832.[140] William Gilmore Simms, editor of the *Charleston Courier* in the early 1830s, addressed the Union and State Rights party in 1831.[141] And John Hemphill, editor of the *Sumter Gazette* (South Carolina) gave a partisan oration on the Fourth of July in 1832 to the unionist celebration in Sumter.[142]

Many editors attended party conventions as delegates and platform writers. M. D. Richardson, editor of the Sumter, South Carolina, *Southern Whig*, helped organize pro-Union (moderate state rights) meetings in the early 1830s and helped draft various resolutions adopted at those meetings.[143] Charles W. Gill, editor of the *Cortland Advocate* (New York), organized a public meeting to protest the Senate's rejection of Martin Van Buren as minister to England.[144] Gill also was a delegate to his county's convention in 1832 and helped draft the convention's resolutions.[145] T. C. Strong, editor of the Geneva *Independent American* was a delegate to the New York State Antimasonic convention from Orleans County.[146]

All the National Republican editors from Boston (from the *Columbian Centinel*, the *Boston Daily Courier*, and the *Advertiser* and *Independent Chronicle*) were delegates to the Massachusetts State National Republican Convention in 1832.[147] Joseph T. Adams, one of the editors of the Boston *Columbian Centinel*, was secretary at a Boston ward meeting of the National Republican party.[148] Across Massachusetts, editors attended party meetings as delegates.[149]

The two leading political editors of the Jacksonian era were Francis Preston Blair, of the Washington, D.C., *Globe*, and Duff Green of the Washington, D.C., *U.S. Telegraph*. Both worked extensively to promote presidential candidates and to coordinate partisan activities nationwide, issuing campaign extras and directing grass-roots organizations.

Green's greatest efforts were on behalf of John C. Calhoun in the early 1830s. Green developed a fairly elaborate strategy to get Calhoun elected president in 1832. He tried to deemphasize extreme state rights issues—specifically nullification, which was so closely tied to Calhoun and unpopular in the North.[150] He nurtured grass-roots political support primarily by establishing pro-Calhoun newspapers in Pennsylvania and Virginia so that the South Carolinian could win the Democratic presidential nomination.[151] And he hoped to win the Antimasonic party nomination for Calhoun for president.[152] When it became apparent by the spring of 1832 that Calhoun could not win any party's presidential nomination, Green supported an anti-Jackson coalition (endorsing no candidate, but just arguing against Jackson) and issued a *Telegraph* extra that assailed the Jackson administration's record.[153]

While Green was working to promote the political fortunes of John C. Calhoun in the early 1830s, Francis Preston Blair was trying to keep the 1828 Jacksonian coalition in line behind the president. Blair's loyalty to the president had been apparent from the first issue of his newspaper in late 1830, and the editor never faltered in his belief that Old Hickory's policies were best designed to keep the country and its citizens free.

Although Blair's prominence derived in large part from his ownership and editorship of the *Globe*, he was much more than just an editor. As William E. Ames writes, ". . . he was primarily a politican who edited a newspaper in order to advance his political party."[154] During his years with the *Globe*, politics and journalism were one and the same. He was interested in the occupation of journalism only as it promoted the political goals that he supported.[155]

As Ames notes, Blair followed the basic patterns of political activism pioneered by Duff Green, and he expanded upon them, emerging as a key confidant and political adviser to President Jackson and the key link between the president and many members of the party.[156]

Blair's political role within the administration was well recognized. Jacksonians in the states turned to Blair with their requests for political appointments,[157] and for help in solving their problems with the federal bureaucracy, particularly with the postal system.[158] Blair helped establish Jacksonian newspapers, loaning $200 to one editor to start an administration newspaper in Raleigh, North Carolina.[159] Other Jacksonians also turned to Blair for help in establishing papers loyal to the president.[160]

In 1832, Blair's major work during the election campaign was the publication and distribution of 30 weekly issues of *Globe* extras "so that the people may know and appreciate the measures and principles which guide Gen. Jackson in the administration of government." These were printed over the course of the six months preceding the election.[161] Blair was highly successful in distributing the extra. One Antimasonic editor in western New York said that "thousands and tens of thousands of extra sheets of this vile electioneering print" are being distributed "to the remotest corners of the Union."[162] Supporters of the Second Bank of the United States lamented the success of the *Globe*. One friend told bank president Nicholas Biddle that "the interior is inundated with official Globes and Jackson papers."[163]

Other issues of *Globe* extras appeared during the battle of the removal of the federal deposits from the Second Bank of the United States (in 1834) and during the presidential campaigns of 1836 and 1840.[164]

Elsewhere in the nation, in cities as well as in small towns, editors served as key political activists. The *Boston Statesman* was the center of the Massachusetts Jacksonian party in the late 1820s.[165] John Brazer Davis, a National Republican editor in Boston, worked to organize not only his own state's allies but also National Republicans throughout the country in the early 1830s.[166] Edwin Croswell of the *Albany Argus* (New York) was prominent in almost all Regency organizational efforts in the 1820s and 1830s,[167] just as Thurlow Weed of the *Albany Evening Journal* dominated Antimasonic party efforts.[168] In South Carolina, Henry Laurens Pinckney was not only editor of the *Charleston Mercury* but also a major political leader in the state legislature in the 1820s and early 1830s.[169] Many of these editors did not seek political office; they seemed content to work as party functionaries. Some were party kingpins, such as Thurlow Weed; others had far less power. All were political activists.

Conclusions

In *The Second American Party System*, Richard McCormick writes that Jacksonian-era political parties had two prime goals: first, to gain power, and second, to keep it. To those ends, American political parties devoted great effort to organization and electioneering. In that activity, newspapers and editors figured prominently.

Politicians and political activists saw newspapers as central to their hopes for electoral success. Martin Van Buren, the foremost political organizer of his day, never forgot that victory at the polls depended on reaching the electorate through political newspapers. Without such newspapers, he said, "we might as well hang our harps on willows."[170]

Van Buren was not alone in this belief. Each party wanted a newspaper in every hamlet, town, and city of the nation, ready to argue and advance party policies and candidates. Politicians and political activists worked hard to assure that the press would serve their needs. They shaped the press, recruiting editors, writing for newspapers, providing information and advice to editors. They also provided money to editors, subsidizing businesses that were often precarious financially.

This financial support, derived from the vision that politicians had of the press, clearly sustained the press. It gave political interest groups great power vis-à-vis the press. Indeed, disloyal editors were replaced, or their crucial subsidies were cut off. More often than not, however, partisan enthusiasms were not impressed upon unwilling editors. Editors themselves were party zealots, eager for patronage, but also eager for party debate and advocacy and for the power that came with victory.

Within this context, news dealt with politics: congressional and state legislative proceedings, partisan essays, profiles of candidates, and reports on party meetings. Despite the emphasis on political victory, these editors and politicians created a press that openly and loudly debated the day's public measures. There's no evidence that these editors engaged in debate because they idealized the *process* of debate. Rather, they engaged in debate in an effort to win elections.

The relatively small financial needs of the press fit well the largesse of the patronage system: a minimal amount of money could go a long way. The sums of money from political patronage in the early nineteenth century were not large, but editors of small rural newspapers found that even two or three dollars cash was a boon. For the newspapers in state capitals, such as Albany, the amounts were much larger. Few editors would become rich or even financially comfortable through the patronage system; for most it was merely a life-sustaining subsidy.

Newspapers were relatively cheap to establish, so political activists started newspapers to advance their beliefs and the candidates of their choice. New parties, such as the Antimasons, established scores of newspapers in the late 1820s. When a political newspaper proved disloyal or unsatisfactory, partisans would establish a new paper to replace it.

Patronage tied press and party together in an intimate fashion in the early nineteenth century. Patronage served as a kind of umbilical cord to the press, and many editors may well have been wary of taking unorthodox or maverick positions vis-à-vis their party for fear of losing that patronage. The extent of self-censorship is difficult to gauge. Certainly it limited press content. Party editors did not detail their opponents' views in any evenhanded way. They skirted discussions that would undermine the power of their political parties.

On balance, what seems more significant is that many editors were themselves party activists or leaders—members of the central committees that set the policies that they later promoted in their newspaper columns. These editors were the party strategists who created coalitions, chose party tickets, and guided campaigns. Parties were not, in a sense, dictating to newspapers; rather newspapers had been integrated into the party apparatus.

Notes

1. John B. Turner to Samuel Breck, October 10, 1832, Misc. MSS, "P," "We The People and Old Colony Press Business Records," American Antiquarian Society.
2. William H. Seward to Thurlow Weed, November 14, 1832, Thurlow Weed Papers, Rush Rees Library, University of Rochester.
3. Roy F. Nichols, *The Invention of the American Political Parties* (New York: Macmillan Co., 1967); Robert N. Elliot, Jr., "The Raleigh Register" (Ph.D. diss., University of North Carolina, 1953), pp. 71–4, 77–8.
4. Richard P. McCormick, *The Second American Party System: Party Formation in the Jacksonian Era* (Chapel Hill: University of North Carolina Press, 1966), p. 343; Cullen B. Gosnell and C. David Anders, *The Government and Administration of Georgia* (New York: Thomas Y. Crowell Co., 1956), pp. 16–17.
5. Ronald P. Formisano has written two of the best studies of state politics in the Jacksonian era. See *The Birth of Mass Political Parties: Michigan, 1827–1861* (Princeton, N.J.: Princeton University Press, 1971), and *The Transformation of Political Culture: Massachusetts Parties, 1790s–1840s* (New York: Oxford University Press, 1983). Also see Arthur B. Darling, *Political Changes in Massachusetts, 1824–1848: A Study of Liberal Movements in Politics* (New Haven: Yale University Press, 1925).
6. McCormick, *The Second American Party System*, p. 344; Formisano, *The Transformation of Political Culture*, pp. 10, 15.
7. McCormick, *The Second American Party System*, pp. 344–5; William N. Chambers and Philip C. Davis, "Party, Competition and Mass Participation: The Case of the Democratizing Party System, 1824–1852," in *The History of American Electoral Behavior*, ed. Joel H. Silbey, Allan G. Bogue, and William H. Flanigan (Princeton: Princeton University Press, 1978), p. 174.
8. Chambers and Davis, "Party, Competition and Mass Participation," pp. 174–5, quoting

Chilton Williamson, *American Suffrage from Property to Democracy, 1760–1860* (Princeton: Princeton University Press, 1960). In New York State, only a third of adult males could qualify for voting for governor in 1820; following constitutional revision in 1821, 80 percent qualified. McCormick, *The Second American Party System*, p. 113.

9. Robert V. Remini, *Andrew Jackson and the Course of American Freedom, 1822–1832*, volume 2 (New York: Harper and Row, 1981), p. 384; Washington, D.C., *National Intelligencer*, October 5, 1832, quoted in Remini, *Andrew Jackson and the Bank War* (New York: Norton, 1967), p. 98. For criticism of self-promotion by candidates, see the *Macon Advertiser* (Georgia), September 30, 1831 (criticizing Wilson Lumpkin for campaigning for governor); Geneseo, New York, *Livingston Register*, September 14, 1825; *Louisville Public Advertiser* (Kentucky), October 3, 1827, July 16, 1828; Baltimore *Niles' Weekly Register*, May 9, 1827, p. 165; *Greensborough Patriot* (North Carolina), June 13, 1829, August 29, 1832; *New Bern Spectator* (North Carolina), July 25, August 1, 1829; Cincinnati *Advertiser*, August 30, September 6, 1828, April 18, 1829; *Penn Yan Enquirer* (New York), November 2, 1831; Batavia, New York, *Republican Advocate*, October 21, 28, 1831; Thomas Ruffin to David L. Swain, October 15, 1829, D. L. Swain Papers, Southern Historical Collection, University of North Carolina, Chapel Hill; Richard Rush to John Binns, October 18, 1828, Society Collection: American Statesmen and Lawyers: Richard Rush, Historical Society of Pennsylvania.

10. Robert V. Remini, *The Election of Andrew Jackson* (Philadelphia: J. B. Lippincott Co., 1963), p. 62.

11. Charles S. Benton to Azariah Flagg, December 12, 1836, Azariah Flagg Papers, New York Public Library.

12. *Greensborough Patriot* (North Carolina), June 13, 1829.

13. *Haverhill Iris* (Massachusetts), January 21, 1832; *Newburyport Herald* (Massachusetts), August 1, 1832; *Newburyport Advertiser* (Massachusetts), November 5, December 14, 1831.

14. *Newburyport Advertiser*, June 22, 1831.

15. Henry Petrikin to George Bryan, January 17, 1823, George Bryan Papers, Historical Society of Pennsylvania.

16. James S. Chase, *Emergence of the Presidential Nominating Convention, 1789–1832* (Urbana: University of Illinois Press, 1973); John C. Vinson, "Electioneering in North Carolina, 1800–1835," *North Carolina Historical Review* 29 (April 1952).

17. In *The Transformation of Political Culture*, Formisano writes that newspapers were essential for parties, facilitating intraparty communication and serving "as a kind of public address system to supporters and sometimes as forums for debating controversial issues." p. 16.

18. Guion G. Johnson, *Antebellum North Carolina: A Social History* (Chapel Hill: University of North Carolina Press, 1937), pp. 95–6.

19. *Louisville Public Advertiser* (Kentucky), June 14, 25, 1828; Concord *New Hampshire Patriot*, August 6, 1828; Harrisburg *Pennsylvania Reporter*, May 25, 1838; *New Bern Spectator* (North Carolina), January 20, 27, 1832; *Savannah Republican* (Georgia), January 20, 1831; Charleston *City Gazette*, December 1, 1830; Winfield Scott to C. K. Gardner, August 7, 1824, Gardner Papers, New York State Library; Theodore D. Jervey, *Robert Y. Hayne and His Times* (New York: Macmillan Co., 1909).

20. Russel B. Nye, *Society and Culture in America, 1830–1860* (New York: Harper Torchbooks, 1974), p. 366.

21. Ibid.

22. Richard B. Kielbowicz, *News in the Mail: The Press, Post Office and Public Information* (New York: Greenwood Press, 1989).

23. Robert K. Stewart, "The Jackson Press and the Elections of 1824 and 1828" (M.A. thesis, University of Washington, 1984).

24. Pinckney was spokesman for the state rights activists in South Carolina; Greene, for the Jacksonian Democrats in Massachusetts.

25. *Proceedings of a Convention of Delegates from the Different Counties in the State of New York, Opposed to Free Masonry, Held at the Capitol in the City of Albany, on the 19th, 20th and 21st Days of February, 1829* (Rochester: Weed and Sprague, 1928), p. 12.

26. Myron Holley to Orville Holley, December 28, 1830, Holly Papers, New York State Library.

27. James Gordon Bennett diary, July 18, 1831, New York Public Library.

28. John C. Calhoun to J. H. Hammond, February 16, 1831, James Henry Hammond Papers, volume 2 (1830–33), Library of Congress.

29. Nicholas Biddle to P. P. F. Degrand, December 22, 1830, Letterbooks, p. 426; Biddle to M. Robertson, April 8, 1831, Letterbooks, pp. 501–2, Nicholas Biddle Papers, Library of Congress.

30. Nicholas Biddle to C. J. Ingersoll, February 12, 1831, Letterbooks, p. 466, Nicholas Biddle Papers, Library of Congress.

31. The median for the five metropolitan newspapers studied here is 50.5 percent of content devoted to politics. A fuller presentation of these data is available in table 1.1 below and in appendix 2.

32. The median for the five newspapers studied here is 22.9 percent of content devoted to business and labor. Please see table 1.1 and appendix 2 for a fuller presentation of these data.

33. Less than half of all revenues derived from advertising. Kobre estimates that about 16 percent of the New York *Courier and Enquirer*'s income came from advertising in the 1830s. Crouthamel estimates that less than 50 percent of the revenues of the leading New York City commercial newspapers (the *New York Daily Advertiser*, the *Commercial Advertiser*, and the *Mercantile Advertiser*) came from advertising. Sidney Kobre, *Development of American Journalism* (Dubuque: Wm. C. Brown Co., 1969), p. 170; James L. Crouthamel, *James Watson Webb: A Biography* (Middletown, Conn.: Wesleyan University Press, 1969), p. 16.

34. Seven of the nine New York City commercial-political papers were Whig in the late 1830s; the others, Democratic. Crouthamel, *James Watson Webb*, p. 84.

35. James Crouthamel writes that in 1832 the New York *Courier and Enquirer*, edited by James Watson Webb, was a "consistent" supporter of Jacksonian policies. "It had not become the power in politics that Webb hoped to make it, but it was influential in party circles. It is no exaggeration to say that Webb managed the nation's largest Jacksonian daily in 1832." *James Watson Webb*, p. 33.

36. *Historical Statistics of the United States, Colonial Times to 1970*, volume 1, Series A57–72, "Population in Urban and Rural Territory by Size of Place, 1790 to 1970" (Washington, D.C.: Government Printing Office, 1975).

37. The definition of a metropolitan area for 1830 is open to discussion, and the figure of 25,000 or more in population is suggested here as one possible definition. The population of the nation's leading cities in 1830 were: New York City, 197,112; Philadelphia, 80,462; Baltimore, 80,620; Boston, 61,392; and Charleston, 30,289. U.S. Census Office, *Fifth Census or Enumeration of the Inhabitants of the United States, 1830*, "Aggregate Amount of Each Description of Persons within the United States and the Territories According to the Census of 1830" (Washington, D.C.: Duff Green, 1832), pp. 17, 51, 65, 81.
     Cities of 50,000 or more held 3.3 percent of the population; 1.5 percent lived in cities of 100,000 or more (i.e., New York). *Historical Statistics of the United States*, Series A57–72.

38. Robert Remini, *The Election of Andrew Jackson*, p. 77.

39. John Eaton to Overton, November 16, 1824, John B. Overton Papers, Tennessee State Archives, Nashville, quoted in Gabriel L. Lowe, Jr., "John H. Eaton, Jackson's Campaign Manager," *Tennessee Historical Quarterly* 11 no. 2 (June 1952), p. 128.

40. Lowe, Jr., "John H. Eaton," pp. 126–8; Remini, *The Election of Andrew Jackson*, p. 49.

41. Nathaniel J. Palmer to W. P. Mangum, October 21, 1831, pp. 414–15, and C. Fisher to Mangum, August 24, 1832, pp. 571–2, Henry T. Shanks, ed., *The Papers of Willie P. Mangum*, volume 1 (1807–32) (Raleigh: State Department of Archives and History, 1950); *Raleigh Register* (North Carolina), September 29, 1831.

42. *Albany Argus* (New York), quoting the *Baltimore Republican*, December 13, 1831; Worcester, Massachusetts, *Worcester County Republican*, March 4, 1829; John Norvell to B. S. Bonsall, June 4, 1832, Benjamin S. Bonsall Correspondence, Gratz Collection, Case 15, Box 2, Historical Society of Pennsylvania; *Greensbourgh Patriot* (North Carolina), November 7, 1829, April 14, 1830, June 1 and November 12, 1831; Herbert Ershkowitz, "New Jersey during the Era of Jackson, 1820–1837" (Ph.D. diss., New York University, 1965), p. 103; Russel J. Ferguson, *Early Western Pennsylvania Politics* (Pittsburgh: University of Pittsburgh Press, 1938), p. 267; Marguerite G. Bartlett, *The Chief Phases of Pennsylvania Politics in the Jacksonian Period* (Allentown, Pa.: H. Ray Haas and Co., 1919), p. 30; *Philadelphia Mercury*, September 29,

1827; Philadelphia *National Palladium*, January 8 and September 26, 1827; *Elizabeth City Star* (North Carolina), January 14, 1832.

43. Milton W. Hamilton, "Antimasonic Papers 1826–1834," in *The Papers of the Bibliographic Society of America*, volume 38 (Chicago: University of Chicago Press, 1938), p. 74.

44. Bartlett, *The Chief Phases of Pennsylvania Politics; Boston Daily Advocate*, January 3 and June 12, 1832; Seth Hunt to Thurlow Weed, March 16, 1831, Thurlow Weed Papers, University of Rochester.

45. F. Whittlesey to Thurlow Weed, December 14, 1831, Thurlow Weed Papers, University of Rochester; Myron Holley to William H. Seward, January 2, 1829, William Henry Seward Papers, University of Rochester.

46. Virginia L. Glenn, "James Hamilton Jr. of South Carolina: A Biography" (Ph.D. diss., University of North Carolina, 1964), pp. 146–7.

47. James Hamilton to Waddy Thompson, June 8 and August 31, 1832, James Hamilton Papers, South Caroliniana Library; H. H. Townes to G. F. Townes, March 10 and June 28, 1832, S. A. Townes to G. F. Townes, June 7, 1832, both in Townes Family Papers, South Caroliniana Library; J. Mauldin Lesesne, "The Nullification Controversy in an Up-Country District," *Proceedings of the South Carolina Historical Association* (1939), pp. 18–19; Harry L. Watson, "Early Newspapers of Abbeville District, 1812–1834," *Proceedings of the South Carolina Historical Association* (1940), pp. 28–9, 31; "Letters on the Nullification Movement in South Carolina, 1830–1834," *American Historical Review* 6 (1901), p. 741; *Greensbourgh Patriot* (North Carolina), December 4, 1830; Camden, South Carolina, *Camden and Lancaster Journal*, March 13, June 22, 1832.

48. *Harrisburg Chronicle* (Pennsylvania), September 10, 1832; Harrisburg *Pennsylvania Reporter*, July 24, 1829.

49. Joseph Sprague to Daniel Webster, January 31, 1830, Daniel Webster Papers, Library of Congress; A. H. Everett to Edward Everett, September 24, 1831, Edward Everett Letters, Hale Family Papers, Library of Congress; Daniel Webster to Edward Everett, August 25, 1831, Edward Everett Papers, Massachusetts Historical Society; *Boston Patriot*, July 20, 1831.

50. S. D. Miller to C. F. Daniels, September 6, 1830, Stephen D. Miller Papers, Duke University. Also see C. F. Daniels to S. D. Miller, September 6, 1830, Chestnut-Miller-Manning Papers, South Carolina Historical Society; C. F. Daniels to James Lawson, November 23, 1830, May 29, 1832, C. F. Daniels Papers, South Caroliniana Library.

51. James L. Crouthamel, *James Watson Webb*, p. 22; Webb to Nicholas Biddle, March 18, 1832, Nicholas Biddle Papers, Library of Congress; John Mumford to Charles Gardner, August 15, 25, 1832, Gardner Papers, New York State Library, Albany; William L. Marcy to Thomas W. Olcott, January 5, 1832, Thomas W. Olcott Papers, Columbia University; John Dix to T. S. Smith, October 20, 1831, John Dix Papers, Columbia University.

52. *Register of All the Officers and Agents, Civil, Military, and Naval, in the Service of the United States on the Thirtieth September, 1833*, comp. William A. Weaver (Philadelphia: Key and Biddle, 1834), pp. 171, 173.

53. William L. Marcy to Martin Van Buren, February 15, 1824, Martin Van Buren Papers, Library of Congress, quoted in Alvin Cass, *Politics in New York State, 1800–1830* (Syracuse: Syracuse University Press, 1965), p. 35; Van Buren to G. Worth, February 22, 1824, Martin Van Buren Papers, Library of Congress; Kalman Goldstein, "The Albany Regency: The Failure of Practical Politics" (Ph.D. diss., Columbia University, 1969), pp. 85–6; *Albany Argus* (New York), June 4, 1824.

54. H. C. Sleight to Henry O'Reilly, March 20, 1873, O'Reilly Collection, Rochester Historical Society, in Milton Hamilton, *The Country Printer: New York State, 1785–1830* (New York: Columbia University Press, 1936), p. 116.

55. *Lynn Record* (Massachusetts), July 17, 1830, November 2, 1831.

56. Herman Norton to Thurlow Weed, March 25, 1829, Thurlow Weed Papers, University of Rochester.

57. Washington, D. C., *Globe*, December 7, 1830; A. C. Flagg to F. P. Blair, January 11, 1832, Gratz Collection, Case B, Box 36, Historical Society of Pennsylvania.

58. Daniel J. McFarland, "North Carolina Newspapers, Editors and Journalistic Politics, 1815–1836," *North Carolina Historical Review* 30, no. 3 (July 1953), pp. 376–7. The best

study of the patronage system is Culver H. Smith, *The Press, Politics and Patronage* (Athens: University of Georgia Press, 1977).

59. *Fayetteville Observer* (North Carolina), June 30, 1834, quoted in Herbert D. Pegg, "The Whig Party in North Carolina, 1834–1861" (Ph.D. diss., University of North Carolina, 1932), p. 42.

60. William R. Ransom to Willie P. Mangum, February 8, 1832, Shanks, ed., *The Papers of Willie P. Mangum*, volume 1 (1807–32), pp. 474–6.

61. Pegg, "The Whig Party," p. 42, quoting the *Carolina Watchman* (Salisbury, North Carolina), May 3, 1845.

62. See the Batavia, New York, *Republican Advocate*, September 28, 1827; *Lyons Countryman* (New York), June 6, August 1, 8, 15, November 14, 1832.

63. Johnson, *Antebellum North Carolina*, p. 806; McFarland, "North Carolina Newspapers," p. 377.

64. Hamilton, *Country Printer*, p. 68.

65. Poughkeepsie, New York, *Dutchess Intelligencer*, July 15, 1829, quoted in Hamilton, *The Country Printer*, p. 121.

66. Thurlow Weed, *Autobiography of Thurlow Weed*, ed. Harriet A. Weed (Boston, 1883; reprinted, Da Capo Press, 1970), p. 78.

67. George Bond to Nathan Appleton, January 26, 1832, Nathan Appleton Papers, volume 5 (1832–39), Massachusetts Historical Society.

68. William E. Ames notes that Congress spent about $2.5 million on printing between 1819 and 1846: $1 million to the *National Intelligencer* (with $650,000 more for the American State Papers); $500,000 to Blair and Rives of the Washington, D.C., *Globe*; $400,000 to Duff Green and $258,000 to Thomas Allen of the *Madisonian*. Ames, *A History of the National Intelligencer* (Chapel Hill: University of North Carolina Press, 1972), p. 282.

69. Remini, *The Election of Andrew Jackson*, p. 84; Culver Smith, *The Press, Politics and Patronage*, p. 71; Edward Everett to Duff Green, September 15, 1832, Edward Everett Papers, Massachusetts Historical Society.

70. *Register of All the Officers and Agents . . . of the United States*, 1833, 1835, 1837, 1839, and 1841.

71. The newspapers receiving the largest sums of executive patronage were: Washington, D.C., *Globe* ($163,222.80 from 1831 to 1841); Concord *New Hampshire Patriot* ($18,112.48, 1831–41); *Boston Morning Post* ($63,339.48, 1831–41); *Louisville Public Advertiser* (Kentucky) ($24,639.09, 1831–41); Columbus *Ohio Statesman* ($25,811.38, 1833–41), and Philadelphia *Pennsylvanian* ($17,526.79, 1831–41). *Register of All the Officers and Agents . . . of the United States*, 1833, 1835, 1837, 1839, 1841.

72. Hamilton, The *Country Printer*, p. 120.

73. *Richmond Daily Whig* (Virginia), April 17, 30, May 2, 5, 19, 25, 28, 30, June 1, 5, 9, 12, 13, 19, 27, July 1, 24, and August 4, 1829, January 5 and June 21, 1830; Cincinnati *Advertiser*, April 15, 18, 29, May 6, June 10, and August 15, 1829; *Greensborough Patriot* (North Carolina), June 6, 13, 27, and August 22, 29, 1829; *New Bern Spectator* (North Carolina), June 20 and August 22, 1829, June 26, 1830; Baltimore *Niles' Weekly Register*, June 5, 1830, p. 271.

74. Carolyn Stewart Dyer, "Political Patronage of the Wisconsin Press, 1849–1861: New Perspectives on the Economics of Patronage," *Journalism Monographs* 109 (February 1989).

75. In addition, the special allocation for the printing and binding of the revised statutes (spread over the three-year period of 1828–31) paid Croswell $15,124.59 ($8,205.84 for printing and $6,918.75 for binding). New York State, Senate, Report of the Comptroller, 66th Sess., January 20, 1843, Doc. 12; New York State, Senate, Report of the Comptroller, 57th Sess., volume 2, March 13, 1835, Doc. 67; Croswell Papers, April 12, 1832, New York State Library.

76. New York State, Comptroller's Office Day Book 22, February 11, 1832–June 6, 1833; New York State, Comptroller's Office Day Book 20, April 7, 1830—September 11, 1830; both in New York State Library Manuscripts and Archives, Albany.

77. A. Z. Flagg to F. P. Blair, January 11, 1832, Gratz Collection, Case B, Box 36, Historical Society of Pennsylvania.

78. Samuel Hazard, *The Register of Pennsylvania* (Philadelphia: W. F. Geddes): volume 1 (January

1828), pp. 59–61; volume 3 (January–July 1829), pp. 193–4; volume 4 (July 1829–January 1830), pp. 409–11; volume 6 (July 1830–January 1831), p. 400; volume 7 (January–July 1831), p. 52; volume 8 (July 1831–January 1832), pp. 405–6; *Harrisburg Chronicle* (Pennsylvania), December 16, 27, 1830, February 10, December 12, 1831, December 10, 1832, December 9, 1833.

79.   Hazard, *Register*, volume 4, p. 317; Harrisburg *Pennsylvania Reporter*, February 29, 1828; *Harrisburg Chronicle* (Pennsylvania), December 16, 1830.
The allocation for three papers was $15 per legislator (totaling $1,995 for both houses of the legislature).

80.   Governor Wolf appointed six printers to various offices in the Pittsburgh area in 1830. The *New Bern Spectator* (North Carolina), March 13, 1830, lists the appointments. Editors usually were justices of the peace or clerks. James A. Kehl, *Ill Feeling in the Era of Good Feeling* (Pittsburgh: University of Pittsburgh Press, 1956), pp. 126, 131.

81.   The payments to the *Journal* from 1828 through 1832 averaged about $6,500 annually. State of Georgia, Senate, Journal, 1829, p. 263; State of Georgia, House, Journal, 1829, pp. 390–1; State of Georgia, Acts of the General Assembly, 1831, Appendix, p. 10; State of Georgia, House, Journal, 1831, pp. 8–10; State of Georgia, Senate, Journal, 1832, pp. 356–7.

82.   Miller Grieve was secretary to Governor Gilmer in 1830–31 and began editing the Milledgeville *Southern Recorder* a month after Gilmer left office. John Cuthbert, editor of the Milledgeville *Federal Union*, took Grieve's position in the next state administration, serving as the governor's secretary (while still editing his newspaper). State of Georgia, House, Journal, 1831, Appendix, pp. 14, 26; A. B. Caldwell, "Miller Grieve," in *Men of Mark in Georgia*, ed. William J. Northen (Atlanta: A. B. Caldwell, 1910), pp. 104–5; *Memoirs of Georgia* (Atlanta: Southern Historical Association, 1895), pp. 266–7; Milledgeville *Federal Union*, January 1, 1830.

83.   *Richmond Daily Whig* (Virginia), June 19, 1829, December 10, 1830.

84.   W. R. Gales to David Swain, September 14, 1823, Swain Papers, Southern Historical Collection, University of North Carolina.

85.   Dyer, "Political Patronage of the Wisconsin Press, 1849–1861:" 1989, p. 26.

86.   Harrisburg, Pennsylvania, *Republican and Anti-Masonic Inquirer*, February 19, 1831.

87.   Hazard, *Register*, volume 3, p. 143; Philadelphia *Democratic Press*, March 14, 19, 1828; Milton Hamilton, *The Country Printer*, p. 131.

88.   Ernest P. Muller, "Preston King: A Political Biography" (Ph.D. diss, Columbia University, 1957), pp. 33–6.

89.   George Bond to Nathan Appleton, January 26, 1832, Nathan Appleton Papers, volume 5, 1832–39, Massachusetts Historical Society; Ershkowitz, "New Jersey during the Era of Jackson," p. 102; E. S. Duryea to David E. Huger, March 24, 1832, Joel R. Poinsett Papers in the Henry D. Gilpin Collection, Historical Society of Pennsylvania.

90.   The political nature of these commercial-political newspapers is demonstrated by the *Boston Morning Post*, which devoted only 40.3 percent of its news columns to politics and 17.7 percent to business issues, but was still clearly the Jacksonian state organ. (See appendix 2: table A2.1.) The New York *Courier and Enquirer*, which devoted 50.5 percent of its space to politics and 22.9 percent to business issues, was deeply involved in national banking debates. The *Charleston Mercury* devoted 48.4 percent of its columns to politics, and was edited in the late 1820s and early 1830s by Henry Laurens Pinckney. Pinckney was a legislator, nullification party leader, and mayor of Charleston during his editorial tenure. *Charleston Mercury*, June 18, August 30, September 8, 11, 1830; February 27, April 16, 1832; *Charleston Courier*, February 4, 1863; Granville T. Prior, "A History of the *Charleston Mercury*, 1822–52" (Ph.D. diss., Harvard University, 1946).

91.   The figure on competition in New York State is derived from Winifred Gregory, ed., *American Newspapers 1821–1936* (New York: H. W. Wilson Co., 1937); also see *Lyons Western Argus* (New York), December 21, 24, 1831, March 7, 1832; *Cortland Advocate* (New York), October 21, November 4, December 2, 1831, February 17, 24, April 20, May 25, August 10, 1832, for a debate with the Cortland *Anti-Masonic Republican*; also *Cortland Advocate*, November 4, December 2, 1831, April 20, May 4, 11, July 13, October 26, November 4, December 2, 1832, for debate with the Homer *Cortland Observer* and Homer *Globe*.

92. J. L. Petrigru to William Elliot, August 25, 1831, J. L. Petigru Papers, South Carolina Historical Society.

93. In 1832, the three major Washington, D.C., newspapers all received governmental subsidies while pursuing quite different political agendas. The *Globe* received presidential patronage ($39,033.42); the *U.S. Telegraph*, congressional printing ($142,778.65); and the *National Intelligencer*, the American State Papers ($67,376.20). During the Twenty-third, Twenty-fourth, and Twenty-fifth congresses, rival editors held the congressional printing contracts (one for the Senate, one for the House). See *Register*, 1831, 1833, 1835, 1837, 1839, and 1841; Ames, *History of the National Intelligencer*, pp. 127, 151, 158–9.

94. *Register of All the Officers and Agents . . . of the United States*, 1833, 1835, 1837, 1839, 1841; U.S. Congress, House, *Examination of the Post Office Department*, 2d sess., 1835, H. Rept. 103, pp. 779–82, 784–86, 788; U.S. Congress, Senate, Committee on the Post Office and Post Roads, 23d Cong., 1st sess., 1834, S. Doc. 422; Joseph T. Buckingham, *Personal Memoirs and Recollections of Editorial Life*, reprinted., volume 2 (New York: Arno Pres, Inc., 1970); *Boston Daily Courier* June 26, 1832; Amasa Walker to Pliny Merrick, February 9, 25, 1830, Pliny Merrick Correspondence, Folder 2, American Antiquarian Society; *Boston Daily Advocate*, January 3, 1832; Boston *Columbian Centinel*, January 4, 1832.

95. *Louisville Public Advertiser* (Kentucky), July 9, 1828.

96. Washington, D.C., *U.S. Telegraph*, October 7, 1828.

97. *Lyons Western Argus* (New York), August 1, 1832.

98. *Greensborough Patriot* (North Carolina), quoted in the *Raleigh Register*, July 6, 1832.

99. Haverhill, Massachusetts, *Essex Gazette*, July 16, 1831.

100. This prospectus was published in the Tarborough, North Carolina, *Free Press*, October 18, 1831.

101. *Boston Morning Post*, November 9, 1831.

102. *Macon Advertiser* (Georgia), August 21, 1832.

103. Ibid., September 4, 1832.

104. Columbus, Georgia, *Democrat*, August 4, 1832.

105. *Macon Telegraph*, March 10, June 2, September 9, 14, 1832.

106. Washington, D.C., *Globe*, August 6, 9, 17, 30, September 5, 11, 15, 17, 26, October 2, 1832; Washington, D.C., *National Intelligencer*, August 2, 7, 11, 16, 21, 25, 30, September 6, 13, 1832.

107. *Harrisburg Chronicle*, April 16, 1830.

108. For debates among these Massachusetts newspapers, see: the Salem *Commercial Advertiser*, April 21, June 2, July 7, 21, August 4, 18, September 5, 8, 22, October 24, 1832; *Essex Register* (Salem), April 9, 30, May 31, June 11, 28, July 5, 9, September 13, 30, November 1, 1832; *Essex Gazette* (Haverhill), August 22, 1831, July 18, September 15, 17, October 27, 1832; *Salem Gazette*, January 24, June 12, September 7, 11, and November 13, 1832.

109. For commentary on the tariff, see: Springfield, Massachusetts, *Hampden Intelligencer*, July 27, 1832; Worcester *Massachusetts Spy*, May 9, September 5, 1832; Boston *Independent Chronicle*, June 27, 1832; Concord *New Hampshire Patriot*, November 21, 1831; *Raleigh Register* (North Carolina), September 2, 1830, November 23, 1832; Charleston *Southern Patriot*, July 10, 1832; *Charleston Mercury*, August 25, 1832.

110. Springfield, Massachusetts, *Hampden Journal*, April 11, October 10, 1832; Philadelphia *Democratic Press*, January 8, 19, February 2, 4, 21, March 6, 13, 14, 19, 21, 26, 1828; Boston *Columbian Centinel*, February 1, 3, 11, March 3, 1832; *Boston Daily Advertiser*, May 5, 1832; *Boston Daily Courier*, May 1, August 16, December 13, 1832; *Savannah Republican* (Georgia), May 19, 1832.

111. Washington, D.C., *Globe*, December 18, 1830, January 12, 19, May 16, 1831, January 12, July 12, October 2, 1832; *Harrisburg Chronicle* (Pennsylvania), February 28, 1831; *Albany Argus* (New York), April 12, 1831, January 1, 31, May 9, 11, 15, 16, 17, 24, August 14, 28, 1832; Athens, Georgia, *Southern Banner*, April 3, August 3, 1832; *Savannah Republican* (Georgia), February 4, March 20, July 21, 1832; *Pittsfield Sun* (Massachusetts), September 6, 16, 1832; *Lowell Mercury* (Massachusetts). June 15, August 31, 1832; *Richmond Daily Whig* (Virginia), May 8, 1830; Charleston, South Carolina, *Southern Patriot*, July 17, 1832; Washington, D.C., *National Intelligencer*, March 12, 19, 25, 26, 1831, June 12,

July 12, 1832; New Bedford, Massachusetts, *Daily Mercury*, May 8, 12, 21, 31, and June 11, 1832.

112. William B. Fraley, "The Representation Controversy in North Carolina, 1787–1835" (Ph.D. diss., University of North Carolina, 1965), pp. 32–5; Harold J. Counihan, "North Carolina, 1815–1836: State and Local Perspectives on the Age of Jackson" (Ph.D. diss., University of North Carolina, 1971), pp. 135–72.

113. *Richmond Daily Whig* (Virginia), February 16, March 9, 1830.

114. License laws: *Boston Morning Post*, November 10, 11, 14, 16, 18, 24, 1831, February 28, 1832; Boston *Columbian Centinel*, February 4, 1832; church and state: Worcester, Massachusetts, *National Aegis*, February 15, 1832.

115. Troupites versus Clarkites: see the *Columbus Enquirer* (Georgia), July 28, 1832; Milledgeville *Georgia Journal*, March 22, 1830, July 7, 28, August 11, 18, September 15, 1831, June 14, 1832; Milledgeville *Southern Recorder*, July 14, August 4, 11, 18, 25, September 8, 15, 22, 29, October 27, November 10, 17, 24, 1831, January 12, 1832. National Indian policy: see the Milledgeville, Georgia, *Federal Union*, September 4, 1830, March 24, 1831; *Augusta Chronicle* (Georgia), June 16, 1832.

116. *Charleston Mercury*, August 27, 1830; Columbia, South Carolina, *Southern Times*, July 19, August 13, 16, 19, 23, 26, September 2, 9, 1830.

117. *Albany Evening Journal* (New York), March 23, April 29, 1831; *Albany Argus* (New York), June 5, 1829, January 9, 1832; Batavia, New York, *Republican Advocate*, October 2, 1832; Geneseo, New York, *Livingston Register*, November 11, 1828, August 11, September 1, 22, 1830.

118. *Louisville Public Advertiser* (Kentucky), October 18, 1828.

119. Springfield, Massachusetts, *Hampden Intelligencer*, May 2, 1832. For other announcements of meetings, see: Penn Yan, New York, *Yates Republican*, February 17, 1829, July 20, 1830; St. Lawrence, New York, *Northern Light*, September 22, 1831, May 24, August 23, September 6, 13, 1832; *Charleston Mercury*, October 6, 1832; *Boston Daily Advocate*, August 2, 1832; Harrisburg, *Pennsylvania Reporter*, August 7, 1829; Charleston, South Carolina, *Southern Patriot*, October 1, 1831, July 25, 1832.

120. Boston *Columbian Centinel*, September 26, 1832.

121. Penn Yan, New York, *Yates Republican*, August 17, 1830; St. Lawrence, New York, *Northern Light*, August 2, 9, 23, 1832; *Boston Daily Advocate*, November 9, 1832; *Charleston Mercury*, August 31, 1831; *Albany Argus* (New York), October 10, 12, 13, 1829, October 11, 1831, September 20, 26, 1832; Worcester *Massachusetts Spy*, November 7, 14, 1832.

122. *Albany Argus* (New York), October 11, 1831.

123. *Charleston Mercury*, February 24, June 6, August 31, 1831; August 6, 17, 18, 23, 25, September 6, 19, 1832.

124. Milledgeville, Georgia, *Federal Union*, August 16, 23, 30, 1832.

125. Concord *New Hampshire Patriot*, February 28, 1831.

126. Worcester *Massachusetts Spy*, October 24, 1832.

127. *Harrisburg Chronicle*, April 26, 1830.

128. Washington, D.C., *Globe*, November 27, 1837, quoting the St. Louis *Missouri Argus; National Intelligencer*, November 20, 1837, quoting the St. Louis *Missouri Republican*.

129. Daniel M. McFarland, "North Carolina Newspapers," pp. 401–2.

130. Z. McLenegan to Joseph Wallace, October 25, 1831; J. R. Roseburg to Joseph Wallace, May 13, 1832; both in the William Macpherson Papers, Historical Society of Pennsylvania.

131. Batavia, New York, *Republican Advocate*, September 15, 29, 1826, June 29, 1827, February 28, May 30, 1828, September 25, 1829, October 21, 28, 1831; Geneseo, New York, *Livingston Register*, September 8, 1830, September 28, 1831, April 25, 1832; Penn Yan, New York, *Yates Republican*, July 22, November 2, 1828, February 17, 1829, February 2, October 19, 1830.

132. *Lyons Countryman* (New York), June 22, October 5, 1830; January 11, July 26, September 22, 1831.

133. Ibid., October 5, 1830, March 15, May 3, July 12, August 22, 1831.

134. He edited the *Le Roy Gazette* in 1827 and 1828, the Herkimer *Republican Farmers and Free Press* in 1830 and 1831, and the Utica *Elucidator* in 1832.

135. Batavia, New York, *Republican Advocate*, June 29, 1827, May 30, 1828, May 7, 1830,

August 14, October 23, 1832; *Lyons Countryman* (New York), March 2, 1830; St. Lawrence, New York, *Northern Light*, November 1, 1832.

136. Lynwood M. Dent, Jr., "The Virginia Democratic Party, 1824–1847" (Ph.D. diss., Louisiana State University, 1974), p. 30; J. C. Calhoun to Francis W. Pickens, March 2, 1832, Pickens Papers, Duke University.

137. Isaac Hill to Levi Woodbury, August 4, 1828, Levi Woodbury Papers, Library of Congress; Col. Henry Orne, *The Letters of Columbus Originally Published in the Boston Bulletin* (Boston: Putnam and Hunt, 1829), pp. 13ff.; *Boston Statesman*, May 11, 13, 1829, November 5, December 3, 1831, March 3, 1832; George M. Dallas to Samuel D. Ingham, February 16, 1825, Dallas Papers, Historical Society of Pennsylvania; *Harrisburg Chronicle* (Pennsylvania), August 27, September 24, 1832, July 29, 1833; Ershkowitz, "New Jersey Politics during the Era of Jackson," pp. 98–102; H. H. Townes to Capt. G. F. Townes, March 10 and August 4, 1831, Townes Family Papers, South Caroliniana Library; Sumter, South Carolina, *Southern Whig*, September 29, 1832; Charleston *Southern Patriot*, September 6, 1832.

138. Harrisburg, Pennsylvania, *Republican and Anti-Masonic Inquirer*, March 6, 1830, June 2, 1831; *Columbia Hive* (South Carolina), September 15, 1832. Editors M. D. Richardson, B. F. Perry, and Richard Yeadon were members of the Union and State Rights party Committee of Correspondence in South Carolina; *Harrisburg Chronicle* (Pennsylvania), August 27, 1832; *Philadelphia Mercury*, January 5, 1828.

139. Worcester *Massachusetts Yeoman*, February 25, 1832; Springfield, Massachusetts, *Hampden Intelligencer*, July 25, August 8, 29, 1832.

140. Samuel A. Townes to G. F. Townes, July 5, 1832, Townes Family Papers, South Caroliniana Library.

141. Henry D. Capers, *The Life and Times of C. G. Memminger* (Richmond, Va.: Everett Waddey Co., 1893).

142. *An Oration on the Fourth of July, 1832, at Sumter Court House* (Sumter, S.C.: Gazette Office, 1832).

143. Sumter, South Carolina, *Southern Whig*, August 9, October 6, 1832.

144. *Cortland Advocate* (New York), February 10, 1832.

145. Ibid., February 3, 17, July 20, 27, August 17, September 7, 29, 1832.

146. *Lyons Countryman* (New York), February 16, 1830.

147. Worcester, Massachusetts, *National Aegis*, September 19, 1832; *Boston Daily Advertiser*, September 11, 13, October 13, 1832.

148. *Boston Daily Courier*, April 23, 1832.

149. Jubal Harrington, editor of the *Worcester Republican*, was a delegate to the Worcester County Jacksonian Convention in 1832; he also served as convention secretary. *Worcester Republican*, October 10, 1832. Charles Green, editor of the *Boston Morning Post*, was a delegate to the Jacksonian state convention in late 1831. *Boston Statesman*, August 20, 1831. John B. Eldridge, editor of the Springfield *Hampden Whig*, served as a delegate and as secretary to the Jacksonian state convention in 1831. *Worcester County Republican*, September 7, 1831. Samuel Bowles, editor of the *Springfield Republican*, was secretary of the Springfield National Republican town meeting and chaired the Massachusetts Young Men's National Republican Convention. Springfield *Hampden Journal*, April 18, 1832. Phineas Allen, editor of the *Pittsfield Sun*, chaired the Berkshire County Democratic-Republican Convention in early 1831. *Pittsfield Sun*, March 10, 17, 1831.

150. Green to Calhoun, May 31, 1831; Green to James Hamilton, Jr., November 9, 1831; both in General Correspondence, volume 5, Duff Green Papers, Southern Historical Collection, University of North Carolina. Calhoun was kept informed of political developments in Washington and throughout the nation by Green's letters. See Green to Calhoun, April 21, July 18, 1831, July 9, August 28, October 9, 1832, volume 5, Duff Green Papers.

151. Green to Stephen Simpson, July 17, 28, 1831, General Correspondence, volume 5; Green to James Hamilton, Jr., July 18, 1831, General Correspondence, volume 5; Green to Judge Semple, February 12, 1832, Letterbooks, volume 4, p. 472; Green to J. S. Barbour, July 22, 1831, volume 4, Letterbooks, p. 438; Green to Richard K. Cralle, August 21, September 5, Nov 1, 11, 12, 1831, February 17, 1832, General Correspondence, volume 5; all in Duff Green Papers, Southern Historical Collection, University of North Carolina.

152. Green to Col. A. Storrow, September 3, 1831; Green to James Hamilton, September 4,

1831; Green to D. Russell, July 12, 1831; all in General Correspondence, volume 5, Duff Green Papers, Southern Historical Collection, University of North Carolina.

153. Green to James M. White, August 30, 1832, General Correspondence, volume 5; Green to Joseph Hixie, September 10, 1832, Letterbooks, volume 4, p. 515; Green to F. Whittlesey, September 12, 1832, Letterbooks, volume 4, p. 520; all in Duff Green Papers, Southern Historical Collection, University of North Carolina; Edward Everett to Duff Green, September 15, 1832, Edward Everett Papers, Massachusetts Historical Society.

154. William E. Ames, "A History of the Washington *Globe*," unpublished manuscript, University of Washington.

155. Ibid., pp. 1–2.

156. Ibid., pp. 126, 224, 228–9.

157. T. B. Barnow to Blair, February 10, 1831; Allen A. Hall to Blair, May 7, 1831; Thomas Crawford to Blair, April 13, 1833; and Michael Crider to Blair, April 22, 1844; all in Blair-Lee Papers, Princeton University.

158. Ames, "History of the Washington *Globe*," pp. 157–9, quoting William Thomas Burke to Blair, July 2, 1833; Richard Newcastle to Blair, November 10, 1832; copies in Blair-Lee Papers, Princeton University.

159. Ames, "History of the Washington *Globe*," p. 156, quoting William S. Ranson to Blair, August 12, 1831, copy in Blair-Lee Papers, Princeton University.

160. Ames, "History of the Washington *Globe*," pp. 156–7, quoting Joseph E. Hinton to Blair, August 26, 1833; Gerard Banks, Jr., to Blair, November 28, 1831; Richard H. Newcastle to Blair, September 3, 1831; copies in Blair-Lee Papers, Princeton University.

161. Washington, D.C., *Globe*, April 10, May 19, 1832; Sen. A. Bucker to Blair, May 10, 1832, Draper Collection, American States, volume 1, Historical Society of Pennsylvania; F. Ewing to Blair, April 20, 1832, Blair-Rives Papers, Library of Congress.

162. Batavia, New York, *Republican Advocate*, September 11, 1832.

163. Thomas C. Clarke, September 12, 1832, Nicholas Biddle Papers, Library of Congress.

164. Ames, "History of the Washington *Globe*," p. 228, quoting Blair to Kendall, December 24, 1842, copy in Martin Van Buren Papers, Library of Congress; also see Ames, "History of the Washington *Globe*," pp. 241–2.

165. F. Lauriston Bullard, "Nathaniel Green," *Dictionary of American Biography*, volume 4, ed. Allen Johnson and Dumas Malone (New York: Charles Scribners' Sons, 1960), part 1, p. 573; Arthur B. Darling, *Political Changes in Massachusetts, 1824–48*, pp. 41–2; John B. Derby, *Political Reminiscences, Including a Sketch of the Origin and History of the "Statesman Party" of Boston* (Boston: Homer and Palmer, 1835), pp. 12–13.

166. "Letters to John Brazer Davis, 1819–31," Massachusetts Historical Society *Proceedings*, volume 49 (Boston: University Press, 1916).

167. Charles G. DeWitt to A. C. Flag, October 6, 20, 1830; S. J. B. Skinner to Flagg, July 31, 1830; Henry O'Reilly to Flagg, November 11, 1829; Michael Hoffman to Flagg, January 2, 22, December 15, 1827; Jonathan DeGraff to Flagg, December 27, 1827; E. Mack to Flagg, Jan 11, 1832; all in the Azariah Flagg Papers, New York Public Library; Croswell to Charles Butler, September 1, 1824, Charles Butler Papers, Library of Congress; Croswell to Levi Woodbury, April 9, 1832, Levi Woodbury Papers, Library of Congress.

168. M. Cadwallader to Weed, December 14, 1829, and March 26, 1830; Herman Norton to Weed, March 25, 1829; both in the Thurlow Weed Papers, University of Rochester.

169. Walter B. Edgar, ed., *Biographical Directory of the South Carolina House of Representatives*, volume 1, *Session Lists, 1692–1978* (Columbia: University of South Carolina Press, 1974), pp. 292, 298, 304, 309, 313, 316, 322, 326; P. M. Butler to J. H. Hammond, November 21, 1831, James Henry Hammond Papers, Library of Congress; *Charleston Mercury*, August 30, September 8, 1830, February 27, 1832; William L. King, *The Newspaper Press of Charleston*, S. C. (Charleston: Lucas and Richardson, 1882), pp. 148–9; David F. Houston, *Critical Study of Nullification in South Carolina* (New York: Longmans, Green and Co., 1896).

170. Remini, *The Election of Andrew Jackson*, p. 49.

Age of Information

INTRODUCTION TO PART FOUR

B Y THE BEGINNING OF THE 20TH CENTURY, technological advances encouraged the dissemination of communication messages to millions of Americans. Daily urban newspapers flourished throughout the country and the development of telephones, radio, film, and photography helped to make communication more timely, accessible and relevant. Yet, the dependence on new public technologies fueled concerns that in an era of endless communication authentic communication was no longer possible.

The growth of daily newspapers in the United States peaked in 1909 at 2,600. By the 1920s, facing escalating costs for machinery, ink and newsprint, and challenges regarding greater efficiency, newspaper publishers began to adopt a variety of business strategies to increase profits including: the creation of monopolies and newspaper groups, aligning themselves with other large employers, and lobbying government for policy exemptions and special privileges. At the turn of the 20th century, individuals or corporations with newspapers in two or more cities owned 10 percent of U.S. newspapers, yet by 1945 40 percent of U.S. newspapers were part of newspaper chains.

Media critics like Edward Alsworth Ross (1918) bemoaned the privilege afforded the "sacred cows" of business, industry and government by the daily press and began to question the suppression and misrepresentation of news and information.

During the first two decades of the 20th century, muckraking journalists sought to educate and inform the public about important social issues. Muckrakers targeted urban, middle-class readers through mass-circulation magazines, newspapers and books, seeking to eliminate public apathy and ignorance by rousing citizens to speak out against abuses of power in society. Crafting approximately 2,000 investigative reports, based on the careful examination of government documents, muckrakers provided evidence of deep alliances between government and business, illustrated deception and corruption of politicians and business leaders, and exposed economic inequities in the United States.

By the 1920s, two types of newspapers based on class divisions flourished in the United States. Gossip-oriented tabloids, emphasizing storytelling and unusual happenings, reflected the experiences of a newly literate urban population. Tabloids such as the *New York Daily News* captured readers' attention with an emotional mix of sex and crime news, sensational photographs, and glaring headlines. In contrast, information newspapers, such as the *New York Times*, remained geared to a middle- and upper-class audience, providing the official record of the governing elite in a rational, logical, and factual format.

A new journalism of interpretation also emerged during the 1920s with the development of news magazines. Publications such as *Time*, founded by Henry Luce and Briton Hadden, focused on politics, economics, culture, and medicine, summarizing news published in the daily press and commenting upon that information. Rejecting any pretense of neutrality or objectivity, *Time* provided readers with commentary on, and interpretation of, current policies and ideas. Written in a flippant narrative style *Time* was geared to upper-class, white, male readers. According to Michael Schudson in *Discovering the News. A Social History of American Newspapers* (1978, p. 149), in critiquing the state of journalism, Luce recommended that newspapers drop its separation of news and editorial in favor of front-page news that joined "intelligent criticism, representation and evaluation of the men who hold offices of public trust."

The development of radio involved a story of technical innovation as well as a battle for control between individual entrepreneurs and corporate interests. Politicians and business leaders envisioned radio as a tool of social influence, while educators debated its usefulness as a teaching tool, and cultural elites worried about its influence on high culture. The Federal Communications Commission, which in 1934 was given the power to grant licenses and enforce legislation related to radio frequencies, ownership practices, and broadcast programming restrictions, addressed challenges of spectrum crowding and poor reception. Providing free entertainment news, and a connection to the larger world, during the Great Depression radio became the dominant form of mass communication. Franklin D. Roosevelt effectively used the new medium during his presidential campaigns and, as president, his national radio addresses urged Congress and voters to accept new proposals for the country. In weekly radio broadcasts known as "Fireside Chats", Roosevelt informed the public about his plans to solve the economic crisis and he later used his radio chats to encourage Americans to support the war effort.

At the height of the depression, in 1933, reporters who were frustrated by low wages and poor working conditions, founded the American Newspaper Guild. Wishing to raise journalistic standards and represent the working interests of its members through collective bargaining, at its first convention, the Guild approved a code of ethics and passed a freedom of conscience resolution considering freedom of the press a right of readers and a responsibility of journalists. Most newspaper editors and publishers soon rejected the Guild, refusing to recognize it as a representative for journalists, and intimidating reporters who dared to join. As resistance to the organization grew, journalists began to rely more on labor union techniques such as picketing, walkouts and strikes, and in 1936 the American Newspaper Guild formally affiliated with the American Federation of Labor.

An 80-year struggle by American suffragists culminated in 1920 with the passage of the Nineteenth Amendment granting all female citizens over the age of 21 the right to vote. In the 1920s, while almost 20 percent of newspaper reporters were women, most of them were confined to working on women's issues and society pages. Of the nearly 12,000 female journalists working in the U.S. during the 1930s, very few were allowed to cover politics, public affairs or other front-page news stories. While during the 1970s, women still earned less than 60 percent of men's pay, they had gained access to all aspects of the news process and female reporters regularly covered front-page news. Yet broadcast news remained a male domain throughout the 20th century. It was not until September 5, 2006, that a woman, Katie Couric, became the first female solo anchor on a network evening broadcast news program.

The first public demonstration of a fully electronic television system began on August 24, 1934, at the Franklin Institute in Philadelphia. Philo T. Farnsworth initially conceived of electronic television as a teenager, and by the early 1930s had patented an Image Dissector and other key aspects of television. In 1935, the U.S. Patent Office awarded him priority of invention for the development of television, yet David Sarnoff and the Radio Corporation of America (RCA), tied Farnsworth and his invention up in litigation for many years. The U.S. government suspended sales of television sets during World War II, and by the end of the war, with Farnsworth's key patents about to expire, Sarnoff and RCA took control of the production and sales of television sets. As Daniel Stashower in *The Boy Genius and the Mogul: The Untold Story of Television* (2002, p. 255) explains, Sarnoff and RCA quickly launched a national public relations campaign to promote Vladimir Zworkin as the "father of television" and Sarnoff as the "clear-sighted and steadfast godfather."

Theatrical newsreel companies initially supplied television stations with early news programs yet technical problems and a dull format resulted in low ratings. "The Camel News Caravan," a 15-minute evening news broadcast sponsored by Camel cigarettes debuted on NBC in February 1949. Narrated by John Cameron Swayze, the Monday through Friday news program provided a model for future newscasts throughout the world. While critics initially dismissed television news, its ability to generate emotion, particularly in coverage of the Civil Rights Movement and the assassination of President John F. Kennedy, helped make television the dominant source for news by the 1970s. The first network devoted exclusively to news, Cable News Network (CNN) debuted in June 1980 with 2,000,000 subscribers. By the mid-1990s, the network reached 62,000,000 U.S. subscribers and had an international audience of more than 67,000,000 viewers.

Manipulating reporters' reliance on objectivity and their reliance on public officials as primary sources of information, during the early 1950s, Senator Joseph McCarthy used innuendo, hysteria, and ad hominen attacks in a witch-hunt against individuals suspected of being sympathetic to the communist movement. Members of the Washington press corps dutifully reported McCarthy's baseless accusations, rarely asking for evidence or investigating his charges. According to David Halberstam (1933, p. 52), with the elite press as his accomplice, McCarthy "crystallized and politicized the anxieties of a nation living in a dangerous new era. He took people who were at the worst guilty of political naïveté and accused them of treason. He set out to do the unthinkable, and it turned out to be surprisingly thinkable" ultimately destroying the lives and careers of thousands of innocent Americans.

During the 1960s and 1970s young people, women, and racial, ethnic, and sexual minorities launched a general revolt against an oppressive, inhumane, and artificial consumer culture. One journalistic response, New Journalism (also known as Literary Journalism), began to revive the 19th-century concept of the journalist as advocate, interpreter, and critic combining the factual authority of journalism with the atmospheric license of fiction. Writers such as Tom Wolfe, Truman Capote, Gay Talese, and Hunter Thompson fused journalistic, cinematic, conversational, and literary writing styles to create more accurate depictions and to tell deeper truths about society.

A variety of underground newspapers also challenged traditional journalism during the 1960s, offering readers an honest subjectivity rather than a traditional understanding of objectivity. Using cheap offset-press technology, and staffed primarily by student reporters, the underground press embraced politics, dissent, popular culture, and experimentation and attempted to remove traditional race, class, and national boundaries.

The journalistic coverage of the Watergate scandal during the early 1970s highlighted traditional journalistic practices related to the notion of objectivity, and reinvigorated the field of investigative reporting. The press's role in exposing a crucial political scandal, which culminated in the resignation of the president, inspired a generation of journalists and offered justification for continued First Amendment protection of the press. Bob Woodward and Carl Bernstein's highly-ranked government source, Deep Throat, provided important background information pivotal to the case. For 30 years, until ex-FBI official Mark Felt revealed himself in 2005, Deep Throat was the most widely debated anonymous source in the history of American journalism. After Watergate, Woodward and Bernstein became folk heroes, penning a bestseller, *All the President's Men*, which codified an ideology of journalism that has framed subsequent understandings of the role of the press in American society.

An anti-labor climate fueled media mergers, consolidations, and deregulation and encouraged the passage of the Telecommunications Act of 1996, which further relaxed ownership rules resulting in a media landscape where a small number of giant corporations now control the vast majority of media content. At the beginning of the 21st century, vast conglomerates such as AOL Time Warner and Viacom emphasize short-term profits over information, gutting newsrooms and foreign bureaus and shutting down newspapers and broadcast programming that do not aid their bottom line. Public skepticism regarding media professionalism and the accuracy and credibility of news is at an all time high and scholars, critics and media practitioners now wonder if there is a future for journalism.

Chapter 20

ROBERT DARNTON

WRITING NEWS AND TELLING STORIES

All the news that fits we print.
From the graffiti in the pressroom of police headquarters, Manhattan, 1964

THIS ESSAY IS A PERSONAL REPORT ON the experience of writing news.[1] It resulted from an attempt to circumnavigate the literature on communication theory, diffusion studies, and the sociology of the media, which I undertook in the expectation of finding a new approach to the French Revolution. As an historian of propaganda and radical ideology, I have always held onto the hope that the social sciences will provide a kind of Northwest Passage to the past. I ran aground, however, while reading "Newsmen's Fantasies, Audiences, and Newswriting" by Ithiel de Sola Pool and Irwin Shulman in *Public Opinion Quarterly* (Summer, 1959). That article touched off an analysis of my earlier experience as a reporter, which I offer with the wish that it may point to some fruitful lines of inquiry, despite its subjective character.

The Pool-Shulman Study

Pool and Shulman got newspapermen to conjure up images of their public through a process of free association. They asked thirty-three reporters to name persons who came to mind as they were going over stories they had just completed. Some reporters named persons whom they liked and whom they expected to react warmly to stories conveying good news. Others imagined hostile readers and took a certain pleasure in providing them with bad news. The comparison of the fantasies about "supportive" and "critical" readers suggested that the affective component in a reporter's image of his public might influence the accuracy of his writing. Pool and Shulman tried to test this distortion factor by supplying four groups of thirty-three journalism students each with scrambled facts taken from stories that communicated both good news and bad news.

Each student assembled the facts into his own version of the story and then listed persons who came to mind while thinking back over the writing. He then was interviewed to determine the degree of approval or criticism that he attributed to the persons on his list, and his story was checked for accuracy. The experimenters found that writers with supportive "image persons" reported good news more accurately than they reported bad news, and that writers with critical "image persons" reported bad news with more accuracy. Pool and Shulman concluded that accuracy was congruent with a reporter's fantasies about his public.

The experiment suggests how current theories about mass communication may be applied to research on the media. Now that sociologists no longer think of communication as a one-way process of implanting messages in a relatively passive "mass" audience, they can analyze the audience's influence on the communicator. Having become sensitive to the importance of feedback and noise, they can understand how a writer's image of his public shapes his writing. But they sometimes fail to take into consideration another element, which is conspicuously absent from the Pool-Shulman study, namely, the communicator's milieu. Reporters operate in city rooms, not in classrooms. They write for one another as well as for the public. And their way of conceiving and communicating news results from an apprenticeship in their craft. Translated into sociological language, those observations suggest four hypotheses: in order to understand how newspapermen function as communicators, one should analyze (1) the structure of their milieu, the city room; (2) their relation to primary reference groups, i.e., editors, other reporters, and news sources; (3) their occupational socialization, or the way they get "broken in" as reporters; and (4) the cultural determinants of their encoding, or how standardized techniques of telling "stories" influence their writing of "news." By ignoring the milieu of the city room and by dealing with students who had not undergone an apprenticeship, Pool and Shulman neglected the most important elements in newswriting. In order to indicate the importance of the four elements named above, I have tried to analyze my recollections of my brief career as a reporter for the *Newark Star Ledger* and *The New York Times* from 1959 to 1964.

The Structure of the Newsroom

Reporters on *The New York Times* used to believe that their editors expected them to aim their stories at an imaginary twelve-year-old girl. Some thought that she appeared in *The Style Book of The New York Times*, although she only existed in our minds. "Why twelve years old?" I used to ask myself. "Why a girl? What are her opinions on prison reform and the Women's House of Detention?" This mythical creature was the only "audience image" I ever ran across in my newspaper work, and she merely functioned as a reminder that we should keep our copy clear and clean. We really wrote for one another. Our primary reference group was spread around us in the newsroom, or "the snake pit," as some called it. We knew that no one would jump on our stories as quickly as our colleagues; for reporters make the most voracious readers, and they have to win their status anew each day as they expose themselves before their peers in print.

There are structural elements to the status system of the newsroom, as its layout indicates. The managing editor rules from within an office; and lesser editors command clusters of "desks" (foreign desk, national desk, city or "metropolitan" desk) at one end of the room, an end that stands out by the different orientation of the furniture and that is enclosed behind a low fence. At the other end, row upon row of reporters' desks face the editors across the fence. They fall into four sections. First, a few rows of star reporters led by luminaries like Homer Bigart, Peter Kihss, and McCandlish Phillips. Then three rows of rewrite men, who sit to the side of the stars at the front of the room so that they can be near the command posts during deadline periods. Next, a spread of middle-aged veterans, men who have made their names and can be trusted with any story. And finally, a herd of young men on the make in the back of the room, the youngest generally occupying the remotest positions. Function determines some locations: sports, shipping, "culture," and "society" have their own corners; and copy readers sit accessibly to the side. But to the eye of the initiate, the general lines of the status system stand out as clearly as a banner headline.[2]

The most expert eye in the city room belongs to the city editor. From his point of maximal visibility, he can survey his entire staff and can put each man in his place, for he alone knows the exact standing of everyone. The "staffer" is only aware of occupying an indeterminate position in one of the four sections. He therefore tries to trace the trajectory of his career by watching the key variable in the functioning of the city room: the assignment. A reporter who keeps a string of good assignments going for several weeks is destined to move up to a desk nearer the editor's end of the room, while a man who constantly bungles stories will stagnate in his present position or will be exiled to Brooklyn or "society" or "the West Side shack" (a police beat now extinct and replaced, functionally, by New Jersey). The daily paper shows who has received the best assignments. It is a map, which reporters learn to read and to compare with their mental map of the city room in an attempt to know where they stand and where they are headed.

But once you have learned to read the status system, you must learn to write. How do you know when you have done a good job on a story? When I was a greenhorn on *The Times*, I began one week with a "profile" or man-in-the-news, which won a compliment from the assistant city editor and a coveted out-of-town assignment for the next day. Half the police force of a small town had been arrested for stealing stolen goods, and I found a cop who was willing to talk, so the story made the "second front," the front page of the second section, which attracts a good deal of attention. On the third day, I covered the centenary celebrations at Cornell. They satisfied my ego (I rode back to New York in the private plane that normally served the president of the university) but not my editor: I filed seven hundred and fifty words, which were cut down to five hundred. Next, I went to a two-day convention of city planners at West Point. Once again my ego swelled as the planners scrambled to get their names in *The Times*, but for the life of me I could not find anything interesting to say about them. I filed five hundred words, which did not even make the paper. For the next week I wrote nothing but obituaries.

Assignments, cuts, and the situating or "play" of stories therefore belong to a system of positive and negative reinforcements. By-lines come easily on *The Times*, unlike many papers, so reporters find gratification in getting their stories past the copy desk unchanged and into a desirable location in the paper, that is, close to the front and above the fold. Every day every foreign correspondent gets his reinforcement in the form of "frontings," a cable telling him which stories have made the front page and which have been "insided." Compliments also carry weight, especially if they come from persons with prestige, like the night city editor, the stars, or the most talented reporters in one's own territory. The city editor and managing editor dispense pats on the back, occasional congratulatory notes, and lunches; and every month the publisher awards cash prizes for the best stories. As the reinforcements accrue, one's status evolves. A greenhorn may eventually become a veteran or embark on more exotic channels of upward mobility by winning a national or foreign assignment. The veterans also include a sad collection of men on the decline, foreign correspondents who have been sent home to pasture, or bitter, ambitious men who have failed to get editorships. I often heard it said that reporting was a young man's game, that you passed your prime by forty, and that as you got older all stories began to seem the same.

Reporters naturally write to please the editors manipulating the reward system from the other end of the room, but there is no straightforward way of winning reinforcement by writing the best possible story. In run-of-the-mill assignments, a voice over the public address system—"Jones, city desk"—summons the reporter to the assignment editor, who explains the assignment: "The Kiwanis Club of Brooklyn is holding its annual luncheon, where it will announce the results of this year's charity drive and the winner of its Man of the Year Award. It's probably worth a good half-column, because we haven't done anything on Brooklyn recently, and the drive is a big deal over there." The editor tries to get the best effort from Jones by playing up the importance of the assignment, and he plants a few clues as to what he thinks "the story" is. A potential lead sentence may actually rattle around in Jones's head as he takes the subway to Brooklyn: "This year's charity drive in Brooklyn produced a record-breaking $ . . ., the Kiwanis Club announced at its annual luncheon meeting yesterday." Jones arrives, interviews the president of the club, sits through a chicken dinner and several speeches, and learns that the drive produced a disappointing $300,000 and that the club named a civic-minded florist as its man of the year. "So what's the story?" the night city editor asks him upon his return. Jones knows better than to play up this non-event to the night city editor, but he wants something to show for his day's work; so he explains the unspectacular character of the drive, adding that the florist seemed to be an interesting character. "You'd better lead with the florist, then. Two hundred words," says the night city editor. Jones walks off to the back of the room and begins the story: "Anthony Izzo, a florist who has made trees grow in Brooklyn for a decade, received the annual Man of the Year Award from the Brooklyn Kiwanis Club yesterday for his efforts to beautify the city's streets. The club also announced that its annual charity drive netted $300,000, a slight drop from last year's total, which the Club's president, Michael Calise, attributed to the high rate of unemployment in the area." The story occupies a mere fourth of a column well back in the second section of the paper. No one mentions it to Jones on the following day. No letters arrive for him from Brooklyn. And he feels rather dissatisfied about the whole experience, especially as Smith, who sits next to him in the remote centerfield section of the city room, made the second front with a colorful story about garbage dumping. But Jones consoles himself with the hope that he might get a better assignment today and with the reflection that the allusion to the tree growing in Brooklyn was a nice touch, which might have been noticed by the city editor and certainly had been appreciated by Smith. But Jones also knows that the story did not make his stock rise with the assignment editor, who had had a different conception of it, or with the night city editor, who had not had time to devote more than two or three minutes' thought to it, nor to the other editors, who must have perceived it as the hack job that it was.

In the case of an important assignment, like a multi-column "take out," the city editor might walk over to Jones' desk and discuss the story with him in a kind of conspiratorial huddle before a sea of eyes. Jones contacts a dozen different sources and writes a story that differs considerably from what the editor had in mind. The editor, who gets a carbon copy of everything submitted to the copy desk, disapproves of the text and has Jones summoned to him by the public address system. After huddling in alien territory, Jones negotiates his way back to his desk through the sea of eyes and tries again. Eventually he reaches a version that represents a compromise between the editor's preconceptions and his own impressions—but he knows that he would have won more points if his impressions had come closer to the mark imagined by the editor in the first place. And he did not enjoy walking the tightrope between his desk and the city editor before the crowd of reporters waiting for his status to drop.

Like everyone else, reporters vary in their sensitivity to pressure from their peer group, but I doubt that many of them—especially from the ranks of the greenhorns—enjoy being summoned to the city desk. They learn to escape to the bathroom or to crouch behind drinking fountains when the hungry eye of the editor surveys the field. When the fatal call comes over the public address system—"Jones, city desk"—Jones can feel his colleagues thinking as he walks past them, "I hope he gets a lousy assignment or that he gets a good one and blows it." The result will be there for everyone to see in tomorrow's paper. Editors sometimes try to get the best effort out of their men by playing them off against one another and by advocating values like competitiveness and "hustling." "Did you see how Smith handled that garbage story?" the city editor will say to Jones. "That's the kind of work we need from the man who is going to fill the next opening in the Chicago bureau. You should hustle more." Two days later, Jones may have outdone Smith. The immediacy and the irregularity of reinforcement in the assignment-publication process mean that no one, except a few stars, can be sure of his status in the newsroom.

Chronic insecurity breeds resentment. While scrambling over one another for the approval of the editors, the reporters develop great hostility to the men at the other end of the room, and some peer-group solidarity develops as a counter-force to the competitiveness. The reporters feel united by a sentiment of "them" against "us," which they express in horseplay and house jokes. (I remember a clandestine meeting in the men's room, where one reporter gave a parody of urinating techniques among "them.") Many reporters, especially among the embittered veterans, deride the editors, who are mostly former reporters, for selling out to the management and for losing contact with the down-to-earth reality that can only be appreciated by honest "shoe-leather men." This anti-management ideology creates a barrier to the open courting of editors and makes some reporters think that they write only to please themselves and their peers.

The feeling of solidarity against "them" expresses itself most strongly in the reporters' taboo against "piping" or distorting a story so that it fits an editor's pre-conceptions. Editors apparently think of themselves as "idea men," who put a reporter on the scent of a story and expect him to track it down and bring it back in publishable form. Reporters think of editors as manipulators of both reality and men. To them, an editor is a person who cares mainly about improving his position in his own, separate hierarchy by coming up with bright ideas and getting his staff to write in conformity to them. The power of editor over reporter, like that of publisher over editor, does indeed produce bias in newswriting, as has been emphasized in studies of "social control in the newsroom" (see the bibliographical note at the end of this essay). But the reporters' horror of "piping" acts as a countervailing influence. For example, an assistant city editor on *The Times* once got an inspiration for a pollution story from his son, who complained that an ice-cream cone had become so filthy as he walked down the street that he had had to throw it into a trash can. The reporter dutifully built the story around the anecdote, adding as an embellishment that the unnamed little boy missed the trash can and walked away. The editor did not delete this last touch. He was delighted with the story, which presumably improved his standing with the other editors and the reporter's standing with him. But it made the reporter's reputation plummet among her peers and served as a deterrent against further "piping" on the other side of the fence.

The peer group's own standards of craftsmanship also pit reporters against copyeditors. Copyeditors tend to be a separate breed among newspapermen. Quiet, intense, perhaps more eccentric and more learned than most reporters, they are cast in the role of being sticklers for language. They go by the book—*The Style Book of The New York Times* on *The Times*—and they have their own hierarchy, which leads from the lowly members of their desk to the "slot man," who apportions the copy among them, to the "bull pen," where the final tailoring of each edition takes place, and ultimately to an assistant managing editor, who in my day was Theodore Bernstein, a man of great power and prestige. Copyeditors apparently think of themselves as second-class citizens in the newsroom: every day, as they see it, they save the reporters from dozens of errors of fact and grammar; yet the reporters revile them. "The game is to sneak some color or interpretation past that line of humorless zombies," one reporter explained to me. Copyeditors seem to view stories as segments in an unremitting flow of "copy," which cries out for standardization, while reporters regard each piece as their own. Personal touches—bright quotations or observations—satisfy the reporter's sense of craftsmanship and provoke the blue-penciling instinct of the copyeditor. Lead sentences produce the worst injuries in the reporter's unending battle with his editors and copyeditors; he may attribute cuts and poor play of his stories to the pressure of circumstances, but a change in his lead is a challenge to his news judgment, the ineffable quality that marks him as a "pro." To reverse the order of a reporter's first two paragraphs is to wound his professional identity. He will even take offense at slight changes of phrasing in his first sentence that he would hardly notice further down in the story. And a really bad lead can damage a man's career. A friend of mine once led a story with a remark about a baby who had been burned "to an almost unrecognizable crisp." It was the "almost" that especially outraged the editors. That lead cost him ten years in the lowliest position of the newsroom, or so we believed.

Reporters are held together by sub-groups, which also mitigate competitiveness and insecurity and influence ways of writing. Clusters of reporters form according to age, life-style, or cultural background (City College vs. Harvard in the early sixties at *The Times*). Some have lunch together, buy each other drinks in certain bars, or exchange family visits. A reporter develops trust in his sub-group. He consults it while working on stories and pays attention to its shop talk. A reporter in my group once had to do a rushed story about a confusing change in the city's incomprehensible welfare programs. Four or five of us went over his material, trying to extract some meaning from it, until one person finally pronounced, "It's a holding operation." That became the lead of the story and the idea around which the entire article was organized. Almost every article develops around a core conception of what constitutes "the story," which may emerge from the reporter's contacts with allies in the city room as well as from his dialogue with the editors. Just as messages pass through a "two-step" or multi-step communication process on the receiving end, they pass through several stages in their formation. If the communicator is a city reporter, he filters his ideas through reference groups and role sets in the city room before turning them loose on "the public."

The adjustment of writer to milieu is complicated by a final factor: institutional history. Long-term shifts in the power structure of a newspaper affect the way reporters write, even though the rank and file does not know exactly what goes on among editors and executives. Many papers are divided into semi-autonomous dukedoms ruled by the city editor, the foreign editor, and the national editor. Each of these men commands clusters of assistant editors and owes fealty to the managing editor, who in turn shares power with other executives, such as the business manager, and submits to the supreme sovereign of all, the publisher. At *The Times*, each editor dominates a certain proportion of the paper, so that in an issue of n columns, the city editor can expect to command x columns, the foreign editor y columns, and so forth. Of course the proportions vary every day according to the importance of events, but in the long run they are determined by the ability of each potentate to defend and extend his domain. Changes in territoriality often take place at the "four o'clock conference" in the managing editor's office, where the day's paper takes shape. Here each editor summarizes the output of his staff and, day after day, builds up a case for the coverage of his area. A forceful city editor can get more space for city-room reporters and can inspire them with a fresh sense of the newsworthiness of their subjects.

City news underwent such a revival during my period at *The Times*, owing to the influence of a new city editor, A. M. Rosenthal. Before Rosenthal's editorship, New York stories tended to be thorough, reliable, conventional, and dull. Rosenthal wanted snappier, more original copy, and he wanted his men to "hustle." He therefore gave the best assignments to the reporters who conformed most closely to his standards, regardless of their position in the city room. This policy infuriated the veterans, who had learned to write according to the old rules and who believed in the established principle that one earned the right to the best assignments by years of solid service. They complained about trendiness, jazziness, superficiality, and sophomorism. Some of them resigned, some succeeded in brightening up their copy, and many withdrew into a world of private or peer-group bitterness. Most of the greenhorns responded by exuberant hustling. An alliance grew up between them and Rosenthal, a poor boy from the Bronx and City College, who had hustled his way to the top of *The Times*. The qualities that had made him succeed—talent, drive, enthusiasm—now made for success in the city room. Of course those qualities were recognized under the old seniority system (otherwise Rosenthal himself would never have had such a spectacular career), but the new editor shifted the balance among the norms: the emphasis on hustling at the expense of seniority meant that achievement outweighed ascription in the determination of status.

The institutionalization of this new value system created more confusion and pain than can be conveyed by sociological terminology. In disturbing the established routes of mobility, Rosenthal did not completely cut himself off from the veterans. He did not interfere with the stars, and he did not win over all the greenhorns. Instead, he produced status anxiety everywhere, perhaps even for himself; for he seemed to have been surprised at the hostility he evoked from men who had been his friends, and he probably had worries about his own standing among the other editors and executives. The first months of his editorship constituted a difficult, transitional period in the city room. While the rules of the game were changing, no one knew where he stood; for standing seemed to fluctuate as erratically as the apportionment of assignments. A reporter might keep a string of good assignments going for a week, while a deadly rain of obituaries fell all around him, but he could also be banished overnight to the obit page or the "caboose" (the last news section of the Sunday paper). Hence the dread character of the summons over the public address system. Eventually, however, a new status system became established according to the new norms. Bolstered by raises and promotions, the bright, aggressive young men set the tone in the newsroom and moved on to more prestigious posts. By now several of them have become stars. Changes also occurred throughout the executive ranks. The paper acquired a new foreign editor, city editor, national editor, Washington bureau chief, and, ultimately, a new managing editor—A. M. Rosenthal. Gossips attributed these changes to personal machinations, but in its brutal, awkward way *The Times* was really rejuvenating itself by putting power into the hands of the generation that was ready and eager to succeed those who had reached their prime during World War II. Institutional evolution—the redistribution of power, the disturbance of role-sets, and the modification of norms—had an important influence on the way we wrote news, even though we were only half aware of the forces at work.

Secondary Reference Groups and the Public

Whatever their subliminal "images" and "fantasies," newspapermen have little contact with the general public and receive almost no feedback from it. Communication through newspapers is far less intimate than through specialized journals, whose writers and readers belong to the same professional group. I have received many more responses from articles in scholarly journals with tiny readerships than from front-page stories in *The Times* that must have been read by half a million persons. Even well-known reporters do not receive more than one or two letters a week from their readers, and very few reporters are really well known. The public rarely reads by-lines and is not apt to know that Smith has taken over the city-hall beat from Jones.

It may be misleading to talk of "the public" as if it were a meaningful entity, just as it is inadequate, according to diffusion studies, to conceive of a "mass" audience of undifferentiated, atomistic individuals. The management of *The Times* assumes that its readers consist of heterogeneous groups: housewives, lawyers, educators, Jews, suburbanites, and so on. It calculates that certain groups will read certain parts of the paper, and not that a hypothetical general reader will read everything. It therefore encourages specialization among reporters. It hires a physician to cover medical news; it sends a future Supreme Court reporter to law school for a year; and it constantly opens up new beats such as advertising, architecture, and folk music. A serious sociology of newswriting ought to trace the evolution of beats and the branching out of specializations. It might also profit from the market research done by newspapers themselves, which hire specialists to devise sophisticated strategies for increasing their circulation.

The tendency toward specialization within newspapers encourages reporters to write for particular publics. City hall took notice when Smith replaced Jones, and Smith expected city hall to give his stories a careful reading. When Tom Wicker was covering the Kennedy White House, he not only knew that Kennedy read his stories attentively, he also knew exactly when and where Kennedy read them. The Pentagon correspondent, I was told, knew that MacNamara read defense stories between 7:00 and 8:00 A.M. every day while being driven to the office. Those reporters must have had vivid images of Kennedy and MacNamara scowling or smiling at their prose at certain times in certain places, and those images probably had more effect on their writing than any fuzzy view of the general public. For a reporter with a beat, "the morning after" begins to exist, psychologically, in the early afternoon, when he turns in a summary of the story he is about to write; for he knows that he must confront his news sources on the next day and that they can hurt his attempt to cover subsequent stories if he wounds them in writing this one. A reporter on general assignment suffers less from anticipatory retaliation, because he develops fewer stable relationships with the subjects of his stories.

I got the impression that newspapermen were very sensitive to the danger of becoming captives of their informants and of slipping into self-censorship. Conventional news sources, especially in government, struck me as being sophisticated about the give-and-take with reporters. Press spokesmen and public relations men are often former reporters, who adopt a tone of "we are all in this together" and try to seem frank or even irreverent in their off-the-record comments. In this way they can influence the "angle" or the "slant" of a story—the way it is handled and the general impression it creates—rather than its substance, which is often beyond their control. They attempt to influence the reporter during the stage before "the story" has congealed in his mind, when he is casting about for a central, organizing conception. If his lead sentence begins "The decline in unemployment . . ." instead of "The rise in inflation . . .," they have succeeded in their task. Some press spokesmen hoard big stories and dispense them to reporters who write favorably; but that strategy can backfire, because reporters are sensitive to favoritism and, in my experience, tend to be cliquish rather than competitive. Outright manipulation may be less effective than the establishment of a certain amicable familiarity over a long period of daily contact. After a year or so on a single beat, reporters tend insensibly to adopt the viewpoint of the people about whom they write. They develop sympathy for the complexities of the mayor's job, the pressures on the police commissioners, and the lack of room for maneuver in the welfare department. The head of the London bureau of *The Times* when I worked there was vehemently pro-British, while the head of the Paris bureau was pro-French. They wrote against each other, while reporting Britain's negotiations to enter the Common Market. *The Times* is so wary of the tendency among its foreign correspondents to develop a bias in favor of the countries they inhabit that it shifts them around every three years. On a humbler level, the veteran crime reporters who dominate the press rooms in most police headquarters develop a symbiotic relationship with the police. In Newark there were four tough old reporters who had done more time in headquarters than most of the cops. They knew everyone of importance on the force: they drank with cops, played poker with cops, and adopted the cops' view of crime. They never wrote about police brutality.

A sociology of newswriting ought to analyze the symbiosis as well as the antagonisms that grow up between a reporter and his sources, and it ought to take account of the fact that those sources constitute an important element of his "public." The reporting of news runs in closed circuits: it is written for and about the same people, and it sometimes is written in a private code. After finishing a story by James Reston, which mentions "concern" about the Middle East situation among "the highest sources," the initiate knows that the President has confided his worries to "Scotty" in an interview. It used to be said that the defense correspondent of the *Manchester Guardian* wrote in a code that could be understood only by the defense minister and his entourage, while the ostensible message of the articles was intended for the general public. The sense of belonging to a common in-group with the persons who figure in their stories—the tendency toward sympathy and symbiosis—creates a kind of conservatism among reporters. You often hear that newsmen tend to be liberals or Democrats, and as voters they may indeed belong to the Left. But as reporters, they generally struck me as hostile to ideology, suspicious of abstractions, cynical about principles, sensitive to the concrete and the complex, and therefore apt to understand, if not condone, the status quo. They seemed scornful of preachers and professors and quick with pejoratives like "do-gooder" and "egg-head." Until some social psychologist devises a way to make an inventory of their value system, I am inclined to disagree with the common contention that journalism suffers from a liberal or left-wing bias. It does not follow, however, that the press consciously favors "the establishment." The "shoe-leather man" and the "flat-foot," the diplomatic correspondent and the foreign minister are bound together by the nature of their jobs, and inevitably develop some common points of view.

The producer-consumers of news who make up the inner circle of a reporter's public also include reporters from other papers who constitute his wider, occupational reference group. He knows that the competition will give his stories a careful going over, although, paradoxically, nothing could be less competitive than a group of reporters on the same story. The greenhorn may arrive on the scene with his editor's injunction to hustle ringing in his ears, but he soon will learn that the greatest of all sins is to scoop the other side, and that the penalty can be ostracization on the next assignment. If he works from a pressroom outside his paper, he may become totally absorbed in a group of inter-paper peers. "Them" then becomes the city desks of all the papers and news services in town, who invade the repose and security of the men on the beat. Under those conditions, the failure to share information is such a crime that some reporters leak "exclusives" to colleagues on their own paper, so that the story will seem to come from "them" and will not disturb relations in the pressroom. In some pressrooms, one man does all the "leg work" or research, while the others play poker. Once he has collected the facts, he dictates them to the group, and each man writes his own version of the story or phones it in to a rewrite man in his city room. If a man is being pushed by his desk, he may by tacit agreement make extra phone calls to dig up exclusive quotes, "color," and "angles," but he would be condemned for doing this digging on his own initiative. An independent hustler can force hustling upon everyone else and will certainly break up the poker game, which is an important institution in many pressrooms. In the old press shack (now destroyed) behind police headquarters in Manhattan, the pot often came to fifty dollars, and the gamblers gathered around it included an assortment of cops and robbers. At critical moments, a cop who had dropped out of a hand would take calls from city desks. Reporters would suppress stories in order to avoid interrupting the game. The group was cohesive enough to keep "them" from discovering the news, except in the case of big stories, which threatened every reporter's security by arousing the appetite for "angles" and "exclusives" among his editors. To protect themselves, the reporters shared leads as well as details of their stories. After a news conference, they would mingle, filtering impressions and sounding one another out as to what the "story" was, until they reached a consensus and were able to file variants on the same lead: "Well, what d'ya think?" "Don't know." "Not much new, was there?" "Naw, that bit about weeding out corruption, he's said that before." "Maybe the part about civilianizing the force. . . ." "Yeah, civilianizing. . . ."

Competitiveness has also declined as a result of the attrition rate among news-papers. Reporters in one-newspaper cities only need to keep ahead of the wire services and television, which represent different genres of reporting and do not provide real competition. But if they work out of an important bureau, they are bound to be read by reporters who cover the same stories for papers in other towns. They know that the way those colleagues judge their work will determine their position in the status hierarchy of the local press corps. Professional reputation is an end in itself for many reporters, but it also leads to job offers. Recruiting often takes place through reporters who learn to respect one another by working together, just as promotions result from impressions created within a reporter's paper. *The Times* has a tenure system: once one has "made staff," he can remain there for life, but many lifers never make it out of the veterans' ranks in the city room. Professionalism is therefore an important ingredient in reportage: stories establish status, and reporters write to impress their peers.

They also get some feedback from friends and family, who look out for their by-lines and who provide such comments as: "That was a nice piece on Kew Gardens. I was down there last week, and the place really is going to hell"; or "Is Joe Namath really as obnoxious as he sounds?" Such remarks carry less weight than the reaction of fellow professionals, but they give reporters a reassuring sense that the message got through. "Mom" may not be a critical reader, but she is comforting. Without her, publishing a story can be like dropping a stone in a bottomless pit: you wait and wait, but you never hear the splash. Reporters also can expect some reaction from special segments of the public—from some readers in Kew Gardens or from some football players. Much of this kind of feedback tends to be negative, but reporters learn to discount for discontent among special interest groups. What they have difficulty in imagining is the effect of their stories upon the "mass" public, which probably is no mass at all but a heterogeneous collection of groups and individuals.

In short, I think Pool and Shulman err in assuming that newswriting is determined by a reporter's image of the general public. Newspapermen may have some such image, though I doubt it, but they write with a whole series of reference groups in mind: their copyreaders, their various editors, their different sets of colleagues in the city room, the sources and subjects of their articles, reporters on other papers, their friends and family, and special interest groups. Which of these readers takes precedence may vary from writer to writer and from story to story. They can make competing and contra-dictory demands upon a reporter. He may even find it impossible to reconcile the con-ception of "the story" that he gets from the assignment editor, the city editor, the night city editor, the copy reader, and his colleagues. Most of the time he tries to minimize "noise" and muddle through.

Occupational Socialization

Although some reporters may learn to write in journalism schools, where Pool and Shulman selected the subjects for the student group in their experiment, most of them (including many journalism-school graduates) pick up newswriting in the course of an apprenticeship. They acquire attitudes, values, and a professional ethos while serving as copy boys in the city room; and they learn to perceive news and to communicate it while being "broken in" as rookie reporters.

By watching the smoke rise from Homer Bigart's typewriter near deadline time, by carrying his hot copy to the editors, and by reading it in cold print on the next day, the copy boy internalizes the norms of the craft. He acquires the tone of the newsroom by listening. Slowly he learns to sound more like a New Yorker, to speak more loudly, to use reporter's slang, and to increase the proportion of swear words in his speech. These techniques ease communication with colleagues and with news sources. It is difficult, for example, to get much out of a telephone conversation with a police lieutenant unless you know how to place your mouth close to the receiver and shout obscenities. While mastering these mannerisms, the copy boy insensibly stocks his mind with values. I remember vividly the disgust on a copy reader's face when he read a dispatch from a correspondent in the Congo that contained some hysterical phrases about bullets whizz-ing through the hotel room. It did not do to lose one's cool. Another correspondent, who had seen some rough fighting during the Algerian revolution, impressed me with a story about a lizard that got caught in the fan of his cooling unit in the Algiers bureau. He did not mention the slaughter of Algerians, but he had a great deal to say about the difficulty of writing while being sprayed with chopped lizard. One does not have to eavesdrop very hard to get the gist of reporters' talk. They talk about themselves, not the personages of their stories—just as history professors talk about history professors, not Frederick II. It takes only a few weeks of carrying copy to learn how Mike Berger interviewed Clare Booth Luce, how Abe Rosenthal anatomized Poland, and how Dave Halberstam scored against the Diems in South Vietnam. In fact, the talk of *The Times* is institutionalized and appears as *Times Talk*, a house publication in which reporters describe their work. So even if you feel timid about approaching Tom Wicker, you may still read his own version of how he covered the assassination of President Kennedy.

Like other crafts, newspapering has its own mythology. Many times have I heard the tale of how Jamie MacDonald covered a raid over Germany from the turret of an R.A.F. bomber and how his wife Kitty, the greatest telephone operator of all time, put Mike Berger, the greatest city reporter, in touch with the governor of New York by establishing a radio link-up to a yacht in the middle of the Atlantic, where the governor was trying to remain incommunicado. The newsroom will not soon forget the day that Edwin L. James took up his duties as managing editor. He arrived in his fabled fur coat, sat down at the poker game that was always under way behind the rewrite desks, cleaned everybody out, and then joined "them" at the other end of the room, where he reigned thenceforth with supreme authority. Reporters sense an obligation to "measure up" to standards set in the past, though they know that they must look small in comparison with their mythical titans. It does not matter that Gay Talese can never write about New York as well as Mike Berger or that Abe Rosenthal can never com-mand the managing editorship with the intelligence and flair of Edwin L. James. The cult of the dead gives life to the quick. We wrote for Berger and James as well as for the living members of the city room.

Reporters' talk also concerns the conditions of their work: the problems of tele-phone and telegraph communication in under-developed countries, the censorship in Israel and the U.S.S.R., expense accounts. (I was so obtuse about filing for expenses in London that I did not even get the point of the classic stories about the Canadian correspondent who put in for a dogsled, or the African correspondent who invited reporters to spend week-ends in his villa and then presented them with fake hotel bills to be filed with their expense accounts. I had to be told that my paltry expenses were lowering the living standard of the whole bureau.) One city room reporter told me that his proudest moment came when he was sent to cover a fire, discovered it was a false alarm, and returned with a story about false alarms. He felt he had transformed the humdrum into "news" by finding a new "angle." Another reporter said that he felt he had crossed the line dividing greenhorns and veterans one day when he was covering the civil war in the Congo. He got an open line to London at an unexpectedly early moment, when he had hardly finished reading over his notes. Knowing that he could not postpone communication and that every minute was terribly expensive, he wrote the story at great speed directly on the teletype machine. Some reporters remarked that they did not feel fully professional until they had completed a year on night rewrite, an assignment that requires great speed and clarity in writing. Others said that they gained complete confidence after successfully covering a big story that broke right on deadline.

Reporters gradually develop a sense of mastery over their craft—of being able to write a column in an hour on anything, no matter how difficult the conditions. The staff in London had great respect for Drew Middleton's ability to dictate a new lead to a story immediately after being awakened in the middle of the night and informed of a major new development. Failure to make a deadline is considered unspeakably unprofessional. One man near me in the city room had missed several deadlines. At about 4:00 P.M. when he had a big story, he would furtively gulp down a Dixie Cup full of bourbon from a bottle that he hid in the bottom drawer of his desk. The copy boys knew all about him. In one sweep of the eye, they could take in the deadline agonies of dozens of men. Their job virtually forces anticipatory socialization upon them, for they have no fixed position but rove all over the city room, working with editors and copyreaders as well as reporters. They quickly learn to read the status system and have no difficulty in choosing positive and negative identity models. By listening to shop talk and observing behavior patterns, they assimilate an ethos: unflappability, accuracy, speed, shrewdness, toughness, earthiness, and hustle. Reporters seem somewhat cynical about the subjects of their stories and sentimental about themselves. They speak of the "shoe-leather man" as if he were the only honest and intelligent person in a world of rogues and fools. While everyone about him manipulates and falsifies reality, he stands aside and records it. I remember how one reporter introduced the figure of the news-paperman into an anecdote about politicians, ad men, and p.r. men: ". . . and then there was this guy in a trench coat." I never saw a trenchcoat anywhere in *The Times*. The reporters tended to outfit themselves at Brooks Brothers, which may have been a sign of ambivalence about an "establishment" that they pretended to despise. But they had a trench-coat image of themselves. In fact, they had a whole repertory of stylized images, which shaped the way they reported the news, and they acquired this peculiar mental set through their on-the-job training.

Standardizing and Stereotyping

Although the copy boy may become a reporter through different rites of passage, he normally undergoes a training period at police headquarters. After this "probation," as it is known at *The Times*, he is supposed to be able to handle anything; for the police story passes as an archetypical form of "news," and he is ready for the White House if he has survived headquarters—a parallel, incidentally, that suggests something of the spirit in which reporters approach their material.

I was inducted at the police headquarters of Newark, New Jersey, in the summer of 1959, when I worked for the *Newark Star Ledger*. On my first day of work, a veteran reporter gave me a tour of the place, which came to a climax in the photographic section. Since a police photographer takes a picture of every corpse that is found in Newark, the police have developed a remarkable collection of pictures of ripped-open and decomposed cadavers (the corpses of drowned persons are the most impressive), and they enjoy showing it off to greenhorns from the press. Press photographers build up their own collections, sometimes with help from the police, who get arrested prostitutes to pose for them. When I returned to the pressroom, a photographer from the *Mirror* gave me one of his obscene mug shots and showed me his homemade pin-up collection, which featured his fiancée. A woman reporter then asked me whether I was a virgin, which produced a round of laughs from the men at the poker game. She was leaning back in her chair with her feet on the desk and her skirt around her hips, and my face changed instantly from green to red. Once the initiation was over, the poker game resumed, and I was left to do the "leg work" for everyone. That meant collecting the "squeal sheets," or summary reports of every action by the police, from an office upstairs. The reporters depended on the police radio and on tips from friends on the force to inform them of big stories, but they used the squeal sheets to check out the odd, man-bites-dog occurrence that has potential news value. Every hour or so I would bring a batch of squeal sheets down to the pressroom and would read them aloud to the poker game, announcing anything that struck me as a potential story. I soon discovered that I was not born with a nose for news; for when I smelled something newsworthy, the veterans usually told me that it was not a story, while they frequently picked up items that seemed unimportant to me. I knew, of course, that no news is good news and that only something awful could make a really "good" story. But it took some time before I learned not to get excited at a "d.o.a." (dead on arrival—a notation that often refers to heart attacks) or a "cutting" (a stabbing, usually connected with minor thefts or family squabbles that were too numerous to be newsworthy). Once I thought I had found such a spectacular squeal sheet—I think it included murder, rape, and incest—that I went directly to the homicide squad to check it out. After reading the sheet, the detective looked up at me in disgust, "Can't you see that it's 'black,' kid? That's no story." A capital "B" followed the names of the victim and the suspect. I had not known that atrocities among black persons did not constitute "news."

The higher the victim's status, the bigger the story: that principle became clear when Newark was lucky enough to get the biggest crime story of the summer. A beautiful, wealthy debutante disappeared mysteriously from the Newark airport, and immediately the pressroom filled with hot-shot reporters from all over the East, who filed such stories as NEWARK HUNTS THE MISSING DEB, FIANCEE DISAPPEARS IN BROAD DAYLIGHT, and FATHER GRIEVES KIDNAPPED HEIRESS. We had not been able to get our desks to take more than a paragraph on the best muggings and rapes, but they would accept anything about the missing deb. A colleague and I filed a long report on HER LAST STEPS, which was nothing more than a description of the airport's floor plan with some speculation as to where the girl could have gone, but it turned out that "side bars" (stories devoted to secondary aspects of an event) about last steps often accompany stories about kidnappings and vanishings. We simply drew on the traditional repertory of genres. It was like making cookies from an antique cookie cutter.

Big stories develop in special patterns and have an archaic flavor, as if they were metamorphoses of *Ur*-stories that have been lost in the depths of time. The first thing a city-room reporter does after receiving an assignment is to search for relevant material among earlier stories filed in the "morgue." The dead hand of the past therefore shapes his perception of the present. Once he has been through the morgue, he will make a few phone calls and perhaps do some interviewing or observing outside the office. (I found that reporters consumed little shoe leather and ran up enormous telephone bills.) But the new information he acquires must fit into categories that he has inherited from his predecessors. Thus many stories are remarkably similar in form, whether they concern "hard news" or more stylized "features." Historians of American journalism—with the exception of Helen MacGill Hughes, a sociologist—seem to have overlooked the long-term cultural determinants of "news." French historians, however, have observed some remarkable cases of continuity in their own journalistic tradition. One story concerns a case of mistaken identity in which a father and mother murder their own son. It first was published in a primitive Parisian news-sheet of 1618. Then it went through a series of reincarnations, appearing in Toulouse in 1848, in Angoulême in 1881, and finally in a modern Algerian newspaper, where Albert Camus picked it up and reworked it in existentialist style for *L'Étranger* and *Malentendu*.[3] Although the names, dates, and places vary, the form of the story is unmistakably the same throughout those three centuries.

Of course it would be absurd to suggest that newsmen's fantasies are haunted by primitive myths of the sort imagined by Jung and Lévi-Strauss, but newswriting is heavily influenced by stereotypes and by preconceptions of what "the story" should be. Without pre-established categories of what constitutes "news," it is impossible to sort out experience. There is an epistemology of the *fait divers*. To turn a squeal-sheet into an article requires training in perception and in the manipulation of standardized images, clichés, "angles," "slants," and scenarios, which will call forth a conventional response in the minds of editors and readers. A clever writer imposes an old form on new matter in a way that creates some tension—will the subject fit the predicate?—and then resolves it by falling back on the familiar. Hence Jones's satisfaction with his lead sentence. Jones began by summoning up a standard image, the tree growing in Brooklyn, and just when the reader began to feel uneasy about where it might be going, Jones snapped it on the "peg" or the event of the day: the man-of-the-year award. "A florist gets a prize for making trees grow in Brooklyn," the reader thinks. "That's neat." It is the neatness of the fit that produces the sense of satisfaction, like the comfort that follows the struggle of forcing one's foot into a tight boot. The trick will not work if the writer deviates too far from the conceptual repertory that he shares with his public and from the techniques of tapping it that he has learned from his predecessors.

The tendency toward stereotyping did not mean that the half-dozen reporters in Newark police headquarters wrote exactly the same thing, though our copy was very similar and we shared all our information. Some reporters favored certain slants. One of the two women regulars in the pressroom frequently phoned around district police stations asking, "Any teen-age sex parties lately?" As the acknowledged expert in her field, she filed stories on teen-age sex that the rest of us would not touch. Similarly, a fire-buff among the Manhattan reporters—a strange man with a wooden leg, who wore a revolver around his chest—reported more fires than anyone else. To remain as a "regular" in a police pressroom probably calls for some congruity in temperament and subject matter, and also for a certain callousness. I learned to be fairly casual about "cuttings" and even "jumpers" (suicides who leap off buildings), but I never got over my amazement at the reporters' ability to get "reaction" stories by informing parents of their childrens' death: " 'He was always such a good boy,' exclaimed Mrs. MacNaughton, her body heaving with sobs." When I needed such quotes, I used to make them up, as did some of the others—a tendency that also contributed toward standardization, for we knew what "the bereaved mother" and "the mourning father" should have said and possibly even heard them speak what was in our minds rather than what was on theirs.

"Color" or feature stories left more room for improvization but they, too, fell into conventional patterns. Animal stories, for example, went over very well with the city desk. I did one on policeman's horses and learned after its publication that my paper had carried the same story, more or less, at least twice during the previous ten years.

By the end of my summer in Newark, I had written a great many stories but had not received a by-line. One day, when I had nothing better to do, I checked out a squeal sheet about a boy who had been robbed of his bicycle in a park. I knew that my desk would not take it, but I produced four paragraphs on it anyway, in order to practice writing, and I showed it to one of the regulars during a lull in the poker game. You can't write that kind of a story straight as if it were a press release, he explained. And in a minute or so he typed out an entirely different version, making up details as he needed them. It went something like this:

> Every week Billy put his twenty-five-cent allowance in his piggy bank. He wanted to buy a bike. Finally, the big day came. He chose a shiny red Schwinn, and took it out for a spin in the park. Every day for a week he rode proudly around the same route. But yesterday three toughs jumped him in the middle of the park. They knocked him from the bike and ran off with it. Battered and bleeding, Billy trudged home to his father, George F. Wagner of 43 Elm Street. "Never mind son," his dad said. "I'll buy you a new bike, and you can use it on a paper route to earn the money to pay me back." Billy hopes to begin work soon. But he'll never ride through the park again.

I got back on the phone to Mr. Wagner with a new set of questions: Did Billy get an allowance? Did he save it in a piggy bank? What was the color of the bicycle? What did Mr. Wagner say to him after the robbery? Soon I had enough details to fit the new pattern of the story. I rewrote it in the new style, and it appeared the next day in a special box, above the fold, on the front page, and with a by-line. The story produced quite a response, especially on Elm Street, where the Wagners' neighbors took up a collection for a new bicycle, as Mr. Wagner told me later. The commissioner of parks was upset and telephoned to explain how well the parks were patrolled, and how new measures were being taken to protect citizens in the Elm Street area. I was astonished to discover that I had struck several chords by manipulating stock sentiments and figures: the boy and his bike, piggy-bank saving, heartless bullies, the comforting father. The story sounded strangely old-fashioned. Except for the bicycle, it might have come out of the mid-nineteenth century.

Several years later, when I did some research on popular culture in early modern France and England, I came across tales that bore a striking resemblance to the stories that we had written from the pressroom of police headquarters in Newark. English chapbooks, broadside ballads, and penny dreadfuls, French *canards, images d' Epinal*, and the *bibliothèque bleue* all purvey the same motifs, which also appear in children's literature and probably derive from ancient oral traditions. A nursery rhyme or an illustration from Mother Goose may have hovered in some semi-conscious corner of my mind while I wrote the tale of Billy and the bullies.

> I had a little moppet [a doll]
> I kept it in my pocket

And fed it on corn and hay;
Then came a proud beggar
And said he would have her,
And stole my little moppet away.

In their original version, nursery rhymes were often intended for adults. When journalists began to address their stories to a "popular" audience, they wrote as if they were communicating with children, or "le peuple, ce grand enfant," as the French say. Thus the condescending, sentimental, and moralistic character of popular journalism. It would be misleading, however, to conceive of cultural diffusion exclusively as a "trickle-down" process, for currents move up from the common people as well as down from the élite. The *Tales* of Perrault, *The Magic Flute* by Mozart, and Courbet's *Burial at Ornans* illustrate the dialectical play between "high" and "low" culture in three genres during three centuries. Of course we did not suspect that cultural determinants were shaping the way we wrote about crimes in Newark, but we did not sit down at our typewriters with our minds a *tabula rasa*. Because of our tendency to see immediate events rather than long-term processes, we were blind to the archaic element in journalism. But our very conception of "news" resulted from ancient ways of telling "stories."

Tabloid stories and crime reporting may be more stylized than the writing that goes into *The New York Times*, but I found a great deal of standardization and stereotyping in the stories of *The Times'* London bureau, when I worked there in 1963–64. Having spent more time in England than the other correspondents in the bureau, I thought I could give a truer picture of the country; but my copy was as stylized as theirs. We had to work within the conventions of the craft. When we covered diplomatic stories, the press spokesman for the Foreign Office would provide an official statement, an off-the-record explanation, and a background analysis for anything we needed to know. The information came so carefully packaged that it was difficult to unwrap it and to put it together in another way; as a result, diplomatic stories all sounded very much alike. In writing "color" stories, it was almost impossible to escape American clichés about England. The foreign desk devoured everything about the royal family, Sir Winston Churchill, cockneys, pubs, Ascot, and Oxford. When Churchill was ailing, I wrote a story about the crowds that gathered outside his window and quoted one man who had caught a glimpse of him as saying, "Blimey he's beautiful." The cockney-Churchill combination could not be resisted. *The Times* put it on the front page, and it was picked up by dozens of other papers, wire services, and news magazines. Few foreign correspondents speak the language of the country they cover. But that handicap does not hurt them because, if they have a nose for news, they do not need a tongue or ears; they bring more to the events they cover than they take away from them. Consequently, we wrote about the England of Dickens, and our colleagues in Paris portrayed the France of Victor Hugo, with some Maurice Chevalier thrown in.

After leaving London, I returned to the newsroom of *The Times*. One of my first stories concerned a "homicidal maniac" who had scattered his victims' limbs under various doorsteps of the West Side. I wrote it up as if I were composing an ancient *canard:* "Un homme de 60 ans coupé en morceaux. . . . Détails horribles!!!"[4] When I had finished the story, I noticed one of the graffiti scribbled on the walls of the pressroom in the headquarters of the Manhattan police: "All the news that fits we print." The writer meant that one can only get articles into the paper if there is enough space for them, but he might have been expressing a deeper truth: newspaper stories must fit cultural preconceptions of news. Yet eight million people live out their lives every day in New York City, and I felt overwhelmed by the disparity between their experience, whatever it was, and the tales that they read in *The Times*.

Conclusion

One man's encounter with two newspapers hardly provides enough material to construct a sociology of newswriting. I would not presume to pronounce on the meaning of other reporters' experience, because I never got beyond the green-horn stage and because I did not work on papers that typify either "yellow" or "quality" journalism. Styles of reporting vary according to time, place, and the character of each newspaper. The American way of writing news differs from the European and has differed throughout American history. Benjamin Franklin probably did not worry about an occupational ethos when he wrote the copy, set the type, pulled the sheets, distributed the issues, and collected the revenue of *The Pennsylvania Gazette*. But since Franklin's time, newspapermen have become increasingly enmeshed in complex professional relationships, in the newsroom, in the bureau, and on the beat. With specialization and professionalization, they have responded increasingly to the influence of their professional peer group, which far exceeds that of any images they may have of a general public.

In emphasizing this influence, I do not mean to discount others. Sociologists, political scientists, and experts on communication have produced a large literature on the effects of economic interests and political biases on journalism. It seems to me, however, that they have failed to understand the way reporters work. The context of work shapes the content of news, and stories also take form under the influence of inherited techniques of story-telling. Those two elements of newswriting may seem to be contradictory, but they come together during a reporter's "breaking in," when he is most vulnerable and most malleable. As he passes through this formative phase, he familiarizes himself with news, both as a commodity that is manufactured in the newsroom and as a way of seeing the world that somehow reached *The New York Times* from *Mother Goose*.

References

1.   This paper was conceived in discussions with Robert Merton, Giddings Professor of Sociology at Columbia University. It owes a great deal to his ideas and criticism and also to the Center for Advanced Study in the Behavioral Sciences at Stanford, California, which made us fellow Fellows in 1973–74 and gave us the opportunity to wander outside our disciplines. My brother John Darnton, a reporter on *The New York Times*, gave the paper a very helpful, critical reading, although he should not be held responsible for anything in it.
2.   The layout and personnel of the newsroom have changed somewhat since I left *The Times*, and of course much of this description would not fit other newspapers, which have their own organization and ethos.
3.   J. P. Seguin, *Nouvelles à sensation: Canards du XIXe siècle* (Paris, 1959), pp. 187–90.
4.   *Ibid*, p. 173.

Bibliographical note

As this essay is not intended to be a formal sociological study, I have not included a bibliography. In fact, I wrote it before reading the sociological literature on journalism; and later while going over that literature, I found that several scholars had made thorough and intelligent studies of some issues I had tried to understand by introspection. Much of their work, however, concerns the problem of how reporters, who are committed to an occupational ethos of objectivity, cope with the political biases of their newspapers. Thus the line of analysis leading from the classic study of Warren Breed, "Social Control in the Newsroom: A Functional Analysis," *Social Forces*, 33 (May, 1955), 326–35, to more recent work: Walter Gieber, "Two Communicators of the News: A Study of the Roles of Sources and Reporters," *Social Forces*, 39 (October, 1960), 76–83, and "News Is What Newspapermen Make It" in L. A. Dexter and D. M. White, eds., *People, Society, and Mass Communication* (New York, 1964), pp. 173–80; R. W. Stark, "Policy and the Pros: An Organizational Analysis of a Metropolitan Newspaper," *Berkeley Journal of Sociology*, 7 (1962), 11–31; D. R. Bowers, "A Report on Activity by Publishers in Directing News-room Decisions," *Journalism Quarterly*, 44 (Spring, 1967), 43–52; R. C. Flegel and S. H. Chaffee, "Influence of Editors, Readers, and Personal Opinions on Reporters," *Journalism Quarterly*, 48 (Winter, 1971), 645–51; Gaye Tuchman, "Objectivity as Strategic Ritual: An Examination of Newsmen's Notions of Objectivity," *American Journal of Sociology*, 77 (January, 1972), 660–79, and "Making News by Doing Work: Routinizing the Unexpected," *American Journal of Sociology*, 79 (July, 1973), 110–31; and Lee Sigelman, "Reporting the News: An Organizational Analysis," *American Journal of Sociology*, 79 (July, 1973), 132–49. Important as it is, the problem of political bias does not impinge directly on most newswriting, except in the case of reporters with political beats; yet general reporting touches on crucial aspects of society and culture. I found little analysis of the socio-cultural aspects of newswriting, and it seemed to me that further studies might profit from continuing the broader, more historically minded approach that was developed by Helen MacGill Hughes in *News and the Human Interest Story* (Chicago, 1940).

The sociology of newswriting could make use of the ideas and techniques developed in the sociology of work. I found the studies inspired by Robert E. Park, a newspaperman turned sociologist, and Everett C. Hughes, a successor of Park in the "Chicago school" of sociology, to be most helpful in analyzing my own experience. See especially Everett C. Hughes, *Men and Their Work* (Glencoe, Illinois, 1958) and *The Sociological Eye: Selected Papers* (Chicago and New York, 1971); the issue of *The American Journal of Sociology* devoted to "The Sociology of Work," vol. 57, no. 5 (March, 1952), Robert Merton, George Reader, and Patricia Kendall, eds., *The Student-Physician; Introductory Studies in the Sociology of Medical Education*, (Cambridge, Mass., 1957), and John Van Maanen, "Observations on the Making of Policemen," *Human Organization*, 32 (Winter, 1973), 407–19.

The works in the burgeoning literature on popular culture to which I feel especially indebted are: Robert Mandrou, *De la Culture populaire aux 17ᵉ et 18ᵉ siècles* (Paris, 1964); J. P. Seguin, *Nouvelles à sensation: Canards du XIXᵉ siècle* (Paris, 1959); Marc Soriano, *Les Contes de Perrault, culture savante et tradition populaire* (Paris, 1968); E. P. Thompson, *The Making of the English Working Class* (2nd ed., New York, 1966); and Richard D. Altick, *The English Common Reader: A Social History of the Mass Reading Public* (Chicago, 1957). For examples of scholarship on nursery rhymes and folklore, see Iona and Peter Opie, *The Oxford Dictionary of Nursery Rhymes* (Oxford, 1966) and Paul Delarue, *The Borzoi Book of French Folk Tales* (New York, 1956), which include primitive versions of "children's" stories. I especially recommend "Where are you going my pretty maid?" and "Little Red Riding Hood."

Chapter 21

WILL IRWIN

THE REPORTER AND THE NEWS

This article deals with the art of reporting, as first worked out by Charles. A. Dana. It shows where journalism blends with literature, and where it stands apart. It shows how necessary is the faculty of accurate and minute observation in artistic reporting, and how the yellow reporter conceals his lack of art by melodrama and faking.

THE REPORTER IS THE SENSORY ANTENNA of the newspaper. As Irwin realized, much of the real power of a newspaper resides in the reporting staff, through its organization, deployment, and skill.

By 1911 the press was already approaching top efficiency in news gathering by means of the "beat system," which allocated reporters to regular coverage of the city's main centers of news. Irwin estimates in this article that probably nine-tenths of the day's news was gathered in that way. The news tip, which sometimes permitted competitors to be scooped or beaten, accounted for the remaining tenth. Even during those years when competing newspapers were most numerous, Irwin seems to be saying, the scoop was of little real use in building a modern newspaper. His comment is all the more interesting in view of today's rather widely held assumption that a strength of the monopoly newspaper situation is the scoop's de-emphasis, which theoretically helps prevent hasty publishing of incomplete stories. If the scoop was of so little real importance in a competitive situation, why is its absence so beneficial in today's non-competitive world?

The beat technique of systematic news gathering is still retained, of course, though better newspapers have come to recognize certain inherent weaknesses and try to compensate for them. Perhaps the chief weakness of the beat method is that it tends to give what may be an unreal or artificial shape to the news. Thus the police reporter may see his product as police beat news (so many crimes, so many arrests, so much progress on this or that investigation) and in the day-to-day writing of these stories may miss the significance of trends over time, or may even reject worthwhile stories because they do not fit within the usual framework he employs. This rigidity in viewing the news can become invested with "tradition" to the extent that the original reason for adopting the beat system (efficiency in news gathering) is no longer the chief consideration in its retention or modification. For it is obvious that today's system of news gathering must be different from the 1911 system. The tremendous growth of the federal government, to cite one example, shows the need for different organization. The federal beat of Irwin's day was infinitely less complex than it now is. Indeed, with the great increase in federal spending at all levels of government, each level—state, county, local, and metropolitan—is now a federal beat. A story written from facts obtained only from the federal building will give only part of the picture. Hence the increase today of news beats that are more topical than geographical: civil rights, higher education, urban affairs, and so on.

Despite the very real differences between today's reporting and that of Irwin's time, the emphasis on artfulness remains. The half-century intervening has seen a stress on "objective" reporting begin, grow to time point where demagogic assertions which assassinated character were printed and then the printing defended as "objective" reporting, and finally diminish in favor of "interpretation." The labels may change, but when Irwin speaks of the need to stalk truth from a point of view, he seems indeed very modern.

In considering the editor's relation to the news, we have seen how the supreme head of a newspaper sets the major point of view for his writing gentlemen, is keeper of their larger ethics. He determines, in his functions of selection and training, whether his newspaper as a whole shall be radical or conservative on public questions, shall treat money and property with exaggerated respect or with scant courtesy, shall make man more important than wealth or wealth than man, shall appeal to the head, the heart, or the lower nervous centers. He can not, however, set for his writers their minor points of view on the little things which come under their notice. If he tries to do so, he tends to destroy all originality and individuality in the product of his force.

What now of the reporter, the newest arm of this newest power in civilization? Here is a young man sent out among the million complexities of the day to find the facts which will interest his world, to see truth for the homestayers, as truth presents itself to his point of view. "He wields," said Dana, "the real power of the press." This is only measurably true, since the editor or publisher should, and generally does, lay out the larger scheme for his reporters. But the fact remains that this prying, romantic individual, wholly an outgrowth of modern life, is a more vital member of the social organism than the philosophers have let themselves admit. Through the glass which he holds up before us, most of us see our times. His product is daily bread of the minds to three-quarters of the population. He is to the individual reader the most important functionary in a newspaper organization, just as the police power is to the humble private citizen the most important function of law. If he write sanely, truthfully, with good taste and art, he cultivates sanity, truth, taste, and sense of proportion in his readers. If he write narrowly, cynically, loosely, and without taste, he correspondingly lowers the intellectual standard of his time. He furnishes the raw material for public opinion. If the strand be shoddy, how can the finished fabric be sound?

There is a craft in reporting and an art; the reporter must first get his material, by burrowing as far as he can through the wrappings which hide fact and truth, and then write it. Each of these activities calls for a separate faculty not always united in the individual. The experienced city editor has this dual function in mind when he speaks of his "break-in reporters" and his "artists" or "writing men." The man who possessed merely the faculty of getting news was all-important in the times which followed Bennett and preceded Dana. Later he divided importance with the news-artist. Yet he who is merely a writer, with no "nose for news" and no knack of getting it, is still less vitally important than the reporter with the mere sense and skill of news-gathering. The supreme reporters are those in whom the two faculties blend. Such were "Jersey" Chamberlin, Stephen Crane, Julian Ralph, John P. Dunning, and Harry Stevens of the last generation; such are Clifford Raymond, the late "Nick" Biddle, E. H. Hamilton, and Frank Ward O'Malley of this.

The first personal question which a layman asks a reporter is usually: "What do you do? Just go out and hang around until you find a piece of news?" That was exactly the method of the earliest reporters, and is still of the country editor. But expansion has brought system into metropolitan journalism. A city is now "covered" by a machine as fine and complicated as a rotary press. The city editor keeps men day and night at the police station and emergency hospitals, these being the points where news of crime and disaster first manifests itself. He has a man or a bureau at the local financial center, whether it be a stock exchange or a banking district. "Routine men" watch the local centers of government, as the City Hall, the courts, and the Federal Building. Others visit daily such institutions as the Public Library, the Chamber of Commerce, and the bureaus of charity. If it be a seaport, each newspaper has a marine specialist at the water-front. Specialists keep in touch with the churches, the labor unions, "society," and the women's clubs. By a similar system the press bureaus keep watch of the wider world.

Probably nine-tenths of the news, and on most days all of it, comes originally from one or another of these sources. For the rest, the original information—the "tip," in trade slang—proceeds generally from some private source, as a gossipy friend of the city editor or of a reporter. In the scope of that narrow tenth lies the "beat" or "scoop," the exclusive piece of news so cherished and esteemed by the older generation and of so little real use to modern newspaper building.

Why Don't Our Newspapers Tell the Truth?

In the larger and more advanced cities these routine activities are taken off the individual newspaper's hands by a news agency, which "covers" the regular sources and rushes the bare information to all its clients at once. Then from his own staff the city editor sends a reporter to look further into the matter and to write the story. Little remains to chance; the machine for news-gathering is as well-ordered as it can be, considering that it must constantly encounter emergencies.

Truth, fogged by the imperfections of human sight, hidden under the wrappings of lies, stands the final aim of a reporter when he goes out on a news tip. It is the working hypothesis of a reporter. "Why don't our newspapers tell the truth?" ask politicians and excellent ladies of women's clubs. Could they only know the difficulty of reaching an approximation to the hidden fact! Accurate perception of the event which has just happened before the eyes of flesh is so exceptional as to be almost unknown. Hugo Münsterberg tried an experiment once before his Harvard class in psychology. As the students settled themselves to the lecture, two men rose from the front seat and started to fight. Others joined in to separate or to assist them. A minute of lively action followed. "Gentlemen," said Dr. Münsterberg, when the disturbance was quelled, "we have only been acting for your benefit, a little drama, rehearsed beforehand. We know, for we followed our lines, just what happened. Please write down all you saw." The resultant papers differed ridiculously from each other; and all differed materially from fact. Later, Münsterberg produced another such drama, this time warning the class, asking them in advance to observe, and to write out their observations. The results were only a little less inaccurate. A professor at a Kansas university, imitating the Münsterberg experiment, staged a pretended "shooting scrape." One of the actors sprang into the mêlée flourishing a monkey-wrench. Not a member of the class but saw it as a pistol. The steamer *Rio de Janeiro* struck the reef off Fort Point in the Golden Gate, ran out toward the sea in the darkness and ebb tide, and sank, blowing her whistle until the water drowned her steam. In the subsequent inquiry the duration of her whistle blasts became important. A company of soldiers was quartered just above Fort Point; most of them heard the blasts. Part of their drill in soldiering had consisted in counting off seconds. Yet some said that the blasts were ten seconds long, some two minutes, and some that there was just one continuous blast.

Now the reporter really approaches accuracy of perception. Daily training has made him so. Had Professor Münsterberg produced his drama before a body of journalists, I venture that their reports would have varied but little in statement of fact; I venture that certain individuals among a body of reporters watching the Kansas experiment, would have detected the monkey-wrench, and that had there been a trained journalist in the barracks over Fort Point we should know more than the Government ever learned about the means the *Rio* took to save herself.

But the reporter sees few of his comedies, tragedies, dramas, and little novels of the street first-hand. He is not there when the trains collide, the maniac shoots, or the thief escapes. He must take his information second-hand from witnesses with untrained and imperfect eyes. The courts, when they come to adjudicate these matters, will have trouble enough and to spare in getting at the probable truth; yet lawyers and detectives have weeks to weigh, sift, and correct by that circumstantial evidence which is often the best evidence, where reporters have but minutes.

This would be difficult enough were all the witnesses of the events which he sets about to chronicle disingenuous and truthful. But no one is so beset by the falsity of man as this same reporter. "Half the population," some one says, "is trying to keep out of the newspapers and half trying to get in." And both these classes lie consistently, or employ press-agents to do the lying for them. In unraveling these tangled things, in arriving at his results—marvel of accuracy in view of his difficulties—the reporter's feet, like Patrick Henry's, are guided by the one lamp of experience. Roughly acquainted with all classes of men, all kinds of human institutions—for each day brings him in contact with a fresh aspect of life—he develops an intuition, which is only crystallized experience, for the probable fact hidden under human contradictions and lies. You, reader, as a consumer of newspapers, do not often see a newspaper story about a little girl lured away from home and imprisoned in a dark cellar by a villain. Yet cases of that kind are commonly reported to the police. Now experience has shown that a certain kind of hysterical girl who has played truant from home for a day or so usually falls back on her Laura Jean Libbey and invents such an excuse to her family. The girl's assertion is uncontradicted; but the reporter, remembering previous cases, does not accept the story unless it has strong circumstantial corroboration. Here we have an obvious case of experience in action.

In this elemental function of finding just what happened, reporters and those editors in most immediate touch with them are, by and large, about as sincere as we may expect imperfect humanity to be. The untruth in our journalism resides elsewhere. William Jennings Bryan once raised the question: "Have we an honest press?" Were news investigation all of journalism, the answer would need be a strong affirmative. Excepting for the very "yellow" reporter, who has lost his sense of truth and proportion, these men are after the fact and nothing else. Indeed, reporting is an unsurpassed training in sincerity. And where news results seem untruthful, the fault lies often with the reporter's judgment, not his intentions. He may accept, in the first excitement following a disaster, the statement of some hysterical official that twenty people are dead, may telephone in this estimate for an extra, and may find later that the victims number only two or three. Here the public is partly to blame, since it demands immediate information. News editors, in throwing out extras while the event is still fresh, generally make allowance for this tendency and cut down the first figures. "Halve 'em," is the rule of a great press bureau. And in late years the roster of victims grows rather than diminishes with succeeding extras.

Again, the layman criticizes, as the reporter writes, from a point of view. Given that Mr. Bryan, for example, is in a political campaign. His picture of himself and of the Democratic cause is not quite that of an unbiased outsider. If a company of archangels, absolute in virtue and holding knowledge of absolute truth, were to become incarnate and write the running story of his campaign, still neither Mr. Bryan nor his partizans would be satisfied; any report which did not lean toward their side would seem to them unfair and dishonest. I have heard the same news report of a political or sporting event criticized as "unfair to us" by both sides. Still more does this apply when the critic is a galled jade. In the height of the Roosevelt war on corporations, I encountered a stranger who denounced with violence and some profanity the "lies" of the American press concerning corporations. To the Washington "Post," I believe, he paid the tribute of exception. For the rest—lies, all lies! "Why, they make you think Roosevelt is a well-intentioned man!" he said. "Why don't they tell the truth and show him up for a demagogue?"

"What is his name again?" I asked when the stranger had gone.

"— of the Salt Trust," came the answer.

Unaware, as most men are, that truth must be stalked from a point of view, he took the variant point of view for deliberate falsehood. The criminal on trial believes that he is "getting the short end of it" from the newspapers, when they are trying fairly to present both sides of the evidence. With much just criticism of the truth in newspapers is mixed always this unjust carping.

Curiously, the falsity in newspaper presentation of the world increases as it rises to the top. It is, in fact, when he passes up from news-gathering to writing, when he sits down to tell in his most interesting fashion the story which he has found, that the reporter meets his greatest temptation to depart from truth. As he reviews the facts on his way to the office, they may seem bare, unilluminating. An imaginary detail here and there, a conjunction of this remote fact with that, a remark taken from its context and thrown to the fore, would give it, he feels, more dramatic, pathetic, or comic force. Few newspaper writers are so conscientious as never to have yielded to this temptation. Yet truth, illumined by a point of view, is the very kernel of the reporter's art, as it is that of his ethics. And this introduces the fact that reporting—contrary to the opinion of Robert Louis Stevenson and his kind—may be dressed out with ornament; that an art akin to Stevenson's own distinguishes the great, smashing, effective news stories from the mere dull tabulation of events. The craft is like to furniture-making and interior decoration. A trade in its mediocrity, it becomes an art at its best. This art is a reporter's special province, as keeping major ethics is that of an editor.

Some Great News Stories

Even in the academic definition of that hazy word, journalism blends with "literature." Living between book covers, passed on from generation to generation, is a great body of English letters written solely for the need of the day. It includes most essays by Addison and Steele, a good part of De Foe, the Junius letters. De Foe wrote "Sunday stuff"; Addison, "features"; Junius, editorial. Further back than that, Pliny's story of the Pompeiian disaster was a news story supremely done. Charles A. Dana used to say with all reverence that the story of the crucifixion in the Gospel according to St. Matthew was the greatest of all news stories. Xenophon wrought but as a reporter when he wrote the immortal "Anabasis" to tell the Athenians what account their ten thousand had given of themselves in Persia. Had Athens possessed daily newspapers, doubtless Xenophon would have published his story in them, instead of on papyrus. In our own time, Mark Twain laid his hand to little more worthy of preservation in his complete works than the news story, done first for a Sacramento daily, of the shipwrecked crew which he found in Hawaii; and Hazlitt's "The Fight" is a sporting report.

Though journalism reaches these immortal heights but seldom, we have produced in this country volumes of matter for the daily press much better by any literary standard than most which we preserve in magazines or embalm in books and call literature. Of such are the unhappy John P. Dunning's account of the Samoan disaster and Lindsay Denison's story of the struggle to rescue Bill Hoar the diver—both lost now in old files, their very dates forgotten.

The Requirements of News Writing

One principal canon governs the art of news writing—severe plainness. The novelist writes to tell an imaginative tale for the reader's leisure; perhaps, going deeper, he writes also to illuminate, criticize, and explain life in bulk. The poet writes to conjure beauty. Seemly for each of these is all proportionate decoration of style and philosophical digression. The reporter is telling a story of the day. He writes in haste; in like haste his patron reads. A swift, rushing narrative, whose movement to an end no ornament dams or delays, should be his aim. He may catch the reader's attention by a trick of style or a turn of wit in the opening sentence, he may carry it on from stage to stage by similar devices, but he can not stop long to moralize or to describe. In the first place, it clogs the story; and the rush of narrative is more important to him than even to the fiction writer. In the second, he has no time to struggle for those decorations which come spontaneously only with leisure. If he follow the right method, this haste need not make him a mere stringer of stock phrases—"still smoking revolver," "mad panic," "prominent citizen"—as so many mechanical reporters are.

Within these seeming narrow limits is room nevertheless for art—wit, humor, pathos, drama—so long as it abides by the journalist's chief ethical canon of truth, and is not merely an invention. A man in New Jersey sat on a hickory limb and sawed between himself and the trunk. He fell forty feet on his head. "Having the kind of head which goes with that kind of trick, he was uninjured," wrote the reporter. That play of wit lay within the canons of his art, even though he showed a brutal attitude toward the victim. A woman left her baby in its carriage at the door of a department store. A policeman found it there, apparently abandoned, and wheeled it to the station. As he passed down the street, a gamin yelled: "What's the kid done?" The reporter put that in; and here again he was within the limits.

Curiously enough, if one look only on the surface, but naturally if one but look deeper, the more artistic a story is, the more it squares with the facts, with the event as it happened—which is perhaps only a fashion of saying that good journalistic writing lies in finding the art in truth.

For imagined details seldom quite fit in a news story. Somehow they stand crudely out from the picture. Critical writers of fiction have observed this principle at work in the reverse process. An actual and remembered incident, incorporated in an imaginary story, usually remains an insoluble lump in the finished product; it is the first thing on which a clever critic lays his finger, saying: "This is incongruous." Just so, imagined detail lumps and mars a good news story. For fiction is the art of lies—often true lies paradoxically—and reporting the art of truth. The greatest reporters, such as Julian Ralph, Harry Stevens, and Stephen Crane, have got their effects from details which they perceived in the event.

How poor, indeed, is the imagining of any ordinary man compared to the detail which surrounds the event itself! If it be great enough to get into the newspapers, it must have personality, atmosphere, a background. Behind every tragedy lies a whole novel, behind every movement for human good a poem. No story so dull, so common-place, that the writer can not get the incident he needs from what he sees.

What he sees—there is the point, there the difference between the mechanic of news and the artist. Those very perceptions which make the good news-getter, applied to a different purpose, make the news artist. Forty reporters met Mrs. Maybrick at New York after her release. One, a woman, saw that she was wearing a ready-made gown. No one else noticed that. Another, a man, saw that for all her nervously erect carriage she showed the stiffening and coarsening of the back which hard labor imprints on woman—mark of her scrubbing at Woking Jail. No one else saw *that*. A man and a woman of my acquaintance, both writing journalists, visited a cheap vaudeville team in their dressing-room. It was a new experience for them both. "What struck you most vividly?" asked the woman afterward.

"The way that stage mother was maneuvering to keep between me and her daughter," he said, "it's a pathetic commentary—shows what they expect of life."

"I didn't notice that," said the woman. "But did you see the baby asleep in the suit-case under the dressing-table?"

"No. I didn't notice that!"

Here was good detail—that of the suitcase almost beyond imagination of the novelist—yet these two pairs of trained eyes saw differently.

In fact, most false, yellow, and unduly sensational newspaper writing is only a confession of lack of art. Let us go back to the type-story which I have already used as illustrating the yellow method with news—the servant girl in cheap clothing who has committed suicide by the park lake. Put an artist in reporting on that. If it strike him on his sympathetic nerve, he will observe the poor, worn hands, the cheap clothes, imagine the struggle against poverty, scorn, and vice to which she has succumbed, and make a story whose pathos will carry it to every one. It is the yellow reporter, untrained to do this, who makes it a "Mystery of the Park," a "Pretty Girl Richly Dressed." By a lie he tries to match the other's skill in truth.

Weddoc of the Chicago "Tribune" had a story one morning about a girl who had gone the easiest way—and turned on the gas. It was a "plain suicide," good for an inch-long item in every other Chicago newspaper except one, which tried to make it a mystery. Weddoc marked the knot of white crape on the tenement-house door, listened to what the neighboring women, gossiping palm to face on the steps, had to say about her case, and wrote a classic. The knot of white crape ran through it like a refrain, as he traced her course from the tough public dance to the gas chamber. And he never once threw in a word to bring his own point of view to the surface—never once raised his voice. Buried in the dusty old files of the "Tribune," it lingers in the memory of Chicago. A child, lost for an afternoon, was found dead in an alley—she had fallen from a roof. That happens commonly in the tenement district of New York. E. C. Hill told exactly what happened, with skilful management of the little details. And what old reader of the "Sun" has forgotten "A Little Child in the Dark"?

The Qualities of a Good Reporter

It may seem that I am treating only of the exceptional man; it may be argued that the rank and file can not hope to be artists. As a matter of fact, such abilities lie hidden in nearly every man who has the sense of romance, the thrill of life and the power of expression which made him a journalist in the beginning. Ignorant, mechanical copy-reading, and a false view of news, have spoiled good reporters by regiments. Dana himself said that he produced his great results with pretty ordinary material. It was not that he got exceptional men, but that by intelligent handling, knowing where to curb the point of view and where to give individuality its head, he made the most of material little above the ordinary. He had unusual assistance in this; Amos Cummings and Chester S. Lord were artists in news, and Selah Merrill Clark, chief school-master to the "Sun," has put genius into the ungrateful task of copy-reading. William R. Nelson of the Kansas City "Star," whose ideas on the journalistic mission differ from those of the "Sun," but whose view on the art in his craft is about the same, makes like comment on his own staff.

"Any one who can write an interesting letter," said Julian Ralph, "has it in him to be a good writer for the newspapers." And any one with that faculty is amenable to training in seeing and recording details. Above that, of course, lies capacity, the qualities of mind and heart which approach greatness; these set off the exceptional reporter. But none who is capable of holding a place on a newspaper need be a mere mechanic.

The Effect of the Atlantic Cable

On his way to Europe after the Civil War, that great old correspondent George Alfred Townsend ("Gath") sighted the steamer which was laying the first Atlantic cable.

"There's the end of newspaper writing," he said. Gath was wrong; we were hardly at the beginning of good newspaper writing, for Dana had not yet acquired the "Sun." But the cable, and succeeding forms of swift transmission, have vindicated his back-thought. For they have introduced a uniformity, a kind of monotony, into the literary form of newspapers. In Gath's time the New York "Herald," the Cincinnati "Enquirer," the Chicago "Tribune," and whatever other great newspaper of the period you may name, sent its own correspondents to the seat of important news, no matter how far away. After the Atlantic cable had finished the application of Morse's invention to journalistic needs, the general press bureaus appeared. Even the greatest newspapers came to rely on them for all but the most important news outside of their own territory; and a press bureau, ministering to all kinds of organs, tries to keep its writing bald and colorless. Telegraph editors can go only so far in rewriting the bare statements of the Associated Press or the United Press, and even then the rewriting avails little, since it is second-hand work. Where the city has a local news bureau, the same tendency is at work with local reports. The best editors and the smartest staffs regard this agency only as a dispenser of "tips," sending their own men to do the investigation and writing. But the more slipshod workmen print the minor news about as the press bureau sends it; and this is another tool bending the newspaper toward standard gage.

The Press Bureaus

In fact, editors are everywhere trying all devices to beat this tendency. The Associated Press and the United Press are the leading news bureaus. The United Press, younger and lesser of the two, runs only an "evening wire." All over the country, editors of important evening papers take both services, for the sake of variety. The New York "Sun," through its Laffan Press Bureau, farms out its own news; this matter, being especially well written, is valuable for enriching interest. The seven English Hearst newspapers have only two Associated Press franchises between them: Hearst has been forced to create a press bureau of his own; and he rents the service to other newspapers outside his territories. Of late, the New York "World," "Herald," and "Times" have taken to farming out their best news stories; they have long syndicated their "features." By picking and choosing among these syndicates, the news editor may create, in stiff mosaic, a picture of his times a little different from that presented by his rival across the street.

So it goes with "features." Once city newspapers outside of the metropolis had their own exclusive humorists and comic artists; the Denver "Tribune" and the Chicago "News" cherished Eugene Field as their property. Except for the cartoonists, who exercise a political function and can not be passed around with apparent sincerity, the "feature-man" appears nowadays only to be swallowed up by a syndicate which sends out his work to twenty, fifty, a hundred newspapers. Such was the early fate of Finley Peter Dunne ("Mr. Dooley"). "Walt Mason" appeared but two or three years since on the Emporia "Gazette." Already, he is in a syndicate. The fine flavor of locality is gone from most city newspapers; one must look far down the scale of population before he finds something which stands out, a distinct personality, like William Allen White's Emporia "Gazette," or Chester Rowell's Fresno "Republican." This but follows the modern industrial law; machine production and easy transportation tend to erode all local customs and peculiarities.

This movement of the times makes against good newspaper writing. It concentrates a few high-priced stars on the press bureaus, where art is limited through the necessary limitation of the point of view, or on such great metropolitan newspapers as farm out their matter syndicate-fashion. And it tends to make the rank and file in the smaller cities mere news machines.

The Effect of the Syndicates

However, another and opposing tendency is at work. As we grow great in wealth, as, having finished the all-absorbing task of breaking industrial ground, we begin to take our industrial leisure, a taste for art and all other fine things inevitably follows. Behold Chicago. Twenty years ago, when she was still plowing new industrial fields, her hideous rawness, her insensibility to the finer life, were a standard American joke. But Chicago established herself, pushed business development to a point near to diminishing returns. "Culture" followed; at first culture by main force, with the teeth clenched, then a dawning appreciation of the gracious and beautiful; and now Chicago is both producing and appreciating her craftsmen and artists. It is no accident—getting back to our own ground—that the Chicago newspapers are technically the best in the United States, and that their local reports are, by and large, the best written.

Chapter 22

TALCOTT WILLIAMS

PAY AND PECUNIARY REWARD

WHEN SIR HENRY IRVING SAID OF the theatre that it must succeed as a business or it could not exist as an art, he aptly expressed the condition of the newspaper. This came with its beginning. Through the seventeenth and eighteenth centuries the newspaper was poverty-stricken. Some newspapers made money, Franklin's, for instance, but he had to eke out its returns by acting as postmaster, running a job office, publishing books—most of them a loss to him—and getting every salary and stipend that came his way. At the beginning of the nineteenth century John Walter, a printer and publisher, put the London *Times* on a solvent basis. Other periodicals made money for a season. This is the only one which had a century of steady profit, until it, too, ceased to be attractive to its family of owners who had lived on it through four generations of its long gain. No newspaper in the United States has had this continuous success. The Chicago *Tribune* comes nearer to this record by public report, but it is not the only enterprise of its owners. Of the dailies in the other cities of the United States, there are few, if any, which have not gone on the "red" in the past fifty years, so far as their yearly profit-and-loss account is concerned. This was true through all the last century. A socio-political economist speaks in a book of a happy past when editors owned their newspapers and made them their "avatars." He instanced Greeley, Raymond, Halsted, no one of whom owned their own papers. In the list he gave there was only one that did. Greeley, himself, after *The Tribune* was ten years old, declared that a solvent newspaper could not be run in New York unless it had official advertising and the favor of a political party. This is no longer true in New York.

It was very nearly true of the first James Gordon Bennett that he won, independent of these aids; but *The Herald* in time ceased, with other dailies, to have the margin of profit needed for a solvent paper. A newspaper, like a theatre, when profitable, is a gold-mine, but, like a theatre, when public support departs, the loss on a daily is sudden and paralyzing. This is true of the whole range of periodicals. The monthly has not had any long business success in the United States. Few have survived the first editor in steady profits. The weekly has been more profitable than the monthly, on the average, taking the capital involved, but no American weekly has yet outlasted two lives except among country weeklies. Some of these admirable papers, which I sometimes think the best product of our America, reflecting and recording the sound life of our American countryside, have been profitable for three lives, but there are not many of these, possibly only four or five.

National weeklies, by which is meant a weekly with a general circulation over the country, have so far had a precarious career. Several of such weeklies in New York, radical or conservative, are subsidized, the annual loss being met by wealthy sympathizers. A paying public they do not represent. Robert Bonner, from 1844 to 1887, made the New York *Ledger* highly profitable, but the secret of its success died with him. This span of years, let us say, from 1840 to 1890, was the period of the weekly. In it the religious weekly rose, flourished, made fortunes for some of its owners comparable to those bequeathed by English bishops a century ago. Their editors often ran their sheets like militant mediæval bishops. The weeklies remain; their old profits and power are gone. This success, for one life only, has attended literary weeklies in this country.

The United States has never produced a critical weekly, like the London *Athenæum*, whose profits and success ran on for eighty years, or *The Spectator*, whose profits have varied, but whose position has been maintained approaching a century. A place on such weeklies is always agreeable and often profitable; but in this country such weeklies have furnished a very precarious livelihood. The two classes of weeklies here offering permanent careers are country weeklies, already cited, and technical journals. These last furnish permanent posts, the pay is as high for many tasks as any daily, and the work is absorbing to those who have the imagination to feel the throb and thrill of finance, of production by field and mine, of great industries, of agencies for transportation or wide-spread distribution. The men successful in these weeklies are almost unknown to the general public; they play a relatively small part in affairs, save in farming weeklies, but when they have ability, prophetic accuracy—a very rare gift—and vision, they exercise a pontifical influence and authority for various trades and industries in creating standards and policies within the fruitful but specialized field they till.

Mr. Bradford Merrill, a journalist of the first rank, a master of the business of the newspaper and an untiring student of the history of journalism, writes me of the daily:

> When the New York *Herald* was founded, only eighty-odd years ago, there were six morning newspapers in New York, every one of which has since died, although one of them, *The Sun*, still shines as an evening paper. In the past fifty years fifteen or sixteen new morning papers have been born in New York City, but all have died except six. Of these papers of general circulation (except one born in the last two years) every one has been bankrupt or on the verge of bankruptcy, and living on private loans at some time in the past twenty-five years.

This experience can be matched in every large American city. Abundant evidence exists and has been presented in court that where an ordinary sound and successful business or manufactory is worth ten or fifteen years' purchase on its profits, a newspaper is not worth over five.

The alternations of the daily from profit to loss and back again are familiar to every newspaperman. This adds to the precarious conditions of the work of the journalist, always under greater risks than other callings of the mind, because journalism is inter-linked with business. There is a wide gap between the steady, continuous impress on the public made by a man holding any staff position on a great daily and the most brilliant writer, even though in constant demand. The essence of the work of the newspaper, as has already been pointed out, is that it furnishes a continuous audience on a scale large enough to be a sensible and effective factor in the society of which it is a part. Unless a man acts through this, he is without the greater weight and influence of the journalist. He is a pamphleteer, even if his organ of expression is a weekly of 40,000 circulation or so. He writes for and is read by a selected, non-political group and not by a general audience.

This, however, is changing. A new phase of journalist has appeared, who practises applied journalism as he might law, medicine, or engineering. Such a man wins vogue for his name. He is known to a wide congregation of readers. He refuses to associate himself with one periodical, daily or other. He places his matter as he writes it, and he gets orders for articles as lawyers are retained. Any expert man who makes his place before the public early finds that he does not have to send his articles in for approval. They are ordered and paid for in advance of publication, a far more agreeable proceeding. Such men are few. For some reason, not easily explained, they wear out their welcome. Their originality becomes exhausted. Most of them finally gravitate to a permanent job. Many have this from the beginning, in various forms. It is a necessary part of a journalist's continuous work, that he gear into a permanent relation to weekly or daily. Unless he has this, however alive he may be and however successful, he is not in real touch with the current situation. He misses that large area of news which does not get printed. As Mr. Dana was fond of saying: "We only get half the news and we do not get the best half."

This remains true. The type of journalist I have been describing, in the past thirty-five years began with "syndicating" by Allen Thorndike Rice and S. S. McClure in the middle of the 'eighties. The increase of this type makes it at least possible that the periodical world of a generation hence, let us say of 1960, will be made up of two sets of newspaper workers—the men who hold regular continuous permanent posts on some newspaper, changing from one to another, and the men and women who have their contracts with some papers and their contributions to and orders from others, who carry on an independent existence. One such man in 1918 made $23,000, though still only a dozen years or so out of college. A pretty large number make from $5,000 to $10,000, and the number grows. Women have, on the whole, succeeded better in this task than in staff positions on daily papers. This is in part because the world is not accustomed yet to women in command, outside of domestic life. This is, of course, nonsense. No end of examples exist to show the executive powers of women. It is an outworn superstition which leads an office to hesitate to make the best reporter in the room—every news man knows cases in which this is a woman—city editor, or select the keenest executive in a newspaper organization for managing editor. Few women edit news, but from the work done in schools of journalism I have no manner of doubt that, ability being equal, a woman would hold down a sheet of manifold on a news desk just as well as any man. This belated restriction on the careers of women and the circumstance that a major share of woman-stuff, always widely salable, is done by women, leads many of them, sooner or later, to the ranks of the unattached. Fashion, "soblets," manners, cooking, and advice on how to make over an old dress or a new husband, these subjects know not politics, cities, or various types of newspaper—like the "comic" daily strip, plain or colored, these have an universal appeal. Very possibly, as the differentiation of the daily goes on, the newspaper will be more and more a forum for many voices and pens, supplying opinion and information on all topics and issues, as each attracts. Selection and direction will be made by a strong selected permanent staff. The general news will be standardized and be the same, substantially alike, in all newspapers, the business office watching circulation and advertising. There is, at present, a tendency in this direction. Just as this is the first American war which has not furnished a general who became President, so it is the first war which has not thrown up a conspicuous American correspondent whom the public of newspapermen recognized as the war correspondent of the day. The war news was more standardized than ever before. City news associations do what individual reporters once did and the reliance on association news of various kinds grows in all the various fields. Syndicates which furnish articles to many newspapers, reaching an audience numbered by millions, pay high prices for articles by well-known writers and to the well known who cannot write.

The newspaperman in his training has, therefore, two types of careers before him, though for seven men out of ten fate decides. Choice is not within their power or powers. Those who have liberty and the personal ability to choose vary temperamentally. There are those who prefer to cross the ocean in a liner with everything found, than to address themselves to a voyage on a single-hander. The gap is not as wide as this, but this comparison illustrates it. On one side there are the daily risks, a sense of personal independence and reputation, and the freer hand; on the other, organization, a wider horizon, and a more constant income and the anonymous life. Large prizes are won in both. Forty years ago a red-headed and hopeful, slender, nervous, and much-be-freckled young man told me in Washington that he was tired of the news game and proposed to see all the world at the expense of the American newspaper. He found that by economy, many stops, and that cheerful readiness to take anything that is coming, which goes with red hair, he could keep moving on fifty dollars a week. He began with an absurdly small grub-stake and started, selling his "stories," as a newspaperman would call his travel-letters, at five dollars apiece. Pretty nearly half this was eaten up by the "overhead." He kept on. You could not open the Sunday papers of any city, large or small, without finding that one of them had his account of strange lands. He worked hard. He read. He carried a weighty load of books and reports on each trip, and he knew his land before he visited it. In time he had a competence. His letters gave him public repute as a geographer, and he issued school geographies that sold and out of which he is said to have received $120,000. A woman of unusual aptitude for advice to women has had for a number of years an annual income of $18,000. Richard Harding Davis went to the Boer War with contracts for $22,000 a year from English and American papers. He would get more now. As the war wore on he was convinced the Boer cause was just, and he threw up his contracts and, at considerable risk of being shot as a spy, crossed over to the Boer lines, and his work there brought him a bare fraction of what he was receiving from the sheets of the more powerful antagonist whose cause he had abandoned.

Victrix causa placuit Diis, sed victa Catoni.

The American newspaper was never able to pay living salaries to its staff until advertising began on a large scale, half a century ago. In 1851 the New York *Tribune* divided the morning-paper field with Bennett's *Herald*, which had two or three times its circulation and business. It had become in ten years, since it was founded, the leading anti-slavery daily and weekly in the country. The first paid nothing, the weekly, before long with 250,000 circulation, was profitable. Horace Greeley was the foremost figure in the newspaper fight with slavery. He received $50 a week in 1851, when *The Tribune* was ten years old and he a journalist twenty years. Snow, the advertising man, had $30; Charles A. Dana, the managing editor, $25; Bayard Taylor, correspondence, editorial, and special articles, $20; and George Ripley, easily one of the five best book reviewers the American press has produced, $15. Greeley received, in addition from dividends on his shares, $7,500 in 1850, and in 1851 about $10,000. His total return was, therefore, at the cost of living, as large as any writing man for twenty years after. He owned only a quarter of the shares, and until he died, in 1872, held his place only through the support of other shareholders. A reporter was then receiving from $5 to $8 a week. By 1875 a reporter just beginning in New York on a daily was paid $15 a week; in two or three years he might expect $25. A city editor had from $40 to $50 a week, a managing editor $75 upward or downward, and an editorial writer of the first rank was paid $100 a week. A dramatic critic received from $40 to $50, but many of the notices were written by men paid from $15 to $20 a week. The notices in the New York *World* in 1876 of Booth's return to the New York stage, when he performed for the first and only time "Richard II," were written by a young man three years out of college, who was paid $20 a week. When Ivory Chamberlain, an editorial writer of the first rank in his calling, went on the New York *Herald* in 1876 to do six editorial articles a week, column and turn—the younger Bennett desiring to set up an editorial page—his pay of $15,000 a year was commented on as phenomenal. The pay of writing men in other American cities ran 20 to 30 per cent below those in New York. There was probably no editorial writer anywhere who received over a third of Mr. Chamberlain's pay. John Hay did not. The largest pay of an editorial writer at present, 1921, is on weekly pay and a sliding contract, running from $200,000 to $300,000 a year, all told.

Through the 'eighties the range of salaries over the United States remained little changed, though an advance took place in Boston and Philadelphia. At the close of the last century an advance came slowly. Mr. Arthur Brisbane, March 26, 1912, published an article, contributed to the *Cornell Era*, in which he said:

> Young men start, as a rule, on a salary varying from $10 to $15 a week— on newspapers in large cities. The salaries that are paid now in newspaper work are very much bigger than they were a few years ago. They run as high as twenty-five and fifty thousand dollars a year for employees. Owners of newspapers sometimes make as much as a million a year and more from one single paper.

Salaries and profits are still higher to-day. The reporter begins in New York at from $20 to $25 a week, if he comes from a school of journalism. An experienced reporter has $75 to $100 a week, often more. A city editor who received $7,500 a year in 1912 when Mr. Brisbane wrote, receives twice as much now. At least five receive this sum in New York. The managing editor who was paid from $10,000 to $12,500 then, receives now from $20,000 to $30,000. There are eight managing editors, three in New York City, nearer $30,000 than $20,000. The income of one managing editor ran recently to $40,000. Three managing editors in New York receive from $40,000 to $50,000 a year. Forty years ago there were some twenty men on New York papers who were paid $100 a week and over. Today a club of upward of 200 members could be gathered of men on the daily and technical press of New York who receive $10,000 a year and more. Among the rank and file, salaries of $60 to $80 a week are frequent.

Salaries like these are paid nowhere else. In Chicago, Boston, and Philadelphia reporters are still beginning at $12, $15, and $20 a week. Men editing news receive $40 a week. A city editor twice or three times this. Editorial writers have not gone much above $100, which were paid in these cities twenty years ago. Managing editors receive $150 to $300 a week. The salaries in lesser cities are small. They are not much above the salaries of thirty years ago in New York. In other cities, like Buffalo, Minneapolis, St. Paul, St. Louis, Kansas City, and San Francisco, the men at the top are paid as much as in larger cities, and the beginner and the men at the bottom less. The poorest return to newspapermen are in cities under 100,000 population. Papers are few. There is no bid for men between the dailies, but much competition between the men. The narrow horizon must be met by courage, thrift, study. Reporters' salaries are deplorably small. Some improvement has been secured in Boston, Rochester, Scranton, and other cities after organizing unions affiliated with the American Federation of Labor. This gave the writing force the support of the mechanical departments in their demands, a very effective alliance. In Rochester after the pay of writers was brought to a level with wages in the mechanical field, the union dissolved. In Australia and New Zealand, newspaper writers have been organized for a decade. Salaries have been advanced, security of tenure gained, and hours reduced. The general standard of work has not suffered. In a number of newspaper offices in this country the average salary of the composing-room and the pressroom is larger than the average in the writing force. These things ought not so to be.

Relative incomes in other callings and in journalism in our larger cities range about as follows, taking the leading men. The successful lawyer gathers the largest professional income. The specialist in medicine comes next. The large corporation manager will rank with these men, but there are fewer large returns of $150,000 and upward, and more managers on $30,000 to $50,000. The architect varies much between different years, but a run of $30,000 to $50,000 a year is gained only by leading men. At this place the journalist comes with a few above $20,000, with executive men at $30,000 to $50,000 a year, and very, very few higher. In cities of 500,000 or more there are cases of clergymen whose salaries and fees together run close to and sometimes exceed the best-paid salaried newspapermen in the place.

In considering the pecuniary rewards of the newspaperman there must be considered both the relatively low return for equal abilities and the hazards of financial risks in the newspaper. The foundering of a newspaper in any city or its consolidation with a rival is like a wreck. The younger men, under thirty-five, acquire new posts with little difficulty, but older men, holding specialized posts after many years of service on one newspaper, often find themselves in very serious straits. There is no calling in which it is more necessary for the young man to insure his life early, at the very start, and to save systematically, steadily, and inexorably. If he does, he can, judging from the number of cases I have known, find himself at the end from $30,000 to $50,000 ahead of the game. This is no large sum, but it is a mighty comfortable proposition when the years begin to slope. There are instances of larger estates left by working journalists, reaching $250,000, but these are rare with men not owners.

If pay be low, hours are long in a journalist's day. The morning newspaperman will have many years in which he does not leave his office until from 12 to 2 A. M. These hours were once even later. A day of ten or twelve hours will be no unusual thing for him, often the rule for weeks together. The evening newspaperman has to begin earlier and bear the heavy burden of the early riser. The afternoon daily has, too, that awful task, the "lobster watch," which begins at midnight, is occupied in diligently conning and collating the morning papers until its luckless holder leaves the office between 8 or 10 A.M., as the rest of the staff arrive.

These hours entail much self-denial. They render any social life very difficult, but this troubles few working newspapermen. There is the terrible legend of the luckless night editor who, going home at gray dawn, was never seen by his children except when they awoke and he was in his pajamas, ready to go to bed. While they were asleep he went to his work. They wholly refused to recognize him when they met him in the ordinary garb of a citizen by day. Unless a journalist marries a woman who adopts his newspaper hours, as the writer is glad and grateful to record has been his supreme good fortune, there will be an inevitable conflict between the household and the professional day. The strain on health in the hours, the exigencies, and the nervous wear and tear of a calling which has its daily crisis in "going to press," calls for physical strength, a sound constitution, and constant care for health, and here again the newspaperman's future will depend on the skill with which he is fed and protected from interruption in his sleep at his home.

These various causes bring it about that those who drop out in journalism are very numerous. Perhaps no larger than in law, but far more, I think, than in the ministry, in medicine, or architecture. It is true of all our professional schools that a very much larger share cease to practise the calling for which they are trained than the public realizes. Possibly professional schools do not sufficiently exclude men unfit for the calling. The "mortality" in the course of preparation is largest in medicine, and it has the most rigorous schooling. All professional schools pass men about whose professional future they are in doubt. Nor are these always the men who fail.

The wraith which stands in the way for all who practise the arts of expression is the short period in which men are at their best. In medicine the end comes first for the surgeon. Wise lawyers avoid this fate by drawing young men into their firms. Unless this is done, as Richard H. Dana's biography shows, clients begin to dry up as sixty is passed. Architects cease as years go to meet immediate and current taste. Landscape-painters are in an art revolutionized every thirty years. The portrait-painter and the statuary last longer. The "dead-line of 50" is familiar in the clergy. The journalist loses his capacity in like fashion and for a like reason. The speaker, the actor, the painter, the writer, the journalist enter active life with a larger number abreast of their way of seeing and depicting, on the onward march, than will keep step with them again. As this host diminishes and new ranks appear in the rear, the message of those older finds fewer who know its meaning. But Mr. Arthur Brisbane has put this conditioning fact better than any one else. He at least has escaped this peril. I first saw him thirty-nine years ago in the New York *Sun* office, a slender youth with a face of high power and pallor, and Mr. Chester G. Lord, the best judge of the young writer I have ever known, pointed him out to me as the ablest young man that had ever entered *The Sun* office. In the years since, those of his craft know how he has kept up his reading, worked at every new subject, multiplied his contact with men, and seen each new cause from afar. His style is a model of the way to reach the vast mass. In the article from which I have already quoted he says:

> And in the newspaper business there exists a condition and a danger unknown in other work. That should be thought of carefully by young men that contemplate newspaper work.
>
> The newspaperman becomes less valuable nine times out of ten as he becomes more familiar with his work—and for this reason.
>
> The value of a newspaper writer—reporter, editorial writer, or whatever—depends upon the strong impression that events make upon him, and upon his ability to express that impression in what he writes.
>
> The longer the ordinary man continues to SEE the less he FEELS.
>
> In the ordinary lines of work diminished emotion is not a detriment, but rather a help.
>
> A young doctor for the first time amputates a leg and suffers torments—his impressions are vivid.
>
> Ten years later he cuts off a leg with no emotion, doing his work carefully and perhaps thinking of the golf game in the afternoon. He cuts the leg off or opens up the human body with no emotion at all—and HE IS A BETTER DOCTOR THAN IN THE DAYS WHEN HE FELT EMOTION.
>
> The young reporter sees his first "electrocution," describes his first great labor strike or fire, is deeply impressed, feels strongly, and writes "a good story."
>
> Ten years later, in nine cases out of ten, he is like the doctor cutting off the leg. He feels nothing—and then he is no longer a good newspaperman. For no man can really pretend to feel when he doesn't. He may not see the difference, and his editor may not see the difference—but the man who reads the newspaper will see the difference at once.

Another difference with the newspaper writer is this:

> He must make his reputation fresh every day. The lawyer of fifty lives perhaps on work that he did at thirty; the work that brought him clients whom he still keeps.
>
> And the doctor at fifty lives on patients whom he gathered about him in his youth and vigor.
>
> Not so the newspaperman. If he cannot do TO-DAY what he did ten years ago or twenty years ago HE IS NOT WANTED TO-DAY.
>
> The newspaperman in that respect is even more unfortunate than the actor. For if the actor loses his power, if the singer loses his voice, the public will still hear with pleasure an old favorite, and the advertising of the name has value. Not so with the newspaperman. When he can no longer act or sing—in his line of work—his day is done.

* * *

However, newspaper work is the best work—since the greatest thing that a man can do is to deal with millions of others. Newspaper power is the greatest power, for it is the power that shapes and directs the thoughts of men. And there is no power but thought.

Newspaper work, though it may not lead to great newspaper success or great financial reward, is a most useful school of experience.

The young man who goes to work as a reporter—and that is the only way to begin—who observes, takes care of himself, keeps out of temptation and all forms of nonsense, is attending a real LIFE college of the highest possible value.

Those who best escape this peril are men who possess the unusual but still not infrequent combination of business capacity and the gift of journalism: the shrewd ability of the profit maker and the penetration of the newspaperman as to the news that is wanted and the opinion which expresses current needs and the demand and duty of the hour. Journalism offers to such opportunities both for fortune and for influence as long as a man keeps himself from holding any political office or entering "politics," the constant temptation and snare spread before such men. Joseph Pulitzer was a crowning example of this combination. As Rodin said, when he modelled the bust of Joseph Pulitzer, a replica of which stands in the School of Journalism of Columbia University, which he endowed, he found himself modelling a man with two sides to his face, one a business American and the other the prophet and poet. When Joseph Pulitzer bought the New York *World*, May 10, 1883, it had made no profits for nine years. In six years it returned a "profit-and-loss-account" profit of $1,018,000. Meanwhile meeting out of the profits the sum required for its purchase, $400,000. To an amazing power of creating circulation and putting a business on a profitable basis within a year, Mr. Pulitzer added the political sagacity which led him to print a platform of ten planks, all of which have been adopted and none of which seemed then likely to command a majority in the United States. What was then both a new declaration, a political principle, or a prophecy has now come to be accepted by every one in substance, if not in detail. Such instances are rare and, least of all, in a metropolitan newspaper. James Gordon Bennett had this specific combination of business and journalism. It is possessed in an eminent degree by Mr. Adolph S. Ochs, of the New York *Times*, and has been exercised by him with constant reference to public duty.

The country weekly furnishes many men who have this unusual combination, because the business problems, while much harder than they seem, are less difficult than the financial responsibilities of a great newspaper. Every State in the Union has a little group of men, not much known to the general public, who edit its country newspapers and make out of the work a fair income, and exert a political influence in the town and county in which they live, and often over their own State, far greater than is usually held by the publisher or editor of a daily, large or small, in a city. Very few forms of success are more tangible and more agreeable than that of an editor of a country weekly who has these twin abilities, and has achieved the success just outlined. The possible profits of a man who has this combination of powers, in a greater or less degree, increases and increases with great rapidity as the circulation of the paper is large and its business issues correspondingly weighty.

As has already been pointed out, a metropolitan daily in a large city generally suffers in circulation, advertising, and influence if its head takes a political post, whether elective or appointed. There are exceptions, but they are few. The editor or proprietor of a daily in a smaller city, let us say of 250,000 population or less, on the other hand, often improves his position before the public and the influence of his paper by taking public office. Senator Gilbert M. Hitchcock, of the Omaha *World-Herald*, is one of the most useful members of the Senate to which he has been elected by a Republican State, though himself a Democrat. His newspaper has steadily gained in circulation and profit during his successful political career. President Harding is a still more notable instance of an editor at the head of a daily in a city of 28,000 reaching the highest position open to an American. Nor was any journalist who knew the Marion, O., *Star* unaware of his ability. The Democratic candidate in 1920, Governor Cox, was also a newspaperman. The country-weekly editor is pretty constantly in politics. Editors in elective and public posts are more numerous now than a generation ago.

The newspaperman who wants a political career should early turn to the weekly or small daily. He may not succeed, but he is almost certain to fail if he seeks political preferment on the big daily of our great cities. The best public service of a newspaper-man comes by keeping out of politics in all the fields of journalism. If he does, be his field large or small, he will suggest legislation and see it pass, expose abuses and force their reform, modify public policy, prevent poor nominations, defeat unfit men, and promote sound selections. No newspaper can always accomplish these ends. Elections do not follow circulation. Newspaper influence is not like the registry of a pressure gauge, moving with every change. It is a constant, continuous work whose harvest may be delayed, but which in time changes the public current. Public men are constantly expressing their disregard of the newspaper in public, but every newspaperman knows their anxiety to be reported, their apprehension at newspaper attack, their fear of opposition to a candidate, and their dread of exposures.

The complete control of a newspaper by one man is only possible where the man himself is able both to manage the newspaper as a business and to write himself upon its editorial page, or has the still more unusual gift of outlining an editorial policy, and persuading other men to express it successfully, without any sense of loss of individual power on their part. Where the publisher cannot write or the editor cannot publish there is certain to be a divided field of authority, and relations between the two men are extremely likely to be the mutual decision of two partners, strong on one side of the business, but quite unequipped on the other.

Another combination of various talents, new and almost as profitable, is presented by the newspaper artist with a gift for humor and the capacity to dramatize picture and text in the old familiar channel of folk-lore. "Mutt and Jeff" are our old friends Don Quixote and Sancho Panza. "Foxy Grandpa" is the "myth of the old man" which has so long ruled society, and to which Mr. H. G. Wells so strongly objects. Various infant prodigies who make game of age, authority, and an array of elderly enemies are but "Jack the Giant-Killer." Nell Brinkley is a newspaper Watteau. The capacity to do this in effective caricature and catchy phrases, in flowing lines and happy suggestion, pays better, just at present, than the American presidency. One such genius climbed in three short years from $15 a week to $50,000 a year, with movie rights to follow. A syndicate nearly always handles this combination of art, dialogue, love, and laughter, supplying sketches and writings to seventy or eighty newspapers. The appetite for folk-lore being just as strong as at the dawn of the race, those who do this work are not only better known to the mass than any other names in our dailies, but a number have guarantees of $50,000 a year under long contracts, and two or three earn over $100,000 a year on salary.

The ballad-maker once had nothing but cakes and ale, but the newspaper poet whose verse appears daily receives $30,000 or more a year. A butt of malmsey Madeira (commuted now to £60 or £70 a year) is all the British crown pays its poet laureate, but democracy has larger and more tangible rewards for the verse-maker who catches its fancy and holds its attention.

Of all the workers on the newspaper these gifts are the most unique and inexplicable. They meet a living human need not slaked by the conventions of art, and no training has yet been found either to develop or discover them. Colored supplements are often called demoralizing; but who can hold an ethical brief for *Grimm's Tales* or the morals of many a fairy-story?

Chapter 23

GEORGE SELDES

THE HOUSE OF LORDS

ONCE EVERY YEAR THE AMERICAN NEWSPAPER Publishers Association, the House of Lords of our press, meets in secret. No one cares to spy on it, no newspapermen are present, no photographers interrupt, no representatives of a yellow journal harass or intimidate the members. It would be useless. If a reporter found out what plans are discussed, what plots are made, what schemes proposed, no newspaper would publish the disclosures, sensational as they might be. Nothing is sacred to the American press but itself.

And yet these secret meetings of our organized publishers rank among the most important actions against the general welfare of the American people ever taken (legally) by any small national group in our time. But since the press publishes the news, true or false or half-way, about everything in the world except itself, the American public knows nothing about what the rulers of public opinion annually decide for it.

Only rarely do the millions learn or sense the truth about the activities of this group of leaders. In the repudiation of the press in the 1936 election there was a symptom of the universal suspicion and growing anger of the public, but this awakening was made possible by the fact that millions were already pledged to the party the majority of newspapers attacked, and the radio was used extensively, and there were other means of breaking the press offensive. In social, rather than political, issues there is no means by which the public can defeat the dictation of the press.

The publishers' meetings are secret because their actions cannot bear the light of publicity. Three hundred and sixty days in the year the publishers speak editorially for open covenants openly arrived at, whether in international relations or in the advertising business, but every April they lock the doors and make a hypocritical paradox out of their own ideals.

We know that in the open meetings they approve annually of "freedom of the press as the bulwark of our civilization," and that in the closed meetings they discuss ways and means of fighting labor and their own employees who demand higher wages or perhaps better light or decent toilet arrangements. We do know that in the open meetings they pledge themselves to honesty and truth and the whole bagful of tricks in the ethical code of their profession, and they also discuss the cost of paper, the ways to increase advertising and gain circulation, and other purely materialistic subjects which are necessary if any press, free or kept, is to survive. But it is somewhat of a shock to learn that in the closed sessions they defend the employment of child labor, they take united action against a Congressional measure which would keep drugmakers from poisoning or cheating the American people, and they gloat over their own strike-breaking department which offers scabs not only to members but to anyone who wants to fight the unions.

One of the most recent secret meetings was devoted to nothing but war on the American Newspaper Guild, the association of newspaper workers which offended the publishers when it joined the American Federation of Labor and drove them into hysterics when it later joined the Committee for Industrial Organization. In all American business and industry today there is probably no instance of such bitterness, such conflict, such hatred, such opposition, and such war to the throat as between the newspaper workers and the newspaper owners. The amusing angle to this story is that the publishers still print that cockeyed falsehood about the interests of capital and labor being identical. It certainly isn't in their own line.

What conspiratorial plans are made to fight labor at the secret sessions we can judge best by what happens. We have seen such united action as an attack on Congress when it considered passing the Wagner Labor Act which is regarded as a Magna Carta of the working people of America. We have watched the press of the country condemn it after it passed. And, moreover, we have seen the publishers openly defy the law, declare it unconstitutional, and, when the Guild took the test case to the Supreme Court and the law was declared constitutional, we have seen the publishers inaugurate a movement to repeal or alter or emasculate this law.

We have seen the publishers declare the National Labor Relations Board unconstitutional long before the Supreme Court declared it constitutional. We have seen the publishers unite to fight any and every attempt to increase taxes on the rich and alleviate the burdens of the poor. All sorts of transcendental humanitarian poppycock has been invented by the highly paid editorial writers and rich columnists to hide this fundamental conflict of the Haves and Havenots in America. But the fact is becoming known to the public that the press lords of America are the champions of the former while still flying the pre-war flag of "service to the common people."

There are of course many men of the highest ideals in the membership. But so far as can be learned they have not been able in the past to gain their points even in the most flagrant cases of violation of journalistic ethics.

The La Follette Civil Liberties Investigation Committee has given documentary evidence that four of the biggest newspapers in the country had employed spies or thugs, but no action was taken by the publishers' association.

Some years ago one of its members was found guilty in a Federal court of theft. His news service had stolen the news from another service. But he was not fired from either the publishers' association or the service which he robbed and of which he is still a member.

Another newspaper was found guilty of blackmailing oil companies for a million dollars. And a third of suppressing the scandal for $92,000. There was some talk of taking action.

Twenty or more of the big newspapers of the country were found by a

Congressional investigation to be secretly controlled by the power and paper trust. Colonel Robert Ewing, publisher of the *New Orleans States*, president of the Southern Newspaper Publisher Association, a component branch of the A. N. P. A., offered, at the convention of the latter, a resolution condemning the power and paper trust's activities. It was tabled. S. E. Thomason, then of the *Chicago Journal*, went Colonel Ewing one better with a resolution that all the great publishers in America make public all their connections with power and paper trusts, with all the banks, and with all the powerful financial institutions which control the country.

The resolution was defeated with a roar of laughter.

On the other hand, when a speaker for the National Electric Light Association— with its $25,000,000 a year fund for influencing newspapers—said at its convention that "There we are, brothers under the skin, utility and newspaper battling shoulder to shoulder. Our most important contact is . . . the American Newspaper Publishers Association," the latter accepted the remark as a compliment.

In fact every annual convention proves more fully than the last the statement made by William Allen White, now president of the editors association, that the newspaper business is a business and nothing more. The code of ethics of the journalistic profession is no longer put into practice. But all the anti-social activities of big business have become the program of the A. N. P. A. In fact it is frequently difficult to distinguish its program from that of the National Association of Manufacturers and the United States Chamber of Commerce.

Heywood Broun, president of the Guild, who attended several open and secret sessions one year, said he was shocked by the smallness "of this collection of very small men so obviously drunk with a smug sense of power and self-righteousness," who "get themselves up as the full and all-sufficient judges of what the public should get in the way of news and of opinion." He listened for days. "The ghost of Thomas Jefferson was sent whirling along the flying trapeze as Bainbridge Colby, exhumed from heaven knows where, uttered dreary tory platitudes about big business and its sacred rights. I was struck by the fact that, with the mild exception of Glenn Frank, all the spokesmen and invited orators of the publishers were old men. And they did not talk of journalism but of the industry. If a man from Mars had happened in, I think he might have spent an hour and still remained puzzled as to whether he had happened in upon a convention of bankers, cotton-mill owners, or the makers of bathroom supplies. . . .

"The publishers decided that they would accept no sort of code of fair practice whatsoever. They decided not to disturb carrier boys between the ages of ten and twelve who are already on the job. They condemned the mild Copeland bill on foods and drugs. H. W. Flagg, of the Philadelphia *Public Ledger*, chairman of the Open Shop Committee, unofficially offered the services of his committee to all publishers, members and non-members, for strike-breaking purposes. And so you see once more the publishers have saved the freedom of the press."

When the National Electric Light Association was engaged in buying the good will of the American press, it also maintained a lobby in Washington for the purpose of using Congressmen for its own commercial purposes. This lobby was never exposed or mentioned.

Other lobbies, notably those which are not in any way affiliated with advertising, have from time to time been the subject of newspaper attacks. They have given the word "lobby" a sinister connotation, associated with such words as "propaganda" and "isms" and other things called "un-American."

But for years there has been a powerful lobby at work in Washington which up to now has been more successful than any except possibly the American Legion lobby. This is the publishers' lobby. It not only is active in making laws, amending laws, and preventing laws, but it has the unique distinction—can it be because of the power of the press?—of recommending that the publishers break the law.

Incidents and illustrations of this group's power are many and important. But before sampling those of New Deal time, I would like to mention an exposure of this lobby which can be found in "62nd Congress, 1st session, Senate Documents, Vol. 6, Reciprocity with Canada Hearings, Vol. 2," because this episode although belonging to another generation nevertheless illuminates not only the means the organization still employs, but also furnishes a clue to subjects of later chapters.

The United States, as many readers may remember, has from time to time been the scene of hefty debate over tariffs on foreign goods. The Republican press has been in favor, the Democratic press has been opposed to them, the industrialist North generally for protection, the agricultural South for free trade, the Republican newspaper propaganda insisting that prosperity and the full dinner pail—what memories these old-fashioned words bring up!—depended entirely upon the tariff wall keeping cheap foreign goods out and the American laborer contented in rich green pastures, the Democrat denying it all at every depression.

At the very time the Republican newspapers were publishing this drivel and propaganda they combined with the owners of Democratic newspapers in lobbying in Washington for the purpose of getting print paper and wood pulp exempt from a proposed severe tariff bill. The matter involved was a mere $5,000,000 per annum for the entire newspaper industry, no awe-inspiring sum in the face of a yearly advertising budget of one and a half to two billions and the fact that more than one newspaper had net annual earnings of five millions or more. Yet for this sum at least half the entire press of the United States was willing to give up its editorial policies regarding tariff and join with its political enemies in a non-partisan bit of lobbying.

Among those who called on the Secretary of State to demand free wood pulp and free print paper was Frank B. Noyes, of the *Washington Star*, one of the founders of the Associated Press, and its president up to April, 1938. Within a few days after this visit the president of the A. N. P. A., Herman Ridder, sent a letter to every publisher, member or not, which after mentioning a saving of five millions added that the bill, if ratified, would also save our forests and remove "a tax upon knowledge"; therefore "will you promptly communicate with your Senators and representatives in Congress and urge favorable action."

So far the activities of the publishers' lobby had been both legal and ethical. But apparently the matter was not going through unopposed, for in the Congressional investigation there was introduced a copy of a confidential telegram which Ridder also sent, saying that "it is of vital importance to the newspapers that their Washington correspondents be instructed to treat favorably the Canadian reciprocity agreement. . . ." This request was a violation of every code of ethics in the history of journalism.

During the course of the debate it was proved that the "tax upon knowledge" was pure hypocrisy. It was purely a savings for publishers. The claim the reader would be benefited financially was proven false: it would take about thirty-three years for one average copy of a daily to consume a ton, and the duty of $3.75 meant ten cents a year more for each subscriber. And when farmers spoke against the tariff cut the Associated Press men took no notes, whereas those who spoke for it made the headlines. When

Melville Stone, head of the A. P., said the press was fair although ninety percent of the publishers were against the tariff, it was proven statistically that the A. P. itself was sending out six times as much pro as anti news, and Mr. Stone was forced to admit that it was due "either to stupidity on the part of the people who were reporting . . . or ordinary weaknesses that attach to human beings."

These human weaknesses eventually rob a nation of a free press as great editors will testify. They are the weaknesses of egotism, of power seeking, of greed for profits, which men in other businesses often admit but which most publishers hide under beautiful words about public service. However, in the actions of the publishers' lobby against all reform legislation in more recent times we can see these motives a little more clearly than in the hypocritical past.

From the earliest days of the so-called New Deal, and immediately following the 1933 pro-Roosevelt parade in which the publishers marched under a friendly banner, their lobby has aimed at getting the press exempt from every law and regulation which affects other businesses and which might also affect their profits. The story is told that Bernard Shaw, leaving an Albert Hall meeting which he had addressed, was stopped by a beggar who held out a tin can. "Press!" said Mr. Shaw, and moved on. Apocryphal as this story may be, it illustrates well the attitude of the American newspaper publishers. In reply to every attempt to apply legislation affecting unionization, child labor, hours, wages, sanitation, working conditions, or other social reforms upon them, they have excused themselves with Mr. Shaw's remark; they have not only whispered, but bellowed "Freedom of the Press!"

The President put them in their place in 1934 when the industrial codes, later outlawed, were hailed as the salvation of the nation. The publishers' lobby favored a code for every business except theirs. But since this could not be, they drew one up which was "the most dishonest, weasel-worded and treacherous document"[1] ever offered to General Johnson. The publishers' lobby code was so designed that it would permit them to escape all the obligations (for promoting prosperity) which they were urging upon all the rest of the nation.

When General Johnson threw the lobby code aside, the lobby replied by publishing a false statement that it had been accepted. When this intimidation failed, the lobby demanded that Postmaster General Farley put pressure upon Johnson. When this also failed, the attack was continued with other weapons, one tabloid going so far as to publish an untrue story about the General and his party crashing a speakeasy. General Johnson went speaking throughout the country. He was bitter against the publishers, and especially the lobby. "They are few in number, but ruthless in method," he declared. "Some of them control powerful newspapers and they are using these papers to mis-represent every development of NRA. It is no longer possible to get a square deal in truth and accuracy . . ." But the betting in newspaper offices was ten to one that "the big steamroller, as represented by the American Newspaper Publishers Association, would crush General Johnson, the President himself, and everyone connected with the NRA." This steamroller is still crushing. In several instances, it is sad but true, the President has given in to the publishers; and the latter repaid him by joining—Democrats and Independents with Republicans—in the vast 1936 campaign against his second election.

In 1935 the publishers' lobby won four of its five campaigns in Washington, and barely lost the last, an exemption from the provision of the Wagner Labor Disputes Bill, where the Newspaper Guild was on the side of labor, as opposed to the publishers who represented the employers. During the Senate hearings Elisha Hanson, attorney for the

A. N. P. A., attacked the bill as a whole, on the ground that it would infringe freedom to print or fail to print what the publishers wished. In the House, the publishers got Representative William P. Connery (Dem., Mass.) to add a proviso which was nothing more than the old "Freedom of the Press" clause always trotted out when profits are at stake. The Guild spokesman, however, exposed this maneuver, and the amendment was out when the bill passed.

It is now well known that the publishers played the strongest hand in defeating the Tugwell Bill. Nevertheless, when the first Copeland Bill, its mild, emasculated successor, was produced in Congress, the publishers joined the Proprietary Association of Drug Manufacturers in defeating it also. The reason for this sanguinary attack on a bill already weakened to please the drugmakers, was the publishers' insistence on clauses putting all the blame for violations on the manufacturers and dealers, none on the advertising agencies and newspapers.

Along came the Agricultural Adjustment Act, and along came the publishers with amendments, one definitely stating that no marketing order could be issued "prohibiting, regulating or restricting" advertising, and providing that no processing tax can be fixed on material to be made into wood pulp, from which newsprint is manufactured.

The Black Thirty-Hour-Week Bill was kept in Representative Connery's labor committee until it emerged with exemptions for banks, newspapers and magazines.

Finally, there was the Eastman Bus and Truck Bill which was sent to the President for signature. It gives the Interstate Commerce Commission power to regulate motor carriers, but makes four commodity exemptions, the first three being livestock, fish and agricultural products, the last being newspapers.

When this list of 1935 achievements of the publishers' pressure lobby was announced the *Guild Reporter* said it was "overcome with admiration." Of course that provision in the last of the laws which sets maximum hours for truck drivers hauling papers in interstate commerce might well be interpreted as an attack on freedom of the press. Naturally, any attempt by Congress to tax wood pulp is a violation of the constitution which grants liberty to publishers. And of course if Congress insisted that the advertisers of worthless drugs tell the same truth in the newspapers which the 1906 law requires them to tell on the labels, that would curtail sales, curtail advertising, curtail profits for publishers and therefore become the most dastardly attack on the American public's inherent right to a free press which our history has ever known. So you see, the lobby has a lot of work.

* * *

It may not be ethical, or decent, or moral in the higher sense, but it is generally legal. The great publishers of America have never been afraid to defy legality when it was to their own benefit to do so. Openly the House of Lords has always stood for law and order so far as others were concerned. Generally speaking the big press of the nation has always accused labor of favoring and originating violence throughout the long and bloody history of the struggle of the working people for a better life. The exact opposite is true. After the daily newspaper has screamed its charge against the unions, the impartial historian has found, too late to be of any practical use, that in some ninety cases out of a hundred it is the employer or the police or the enemies of labor who are guilty of favoring and initiating violence.

And when it comes to lawbreaking or defiance of the law, actions which are generally charged only to criminals, the publishers have a great advantage when they do so because there can be no "public outcry" against them, no protest, no "vox populi," no "wave of indignation," nor any of the other movements they frequently invent, knowing they themselves are the only channel for such movements.

Here are, for example, two forces which affect the newspapers—and their profits. Despite publishers' opposition the Wagner Act was passed, the National Labor Relations Board came into being. Manufacturers did not like it but they obeyed it. Not so the publishers.

"If," said Elisha Hanson, chief counsel for the A. N. P. A., "the NLRB issues an order in this case, Mr. Hearst will not comply with it."

In October 1936 this same Hanson sent out a general statement to the publishers telling them not to obey the rulings of the same board because, he, Hanson, thought they were unconstitutional. "Publishers from now on," he ordered, "should flatly refuse to have anything to do with the National Labor Relations Board other than to notify it is without power under the constitution to interfere with their business. . . . In so far as the newspaper business is concerned, I am convinced no order of the Board directed to a publisher requiring him to comply with a decision thereof will, if it is contested, be upheld in the courts."

The order under discussion (the Watson case) was upheld.

The NLRB law was upheld.

In other lines of business the government and its laws have also been challenged—but not defied. Government laws and regulations have been obeyed pending the institution of suits to test constitutionality, but in no important instance has there been defiance, as in the case of the publishers. Replying to Hanson's orders to the publishers the *Guild Reporter* called the lawyer an anarchist. Of his opinion it said (October 15, 1936): "All concern for the general welfare, all respect for the right of Congress to establish public policies which it deems to be essential for the country, have been abandoned in this document which its board sponsors. A law that most of the millions of workers of the country believe is needed to protect them in their right to earn a decent livelihood, treads to some extent on the interests of 1,200 publishers. Out with it! Ignore it!"

From the very first days of the New Deal—under which incidentally newspaper workers were first enabled to organize—until the present, the American Newspaper Guild has charged the publishers with violating not only the spirit of the law but the laws themselves. The publishers' proposed code was "treacherous and dishonest" but legal; but the subsequent "dark maneuverings," said the Guild editorially, proved that "the A. N. P. A. undertakes to set itself above Congress and the President." The Guild "questioned the sincerity of the publishers in their sanctimonious espousal of the freedom of the press. . . . The American Newspaper Guild has been the only organization in the country with the courage to bring the lawless spirit of this self-appointed oligarchy out into the open and denounce it. . . . A truly free and honest press is of more importance to the members of the American Newspaper Guild than any immediate economic interest."

Only one brave publisher agreed with the Guild. J. David Stern, of the *New York Post, Philadelphia Record, Camden Courier* and *Camden Post,* withdrew his membership in the House of Lords.

"We are resigning," he wrote the A. N. P. A., "because your association, founded to benefit and strengthen the daily newspapers of this country, has in the past few years so conducted itself as to lower American newspapers in popular esteem, to endanger the freedom of the press, and has even gone so far as to urge its members to breach the law. . . .

"I do not see how a law-abiding newspaper can consistently retain membership. . . .

"Your board recommended to its membership that no agreement be entered into with any group of employees. As we understand the Wagner Act it is obligatory upon employers to negotiate with representatives of a majority of employees. . . .

"Ever since the NRA code, the A. N. P. A. has been using the pretext of protecting the freedom of the press to gain special privilege in purely business obligations.

"That is why I say you are endangering the freedom of the press, and one of the most important essentials of democracy. . . ."

Mr. Stern's *Philadelphia Record* quit the A. N. P. A.; his *New York Post* had never been a member. Within a year from that date no less than twenty-nine charges of violation of the Wagner Act and other laws which not only the Supreme Court but even the publishers' association admit are legal, were made against as many publishers.

There were seventeen instances of intimidation, coercion and actual discharge of employees for utilizing the clauses in the Wagner Act which permit unionization; in six instances the publishers were accused of breaking the law by refusing to bargain with their employees; in two instances the publishers were accused of forming company unions, all these episodes forming a record which the official organ of the newspaper writers called "irresponsible, unscrupulous and contemptible."

Among the newspapers against which charges were filed were (Gannett's) *Knicker-bocker Press* and *Albany News, Boston Herald, Boston Traveler*, (McCormick's) *Chicago Tribune, Detroit Times*, (Hearst's) *Los Angeles Examiner*, the Associated Press in New York, (Hearst's) *New York Daily Mirror, Seattle Post-Intelligencer, Seattle Star*.

With the exception of only a handful of liberal newspapers, the press of the country, which first failed to get a clause exempting itself from the Wagner Act, then defied the law, later in many instances violated the law, is today producing bitter and unfair editorials demanding that this measure—and in fact all measures which favor labor rather than capital—should be repealed.

Accused in numerous cases of discharging men for no reason but legal union activity, many publishers have sought to hide their prejudices by posting a "firing code" sent them by the A. N. P. A., and consisting of sixteen "grounds" for discharge, one of which is the failure to return a book to its proper place in the bookshelf before going home. Or leaving the electric bulb turned on over one's desk while going to the toilet. Or scratching the furniture.

The leader in the anti-labor movement of the A. N. P. A. has been its president, James G. Stahlman, publisher of the *Nashville Banner*. He is one of the minor press lords of America, and the story of his battle with the unions, his red-baiting, the sensational-izing of anti-C. I. O. news in his paper and the suppression of news favoring labor, will be found in a later chapter. The man chosen to lead the great publishers of America in their oft-announced fight for the freedom of the press is the same James G. Stahlman who, addressing the members of the Belle Meade Country Club, recently[2] said:

"If I had my way I would get me six husky policemen, take these labor organizers outside the city limits, and tell them it wouldn't be healthy for them to be seen in the vicinity again."

* * *

The foregoing are some of the subjects which the men who do a large part of the thinking, the leading or the misleading of the nation, discuss in their secret meetings. In the open meetings it is of course the welfare of the public, the freedom of the press, with only an occasional word about advertising money.

Strike breaking, the suppression of the labor movement, the maintenance of child labor, the mistakes of its counsel which sought to destroy the NLRB in the Watson case, and all general topics which are not concerned with public welfare, but with that of the pocketbook, make up most of the four days of the secret meetings which occur every year and the special Chicago meeting which was devoted to nothing but an attempt to destroy the Newspaper Guild. At that time an anonymous reporter wrote the "March of the Publishers":

> On to Chicago to fight for our freedom—
> Freedom to hire men, work 'em and bleed 'em—
> Freedom to chisel to heart's content—
> Freedom to make thirty-seven per cent.
> On to Chicago—but don't fail to stress—
> That our battle, of course, is for freedom of the press.

In the following chapters some of the individuals, all but one or two little known to the people of the country whose minds they rule, will be discussed at some length, and the common denominator of their power and their motives suggested. The reader may then judge whether or not the most powerful anonymous group of men in America can be classified as the friends or enemies of the American people.

It is the writer's intention to "let the facts speak for themselves," as Euripides suggested, and if there is criticism, expressed or implied, the reader will please remember that nothing that will be said can equal in severity that which has already come from within the ranks of the profession, from the very small minority, it is true, who still uphold the traditional journalistic liberalism of America. It is William Allen White, now president of the national editorial association, who first pointed out that the newspapers have degenerated from a noble profession to an eight percent investment, and who now states they are dominated by the "unconscious arrogance of conscious wealth," and it is J. Roscoe Drummond, executive editor of the *Christian Science Monitor*, who writes that freedom of the press "is not an end in itself. . . . A free press in the United States is not, I believe, in danger from without. It is always in danger from within. A truly free press requires . . . free men to give it life. Free men require free minds—minds intellectually honest, intellectually open, and intellectually eager. The press of the United States . . . needs . . . a leadership dedicated to the service of democracy."

The press lords of the United States in one year made this great record:

1. Fought all issues where their profits were involved.
2. Led the attack against a real pure food and drug law.
3. Opposed the Wagner Act, the Magna Carta of labor.
4. Urged amendment of proposed social insurance legislation putting newspapers in a special class.
5. Proposed compulsory arbitration of labor disputes with the outlawing of strikes.
6. Favored child labor.
7. Frowned at the Securities Act.

In its 1935 report which urged members to fight food, drug and cosmetics bills, the Wagner-Connery Law, the Thirty-Hour Bill, Social Insurance and laws "affecting the newspaper business," A. N. P. A. publishers were told to "be constantly alert and vigilant if their properties are not to be destroyed or irreparably injured."

Property, not public welfare, is the program of the A. N. P. A.

Their interests, says Alfred McK. Lee, historian of our present journalism, differ little from that of other industries; the A. N. P. A. "has sometimes been a powerful adjunct in legislative circles to the lobbies of the United States Chamber of Commerce, the National Association of Manufacturers and the trade associations of specific industries."

The press needs free men with free minds intellectually open; but its leadership consists of moral slaves whose minds are paralyzed by the specter of profits. The publishers are not leading the American people forward. They are not facing the social issues. Whether more often they are falsifying the social issues the reader may perhaps judge from the following documentation.

Notes

1.   So reported by Washington Correspondent P. Y. Anderson.
2.   *Guild Reporter*, August 30, 1937.

Chapter 24

SILAS BENT

A NEGLECTED STORY

IT IS SINGULAR THAT NEWSPAPERS, seldom bashful about their virtues, have made so little to-do about their achievements in crusading. As champions of reforms, as defenders of individuals, as protagonists of their communities, they have exercised influences, I venture to believe, quite as important as the transmission of information and the expression of opinion.

Yet this has been written only in fragmentary form. Historians of daily journals, biographers of newspaper publishers and editors, and occasionally an instructor in a school of journalism, have dealt with it in particular, sometimes in its larger aspects, but not sweepingly. A treatment at once minute and comprehensive, indeed, is impossible within the scope of a single volume, such is the wealth of material available. What is presented here must attempt a representative selection.

More than once a newspaper, at the conclusion of a successful campaign, has preened itself or has paid tribute to a fellow; by and large our most articulate institution, sometimes almost as vainglorious as politics (God save the mark!) has been surprisingly reticent about one of its primary responsibilities. Yet it has recognized crusading as a natural function and as a responsibility, and has discharged it for the most part admirably, sometimes at severe sacrifice. That there has been default in certain areas none can deny, but the account balances heavily to the credit of the press and to the benefit of its public.

Here lies the best argument for newspaper freedom not only from governmental interference but from the coercion of a capitalist economy. The history of our press since Colonial days is shot through with the struggle for unrestricted critical activity and the right to crusade. Every crusade implies, to be sure, the expression of opinion or of an attitude, but it involves more than that. It means also a willingness to fight if need be. It means, according to my dictionary, "to contend zealously against any evil, or on behalf of any reform."

To contend zealously must mean surely to struggle with ardent devotion. The zeal which fires a crusading editor may bring him to the boiling point of fanaticism, and has done it time and again. None who has undertaken a campaign in the certainty that it would entail loss of circulation and advertising, perhaps permanently, but was a fanatic, just on the sunny side of lunacy. Skeptics who deny that campaigns are ever undertaken for other than sordid motives may disabuse their minds by examining the record. If newspapers have faced actual losses in the discharge of their duties as public servants, then they have an unmistakable claim to the guaranty of the First Amendment.

Yet the daily press almost never advances crusading as proof that it should be free of restrictions. We may accept as a fair expression of its attitude the report adopted unanimously by the American Society of Newspaper Editors, at its 1938 session, declaring that the public lacked appreciation of "the true value and true functions of a free press." What is this value, and what are the functions?

> Unfortunately all citizens do not think through the meaning of a free press [said the report]. Too many regard it merely as the profitable privilege of publishers, instead of the right of all the people and the chief institution of representative government. A free press is that privilege of citizenship which makes governmental dictatorship impossible. When editors fight for the liberty to speak and write, they fight for the greatest of all human rights under government. He is not thoughtful who cannot see that democracy cannot exist except through the maintenance of a channel through which information can flow freely from the center of government to all the people and through which praise and criticism can flow freely from the people to the center.

Our editors, it seems to me, overstated the case when they said too many regarded journalistic freedom merely as a profitable privilege. Newspapers can fatten as well financially under a dictatorship as in this country; and since the daily press here is published for private profit, there can be but few who regard the cash register as the basis of free opinion, or suppose that dividends should guarantee a privileged vantage point. There are millions, to the contrary, who echo (as our editors did, with an air of saying something not usually known) the Jeffersonian dicta that "our liberty depends on the freedom of the press, and that cannot be limited without being lost"; or that "no government ought to be without censors, and where the press is free, no one ever will be." These arguments, and the importance to democratic processes of a free flow of information and criticism, have been familiar to the American public for nearly three centuries.

Not one word in that report, be it noted, about the power of newspapers to correct abuses when they leave the field of obvious comment and sally forth from routine news to rebuild and regenerate through volunteer criticism and the creation of news.

* * *

William Allen White, elected president of the society at that session, spoke his mind candidly, according to his wont, a few days thereafter. He was talking to students of the Wharton School of Merchandising about "Merchandising News in a Machine Age," and touched trenchantly both upon crusading and freedom of the press.

"The problem of the American newspaper today," Mr. White said, "is to open its channels of cordial reception to new social ideals and to insure fair treatment for any reform or any reformer who is obviously honest, reasonably intelligent, and backed by any considerable minority of the public." He suggested that to become open-minded the newspapers "might try intelligence"; and, as a corollary: "They might try to hire as doorkeepers in the house of the Lord on copy desks and in editorial chairs men who are free to make decisions about newspaper copy."

By indirection Mr. White reverted presently to the old what-the-public-wants theme. "The newspapers," he said, "will broaden their sphere of influence and will come out of the present shadow only when liberal, open-minded opinion in the middle class demands a really free press." He thought that class consciousness was discrediting the press, especially in the English-speaking democracies. "It is not the department store but the country club that has discredited the American newspaper in so far as it has lost caste with the American people." But he said also that in newspaper offices "the sense of property goes thrilling down the line," and that to a wide circle "we are 'the capitalist press'."

An uneasiness about "lost caste" runs through newspaper men. More than one of them had used that precise phase in talking with me long before Mr. White delivered his homily. Prof. Harold L. Cross has listed five major causes of this, in his work at the Graduate School of Journalism at Columbia University; the causes range from partisan-ship to the invasion of privacy. James G. Stahlman of the Nashville *Banner* has declared that the public "is fed up with week-kneed, namby-pamby editorial policies. They are tired of sloppy editing, canned bunk, and pornographic filth." *Editor and Publisher* has sounded a warning to its audience that "their every move is being watched." S. E. Thomason of the Chicago *Times* has conceded that the public was "to put it conserva-tively, unimpressed with all the battle cries for a free press." Karl von Wiegand, foreign correspondent, visiting these shores, said he was "distressed to find that the newspapers of our country are steadily and increasingly losing their influence and prestige in the public mind." So it ran, through all ranks.

If, instead of writing a new book of lamentations, newspaper men had scrutinized the record of their fraternity in crusading, they might have thrown out their chests in a better opinion of themselves. To a man who mistrusted his own powers Goethe said: "Ach! You need only blow on your hands!" Forgetting caste and prestige, newspaper men might well blow on their hands and attend to a vitally important job; then the caste and prestige would take care of themselves.

* * *

A little blowing on the hands instead of blowing about a free press would help. Does the First Amendment guarantee freedom from taxation? One might suppose so. A Hackensack daily which spent a deal of money investigating township expenses, in a campaign to have them reduced, sought to have that sum deducted from its taxes (thus denying by implication that such an investigation was obligatory), and Washington properly refused. The publishers of the Arizona *Republic* and the Phoenix *Gazette* pro-tested the right of the State to impose a license fee of $1 and a tax of one per cent upon gross income. Their attorney declared in the Federal Courts that this would give the legislature power to control the press of the State and even to destroy it. *Editor and Publisher* echoed with the discredited old maxim of Chief Justice Marshall that "the power to tax is the power to destroy." Taxes, a modern Justice of the Supreme Court said, "are the price of civilization." The Arizona papers carried their fight to the Supreme Court, which heartlessly upheld the tax.

Does freedom of the press include the right to publish in advance material that might obstruct justice? This question arose when L. G. Turrou resigned from the Federal secret service during its investigation of spy activities in this country, and made a contract with J. David Stern, publisher of the New York *Post*, to sell him articles about the confessions of four suspects who were awaiting trial.

Washington, contending that publication in advance would hamper the investigation still under way and make prosecution of the suspects difficult, sought to enjoin the projected series. Turrou vowed that he was animated by the highest patriotic motives; Mr. Stern said that the Government's move was "an unprecedented attempt to erase freedom of the press from the Constitution." *Newsdom*, a periodical of the trade, commented that although Mr. Stern was willing to accept financial responsibility, "the injury that publication of these articles might do the Government would hardly be compensated for by fines, jail sentences for contempt, or the like." *Editor and Publisher* observed that twenty years earlier it would have been "unthinkable for a newspaper to have entertained the notion of publishing the evidence which underlay an indictment not yet brought to trial." The St. Louis *Post-Dispatch*, to my way of thinking the greatest newspaper now functioning in this country, said:

> We regret to see Mr. Stern raising the cry of freedom of the press in this case. Too often it has been a false alarm—an alibi, not a genuine grievance. As we have said before, the cry of "wolf" can be used so often by publishers that it will meet only disbelief if and when the real wolf appears.

Reluctantly and with bad grace Mr. Stern abandoned his championship of freedom for the press, and agreed to postpone the articles.

When three-fourths of the revenue of the daily press was derived from the sale of space for advertising, I described freedom of the press as "an adored fiction," because, although I denied the power of the individual advertiser to influence or suppress news save in rare instances, I believed that the general pressure for the maintenance of the status quo was too strong for free expression. As this is written the revenue from advertising in proportion to that from circulation is about sixty-forty, so that the pressure has relaxed somewhat. But even when it was severest, the advertiser seldom held a whip over the crusading editor.

At the very outset, most crusades are likely to offend the advertising fraternity on the general ground that they tend to stir up the menagerie and disturb the placid purchaser. Sometimes objection is raised on the particular ground that a campaign invades the entrenchments of a favored group. It may be that in some instances newspapers have closed their eyes to situations which cried out for exposure on account of these objections; but Richard Lloyd Jones, while editor of the Tulsa *Tribune*, described the paper which would not search out facts and publish them boldly as "an enemy of society." He suspected that some of them exercised a form of self-censorship by dodging troublesome issues. We are accustomed to speak of criminals as enemies of society, and doubtless Mr. Jones thought that his fellows who neglected to crusade were tainted with felony. Certainly it is true that merely to print a great quantity of colorless news, however well arranged and ably presented, is not enough to acquit any newspaper of its duty. Until it has let the light into dark places, served as a cleansing agency, and manifested a valiant spirit, it has neither fulfilled its obligation to society not earned its privilege of freedom.

*   *   *

Richard Lloyd Jones was not alone in his doubt about the militancy of his fellows. There is a widespread impression that newspapers are no longer good crusaders, and I myself entertained it, regarding most of them, when I began gathering material for this book. I soon found out better; and so I felt impelled to write to the *New Republic* of June 1, 1938, a letter setting it right on this point, which may be worth repeating in part:

> Sir: In your editorial paragraph of May 11, dealing with the Pulitzer award to Raymond Sprigle, you say: "American journalism is not in a crusading mood these days; few campaigns of any sort are undertaken, a fact which may help explain the award to Mr. Sprigle."
>
> When Whittlesey House assigned me to prepare a book about newspaper crusades, some six weeks ago, I said much the same thing; but when I began nosing around. I found, first, that scores of recent campaigns were fully documented at the Pulitzer School of Journalism, so that your explanation of the award to Mr. Sprigle is cockeyed; second, that there had been at least two score noteworthy crusades this year and last. Even the sobersided Chicago *Daily News* had put its foot down on extortionate receivership fees, and other papers elsewhere had followed suit. One daily, espousing an unpopular cause, had lost nearly half its circulation but had stuck to its guns and carried the day. The wide range of voluntary service for the protection of the public was astonishing . . .

The magazine insisted that its statement was true, and that I would find it justified by a comparison of "the total number of important campaigns now as compared with the number some years ago." Quite aside from the fact that every newspaper campaign tends to reduce the opportunities for campaigning in its field, this impressed me as saying that if a man, having eaten a fuller lunch than usual, was rather sparing at dinner, then he must have lost his appetite. Moreover, the total number of campaigns now does compare favourably with the number "some years ago," whatever the *New Republic* may mean by that.

Bruce Bliven, a former newspaper man, was editor in chief of the *New Republic* when that paragraph appeared, and one might have expected him to know better. Ferdinand Lundberg, a former newspaper man, wrote "America's Sixty Families," and we find him saying:

> The class inhibitions which haunt the contemporary press under its millionaire ownership are responsible in large measure for the neurotic character of American newspapers. Because so many fields of editorial investigation and exposition are taboo, the press as a whole must confine itself to a relatively restricted "safe" area . . . The pecuniary inhibitions that rule the press like a Freudian complex have brought such discredit upon newspapers that they are no longer trusted by informed persons or even by business interests.

Mr. Lundberg was making the point that his sixty families controlled the daily press in this country, and that on their account the press must play safe. His group did not include the Pulitzers, and he could give no account or explanation of the fact that the elder Joseph Pulitzer, after he had become a multimillionaire outranking in wealth some of Mr. Lundberg's families, continued unabated his fight for the underdog. Probably the greatest crusader the world has seen, he continued to direct the fight even after his health was broken and his eyesight had failed. E. W. Scripps was another—not listed among the sixty—who fought as a newspaper owner for the underprivileged even after he had become a multimillionaire.

One is taken somewhat aback to find R. E. Wolseley, lecturer in journalism at the Medill School of Northwestern University, joining the chorus. Mr. Wolseley contributed to the *Commonweal* of July 29, 1938, an article, "Newspaper Editors are Sissies," in which he said:

> Today a thousand causes go unpublicized in the majority of American newspapers . . . How about a few really big drives against munitions makers who profit from the deaths of Japanese, Chinese, and several kinds of Spaniards? Or a campaign against lynch law? Against waste of natural resources by private business as well as by government? Against Frank Hague's fascism? Against municipal corruption in dozens of cities?

These questions will be answered, for the most part, a little later. As for the campaign against lynch law, it is one of the finest pages in the history of American newspapers. As for Frank Hague's fascism, newspapers were barred from sale in Jersey City because they were exposing Mayor Hague's violation of civil rights. It would have been more to the point if Mr. Wolseley had asked why newspapers had not fought for the child labor amendment, why they had not demanded that the United States free the Philippines according to its promise, why they had closed their eyes to the meretricious Pullman Company, our last unchallenged monopoly, why they continued to print patent medicine advertisements and refused to support bills for better foods and drugs.

* * *

It must be admitted that there is a gap between the ideals and the performances of newspapers, just as there was a hiatus between the theory and the practices of medieval Crusaders. In that older day there was a Christian ideal and there was the ideal of a warrior aristocracy; the knight stood for the use of force, but his faith put the use of force on the side of humanity and justice. Yet only Sir Galahad was noble and pure, and he was a figment of the imagination. The knights who sought to wrest the Holy Sepulcher from the Saracens were not above reproach; of the seven Crusades, the first only, which resulted in the capture for a time of Jerusalem, was idealistic and truly religious. The others were tainted with commercialism and imperialism. But at any rate the returning Crusaders brought to Europe the bathtub.

Bearing in mind this lapse between the professions and the practices of crusaders, medieval and modern, let us see whether newspaper campaigners are quite as bad as sometimes they are painted. Here I find H. L. Mencken saying, in the pages of the *Atlantic Monthly*, that the primary purpose of a newspaper crusade is to "give a good show to the crowd," and that the way to do this is "by first selecting a deserving victim and then putting him magnificently to the torture." Even the campaign for good government, he vows, is conducted "in exactly the same way," "dramatizing and vulgarizing it." The editor, he explains, is a "mobmaster."

Never, Mr. Mencken declares, is the crusading appeal to "the educated and reflective minority of citizens, but frankly to the ignorant and unreflective majority." Hear now his confession of faith: "For morality, at bottom, is not at all an instinctive matter, but a purely intellectual matter." I am reminded of a conversation with Theodore Dreiser in which this question came up, and in which he threw a lightning flash upon it. "Read Villon's poetry," he told me; "marvellous! And yet France hanged that bastard for a good reason." There is some doubt, I believe, as to whether Villon was hanged, but there is no doubt that he merited it, nor is there any doubt as to his intellectual grasp.

Newspaper crusading, according to Mr. Mencken, is "a popular sport" for the ignorant masses, "always far more orgiastic than reflective." The crusade against William M. Tweed, corrupt boss of Tammany Hall, "shook the whole nation, for he was a man of tremendous power, he was a brave and enterprising antagonist." Thus is one of the most celebrated newspaper campaigns dismissed airily with praise for the "deserving victim" who was put "magnificently to the torture."

There is good reason to doubt whether any magazine less gullible than the *Atlantic Monthly* would have sponsored an outgiving so false. Mr. Mencken at that time, to be sure, was editor of the Baltimore *Evening Sun*, and the editors of the magazine may have supposed in their innocence that he voiced the views of newspaper men everywhere, instead of the policy of a journal, once liberal, which had turned reactionary. I cannot be sure of this, for the same editors ran a series of "articles" about corporations, written by Arthur Pound, which in fact were paid advertisements. But at any rate the *Atlantic Monthly* made amends to the extent of giving space to a reply to Mr. Mencken by Ralph Pulitzer, then president of the New York *World*.

Commenting on Mr. Mencken's "very unfortunate class arrogance," Mr. Pulitzer said: "A great many persons of guaranteed education are sadly destitute of any reflectiveness whatsoever, while an appalling number of 'the ignorant' have the effrontery to be able to reflect very efficiently. This is apart from the fact that the general intelligence among many of the ignorant is matched only by the abysmal stupidity of many of the educated."

But what about Mr. Mencken's charge that newspapers fight even their "constructive campaigns for good government in exactly the same gothic, melodramatic way"? Said Mr. Pulitzer:

> Now "muck-raking" rather than incense-burning is not a deliberate aim so much as a spontaneous instinct of the average newspaper. Nor is there anything either mysterious or reprehensible about this. The public, of all degrees, is more interested in hitting Wrong than in praising Right, because fortunately we are still in an optimistic state of society, where Right is taken for granted and Wrong contains the element of the unusual and the abnormal. If the day shall ever come when papers are able to "expose" Right and regard Wrong as a foregone conclusion, they will doubtless quickly reverse their treatment of the two. In an Ali Baba's cave it might be natural for a paper to discover some man's honesty; in a *yoshiwara* it might be reasonable for it to expatiate on some woman's virtue . . .

Space does not permit me to quote much further, but I must select part of another paragraph:

> If Mr. Mencken's ideal is a nation of philosophers calmly agreeing on the abstract desirability of honesty while serenely ignoring the specific picking of their own pockets, we have no ground for argument. But until we reach such a semi-imbecile Utopia, it would seem to be no reflection on "the people's" intellectual or moral concepts that they should refuse to excite themselves over any theoretical wrong . . .

Mr. Pulitzer, in short, exposed Mr. Mencken's fallacies and misstatements mercilessly, punctured his supercilious pretensions, and left him on the field completely deflated. The chastening effect of this salutary drubbing was apparent in a subsequent statement Mr. Mencken gave to *Editor and Publisher:*

> The newspapers, fortunately, are still more or less free, and can thus speak plainly. They constitute the last defense of common honesty, common decency, and common sense. It is their highest function to scrutinize the acts of all public officials, high or low, with the utmost diligence, and to denounce instantly every sign of stupidity or false pretenses.

From terming the crusading editor a "mobmaster," and asserting that campaigns for good government were conducted by "dramatizing and vulgarizing" them, Mr. Mencken has been converted to regarding such campaigns as the editor's "highest function" and urges him to utter instant denunciation. Long ago it was apparent to everybody else that American newspapers could not qualify, even at their worst, for all the nasty adjectives he found in his thesaurus; maybe it has become apparent to him, too.

Let me set down here a sketch of what seems to me a perfect crusade, worthy of a very Galahad. It was not the work of a newspaper but of an individual, and its value therefore is solely illustrative. Behind it was no motive of publicity or of financial gain or of personal aggrandizement. By this even if for no other reason John Jay Chapman deserves to live as one of our immortals.

In Coatesville, Pennsylvania, on August 13, 1911, a Negro was hideously burned to death. He had been drinking, and in his exhilaration had fired three shots according to his own account, near the plant of the Worth Brothers Steel Company. Arrested by a special policeman, he tried to pull away and then, in self-defense, so he said, killed the man. As he fled he was wounded and lodged under police guard in the Coatesville Hospital. A mob, apparently without resistance by the police, dragged him out bound to his cot, and set it on a pile of rubbish.

"Don't give me a crooked death because I'm not white," the Negro pleaded.

Fire was set to the rubbish, and the victim was done jubilantly to death.

On the following day New York newspapers carried stories of the horror. M. A. DeWolfe Howe tells us, in "John Jay Chapman and His Letters," that these "were indeed enough to stir a man of Chapman's sensitive fibre to the deepest feeling." As the anniversary of the event approached he said that "my inner idea forced me to do something." He considered organizing a committee and inviting protestants from far and wide to go with him to Coatesville, but he decided to go with but one friend, a woman, to hold a memorial prayer meeting, "not for condemnation but for intercession." He felt that if this outrage were permitted to lie fallow it would do an irreparable injury to his country's people, but that a single protest might serve somewhat as an expiation.

One may fancy how a community in the Deep South would have received an outsider who came to protest a lynching; Yankee Coatesville did no better. No public hall could be rented, but an empty shop was procured. The Coatesville *Record*, after a good deal of hesitation and questioning, permitted the insertion of a paid notice of the meeting. Beside Mr. Chapman's friend, only two auditors were present: an aged Negress from Boston and a man who served apparently as an outpost or spy. Nevertheless Mr. Chapman held his meeting, with Bible readings, a brief talk, a prayer, and silent prayer.

Elsewhere I shall wish to quote from the talk Mr. Chapman made. Mr. Howe is justified in speaking of its "austere restraint and tragic beauty." Here it is enough to say that something of the noble and fearless spirit which animated that obscure pilgrimage has flamed more than once in newspaper editors during their crusades. Mr. Chapman's move was stripped bare of any desire for applause, or any feeling that ultimately it might pay dividends in respect and good will. His was a voice crying in the wilderness. Mrs. Chapman feared, with good reason, that he was taking his life in his hands, but he derided the notion. It is certain that more than once crusading editors and reporters have risked their lives and in some instances have lost them.

*   *   *

Oftenest the risk has come through the exposure of political corruption. Let me say at once that this form of campaigning, with which most of us associate newspaper crusades, is not my sole topic. No, the crusades with which I shall deal cover a surprising territory, ranging through the fight against racial and religious intolerance, the integration of communities, the liberation of persons unjustly imprisoned, the rehabilitation of a city's reputation and fortune, the reduction of taxes and the rates charged by public utilities, the improvement of working conditions, to the reformation of State prisons and institutions for the insane. Governmental housecleaning has been more spectacular than some of these, but not always of greater reach in social betterment.

After sketching the achievements of a few of our most famous crusaders, in order to look at their methods and their motives, I hope to chronicle briefly the part Colonial newspapers played in preparing for the revolution against George III. That rebellion could not have been fomented solely by pamphleteering and from the soapbox; it would have been impossible without the spur of the press. I would like to tell about the attitude of these newspapers toward the Constitution, toward the abolition of human slavery, and toward various matters of national import after the Civil War. It is a record, by and large, of which all of us may be proud; for it vindicates the privileges we have accorded in this republic to one of our greatest institutions.

Chapter 25

OSWALD GARRISON VILLARD

THE DISAPPEARING DAILY

THE OUTSTANDING FACT IN ANY SURVEY of the American press is the steady and alarming decrease in the number of dailies. Consolidation, suppression, and a strong drift toward monopoly are taking their toll. With an increase in population to more than 130,000,000, with world-shaking events of almost daily occurrence and the need for detailed, printed information greater than ever in the battle for human liberty, there are at this writing but 1,754 daily English-language journals in the great American nation as against 2,042 in 1920, and 1,933 in 1930. The decrease has been marked throughout this century. No less than 104 dailies died or were amalgamated between September 30, 1941 and March 31, 1943, although this period, except for the first two months, was distinguished by the attack on Pearl Harbor and the startling developments of our second World War. Not only were the factors making for the decrease of the dailies not offset by these thrilling events in all quarters of the globe, but there was almost no evidence of any desire to start new journals. Moreover, the war added to the difficulties of the weaker dailies through increasing costs, scarcity of labor, lack of paper, and a large decrease in advertising, such as automobile announcements, though others showed striking increases. Today there are no less than 1,103 towns and cities with only one newspaper, and in 159 large towns and cities having more than one daily there is complete ownership of the local press by one man or one group.

It is true that, according to figures compiled by *Editor and Publisher*, English-language daily newspaper circulations increased approximately four per cent during the period from Pearl Harbor to March 31, 1943, the total daily circulation for all the newspapers being 44,392,829 copies. This is the highest figure recorded in the history of the American press, and this despite the loss in the number of newspapers. But this gain in total sales by no means offsets the loss of many organs of public opinion. There are still 11,474 weekly papers (though here, too, there is a marked decrease), and some of these carry considerable weight in their communities by trying to print more news, and in some cases even taking over standard features, such as the work of some of the columnists. In the weekly field there are few signs of vital growth if by that is meant the entrance into the business of vigorous young personalities with a message to impart. The case of the newspaper proprietor in the large towns and small cities also becomes more and more difficult because of those increasing costs of conducting the modern newspaper with its expensive machinery—the New York *Times's* newest press is valued at more than $1,000,000—and its more and more elaborate means of acquiring and receiving its news. Only in periods of intense financial depression is there any slackening of the mounting costs of producing a daily, whose owners are often at the mercy of the inventor of a labor-saving or time-saving device, however expensive. Finally, in war-time the limitation of the supply of paper comes into the picture. Thus on a single day in October 1943 one of our largest newspapers was forced to omit 125 columns of advertising, and this was not even a Sunday issue.

Few laymen understand that in the smaller communities in particular there is a definite limitation of the possible support to be had for a daily. While there exists, of course, a large volume of what is known as "national advertising," paid for by concerns marketing goods or services in which all communities are more or less interested, the main support of a daily usually comes from the merchants of the place of publication. These sellers of goods not only do not oppose the newspaper trend to monopoly, but encourage it on the ground that if they advertise in only one daily they will save time and labor in the preparation of their announcements and have much less to pay out. What they and the proprietors of newspapers who seek monopolies overlook is that the newspaper business is unlike most others in that it is "affected by a public interest." It is a vital public need that the people in a democracy shall have the news and the opportunity to read all sides of political debates of the hour. As Thomas Jefferson put it, the best way to head off unsound opinion in a democracy is "to give them [the people] full information of their affairs thro' the channels of the public papers and to contrive that these papers should penetrate the whole mass of the people." To establish a press monopoly in a locality is to restrict the field of public information or to narrow its vision, or even perhaps to put an end to the presentation in the remaining dailies of anything but a partisan aspect of the national political or economic situation—and this despite the coming of the radio. Yet every successful publisher is beset by the temptation to increase his power and to make sure of financial profit by eliminating competitors.

From the point of view of economy and avoiding duplication of labor and editorial effort, a case can be made for the realization of the average newspaper publisher's dream of only one morning and one evening newspaper in each large city, and only one daily in all cities having 100,000 or fewer inhabitants. But aside from special influences in the newspaper business, there never was any reason to believe that the newspapers, having changed from a profession open to men of small means into a business requiring millions and therefore possible for only the very wealthy, could escape those economic tendencies which, notably in America, have more or less affected all other large industrial enterprises. Since no one would dream of starting a metropolitan newspaper with less than ten or even fifteen millions in the bank, the daily everywhere takes its place as an important industrial enterprise, a big business whose proprietors are entitled to rank among the foremost mercantile leaders of the community. Their tendency is naturally to think and act as do the members of the economic group to which they belong, and to drift steadily away from the plain people and especially from the workers. Just as the profession of journalism has changed into a business, so there is every temptation for the proprietor to consider all political and economic questions from the point of view of those who have very large economic stakes and to look with alarm upon all proposed social and political reforms. The newspaper owner feels that he belongs in the Chamber of Commerce and the merchants' associations more naturally, perhaps, than anybody else except the heads of the public utilities. His property ranks with those powerful business corporations which in every American community dominate its economic and financial life, whose officials and their wives set the "society" tone and too often control all social progress.

Other important changes in the evolution of the dailies are their increasing standardization, their continuing change from a purely informative and news-printing medium into an organ of entertainment as well, and their great loss of political and editorial influence. As for standardization, that is so obvious as to need no stressing. It is naturally increased by the existence of chains of dailies under one ownership. When one travels through the country on a fast train and buys successively the newspapers of larger cities, one is struck by their similarity. One finds the same comics, the same special features in almost all, the same Sunday magazine and financial section, and precisely the same Associated Press or United Press news. I have looked through the Sunday editions of nine large Eastern and Midwestern newspapers; a cursory examination of the Philadelphia *Inquirer* revealed twenty features that were also in the other eight newspapers. Today whenever a journal discovers a new feature, there is a widespread rush to copy it; the competition for a popular comic strip or its imitation is the clearest testimony on this point. There is no copyright to bar the adoption of new trade devices if they are dressed anew.

The newspaper of striking individuality has yielded to the desire to print everything offered by one's rivals. Almost nobody among present-day journalists sets any store by beauty of type and originality of appearance. There are still striking exceptions, like the *Herald Tribune*, the *Christian Science Monitor*, the Cincinnati *Enquirer*, and some Southern newspapers; but with the coming of mass production of dailies the desire for originality seemed to pass. Moreover, the columnists and the "canned editorials," the syndicated articles, and even the latest mechanical developments all make for similarity. When the teletypesetter came in, Frank Gannett, one of its backers, wrote that it would "work towards standardization," saying: "It will be necessary for newspapers that intend to go in a circuit to standardize their grammatical style, width of column, and the size of type used. It will also tend to standardize our news services." There are hundreds of newspapers that receive their editorials from one source, such as the Newspaper Enterprise Association. I have received as many as sixty clippings from as many small dailies all over the Union containing editorial comment upon some words of mine—all alike, all from the same source, the facts and opinions given being accepted by the editors receiving them without any critical examination whatever as to their correctness.

Indeed, nowhere is the drift toward standardization more marked than in the editorial pages, unless it be in the first pages, where, in the smaller cities particularly, one often finds slavish copying of the headlines and make-up of the large city dailies. Just as there is no longer any desire to make newspapers distinctive for individuality and for originality in the presentation of news, so many of the proprietors are influenced by this trend not to have striking personalities in charge of their editorial pages. The conservative owner does not want a powerful leader-writer to "ride hobbies or antagonize whole groups of readers," as one of them remarked to me. Curiously enough, he sticks to this although he is often aware of the lack of influence of his editorial page, for he frequently sees no inconsistency in spreading upon the first page of his daily editorials he specially wishes to have read. He even signs them himself in order to win the attention of politicians and public. At the same time he pays large sums to writers of distinction to take over his sports pages or contribute daily columns under their own signatures.

It has not been at all difficult for the dailies to swing over to the amusement side. Indeed, many have been compelled to do so and owe their continued existence to the comics, the illustrations, the puzzles, the fiction, the sports news, and the personal gossip they print. Thus, in order to keep alive, they enter fields of activity which seemed wholly outside of the scope of the newspaper until a few decades ago. Even when empty cupboards have not driven the owners along this road to success, many have realized the tremendous interest of the masses in the amusements which are their escape from their work and the routine of their lives, and, in war-time, from the nerve-racking strains to which most people are subjected. Some dailies, like the New York *Times*, to their infinite credit have refused to yield; but it has not been necessary for their financial welfare to do so. Here, as in so many other cases, we have a world-wide phenomenon.

Sir Philip Gibbs, for example, in discussing the sad plight of the British press, appealed for "less pandering to the gallery of human nature," in addition to his demand for more newspapers to offset the increasing monopolies, and for more responsibility and reliability because the press as a whole has lost its power, because "its word is no longer accepted as gospel." Few newspaper managers care for this loss of standing if they can add to their readership by printing pages and pages of comics, hints to the lovelorn, canned advice to parents, syndicated recipes for the housewife, widely marketed cuts of the coming fashions for women young and old. As long as such features make a popular appeal the modern proprietor does not care in how many other dailies they appear or how trivial and banal or vulgar they may be. He is competing with the movies, with the radio, with the legitimate stage. Hence he is sure that his greatest appeal to his readers is to be found in his "funnies" and his sensational pictures.

The commercial proprietor of this type is, therefore, little affected if he is told that he is not living up to his duty as the mentor and critic of our political and economic life. It is his income that is at stake. He is not worried when he reads a criticism like that of Irving Brant, the head of the editorial page of the St. Louis *Star-Times*, who has declared that: "Taken as a whole, the newspapers of America furnish no driving force for social reform. They are a positive handicap in economic reform. . . . It is impossible to point to one important constructive step in the last eight years which represents either the inventiveness the initiative, or the supporting activity of the American press."[1] Mr. Brant, an ardent champion of the New Deal, says that for a few months in 1933 there was an emotional press response to the initiative and leadership of President Roosevelt, but that the metropolitan newspapers have been "substantially regimented against the New Deal" from the day "they were asked to limit the hours of their employees to forty per week and to pay reporters a minimum wage of $25, from the day they were told that the law guaranteed newspaper employees the right to organize for collective bargaining."

Largely because of this changed attitude of the press, it is a fact that its loss of prestige and influence is appalling and overshadows every other development except its decrease in numbers. The newspaper reader pays less and less attention to what the editors are saying and to their advice on the conduct of the nation's affairs. Here the outstanding proof is afforded by the results of the Presidential elections of 1936 and 1940. In both cases the vast bulk of the press opposed the re-election of the President. Indeed, the opposition was so overwhelming that the election of 1936 was called a vote against the newspapers, a "judgement day for America's daily press." The electorate went to the election booths under the strongest impression not only that the press was mainly Republican, but that it was fighting not for the country as a whole but for its own personal interests. They felt so keenly that it was a hostile force that in Chicago the crowds cheered attacks on their anti-Roosevelt dailies as the returns came in. In 1896 the press threw itself overwhelmingly into the fight against Bryan and stopped at nothing to accomplish its purpose. It showed its power and won. In 1936 and in 1940 it failed.

In an extraordinarily able article after the 1936 election, the editors of the *Christian Century* indicted the press for "its arrogance, its tyranny, its greed, its scorn of fairplay." They declared that every variety of political liberalism, in addition to organized labor and the organized farmer, had definitely come to the point where "they no longer hoped to be given just treatment" in the columns of the newspapers. Undoubtedly the intensity of this feeling, which still persists to a remarkable degree, was due to the opposition of the press to the NRA, and its long-continued refusal to accept a code for itself. Its challenging—and defeating—the child-labor constitutional amendment lest it be deprived of its newsboys, and its hostility to unions among its own workers, were both accepted as further proof that the press had cast aside all pretense that it was governed by devotion to the public welfare. Many a critic besides the *Christian Century* saw in this vote a branding of the press for its "social malfeasance," for its carrying on merely as the property of rich men, as a dangerous enemy in "the ultimate issue in a democracy, wealth versus commonwealth." Whatever the exact delinquency of the press in 1936, it cannot deny that Roosevelt carried the country by a 10,000,000 plurality, polling 27,000,000 votes.

The editors of the *New Republic* made a special study[2] of fifteen cities in connection with the 1936 Presidential election. Approximately 71 per cent of the total newspaper circulation of the fifteen cities, excepting those newspapers which were for neither Roosevelt nor Landon, was hostile to the Roosevelt candidacy, but in those cities only 31 per cent of the voters cast their ballots for the Republican candidate. In Boston, for example, there was a pro-Landon circulation of 1,158,352, yet there were only 96,418 votes cast for him. In Los Angeles the pro-Roosevelt newspapers sold only 74,252 copies, but there was a Democratic vote of 757,351, which was exactly 400,000 more than the Republican vote. In Detroit not a single newspaper advocated the re-election of Roosevelt, but he carried the city by 404,055 to a Republican vote of 190,732. The *New Republic's* editors felt that the unfairness of some of the newspapers to Roosevelt's candidacy during the campaign showed that the press was getting worse and not better, and that the decay of the editorial page was more and more marked. They charged that the Chicago *Tribune* and the Hearst chain were the worst offenders because they "not only prevaricated editorially, but distorted and discolored news."

Were there any doubt as to the reactionary and selfish character of much of the press, it would be ended by a study of the policies of the American Newspaper Publishers' Association, which speaks largely for it. The Association not only opposed the NRA, the newspaper code, the coming of the newspaper guilds, and the child-labor amendment, but has also attacked the National Labor Relations Act, and stood against the advance of labor all along the line. If many of the individual newspapers allow themselves to be controlled by the Association, then we have here a very grave threat to freedom of the press. As Mr. Brant has said, the objection to such control lies not in the fact that it is conservative, for it would be just as serious if it came from liberals on behalf of a liberal program. It lies in the truth that any attempt at a centralized control of newspaper opinion is an attack upon a fundamental freedom and "weakens the basis of our American democracy."

The loss of influence by the newspapers is also in large measure due to the belief that much of the local reporting is onesided, biased, and inefficient. Every large community knows how many of its activities go unrecorded, and many of its citizens are aware by personal experience of the too frequent misrepresentation of what does happen. Often the public errs in its judgment of what should and could be reported of a city's life, even by the greatest newspapers. But those citizens who in every municipality are struggling to rectify misgovernment, to apply social curatives, and to improve civic methods know all too well how difficult it is to win and to hold the attention of the dailies. The reformers' programs are usually not sensational and are often not well presented, even when there is a "human interest" side to what they have to offer. When they are told that the lack of space makes it impossible to give room to their activities, yet see columns and columns given to gossip, scandal, and crime, they naturally believe that they have been deceived. They cannot understand it when the editor or publisher tells them he must print discussions of sports, crimes, fiction, "society" and club events, and so on, in order to hold the attention of so diversified a group as any aggregation of newspaper readers.

As one who has been on both sides of the fence, for many years on one side as a reporter and editor, and on the other as a lecturer, author, and protagonist of many causes, I can come to no other conclusion than that there has been a marked deterioration in the character and quality of the average reporting. There are brilliant exceptions—dailies earnestly seeking to be accurate—but in the main the reliability of news accounts is far below what it was years ago, and the chance of misrepresentation through unintentional misquotation as well as carelessness is so great that it is frequently necessary for speakers to safeguard themselves by preserving a copy of their statements, or by preparing in advance a "hand-out" for the reporters. Too often the reporter sent to interview the visitor in town knows nothing about the subject he asks his victim to discuss. Distinguished authors from overseas find themselves cross-examined by high-school graduates who have not the faintest idea of the background or the achievements of the men whom they are undertaking to report and to describe, or just what makes the visitors at that moment "good copy." "Where do you live and how many books have you written?" is hardly the best way to greet a man whose name is known all over the Anglo-Saxon world.

In my small sphere I have encountered reporters who admitted that they did not know whether I was an editor or a hardware merchant or a politician and had no conception of the purpose of their errand. Others could not understand the simplest developments in international affairs and showed their ignorance of outstanding men in American political life. Everyone who has traveled much and attracted the notice of the press will recall his unutterable relief on meeting a reporter who was intelligent, informed, and eager to be accurate. When one has the remarkable experience of having one's remarks recorded with stenographic accuracy and complete understanding, one naturally sends an immediate letter of thanks to the editor and the reporter. I am sure that many besides myself, so far from looking eagerly for the reproduction of an interview, have turned to it only with a wonder as to how bad the misrepresentation would be that time, or have felt relief if no interview was reported at all, or if what appeared was boiled down to a couple of "stickfuls."

On behalf of the reporters it should be said that they are as much sinned against as sinning. It is constantly dinned into their ears that when they go to public meetings or to interviews they must look for something "spicy," something to warrant a smart head-line, something unexpectedly sensational or controversial. There must always be a bright, snappy "lead." So happenings of no real importance are constantly "played up" and really valuable statements or actions overlooked. A controversy between two speakers is particularly beloved, or an interruption from the audience. American assemblies and speakers in a joint debate are so unused to heckling and interrogations that when anyone does speak up, it becomes something extraordinary—to be "featured."[3] So the reporter is trained to look for the bizarre as all-important. If nothing exciting happens and the reporter does not bring out valuable points, or it is a crowded night at the office, his whole report is thrown on the floor. Indeed, what often puzzles the public is to see a group of reporters at a meeting and then to search in vain the next morning for one word of the happenings, or to find only a few skimpy lines. "Why was the reporters' time wasted?" the public asks. "Who called them off?"

One Washington meeting comes to mind, held during mid-summer of 1942 to protest against conditions in India and to demand India's freedom. The hall was crowded to suffocation, despite dreadful heat, and hundreds were turned away, even from an overflowing meeting. The speakers were of good standing and reputation, one a national figure. The reporters' table was crowded, and the next day—not a word anywhere except a complete misrepresentation of the meeting in an evening news-paper! The speakers had been scrupulously polite to the British, but had any one of them made a violent attack upon Lord Halifax or Winston Churchill, or somebody else, the meeting would have made the front pages. I asked the owner of one of the Washington newspapers why his daily had suppressed the news of so large a meeting on so vitally important a war subject. He said he did not know why, but that he was sure that it was due to the shortage of paper and lack of space and not to any deliberate effort to suppress criticisms of English policy. To the question why, if there was so little space, the newspapers wasted time and money in sending reporters out to do nothing and print nothing, he had no reply.

In the case of this Washington meeting the reporters were obviously not respon-sible for the failure of their "stories" to appear. The night make-up editor holds the final say, unless overruled by superior authority. Indeed, the modern reporter is blamed frequently for the errors and the stupidities of the copy-readers. There can be no question that there has been a marked deterioration in the technical handling of "copy" and news dispatches. The newspapers of the 1890s and the first two decades of this century prided themselves upon the accuracy of their reports, and were zealous in their efforts to catch blunders, bad English, and inaccurate descriptions. Today a veteran journalist writes me that "sloppiness in product is the outstanding phase of the Manhattan newspapers in 1943. Nobody seems to be concerned about the real meaning of words. The city and copy desks no longer care about blunders. The old zealot pride in Tiffany-grade craftsmanship seems moribund. Showmanship has replaced reportorial accuracy and ability. How can an eager cub develop into an ace when he lacks persistent coaching in the fundamentals of his profession? I have just read this morning's news-papers and gagged over their inexcusable sloppiness." The above cited ignorance of the average reporter as to recent history, political and other personalities, and current events is too often reflected on the copy-desk.

The readiness of the American daily to drop local happenings on any excuse affects not merely meetings and causes, but accounts of notable events. So marked has this been for some time that the late Frank Vanderlip once declared that if he were a younger man he would launch a new-type daily, one that would contain no news dispatches except those from Washington relating directly to the welfare of the city in which the paper was published. Everything else would be news of local affairs. Yet home coverage used to be the groundwork of every newspaper, and notably of the small country weeklies and dailies with their printing of "personal mentions" to take the place of local events of importance when those were not forthcoming. It will be regrettable indeed if after this war the press does not return to its prime duty of reporting the progress, or the retrogression, or the ambitions of its home communities.

One may well wonder if many proprietors and editors have seriously studied the exact division of their daily's space, or really sought to find out if the city's feelings, as indicated by the public's expression of its views, are adequately covered by their publications. Yet there are few things that have done so much to destroy faith in the press as inexact reporting. It is especially dangerous because persons present at events reported testify widely to the failure or the bias of the press. Here again it must be repeated that there are brilliant exceptions. This is, however, one of the many reasons why people no longer say: "I saw it in the newspapers, and so it must be true," but "Oh, you can't believe what you see in the dailies." Yet the former phrase was on the whole well earned by the press during the generations when the reporting—even in the 1850s—was far superior in detail and accuracy to that of the general run of today's. The New York *Herald*, for example, during the anti-slavery struggle, reported an Abolition meeting with stenographic fidelity even when it was entirely opposed to the purposes of the meeting, and, as in the case of one address by Wendell Phillips, had actually hired a mob to break up the meeting; its verbatim report was superior to that of the Abolition *Tribune*. It is true that in those days there was plenty of space and relatively little news. Today the demands on space are tremendous, but the selection of what is to go into it is too one-sided, too often, as said, guided by the search for sensation, by likes and dislikes.

When we turn to the field of labor it is not difficult to understand why the great body of workers believes the newspapers to be their most potent enemy. This is because of their ability, when strikes and other labor troubles occur, to judge newspaper accounts by their own experience and knowledge. Usually the press is against them and presents colored editorial opinions and misleading or false newspaper reports. However in the wrong and unjust the employers may be, or how partisan the conduct of the authorities and the police, it is rare indeed that a newspaper holds the scales even or leans to the labor side. Of late years the New York *Times* and some other strong newspapers have set an admirable example in appointing special labor reporters, like Louis Stark of the *Times*, and have given them free rein to report what is actually going on within the unions and to portray truthfully the labor point of view. But in the main the tendency to take sides with passion and hostility against labor, and particularly any such unpopular labor leader as John L. Lewis, renders any fair reporting out of the question in the bulk of the press or by the press associations.

Certainly no one would allege that the press as a whole has even begun to do its duty in reporting the unfair practices of employers and public authorities such as have recently been brought out by Senator LaFollette's inquiry into them through his special Committee on Civil Liberties in connection with labor troubles. The ordinary tendency is to uphold the police, however lawless and brutal its actions, however ghastly its slaughter of the workers, such as took place in Chicago during the great strike at the Republic Steel Company's works when the police interfered with a murderous brutality surely not exceeded except by Hitler's S.S. Moving-picture films proved the scandalous conduct of the police, and some corrective measures were taken by the authorities. But if anybody should need further proof of how lawless the press and the police can be, he should turn to the trouble in San Francisco in 1934 which took on the character of a general strike. This is one of the very few cases in which the charge of a newspaper conspiracy can be brought against the dailies. The San Francisco newspapers formed the "Newspaper Publishers' Council" so that they could act together. Their first important effort was to prevent the declaration of martial law on the ground that if order was maintained—and therefore the strike was not illegally interfered with—"the announced objective of the general strike" would have been aided. They were successful in this, and next printed on their first pages editorials stating that radicals had got control of the unions and "that the general strike was a revolution against constituted authority," which it was not in the remotest degree.

Then General Hugh Johnson, the head of the NRA, arrived in San Francisco. Eager to "grant the request of the general strike committee that the longshoremen's demands for complete control of hiring halls be accepted as a condition before any discussion of arbitration should occur," he declared that the shipowners were "anti-social," because "labor is inherently entitled to bargain collectively through leaders of its own choosing," and because "in the American shipping industry, including the loading and unloading of ships, this right has not been justly accorded." He went on to say that because of this the responsibility "for anything that may happen here" would be "on the head" of the shipping managers. Then the Publishers' Council got to work on him and kept at him until three a.m. When the next dawn came he announced that the workers whose cause he had just justified constituted "a threat to the community," planning "civil war," "bloody insurrection," "a blow at the flag of our common country." More than that, he declared that if the government did not act, the people would. This was immediately followed by the appearance of "vigilantes," who, with the police following and abetting them, were soon smashing private property, entering private premises without warrant, and destroying the contents of the headquarters of unions, Communists, and radical newspapers.

The police arrested hundreds of people—again without warrant—and, without the excuse that mob violence was going on, beat them up and threw them into jail. One San Francisco judge alone released eighty men against whom, he said, no shadow of a charge of lawless conduct could be brought. In all of this the newspapers, always with the admirable exception of the Scripps-Howard *News*—which was not in the Council—continued to play a despicable part, inciting by their headlines to public excitement and disorder. They pretended that union men made the raids, which was not true, for, according to reliable witnesses, the police themselves were the most lawless and the most guilty. What can be said of the mentality of those publishers who could not see that offenses by officials under oath to uphold and defend the laws and the rights of the individual constitute vastly more dangerous blows to our American institutions and our Constitution than could the activities of the few really "radical" leaders in San Francisco? Was it any wonder that thereupon the San Francisco unions voted to boycott all the newspapers except the *News*?

It is hardly surprising in the light of this, and any amount of similar evidence, that the workers have no faith whatever in the daily press, that in 1936 and 1940 they loved Mr. Roosevelt for his newspaper enemies. Whatever else may be said of Mr. Roosevelt—and I am entirely opposed to his continuance in office—the workers believed rightly that the New Deal gave them their only hope of the improvement of their social and economic position—until Mr. Roosevelt himself betrayed his creation. The public is buying more newspapers as the quoted figures show, partly, of course, because we are in the greatest of wars. The readers want their comics, they want their sports, they want news of Hollywood, and they want the news of our steady progress in the war. Especially they want the radio timetables that they may hear not only the entertainment features offered by the stations, but important public addresses and "flash" news bulletins. But the people buy the newspapers not for their counsel or their leadership, not for any inspiration, nor in any expectation of finding them championing any far-reaching, fundamental reforms or leading them toward a better era.

Finally, in this survey of the trend of American journalism during the last twenty years, it must be stressed again that the tendencies cited are to be found not merely in the United States, but in other freedom-loving countries. They are part and parcel of the evolution of this capitalistic age, which, through its failure to head off the second World War, has invited its own destruction. In my judgment, the burden of guilt upon the press of the world for the coming of this war is second on the Allied side only to that which rests upon the shoulders of the statesmen of Belgium, of France, of England, for their refusal to see from 1920 on whither the Treaty of Versailles was leading us, their unwillingness to aid the German Republic and the democratic forces supporting it, their failure to prevent the rearming of that country by Hitler, their giving him the right to re-create a navy, and their appeasing of the German dictator.

That a very considerable portion of the press in both England and the United States foresaw what was coming and repeatedly warned against it and encouraged their foreign correspondents to portray what was actually happening, does not mitigate the dreadful failure of the newspapers as a whole to prevent the coming of the greatest catastrophe in human history. But the governments were too shortsighted, composed of men too small mentally or too stupid, too steeped in worn-out diplomatic and power-political conceptions, to heed. And the editors were neither sufficiently united nor powerful enough to arouse a compelling public opinion on their side. It unfortunately cannot be added that the press, both here and abroad, is redeeming itself by its presentation of the war news, or by its editorial leadership in this struggle. Indeed, it is constantly misleading by wrongful emphasis, notably in the headlines, in failure to hold the news-scales evenly and objectively. There seems to be as little statesmanship in the editorial offices as in the chancelleries here or abroad. All of this may be playing its part in the disappearance of the American daily.

The Freedom of the Press

It is one of the bright spots in the current press picture that the newspapers of today are alert to the dangers to their freedom of utterance inherent in the war and in the great concentration of governmental power in Washington during the last few decades. That this awareness has its limitations is true, and so is the criticism that few publishers are as concerned to see that others are also assured of their full liberties under the Constitution, although restriction of the freedom of one group in our national community imperils the liberties of all. Many critics of the press insist that by keeping silent on many wrongs the newspapers deliberately aid the forces of reaction in depriving the disadvantaged of their rights and privileges. As for the existing shackles upon the freedom of expression of the newspapers, no one can deny that many of them are self-assumed because of the profit motive of their owners. Where that motive controls, advertisers become a great danger to a newspaper's freedom. When a newspaper is weak or conscienceless, fear of offending readers and advertisers is a powerful fetter. But however open to censure in this respect the press may be, whenever it does speak out for the preservation of its liberties from public attack it deserves praise. For we live in a totalitarian age, and it cannot be denied that moves to restrict utterances in the press and over the air were evident in Washington, and in some of the individual states, before the coming of the present war!

The attack of the government upon the Associated Press is discussed elsewhere in this volume. The Minnesota gag law which resulted in the suppression of a newspaper active in revealing political corruption is the most striking case of a deliberate effort by an American state to limit the freedom of the printed word. Another serious move during the regime of Huey Long in Louisiana was also thwarted, and various efforts by the courts to enjoin editorial utterances have been repelled. One difficulty in keeping public opinion alert to the danger of suppression lies in the mistaken belief that there can be safe restrictions upon freedom of publication beyond the laws of libel and those relating to the printing of obscenity. Few Americans really understand that liberty of the press means *license* and means *abuse* of that liberty. This is the price which must be paid for the enjoyment of freedom; that was realized by all the Founders, and notably by Thomas Jefferson. Yet the tendency is to say "I believe in freedom, but . . ." and then to proceed to urge deadly blows at that freedom because some editors are guilty of bad manners or the use of intemperate language, or otherwise offend. There can and must be no restrictions whatever beyond those of libel and obscenity. The minute anything else is attempted, the way is open to serious infractions of liberty. Hence, whatever their own fallibility, the press owes it to the country to attack every governmental move which even remotely suggests the control or limitation of the radio or of its own activities.

A growing fear of constituted authority is one of the press's weaknesses. Most of our dailies have a seriously mistaken idea of what constitutes their patriotic duty to the government, so that even in peace-time they are often afraid to incur the ill will of officials. They dread denunciation and attack by the government. They recall that the New York *World* was at one time attacked and taken into court by the Theodore Roosevelt Administration because of its revelations of the circumstances surrounding the American government's theft of territory from Colombia to set up the bogus Republic of Panama and to build the Panama Canal. This was a most deliberate governmental move to end freedom of press criticism, which the courts soon quashed. In war-time the dangers to free expression need no stressing. Yet it is at just such a period that the press can perform its greatest service to our democracy. In every war the one safeguard to prevent the civilian and military leaders from endangering the liberties of the people has been the press. If it has often erred in war-time in seeking to dominate military moves and governmental policies, it has none the less earned its characterization as the Fourth Estate by its ability to check and to criticize. We have gone far enough in the present war to prove the very parlous state the people's liberties would be in at the hands of the Roosevelt Administration had the newspapers not been able to ridicule, criticize, denounce the absurdities, the follies, and the blunders of the Roosevelt government on the civilian administrative side.

Curiously enough, the press was itself faithless before we entered the struggle in accepting the so-called voluntary censorship demanded and obtained by the Secretary of the Navy, Frank Knox. This was an unprecedented request, and one that should never have been listened to short of an act of Congress. It is true that we were then on the highroad to war, deliberately put on that road by various governmental actions and laws passed by Congress under the false excuse that those measures would keep the country at peace. Mr. Knox appealed to the editors as patriots. The reply should have been that the primary duty of the press was to uphold freedom of utterance until the highest legislative authority approved war-time limitation. Instead, the newspapers rushed to put on the collar of censorship, which was none the less a censorship because it was voluntarily assumed. By means of that censorship the government successfully concealed from the American people military and naval actions that were little short of acts of war, if not actually such acts. It meant the withholding from the public of vital facts which the people were entitled to have if they were to control the acts of the government and to govern policies. From this point of view the voluntary censorship was an indisputable betrayal of the people's interest and their freedom of action. Since we entered the war the conduct of the newspapers in accepting restrictions has been exemplary. Indeed, it has gone too far; they should have demanded, and could have obtained by united action, the ending of numerous absolutely unnecessary suppressions by both army and navy—suppressions denounced by all the leading military and naval writers. Our government has given the American people far less information about what has been going on than the Churchill administration has vouchsafed to the British public. The English press, be it noted here, has on several occasions, notably as to North Africa, protested against the failure of the American authorities properly to inform it as to American moves while also keeping the American press in the dark.

There is also the grave question whether the press has not erred in this way in allowing too much authority to military and naval officials in other directions than the handling of the news. It has been Mr. Roosevelt's deliberate policy to turn over the conduct of the war almost completely to the generals and admirals, a policy acclaimed by many and held to have been responsible for many of the gratifying successes achieved up to the time of this writing. None the less, the dangers in granting such powers without civilian control, in accordance with what has been the hitherto unbroken American policy, have been well voiced by Wendell Willkie in his charge that the war was being entirely too much engineered by the fighting services, and has been illustrated further by the cruel and morally indefensible, and surely unconstitutional, removal of American citizens of Japanese ancestry from their homes on the Pacific coast by the fiat of the commanding military officer. There is no other safe way for a democracy in war-time than to insist that the military shall be fully subordinated to the civilian authorities. In such matters as what should be our policy for Italy, North Africa, and the other countries we may take over, the press must watch and control day by day the actions of the executive branch of the government.

Alexander Hamilton pointed out in one of his *Federalist* papers that in the end freedom of the press will depend not on any constitutional guarantee, but on public opinion, and, he might have added, on the zealousness of the press itself. As for any constitutional guarantee, he said that it amounted to nothing, using these words: "What signifies a declaration that 'the liberty of the press shall be inviolably preserved'? What is liberty of the press? Who can give any definition which would not leave the utmost latitude for evasion? I hold it to be impracticable; and from this I infer that its security, whatever fine declarations may be inserted in any constitution respecting it, must altogether depend on public opinion, and on the general spirit of the people and of their government. And here, after all . . . must we seek for the only solid basis for all our rights." Since the press to such a considerable degree controls public opinion, it plainly has in its own hands the safeguarding of its liberty.

This applies not merely to the danger of governmental and judicial interference, but also to those other shackles already mentioned, the self-imposed ones, and those that are ingrained in the present economic situation of our dailies. Those newspapers that surrender their right of free opinion to advertisers, or live in terror lest they offend large groups of readers, are playing into the hands of the reactionaries and the totalitarians, if only because they weaken their prestige and the standing of the newspaper business in the eyes of the public. If they blindly accept such reactionary leadership as has been given by the American Newspaper Publishers' Association, they will find it much more difficult to fight for freedom of the press. To safeguard its liberties they must also face squarely the import of the tremendous economic and social revolution in which we find ourselves, a revolution which is threatening to destroy traditional and vitally important educational and political principles and ideals. No press can preserve its power or its liberty if as a group it sets itself deliberately to block political revolution.

Its only hope lies in sympathetically understanding and interpreting this great tidal wave of change which is sweeping us whither no man knoweth, to guide it into wise channels, and to prevent its going beyond wise bounds and thus submerging the rights of the individual. It will lose its usefulness to the public still more, be definitely aligned as an enemy of progress with the worst reactionaries, and find it more and more difficult to maintain an independent economic status if it does not seek leadership, as well as dispense wisdom and tolerance, in the struggle that is going on and the larger struggle still to come. This is vital to the maintenance of American freedom and American institutions—unless leadership is taken over by other means of communication and the newspapers become "as dead as mutton."

As for the outlook, it cannot be said that it is too cheerful. Not only is the daily press vanishing, but other journals of opinion are not showing signs of growth. The weekly political journals do not increase in numbers, do not maintain themselves; and their readership has not been enlarged during the last twenty-five years—the *New Republic*, for example, probably has only about half the subscribers it had in 1917. To float such a weekly journal of opinion calls for hundreds of thousands of dollars; as business propositions they are incapable of success. There are relatively few small publications of protest and propaganda, and their range is extremely limited. The great new weeklies, like *Time* and *Life*, are the creations and the mouthpieces of a man grown very rich; *Life* from the beginning called for the expenditure of millions before achieving its great success, and the most widely read publication of all, the *Reader's Digest*, influences public opinion almost wholly by choice of articles from other publications. There is no strong labor press coming to the front, and no sign of one—nothing to correspond to the London *Daily Herald*, the popular organ of the Labour Party. The vernacular daily Jewish press deteriorates, and in the long run will have to turn to the use of English.

Only the Negro press has developed by leaps and bounds—a most remarkable phenomenon, with many of the editors showing great ability and power. Its growth in numbers and in the extent of its support by members of the race is astounding to many who have not been aware of the seething currents of discontent and anger among our colored millions at the injustices and the discriminations against them. Born of these bitter passions, the new Negro press speaks with vigor, and far too often with a violence, that have startled the whites who have suddenly been brought into contact with it. It is not cowed because this is war-time; it does not tremble before authority. It uses little or no restraint in discussing the refusal of this government to grant to our Negroes not only their constitutional privileges, but full equality in the army and the navy, the right to fight for their country on equal terms with white citizens. It scorns the pretense that this country is fighting this war for the Four Freedoms as long as 13,000,000 people here at home are denied their rights because of the color of their skins. These militant newspapers are both creators of the suddenly developed Negro sense of solidarity and themselves an index of a developing race consciousness and unwillingness to remain in a subordinate position, a helotry in a democracy. It is unfortunately true that many Negro dailies and weeklies go to censurable excesses and injure their case by the violence of their unbridled attacks in this extremely explosive period of our days. The responsibility for this, however, lies primarily upon those whites who have believed, or pretended to believe, that this democracy could exist part servile and part free.

Perhaps this startling evolution of the press of one great group out of the depth of its feelings as to its own status, its own injustices and wrongs, may be a portent that in the immediate future the issues confronting the American people, especially after the war, will be so vital, so revolutionary, so all-embracing that the white daily press will similarly catch fire. If H. G. Wells is correct in saying that the only way out of the newspaper impasse is pamphleteering, then conditions may soon be ripe for a return to this medium of expression on this side of the Atlantic. The pamphlet offers a vehicle of protest which one can create and use without being wealthy. Its disadvantages are obvious. The great strength of a daily lies in its power of iteration and reiteration, its ability to drive home its points day after day, to uphold and to portray a cause from its every facet. The pamphleteer must be gifted indeed to win a large audience, as did the brilliant sixteen-year-old Alexander Hamilton in the days leading up to the Revolution, for the author of a tract is at a loss how to advertise the product of his pen unless he can fall back upon the daily press. A new Tom Paine could gain and hold a large audience. What of the lesser lights? And how should we check the too frequent tendency to compose long documents, too long for the overburdened modern to read and digest? Surely there would have to be great political excitement for tracts to reach large numbers of readers in an audience of more than a hundred million. Yet it is one of the few possible remedies for a failing press.

When the editors of the *New Republic* made their already cited study, "The Press and the Public," they admitted at once that "it is always easier to draw up an indictment than to suggest practicable methods of reform. One thing, however, is certain: the press will not reform itself." They turned to the old stale suggestion of endowed newspapers seeking only enough money "to cover their operating expenses," and "conducted primarily for the good of the community." But the *New Republic* itself has long been an endowed journal, and has certainly never made both ends meet. Who would control the board of trustees of an endowed newspaper? Would not the very trusteeship involved in the handling of a great endowment and of safeguarding it inevitably ensure an ultra-conservative management no more inclined to progressive leadership than is the New York *Times*? Next these editors thought of a ten-cent newspaper without advertising, and discarded it. So they fell back upon that glittering old generality that the readers themselves can control a newspaper and make it conform to their wishes. Even this position is untenable. The simple fact is that when a conscientious, progressive owner finds that he cannot carry on his paper, it ceases publication or passes into other hands. If another type of newspaper cannot make both ends meet, it too, dies or is amalgamated. I do not know of a single case in which public opinion has compelled any radical alteration in the mental attitude and policies of a daily journal. The *New Republic's* final hope that labor might perhaps come to be a dominating factor and crack the whip which is to make the whole press free, honest, progressive, and sympathetic with the masses, is as idle as its other suggestions.

As for other means of offsetting the commercialization of the press, if there were more journals like the *Christian Science Monitor*, which is without the profit motive because of its being sponsored by a religious organization, and if there could be experimentation with English-language dailies along the line of the non-profit-making Jewish *Forward*, there would be a marked advance. Twenty years ago there was in existence the Minnesota *Daily Star*, the "newspaper with six thousand owners," described by me in an earlier volume. Unfortunately, it soon failed needlessly, because of unskilled and inefficient business management, and so we learned nothing from this co-operative venture to establish group ownership of a daily and thus escape the evils of one-man control. Still another interesting experiment, Marshall Field's *PM*, "the daily without advertising," has also unfortunately got off to a very bad start and, as set forth in another chapter, may not live to demonstrate whether a well-run and honest daily of this type can be made to pay without advertisements. This is a misfortune because information on this point would be extremely valuable. There are no other experiments which offer any promise of an amelioration of the parlous conditions of the press or an offset to its steady decrease in numbers.

There remains the coming of the radio, as to the value of which in the formation of intelligent public opinion there can be no question whatever. When it first came upon the scene, the newspapers mistakenly looked upon it as an enemy and did everything in their power to prevent the broadcasting of news, fearing that that would cost them many readers. They recognized that their competitors on the air had possession of a weapon more potent than theirs. In time, however, the newspapers learned that this competitor not only did not destroy their circulations but in all probability helped them, since it is a human characteristic to wish to see in print, if possible, what one has seen with one's own eyes or has heard. It seems ridiculous now to read that in 1936 the chairman of the radio committee of the American Newspaper Publishers' Association declared that "the sale of news to any broadcasting station or to any advertiser for sponsorship over the air is just as unsound as if the newspapers sold news to their advertisers and then permitted them to commingle this news in their advertising copy. How long would the newspapers hold the confidence of the public as media for the dissemination of information if they adopted such a policy?" They adopted it soon thereafter.

Like the newspapers, radio is "an instrument that can enslave or free." It is in even greater danger from censorship because of the constant and dangerous supervision of the Federal Communications Commission, which leads the broadcasters to supervise and edit any statement or manuscript of a controversial nature. Ruth Brindisi in her study of broadcasting has pointed out that news is now hourly interpreted by men who receive their weekly pay checks from the business rulers of America. It is probably a cause for congratulation that there are few charges that news is mishandled, but it would be impossible to assert that it is always free from color, especially as it is so easy in speaking to slur over some things and to stress and emphasize others and because radio is the happiest vehicle for propagandists. But every allegation of this kind brought against the radio can, of course, be paralleled by similar charges against the dailies.

After the first period of hostility to the radio passed, many newspapers themselves entered the field and purchased or set up stations of their own. Undoubtedly in some few cases there is a considerable advantage in this, but Hearst has sold some of his stations, and the move in this direction seems checked. The New York *Times* could, of course, have entered this field immediately, but refused to do so. It now hires time from a New York City station to give out hourly news bulletins, something that would have seemed treason to the press ten years ago. It is beyond question a service to the public, notably in war-time, and an excellent advertisement for the *Times*. Whether in due course the government will not demand a separation of the newspapers from the radio stations is an open question. There are parallels in other fields pointing this way. In the main, however, it must be stressed again that the coming of the radio has been a great boon to the American democracy, and radio will remain its chief source of news since it penetrates into millions of homes, many of which cannot obtain a daily newspaper. If the press continues to decrease in numbers and influence, the necessity of the radio for informing the people will hourly become more apparent.

Today perhaps the only hope for the press is, as has been suggested, such a development of the affairs of the world and of the present world-wide revolution as will again bring to the editorial chairs men of fire and passion, with programs to further and vital, stirring causes to lead. They will find their tasks even more difficult than those which confront the editor of today. As has been said, "the world has become a vast sounding board of conflicting voices." Everything is in flux, in conflict, and there is not the slightest sign that after this global war is over, business will be as usual in any market-place in the world. The present day editor is overwhelmed by the magnitude of the problems with which he is confronted, for the solution of which he is supposed to give leadership. But the task cannot be shirked if the press is to survive as a leader. After all, there are principles of human life and human conduct long tested and beyond question, just as the tenets of democracy are proving in this struggle that they are surviving, while the new totalitarian doctrines are largely going down to defeat. It is by the principles of liberty that free editors must be guided in their fight, not only for the Four Freedoms, but for all of them.

The editor will always have a great advantage over his competitors for leadership on the platform, in the senates, over the air, for the printed word *is* superior to the spoken. It is far less perishable. If it has beauty, as has been written by a veteran editorial writer of the *Herald Tribune*, Roscoe C. E. Brown, that beauty is far more certain to survive. If it has wisdom, it is at least temporarily "engraved upon tablets" and capable of enlightening men's minds and stirring men's emotions, even when the last of those who heard the spoken word have perished from the human scene. The editor's is the power to write day by day with unyielding emphasis. If he is a free man and his soul is his own, he is among the most fortunate of men, for the spiritual fight to better human conditions brings more joy and balm to the soul than any other. No one who has ever had the power to fight unceasingly in a printed page, with absolute freedom, for the oppressed, the disadvantaged, the victims of human greed, can ever be willing cheerfully to give up the opportunity to battle on. There may be times when he will recall Isaiah's saying: "The voice said, Cry. And he said, What shall I cry?" But if he is true to his ideals he will always know what to say, and whatever the obstacles he will find a medium in which to say it.

Notes

1.   "The Newspaper in Public Affairs," an address at the University of Colorado College of Journalism on May 8, 1937.
2.   Issue of March 17, 1937.
3.   Colonel Henry W. Nevinson, the great English journalist and war correspondent, once said to me, after a meeting in New York at which he had spoken, that he knew he had made a bad speech because no one had interrupted or heckled him!

Chapter 26

ERIK BARNOUW

VOICES

> *broadcast* . . . act or process of scattering seeds
> *New National Dictionary*, 1901

> *broadcast* . . . to scatter or disseminate . . . specif., radio messages, speeches, etc.
> *New Century Dictionary*, 1927

THE AGE OF BROADCASTING WAS FORESEEN, at least by some, almost from the moment that Alexander Graham Bell demonstrated his telephone. His revelation in 1876 stirred astonishing visions of things to come. An artist for the New York *Daily Graphic*, in the issue of March 15, 1877, depicted what he called "Terrors of the Telephone." He showed an orator at a microphone heard by groups of people throughout the world.

In the same year a popular song, "The Wondrous Telephone," published in St. Louis, described the glories of the invention in these terms:

> You stay at home and listen
> To the lecture in the hall,
> Or hear the strains of music
> From a fashionable ball![1]

In 1879, in *Punch*, the artist George Dumaurier took a further forward leap—into the age of television. He showed two people by a fireplace, watching a sporting match on a screen above the mantel. Sounds were transmitted by a telephone.

Bell himself visualized diverse uses for the telephone, which his patent application called "a method of, and apparatus for, transmitting vocal and other sounds telegraphically." Starting that spring, he gave lecture-demonstrations in which he always included music as well as speech. The Boston *Evening Transcript* described him as demonstrating "telephony, or the telegraphing of musical sounds."[2] On one occasion a band playing

"The Star-Spangled Banner" in Boston was heard by an audience of 2,000 in Providence. On another, a singer performing selections from *The Marriage of Figaro* in Providence was heard by an audience in Boston. Another program included an exhortation by the evangelist Dwight L. Moody with a gospel hymn sung and played by Ira David Sanky. When Bell exhibited his invention at the Philadelphia Centennial Exposition during the summer of 1876 he included a reading of "To be or not to be." The following summer his demonstrations for Queen Victoria at Windsor Castle offered transmissions from various points and included bugle calls, organ music, and a young lady singing "Kathleen Mavourneen." Her Majesty and royal household "evinced the greatest interest."[3]

During the following years such possibilities were not developed in a significant way but were not forgotten. In the summer of 1890, at the Grand Union Hotel in Saratoga, eight hundred people were provided with a concert by telephone wire from Madison Square Garden, as well as entertainment from other points, including dance music and a recitation of "The Charge of the Light Brigade." The program was also heard by a gathering at the home of a telephone executive in New Jersey, where guests danced "with perfect ease" to the music. Both here and at Saratoga regular telephone receivers were used—with an improvised addition:

> The orchestral music was listened to at Saratoga by means of sets of hand telephones, and every note was heard distinctly, even to the applause of the audience gathered at Madison Square Garden. Some of the songs and solos and the recitation were heard all over the room at Saratoga by means of a single loud-speaking receiver provided with a large funnel-shaped resonator to magnify the sound.

Significantly, the magazine which reported this event, *Electrical Engineer*, felt that the American Telephone and Telegraph Company was not doing enough to exploit the possibilities of "furnishing of musical and other entertainments by wire at the fireside."[4]

The truth was, the telephone company was finding it profitable to concentrate on what had become its special function, a link for two-way talk. It saw for the moment little reason for digressing into what must have seemed, at best, side-show possibilities. But when the wireless age dawned, such dreams stirred again.

The inventions that marked the road to radio and television have often been traced and are not our main concern. But almost every invention became the property of a company, and eventually a weapon in titanic struggles, deals, and mergers, bearing on control of the broadcasting media. These maneuvers, in which the stakes were high, were to have a profound effect on the shape of broadcasting in the United States, and must be reviewed to lay the groundwork for our story.

There is a direct line of descent from the youth Marconi, who received a patent at the age of twenty-three, to the Radio Corporation of America and its subsidiary the National Broadcasting Company. This and other lines must now be followed.

The Black Box

By the early 1890's the waves we call radio waves were already a subject of intense speculation and experiment. Because it was Heinrich Hertz of Germany who, during the years 1886–89, had clearly demonstrated their nature, they were at the moment called "Hertzian waves." He had shown how to set them in motion and how to detect them.

The fact that some of these waves could pass through fog and solid objects was especially provocative. Sir William Crookes, in a widely read article in the London *Fortnightly Review* in 1892, discussed the implications:

> Here is unfolded to us a new and astonishing world. . . . Rays of light will not pierce through a wall, nor, as we know only too well, through a London fog. But the electrical vibrations of a yard or more in wave length . . . will easily pierce such mediums, which to them will be transparent. Here, then, is revealed the bewildering possibility of telegraph without wires, posts, cables or any of our present costly appliances. Granted a few reasonable postulates, the whole thing comes well within the realms of possible fulfillment. . . .
>
> This is no mere dream of a visionary philosopher. All the requisites needed to bring it within the grasp of daily life are well within the possibilities of discovery, and are so reasonable and so clearly in the path of researches which are now being actively prosecuted in every capital of Europe that we may any day expect to hear that they have emerged from the realms of speculation into those of sober fact.[5]

Among the many pursuing these reasonable, bewildering, astonishing possibilities were Oliver Lodge in England, Alexander Popov in Russia, Adolphus Slaby in Germany, Edouard Branly in France. Alternative avenues to wireless communication were also being explored, both in Europe and America.

Guglielmo Marconi was at this time a youth in his late teens, living with his family in a villa near Bologna. His mother was an Irish girl who, before she was of age, had fallen in love with an Italian gentleman, older and already a widower and a father. Her parents forbade an engagement. Biding her time until she was twenty-one, she crossed the Channel and married him, and they went to Italy and settled at the Villa Grifone; in due time she bore two sons, Alfonso and Guglielmo. For years she did not see her homeland.

Guglielmo became a thin, intense youth, who read all the scientific books at the villa and revered Benjamin Franklin and other giants of electricity. Much of his education was provided by tutors. Even at mealtimes he often got lost in thought. The elder Marconi, who believed in instructive discourse during meals, found this irksome, especially when Guglielmo would suddenly ask a question having nothing to do with the topic at hand. In the summer of 1894, Guglielmo and his half-brother Luigi took a vacation trip to the Italian Alps, where Guglielmo picked up a periodical with an article on Hertzian waves. From that moment on, he was like someone possessed. His brother found him constantly sketching strange diagrams, making calculations. On returning to the Villa Grifone, he practically confined himself in a third-floor room that had become his workshop. For long stretches the door stayed locked. His mother, worried about his thinness, took to carrying trays upstairs and leaving them on the landing outside the locked door. His father fumed: the boy was wasting irreplaceable years.[6] The first experiments were clearly failures, but experimenting continued. In due time the family was allowed a look. Guglielmo had reached a point at which, via Hertzian waves, he could ring a bell across the room, or even downstairs. He knew he was only beginning. He hardly dared open an electrical journal lest he read that the goal, so clearly defined by Sir William Crookes, had been reached. Was it possible that those famous men in all the capitals of Europe had not yet found it? Guglielmo introduced a Morse key into his circuit. "From the beginning I aimed at . . . breaking the emission up into long and short periods so that Morse dots and dashes could be transmitted."[7] The tests now extended to the outdoors; his older brother Alfonso became his helper.

To actuate his waves, Guglielmo used the method Hertz had used: a spark leaping across a gap. His receiver was a device developed by Lodge, from an idea by Branly. Branly had found that certain metal filings would *cohere* when Hertzian waves struck them. Filings in a glass tube could thus be used as a detector. A tap was needed to loosen the filings for the next dot or dash. Morse key, spark, coherer, tapper; to these essential elements young Marconi now made crucial additions: something he called an *antenna*, and a grounding at each end of the operation.

Young Marconi knew that success required distance, and clear demonstration that the waves would overcome obstacles such as hills and mountains. During 1895 the tests moved forward. Family tradition described them as follows:

> The handkerchief was adequate to signal success from the fields in front of the Villa Grifone. It would not be seen if Alfonso went to the far side of the hill behind the house. For this he was armed with a hunting rifle and he marched sturdily off, up the narrow path past the farm buildings. It was the end of September now and the vines were heavy with purple grapes, the air golden. The walk over the rim of the hill took twenty minutes. Alfonso led, followed by the farmer Mignani and the carpenter Vornelli, lugging the antenna. Finally, Guglielmo, watching tensely from a window, lost sight of the small procession as it dropped over the horizon.

Marconi himself has told the rest of the story. "After some minutes I started to send, manipulating the Morse key . . . In the distance a shot echoed down the valley."[8]

The elder Marconi for the first time began to take the events seriously. The parish priest and family doctor were consulted. The priest listened to the whole story, nodding thoughtfully. Finally a letter was dispatched to the Italian Minister of Post and Telegraph. When the reply came, saying the government was not interested, his mother made a prompt, resolute decision: she and Guglielmo would go to England with the invention. Perhaps she was homesick; perhaps she was protecting her son against the hurt of rejection. But she could not have made a sounder decision. The British empire, held together by thin lines of ships and threads of ocean cable, could use such a means of communication better than any other world power. Her virtual control of ocean cables, important as it was, was of uncertain military value; what would become of them in war was not yet known.

Young Marconi himself carefully packed, locked, and carried the black box that held the invention. In February 1896 they set sail for England: the mother, beautiful and aglow with anticipation; he, thin and primly dressed in dark suit and a high-collared shirt. To offset his youth, he "drew a cloak of dignity around himself." The black box at once aroused the suspicion of British customs officials. Only two years earlier, the French President had been killed by an Italian anarchist. In the box were wires, batteries, dials; smashing it seemed the wisest policy, and this the officials did. On arrival in

London, Marconi had to begin by rebuilding it. But meanwhile a relative, to whom his mother had written ahead, was putting them in touch with one of London's best patent attorneys. While the patent procedure went forward, they were also calling on Sir William Preece, chief engineer of telegraphs in the British Post Office system. In all this they were fortunate. Preece had himself experimented in wireless—with success, but without achieving a useful distance. He was able to appreciate what Marconi had done. Tests began in rooms of the London Post Office, then moved onto Salisbury plain, reaching a hundred yards, then one mile; then six miles, nine miles. Marconi later recalled: "The calm of my life ended then."[9]

Marconi received his patent July 2, 1897, and in that same month a small, powerful British group joined with him to form Wireless Telegraph and Signal Company, Ltd., later renamed Marconi's Wireless Telegraph Company, Ltd. It was capitalized at £100,000 and acquired Marconi's patents everywhere except in Italy and dependencies. Marconi received half the stock and £15,000 in cash. He became one of six directors, in charge of development. He was twenty-three.

For years the pace of events was not to slacken. As soon as the company was formed, Marconi moved to the coast. Setting up equipment on the Isle of Wight, he communicated with the mainland 14 miles away, then with a ship 18 miles away, penetrating fog and rain. The tests caused international excitement. Newspapers throughout the world carried accounts. Foreign observers arrived, especially naval and military observers. In 1898 the new company received its first revenue: wireless equipment was ordered for several lighthouses. In a comic-opera development, Queen Victoria entered the wireless story—as she had the telephone story. The Prince of Wales had wrenched his knee and was recuperating on a yacht, perhaps to get away from his anxious mother. The Queen's entourage contrived a countermove—wireless. Marconi was enlisted to keep her informed. He fitted the ship with an antenna and built a land station at Osborn House, where the Queen was staying. Marconi, wandering about the garden to find the best location for his antenna, was stopped by a gardener. He had apparently intruded where servants were not to go. Marconi ignored his warning and the incident was reported to the Queen, who was affronted by Marconi's behavior. "Get another electrician," she instructed, but was told that alas, England had no Marconi. Before long, however, bulletins began to arrive from the yacht: "H. R. H. the Prince of Wales has passed another excellent night . . . the knee is most satisfactory."[10]

Meanwhile, Marconi had undertaken another assignment as ephemeral in content, and as certain to thrust him onto the international scene. The Dublin *Daily Express* requested a minute-by-minute wireless account of the Kingstown Regatta. A steamer, chartered to follow the racing yachts, was fitted with a 75-foot antenna. The details of the race, received at a shore station, were telephoned to the newspaper and were in print before the ships had returned to port.[11] The feat was dazzling and brought an invitation from the New York *Herald* to report the *America*'s Cup Race in the United States in October 1899. Marconi and his associates saw the invitation as a timely opportunity for overtures to the American navy.

During 1899 Marconi equipment was being installed on three British battleships and was used during naval maneuvers. Demonstrations were also made across the English Channel, and these brought Marconi his first contact with French officials. Now the Marconi directors were thinking about the United States. To exploit the possibilities there, they planned to form an American subsidiary. All this was part of the plan, as Guglielmo Marconi accepted the invitation of the New York *Herald*.

Large-scale international rivalry and intrigue were already afoot. We have mentioned Adolphus Slaby of Germany and Alexander Popov of Russia as early experimenters in wireless communication. These and many others—on both sides of the Atlantic—were now involved in efforts to catch up with and surpass the achievements of Marconi.

Slaby, who had studied with Heinrich Hertz, had actually witnessed some of the Marconi demonstrations in Britain. In the April 1898 issue of *Century*, he wrote:

> . . . when the news of Marconi's first successes ran through the newspapers, I myself was earnestly occupied with similar problems. . . . Quickly making up my mind, I traveled to England, where the Bureau of Telegraphs was undertaking experiments on a large scale. Mr. Preece, the celebrated engineer-in-chief of the General Post Office, in the most courteous and hospitable way, permitted me to take part in these; and in truth what I there saw was something quite new.

Slaby presently returned to Germany, continued his research, and was soon awarded several patents. In collaboration with Count Arco he developed the Slaby-Arco system, the foundation of Telefunken. Soon Slaby-Arco representatives would be submitting equipment and bids to the U. S. Navy Department, with considerable success.

Alexander Popov's interest in electromagnetic theory had already taken him to the United States. In 1893, representing Russia's Torpedo School at Kronstadt, he had gone to Chicago to see the World's Columbian Exposition, and also to attend an electrical congress presided over by Helmholtz, in which there was intense discussion of Hertzian waves. Popov was caught up in the same excitement that had possessed Marconi. Returning to Russia, he pursued similar experiments at the Torpedo School, which was destined to become Russia's "cradle of radio." He too used the spark transmitter with a coherer. On May 7, 1895, he read a paper reporting on the ringing of a bell by these means.[12] Popov subsequently developed equipment which was used by the Russian navy and to some extent by the French navy. Soon other French experimenters were demonstrating equipment for the French navy, as well as for the American navy. The Italian navy was by now dealing with Marconi. The rivalry was international.

It was, in various ways, the perfect moment to approach the United States armed forces on the subject of wireless. When Guglielmo Marconi arrived in New York City on September 11, 1899, aboard the *Aurania*, the city was preparing a spectacular welcome not for him but for the hero of Manila Bay, Admiral George Dewey. Overshadowed too were Sir Thomas Lipton and his *Shamrock*, arriving for the *America*'s Cup Race. It was an hour bursting with manifest destiny. The American republic had suddenly turned empire, with overseas possessions. There were protests, like those of the Anti-Imperialist League; one of its spokesmen, William Jennings Bryan, would soon be campaigning for the presidency as an anti-imperialist. But he was already being reviled as wanting a "small" instead of a "big" America. The prevailing mood was more muscular and arrogant. The building of frenzy and newspaper circulation had gone hand in hand; aided by these, navy and army appropriations slid swiftly through Congress. Those with overseas interests were not averse: protected bases, harbors, coaling stations, were needed by a great and expanding power. Such a nation would also, like the British empire, have to think about communication. In the "splendid little war," as John Hay had named it, there had been some difficulties in communication. According to navy annals, it had been splendid within naval squadrons but unsatisfactory between army and navy, and between the field forces and Washington. In fact, to inform Washington of his victory and subsequent actions at Manila, Admiral Dewey had had to send dispatch boats to Hong Kong, whence the news was telegraphed westward, going over British-controlled cables via the Indian Ocean, the Red Sea, the Mediterranean, and the Atlantic Ocean.[13] Somehow, it didn't fit with the new world posture. At this juncture Guglielmo Marconi arrived in America.

Beginning October 16, 1899, the races between the *Shamrock* and *Columbia* were duly reported by wireless and acclaim was distributed—to the *Herald* for vision, to Marconi for genius, to America for seamanship, to Sir Thomas for sportsmanship. Army and navy officials watched with interest and excitement. Remembering Guantanamo, a navy observer wrote: "If we could only have had this last year, what a great thing it would have been." After the races there were special tests for the navy; off the New Jersey coast messages were sent and received by ships and a shore installation. Along with this there was historic legal business: on November 22, 1899, the Marconi Wireless Company of America was incorporated under the laws of New Jersey, to exploit Marconi patents in the United States and various possessions including Cuba. Authorized capital of $10,000,000 was covered by two million shares with a par value of $5. Many of these shares went back to England, 365,000 being held by the parent firm, and 600,000 assigned to Marconi.[14] Two decades later, in a new incarnation, this company would become the Radio Corporation of America.

As the new century dawned, the equipping of ships with wireless proceeded at a rapid and quickening pace. The parent Marconi company and subsidiaries organized themselves to supply the need, while building shore stations to communicate with the ships. Other companies labored to the same end. Marine disasters anywhere speeded the process. The life-saving aspects of wireless were constantly discussed, but its adoption also dovetailed with the needs of trade, the zeal for empire, the burgeoning of military budgets. The new medium would grow on those budgets, and they would shape its youth.

The spirit of the time was symbolized by the hasty departure of Marconi for England before the naval demonstrations were even finished. It was explained that England had requested his return to prepare apparatus for use in the Boer War.[15]

In spite of the enthusiasm that surrounded the navy tests, official reports had a restrained tone befitting seasoned officials. It was recommended that the navy give the invention a trial, but reservations were mentioned. The drama of the bluish spark, crashing noisily across its gap, had left afterthoughts. "The shock from the sending coil," said the report, "may be quite severe and even dangerous to a person with a weak heart." However, "no fatal accidents have been recorded." But the effects of rolling and pitching were not yet known. And the apparatus might "injuriously affect the compass if placed near it." Behind such objections appear to have been fears of some officers that their authority at sea would be undermined by the new invention. But the navy hierarchy had other objections. They had asked Marconi and his associates about senders interfering with each other, and had found the answers evasive. Here Marconi had, in fact, reason to be guarded. He was hard at work on the principle of tuning to different wave lengths. Need for such a provision had already been foreseen by Sir William Crookes in 1892. Without it the air would become chaos. Marconi felt he had solved the problem, but he did not receive a patent until later—in April 1900. Meanwhile the U. S. Navy was nettled by his answers, which one officer thought were "intended to mislead."[16]

A more serious cause of friction was coming between the navy and Marconi—with far-ranging results. Marconi's first income had involved outright sale of equipment, but a new policy was evolving. It paralleled the policy pursued by telephone companies: the Marconi companies would not sell equipment but *communication*. In dealings with commercial shipping companies, the policy worked in this way. A Marconi company would install equipment on a ship and furnish a man to maintain and operate it. The equipment would remain Marconi property, and the man a Marconi employee. An annual fee to the Marconi company would cover use of the equipment and the services of the operator.

Aboard ship Marconi operators would transmit "marconigrams" to and from passengers at rates to be established; company and officers would be served at a much reduced rate. Meanwhile Marconi shore stations would be maintained at various points to provide the Marconi-equipped ships with shore communication. For a time these shore stations communicated freely with wireless operators on any ship, but in reaction to growing competition, this practice was abandoned. Why should the Marconi companies maintain shore stations for the convenience of ships equipped by rival companies? It became the policy of Marconi shore stations—except in emergencies—to communicate only with Marconi-equipped ships; communications from non-Marconi operators and equipment were, by and large, to be ignored.

While such a plan could not apply to naval forces, a variation was worked out for them. In proposals made to the U. S. Navy Department at the end of 1899 the Marconi representatives offered to equip twenty vessels for a lump sum of $10,000 plus a royalty of $10,000 per year. Navy personnel would be permitted to operate the equipment, but it must be agreed that they would not communicate with non-Marconi shore stations except in emergencies. The navy was offered special low rates at Marconi stations so that it would not need to build shore stations of its own.

The navy reacted to these terms with indignation. It considered the royalty plan illegal and the other proposals a high-handed attempt to establish a world monopoly over wireless.

The Marconi policy became ammunition for rival companies. That the Marconi companies were instruments of "British monopoly," an attempt to extend to wireless the control already exercised by the British over cables, became a favorite theme among the rival companies and among navy officials. It had an important effect: it briefly slowed the surge of the Marconi companies, at least in their relations with the United States government. Turning away from Marconi, the navy would establish its own shore stations, and buy equipment from other experimenters. This, incidentally, would precipitate years of patent disputes. But meanwhile the spotlight would turn to these other experimenters—including many in the United States.

On Native Soil

Before Marconi seized world attention, native experimenters in wireless communication had generally worked in obscurity, getting newspaper attention only as items of the bizarre, like the finding of dinosaur eggs. Later years brought to light that there had been a number of such experimenters; just what they had done was by that time difficult to determine.

There was a Dr. Mahlon Loomis, who had experimented in the Blue Ridge Mountains in Virginia. Raising kites from two mountain peaks 14 miles apart, he is said to have sent "intelligible messages" between them in October 1866.[17] In 1872 he obtained U. S. Patent No. 129,971 for an "improvement in telegraphing."

There was Professor Amos Dolbear of Tufts College, who had been a telephone experimenter before Bell and later became an early wireless experimenter. In 1886 he obtained U. S. Patent No. 350,299 for an "induction" system of wireless telegraphy. It apparently did not achieve notable distances, but on the basis of the patent he threatened for a time to restrain Marconi from reporting the *America*'s Cup races by wireless. He later changed his mind.[18]

There was the mysterious figure of Nathan B. Stubblefield, whose gravestone in Murray, Ky., names him the Father of Radio Broadcasting. He is said to have transmitted voice as early as 1892 and made public demonstrations in 1902, including one in Philadelphia and another near Washington. His U. S. Patent No. 887,357, obtained in 1908, was the subject of long litigation, which won him victories but no revenue. He died of starvation in 1928 in a shack in Kentucky.[19]

These were early starters, pre-Marconi. Now, with wireless a center of attention, there would be experimenters by hundreds and by thousands. For a number of these the dream would be different: speech and music. With them a new era began, associated with the terms *wireless telephone . . . radio telephone . . . radiophone . . . radio*. On the heels of Marconi's recall to England it began.

Voices in the Night

One of its first leaders was Reginald Aubrey Fessenden, a Canadian, who had worked for Thomas Edison at his New Jersey laboratory and for the Westinghouse company in Pittsburgh. In 1893 he had become professor of electrical engineering at Western University—later renamed University of Pittsburgh—where he had experimented with Hertzian waves. In 1900 the Weather Bureau of the U. S. Department of Agriculture, stirred by the Marconi excitement, employed him at $3,000 a year to test the idea of disseminating weather information by wireless.[20]

Already Fessenden had his mind on voice transmission. To accomplish this, he proposed a heresy. The wave sent out must *not* be—as in the Marconi system—an interrupted wave or series of bursts. Instead it must be a *continuous* wave, on which voice would be superimposed as variations or modulations. This heresy became the foundation of radio.

In 1901, using a telephone microphone, Fessenden superimposed a voice on such a wave. Now he needed a detector more sensitive than the primitive coherer. By 1902 he had one, an "electrolytic" detector. This and similar detectors soon came into fairly wide use.

Fessenden's ideas went beyond the aims and funds of the Weather Bureau; and, moreover, Fessenden was nettled by a government tendency to consider all his findings its property. But two Pittsburgh financiers, T. H. Given and Hay Walker, Jr., now decided to back his experiments. The National Electric Signaling Company was formed, to which they contributed cash—eventually almost $1,000,000[21]—and Fessenden his patents and services. He moved to the shore, first to Chesapeake Bay, then to Brant Rock, Mass. He turned to General Electric in Schenectady to construct for him the kind of alternating-current generator he felt was needed for his transmission. At General Electric the regular designers considered his ideas absurd, and they gave the task to a recent immigrant, Swedish-born Ernst F. W. Alexanderson, who had studied with Professor Slaby in Germany; the newcomer was "crazy enough to undertake it."[22] After many difficulties the needed "alternator" was installed at Brant Rock.

A climax to these events came on Christmas Eve, 1906. Over a wide area ship operators, with earphones to head, alert to the crackle of distant messages, were snapped to attention by a "CQ, CQ" in Morse code. After a moment they heard

> a human voice coming from their instruments—someone speaking! Then a woman's voice rose in song. It was uncanny! Many of them called their officers to come and listen; soon the wireless rooms were crowded. Next someone was heard reading a poem. Then there was a violin solo; then a man made a speech, and they could catch most of the words.[23]

They were hearing a Christmas Eve broadcast. The violin solo was played by Fessenden himself (Gounod's "O, Holy Night") and he also sang a few bars and read verses from Luke. The woman's voice came from a phonograph recording of Handel's "Largo." At the end Fessenden wished his audience a Merry Christmas and promised another broadcast on New Year's Eve. Those listening were asked to write to R. A. Fessenden at Brant Rock, and many seem to have done so. The New Year's Eve program, of similar pattern, was heard by ships as far away as the West Indies, including banana boats of the United Fruit Company.[24]

All this had an immediate result. The United Fruit Company was already experimenting with wireless, by which perishable cargoes could be directed to profitable markets, and scattered plantations could be co-ordinated. Spurred by the Fessenden successes, it now bought a quantity of his equipment and assumed a pioneering role throughout the Caribbean—first in dot-and-dash wireless, eventually in voice transmission.

But meanwhile the big wireless push took other directions. For many experimenters, including Marconi, the obsession was not voice but *distance*—especially the crossing of oceans. In 1901 the letter S, sent from Cornwall by Morse code, had been received in Newfoundland via a kite antenna and heard by Marconi on an earphone. On the strength of this, transatlantic stations were built. On January 19, 1903, a greeting from President Theodore Roosevelt to King Edward VII was hurled out in noisy dots and dashes by a Marconi station at South Wellfleet on Cape Cod, and a reply was received. These stations were erratic, unreliable; often, for hours, not an intelligible signal came through. Yet they could be seen as eventual competitors to the lucrative cables. Fessenden too worked in this direction, with successes followed by exasperating failures. But his great goal was to include speech and music. Why? To many it seemed a frill, economically unpromising. But Fessenden was stubborn and continued. Others followed.

Mission in the Ether

Lee De Forest was born in 1873 in a parsonage in frontier Council Bluffs, Iowa, where his father, a minister, had married the young choir leader. They soon moved to Alabama, his father to head Talladega College, which had been founded by missionaries after the Civil War to educate the "freedmen." Resented as northern meddlers, the De Forests found themselves ostracized by the white citizens of Talladega. Their life revolved around the Negro college, where young Lee spent hours in the library, poring over the *Patent Office Gazette*, fascinated by its mechanical drawings. At home he read the Bible from cover to cover. But the unforgettable times were the parlor musicales arranged by his mother, a soprano and pianist. Lee himself took cornet lessons.

The Talladega atmosphere never left De Forest. Throughout life he had a sense of isolation, and at the same time addressed the world in statements with a biblical ring. In his diary, begun when he was seventeen, he constantly seemed to see himself as a figure in an epic pilgrimage, struggling up a steep and difficult road; in many an entry he exhorted himself to sterner effort. Though he rejected his father's pleas to become a minister, the mission he found among Hertzian waves seemed to become for him a new evangelism, in which he, like his father, constantly had a soprano at his side.

Though his school preparation was biblical and agricultural, he passed examinations which admitted him, in 1893, to the Sheffield Scientific School of Yale University. Before starting his studies he headed for Chicago and its World's Columbian Exposition, getting a job as chair pusher at $8 per week and sleeping at a farm for fifty cents a night.[25] Whenever his customers agreed, he steered them to Machinery Hall, where he saw the electrical exhibits again and again.

He owed his job to a strike of the Amalgamated Order of Chair Pushers, which meant that he was a strike breaker; this troubled him, a diary entry tells us, but to leave would have been like "leaving heaven."[26] Among the innumerable customers he wheeled to Machinery Hall may have been the man who became Russia's "Father of Radio," Alexander Popov, sent as observer from Kronstadt.

At Yale, Lee was a lonely figure. He could spend only fifteen cents per meal and often got up at 4 A.M. to mow lawns. When he lost time, he reprimanded himself in his diary. "The morning wasted, bitterly will its hours be craved, but no tears of remorse avail to bring back one golden moment." When other students scattered for Christmas he stayed, working ceaselessly on a design for an underground trolley, for a $50,000 prize offered by *Scientific American*. When he finished, he could not conceive of the possibility of not winning the prize. "I felt so supremely happy I could have shouted . . . I vowed to give $5,000 to the Lord if I won . . ." He did not win. Nothing he did at Yale quite worked out. Meanwhile his readings in Darwin made him anxious, undermining the faith of his upbringing; he tried consciously to find a religious dimension in his study of science. He won his undergraduate degree in three years. His classmates voted him Nerviest and also Homeliest.[27] Perhaps his dedication to great ends invited retaliation.

De Forest stayed on for his Ph.D., earned in 1899 with a dissertation on *Reflection of Hertzian Waves from the Ends of Parallel Wires*. Then he headed back for the Chicago area, where he held several jobs over a two-year period. One was with Western Electric, where he managed to be transferred to the telephone department, "goal of my hopes." In his diary he wrote: "What finer task than to transfer the sound of a voice of song to one a thousand miles away. If I could do that tonight!" His one indulgence in Chicago was an occasional twenty-five-cent balcony ticket for the Castle Square Opera Company; he gloried in its music. Most of his evenings were spent experimenting in his rented room. He had decided, along with many others, that the coherer was the weak link in the Marconi system, and he was developing an alternative which he called a "responder." The work that went into it diverted cash from food and clothing. When his employers gave him a $10 a week raise he was ecstatic. "Never again shall I . . . wear the same collar longer than three days." With two other experimenters he tested his responder from rooftop to rooftop. De Forest stood in the rain on top of the Lakota Hotel with his heart pounding. The results were so good that he felt his hour had come. That year, 1901, there would be a new international yacht race off Sandy Hook. They must go to New York and report it by wireless. "Emboldened . . . I forced the hands of my confreres."[28] After the trip to New York by day coach, De Forest was taken aback to learn that the New York *Herald* and the Associated Press had already contracted with Marconi to report the races. But De Forest managed to obtain a commission from the lesser Publishers Press Association. On the strength of this contract, he raised $1,000 to prepare equipment. De Forest and his associates had endless difficulties but worked day and night, hardly eating. Before they were ready, Lee De Forest collapsed and was taken to a hospital. They were saved from disaster by a grisly event. The assassination of President McKinley resulted in postponement of the yacht races; the extra time allowed De Forest to recover and prepare the equipment. Meanwhile, still another wireless entrepreneur, though without sponsor, announced that he would report the events by wireless.

The races began. From three transmitters along the route the reports crackled into the air, producing chaos. Navy observers were on hand; not a signal was intelligible. Each transmitter completely blotted the others. The fiasco could not have been more total.[29] But the enterprising, competitive spirit of the press saved the day for De Forest. Newspapers, which had taken the precaution to get results by semaphore, blandly announced that they had the news "by wireless." De Forest's name was in the paper; he was being mentioned along with Marconi; people began to pay attention. De Forest met a promoter, a "very personable Wall Street character," Abraham White, who in one afternoon became extremely interested and said he would back De Forest. Before leaving him that day, White slipped him a $100 bill, because the young man would need pocket money.[30]

Early in 1902 they incorporated the De Forest Wireless Telegraph Company, with capitalization of $3,000,000. De Forest received a block of stock, a salary of twenty dollars a week, and a chance to continue experimenting. Almost immediately, through a demonstration for the Signal Corps, the company made a sale to the War Department. And the navy decided on a small purchase for testing purposes.

But White, unlike Fessenden's backers, wanted to sell stock to the public: this was his main intention. One of De Forest's functions was to help him do it by staging demonstrations, dramatizing the new era. De Forest entered enthusiastically into all this. With the flamboyance of White and the technical skill of De Forest, the company became known for dazzling salesmanship. Paul Schubert, in *The Electric Word*, writes:

> A "latest model" 1902 automobile ran about the streets of New York carry-
> ing a demonstration De Forest apparatus; its spark gap crackled daily before
> gaping crowds, and every afternoon it invaded Wall Street and stopped
> before the Stock Exchange to telegraph the "closing prices" to mythical
> listeners. At Coney Island, the city's amusement resort, a high mast went
> up and there, too, hundreds were introduced to the new telegraphy.[31]

The public was buying the stock. White decided that $3,000,000 wasn't enough. In a reorganization, the capitalization was set at $15,000,000[32] and the pace of stock-selling stepped up. White was living in a splendid style and shopping for a Long Island mansion. The company put out grandiose brochures, envisaging a world-wide chain of De Forest stations. Through these the Caribbean would be firmly welded; the Pacific would become "an American lake."[33]

At the 1904 St. Louis world's fair—the "Louisiana Purchase Exposition"—Lee De Forest and his wireless tower became a star attraction. In a glass house the chair pusher of yesterday was on view to thousands. "The staccato crackle of our spark, when purposely unmuffled, brought them swarming."[34]

No doubt such occasions had, for De Forest, a quality of evangelism. He was a prophet pointing to a promised land. To some people the circus promotion, coupled with the financial manipulations of White, were giving the company an air of chicanery. But De Forest allowed himself to feel that things were going well. At the company plant in Newark equipment was being made and sold. Shore stations were being built. In ship-to-shore communication, especially in coastal shipping, the company was competing successfully with American Marconi. In 1903 it merged with another company, increasing its shore stations. Best of all, De Forest was getting the chance to continue research, aiming at his real goal: transmission of speech and music. In this, momentous things were about to happen.

In 1904 in England, Professor John Ambrose Fleming, utilizing an observation made by Edison years earlier during work on the incandescent lamp, developed a glass-bulb detector. Fleming was working for the Marconi company, which obtained the patents—in 1904 in England, in 1905 in the United States. That same year De Forest carried this work an historic step forward. He added a third element or "grid" in the vacuum tube, enormously increasing its effectiveness as detector and amplifier. The "Audion," as he called it, was patented in 1906. Here was one of the key elements on which radio, and the whole electronics industry, were to grow. "Unwittingly then," wrote De Forest in his diary, "had I discovered an Invisible Empire of the Air."[35]

Early in 1907 he formed the De Forest Radio Telephone Company; in New York he began intensive tests to demonstrate his Audion. It was used in receiving, and later also in sending. On March 5, 1907, he wrote in his diary:

> My present task (happy one) is to distribute sweet melody broadcast over
> the city and sea so that in time even the mariner far out across the silent
> waves may hear the music of his homeland . . .

At first Columbia phonograph records supplied the music, but De Forest now began to invite singers to his laboratory. Leading the way was a Miss Van Boos, who sang "I Love You Truly" and was heard by two operators at the Brooklyn Navy Yard.[36]

Most of these experimental broadcasts were done from the top floor of the Parker Building, on Fourth Avenue at 19th Street. Among De Forest's listeners, growing in numbers, were two inventors working nearby. In the Metropolitan Life Building was Miller Reese Hutchinson, who was trying to improve the klaxon; in Madison Square Tower, Peter Cooper Hewitt, inventor of a mercury-vapor light. Both were wireless enthusiasts and experimenters. De Forest often alerted them by phone when ready to test; they would signal results. People in the streets below were sometimes puzzled to see a man waving a towel from a high window of the Metropolitan Life Building.[37]

People often asked De Forest, what was the use of all this? In the New York *World*, De Forest answered with rhetorical questions.

> What is the use . . . of attuning a new Aeolian harp and having it
> vibrate . . . to the rhapsodies of master musicians played in some
> far-distant auditorium?[38]

The broadcasting idea became a grand obsession, marred only by a growing stench from the manipulations of Abraham White. White and others formed a new corporation, United Wireless Telegraph Company—capitalized at $20,000,000—which took over the activities of the De Forest Wireless Telegraph Company. White, controlling both companies, arranged this in a way that was completely to the advantage of the new company, and left nothing to the stockholders of the older company, including De Forest.[39] The inventor found himself powerless, with a block of almost worthless stock. Dismayed and infuriated, he had seen a paper fortune vanish. Fortunately he had hung onto his Audion and radio telephony, and these became his means to rebound. In the navy a number of officers were rallying enthusiastically to the radio telephone. Most early navy orders had gone to Slaby-Arco; the navy had usually shied away from De Forest, for reasons that included excessive stock promotion and untidy management. But now, for a proposed round-the-world cruise of an American squadron—a bid for world prestige—the radio telephone seemed essential. An order for twenty-six sets of De Forest equipment was placed.[40] For De Forest disaster was averted, but his De Forest Radio Telephone Company was still on thin ice. The panic of 1907 created unpromising prospects. What was needed, De Forest felt sure, was promotion—and sale of stock to finance further development.

He was falling in love with a lady pianist living in the apartment next to his. He had admired her playing through the wall, even before meeting her. "Propinquity led to acquaintance." Nora Blatch soon shared his excitement over the quixotic idea of broadcasting. She married him, and early in 1908 joined him in one of the most spectacular of De Forest promotions. They went to Paris and secured permission to broadcast from the Eiffel Tower. All one night they shared the work of feeding discs to a Pathé phonograph. Later they learned they had been heard 500 miles from Paris. De Forest returned to New York in an aura of celebrity, which helped to dispel somewhat the United Wireless scandals. The messy affairs of that company would in time be aired in the courts. Meanwhile De Forest pursued tenaciously his broadcasting ideas, which now included more than "sweet melody." In 1909 Mrs. Harriet Blatch, his mother-in-law, was invited to send into the ether a plea for woman suffrage, marking a broadcasting milestone of a sort.[41]

The following year came a more astonishing achievement: a broadcast with Enrico Caruso direct from the stage of the Metropolitan Opera House—January 13, 1910. It was a double bill of *Cavalleria Rusticana* and *Pagliacci*. Two microphones were used, one on stage, the other in the wings. A 500-watt transmitter was installed in a room at the top of the Opera House. The antenna, suspended from two bamboo fishpoles, led to an attic room off the ballet rehearsal room.

Groups of listeners, passing earphones around, were assembled at the Newark plant and at several points in New York City, including De Forest's laboratory and the Metropolitan Life Building. The broadcast was also heard by ship operators and amateurs.[42]

Excitement prevailed, but scoffers were also heard. Interference from other stations, including code transmissions and snatches of ribald talk between unidentified operators, caused some difficulty. And there was fading. The "homeless song waves," as the New York *Times* put it, kept losing their way. According to its report, one listener, when asked if he heard the singing, replied that he could occasionally "catch the ecstasy."[43]

What did it all amount to? The importance of this, as of other De Forest experiments, was only partly in the technical study involved. Equally important was the bond it provided for a growing brotherhood, scattered far and wide, that already numbered thousands; a host of experimenters, of every age and status; of listeners who didn't merely listen but communicated feverishly with each other; of enthusiasts who, for want of better terminology, were called amateurs. Their importance, at this juncture of the broadcasting story, must be made clear.

The Greatest Bunch of Junk

In the wake of Marconi, zealous followers sprang up everywhere. They were of all ages, but mostly young. Marconi's youth acted as a spark. The fact that he had used materials available to anyone was additional incentive. Some experimenters worked alone, others jointly. At schools and colleges, groups in electricity clubs defected and formed wireless clubs, and later radio clubs. Some assisted, and also prodded, faculty experimentation. Boys—and men—were constantly filing down nickels to make coherers, or winding wires around round objects—broken baseball bats or, later on, Quaker Oats boxes. In attics, barns, garages, woodsheds, apparatus took shape. Because of the noise and other menaces and hazards, real or imagined, the activity was for a long time banned from living quarters. Some people were drawn by the drama that awaited them in the airwaves, others by technical fascination. Most started with a receiver, with transmission as the next step. For each one who was already transmitting there were always many who had not yet reached this stage.

These experimenters, in city and country, were not only the beginning of what became the radio audience; they were also the cadre from which many broadcasters were to spring. Many of those who started and directed radio broadcasting stations in the 1920's—and, in many cases, television stations later—were "amateurs" in the fertile time before World War I.

Edgar Felix, who in 1922 was to become a staff member of WEAF, New York—a station playing a pivotal role in broadcasting history—got acquainted with wireless in 1904 when he paid a visit to an amateur's "table-top spark coil radio transmitting and receiving station." He would never forget "the Leyden jars which lighted up" when the key was pressed, and the "brilliant flash of the spark."[44] Soon afterwards he built his own first receiver, following directions in a Boy Scout manual.

About 1910 he visited "that great emporium of the amateur world, Hugo Gernsback's Electro Importing Company, under the 'El' at Fulton Street," in New York. Here he bought headphones. In this he differed from others; many an amateur got his from a phone booth. Felix also visited Eimer & Amend, on Third Avenue in New York, and for about half a dollar bought an assortment of crystals—galena, silicon, iron pyrites, perikon.[45] It had been found—at about the time that De Forest was developing the Audion—that each of these crystals could likewise, in some mysterious way, "detect" radio waves, and transform them into electric current if touched in the right spot with a thin wire (or "cat's whisker," as the amateur called it). The received current was feeble but could be made audible with the help of headphones. The crystal thus became the poor man's Audion, more limited in range, erratic, but nonetheless a thing of miracles. Because of low cost its use spread rapidly, especially among amateurs.[46]

Summering in the still sparsely settled area of Greenwich, Conn., Felix found he could pick up navy stations at Portsmouth, Boston, New London, Brooklyn, Philadelphia—and at times even Charleston, Guantanamo, Colon. Rolling a newspaper into a cone, he made a loudspeaker; at noon all members of the household were summoned to set their watches by the daily time signals from navy station NAA at Arlington. He also listened to the Marconi station at South Wellfleet on Cape Cod, which broadcast news to ships several times a day and produced an extraordinary "musical roar . . . rhythmic and beatiful." Distress signals were a collector's item. In 1909 the few boys at school who had heard the distress signals from the S. S. *Republic*, when it was rammed by the *Florida*, were local heroes, winning new converts to amateur radio. Since all but two aboard the *Republic*—which sank—were rescued, the event was also a strong boost for ship wireless.[47]

Drama awaited the amateur along the coast. Stanley R. Manning, who was to play a pioneer role in Detroit during the broadcasting boom of the 1920's, grew up in Irvington, N.Y. Here he built his first receiver in 1909. He soon received a letter from the Brooklyn Navy Yard, complaining that he was blanketing out its operators when they were trying to talk to ships at sea.

> They wanted me to lay off when they were on the air. I wasn't perturbed about it because there weren't any laws, rules, or regulations in those days. All they could do was ask me to be careful about it, which naturally I was, too.

Manning, like Felix, made a pilgrimage to the Electro Importing Company run by Hugo Gernsback, who sold "the biggest bunch of junk you ever saw." Manning did not buy his headphones there. "Where I got the headphones I'd rather not say." In 1912 his father gave him $15 to buy a De Forest Audion, a fabulous treasure.[48]

The appearance of speech in the ether generated enormous excitement. Listeners had long used headphones because they made it possible to catch weak signals. An operator expecting dots and dashes would occasionally hear on his phones a voice or fragment of music. Such episodes were reported in the newspaper and not quite believed. Then one day, it happened to oneself. Manning caught a test by Fessenden—some talk and music.

> When I heard it I thought I was going crazy . . . I had never heard anything like it. I was living in a rooming house up on 72d Street—I believe—at the time and I called in several people, and they heard it, so it was real.[49]

John A. Fetzer, who was to become a midwestern broadcasting pioneer and, during World War II, chief radio censor in the U.S. Office of Censorship, had a similar boyhood experience in Lafayette, Ind. His brother-in-law, a dispatcher on the Wabash Railroad, had interested him in telegraphy and in 1913 helped him start in wireless. They built a 70-foot antenna, which could pull in the time signals from NAA, Arlington. "Every night . . . we would set our clocks with great satisfaction, always marveling at the ability of man to conquer distance." Then, on a night in November 1913, we were suddenly startled to hear violin music bursting forth from the headphones . . . as far as we were concerned, a miracle never to be explained. This phenomenon occurred for fully twenty minutes. The headphones were passed around . . . We called in the neighbors, all of whom agreed that not a single one of us was having day-dreams.[50]

Such experiences gradually, very gradually, became more frequent. They also had their variations. Everett L. Bragdon, who was to become radio editor of the New York *Globe* in 1921—one of the first on a daily newspaper—began wireless experimentation in 1907 in Westbrook, Me. He was the only amateur in town. Two brass spheres from an old bedstead were his spark gap. The 250 watts jumping across this gap made thunderous noises. He listened on headphones for hours every day. One stormy day, the first sound he heard was not code but a woman's voice. Struck with the proper amazement, he then recognized the voice as that of the lady across the street, apparently in a phone conversation. The wetness of phone wires and insulators may have created a leak, which never recurred.[51]

The relation of amateur to governmental authority was a topic of growing interest during the years 1907–12, when Bragdon was experimenting in Maine. Ship traffic off the Maine coast was heavy, and included navy ships moving in and out of Portland. Every amateur "felt that the world was his to explore," and that he had the right to talk with anyone he could reach. Bragdon in Westbrook and two or three experimenters in Portland spent night after night "going up and down the dial" trying to talk to the steamship *Belfast* on her way east along the coast or the *North Star* out of Portland en route to New York. For a time there seemed no limit to the readiness of ship operators to converse. But so many official messages were blotted out that naval authorities became increasingly testy, and then indignant, about amateur interference. Most amateur transmitters were not sharply tuned, and this added to the problem.

We might think we were on 200 meters but we were probably just as powerful on 300 meters, possibly on 500 meters. Thus, no matter how selective the Navy equipment, they still couldn't escape us.[52]

According to Alvin F. Harlow, in *Old Wires and New Waves*, the fleet returning from its world trip under Admiral Evans was unable to communicate with Portsmouth Navy Yard "because of amateur clamor." In some cases, amateurs are said to have broadcast fake orders to naval vessels, purportedly from admirals.[53]

It was perhaps not surprising that the armed forces—and especially the navy, which had the larger stake in radio, and was given the leading role in it as a matter of government policy—began to demand regulation. The amateurs rose in righteous anger, but to no avail. In 1912 the first radio licensing law was passed by Congress and signed by President Taft.[54] It remained the basic radio law of the land until 1927. Although written and passed without thought of the possibilities of broadcasting, it was to be the law under which the first years of the broadcasting era would be governed.

To many in the scattered brotherhood, it seemed the end of freedom. But in practice the law introduced only minor restraints. For transmission a station license was now required; it was available on application from the Secretary of Commerce and Labor. It was also now required that transmission be done or supervised by someone with an operator's license; this license would be awarded on the basis of an examination.

In granting station licenses the Secretary of Commerce and Labor—after 1913 the Secretary of Commerce—could assign wave lengths and time limits, but he apparently could not refuse a license. Such details would in time cause difficulties—in fact, chaos.

A person had to be an American citizen to obtain a station license. However, a company incorporated under the laws of any state could also obtain a license, and this meant that subsidiaries of foreign corporations could get licenses. This too would become an issue.

The new law began an attempt to divide the spectrum by function. Ship, amateur, and government transmissions were to be kept apart. Amateurs were to stay at 200 meters or above. The law also contemplated special "experimental" allocations.

The enactment of the law was quickly followed by the licensing of almost a thousand existing transmitters. These included transmitters at a number of schools, colleges, and universities, some of which already had years of experience behind them.[55]

In addition to those licensed under the new law, we can assume there were a number who continued to send without a license. Among them was Edgar S. Love, an amateur near Pittsburg, who eventually became head engineer of WWJ, Detroit. He knew there was some sort of law, but felt it wasn't meant for him. Among his friends "nobody . . . knew anything about licensing."[56] And nothing happened.

We can also assume that the number receiving but not sending—therefore not needing a license—far exceeded the licensed senders. The non-sending listeners may have numbered many thousands.

In spite of the cries of doom with which amateur experimenters greeted the new law, they continued to grow rapidly in number. By 1917 they held 8,562 transmitting licenses.[57] In many instances, amateur activity developed into professional work that, in one way or another, built foundations for the broadcasting age.

Builders

In Detroit, Thomas E. Clark, who ran an electrical appliance store, began about 1899 to experiment with wireless. He put an antenna on the Banner Laundry building on Michigan Avenue opposite the old Cadillac Hotel, and another on the Chamber of Commerce building at Griswold and State streets,[58] and began to amaze his friends and acquaintances with demonstrations. Before long he was equipping lake steamers—the *Garland*, the *Sappho*, the *Promise*—and launching a wireless service for the Great Lakes under the name Clark Wireless. By 1903 he was calling this company the Thomas E. Clark Wireless Telegraph and Telephone Company[59] and beginning experiments with voice transmission.

In 1902 James E. Scripps, founder and owner of the Detroit *News*, visited the Banner Laundry station with his nineteen-year-old son William. With flashing of sparks, a message was wirelessed by Clark to the Chamber of Commerce building, and the inconclusive answer came back in Morse code: "We received your message by wireless." The younger Scripps hardly knew what to make of it, and peered behind a curtain, which hid more equipment. The elder Scripps made no comment but asked Clark to stop at the house some evening. When he came, Mr. Scripps wrote out a check for $1,000, saying he merely wanted to help the experiments.[60]

Clark built transmitters in a number of port cities on the Great Lakes, equipped more steamers, and in 1906 contracted to broadcast election returns to them.[61]

He later began to broadcast phonograph music; on the steamers four or five people could listen on a telephone receiver.[62] He had expansion plans, but in 1911 another company, blanketing his transmissions, put him out of business. Meanwhile young William E. Scripps, on the death of his father, had become publisher of the Detroit *News*, and developed an increasing interest in radio. Some years later he sought out Clark for advice on the starting of a Detroit *News* station, which began under an amateur license but became WWJ—an historic Detroit station.

In San Jose, Cal., "Professor" Charles D. Herrold or "Doc" Herrold, a genius without formal qualifications, started in 1909 a College of Engineering in which radio became the main attraction. He began transmitting from the Garden City Bank building in San Jose in that same year, and promptly took up voice experiments. Wireless students assisted, and of course learned from the activity. Some twenty amateurs in the Santa Clara Valley became a faithful following; Herrold had helped many of these install crystal detectors for voice reception. They would often call on the phone to ask when he would be on the air again. One of the followers, Ray Newby, a seasoned experi- menter—his first antenna had been knocked down by the San Francisco earthquake in 1906—became an assistant to Herrold.[63] Schoolteachers from the area brought classes to see the station in operation; some of the children later became students of Herrold. The voice experiments grew into weekly programs—each Wednesday evening, with news bulletins, and phonograph records provided by a San Jose music store, which received a mention. It became "almost a religion" with Herrold to be ready on Wednes- days, with his records laid out. Occasionally a singer was brought in. According to a listener of 1912—Joseph Cappa—the quality was always fine at the start of a program, but got "mushy" as Herrold's carbon microphone "burned up on him . . . it would be so mushy and so bad that he'd shut down and be off the air." Next Wednesday he would apologize for the way it had ended. "Then he would say he would try to give a program if his microphone would hold out," but it would often end the same way. As time went on, the programs gathered listeners far beyond the valley. A group of experimenters at the Fairmont Hotel in San Francisco, some forty miles away, heard them and conversed with Herrold. In 1913 Herrold married a young lady who acquired virtuosity in Morse code, and began teaching the introductory course in code transmission—in the dining room at home. Around the dining table eight Morse keys and eight receiving headsets were arranged. Sybil Herrold had never before seen a house with an aerial, but Herrold told her all homes "would have these poles." When their first child was born in 1914, she held it up before the microphone so that friends in the Fairmont Hotel could hear the cries. In 1915 the Panama Pacific Exposition at San Francisco featured radio exhibits by the federal government and by Lee De Forest. At both exhibits listeners heard, on headphones, programs from the Herrold station, which gave daily broadcasts during the fair for this purpose. For New Year's Eve that year Herrold announced a stunt: at midnight he would shoot a gun before his microphone—"the shot heard round the world." He used a blank cartridge in a 45-caliber army pistol. Listeners heard a *whsst*, and Doc Herrold was off the air again.[64]

Herrold would do anything for his station and school. During the night, for long-distance tests, he began to appropriate power at 600 volts from the Street Railway Company, tying onto trolley lines from the roof of the bank building by means of a long bamboo pole with a hook at the end. He also strung an antenna between two mountain tops and took his students, "his boys," into the hills to test reception at a radio-equipped shack with four bunks. The war stopped Herrold's operation. He tried to revive it after the war but couldn't manage, and sold the station to the Second Avenue Baptist Church, which ran it as KQW. The church later turned it over to a commercial operator, who sold it to another, who sold it to the Columbia Broadcasting System, which made it KCBS, San Francisco—50,000-watt descendant of a 15-watt school station of 1909.[65]

Harold J. Power, a student at Tufts College, near Boston, was an avid wireless experimenter in the early 1910's and organized the campus radio club. In the summer of 1913 and again in 1914, after graduation, he had a job as wireless operator on J. P. Morgan's yacht, *Corsair*. This led to a long talk with J. P. Morgan; Power told him he believed in *broadcasting:* eventually everyone should have a receiver. The financier shrugged his shoulders. How could an ordinary person run a radio set? "You've got to be an engineer." Not so, Power told him. As with automobiles, this would be a passing phase. Simple, complete sets could be built. As Power explained his views, Morgan began to show interest. Power said he hoped to go to Harvard for a year of graduate work, study the idea, and draw up a plan. "How much do you need?" Morgan asked. For a year at Harvard, said Power, just $500. Morgan said, "You can't do anything with $500." Power explained that he could attend Harvard for that, if he also gave lessons in radio. Morgan opened his wallet and gave him a $500 bill. A year later Power returned with a complete plan. He wanted to start a station. He had developed a saying: "To get broadcasting started, you have to start broadcasting." Along with that, there must be a laboratory to develop equipment. Power had a budget prepared: the whole thing could be started for $25,000. Morgan said, "I don't think you can do much with that." But Power said he could start it with that, so the financier said, "See my lawyers and organize the corporation."[66] They built a great antenna tower, on land made available by Tufts, and in 1915 organized AMRAD, the American Radio and Research Corporation. The station began a schedule of news bulletins and phonograph records, "for the entertainment of ships at sea." All members of the Tufts Radio Club worked at the station. But the war diverted the plans. Instead of receivers, they were enlisted to make cart transmitters and trench transmitters for the Signal Corps—barbed wire could be used as an antenna.[67] Broadcasting was halted. After the war they started up again; in 1922 the station became WGI, Medford Hillside, Mass. But the laboratory, expanded for war work, was in financial trouble as the work ended. J. P. Morgan kept tiding them over, but presently they sold out to Crosley, and became part of the manufacturing and broadcasting empire of the Crosley Radio Corporation.

These capsule chronologies will suggest how amateur ventures became professional pursuits that led by circuitous routes toward something new. What the new might be, none on the way could be sure. Some had a destination in mind, without knowing how to reach it. Meanwhile they shared the excitement of the journey.

On the eve of World War I the air crackled with code, with people here and there—for one reason or another—talking, playing a phonograph record, reading a poem, singing a solo, making a speech, giving a time signal, predicting the weather. Almost everything that became "broadcasting" was being done or had been done. The experimenters talked about the broadcasting idea, some with a sense of mission. The periodicals they read—such as *Wireless Age*, launched in 1913 by American Marconi— discussed it occasionally. But while the broadcasting devotees excited themselves and each other, they had so far made little impact on the general public. Many people looked on broadcasting as a slightly eccentric activity. The pronouncements made by De Forest and others seemed merely impractical. The devotees themselves must sometimes have wondered whether the idea wasn't irrelevant. Events of the day seemed to proclaim its irrelevancy. As war grew imminent, military uses usurped attention. When war came, everything changed.

We have mentioned that Edgar Felix, experimenter in the countryside near Greenwich, Conn., used to listen to the Marconi station at South Wellfleet, with its beautiful, rhythmic roar, as it wirelessed news to ships at sea. That is how he learned one day that war had begun in Europe. He told neighbors, who seemed unsure whether to believe him. Half a day later a boy on a bicycle, carrying an "extra," brought confirmation.[68] The episode must have been duplicated in hundreds of wireless-equipped households.

From that moment the amateur experimenters knew their days were numbered. A clause in the 1912 law provided that "in time of war or public peril or disaster" the President might close or seize any radio apparatus.[69] For a while the amateurs continued to send and listen; in many ways, these were the most exciting months. Then, on April 6, 1917, the blow came. A state of war existed with Germany. That same day, all amateur radio apparatus was ordered shut, dismantled, sealed. Next day commercial wireless stations such as ship-to-shore stations were taken over by the navy. Almost all stations still in operation were now under navy or army control.

A number of campus radio units had already been taken over for training, and others were reopened for similar use. Trainees began to pour into such units on the Arkansas, Harvard, Loyola, Ohio, Wisconsin and other campuses. Broadcasting was forgotten.

Two or three years later it would be said that broadcasting had been tried by De Forest and others but "nothing came of it."[70] It would seem a discredited notion, belonging to yesterday.

The amateur experimenters gave little thought to this change of direction. There was suddenly a great deal for them to do. The armed forces were seeking them out. Their special knowledge was in demand. Some were being sent overseas. Others would follow.

Notes

1. Quoted, Banning, *Commercial Broadcasting Pioneer*, p. 3.
2. Rhodes, *Beginnings of Telephony*, pp. 26–30.
3. Harlow, *Old Wires and New Waves*, pp. 265, 372.
4. Quoted, Banning, *Commercial Broadcasting Pioneer*, pp. 4–5.
5. *Fortnightly Review*, February 1, 1892.
6. Degna Marconi, *My Father Marconi*, p. 12.
7. Quoted, Dunlap, *Marconi*, p. 18.
8. Quoted, Degna Marconi, *My Father Marconi*, p. 30.
9. *Ibid.* pp. 36–46.
10. *Ibid.* pp. 66–7.
11. Schubert, *The Electric Word*, p. 24.
12. For this reason May 7 is celebrated as Radio Day in the U.S.S.R. See Radovsky, *Alexander Popov*, p. 50.
13. *History of Communications-Electronics in the United States Navy*, p. 13.
14. *Ibid.* pp. 27, 35.

15. The Boers also sought and obtained wireless equipment. The British captured equipment apparently made in Germany, similar in design to Marconi equipment. New York *Herald*, December 31, 1899.
16. *History of Communications-Electronics in the United States Navy*, pp. 28, 34.
17. Young, "The Real Beginning of Radio," *Saturday Review*, March 7, 1964.
18. *History of Communications-Electronics in the United States Navy*, p. 26.
19. Johnson, *Address to Kentucky Broadcasters Association*, 1961.
20. Helen M. Fessenden, *Fessenden*, pp. 76–7.
21. *Ibid.* p. 116.
22. Alexanderson, *Reminiscences*, p. 16.
23. Harlow, *Old Wires and New Waves*, p. 455.
24. Helen M. Fessenden, *Fessenden*, p. 153.
25. De Forest, *Father of Radio*, pp. 62–3.
26. Carneal, *A Conqueror of Space*, p. 3.
27. De Forest, *Father of Radio*, pp. 67–82.
28. *Ibid.* pp. 104–23.
29. *History of Communications-Electronics in the United States Navy*, p. 38.
30. De Forest, *Father of Radio*, pp. 126–9. Carneal, *A Conqueror of Space*, p. 144.
31. Schubert, *The Electric Word*, p. 51.
32. *Success Magazine*, June 1907. Quoted in *History of Communications-Electronics in the United States Navy*, p. 48.
33. Schubert, *The Electric Word*, p. 51.
34. De Forest, *Father of Radio*, p. 165.
35. *Ibid.* p. 4.
36. *Ibid.* pp. 225–33.
37. Carneal, *A Conqueror of Space*, p. 206.
38. New York *World*, April 7, 1907.
39. De Forest, *Father of Radio*, p. 217.
40. *History of Communications-Electronics in the United States Navy*, p. 136.
41. De Forest, *Father of Radio*, pp. 222–49.
42. Carneal, *A Conqueror of Space*, p. 232.
43. New York *Times*, January 14, 1910.
44. Felix, *Reminiscences*, p. 1.
45. *Ibid.* p. 3.
46. One of the developers of the crystal detector, J. G. Pickard, formed the Wireless Specialty Apparatus Company to exploit it; in 1912 the company was bought by United Fruit and became its radio-equipment subsidiary.
47. Felix, *Reminiscences*, pp. 3–5.
48. Manning, *Reminiscences*, pp. 2–5.
49. *Ibid.* pp. 5–6.
50. *Ibid.* pp. 2–3.
51. Bragdon, *Reminiscences*, p. 4.
52. *Ibid.* pp. 5–6.
53. Harlow, *Old Wires and New Waves*, p. 469.
54. See Appendix B. Earlier radio laws, passed in 1910 and 1912, had the purpose of requiring ships of specified types to carry wireless equipment and adequate operating personnel.
55. Among them were the University of Arkansas, Cornell, Dartmouth, University of Iowa, Loyola (New Orleans), University of Nebraska, Ohio State, Pennsylvania State College, Philadelphia School of Wireless Telegraphy, St. Joseph's College (Philadelphia), St. Louis University, Tulane, Villanova, University of Wisconsin, Wittenberg. Many additional licenses were issued subsequently. See Frost, *Education's Own Stations*.
56. Love, *Reminiscences*, p. 6.
57. *Wireless Age*, February 1919.
58. Clark, *Reminiscences*, p. 5.
59. *Western Electrician*, May 1, 1903 (advertisement).
60. William Scripps, *Reminiscences*, pp. 19–20.

61.   Letter of agreement, Detroit and Cleveland Navigation Company, October 9, 1906 (see Plate 2). Clark, *Papers*.

62.   Clark, *Reminiscences*, p. 21.

63.   Newby, *Interview*, pp. 1–11. The interviews here cited were recorded by Gordon B. Greb in 1959.

64.   *Interviews* with Cappa, Newby, De Forest, True. The last-mentioned is with Mrs. Herrold— Sybil True by a later marriage.

65.   Interviews with Newby, Cappa. See also Greb, "The Golden Anniversary of Broadcasting," *Journal of Broadcasting*, Winter 1958–59.

66.   Dunham, *This Is the AMRAD Story*, pp. 2–20; this paper includes the texts of interviews with Power and various associates recorded by Dunham in 1964.

67.   *Standard Book of Reference*, Section 9A, pp. 11–12.

68.   Felix, *Reminiscences*, p. 5.

69.   Public Law No. 264, 62nd Congress, Sec. 2.

70.   Allen, *Only Yesterday*, p. 13.

Chapter 27

DANIEL J. LEAB

THE BEGINNINGS

"IT WOULD BE SIMPLE TO SAY that the Depression drew the curtain on irresponsible individualism [in the newspaper business], that the New Deal set the stage for . . . reform, that Heywood Broun stepped from the wings to fill the leading role, and that events wrote the lines." It would be simple, and as Kenneth Stewart, a veteran newspaperman turned journalism teacher, concluded in his memoir, "all true, but too rational."[1]

The organization of newspapermen in 1933 took place in chaotic and confused fashion. Editorial workers across the United States, often quite ignorant of similar activities elsewhere in the country, responded to the exhortations of some of their number. Many local groups were formed as strong feelings of discontent broke through the newsmen's usual inertia. The underlying causes were many, ranging from extreme economic dissatisfaction to professional pride, but the organization movement received most of its initial stimulus from the publishers' unfriendly reactions to the attempts of the National Recovery Administration (NRA) to do something for the editorial employees.

For a time the major vehicle in the New Deal's drive to achieve economic recovery, NRA had been created, in President Franklin D. Roosevelt's words, "to obtain wide re-employment, to shorten the working week, to pay a decent wage for the shorter week, and to prevent unfair competition and disastrous over-production."[2] Under NRA aegis each of the nation's more important industries through its trade associations or similar groups would write for itself a code, subject to federal government approval, that would enable the industry to attain the President's goals. Each of these industries also would organize an "authority" to regulate itself under the code. If self-regulation failed, the President could license business enterprises. Employees were guaranteed "the right to organize and bargain collectively through representatives of their own choosing" by Section 7a of the bill creating NRA.[3] This measure, submitted to Congress on May 17, 1933, had received Congressional approval by June 13. Three days later, the President signed it into law and appointed General Hugh S. Johnson, one of the authors of the legislation, Administrator for National Recovery.[4]

Johnson, a sentimental, tough-talking, former idea man for Bernard Baruch, had helped organize the draft during the First World War and had served as a liaison between the Army and the War Industries Board, a predecessor of NRA in government-business economic cooperation and planning. Even before NRA's official launching, Johnson had begun working on the codes. But their promulgation came slowly; at the end of NRA's second month only eight codes had been approved. Many major industries hesitated. Less important industries sent draft codes to NRA in such numbers (144 in the last half of July alone) that Johnson and his staff were swamped.[5] Desiring to get NRA operative as quickly as possible, Johnson embarked on a sweeping national campaign to get, in his words, "individual employers to make AGREEMENTS WITH THE PRESIDENT HIMSELF to do their part . . ." pending the adoption of codes for their industry. By July 29 employers throughout the United States were receiving in the mail copies of the President's Re-Employment Agreement (PRA), which bound its signers until the end of the year to employ no child labor, to accept Section 7a, and to establish recommended maximum hours and minimum wages (for the editorial employees in the larger circulation areas, the bulk of the editorial workers in the industry, this would mean a five-day, forty-hour week at a weekly salary of at least $14.50). In return, the PRA allowed the employer to display the Blue Eagle, the NRA emblem. Compliance was voluntary, but in a campaign which one historian has called "unabashed revivalism" Johnson succeeded in so arousing public enthusiasm that initially no employer could avoid at least superficial compliance.[6]

With few exceptions, American newspaper publishers enthusiastically supported the Blue Eagle campaign but proved hesitant about entering into agreements with NRA. As one student of the newspaper code negotiations has pointed out, the publishers "wanted the national economy salvaged, but they doubted that they cared to be rescued themselves" by the Federal government.[7] Their reluctant attitude had already begun to take shape before NRA had been established, first being expressed at a publishers conference which met June 9, the day before the Senate voted on the NRA bill. This meeting had been called by the American Newspaper Publishers Association (ANPA). The 15 men who attended included ANPA officers and directors, presidents of regional publishers associations, representatives from the Hearst chain and from Westchester County Publications, and the president of the National Editorial Association (an organization representing several hundred newspapers, most of which were published in small communities). They unanimously declared themselves "in sympathy" with NRA's proposed objectives, but concluded nevertheless that newspapers should not come under its jurisdiction, stating as their reason the agency's "powers to license [which] gives the power to control and such power potentially completely abridges the freedom of the press."

In the newspaper industry's lengthy, strained negotiations with NRA, the ANPA, asserting itself as never before, took an increasingly prominent role. Its leaders, deciding—in the words of the association's historian—"that there was work to be done to protect newspapers from the NRA legislation . . . ," took the lead in dealing with the government and in drawing up for the daily newspapers business the code that they believed publishers wanted. Although the ANPA—the sole national publishers association—numbered publishers of small dailies among its members, it mainly represented the larger circulation newspapers. The 431 ANPA members in 1933, though representing only about 20 percent of the English-language dailies published in this country, used about 80 percent of the newsprint newspapers consumed in the United

States, employed about the same percentage of newspaper employees, and accounted for more than 75 percent of the total daily circulation.[8]

Initially, the newspaper publishers could not avoid uncertainty about the Roosevelt administration's expectations concerning their industry and NRA. Johnson, at his first press conference, on June 20, said that though he had no knowledge of the position the newspaper industry would take, he did not "know why newspapers would not want to come in. . . ." Three weeks later, *Editor & Publisher*'s Washington correspondent described the Roosevelt administration as being more than anxious that the newspapers come forward with a code. But the ANPA history of the code negotiations declares that during this time; despite extensive speculation in the nation's press, the newspaper publishers had no intimation from official sources about their status under NRA. ANPA leaders on July 13 decided that it would be desirable to obtain direct information and arranged, with the assistance of Bernard Baruch, for a private meeting with Johnson. An ANPA committee—led by Howard Davis, the conservative, forceful business manager of the *New York Herald Tribune* who then was ANPA president—held a dinner conference with Johnson in Washington on July 18. After an extensive discussion about the press and NRA, Johnson cordially bade them goodbye, with the wish that he "might never see them again except socially." Although Johnson added that "certain things are in the fire which if cooked up will bring you back sooner than you expect," the ANPA group left the meeting with what they considered to be a mutual understanding that until the government took further action, newspaper publishers would not undertake to write a code for their business.[9]

Never again would NRA-ANPA relations be so amicable. On July 21, the day the nation's press carried Johnson's announcement of the PRA, the ANPA sent out a special bulletin to its members invoking the issue of freedom of the press and recommending that the newspaper publishers "not at the present time prepare to subscribe to a code. . . ." The bulletin also stated that a survey of wages and hours would be undertaken at once. The vast majority of the nation's press followed the ANPA's recommendations. Many newspaper publishers were troubled by aspects of both the PRA and NRA, including the abolition of child labor (which would eliminate newsboys), the licensing provision (which, it was argued, would end freedom of the press), the necessity to allow unionization under Section 7a, the government demands for reduced hours and increased wages (which, it was believed, would upset existing union contracts and increase costs), and the President's ability to impose new regulations even after agreement upon a code had been reached.[10]

Almost immediately after the issuance of the bulletin, however, the ANPA leadership realized that, given the enthusiastic public support of the Blue Eagle campaign to implement the PRA, newspaper publishers would not be able to remain aloof. Moreover, some important dailies, among them the *Christian Science Monitor*, the *Milwaukee Journal*, and the Philadelphia *Record*, quickly had subscribed to the PRA, including the provision which would give editorial employees a five-day, forty-hour week. Indeed, the *Journal* editorially attacked the ANPA on July 25 for "its self-centered and self-seeking . . . special pleas" in asking the newspapers of the country "to stand aside and apart from a movement for general recovery in the sacred name of freedom of the press." Although the smaller circulation dailies had more to fear economically from the government's attempts to boost wages and cut back hours, among the publishers of these newspapers some dissenters from the ANPA position could be found. Typical was Lee Drake, publisher of the Pendleton, Oregon, *East Oregonian*, who remarked to his business manager that the PRA would bring new advertising and that regulation of hours and wages would not hurt the newspaper.[11]

Anxious to avoid embarrassment, the ANPA moved swiftly to neutralize its critics. On July 24, a day before the *Journal* editorial appeared, Davis had a long telephone conversation with a noncommittal Johnson in an attempt to find out whether newspapers which subscribed to the PRA could be exempted from some of its provisions. Three days later, a joint meeting of ANPA officers and directors, its Committee on Federal Laws, and representatives of various regional and state publishers' associations took place. This group of twenty-five during its five-day session transformed itself into the Daily Newspaper Code Committee and appointed a three-man subcommittee composed of Davis, John Stewart Bryan (a former ANPA president and publisher of the Richmond, Virginia, *News Leader*), and Amon G. Carter (publisher of the Fort Worth *Star-Telegram*) to conduct negotiations with NRA. ANPA counsel Elisha Hanson served as counsel for the subcommittee.[12] Hanson, who, according to a former ANPA general manager, "maybe more than anyone else . . . provided the cogent, forceful, unyielding course that the vast majority of daily newspapers pursued in . . . the NRA code fight," served as a vigorous spokesman for the publishers in their bouts with the government and the American Newspaper Guild throughout the 1930s. A one-time reporter for the *Peoria Journal* and a former Washington correspondent for the Lee Syndicate, Hanson always maintained that editorial employees deserved better treatment, but he bitterly opposed their achieving it through organization—which he considered a threat to freedom of the press—and he proved to be an implacable and hardy foe of the American Newspaper Guild.[13]

By the end of July, Hanson and the subcommittee had begun negotiations with NRA. Johnson, busy with the drafting of more important codes, delegated the handling of the newspaper code to Dudley Cates, an old associate who had left a Chicago insurance company vice presidency to become NRA Assistant Administrator for Industry. Cates held a number of conferences with the publishers' group and, although the talks went on in what *Editor & Publisher* termed "an atmosphere of the greatest secrecy," news of the issues being discussed leaked out, including the problem of exempting editorial staffs from the forty-hour-week provision of the PRA. On this issue, as on most others, Hanson, Davis, Carter, and Bryan refused to compromise. They informally presented their draft proposal on August 7 to Johnson, who said he felt like "a yellow dog" when he read it. Although the publishers' group did concede to call the draft a code rather than merely an agreement, they met none of Johnson's other objections; the next day, August 8, they formally submitted the document to NRA and released it for publication.[14]

An irate Johnson accurately described the draft code when he exclaimed to Hanson and the subcommittee "why this thing is nothing but an exception."[15] It provided for an open shop, exempted newsboys from child labor provision of the PRA, repeated the rights guaranteed the press in the First Amendment to the Constitution, and designated editorial employees as "professionals" so as to take advantage of Section 4 of the PRA, which exempted from the maximum hour regulations "professional persons employed in their profession."[16]

Before the government could take any action whatever on the draft code, publishers began announcing their approval of it. Within two days the Gannett, Hearst, and Scripps-Howard chains, as well as many large metropolitan dailies and small-town newspapers, had indicated their adherence to the draft code. But Johnson balked.

Taking personal charge of the negotiations, he held a number of meetings and at one point confronted Hanson and Davis with a draft newspaper code prepared by his office staff. But neither with bluster nor with diplomatic entreaties could the general make very much headway. A new draft code, which the subcommittee presented to Johnson on August 14 and which he approved as the temporary newspaper code the following day, contained few of the modifications he had desired. Johnson, fearful of losing all cooperation from the newspaper publishers, had conceded to the subcommittee a code not much different in principle from their first draft. Moreover, the section devoted to the guarantee of press freedom had become much more intricate. Drafted by someone on the NRA staff and designed to appease the publishers' group, this section of the code stated that the newspaper publishers could not be compelled by the President, regardless of the powers invested in him by the NRA law, "to comply with any other requirements than those herein contained [i.e., within the code] or waive any right to object to the imposition of any further or different requirements, or waive any constitutional rights. . . ." The use to which publishers put these concepts—embodied in somewhat different language in the final newspaper code—would cause considerable difficulties when later (before the demise of NRA), the first National Labor Relations Board attempted to deal with disputes involving the American Newspaper Guild. Nor did the editorial employees fare well in the draft accepted by Johnson. Not only did the temporary newspaper code continue to exempt "professionals" from the maximum-hour regulations, but also it specifically exempted from the forty-hour week and classified as "professional" reporters earning more than $35.00 a week.[17]

The question of whether editorial employees were professionals exempt from maximum hour regulations had been raised even before the newspaper code negotiations started and, naturally, had proved to be a topic of keen interest to many newspapermen. As early as July 28, NRA general counsel Donald Richberg, at a press conference had side-stepped a question about whether NRA considered newspapermen professionals, telling the reporters, "well, I've heard it argued both ways, but I'll leave it to you to decide." A NRA press release on July 31 declared that newspaper reporters, editorial writers, rewrite men, and other members of editorial staffs would be treated as "professional persons" not subject to work-hour limits, but the next day Johnson said that the release had been a "slip" which could be "revised." On August 4, in what appears to have been a publishers' trial balloon, an Associated Press dispatch stated that the administration intended "leaving to each publisher the decision on bringing his news force under a work-week limit."[18]

Editorial employees reacted to these varying statements in several ways. Those few newsmen who had the opportunity attacked the publishers' position in print. Paul Y. Anderson, Pulitzer Prize-winning Washington correspondent for the *St. Louis Post-Dispatch*, in his weekly Nation column characterized the publishers' proposals as "dishonest, weasel worded, and treacherous . . . carefully designed to enable the newspapers to escape the obligations which their editorial pages were clamorously urging all other employers to assume." Anderson, considered by Johnson "one of my best friends . . . among the Washington newshawks," also tried to use his personal contacts to offset the publishers' pressure on the administration, as did other newspapermen close to the New Dealers. Heywood Broun in his syndicated daily column asserted that the publishers called for "far too many exceptions" and, commenting specifically on the exemption of professionals from work-hour regulations, said that "the word 'professional' is stretched in this application." Other newspapermen, not so influentially situated and unable to place their objections before the public, wrote to Johnson directly. Richard Cornish, a Philadelphia newspaperman later active in the American Newspaper Guild, wrote to criticize the August 8 proposal of the publishers, concluding his letter with the hope that other newspapermen also wrote Johnson, "for we have no union and this is the only way we may express ourselves." A. F. Finestone, a veteran newsman from Kansas City, Missouri, wrote the general that the newspaper code must protect the editorial employees from exploitation, for "we have no labor organization to protect our interests."[19]

Even before the NRA legislation had been introduced in Congress, the hearings of a House of Representatives committee taking testimony on a bill limiting all industries involved in interstate commerce to a five-day, thirty-hour week in the hope of spreading employment had made clear to a number of newspapermen the necessity of having some kind of organization to protect their interests. On April 28, Congressman William P. Connery, Jr. (D.-Mass.), chairman of the committee, had interrupted the testimony of ITU representative Edward F. Cassidy to declare that "I have taken occasion to say to newspapermen, such as we have here today [reporting the hearings], that if they had the kind of organization among their reporters that you have, the publisher could not fire them and could not cut their wages twenty-five percent without any say on their part. . . ." On May 4, at the conclusion of a forceful presentation by a publishers' spokesman of their views, Connery demonstrated the validity of his statement with respect to yet another area—federal regulation of newspapermen's hours and wages—when he declared that the bill did not apply to reporters and that he accepted the publishers' contention that newspapermen are specialists impossible to include in any general legislation. Only a few newspapermen were aware of these statements, but for them, according to one historian of the ANG's early days, "the unopposed exposition of the publishers' point of view made them [i.e., the editorial employees] acutely aware that their story was not being told at all . . . [and] made the need for editorial employee organization . . . obvious."[20]

The newspaper code negotiations received much more publicity than had the thirty-hour-week bill hearings, and many editorial employees—dissatisfied with their treatment under the temporary code—determined to take action so that the final newspaper code would not neglect them. The more energetic of the newsmen decided to take advantage of the provisions in the NRA code-making process which allowed all interested parties to state their objections or offer their own proposals at the public hearings held before the completion of each final code. The desire to have a say at the hearings and in the negotiations that would follow initially motivated most of the newspapermen who became involved in organizational activities during the late summer and early autumn of 1933, but a goodly number had other aims. Some newspapermen, in addition to establishing a body which would deal with NRA, wanted to create a professional society, similar to the medical and bar associations, which would not only improve conditions economically but also set up professional standards, thereby gaining respect for their craft. Some planned to utilize the general unrest among editorial employees to develop a trade union which, using tactics similar to those of the mechanical workers' unions, would improve hours, wages, and working conditions. Some hoped that the editorial workers, once organized, would free the press from the restricting influences of advertisers and politicians. A few, subservient to Communist discipline, schemed to use the newly formed groups for the party's political ends.

On newspapers across the country, editorial employees banded together. In many localities, editorial departments joined forces on a city-wide or multi-newspaper basis. However, traditional newspaper rivalries persisted in some areas and, despite the shared antagonism to the publishers' actions, the editorial staffs of competing dailies organized independently of each other. The rapid multiplication of these groups made it impossible for all of them to present their views, and representatives from a few of the larger, better organized groups came to be considered spokesmen for all. Until December, 1933, although almost no formal organization existed beyond the local level, some newspapermen, already organized, advised or assisted others nearby, and some of the groups distant from one another exchanged ideas and information through correspondence. In these activities the New York City editorial employees' organization—correctly described by one writer as "the heart of the movement that by the end of 1933 had burgeoned into the American Newspaper Guild"—played an increasingly important role because of its large membership, because of its contacts in the Roosevelt administration, and because of the outspokenness of its leaders, especially Heywood Broun.[21]

By any standard Broun must be considered a most unlikely figure to have become the moving force behind a national editorial employees organization. Described in a *Nation* profile as "a natural and prominent habitue of the theatrical and journalistic Bohemia whose capital was the Algonquin Hotel," Broun was at the time one of the most widely read and highly paid syndicated newspaper columnists in America. Newspapermen generally admired his talents and respected the man despite his idiosyncracies. A hulk of a man, pugnacious and sentimental, lazy, amiable, extremely afraid of death, capable of great compassion and excessive generosity, overly fond of good food and drink, Broun—whose personal sloppiness and sartorial defects once had cause his appearance to be likened by Alexander Woollcott to that of "an unmade bed"—drifted into being a columnist after a short but varied career that had run the gamut of newspaper work. His experience included some straight news reporting, sports writing, drama criticism, book reviewing, and a brief turn overseas in 1918 as a war correspondent with the A.E.F. After his participation in the final attempt to save Sacco and Vanzetti from the electric chair in 1927, Broun, who like most of the Algonquin crowd had been liberal in a generalized sense, moved steadily leftward politically. By 1933 his column, "It Seems to Me," once noted for its bonhomie, increasingly dealt with economic and social issues. This many-faceted, complex man was aptly characterized by one of his contemporaries: "He wasn't a Communist, he wasn't a slob, he wasn't a drunk—he was simply Broun."[22]

In his column of August 7, 1933, Broun, then 44 and at the height of his powers and popularity, called for "A Union of Reporters."[23] He disparaged the newspapermen's traditional individualism as unrewarding and criticized the publishers' code for classifying editorial employees as professionals not subject to maximum-hour regulations. Broun admitted that he had little to fear from his employers in calling for the formation of an editorial workers' union because "fortunately columnists do not get fired very frequently." He also acknowledged that he had no complaints about his working hours, for "no matter how short they make the working day it will still be a good deal longer than the time required to complete this stint." Nor did Broun find it easy to accept in the newspaper business "the conception of the boss and his wage slaves," since among his many bosses there had been "not a Legree in the lot." But, he said, the sight of other newspapermen "working too hard" made him feel "self-conscious" and the thought of the many newspapermen "not working at all" embarrassed him even more. Broun believed that the time had come to organize a newspaper writers' union. And he concluded with the declaration that "beginning at nine o'clock on the morning of October 1, I am going to do the best I can to help in getting one up."

It is difficult to gauge just how much of a change in Broun's thinking this column represented, although there can be no doubt that it reflected a shift from his previous attitudes. Broun had done little more for the New York Presswriters Union of the early 1920s than serve as a name on a letterhead. Only 18 months before the publication of this column, he had ignored an appeal to lead the editorial workers of the country in a fight for their rights. In February, 1932, *Newsdom*—a weekly trade paper which at the time maintained that editorial employees must organize and fight "to protect their jobs" or "be nothing but alot of doormats for publishers to step on"—addressed an editorial open letter to Broun asking him to lead the fight.[24] In what proved to be a very accurate prediction, the open letter declared that Broun "in that city room which stretches from coast to coast . . . [would] find a public that's ready to listen . . . and perhaps to take heed." If Broun knew about the open letter, he did not react to it. Hyman Wishengrad, its author and then the managing editor of *Newsdom*, said that he never got any direct response from Broun.[25]

The immediate inspiration for Broun's column was the anticipated publication of the publishers' code, but what motivated Broun to call for a union remains a subject of some disagreement. Broun's friends and associates agree that he sincerely believed what he wrote in that column, but their interpretations of his motives for writing it vary considerably. Morris Watson, an early ANG "martyr," believes that Broun really wanted to help newspapermen better themselves but did not expect his column to be accepted at face value. Broun's secretary Luella Henkel has no doubts that Broun wanted to organize a union to obtain improved working conditions for the press. Doris Fleeson, a newspaperwoman who later assisted Broun in presenting the editorial employees' proposals to NRA, maintains that he wanted to do something for the newspapermen, whom, he feared, the code would neglect. Broun's attorney, Morris Ernst, questions whether the columnist realized immediately that he had committed himself. George Britt, an experienced reporter who in 1930 had collaborated with Broun on a study of discrimination against Jews in the United States, believes that Broun, becoming more and more committed to working for causes, at this time had assumed an "evangelical attitude" toward helping the editorial employees to improve their lot.[26] It seems to me in light of Broun's later actions in regard to the American Newspaper Guild that he acted on the spur of the moment and probably for a combination of all these reasons. His social awareness had increased greatly over the preceding few years; given his disappointment with the forthcoming code and his enormous emotional capacity, he probably decided that the time had come to do something and used his column, his most immediate avenue of expression.

Broun's column affected newspapermen across the country like a bugle call in the night. By the dozens, from Boston to Honolulu, they wrote to him outlining the newspaperman's depressed economic situation in their areas, stressing its seriousness, expressing agreement with Broun's criticisms of the publishers' code and with his intention to form a union. As knowledge of what Broun had said spread to cities whose newspapers did not subscribe to Broun's column, the number of letters to him increased steadily. Typical of his mail was the letter from H. B. Slocum of the *Schenectady Union-Star*, who wrote "just a word to tell you that your column . . . was a PIP. . . . I have read it several times as well as have the other boys here. . . . I can assure you that they heartily agree with you, in fact are tickled to death to see someone tell the story. . . ."[27]

The strong response to his column forced Broun to take action much earlier than October 1, but although he and other interested New York City newspapermen took a very active part in the negotiations for the final newspaper code, until mid-September, 1933, when a public meeting laid the basis for a Newspaper Guild of New York, the organizational initiative lay elsewhere. In fact, except for his August 7 column, Broun did not write again about NRA and the editorial workers until after the hearings on the final code, held September 22–23. Nevertheless, his August 7 column came to serve as a touchstone for many of the newspapermen's groups then being organized in various parts of the country.

During the week of the August 7 column, several groups of editorial employees in different parts of the country took steps to ensure that NRA would be informed of their point of view. In Rockford, Illinois, newspapermen held meetings to discuss ways of protecting their interests. The *Editor & Publisher* story that reported Broun's call for a union told in its concluding paragraph of newsmen in Texarkana, Arkansas, forming the Texarkana News Craft "as a means of obtaining a voice in the drafting of the NRA code for newspapers." No doubt hopeful that NRA's avowed aim of spreading employment would mean a shorter work day, the Texarkana News Craft sent telegrams to Johnson and other government officials asking that the final newspaper code be worded so as to spread employment among as many newspapermen as possible.[28]

In Philadelphia, and just across the Delaware River in Camden, New Jersey, within a few days after publication of the August 8 publishers' code some editorial employees had drawn up a set of counter-proposals that included a five-day, forty-hour week for almost all newspaper workers, an eight-hour work day except in emergencies, working schedules that banned staggered hours, compensation for overtime either by pay at time-and-a-third or by time off equal to the extra duty, and "restoration of pay cuts" (which on some newspapers in the two cities had reduced salaries almost 25 percent) as soon as possible. These proposals originated with a few staff members of the Philadelphia *Record*, whose owner, J. David Stern, a self-styled "maverick" who within a year would become the first major publisher to sign a contract with a chapter of the American Newspaper Guild, gave tacit approval to his editorial workers' activities. At a meeting on August 13, representatives from the editorial departments of all the Philadelphia and Camden English-language dailies decided to present their proposals formally to NRA with the recommendation that they become "an integral part" of any newspaper code. Before being presented at the NRA hearings on the final code, these proposals, representative of the aspirations of most American editorial workers, had been endorsed by more than 200 Philadelphia and Camden newspapermen (a majority of the editorial employees in the two cities). However, some publishers in the area already had exhibited the intense opposition that most American editorial workers would face in the next few years as they attempted in concert to improve their situation; at some of the Philadelphia and Camden newspapers, management pressure, despite public statements to the contrary, resulted in few or no signatures being collected in the editorial departments of these dailies. For example, according to Andrew M. Parker, a *Record* newsman who had been the driving force behind these proposals and who had been authorized to act as spokesman for the newspapermen supporting them, "at the *Evening Bulletin* . . . orders came from the top 'No Signature' [and] the men in fright destroyed the lists already made. . . ." Although the "Philadelphia code" received considerable support in the two cities, attempts then to organize on any sort of permanent basis had little success. Before the late September NRA hearings on the code took place, two organizational meetings had been called and both times only about a dozen newspaper-men attended; no formal organization would be achieved in Philadelphia and Camden until early December.[29]

In Cleveland some newspapermen, believing that publishers' proposals would not extend many benefits to the working press and desiring to back up any protest with the force of numbers, in the first weeks of August undertook to bring together the city's editorial workers for joint action. The resulting Cleveland Editorial Employees Association marks the formal start of the American Newspaper Guild, and after the December 1933 founding convention the officers of the newly established ANG designated the Cleveland group Chapter I.

The organization of the Cleveland newsmen, the beginnings of which antedate Broun's column by a few days, received its impetus from the efforts made by Garland Ashcraft, a well-paid rewrite man and general assignment reporter on the Scripps-Howard *Cleveland Press*, to marshal some kind of protest against a publisher code. Ashcraft, a veteran newsman long since disabused of any notions about the romance of newspapering, had begun agitating among his fellow editorial workers on the *Press*, urging that something be done to protect the newspaperman's economic rights. He found a receptive audience in the *Press* editorial staff, for, as Robert Bordner, then an art editor and copy reader on the *Press*, recalls, "we were good and sore about the possibility of being left out in the cold."[30]

On August 2, some of the *Press* staff, including Ashcraft, Bordner, and labor editor Lloyd White, chipped in a dollar each to send a telegram to Johnson. This wire, apparently signed by Ashcraft alone, though some of the other participants are not sure of this, criticized the publishers for "welching on NRA," said editorial workers should have a five-day, forty-hour work week, and asked that NRA not neglect the working press. The next day, according to Ashcraft, "all the editorial rooms in town were buzzing" about the sending of the wire, and "men discussed the matter on assignment." That night a handful of newsmen from the *Press* and a few from the *Cleveland News* met in the apartment of John Goski, a *Press* photographer. At this meeting, the first of almost nightly discussions for the next two-and-a-half weeks, the newsmen considered ways of drawing NRA's attention to their wants. One of the ideas put forward was unionization. Within a few days, other editorial workers from the *Press* and the *News* as well as some from the *Plain Dealer*, which had the most conservative editorial staff of Cleveland's three English-language dailies, had begun participating in these meetings. At this stage, the organizers of these discussions virtually ignored the editorial workers employed by the foreign-language newspapers and the press associations. When the meetings grew too large for Goski's apartment, the newsmen met elsewhere, often in speakeasies.[31]

Realizing the ineffectiveness of long-distance protest no matter how many newsmen sent or signed telegrams, Ashcraft at these nocturnal meetings urged that Cleveland newspapermen send an attorney to the forthcoming final code hearings who would not only protest the publishers' code but also present the editorial employees' views. Ashcraft would have liked to have gone further and called for immediate formation of a union, but, according to one participant in many of these discussions, Ashcraft "said nothing . . . apparently because he believed that it was premature and that the effort might die aborning."[32]

Petitions authorizing an attorney to speak for the signers had been circulating for a few days when, on August 15 at a small dinner meeting, I. L. Kenen, a political writer for the *News*, declared that no further time should be wasted on petitions. He put forward the idea (which had been proposed and dropped earlier) that on the following Sunday, five days later, a mass meeting of all the interested newspapermen in town be called in order to form a union which would strive to obtain better working conditions for editorial employees as well as serve to protect them from unfair treatment by the NRA code. That afternoon he had outlined his proposal to an old associate, Ralph J. Donaldson, a veteran political writer for the *Plain Dealer* who earlier had discussed with Kenen the possibility of forming a newsmen's organization. Donaldson thought it "probable" that the majority of the *Plain Dealer*'s editorial employees would "go along" with the union idea. Kenen got a much warmer response from the dinner group, which included Ashcraft; Goski; Elmer Fehlhaber, another political writer for the *News*; A. L. Roberts, assistant city editor of the *News*; and three or four others. According to Kenen, they all went along with his proposal and "talked about the name and other details . . . [and decided] to call it an association, since the word union might repel some of the more conservative men." Lloyd White recalls some discussion of the word "guild," but that term "was discarded as too fancy." In the next few days this little group (augmented by a few others) personally sounded out enough Cleveland newspapermen to be sure that a mass meeting would have a broad base of attendance; and the meeting was set for Sunday afternoon, August 20, in the auditorium of the Hollenden Hotel. Nine men signed the call for the meeting: John Haas, Frank O'Neil, and Roberts from the *News*; Donaldson, W. G. Lavalle, and Chad Skinner from the *Plain Dealer*; and Ashcraft, Goski, and White from the *Press*.[33]

It took considerable courage for these newsmen to act as they did. In 1933 news-paper jobs were very scarce and the men involved in organizing the Cleveland editorial workers had no job protection whatsoever; as Robert Bordner points out, "nobody knew whether the axe would fall. . . ." The *Press* management, noted for its generally liberal editorial stance, had reacted in ambiguous fashion to so simple an action as the sending of the wire to Johnson. Almost immediately after its dispatch, its contents had become known to Louis Seltzer, the editor of the *Press*; his brother, a news assistant who happened to be in the city room when the message was typed out, brought him a carbon copy. Late that night the editor called Ashcraft, whom he considered the prime instiga-tor, berated him for blackening the good name of the Press, and told him to report to the front office first thing in the morning. The next day when Ashcraft went to see Seltzer, rumors of dire consequences for the newsman spread through the *Press* city room, but nothing happened. Ashcraft remembers that he and Seltzer chatted about working conditions and that the editor told him that he had thought the matter over and had decided the whole affair might just as well be forgotten. This incident seems to have had a double effect: encouraging some to act, instilling fear in others. Certainly this fear partially accounts for the fact that only about a third of the editorial workers employed by the city's three dailies attended the August 20 meeting.[34]

Each of the 102 newsmen present at the Hollenden Hotel that afternoon received a copy of the manifesto "For Your Information," which had been mimeographed secretly by the organizers of the meeting on the advertising department machines of the *Press*. This manifesto, after outlining many of the editorial employees' grievances, argued that "it is now time that local room staffs start living and working for something more than the by-line and the pat-on-the-back. NRA holds out . . . [the] first bonafide opportunity to go after realities." The manifesto concluded by enumerating the meeting's aims: (1) a "free and frank discussion" of the general situation of Cleveland newspapermen; (2) a "vote on the question: SHALL WE ORGANIZE?"; (3) should the vote be favorable, the granting of authority to a committee "to study the problem, [and to] draft alternate plans of organization." The meeting's organizers also wanted approval for a plan "to present at the next meeting alternate proposals whereby we should present our side of the code proposition at the final hearings. . . ." In a session that lasted about an hour—including speeches by White (discussing NRA and the newsmen), Ashcraft (outlining what he considered the victimization of newspapermen by publishers), and Kenen (expressing the need for a union)—the assembled newsmen, without so much as a word of dissent, voted unanimously in favor of a motion made by Kenen which embodied the manifesto's proposals and which called for the formation of a Cleveland Editorial Employees Association. The nine-man committee which had signed the call for the meeting was authorized to present at another mass meeting set for the following Sunday afternoon a constitution and bylaws for such an association.[35]

Heywood Broun's August 7 column urging that reporters form a union had helped mobilize the necessary support for such an organization as the Association. Thomas Q. Lempertz, then on the *Plain Dealer* staff, wrote Broun a few months later that "the bulletin board in the news room was plastered with your . . . wisecracks aimed at the publishers. . . . In the case of the *Plain Dealer* I KNOW that your word carried a great deal of influence." Kenen believes that Broun's column stirred up a great many Cleveland newspapermen and made them suddenly very conscious of their situation. Roberts, immediately after the August 20 meeting at which he presided, sent Broun a telegram that concluded, "UNKNOWN WHAT OTHER CITIES DOING BUT HOPE TO TAKE LEAD AND HOPE YOU WILL TOO STOP THIS WIRE MAKES YOU INTERNATIONAL PRESIDENT PRO TEM. . . ." In an air-mail letter sent that night, Roberts outlined for Broun in greater detail what happened at the meeting, asked him to come to Cleveland (all expenses paid) to address a gathering of newsmen the following Sunday, and told the columnist that "Cleveland editorial men appreciate your efforts and expressions on behalf of the local staffs of the country. You offered us leadership. . . . You called. We're answering 'present'." And after announcing once again to Broun that "so far as we are concerned you are already our international president," Roberts ended with the declaration that "the Cleveland Boys are behind you."[36] The Cleveland newsmen received an encouraging reply from Broun.

The next meeting, held on the afternoon of August 27 at the Hollenden Hotel, drew 112 newspapermen and brought the Cleveland Editorial Employees Association into formal existence. The constitution and bylaws provided for three chapters, one from each daily. All editorial employees of the three dailies were eligible for membership except managing editors, editors in chief, and "those performing the same duties but under other titles."[37] No provision was made for membership of Cleveland editorial workers not employed by the *News*, the *Plain Dealer*, or the *Press*. Every chapter elected three members to the executive committee from which the membership in a general meeting would choose by secret ballot a president, a vice president-treasurer, and a secretary, no more than one officer coming from a single chapter. Each chapter would carry on its own bargaining, although members also could negotiate as individuals if they so desired. As outlined in the constitution, the purposes of the Association were twofold: "to preserve and protect the economic and professional interests of the membership through collective bargaining" and other means, and to "establish and enforce standards of ethics and craftsmanship" among the members. The word "strike" appeared nowhere, but the bylaws did say that no employee could be called upon by the Association "to withhold his services" from his newspaper unless his chapter approved such action by a majority vote. Should such withholding of services become necessary (either because of a strike or a lockout) however, it was stipulated that Association members upon pain of expulsion not give "moral, financial, or professional assistance to the employer in question." To prevent domination of the Association by persons controlling editorial jobs or assignments, any editorial worker "who in his employment has authority over three or more persons" was barred from all executive positions. The constitution did not provide much of an independent financial base for the Association; it set the initiation fee at $.50, called for $.20 monthly dues, and provided that special assessments could be levied only by a two-thirds vote of the whole Association membership.

The cult of the individual, as well as traditional rivalries between editorial staffs, died hard in the newspaper business and the Cleveland Association's constitution and bylaws reflected this, as would the working rules of many of the other editorial workers' groups that sprang up in 1933. Though the Association's constitution and bylaws created neither a powerful nor a militant organization, stormy arguments—both in the committee sessions and at the August 27 mass meeting—marked their drafting and adoption. And within three weeks, except for a few men, the *Plain Dealer* workers had decided to go it alone as the Plain Dealer Editorial Employee Association. Ideological and personal differences, exploited to some extent by the *Plain Dealer* management, had led to the quick destruction of the unusual, new-found unity of the Cleveland newspapermen. The differences which plagued the Cleveland Association, centering on divergences of opinion about the aims, methods, and extent of organization, also proved to be stumbling blocks for many other local newsmen's groups, both those which came into being in 1933 and those established thereafter.[38]

The majority of the *Plain Dealer* editorial staff had shown only slight interest in the drive for a five-day, forty-hour week and the proposal for continued agitation against a publishers' code. As one of their number said, "our chief object was to provide a mechanism for collective action on general wage increases or reductions." During the first week of September the managements of the *Plain Dealer* and the *News* restored much of the wage cuts their newspapermen had suffered, and on the *Plain Dealer* discontent and unrest decreased greatly. Moreover, most of the *Plain Dealer* editorial staff considered themselves professionals and, as self-styled gentlemen of the press, cared little for the idea of developing a union. On the other hand, the organizers of the Association from the *Press* and *News* had in mind more than just a professional society which had no economic purpose beyond a limited interest in wages. Ashcraft wanted a strong organization which would be "a broad craft proposition." Bordner hoped to set up "a vertical form of organization for all newspaper workers," including the business, circulation, and advertising departments. Even White, one of the least radical of the original organizers and a man interested only in "obtaining the possible," thought in terms of a union.[39]

The leaders of the *Plain Dealer* chapter, having failed to get their own way at the sessions of the committee drafting the constitution and bylaws, tried at the August 27 meeting and at another one on September 2 to have the Association accept their ideas. Both times they proposed constitutional amendments which would have transformed the new organization into three separate groups, loosely federated and not economically oriented; at both meetings the assembled membership voted down the amendments. Realizing the danger to the Association posed by the dissension these *Plain Dealer* proposals represented, Kenen, White, and a few others had attempted to work out some form of compromise. They failed, but they did manage to keep the *Plain Dealer* chapter from withdrawing from the Association until September 10. That afternoon at an acrimonious general membership meeting whatever chance there had been for unity among the Cleveland newsmen was destroyed. The quick-tempered Ashcraft, who resented the attempts to placate the *Plain Dealer* newsmen because he believed that this would undermine the Association, scotched a possible settlement when he accused Donaldson of being a company stooge. Donaldson retorted in equally bitter language. Insults flew back and forth, and more newspapermen became involved in the argument. Finally, most of the *Plain Dealer* newsmen walked out, and at a caucus three days later they determined that their chapter should become an independent organization.[40]

The meeting resumed after the walk-out of the *Plain Dealer* newsmen, and officers were elected. White was chosen president, major factors in his selection being his trade-union experience and his knowledge of NRA's labor policies. Most of the Association membership had at best a rudimentary understanding of the management and functions of a collective bargaining association. Accordingly, they voted for White, a former journeyman printer and ITU member who had worked his way through college in the printing trades and who as labor editor of the *Press* had kept well informed about the relationships between NRA and labor.

The managements of the three Cleveland dailies had not yet taken any strong public stand on the activities of their editorial workers. Seltzer's outburst aside, the only important public reaction by a representative of management was a statement by Paul Bellamy, editor of the *Plain Dealer* and president of the American Society of Newspaper Editors (ASNE). He said that under NRA the newspapermen had a guaranteed right to organization and that he, for one, hoped that some good would come of it. Bellamy's statement notwithstanding, the Association's organizers believed that he and other front-office officials on the three newspapers worked against them, for instance influencing the *Plain Dealer* editorial workers in their divisive stand.[41]

Despite the division among the editorial workers on Cleveland's three English-language dailies, the Association grew rapidly and continued its activities unabated. By mid-October it had more than 200 members (102 out of 104 *News* and 104 out of 107 *Press* editorial employees having signed membership cards) and had begun making arrangements to take in feature syndicate and press association writers working in Cleveland as well as the editorial employees staffing the area's foreign-language and suburban newspapers. As early as August 27, information had been supplied by members of the Association to a Cincinnati newsman who had written for advice on how to proceed with organization, and he was but the first of many who wrote and received assistance; the Association, using newspaper office supplies and machines, mimeographed its constitution and other materials, which were sent out in reply to the numerous inquiries it received. In the following two months the Cleveland newsmen, accurately described by White as "furious letter writers," contacted friends and acquaintances across the country in a drive to interest them in organization; this letter writing campaign received an enormous boost from the fact that the *Press* served as a training ground for the Scripps-Howard chain and that former *Press* editorial staffers could be found in widely scattered newspaper offices. Also, representatives from the Cleveland Association went to Akron, Columbus, Toledo, and Youngstown, Ohio, and to Rockford, Illinois, helping newspapermen there to organize. Moreover, the Association sent two spokesmen to Washington, D.C., to participate in the September hearings by

NRA on the final newspaper code; the proposals they presented differed little from the code drawn up by the Philadelphia newsmen.[42]

Although the Cleveland group made very important contributions to the creation of the American Newspaper Guild, the major effort came from the New York City editorial workers, then perfecting their own organization. For several reasons the organizational idea enjoyed greater success in that city than elsewhere. The goal of most newspapermen, New York attracted a larger proportion of intelligent and energetic newsmen capable of developing an idea into reality. Also the size of the editorial working force necessary to produce the many dailies then published in New York meant that the organizers of the city's newsmen, though faced with some extra organizational problems because of sheer numbers, had a larger core of articulate and militant newspapermen to build on. In addition, this size assured the organizers that, with any success at all, they would have considerable support both in numbers and in funds (from dues). There is some indication, furthermore, that prior to 1933 many New York newsmen had contemplated organization as a solution to their economic woes. An English correspondent who had been stationed in New York for many years—during a talk in 1929 to the American Society of Newspaper Editors on the British Institute of Journalists— told the assembled editors that, based on his New York experiences, if conditions of newspaper employment did not improve, newsmen would organize to help themselves.[43] In early 1932 *Newsdom*'s bitter stories and editorials about the plight of newspapermen (which had concluded with the publication of the open letter to Broun) evoked strong reactions from New York editorial workers. One, who summed up the general tenor of the correspondence *Newsdom* received on this issue, wrote: "Allow me to suggest a constructive measure you could advance . . . unionizing the city rooms and other editorial rooms of newspapers. . . . I am not suggesting anything drastic. The important thing right now is the creation of an organization."[44] Finally, New York City was the home base of Broun, and he gave generously of his time and money, badgered his friends and contacts, and lent his prestige to the cause.

Immediately after publication of his August 7 column calling for a union of reporters, Broun told an interviewer that he was really "very serious" about the matter and was thinking over the best way to proceed. He added that he had chosen October 1 as the target date for the beginning of the organization drive because he wanted to wait until the New York City election had been held so that he would not have to divide his time between politics (he supported La Guardia) and organization work.[45] Seeing that election day in 1933 was November 7 and that La Guardia did not have to run in the September primaries, why Broun chose October 1 remains a mystery that even his closest associates could not explain.[46] In any event, the October date almost immediately became meaningless because Broun began holding at his home informal meetings which had the dual purpose of drawing up some kind of protest to the publishers' code and laying the groundwork for an organization to better newsmen's working conditions. No doubt, one reason for Broun's disregard of the October date he had set was the enthusiastic response his column engendered. Another reason lies in the character of Broun himself. A man of great enthusiasms, he could not wait that long to test his ideas. As Leon Svirsky, at that time a colleague of Broun on the *World-Telegram*, has suggested, the columnist could not resist talking about a union or a protest against the publishers' code, finding out who would support him, how this would be done.[47]

The precise date of the first of these meetings cannot be determined. On September 15, 1933, Broun told *Editor & Publisher* that meetings had been held during the past four or five weeks. George Britt remembers that Broun asked him to the first meeting, which took place a few days after Britt's return to New York on August 10 from a reporting trip abroad. Morris Ernst, who attended a few of the meetings, recalls only that some took place in mid-August. On the reverse side of Roberts' August 20 telegram to Broun informing him about organization in Cleveland, the columnist's secretary Luella Henkel had jotted down in shorthand the basis for the reply Broun wanted sent, which indicated that at a meeting on August 23 an attempt would be made to establish some form of temporary organization in New York City.[48] From these shorthand jottings it can be inferred that some meetings had been held earlier to lay the groundwork for this action.

Confusion also exists about who attended these early meetings in Broun's apartment and how many took place. Any written records that might have existed seem to have disappeared, and memories have faded, often resulting in conflicting recollections of who was there and precisely what was said. Myths have grown up about these meetings and the number of newsmen who claim to have attended has become legion. Wilbur E. Bade, a former ANG official, has commented sarcastically: "There were 5,000 [at those meetings] . . . counting all the guys I've heard say they attended." The composition of the group varied from meeting to meeting. Conflicting assignments, vacations, and occasional trepidation caused a considerable turnover. Altogether, according to Carl Randau, one-time president of the New York Guild, some fifty men and women attended at least one session at Broun's. Among those who are remembered by more than one participant as having taken part in at least one of these meetings were some of the city's most respected editorial workers, including Edward Angly, George Britt, Jonathan Eddy, Doris Fleeson, Lewis Gannett, James Kieran, Joseph Lilly, Carl Randau, Allen Raymond, Leon Svirsky, and Morris Watson. From all available accounts, it seems that four or five meetings were held at Broun's home.[49]

These evening meetings took place in the columnist's cluttered, book-lined study, a not overly large room which could accommodate about 15 to 18 people comfortably. To the first meeting Broun invited not more than ten people, chosen because he knew them well, most of whom were editorial workers of some prominence. Discussion focused less on establishing a union than on obtaining a fair shake from NRA for newspapermen. At the end of the evening, Broun suggested that each of those interested in what had been discussed return a week later with two or three others from his newspaper who might help in the formulation of plans. The tenor of the meetings was very informal; some participants sat on the floor, others sprawled on available furniture. Broun would broach his ideas, asking "will you come along"; others outlined their points of view. Although there was general agreement that action must be taken to protest the inequities of the publishers' code and the general policy of the publishers, even at this embryonic stage there existed among these few newspaper workers a sharp division of opinion about whether any prospective organization should be a union or a more exclusive professional association with limited aims. Doris Fleeson remarked a short time later that "we debated prayerfully whether our pallid infant organization should be named guild, union, or institute." Some suggested that the word union might be too strong, and finally the little group settled on the term guild as a compromise name that would reconcile the differing schools of thought. The full title decided on was Guild of New York Newspaper Men and Women. Precisely who first suggested the use of the word guild is not known. Without presenting any kind of documentation, Broun's biographer claims the honor for him. Lewis Gannett believes that a *New York*

Times newsman first proposed using the term, and Lloyd White recalls being told that Edward Angly of the *Herald Tribune* had suggested the name. Others recall various persons introducing the word at several meetings.[50]

There was little of the conspiratorial about these meetings; although fear of the publishers existed, the evening gatherings were by no means a tightly held secret. Knowledge about them spread by word-of-mouth to the offices of all newspapers in the city. According to some reports, more than 200 New York City editorial workers had endorsed the guild's program before its first formal organization session. This program, developed by the guild's organizers, differed from the stated aims of the Cleveland and Philadelphia newsmen only in that it was more ambitious. As outlined in a flier distributed before the first mass meeting, it called for: (1) a five-day, forty-hour week with consecutive days off; (2) paid vacations; (3) a minimum wage of at least $35 a week to newsmen who had one year or more newspaper experience; and (4) dismissal notice on a graduated basis (ranging from one month's notice for newsmen with three years' service on the same newspaper to six months for those with eight or more years' service). The program also took into account a more important future role for the guild in demanding the elimination of Section 14 in the temporary newspaper code, which stated that contract bargaining between newsman and publisher "free from the interference of any third party shall not be affected by this code" and that nothing in the code would necessitate that an employee must "join any organization or refrain from joining . . . in order to secure or obtain employment."[51]

On September 7 NRA had announced that hearings on the final newspaper code probably would begin September 22. Broun and his colleagues decided to call a general meeting of the city's newsmen, believing that the time had come to mass support publicly for their program. On September 14, notices on New York City newspaper bulletin boards announced that on Sunday night, the 17th, at 10 p.m. there would be an open meeting at the City Club to consider a code for newspapers and to select a committee to go to the NRA hearings to oppose certain provisions of the publishers' code.[52]

About 300 attended the meeting, chaired by Joseph Lilly, a respected *World-Telegram* reporter. Lilly defined the objectives of the gathering, adding cautiously that "we are not meeting in any hostility to publishers." The other speakers at the meeting concerned themselves principally with the newspaper code. Broun, introduced as "the only person connected with a New York newspaper who had the courage to start this thing," attacked the publishers' code and urged cooperation with newsmen elsewhere who planned to send representatives to the hearings. Paul Y. Anderson, an outspoken critic of the publishers' code, answered questions about NRA and the newspapermen. He said that newsmen need not be afraid of prosecuting their interests at the hearings because "the law protects you, [and] if anyone attempts to punish you he is going to have a lot of trouble." Anderson's attitude can be summed up by his statement that "the people who holler the loudest are going to get the most." Edward Angly briefly outlined the deliberations that had gone into the drafting of the program. W. Ian Mack, a *World-Telegram* financial writer, concluded the evening's planned oratory with a description of the operations of the Scranton Newswriters Union.[53]

Even though it was a sultry night, discussion in the crowded meeting room lasted well past midnight. Although many spoke, little argument took place. "Few hints were heard that night," recalled Kenneth Stewart, "of the sharp differences that would split us later, the political charges and countercharges, the personal antagonisms." The editorial workers who attended the meeting generally shared the same vague feelings about the

announced objectives, and the question of tactics (which soon proved to be an important divisive factor) received very little attention. Unsure of the publishers' reaction to
their activity, the newspapermen decided, in order to avoid possible retribution, that,
except for the organizers, speakers did not have to state their names or newspaper
affiliations. Before the gathering adjourned, Angly, Broun, Fleeson, and Lilly were
selected to serve on a committee that would represent the New York newspapermen
at the NRA hearings. Disagreement about who should be the fifth member led the
assembled newsmen to give the committee the power to decide this; after the meeting
the committee enlarged its number by including Morris Watson, an Associated Press
correspondent; James Kieran, a *Times* reporter with ties to President Roosevelt; and
Francis Emery, a *Brooklyn Eagle* newsman. The meeting also empowered the committee
to serve as a steering group in the formation of a permanent organization. Morris Ernst,
Broun's friend and attorney and a very active, tough-minded liberal lawyer, was chosen
at the meeting to serve as the committee's legal adviser. The assembled newsmen also
passed by an overwhelming margin two resolutions. One assessed all present a dollar each
to help defray the expenses of the committee's trip to Washington. The other praised
the *Daily News* and the *World-Telegram* for going beyond the letter of the temporary
newspaper code and extending additional benefits to editorial workers.[54]

This September 17 meeting elicited little overt reaction from publishers. One told
Marlen Pew that the organization movement "makes just another publisher problem"
and that he had no objection to groups such as the New York Guild if organized
newsmen "would remain as free and loyal as they are as individuals."[55] His seeming
disinterest and lack of opposition obviously stemmed from the anticipation that the
guild and its counterparts in other cities, if they survived, would be little more than
social or fraternal organizations. The New York *Daily News* took a different tack. In a
lengthy editorial the newspaper admitted that it did not like the prospect of having to
deal collectively with its editorial workers. However, the editorial declared, given the
publishers' evasions and twisted interpretations of the code, the newspapermen could
not be blamed for organizing to protest actions contrary to the spirit of NRA.[56]

In general, from the time of the Cleveland Association's creation until just before
the NRA hearings, the publishers—if the trade press can at all be considered an accurate barometer of newspaper industry sentiment—had viewed the organization movement with considerable interest but with only a modicum of fear. The most important
trade publication of the newspaper industry, *Editor & Publisher*, stressed the editorial
employees' importance and declared that their protests had some justification. About
the Cleveland Association it said that "the association . . . has served salutary notice and
good may come of it." A month later it made a similar statement about the New York
Guild and the other editorial groups that had sprung up, adding that while it had
heard of no publisher resistance, the publishers evidently were divided on the question
of editorial organization. *The American Press*, which addressed itself principally to small-
town and rural newspapers, stressed a different point of view, one which received
considerable emphasis in the following months. In the magazine's September issue
(distributed about the middle of the month), a statement signed by editor Frank Parker
Stockbridge declared that everyone engaged in the business of journalism, from publisher to copy boy, could "without compromising a single principle or sacrificing their
dignity or importance subscribe to a program or organization on strictly professional
lines, having for its purpose the elevation of professional standards of competence and
ethics." Stockbridge concluded, however, by declaring that establishing a union would

be a distinct step backwards. *Newsdom*, New York oriented but nationally distributed, concentrated on explaining the evils of editorial unions and asserted in its September 9 issue that a good editorial worker did not need a union to protect him.[57]

An increasing number of editorial workers, however, believed it necessary to organize in some form. In the week just prior to the NRA hearings Newark newsmen (aided and strongly influenced by their New York colleagues) established the Guild for Newark Newspaper Men and Women, Buffalo editorial workers at a general meeting considered forming an association, and a group of Twin Cities reporters and desk men called a meeting for the purpose of organizing. During the first few days of September, the Rockford, Illinois, newspaper staffs (aided by representatives of the Cleveland group) had organized as the Rockford Editorial Employees Association. An *American Press* survey conducted by mail at the beginning of September, although limited in scope, gives some idea of how newsmen across the country at this time felt about organization and what they hoped to achieve. Of 500 replies to a questionnaire (which went to a cross-section varied enough to include a Philadelphia reporter, a Kansas City deskman, an Eastern publisher, and a New Jersey managing editor), 76 percent favored organization; of those opposed, two-thirds were either publishers or editors in chief. Almost every reporter or desk man responding wanted closer ties among editorial workers; 20 percent would have had journalists form a union, 40 percent preferred organization along professional lines, and the rest saw merit in a combination of these two methods. Only 4 percent of all those answering had any interest in an organization of newspaper workers that dealt solely with wages; 20 percent considered the securing of job tenure the most important objective an organization could have; 32 percent (a figure slightly higher than the percentage of executives in the sample) stressed the elevation of professional standards; the remainder held all three aims as goals of equal importance. Of all the newsmen polled, 60 percent firmly believed that their newspaper bosses would strongly oppose any movement to fix minimum salaries and maximum hours or to secure job tenure. Indications of the accuracy of this belief came almost immediately at the NRA hearings—the first real public confrontation of the publishers and representatives of the editorial workers.[58]

In effect the publishers brought about this open clash. Despite their editorial praise for NRA, many of them resisted its attempts to work out any but the loosest kind of code for the newspaper business. Pleading freedom of the press and tenaciously making use of all the power the industry commanded, the publishers' representatives succeeded in obtaining a temporary code replete with special concessions, a number of which disappointed editorial employees who had hoped it would result in improved working conditions. Although disappointed, the majority of editorial employees retained their faith in NRA, believing that if they presented a forceful enough case something would be done about the concessions before the code became final. Even before the temporary code's provisions had become known, in various areas some newspapermen— disconcerted by the attitude the publishers had displayed—discussed banding together. In advancing this course of action, which rarely envisioned organization on more than the local level, these newspapermen argued that an organized group would have a more powerful voice than a series of individuals. Brouns' column advocating a "union of reporters" accelerated the interest in organization albeit not exactly in the direction he had indicated. Comparatively few newspapermen had any real interest in a union; indeed, most of those who accepted the need for organization did so mainly because they thought it would lead to a code more beneficial to editorial workers. The old rivalries and myths lived on, often hampering organization, but by mid-September (after just a few weeks of organizational effort) editorial workers, most notably in Cleveland, on the local level had joined together as never before. Even if not quite ready, they stood willing to challenge at the NRA hearings on the final code the publishers, whose reluctance to give even a little had resulted in this confrontation.

Notes

1.   Stewart, *News Is What We Make It*, p. 133.
2.   Quoted in *Handbook of NRA Laws*, p. 1.
3.   *Ibid.*, p. 9.
4.   Schlesinger, Jr., *Coming of the New Deal*, pp. 98–102.
5.   Lyon et al., *National Recovery Administration*, p. 52.
6.   Johnson quoted in *Handbook of NRA Laws*, p. 276; Leuchtenburg, *Roosevelt and the New Deal*, p. 65.
7.   Boylan, "Daily Newspaper Business," p. 6; "Publishers Activities," ANPA *Bulletin*, XLVII (June 15, 1933), 372.
8.   Emery, *ANPA*, p. 224; "Newspapers and the N.R.A.," Chapter 2, *passim*; Burns, "Daily Newspapers," in *How Collective Bargaining Works*, p. 43.
9.   E&P, June 24, 1933, p. 26, July 15, p. 5; Johnson, *Blue Eagle*, p. 310.
10.   "Federal Laws," ANPA *Bulletin*, XLVII (July 21, 1933), 419; Boylan, "Daily Newspaper Business," p. 12.
11.   Quoted in E&P, July 29, 1933, p. 6; *Ibid.*, p. 20; Lee Drake to Fred Lamplin, Aug. 1, 1933, Lee Drake Papers, Box Two, Income and Expense Folder.
12.   Later, Charles R. Butler was added to the subcommittee. He was the publisher of the Mankato, Minn., *Free Press* and president of the Inland Daily Press Association, the oldest and largest of the regional publishers associations.
13.   Boylan, "Daily Newspaper Business," p. 12; "Newspapers and the NRA," Chapter 4, pp. 1–4; "Tribute to Elisha Hanson," ANPA *Bulletin*, LXXVII (May 9, 1962), 65; "Legal Ajax," *Literary Digest*, CXXI (Apr. 18, 1936), 45.
14.   Manning, "Johnson Says Labor Contracts Stand," E&P, Aug. 5, 1933, p. 7; Johnson, *Blue Eagle*, p. 213; NYT, Sept. 2, 1933, p. 2; Johnson quoted by Richberg in E&P, Nov. 18, 1933, p. 14; "National Industrial Recovery Act," ANPA *Bulletin*, XLVII (Aug. 10, 1933), 449–50.
15.   "Newspapers and the N.R.A.," Chapter 4, p. 8. Indicative of many publishers' attitudes is the reply to Johnson's outburst by Bryan, who asserted that conditions in the newspaper business were so different from those in manufacturing and commercial that the press required exceptional treatment. (*Ibid.*)
16.   Case, "History of the Code," pp. 4–8.
17.   Perry, "Codes for Dailies Filed at Washington," E&P, Aug. 12, 1933, p. 3; NYT, Aug. 9, 1933, p. 2; "Newspapers and the N.R.A.," Chapter 6, p. 8; Boylan, "Daily Newspaper Business," p. 20; Anderson, "Johnson and the Freedom of the Press," *Nation*, CXXXVII (Aug. 30, 1933), 235; "The Newspaper Code," ANPA *Bulletin*, XLVII (Aug. 16, 1933), 461; *Handbook of NRA Laws*, p. 326.
18.   NYT, July 29, 1933, p. 1, Aug. 1, p. 10, Aug. 2, p. 10, Aug. 4, p. 9.
19.   NYHT, Aug. 9, 1933, p. 17; Richard Cornish to Hugh Johnson, Aug. 8, 1933, A. F. Finestone to Johnson, July 26, 1933, NRA, Box 1931; Johnson, *Blue Eagle*, p. 308.
20.   U.S., Congress, House of Representatives, Committee on Labor, *Hearings on 30-Hour Week Bill*, pp. 203, 699; Moskin, "Origins of the American Newspaper Guild," pp. 23, 27.
21.   Moskin, "Origins of the American Newspaper Guild," p. 48.
22.   Marshall, "Columnists on Parade VII: Heywood Broun," *Nation*, CXLVII (May 21, 1937), 580; Kramer, *Heywood Broun*, passim; Woollcott quoted in Reynolds, *By Quentin Reynolds*, p. 34; Ashcraft, "25th Anniversary Notes."
23.   NYWT, Aug. 7, 1933, p. 21.

24. *Newsdom*, Jan. 9, 1932, p. 4, Feb. 6, p. 4. *Newsdom*, "edited and published by and for newspaper workers," began publishing on a weekly basis August 23, 1931, staffed mostly by former members of the New York *World* who helped to make it a trade weekly describing personal events in the business. For a while in 1931–32 it became a very strident recorder of the hard times New York newspapermen experienced, and attempted to defend their interests. Never financially secure, the newspaper by 1933 had come to depend heavily on the support of public utilities operator H. L. Doherty, who changed the staff and the format, and soon turned *Newsdom* into a more conservative, less comprehensive version of *Editor & Publisher*. The weekly survived Doherty's death in December, 1939, by less than a month.

25. Interview with Wishengrad, May 2, 1965. *Newsdom*'s very limited circulation made it doubtful that Broun saw it, yet it is hard to believe that nobody called his attention to this appeal. Moreover, at ANG headquarters in Washington, on the last page of a scrapbook of clippings by and about Broun, there is a copy of the *Newsdom* open letter. Alexander Crosby, who went through this and other Broun scrapbooks to cull the columns and stories that made up the Broun compilation published in 1935, doubts that Broun personally kept any scrapbook, though he knew about them. (Interview with Crosby, Oct. 12, 1965.) The person most likely to have kept the scrapbook, Luella Henkel, had no recollection of the *Newsdom* open letter. (Interview with Miss Henkel, Oct. 12, 1965.)

26. Interviews with Watson, Oct. 12, 1965, Miss Henkel, Oct. 12, 1965, Miss Fleeson, Aug. 2, 1965, Ernst, Oct. 8, 1965, and Britt, July 12, 1965.

27. H. B. Slocum to Heywood Broun, Aug. 9, 1933, ANG.

28. Lee, *Daily Newspaper*, p. 678; E&P, Aug. 12, 1933, p. 4.

29. E&P, Aug. 19, 1933, p. 6, Sept. 23, p. 37, Dec. 9, p. 16; Stern, *Memoirs*, p. 285; printed open letter to Johnson, dated Aug. 14, 1933, ANG; Moskin, "Origins of the American Newspaper Guild," p. 48; Andrew Parker to Heywood Broun, Aug. 17, 1933, ANG.

30. Interview with Bordner, June 14, 1965.

31. Interviews with Ashcraft, Oct. 20, 1965, White, Oct. 27, 1965, and Bordner, Oct. 28, 1965; Stolberg, *Story of the C.I.O.*, p. 246; Ashcraft, "Guild's First Chapter Takes a Bow," GR, Dec. 15, 1934, p. 10; "It Got Hot in '33," *Cleveland Newspaper Guild Page One Ball Year-book*, 1953, p. 9; Goski, "First Member of First Guild Unit Tells How and Why It Started," GR, Feb. 15, 1944, p. 7. Ashcraft—who says, contrary to what has been written in many articles and books, that none of these organization meetings took place in his home—also believes that many writers have given too much emphasis to the location of the speakeasy discussions (Ashcraft interview, Oct. 20, 1965).

32. I. L. Kenen, a founder of the CNG, to Clyde Beals, editor of GR, Aug. 21, 1938, p. 1 of a 16-page letter outlining the Guild's origins in Cleveland and elsewhere (hereafter referred to as Kenen to Beals), Kenen papers.

33. *Ibid.*, p. 2; letter from Lloyd White, July 18, 1966; Ashcraft, "Guild's First Chapter Takes a Bow," p. 10; interview with White, Oct. 27, 1965; E&P, Aug. 26, 1933, p. 6.

34. Bordner, "Another Footnote to Guild History," GR, Jan. 1, 1944, p. 5; interviews with White, Oct. 27, 1965, Bordner, Oct. 28, 1965, and Ashcraft, Oct. 20, 1965; Stolberg, *Story of the C.I.O.*, p. 246.

35. E&P, Aug. 26, 1933, p. 6; Kenen to Beals, pp. 3–5.

36. Thomas Lempertz to Heywood Broun, Oct. 9, 1933, A. L. Roberts to Broun, Aug. 20, 1933, ANG; interview with Kenen, Aug. 15, 1965.

37. Both quoted in full in E&P, Sept. 2, 1933, p. 9.

38. The differences, in fact, have never been completely resolved, and they remain a problem for the Newspaper Guild to this day even though after long and hard-fought debate its membership voted in 1937 to extend jurisdiction to include the business, advertising, and circulation departments as well as most other kinds of non-mechanical, non-editorial newspaper employees. An interesting exposition of these divergences of opinion appearing 25 years after they were voted on and supposedly settled is Bracker, "Dilemma of a Guild Reporter," *The Reporter*, XXVIII (Jan. 17, 1963), 31–4.

39. Porter, "Cleveland Newspapermen Split," *The American Press*, LII (Oct., 1933), 3; interviews with Bordner, June 14, 1965, and White, Oct. 27, 1965; Kenen to Beals, p. 11; Ashcraft, "Guild's First Chapter Takes a Bow," p. 10; Bordner, "Why We Organized," *The Quill*, XXI (Oct., 1933), 6.

40. Kenen to Beals, pp. 8–11; E&P, Sept. 7, 1933, p. 17, Sept. 16, p. 10; interviews with White, Oct. 27, 1965, Kenen, Aug. 15, 1965, and Bordner, Oct. 28, 1965; letter from Garland Ashcraft, Dec. 27, 1965.

41. Kenen to Beals, pp. 7–8; E&P, Aug. 26, 1933, p. 6.

42. E&P, Oct. 21, 1933, p. 18; interviews with White, May 24, 1966, and William Davy, first executive secretary of the CNG, May 29, 1966; "It Got Hot in '33," p. 10.

43. American Society of Newspaper Editors, *Problems of Journalism* (1929), p. 110.

44. Letter from Jonathan Edwards, *Newsdom*, Jan. 16, 1933, p. 5.

45. E&P, Aug. 12, 1933, p. 4.

46. No answer as to why Broun chose October 1 came from the people interviewed. An unsigned obituary in the ANG newspaper concluded that "whatever the reason Broun had . . . it is at present blurred." (GR, Jan. 1, 1940, p. 2.)

47. Interview with Leon Svirsky, Nov. 14, 1965.

48. E&P, Sept. 16, 1933, p. 42; interviews with Britt, Nov. 14, 1965, and Ernst, Oct. 8, 1965; A. L. Roberts to Heywood Broun, Aug. 20. 1933, ANG. Miss Henkel, who wrote and signed almost all of Broun's correspondence at this time, used a shorthand system of her own invention. She does not remember the meanings of all the symbols she used, and her transcription of the jottings reads: "We are having a meeting Wednesday night and will endeavor at that time to get up (?) some temporary New York organization. I am (all, also?) for such a movement." (Miss Henkel to author, Oct. 10, 1965.)

49. Bade quoted in Kramer, *Heywood Broun*, p. 145; Randau, "It Happened One Day in September 14 Years Ago," *Frontpage*, Sept.–Oct., 1947, p. 6.

50. Fleeson, "Our Guild," *The Matrix*, XIX (Apr., 1934), 5; interviews with Britt, July 12, 1965, Svirsky, Nov. 14, 1965, and Jonathan Eddy, first ANG Executive Secretary, Aug. 15, 1965; Gannett, "1933—When the Guild Was Very Young," GR, Dec. 26, 1958, p. M-4; Randau, "It Happened One Day"; letters from Morris Watson, Dec. 2, 1965, Lewis Gannett, May 24, 1965, and Lloyd White, July 20, 1966; Kramer, *Heywood Broun*, p. 245.

51. Perry, "New York News Writers Organize," E&P, Sept. 23, 1933, p. 7; Watson, "History Is Now Being Written Behind Nation's Front Pages," GR, Nov. 23, 1933, p. 1; Section 14 quoted in E&P, Aug. 19, 1933, p. 7.

52. E&P, Sept. 16, 1933, p. 42.

53. Perry, "New York News Writers Organize," 7; NYT, Sept. 18, 1933, p. 4.

54. Stewart, *News*, p. 132; Perry, "New York Writers Organize," 7, 42; Watson, "History," p. 1.

55. Quoted anonymously in Pew, "Shop Talk at Thirty," E&P, Sept. 23, 1933, p. 44.

56. New York *Daily News*, Sept. 19, 1933, p. 23. Captain Joseph Patterson had instituted the five-day, forty-hour week on his *Daily News* in 1932. Doris Fleeson, then a correspondent on that newspaper, believes that Patterson, whose sensational tabloid was constantly being attacked as scandalous by other newspapers, supported the editorial workers not only because he felt they deserved support but also because he enjoyed exposing the hypocrisy of the publishers who had been baiting him (interview with Miss Fleeson, Aug. 2, 1965).

57. E&P, Aug. 26, 1933, p. 30, Sept. 23, p. 24; Stockbridge, "A Question of Leadership," The *American Press*, LI (Sept., 1933), 1; "Editorial Union Evils," *Newsdom*, Sept. 9, 1933, p. 4.

58. E&P, Sept. 23, 1933, pp. 6, 37; E. N. Pomeroy to Broun, Sept. 21, 1933, Herman G. Nelson, secretary of the Rockford Editorial Employees Association, to Newspaper Guild of New York, Dec. 4, 1933, ANG; Stockbridge, "Professional Association or Trade Union," *The American Press*, LI (Sept., 1933), 1–2.

Chapter 28

DAN SCHILLER

DEMOCRACY AND THE NEWS

CRIME NEWS SERVED AS A CONCRETE indicator of the vitality of the principle of natural rights at a time of rising class tension. From the reports on the trial
of Richard Robinson for the murder of Helen Jewett to the sustained, broad coverage of
crime in the *National Police Gazette*, the young commercial newspapers continued to use
this test and its results to cultivate a new social role for themselves as the foremost
defender of the public good. The press owed most of its success in its new role to the
acceptance of natural rights—in particular, the right to property—by the recently
emergent public of journeymen and mechanics. Such acceptance lent the small papers
crucial leverage in their earliest years. *Before* the antagonism between capital and labor
took a modern form (*before* workers confronted capitalists as propertyless proletarians),
the penny press acted as an authentic, albeit a fundamentally self-interested, voice of the
artisan public.

Each New Year's Day, following a practice that reached back to the Colonies,
newspapers of the antebellum era published broadsheet addresses to their patrons.
These addresses might recapture important events of the past year, or present a more
general statement of principles. The second course was chosen by the Philadelphia
Public Ledger ("Address of the Carriers of the Public Ledger 1839"):

> How blest thy lot, to feel no bondage gall,
> No bigot's blighting breath, no despot's thrall!
> Whose laws, designed to fence the rights of man,
> Have ne'er been equalled since the world began!
>
> . . . .
> The press, designed for freedom's best defence,
> And learning, morals, wisdom to dispense,
> Perverted, poisoned, lost to honor's rules,
> Is made the sport of knaves, to govern fools.
>
> . . . .

Yet is this noble state by factions vexed,
On every side by demagogues perplexed.

. . . .

   How shall our city from these ills be freed?
How from this downward march of crime recede?
Sustain your laws! Let all their vengeance fall
On those who dare to mock them great or small.
No more rogues in ruffles flaunt secure,
While rogues in rags each penalty endure.

. . . .

We strike for right, and will not spare a blow,
In bold defiance still our ensign show;
All cliques, all sects, all parties we despise,
Above all partial motives proudly rise;
The laws our guide, the good of all our aim,
We yield no principles for transient fame.

With widening class divisions and the transformation of handicraft production, widespread hostility to elite mercantile and political papers found expression in an emergent labor press. The latter, an organizational forum for developing trade unions as well as for the education of the journeymen, did not, however; survive the hard times of the latter 1830s. In the interval between the founding and demise of the labor press, the commercial penny papers arose, boasting of their mass circulation and equating this with a successful defense of public good. If the journeymen complained of unjust monopolies in the three spheres of property, power, and knowledge, these penny papers spoke directly to their grievances. Against unjust concentration of power in the government, the commercial press poised itself as a watchdog in wait for corrupt judges, dishonest police, and venal officials. Against the pretensions to knowledge offered by the sixpenny press, the cheap papers offered "common sense," both popular and scientifically ordained. And, in regard to unjust monopolies of property, the penny press offered entrepreneurial equal rights and an unfocused suspicion of upper-class manners and airs combined with a steadfast commitment to individual property.

In support of its defense of public good, the cheap press invoked journalistic objectivity. It was able to do so successfully, indeed "naturally," because of the pervasive hold of science over the public imagination, a grip made firmer still by photographic realism. "Truth, public faith and science," to use Bennett's terms, commanded that the cheap papers prevail. With advertisers clamoring to take advantage of their exploding circulation, who could disagree?

Yet it is ironic that the American public sphere as it developed in these formative years was directed primarily at absolutist political domination and social privilege (cf. Hohendahl 1979:96–97). Monarchy and aristocracy were left behind forever in the War of Independence, but, in the 1830s, defense of natural rights, public good, and the republic appeared vital in halting a backslide into monarchy and special privilege. This legacy, as we have seen, suffused the young commercial press, especially the *Police Gazette*. It can be glimpsed everywhere: in railings against aristocracy, in hostility to vestiges of English monarchy, which had been smuggled illicitly into the law of the American republic, in generalized suspicion of arbitrary power, in the sustained focus on equal rights of opportunity—in politics, in the economy, and in the public sphere.

Objectivity invoked alongside and in support of natural rights became coextensive with resistance to encroachment by longstanding European corruptions. With its universalistic intent, its concern for public rationality based on equal access to the facts, objectivity harbored a profoundly democratic promise. From the 1830s the informational system was not to be the exclusive preserve of a king, a baron, a president, or a class but rather, as it seemed, of the political nation itself.

The *economic* nation was continuing on its course of dynamic change. The public of artisans was gradually destroyed. Factories moved from rural and suburban rivers into the heart of the city; an unskilled work-force, fed by immigrants hungry for work, was created. Changes in urban spatial organization and in the supervision of public order also contributed to a transformation of artisan culture that paralleled the transition to a more fully industrial capitalism. Throughout this complex process, the characteristic tensions of the penny press—between recognition of class as an intrusive force and adherence to individual property, between constant anxiety over "faithless power" and support of the American state—were decisively inclined toward the progressive strengthening of the hand of capital. Technological improvement of printing processes, an extraordinary increase in capital costs, the broadening of the division of labor, and the widening of the market all changed the social constitution of the newspaper and, indeed, of "the facts" themselves.[1]

Some of the main features of the commercial newspaper's emerging role may be briefly outlined. In general, *formal* equality of access to news reports came increasingly to mask *substantive inequality* in public access to information. Members of the public were free to read what was in the paper, but what was in the paper was not to be decided upon by the citizenry or its delegated representatives. Purported equality of access to news concealed, and left to the discretion of news-gathering organizations, the question of which facts would take the measure of the world each day. "Public opinion" began to conceal the unequal strengths of entities in the marketplace of ideas. Individuals who were largely barred from substantive decisions about news were lumped together with governmental and corporate institutions that exercised a direct and powerful interest in the same sphere. News quickly became a language of power, an idiom through which the correspondence between the public truth of events and the social power of their perpetrators was routinely renegotiated.

The tacit formalization of reporting that occurred beneath this veneer of universal facticity deserves brief mention. So that their articles would not " 'clash' and be contradictory," wrote W. Shanks of the *Herald* shortly after the Civil War, journalists should be " 'well trained,' and have learned by long intercourse the ideas, and caught something of the peculiar style, of the Editor-in-Chief" (1867:521). Outlining his strategy for achieving such uniformity, editor Henry Watterson bluntly confirmed that "two minds are better than one if they can be made to go the same way" (in Wingate 1875:22). The advantage of habitually "discussing matters with my subordinates," Watterson found, was that "they get, somehow, into my own way of thinking." On the job training was best in inculcating what was widely termed "the news sense." "To make proper and pleasing selections," wrote a Western journalist, "requires a rare tact, a sort of sixth sense, which is acquired only in the school of experience" (King 1871:9). Organizational imperatives thus substituted for independent professional expertise. By 1906 the author of a textbook for aspiring journalists could charge reporters generally to "cultivate the friendship of influential citizens" (McCarthy 1906:14) and point out matter-of-factly that "rank and social position add to the importance of news." "The mere killing of a mechanic or day laborer seldom gets more than a paragraph unless the circumstances are extraordinary," he intoned, "but if the King of England or the German Emperor falls down and fractures the royal ankle the incident is worthy of note and is considered a good story. It is easy to see why this is so" (ibid.:16). This indifference to certain social groups was not idiosyncratic: hierarchical news-gathering routines "mirrored" hierarchical social relations; the news net was cast, and a day's catch reflected reality as it had been defined by powerful social actors. New York *Sun* correspondent Julian Ralph mentioned a negotiation between a journalist and an important official, who together decided "to publish or not to publish, as the two agree" (Ralph 1903:184). He conceded that a "beat," as an exclusive news story was often called, was "growing to be more and more a product of intimate acquaintance with public men, and less and less a result of agility of mind and body" (ibid.:193). The simile Ralph chose to illumine the practices of contemporary journalists is striking:

> No one looks for news anymore. That is an old-fashioned idea which outsiders will persist in retaining. News is now gathered systematically by men stationed at all the outlets of it, like guards at the gate of a walled city, by whom nothing can pass in or out unnoticed. (Ibid.:10–11)

Ralph's confident acceptance that news had been definitively nailed down was congruent, paradoxically, with an enduring and prevalent journalistic belief in crude objectivity, or what Schudson (1978) labels "naive empiricism." "Make rules for news?" queried the official biographer of the New York *Sun*. "How is it possible to make a rule for something the value of which lies in the fact that it is the narrative of what never happened, in exactly the same way, before?" (O'Brien 1928:156). Editor Charles Dana believed that "whatever the divine Providence permitted to occur I was not too proud to report" (1895:12). Sufficiently open-ended to give maximum flexibility to market-hungry journals, Dana's conception of news dovetailed with his notion that "there is no system of maxims or professional rules that . . . is laid down for the guidance of the journalist." News was to be a strict and universal reflection of an objectively visible world. Dana thus contrasted the journalist with the physician, with "his system of ethics and that sublime oath of Hippocrates," and with the lawyer, who "also has his code of ethics . . . and the rules of practice which he is instructed in," and noted that he had "never met with a system of maxims that seemed to me to be perfectly adapted to the general direction of a newspaperman" (ibid.:18). For the majority of journalists, or at least for those who found publishers for the autobiographies they also had time to write, objectivity and organizational routine were unproblematic synonyms. By 1900, however, this easy identification was beset by unprecedented problems and tensions. The society in which newspapers were published had changed radically, molding key aspects of journalism and creating dynamic issues and conflicts that the producers of any major public cultural form of necessity had to face.

Even by the 1870s, newspapers had become big business and remained so. Cochran observes that at this time the biggest dailies, reaching circulations of up to 200,000, were worth one or two million dollars—"amounts exceeded by only a few other manufacturing companies" (1975:156). In the mid-1890s Pulitzer's New York *World*, in the forefront of the cut-throat journalism of the era, was worth ten million dollars and brought in a million in profit annually (Emery and Emery 1978:231). A list of the 500 largest American industrial companies in 1917 includes Hearst Publications, the

Chicago Daily News, and E. W. Scripps (not to mention auxiliary producers of basic newspaper needs like International Paper and American Type Founders, or the gargantuan electronics firms like General Electric, Westinghouse, Western Electric, and Marconi, which were shortly to launch broadcasting as a social and cultural form) (Navin 1970). "To-day a million dollars will not begin to outfit a metropolitan newspaper," wrote a founding pioneer of American social science, Edward Alsworth Ross (1910:303). The owner of the major urban daily, Ross claimed, was more and more frequently "a business man who finds it hard to see why he should run his property on different lines from the hotel proprietor, the vaudeville manager, or the owner of an amusement park." In contrast to the recent past, "now that the provider of the newspaper capital hires the editor instead of the editor hiring the newspaper capital, the paper is likelier to be run as a money-maker pure and simple—a factory where ink and brains are so applied to white paper as to turn out the largest possible marketable product." This accumulation of "ultimate control" by men with "business motives" Ross termed "the commercialization of the press" (1910:304).

The commercialization of the press brought in-house changes in its train. By 1891 the International Typographical Union had amended its constitution to authorize the issuance of charters to reporters and editors (Quinn 1940:5), and a wave of twenty-one short-lived locals broke and spent itself between 1899 and 1904. Although no truly successful national union was formed before the American Newspaper Guild in 1933, agitation for unions was sporadic on a local scale through the opening decades of the twentieth century. Aside from arduous, unpredictable, long hours and notoriously low pay, a major incentive for unionization was the concentration of ownership within the industry. After 1900, the number of newspapers in operation began a long-term decline; while chain-owned papers burgeoned from 10 percent of total daily circulation in 1900 to 43 percent in 1930 (Sterling and Haight 1978:83). Closure of newspapers and staff reorganization made work tenure precarious for some journalists (Quinn 1940:8; Perry and Perry 1963:210, 476–9).

The rise of mass consumer advertising (cf. Ewen 1976) also directly affected a brand of journalism that had never questioned the essential legitimacy of advertiser support. Whereas in the mid-nineteenth century relatively unorganized advertising by relatively small companies did not exert decisive control over newspaper content (Atwan 1979:16–17), by the turn of the twentieth century both the size and the increased expenditures of advertisers changed this. Estimated advertiser expenditures in 1890 accounted for some $300 million, but by 1909 they reached a billion dollars annually (Sterling and Haight 1978:121). Advertising revenues furnished proportionately more, too, of daily newspaper earnings; and public patronage was less vital now than public attention per se: "The readers are there to *read*, not to provide funds," wrote one observer (Ross 1910:304). To collar a share of growing advertising budgets, the newspaper was prepared to make concessions. Stunts, gimmickry, sensation, flagrant self-advertisement, aggressive investigative campaigns, and yellow journalism were used to wrest readers from other activities and to seize their attention for advertisers. Critics complained that news columns and editorial pages had been subordinated to the profitable sale of editorial space; therefore, wrote one, "it is strictly 'businesslike' to let the big advertisers censor both":

> The immunity enjoyed by the big advertiser becomes the more serious as more kinds of business resort to advertising. Formerly, readers who

> understood why accidents and labor troubles never occur in department
> stores, why dramatic criticisms are so lenient, and the reviews of books
> from the publishers who advertise are so goodnatured, could still expect
> from their journal an ungloved freedom in dealing with gas, electric,
> railroad, and banking companies. (Ross 1910:304–5)

The startling rise of huge industrial combines with their extensive consumer-demand management implied to critics that, in the news columns of the sheet "that steers by the cash-register," every concern "that has favors to seek, duties to dodge, or regulations to evade, will be able to press the soft pedal." Cross ownership and trusts also took their toll: "when the shares of a newspaper lie in the safe-deposit box cheek by jowl with gas, telephone, and pipe-line stock, a tenderness for these collateral interests is likely to affect the news columns" (ibid.:305).

Turn-of-the-century America was indeed a heady time for what President Grover Cleveland, in his annual message to Congress in 1888, called "aggregated capital"—the "trusts, combinations and monopolies," such as United States Steel, the Pennsylvania Railroad, or Standard Oil. We cannot linger on the massive and sudden centralization and concentration of capital that occurred around 1900 (cf. Chandler 1977). Nor can we adequately chart the rise of militant reaction, through unionism and radical politics, to what both President Cleveland and the socialist writer Jack London called "an iron heel" of unchecked corporate capitalism. It was a time of savagery in labor relations, when railroad magnate Jay Gould might boast "I can hire one half the working class to kill the other half" (in Boyer and Morais 1972:65). His sentiments and others of the same sort were not lost on many workers. Between 1897 and 1920 union membership expanded from 450,000 to five million. The American Federation of Labor led by Samuel Gompers numbered a million and a half workers by 1904. Not all unions were radical in their challenge to the American state, but the emergence of union power was itself unprecedented. It was also a time of bitter and well-remembered strikes, particularly as World War I drew nigh: strikes led by the Industrial Workers of the World in Lawrence in 1912, and at Paterson in 1913; the Ludlow Massacre in 1914; the Los Angeles *Times* protest, climaxing in the dynamiting of its building in 1910; the steel strike of 1919. Gains were registered by employees—workmen's compensation, laws for factory safety, legislation on maximum hours for women and children may be mentioned (cf. Derber 1970), but conflict continued to escalate. In 1915 1,246 strikes were called, affecting some 470,000 employees. In 1917, 4,233 strikes involved 1,200,000 workers. In 1919, when conflict reached fever pitch in the Pittsburgh area over the steel strike, 3,253 strikes shot through the lives of 3,950,000 workers (Bing 1921:293). It was the heyday of the Socialist Party; while, further to the left, the Wobblies waged free speech fights and attacked "the prostituted press" as a fearsome head of that Hydra, capitalism (*Solidarity*, 7 July 1917; in Bing 1921:256). In a context such as this, any account of working conditions or strike report in the metropolitan press was likely to be caught, framed, and illuminated by the stark contest between organized capital and organizing labor—with consequences to be explored momentarily.

From the vantage point of concerned journalists, advertiser control and the rise of public relations, set against the contrary notions of an often indignant and even militant public, were nothing short of catastrophic. Frank Cobb of the New York *World* stated in 1919 that many of the direct channels to news have been closed and the information for the public is first filtered through publicity agents. The great corporations have them, the banks have them, the railroads have them, all the organizations of business and of social and political activity have them, and they are the media through which the news comes. Even statesmen have them. (In Schudson 1978:139)

The "walled city" of which Julian Ralph had earlier written was creating problems of access in a society that protected those whose motivating principle was self-interest and whose interests had grown into powerful institutions. Unless a reporter knew that news "almost always starts from a special group," warned Walter Lippmann in 1920, "he is doomed to report the surface of events. He will report the ripples of a passing steamer, and forget the tides and the currents and the ground-swell. . . . He will deal with the flicker of events and not with their motives" (1920:87). Intertwining with an informational system that followed the curves of social power, blind adherence to the earlier form of objectivity allowed the emergence and phenomenal expansion of what has since been termed news management (cf. Schudson 1978; Raucher 1968). The power of institutional sources to mold versions of events pushed or pulled into the public sphere had become glaringly apparent.

This was so evident by the turn of the century that a stream of harsh criticism began to descend on the practice of journalism. As early as 1890, an article entitled "An Inside View of Commercial Journalism" demonstrated starkly how Nebraska newspapers had uniformly consented to sell their news and editorial columns to advertisers (Bishop 1890). In the *Nation* and the *New Republic*, especially, complaints over the character of the changing public sphere were loudly voiced. One article excoriated statesmen whose first thought was "not how can I keep this from becoming known, but how can I make it known so as best to work out to my advantage, or that of my party?" (*Nation*, 17 December 1908, p. 594). Hearst's papers were alternately condemned for a rampant lack of "accuracy" and for the mighty editorial and political clout they collectively exercised (*New Republic*, 5 June 1915, p. 105; *Nation*, 10 September 1908, p. 229). Long before communications researchers got wind of the idea, detailed exposures of the techniques whereby journalists were subordinated to private interest, through "the blue pencil" (*New Republic*, 14 December 1918, pp. 192–4), the bribe, and the sack (Sinclair 1919), were common. *Harper's Weekly* (25 July 1914) joined in with revelations about Hearst's brand of journalism; the *Atlantic Monthly* gave space to sociologist Ross's thesis entitled "The Suppression of Important News" (Ross 1910). In their widely remembered essay, "A Test of the News," Lippmann and Merz presented devastating evidence to support their conclusion that "from the point of view of professional journalism the reporting of the Russian Revolution is nothing short of a disaster" (1920:3). Why? Because the *New York Times*, the focus of their study, had been "seriously misled" in its reliance "upon the official purveyors of information":

It indicates that statements of fact emanating from governments and the circles around governments as well as from the leaders of political movements cannot be taken as judgments of fact by an independent press. They indicate opinion, they are controlled by special purpose, and they are not trustworthy news. (Ibid.:41)

Men were wondering, Lippmann announced, "whether government by consent can survive in a time when the manufacture of consent is an unregulated private enterprise" (1920:5). "Not hyperbolically and contemptuously, but literally and with scientific precision," chipped in the gadfly Upton Sinclair, "we define Journalism in America as the business and practice of presenting the news of the day in the interest of economic privilege" (1919:222).

What had changed decisively over nine decades was the definition of corrupting private interest—it now stood revealed as "economic privilege." Such resounding denunciations brought the hopes and fears of the 1830s into a new time: "So long as there is interposed between the ordinary citizen and the facts a news organization determining by entirely private and unexamined standards, no matter how lofty, what he shall know, and hence what he shall believe, no one will be able to say that the substance of demo-cratic government is secure" (Lippmann 1920:12–13). The language of public good against private interest was renewed and made ready for another round. "There is every-where an increasingly angry disillusionment about the press, a growing sense of being baffled and misled; and wise publishers will not pooh-pooh these omens," Lippmann charged (ibid.:75–6). In turn, the newspaper, the journalistic occupation, and the con-ventional practice of objectivity were again transformed in a crucible of social conflict.

Lippmann identified a "crisis in journalism" (ibid.:5) that stemmed from a resur-gence of open class antagonism in society. In testimony before the Senate Commission on Industrial Relations, John L. Matthews, editor of the *Paterson Press*, conceded that passages such as the one below were common in his paper during the agitation in 1913 by the Industrial Workers of the World:

> Akron could not find a law to banish this dangerous revolutionist and his cohorts, but a citizens' committee of 1,000 men did the trick in short order. Can Akron accomplish something that Paterson, N.J., can not duplicate? This Paterson Press dislikes to believe it, but time will tell. (1916:3:2582–4)

The San Diego *Tribune* of 4 March 1912 was less restrained: "Hanging is none too good for them. They would be much better dead" (in Boyer and Morais 1972:173). When the I.W.W.'s Frank Little was murdered in Butte, Montana, the Boston *Transcript* said that it knew "of millions of people who, while sternly reprehending such proceedings as the lynching of members of that anti-patriotic society (the I.W.W.), will nevertheless be glad, in their hearts, that Montana did it in the case of Little" (in Bing 1921:249).

This list of vituperation might be expanded at will. More to the point is that such utterances as the ones just cited were "spread far and wide by the radical press" (Bing 1921:250). The Wobblies' *Solidarity* and the Socialists' New York *Call* devoted much space to reprinting and condemning the violent language of innuendo and outright incitement common to much of the commercial press. After a particularly flagrant instance of abuse by the commercial press in a full-page advertisement in the Seattle *Post-Intelligencer* on 18 November 1919, the employees of the paper met and refused to continue work until the advertisement was removed. The resolution of protest the employees adopted is worth reproducing:

> We have been patient under misrepresentation, faithful in the face of slander, long suffering under insult; we have upheld our agreements and

produced your paper, even though in so doing we were braiding the rope with which you propose to hang us; day after day we have put in type, stereotyped, printed and mailed calumny after calumny, lie after lie, insult after insult. . . . So long as these things appeared to be a part of your unfair fight against organization—our organization and others—we have been able to endure them in the hope that at last truth must prevail. But there must be a limit to all things. In the page advertisement, purporting to have been written and paid for by one Selvin, but which had as well have occupied the position in your paper usually taken up by your editorial page, your utter depravity as a newspaper, your shameless disregard of the laws of the land, your hatred of opposition, your reckless policy of appeal to the passions of the citizenry, reached depths of malice and malignancy hitherto unbelievable. It is nothing less than excitation to violence, stark and naked invitation to anarchy. If your business management cannot demonstrate its capacity and sagacity, if your editorial directing heads must remain blind to the things they are bringing us to; if, together, you cannot see the abyss to which you are leading us—all of us; if you have no more love for our common country than is manifested in your efforts to plunge it into anarchy, then as loyal American citizens— many of us ex-service men who very clearly proved our faith in America and its institutions—we must—not because we are unionists, but because we are Americans—find means to protect ourselves from the stigma of having aided and abetted your campaign of destruction. (In Bing 1921:250–1)

We are once again in the midst of a fiercely conservative appeal to the common good. A similar spirit pervaded the *New Republic*'s critique of the *New York Times* (18 September 1915), when the latter supported the barring of I.W.W. speakers from strike-ravaged Paterson: "It [the *Times*] admits 'that free speech is a noble and indispensable right.' But in view of the fact that the I.W.W. speakers are 'spouters' and 'ranters' and 'rattle-snakes,' and because Paterson lost fifteen million dollars in the recent strike, the authorities are justified in breaking the law and violating the letter and spirit of the Constitution of the United States." The journal went on: "Is the *Times* in favor of the Constitution only when it protects property rights? Is it against the Constitution when it protects the rights of 'spouters' and 'ranters'?" The longstanding concern about private interest and monopoly, revised according to changing circumstances, now assumed a marked economic accent. And when newsstand distributors Ward & Gow broke their contract with the radical *Masses* magazine, the *New Republic* commented: "When a private corporation which monopolizes one important avenue through which news is distributed sets up a censorship it creates an intolerable condition" (29 January 1916, p. 319).

The critique of journalism as a class practice fanned out to challenge hierarchical news values. After the Industrial Relations Commission investigation of tenant farmers in Texas, the *New Republic* observed that only the Socialist New York *Call* had paid any heed to its report.

> The other papers have evidently not regarded the plight of the tenant farmers as very important news. The vaudeville performance of

> Mr. Carnegie was worth columns of space and elaborate editorials. But the rural slums of the Southwest are not headline material. . . . And then people are distressed by agitators. (27 March 1915, p. 191)

One journalist felt threatened enough by the crisis in journalism to protest, in an article appropriately entitled "In Defense of Reporters," that the public must not think that the "fact-loving, truth-serving, intelligent reporter" was a thing of the past. *Publishers* with these qualifications, he admitted, were, however, rarely to be found (*New Republic*, 10 June 1916, p. 147).

Lippmann's argument that "the present crisis of western democracy is a crisis in journalism" (1920:5) was not a mere figure of speech. Escalating social conflicts were putting pressure directly on the practice and characteristic forms of commercial journalism. This is nowhere more obvious than in the analysis written by journalist M. K. Wisehart entitled "The Pittsburgh Newspapers and the Steel Strike" for the Interchurch World Movement (1921).

On 22 September 1919, launching one of the bitterest strikes of the century, 350,000 steel workers around the nation walked off their jobs. The reasons for their strike, the conditions in the steel industry, and the level of militancy among strikers have been discussed elsewhere (cf. Brecher 1972: 118–28). In western Pennsylvania, the heart of the industry, the strike met a particularly fierce response from employers. Pittsburgh newspapers were evidently deeply implicated in this reaction. Documenting his extensive critique with eighty-odd pages of examples taken from the press, Wisehart reached this conclusion:

> It is inconceivable that the public which relied on the Pittsburgh newspapers could, by any human method of reading newspapers and allowing both for exaggeration due to bias and inaccuracy due to haste, have understood either the causes of the steel strike or the significance of its incidents. (1921:147)

A "policy of antagonism to the strike" had been manifested and sustained in the press and related directly to its adherence to long-touted, standard reporting practices. The context of the strike was so highly charged as to make these standards dramatically inadequate. Wisehart claimed that the press's flagrant abuse had been occasioned

> (c) by silence as to actual industrial grievances and by publishing statistics in a misleading way.
> . . . .
> (e) by accepting and publishing accounts of violence and disorder from the employers' and officials' point of view without investigation of such incidents.
> . . . .
> (g) by effectual suppression of news whose tendency would have been to inspire a fair-minded examination of repressive conditions in the Pittsburgh district. (Ibid.:147–8)

The only unprecedented feature of any of this was that in the pitched battle the conventions of objective reportage were shown to be glaringly inappropriate. "The newspapers accepted such accounts," stated Wisehart in retrospect "as were given by the police or other authorities" (ibid.:148). And it was even possible for this Church-sponsored investigator to charge that

> there were no headlines such as: "Steel Workers say they work 7 days a week"; or "Half the Steel Workers are on the 12-hour day"; or "Steel Common Laborers declare they cannot earn enough for families"; or "Workers demand right to hold union meetings." (Ibid.:153)

He continues in the older tradition of investigative journalism (and also in the more modern tradition of naturalist description in novel and drama): "And yet these things were facts, they were news, they constituted the news which explained the strike, they were the 'news peg' of daily happenings, and they were all more or less accessible to reporters." The most damning indictment that Wisehart could make was that "the essential facts, *which were found by others during the strike*, could have been gathered at the time by investigating newspapermen, if searching investigation had been what the newspapers wanted" (ibid.). In a context of apparent class war, objectivity was hidebound.

   With conflict both so intense and so focused, it was not easy to hold, with naive objectivity, that the facts were unproblematic. During the steel strike, unions in Wheeling, West Virginia, resolved: "We have knowledge that the Public Press fear to be impartial in this strike and give an unbiased, true account of actual conditions" (ibid.:154). Immediately following the strike, which the employees lost in January 1920, labor unions made determined attempts to launch their own national news service and to establish their own daily press (ibid.:89). "I propose," declared Upton Sinclair, "that we shall found and endow a weekly publication of truth-telling, to be known as 'The National News' ":

> This publication will carry no advertisements and no editorials. It will not be a journal of opinion, but a record of events pure and simple. It will be published on ordinary news-print paper, and in the cheapest possible form. It will have one purpose, and one only, to give to the American people once every week the truth about the world's events. It will be strictly and absolutely nonpartisan, and never the propaganda organ of any cause. It will watch the country, and see where lies are being circulated and truth suppressed; its job will be to nail the lies, and bring the truth into the light of day. (1919:438–9)

Here as virtually everywhere, even during the most polarized period of the early twentieth century, *the ideal* of unitary truth with universal application continued to be uncontested. Lippmann hammered home the same point in arguing that "opinion could be made at once free and enlightening only by transferring our interest from 'opinion' to the objective realities from which it springs" (1920:97). "The real enemy is ignorance," continued this advocate of refereed pluralism, "from which all of us, conservative, liberal, and revolutionary, suffer. . . . We must go back of our opinions to the neutral facts for unity and refreshment of spirit" (ibid.:98–9). His use of the first-person plural was revealing; ideological disagreement was contained only by the purportedly ideal neutrality of the facts: "In going behind opinion to the information which it exploits, and in making the validity of the news our ideal, we shall be . . . protecting for the public interest that which all the special interests in the world are most anxious to corrupt" (ibid.:70). Lippmann therefore again hoped for the formation of a news agency backed by "those whose interests are not represented in the existing news-organization"—"organized labor and militant liberalism" (ibid.:99, 101). The organization would be one "in which editorial matter was rigorously excluded" (ibid.:103; cf. Ross 1910:310–11).

In such proposals the ideal of a unitary and universal truth was used explicitly to cultivate a single community in the face of sustained discord. The long-declared commitment of institutional journalism to the segregation of fact from value now became the peculiar warrant of the journalistic *profession* (cf. Schudson 1978). "If the news agencies fell into the hands of pacifists the whole complexion of facts would be different," charged the *New Republic* (24 April 1915, p. 290). Such sentiments as this in no way undermined the ideal of objectivity but rather gave it a new twist. Because of social polarization, it was imperative that journalism become "a specifically trained profession, for in schools of journalism there is an opportunity to train that sense of reality and perspective which great reporting requires." Indeed, the journal continued,

> There is an opportunity to create a morale as disinterested and as interesting as that of the scientists who are the reporters of natural phenomena. News-gathering cannot perhaps be as accurate as chemical research, but it can be undertaken in the same spirit. (Ibid.)

Scientific expertise mustered in support of what Gans called "responsible capitalism" (1979:206) was hailed in journalism as well as in other spheres of Progressive reform (cf. Derber 1970). What the *New Republic* frankly recognized as "the fundamental conflict between the economic interests" of wage earner and capitalist could and should be tempered by organized "arbitration" (21 October 1916, p. 283). Otherwise, "class suspicion and hatred" would drive labor "to meet force with force" (ibid:285). As was plain to many, however, this "spirit of arbitration" had been betrayed repeatedly by press coverage of labor. "If the principle of arbitration is to prevail," the magazine asserted, "facts must take the place of special pleading." And, finally, "for help in the accomplishment of this great transformation," it was imperative above all "to rely upon the conscientious sobriety of the daily press," with its capacity to lead "an enlightened public opinion" (ibid.:283, 285). With science for its ideal, what Lippmann termed "a sense of evidence" and a pragmatic "working knowledge of the main stratifications and current of interest" would serve as the best method of journalistic practice (1920:87). When Joseph Pulitzer drew up plans to establish a school of journalism at Columbia University in 1902, he distinguished sharply between business and editorial imperatives and signaled out "the Editorial point of view," with its special emphasis on accurate and reliable reporting, as the fundamental concern of the proposed academic venture (Baker 1954:23–4). In the divisive two decades that followed, Lippmann's belief that training for journalists must be so designed that "the ideal of objective testimony is cardinal" took clear shape (in Schudson 1978:152).

The ensuing subordination of journalists to an explicit objectivity established a new legitimacy for the entire news-gathering system in the form of a standard that implies in its application a probing of "the validity of the news." By charging individual journalists with responsibility for mistakes and prejudices, the systemic biases of news-gathering organizations (the actual weave of the news net, to invoke Professor Tuchman's [1978a] phrase) might be implicitly avoided and displaced. Journalistic professionalism, accordingly, now might assist in reclaiming the commercial newspapers' earlier role of the defense of public good by demonstrating that the century-old ideals of the commercial press were being adhered to.

The forces that made "the validity of the news" a major concern also brought about a major change in the definition of objectivity. Objectivity was now invested with widely discrepant meanings by different, or opposed, social actors. One catches a glimpse of this in the American Newspaper Guild's code of ethics, as stated in 1935 (during another wave of social turmoil) before the U. S. Senate Committee on Education and Labor; the Guild believed

> (1) That the newspaperman's first duty is to give the public accurate and unbiased news reports. (1935:727)

Thus the Guild enshrined its adherence to the ideal of objectivity. Yet its concern with "the validity of the news" was also given dramatic and substantial expression:

> (2) That the equality of all men before the law should be observed by the men of the press; that they should not be swayed in news reporting by political, economic, social, racial, or religious prejudices, but should be guided only by fact and fairness. (Ibid.)

More specifically, the union held

> (4) That the guild should work through efforts of its members, or by agreement with editors and publishers, to curb the suppression of legitimate news concerning "privileged" persons or groups, including advertisers, commercial powers, and friends of newspapermen. . . .
> . . . .
> (6) That the news be edited exclusively in the editorial rooms instead of in the business office of the daily newspaper. (Ibid.)

In two codicils the Guild added to its challenge of established practices a dual condemnation:

> (1) The carrying of publicity in the news columns in the guise of news matter.
> (2) The current practice of requiring the procuring or writing of stories which newspapermen know are false or misleading and which work oppression or wrong to persons and to groups. (Ibid.:728)

Yet, hearing this code of ethics read out, Senator Clark of the Committee asked blandly: "As I understand, that requires that they tell the truth?" "Yes sir," responded Newspaper Guild Vice President Robert M. Buck, tersely switching codes, "that is it, Senator" (ibid.). My point in elaborating this exchange is that objectivity had become polysemic: its universality as an ideal might shield open disparities in its application and interpretation. Objectivity was now nothing less than a socially patterned and stratified cultural resource. The captains of the newspaper industry were thus able to invoke the same ideal to a very different end when they attacked the Newspaper Guild's stand in favor of a closed shop. The Guild, said *Editor and Publisher* in its issue of 3 March 1934, "would defeat the right of the public to enjoy the interests of free, non-partisan disinterested news reporting":

> It is a simple minded notion that reporters and editors, sufficiently imbued with class conscious spirit to join a union and affiliate with other unions would continue to treat news from the viewpoint of impartial observers. They sacrifice neutrality and admit partisanship by their very act. (In Quinn 1940:48)

It was the journalist's job, the publishers insisted, to report controversy "not as a partisan but as an objective observer" (in Schudson 1978:157). In the 1830s apparent class divisions had led the penny papers to claim a universal truth based on natural right. A century later class divisions highlighted the boundaries of objectivity. The practice of objectivity had become open to fundamental dispute.

Disagreement over the substantive character of objectivity itself, however, has tended to be sharply limited. Instead, social conflicts have been disguised, contained, and displaced through the imposition of news objectivity, a framework legitimating the exercise of social power over the interpretation of reality. Those without institutionalized resources have, time and again, found themselves pilloried and marginalized in the press, while crucial issues have been amplified in such a way as to lead the general public to accept institutional control. McCarthy and his heirs found the press a willing partner in the adroit manipulation of the public (cf. Caute 1978:446–56). Routine reliance upon accredited sources permitted news management of the Vietnam war to sustain what may be termed "public opinion from above" (cf. Chomsky and Herman 1979). Today, the horrific and still largely untold story of nuclear power furnishes yet another dramatic example. Keller (1980) quotes ABC's Vice President for Program Development, Av Westin, as saying that, for years before Three Mile Island, "a general good will existed between the nuclear industry and the network news departments, whereby we all accepted the initial safety arguments for nuclear energy." The consequence of this friendly feeling, which was buttressed by expensive public relations efforts, was that for subjects critical of nuclear power a higher standard of proof came into play. In Westin's terms, those who opposed nuclear energy "were forced to prove their case more than those who supported it" (ibid.:16). This sort of abuse occurs, not through the mistakes or biases or corruptions of individual reporters, but because the press is institutionally placed to be used in this way. It is objectivity that protects journalists in their role as "the strongest remaining bastion of logical positivism in America" (Gans 1979:184), and whose scientist aura sets up a formidable barrier to comprehension of actual news values. News remains credible in its insistence that, in ideal principle, it animates and displays no values whatsoever.

Scholars as well as lay activists also continue, on the other hand, to pierce objectivity's scientific veneer and have amply demonstrated the social, organizational, ideological, and occupational constraints on the press and its invisible frame. Their critique points to renewed understanding of our common need for democratic public information, an ideal that returns at once to what is still valid and useful in the historic birth of the popular press. We must redeem the democratic promise that has, since the 1830s, been latent in the American information system. We must strive for a public sphere in which the people themselves rather than undelegated groups from their midst will be lord of the facts.

Note

1.   This formulation is borrowed from James W. Carey (personal communication).

Bibliography

Contemporary Publications

Carriers of the Public Ledger 1839. Address of the Carriers of the Public Ledger. Printed for the Carriers by Wm. F. Rackliff, South-West Corner of George and Swanwick Streets.

Bing, Alexander M. 1921. *War-Time Strikes and Their Adjustment*. New York: E. P. Dutton.

Bishop, J. B. 1890. "An Inside View of Commercial Journalism." *Nation*, 12 June 1890, pp. 463–4.

Dana, Charles A. 1895. *The Art of Newspaper Making*. New York: D. Appleton.

King, Henry 1871. *American Journalism*. Topeka, Kansas: Commonwealth State Printing House.

Lippmann, Walter 1920. *Liberty and the News*. New York: Harcourt, Brace and Howe.

Lippmann, Walter, and Merz, Charles 1920. "A Test of the News." *New Republic*, 4 August 1920, pt. 2, 1–42.

McCarthy, James 1906. *The Newspaper Worker*. New York: The Press Guild.

O'Brien, Frank M. 1928. *The Story of the Sun*. New York: Greenwood Press.

Quinn, Russell 1940. *History of the San Francisco–Oakland Newspaper Guild*. Works Projects Administration 10008 San Francisco, August. O. P. 665–08–3–12. (History of San Francisco Journalism Series, vol. 3, E. L. Daggett, Supervisor.)

Ralph, Julian 1903. *The Making of a Journalist*. New York: Harper and Brothers.

Ross, Edward Alsworth 1910. "The Suppression of Important News." *Atlantic Monthly* 105 (March):303–11.

Shanks, W. F. G. 1867. "How We Get Our News." *Harper's New Monthly Magazine* 34 (March):511–22.

Sinclair, Upton 1919. *The Brass Check*. Pasadena: Published by the Author.

United States. Congress. Senate 1916. *Final Report and Testimony Submitted to Congress by the Commission on Industrial Relations*. vol. 3. 64th Congress, 1st Session. Document no. 415. Washington: Government Printing Office.

United States. Congress. Senate 1935. *Hearings before the Committee on Education and Labor on S. 1958*. pt. 3. 74th Congress, 1st Session. Washington: Government Printing Office.

Wingate, Charles F. (ed.) 1875. *Views and Interviews on Journalism*. New York: F. B. Patterson.

Wisehart, M. K. 1921. *Interchurch World Movement Report on Public Opinion and the Steel Strike*. New York: Harcourt, Brace & Co.

Newspapers

London
   Police Gazette; or, Hue and Cry (1826)
New York City
   Herald (1835–36)
   National Police Gazette (1845–50)
   New York Times (1851)
   Sun (1833–34)

Philadelphia
  Public Ledger (1836)

Magazines

Harper's Weekly (1914)
Nation (1865, 1870, 1890, 1908)
New Republic (1915–20)

Secondary Works

Atwan, Robert 1979. "Newspapers and the Foundations of Modern Adveristing." In *The Commercial Connection*, ed. John W. Wright, pp. 9–23. New York: Delta.

Baker, Richard Terrill 1954. *A History of the Graduate School of Journalism, Columbia University*. New York: Columbia University Press.

Boyer, Richard O., and Morais, Herbert M. 1972. *Labor's Untold Story*. New York: United Electrical, Radio and Machine Workers of America.

Brecher, Jeremy 1972. *Strike!* Boston: South End Press.

Caute, David 1978. *The Great Fear*. New York: Simon and Schuster.

Chandler, Alfred D., Jr. 1972. "Anthracite Coal and the Beginnings of the Industrial Revolution in the United States." *Business History Review* 46 (2):141–81.

Chandler, Alfred D., Jr. 1977. *The Visible Hand*. Cambridge, Mass.: Belknap Press.

Chomsky, Noam, and Herman, Edward S. 1979. *The Washington Connection and Third World Fascism*. Boston: South End Press.

Cochran, Thomas C. 1975. "Media as Business: A Brief History." *Journal of Communication* 25 (4):155–65.

Derber, Milton 1970. *The American Idea of Industrial Democracy 1865–1965*. Urbana: University of Illinois Press.

Emery, Edwin, and Emery, Michael 1978. *The Press and America*. 4th ed. Englewood Cliffs, N.J.: Prentice-Hall.

Ewen, Stuart 1976. *Captains of Consciousness*. New York: McGraw-Hill.

Gans, Herbert J. 1979. *Deciding What's News*. New York: Pantheon.

Hohendahl, Peter Uwe 1979. "Critical Theory, Public Sphere and Culture: Jurgen Habermas and His Critics." *New German Critique* 16 (Winter):89–118.

Keller, Edward 1980. "Television's Coverage of Nuclear Energy." Unpublished manuscript.

Navin, Thomas R. 1970. "The 500 Largest American Industrials in 1917." *Business History Review* 44 (3):360–86.

Perry, Louis B., and Perry, Richard S. 1963. *A History of the Los Angeles Labor Movement, 1911–1941*. Berkeley and Los Angeles: University of California Press.

Raucher, Alan R. 1968. *Public Relations and Business 1900–1929*. Baltimore: Johns Hopkins Press.

Schudson, Michael 1978. *Discovering the News*. New York: Basic Books.

Sterling, Christopher H., and Haight, Timothy R. 1978. *The Mass Media: Aspen Institute Guide to Communication Industry Trends*. New York and London: Praeger.

Tuchman, Gaye 1978a. *Making News*. New York: The Free Press.

Chapter 29

DANIEL J. CZITROM

DIALECTICAL TENSIONS IN THE AMERICAN MEDIA, PAST AND FUTURE

WE MAY THINK OF THE POST-McLUHAN era as one characterized by a deeper and more sophisticated consciousness of the enormous role played by modern communication in everyday life. But the semantic ambiguities once associated with the word *communication* now seem to have regrouped around that increasingly opaque term, *the media*. Much of the discourse about the media, in learned journals as well as informal conversation, suffers from fuzziness, lack of clarity, and a jumble of definitions. Think, for example, of the ways in which the noun *media* finds growing expression as an adjective, as in "media event," "media people," or "media hype."

Think, too, of the various usages of the noun form. The modern sense of the word dates, interestingly enough, from its use in advertising trade journals of the 1920s, as in the phrase "advertising media." But today the term is used interchangeably with the press or the journalistic profession, especially in the sense of investigative reporting. At the same time, *media* is often used to distinguish nonprint forms of communication, such as film and broadcasting, from print. It may connote the larger realms of entertainment and show business. Denunciations of the media as too liberal, too permissive, too conservative, or too manipulative invoke the term as a moral or political category. Most everyone engages in damning the media for glorifying, exaggerating, or even causing some particularly odious feature of modern life.

Confusion of the singular and plural forms, *medium* and *media*, surely reflects a popular perception of the incestuous relations among the various mass disseminators of words and images. Media content is remarkably reflexive; each medium is filled with material from and about other media. Over the past twenty years, a virtual fusion of the techniques, style, and subjects of entertainment programs and news programs has taken place. On the level of public awareness, this superheated reflexiveness takes some curious forms. Television rating wars between the networks are now treated as hard news; film and broadcasting executives enjoy an exalted status as celebrities, cult figures, and creative auteurs in their own right.

The bourgeois commercial nexus at the center of the American film, broadcasting, and press industries clearly encourages this situation. It also promotes the media as a total, unchanging, "natural" part of modern life. Indeed, the everywhereness, all-at-once-ness, and never-ending-ness of the media are powerful barriers to understanding, or even acknowledging, their history.

The diverse meanings evoked by the term *media* represent a linguistic legacy of the contradictory elements embedded in the history of all modern means of communication. For each medium is a matrix of institutional development, popular responses, and cultural content that ought to be understood as a product of dialectical tensions, of opposing forces and tendencies clashing and evolving over time, with things continually giving rise to their opposite. Broadly speaking, these contradictions have been expressed in terms of the tension between the progressive or utopian possibilities offered by new communications technologies and their disposition as instruments of domination and exploitation.

One finds parallels or refractions of this dialectic in the thought of American communications theorists. Within the tradition as a whole, Harold Innis and the later McLuhan represent opposite poles. Charles H. Cooley and John Dewey shared affinities with McLuhan's more utopian outlook, although they started from quite different premises. The emphasis among the Frankfurt group on the media as primary agents for maintaining the dominant monopolies of knowledge and power echoed the profound pessimism of Innis, but from quite another political and cultural vantage point. To varying degrees, several individual thinkers, notably Robert Park, encompassed these tensions within their own work. And the career of Paul Lazarsfeld, key figure in the empirical and behavioral tradition, exemplified the intellectual dialectic, for the refugee who survived by juggling market research contracts also gave T. W. Adorno his first job in America.

What I would like to stress here is the need to recover the historical elements of an as yet uncompleted dialectic in order to further understand the present configuration of American media, to suggest avenues for future research, and to perhaps make sense of the upheaval currently being wrought by new cable, video, and satellite technologies. What follows is an historical sketch of some dialectical tensions in American media as viewed from the three related standpoints of early institutional developments, early popular responses, and the cultural history of media content. Examples are taken mainly from the three media whose histories have already been discussed: the telegraph, motion pictures, and radio.

If the schema presented below seems to have naively favored the utopian side of the dialectic, I can only point to the present dearth of knowledge. We need to redress an imbalance in our historical thinking, to recover a hidden side of media history. At the same time, I have suggested a few nodes on the grimmer side that might prove fertile territory for investigation, areas where the media operate as the excrescence of commercial capitalism.

Finally, I have offered some thoughts on how the historical perspective may help us gain some insight into the latest rash of technological breakthroughs. Here I am less interested in presenting a static, grand theory than in stimulating discussion and action concerning the new fields that are now opening up in three main areas: decentralized distribution networks, greater individual control of hardware, and opportunities for innovative programming.

* * *

Considered as an institution, each medium that evolved from the work of individual inventors and entrepreneurs was later subsumed into larger corporate or military contexts. The key roles played by small concerns and amateurs in the early history of new communications technologies are too often forgotten. Yet the importance of corporate and military settings for technological progress and of the accompanying support by large capital investments and highly organized research teams clearly intensifies the closer one gets to the present.

Samuel F. B. Morse's perfection of a practical electric telegraph was a lonely and poverty-stricken venture. For six years after the 1838 demonstrations of a workable instrument, Morse failed to obtain any government or corporate subsidy for his work. Congress finally authorized a thirty-thousand dollar appropriation to build the first telegraph line in 1844. However, in refusing Morse's offer to buy him out, Congress thwarted his wish that the government control future telegraph development. The ensuing twenty-five years of wildcat speculation and construction, both fiercely competitive and wasteful, finally ended with the triumph of Western Union, the first of several communications monopolies owned by private enterprise.

In the case of motion pictures, one finds a larger group of individual inventors and small businessmen acting as prime catalysts for technological innovation. The variety of cameras and projectors used in the early years reflected the contributions of numerous inventors from around the world. In the early industry, capital investment as well as creative energy came largely from Jewish petit bourgeois immigrant exhibitors and distributors. They were eager to invest in the new business that was beneath the dignity of traditional sources of capital. With roots deep in the urban thicket of commercial amusements, motion pictures found their first audiences mainly in the ethnic and working-class districts of the large cities.

Each early attempt to standardize or license equipment, films, and distribution was undermined by successive waves of independents. The Motion Picture Patents Company, heavily capitalized and dominated by the Edison interests, looked invincible when formed in 1909, but it lasted only a few years. The Hollywood film colony, later the symbol of authority and rigid control, was originally founded by independents seeking to escape the grip of the patents company. The fluidity of the movie industry congealed after the introduction of sound in the late 1920s. "Talkies" helped solidify the hold of a few major studios as the technological complexity of sound production precluded the sort of independent activity characteristic of the early years.

Individual inventors and amateurs figured prominently in the first years of radio as well. Pioneers such as Marconi, De Forest, and Fessenden laid much of the foundation for wireless technology in small, personal research settings. The technological sophistication required for wireless telephony, as well as the needs of the military in World War I, encouraged more systematic and heavily financed research and development. Still, it is worth remembering that an important part of the strategy of large corporations such as A T & T and GE involved buying out and intimidating individual inventors, the most famous case being the notorious dealings of A T & T with Lee De Forest.

World War I had encouraged a boom in radio research, with close cooperation between A T & T, GE, Westinghouse, and the federal government, and it had led directly to the creation of RCA. But the emergence of broadcasting in 1920 came as a shock. Virtually no one had expected broadcasting, the sending of uncoded messages to a mass audience, to become the main use of wireless technology. By 1926 corporate infighting in the radio world resolved itself, leaving in its wake the basic structure of today's commercial television. A T & T agreed to abandon direct broadcasting and sold its station WEAF to RCA. A T & T then won RCA's assurance that it would drop plans to build an independent long-line system of wires. In addition, RCA, GE, and Westing-house set up the National Broadcasting Company to exclusively handle broadcasting and contracted to lease the A T & T web of wires. NBC, with this powerful corporate backing, began to offer the first regular national broadcasting over two networks based in New York.

*   *   *

The dream of transcendence through machines is an ancient one, and the urge to annihilate space and time found particularly intense expression through new communi-cations media. Overcoming the old constraints of time and space implied a great deal more than mere advances in physics. Generally speaking, popular reactions to dramatic improvements in communication emphasized the possibilities for strengthening a moral community and celebrated the conquering of those vast social and cultural distances that had traditionally kept the large majority of people isolated.

An especially strong utopian cast marked contemporary responses to the telegraph and the wireless. The public greeted the first telegraph lines of the 1840s with a combination of pride, excitement, sheer wonder, and some fear. As telegraph construc-tion proceeded quickly in all directions, doubters, believers, and curious bystanders in dozens of cities and towns flocked to get a firsthand look. In 1844 Alfred Vail, Morse's assistant, reported that at the Baltimore end of their experimental line crowds besieged the office daily for a glimpse of the machine. They promised "they would not say a word or stir and didn't care whether they understood or not, only they wanted to say they had seen it." The first telegraph offices had to take these excited crowds into account. Walling off inquisitive onlookers with glass partitions, an early Pittsburgh office announced: "Ladies and Gentlemen, visiting the room merely as Spectators, are assigned ample space, as the most Perfect Order is desirable for the convenience of the public as well as of the Telegrapher."[1]

Successful completion of the first Atlantic cable in the summer of 1858 inspired wild celebrations around the country. Such intense public feeling about a technological achievement appears rather strange to us now; certainly it is difficult to envision such a reaction today. Bonfires, fireworks, and impromptu parades marked the occasion across the nation. New York City held a huge parade, which was described as the city's largest public celebration ever. Over fifteen thousand people, from working men's clubs, immigrant societies, temperance groups, and the like, marched in a procession that revealed the strength of the telegraph's hold on the public imagination.

A widely evinced sentiment held that "the Telegraph has more than a mechanical meaning; it has an ideal, a religious, and a prospective significance, far-reaching and incalculable in its influences." The subtle spark of electricity, one of the fundamental, if dimly understood, creative forces of the universe, was now at man's disposal. The telegraph applied that "marvellous energy to the transmission of thought from continent to continent with such rapidity as to forestall the flight of Time, and inaugurate new realizations of human powers and possibilities." The divine boon of the telegraph allowed man to become more godlike. "It is the thought that it has metaphysical roots and relations that make it sublime." Such paeans rhetorically united the technological advance in communication with the ancient meaning of that word as common participation or communion. They presumed the success of certain Christian messages; but they also suggested that the creation of a miraculous communications technology was perhaps the most important message of all.[2]

One can discern a direct link between the more spiritually toned early responses and the boom in electronic revivalism today. There seems no doubt in the minds of contemporary evangelists about the answer to Morse's query, "What hath God wrought?" The most effective and avant-garde use of the latest communications technologies is probably being made by the various evangelical preachers who regularly "thank God for television" as they broadcast revivals over vast cable and satellite hookups. As Bishop Fulton J. Sheen, a pioneer in the field, once remarked: "Radio is like the Old Testament, hearing wisdom, without seeing; television is like the New Testament because in it the wisdom becomes flesh and dwells among us."[3]

There were secular prophets as well, equally awed by the transforming potential of instantaneous communication. "I see the electric telegraphs of the earth/I see the filaments of the news of the wars, deaths, losses, gains, passions of my race," sang Walt Whitman in "Salut Au Monde" (1856). We know, of course, that those telegraphs ultimately were appropriated by the corporate power of Western Union and the Associated Press. But perhaps Whitman used "filaments" in a double sense, including its traditional meaning as part of the reproductive organs of a flower. If so, he conjured a potent predictive insight. For the telegraph, which we might take as an historical synecdoche for all the electronic media that followed, did more than carry the news. It helped create novel ways of chronicling, reporting, and dramatizing the "wars, deaths, losses, gains, passions" of the society. Our historical knowledge of these forms and their internal relations—from wire service reports and syndicated columns through tabloids, newsreels, and network news—remains surprisingly skimpy.

A more privatized type of utopian response greeted the first wireless devices of the 1890s and early 1900s. In the writings of scientists, amateur enthusiasts, and trade publications, one finds repeated projections of how wireless technology would soon be tailored to fit the personal needs of operators. Many observers of the rapidly advancing scene believed "we shall talk with our friends at sea or from sea to land, or from New York to Peking almost as freely as we now talk to our neighbors in the next block. An opera performance in London or Berlin will be caught up by this new transmitter set about the stage and thrown into the air for all the world to hear . . . it may be that no farm or fireside will be without one."[4]

Today we think of radio as synonymous with broadcasting, but in the first years after the earliest broadcasts the amateur wireless community scoffed at the idea that radio ought to be dominated by a few big stations. The activity of wireless amateurs from around 1905 through the late 1920s is too often neglected as a factor in the history of radio. The "hams" provided a crucial demand for wireless equipment, supplying the original seed capital and audience for the radio industry. They bought radio equipment and kept up with the latest technical advances before and after the first broadcasting. This group numbered perhaps a quarter of a million around 1920, including some fifteen thousand amateur transmitting stations.

Throughout the 1920s radio mania remained an active, participatory pastime for millions. One had to constantly adjust and rearrange batteries, crystal detectors, and vacuum tubes for the best reception. For numerous radio fans of all classes, the excitement lay precisely in the battle to get clear reception amidst the howling and chatter of the crowded ether. The cult of "DXing," trying to receive the most distant station possible, remained strong for years. In 1924 one newly converted radio fan wrote, not untypically, that he was not especially interested in the various programs. "In radio it is not the substance of communication without wires, but the fact of it that enthralls. It is a sport, in which your wits, learning, and resourcefulness are matched against the endless perversity of the elements. It is not a matter, as you may suppose, of buying a set and tuning in upon what your fancy dictates."[5]

By the end of the 1920s, however, the ascension of corporate-dominated commercial broadcasting radically curtailed this sort of radio activity. Broadcasting, originally conceived as a service by manufacturers for getting people to buy surplus radio equipment, eventually shoved aside the very people who had nurtured it. In its mature state, radio succeeded not in fulfilling the utopian visions first aroused by wireless technology, but rather in incorporating those urges into the service of advertising. First in radio and then in television, commercial broadcasting became the cutting edge of a technologized ideology of consumption. Consumer goods promised to make one happy by returning what had vanished. "Nostalgia," originally a painful melancholy caused by absence from one's home or country, has acquired a primarily temporal sense since the rise of broadcasting. One has nostalgic, bittersweet longings for earlier, "simpler" times, and these times are most frequently signified by a "golden age" of radio, movies, popular music, and so forth. Commercial broadcasting wedded the advertiser's message to older popular cultural forms that were transferred to the new home environment of radio.

Today, the advertising and marketing axis that grew up with radio has made audience demographics the crucial template for the production of most of our culture's symbolic forms of expression. The term *life-style* best captures the essence of the current version of this ideology of consumption. A catch-all description for everything from one's clothing, work, or furnishings to preferred leisure pursuits, entertainments, and inebriates, this phrase already seems to have achieved saturation. It reduces all life to a style, equating how one lives with what one consumes. The post–World War II perfection of demographics as a predictive science and as a producer of crucial cultural maps is a story that remains to be told.

*   *   *

The cultural history of modern media, that is, the evolution of their content and the relation of that content to the larger popular culture, reveals another set of contradictions at work. To the extent that popular culture may be equated with the popular arts, modern media have operated mainly as business enterprises intent on maximizing profits. Especially within the broadcast media, the authority of advertising has been paramount in the establishment of cultural parameters and in the promotion of the consumption ethic as the supreme virtue. But this hegemony has never been as complete and total as it seemed on the surface. The media have not manufactured content out of thin air. Historically, the raw materials for media fare, as well as its creators, have been drawn from an assortment of cultural milieus.

The cultural histories of American film, radio, and television, particularly in their early years, could arguably be written entirely from the point of view of the contributions of "the others," immigrant, ethnic, and racial minorities in particular. The critical part played by immigrant audiences and Jewish immigrant entrepreneurs in the rise of the movie industry is well known. Slapstick comedy, raucous, vulgar, and universally appealing, was the first style to pack audiences in. It was also the first style to be identified as uniquely American around the world. Only in Hollywood could a Fatty Arbuckle be transformed in three years from a semiskilled plumber's helper into a comedy star making five thousand dollars a week. When the Warner brothers made the great leap into the sound era in 1927, it was not by accident that they chose *The Jazz Singer*, starring Al Jolson, as their vehicle. Its story of how a cantor's son renounces his father's religion for a career as a popular singer encapsulated both the history of the movie industry itself and the rapid secularization of Jewish life in America. The early film industry was energized in large part by a projection of the powerful urge toward collective representation so prominent in Jewish culture. The Jewish moguls reinvented the American dream in the course of creating the Hollywood mythos.

In the case of broadcasting, the exigencies of advertising demanded that programming present an aura of constant newness. Yet the content relied heavily upon traditional forms. Variety shows, hosted by comedians and singers, became the first important style on network radio. Drawing heavily upon the vaudeville format, these shows remained quite popular through World War II; many of the stars continued their success on television. The master of ceremonies served as a focal point for activity and as a means of easy identification with a sponsor's product. Most of the variety stars had long experience in earlier stage entertainment; ethnic and regional stereotypes, dialect stories, and popular song, all staples of vaudeville and burlesque, easily made the transition to broadcasting. So too did the pre–Civil War form of minstrelsy. The characters in radio's first truly national hit show, "Amos n' Andy" (1928), were direct descendants of blackface minstrel show figures.

These entertainments, and radio in general, seemed to have played a significant mediating role for certain audiences. There is intriguing fragmentary evidence suggesting that, in the early years of radio at least, children of immigrants, particularly in cities, were more likely to own radios than any other group. The census of 1930 revealed that 57.3 percent of the children in families of foreign or mixed parentage owned radio sets, as compared with 39.9 percent in families of native parentage. Among urban families, the figures were 62.8 percent (highest of any group) and 53.2 percent, respectively. The historical relation between "media mindedness" and "cultural otherness" is still largely unexplored, beyond a facile notion of "Americanization."[6]

The history of American popular music in this century offers perhaps the clearest example of how media content has been continually invigorated and revitalized by forms, styles, entertainers, and artists from outside the mainstream. The growth of radio broadcasting and the recording industry in the 1920s hastened the cross-fertilization of popular (but hitherto localized) musical forms. America's rich racial and geographical diversity of authentic folk musics—country, "mountain music," blues, jazz—became commercialized and available to much broader audiences. The new media allowed audiences and artists exposure to musical forms previously unknown to them. The post–World War II rise of rock 'n' roll, closely allied to the more general phenomenon of youth culture, reflected a vital new amalgam of white country music, black blues, and traditional Tin Pan Alley show music.

Recent infusions of Third World musics such as reggae, ska, and salsa point to the growth of an international, multicultural style in popular music. Beneath all its glitter and flash, the disco boom is fundamentally based on the popularization of Latin dance rhythms, spiced with the urban gay sensibility. The power of the recording and radio industries to standardize and exploit popular music, to hype stars and trends, ought not to be ignored or minimized. But denial of the authenticity at the core of much popular music grossly simplifies the complex tensions existing within our popular culture.

* * *

Before I discuss several of the latest developments in communications technology, it might prove instructive to cast a fleeting look backward at two early media dreamers, Edward Bellamy and Hugo Gernsback. In 1889 Bellamy, America's preeminent utopian, elaborated an idealized vision of future communications in his short story "With the Eyes Shut." He described the dream of a railroad passenger suddenly transported into a whole new world of media gadgets. Phonographed books and magazines have replaced printed ones in railroad cars. Clocks announce the time with recorded sayings from the great authors. Letters, newspapers, and books are recorded and listened to on phonographic cylinders, instead of being read. With a slide-projecting phonograph, one can even listen to a play while watching the actors. Everybody carries around an indispensable item, a combination tape recorder and phonograph. Bellamy seems most concerned that the sense of hearing threatens to overwhelm that of sight. But what stands out in his fable is the limitless choice of programming available to the individual in a private setting.

Whereas Bellamy's fantasy spun images of inexhaustible "software," Hugo Gernsback, science-fiction writer and wireless enthusiast, was captivated by the radical potential of radio "hardware." In the early 1900s Gernsback tirelessly promoted amateur wireless activity in his own magazines and others. The culmination of this work came in his book *Radio For All* (1922), which projected "the future wonders of Radio" fifty years hence. Gernsback predicted the coming of television, videophones, telex, and remote-controlled aircraft. He managed to think up some devices we seem to have missed: radio-powered roller skates, radio clocks, even a "radio business control" console. As the frontispiece to Gernsback's book shows, he envisioned a future where an individual's radio equipment would be at the very center of business and social life.

Atavistic expressions of the utopian urges given voice by Bellamy and Gernsback appear all around us today. Only now, with the advent of new satellite and video technologies, their fantasies have a firmer material base. Of course, Bellamy's "software socialism" and Gernsback's "hardware socialism" hardly appear to be lurking around the corner; corporate capital has enormous resources invested in the expansion of that material base. The press is filled with stories detailing the maneuvers of RCA, Warner Communications, MCA, SONY, and all the rest in the scramble to get a piece of the new action. No one can deny the central position of big capital in the new advances. But the recent developments may still promise in essence what they appear to deny in substance.

The accelerated evolution of media hardware and software has been fueled largely by the persistence of utopian urges in the population at large. With the impending spread of cheap video hardware to large numbers of people—video cameras, cassette recorders, video disc players, and home computers—the potential exists for individuals and collectives to become producers as well as consumers. The historical gap in broadcasting between the oligopoly of transmission and the democracy of reception may thus be drastically reduced. It is important to see the interaction between the corporate giants and the deep and genuine desire on the part of people to gain more direct control over the means of communication and the content of communications. The recent revival of the cable television industry is a good case in point.

The decentralizing capacity of cable television has long been recognized, if not actually realized. Indeed, by the early 1970s, the "blue-sky" predictions that ended nearly every discussion of cable in the 1960s seemed laughable. The cable industry was in a great depression, with very little wiring of communities taking place. All the talk about public access channels, two-way hookups, video telephones, home computer terminals, and so forth seemed quite hollow because scarcely any cable companies could get financing to wire homes. Even in New York City, potentially the most lucrative market, both cable franchises were losing millions each year. But two new factors added to the scene in the last five years or so have rejuvenated the industry and freed venture capital.

First, the rise of pay cable services such as Home Box Office (HBO) and Showtime revealed an extensive latent demand for alternative programming. These channels charge a premium each month above the basic cable rate. HBO, owned by Time-Life and the dominant force in pay cable, began with a simple formula of old movies and live sports. It is now moving rapidly toward providing more original programming, such as entertainment specials, comedy shows, plays, and even something it dubs "docutainment," which sounds rather like a modern version of the old "March of Time" newsreels.

Second, the success of RCA's and Western Union's communication satellites has created viable distribution networks for the cable companies. Earth station receivers, costing anywhere from two thousand to twenty thousand dollars, allow cable operators to "get on the bird." Programmers are now busily putting together new networks and pay services aimed at reaching the growing cable audience. The availability of new and specialized programming in turn has stimulated a new demand for cable systems in various communities. Presently, about fifteen million American homes are wired for cable; some industry analysts think the figure could be 80 percent of all television homes by 1990.

Insofar as the power of commercial network television is based on its ability to deliver mass audiences to advertisers, its strength may soon be challenged by the decentralizing trend in cable. Several new networks aimed at specialized audiences have been created already: children, Hispanics, senior citizens, sports junkies. Cable and its attendant new video technologies will, at the very least, mean the decline of mass market television, breaking the thirty-year-old grip of the three commercial networks. The potential for eventual direct satellite transmissions to homes, bypassing local stations and cable systems alike, is also very real. The technological stage is now set for the postbroadcasting era.

Many cable programmers hope to profit in much the same way as special interest magazines, by precisely targeting a well-defined fraction of the population that certain advertisers wish to reach exclusively. The concept is known as "narrowcasting." One might legitimately ask what is so promising about these developments; the specter of "demographic" cable programming is rather depressing. For the present, however, one could argue that the revival of the cable industry itself has been a positive development, spurred by the push and pull between people who want alternative programming and programmers who want to see a greater cable market before they invest. There is no doubt that the hardware is now far ahead of the software. The crucial question has become, can imaginative and innovative programming be created to take advantage of the new technologies?

The key point is that all of the independent program developers, artists, and political activists, who for years have been thwarted by the current system and could never get on the networks, now have a potential way to reach large audiences. A show that reaches twenty million people over network television today is considered a failure; this sort of standard will of necessity change. The new networks of distribution provide possible entry points for independents to reach viewers. Perhaps the most promising new nodes will be local cable and video discs.

Local cable companies all provide a surfeit of channels, including public access and leased channels. For a very small fee, public access channels allow total freedom for live, local programming. Most cable systems also have channels that can be leased by local groups who have lined up sponsors for their program. This whole area is currently in an embryonic state of development, although some communities are farther advanced in exploiting the potential for grass-roots programming.

There are still large unanswered questions about the video disc, which has just begun to be mass marketed. Video discs represent a more passive activity than video cassettes in that one will not be able to make one's own discs; video disc is to video cassette as phonograph records are to tape. The advantage of video disc, however, is said to be its superior quality of picture and sound and its lower cost. The big guns in the field have invested heavily in the home video market of nonbroadcast television. RCA's Selecta-Vision system reportedly represents its largest investment ever in a single product; it has also made a long-term deal with CBS to provide additional disc software. Similarly, N. V. Philips, the Dutch conglomerate, has contracted with MCA to provide software for its Magna-Vision home video center. These kinds of arrangements are likely to increase, but the outlook for software supply, as all concerned agree, leaves more room for independent activity. Local and national networks for video disc rental, sales, and production are already being formed.

Despite all of the high-powered market research and corporate wheeling and dealing, no one is quite certain how the video disc phenomenon will evolve. Incredibly, RCA projects a $7.5 billion video disc market by 1990, but capital could be wrong. Two crucial jokers in the deck are the incompatibility of various disc systems and, more importantly, the increasingly shaky state of the American economy. Will new communications hardware be affordable?

Given the nature of the continuing energy crisis, one could argue that in a broad sense communication must gain primacy over transportation in our society. An awareness of the dialectical tensions within the American media may explain why it is possible to criticize the worst tendencies of modern media—banalization, encouragement of the commodity fetish, the urge toward global hegemony—but at the same time to hold out real hope for future promise. It is less important to curb futurist fantasies than to continually attempt to expose the hidden political and social agenda attending techno-logical progress. The recovery of historical perspective, bringing the contradictions within American media into sharper relief, can perhaps help us to remember the future of modern communication.

Notes

1.   Alfred Vail to Samuel F. B. Morse, 3 June 1844, quoted in Robert L. Thompson, *Wiring a Continent: The History of the Telegraph Industry in the United States, 1832–1866* (Princeton: Princeton University Press, 1947), p. 25; regulations posted in Pittsburgh office of

the Atlantic and Ohio Telegraph Company, in the Henry O'Reilly Collection, First Series, vol. 1, New York Historical Society, New York, NY.

2.   Charles Briggs and Augustus Maverick, *The Story of the Telegraph and the History of the Great Atlantic Cable* (New York: Rudd and Carleton, 1858), pp. 21, 14; *New York Times*, 9 August 1858.

3.   Bishop Sheen quoted in Michael E. Starr, "Prime Time Jesus," *Cultural Correspondence*, no. 4 (Spring 1977): 21.

4.   Carl Snyder, "The World's New Marvels: The Wireless Telephone," *Collier's Weekly* 52 (25 October 1913): 23.

5.   Howard V. O'Brien, "It's Great to Be A Radio Maniac," *Collier's Weekly* 74 (13 September 1924): 16.

6.   U.S. Bureau of the Census, *Fifteenth Census of the United States, 1930*, Population, vol. 6, *Families*, p. 33.

Chapter 30

DAVID R. SPENCER

FACT AND FICTION

IN QUIET AND SOMETIMES POLITE CIRCLES of mainly local and amateur historians, it has often been said that facts should never interfere with the telling of a good tale. Both Joseph Pulitzer and William Randolph Hearst must have been listening at the keyhole when such pronouncements were solemnly declared. After all, both were in the business of commercial newspapers, and their ability to continue to feed any form of public frenzy over scandal, crime, and sensational scientific discoveries depended on money. Pulitzer did not have access to a family fortune as did Hearst, and therefore, the immigrant publisher was obliged to depend on newspaper sales and advertising. These men had some experience in tapping the constituent imagination, so what took place in regard to both their papers and Yellow Journalism in New York in the closing years of the nineteenth century should have been no surprise to anyone with any observational skills regarding the state of American media.

Of the two men, Hearst proved to be the most accurate harbinger of things to come when, as chief arbitrator of bad taste in the big-city press in 1892, he took on Charlotte Perkins Gilman, a leading American feminist and notorious husband collector. Gilman was known as one of the leading icons for instability in family relationships at a time when divorce was still considered a moral scandal. In the *San Francisco Examiner* in 1891, a full-page and exceptionally inflammatory discussion was presented on the latest peccadilloes of the flamboyant Gilman, much to her distress. So, when a Hearst reporter appeared on her doorstep a year later to gather some comments about the whole business of getting divorced, Gilman would not cooperate. After she refused to consent to a formal interview, the reporter attempted to extract commentary by reverting to a casual conversation. When this did not achieve the desired results, he offered to pay Gilman; then, having had no success, he threatened to smear her name in the newspaper. But Gilman did not bend,[1] and the reporter left her doorstep empty-handed.

Gilman's encounter with Hearst over her divorce scenarios led to her lifetime boycott against any Hearst publications, even though many an editor assured her she would not have to face the owner himself if only she would agree to publish in one of his journals. Speaking of the Hearst brand of journalism, Gilman wrote:

> [It] frankly plays on the lowest, commonest of its traits: tickling it with salacious detail, harping on those themes which unlettered peasants find attractive, and for which most people retain an unadmitted weakness. This is the secret[2] of our "Yellow Press" and of the strange prominence given to unimportant stories of vice even in the mildly cream colored variety.

In Gilman's analysis of the Yellow Press, merely being associated with the likes of Hearst was grounds for condemnation. She took on the venerable Ambrose Bierce when he refused to stop writing rude remarks about the Pacific Coast Women's Press Association; she was particularly grieved when Bierce directed his attacks against the individual female members of the organization. She responded[3] to his verbiage by noting, "That man ought not to go unwhipped." Gilman's distaste for Hearst continued to be expressed even after she took her own life in 1935. Her agent, Willis Kingsley Wing, attempted to abscond with her autobiography, which he wanted serialized in the Hearst-owned publication *Cosmopolitan*. Wing received a curt letter and direction from Gilman's daughter, Katherine Stetson Chamberlin, that even though her mother was now deceased, the boycott against Hearst would continue.

So, just what type of journalistic culture encouraged the kind of misbehavior that troubled Charlotte Perkins Gilman and those who agreed with her assessment of the late Victorian press? As historian Fred Fedler and others have noted, the demographic class occupied by working journalists was not far from the bottom of the social ladder. Most journalists were underpaid, drank too much, and were rude and ruthless and fundamentally dishonest. They could not hold a job and drifted from city to city, constantly looking for work. They struggled through long and exhausting hours of labor and lived in hovels on the wrong side of the tracks, often having only the local saloon as a place of comfort.[4] As journalism history professors Steven Vaughan and Bruce Evenson discovered in their study of journalism on film, such images of journalists persisted well into the 1930s, as seen in Ben Hecht's play *The Front Page*. It was only when the American Newspaper Publishers Association began to complain that revisionist histories,[5] such as *His Girl Friday* and the 1940 remake of *The Front Page*, began to soften the image of the hardened journalist.

One of the key problems affecting the journalistic era of Pulitzer and Hearst was dishonesty. When pursuing a story, many reporters refused to identify their profession to potential sources. Prominent individuals frequently woke up to their morning coffee and papers and found themselves quoted, often in a very unflattering light. Journalists typically defended the use of this kind of deception as the only way a reporter could gain access to the facts of a particular case. One editor even boasted that no reporter who was *not* dishonest could succeed in the profession. Needless to say, the journalists' enthusiastic defense of the practice did not cut any ice with Gilman and those who thought like her. And not only did journalists routinely lie to get a good story, they also accepted bribes, eavesdropped on potential sources, and stole pictures and documents from reporters who worked on competitive papers. Hearst newspapers in both New York and Chicago were known for grabbing suspects[6] off the street and grilling them in order to obtain good copy before turning them over to the police.

The problem of dishonesty existed not only in collecting information but also in publishing it. It was well known that many journals that followed Hearst's example printed material that was factually untrue. One of Hearst's most vocal opponents, E. L. Godkin, editor of the New York newspaper *The Nation*, pointed to the coverage of a theatrical event as handled by three different newspapers. The first account noted that the lower floor of the theater was almost completely filled and that the first balcony had three to four rows of chairs. The second reviewer proclaimed that the theater was only about a third filled. And the final account had the place packed, with no room left[7] for anyone wishing to sit. Of course, deceptive and dishonest reporting reached its peak during coverage of the Spanish-American War, which will be dealt with in a later chapter.

The deceptive practices of the journalistic community were well known among those whose circles included individuals with little respect for the law. On July 17, 1890, the *New York Times* printed an article cautioning local merchants about an elaborate swindle being perpetrated by a person using the newspaper's name. Apparently, this man would approach a business and identify himself as a *Times* reporter. In one case, he interviewed an eyeglass manufacturer and wrote a very flattering article on the man's business. He then told the businessman that the *Times* would publish the article if it was paid $10. The businessman felt that he had accomplished his goals when he bartered the swindler down to an $8 sum. The phony reporter left the premises[8] with the money and the article, which, of course, never saw the light of day.

Why was there no wholesale rebelling against this kind of dishonesty? One factor was that people believed the press was simply in the business of being in business and that truth had to be sacrificed if the journalistic community wanted to continue to sell newspapers. In other words, scandal was profitable, and as long as money remained the root of the evil, the evil would continue to exist. The other factor was entertainment. Not only did the Yellow Press consolidate its readership in the lower segments of American society, it also appealed to the middle and upper classes. It seems that everyone in the new industrial America needed a diversion[9] from the tensions of everyday life, and folks such as Pulitzer and Hearst were more than willing to provide the product. Their approach was not without controversy.

In spite of the popularity of the genre, the Yellow Press had its critics in the community at large. It was one thing for a member of the journalistic establishment such as Godkin to spout invective against Pulitzer and Hearst, but it was quite another to have criticism arise among other prominent community members, especially those who were generally regarded as leaders in Victorian society. The Yellow Press was not the first institution to draw attention from one of its own. In 1859, Lambert A. Wilmer's book *Our Press Gang, or, A Complete Exposition of the Corruptions and Crimes of American Newspapers* appeared in American bookshops. The volume did little to halt the march of sensationalism that most people at the time would argue had begun with Benjamin Day[10] and his *New York Sun* of the 1830s.

A number of critics contended that in its extravagant detailing of the most heinous of crimes, the Yellow Press was actually providing a how-to handbook for young criminals. Some of the critics declared that the press did more than provide detailed methods by which successful criminal activities could take place: it actually, they said, encouraged those with no respect for the law to take up a career in crime. As one Baptist minister put it: "Do you suppose that your sons and daughters can grow up pure-minded and clean[11] if their minds are fed on such filth in the formative period of their existence?"

Prominent academics regularly explored what they saw as the irrefutable link between sensationalist reporting and urban crime. In one article, the authors argued that the lower classes, by the very nature of their respective existences, were naturally prone to criminal behavior. These citizens were deemed far less advanced intellectually than those who held the levers of power, and they were considered more impressionable as well. In the age of eugenics, this was not an uncommon position. And where, according to the experts, did these underlings get their views on society? The Yellow Press, naturally.

The Yellow Press found itself in the moral crosshairs of Anthony Comstock, the notorious self-appointed guardian of the moral community in the nineteenth century. Comstock trotted out statistics that proved, in his mind at least, a definite connection between the kinds of stories that appeared in the Yellow Press and proven crimes. As journalism historian John Ferré discovered, the list of crimes[12] was (as one might suspect) comprehensive, including arson, burglary, counterfeiting, assault, forgery, grand larceny, highway robbery, housebreaking, attempted murder, murder, perjury, petit larceny, drunkenness, and attempted suicide.

Any number of crusades were directed at the Yellow Press in the closing years of the nineteenth century. There were campaigns to limit the profits pouring into the coffers of Pulitzer and Hearst. None worked. Some opponents argued that establishing endowments similar to those enjoyed by universities, hospitals, and charitable organizations could lead to a cleaner and more responsible journalism. The concept was quite simple: if one freed the press from the basic need to attract advertisers, the quest for constant circulation increases could be dealt with. Steel magnate Andrew Carnegie called upon his friends to undertake such a course, but alas, the thought of placing their millions into a potential sinkhole was unappealing. So, too, was the campaign to buy out both Pulitzer and Hearst. In the final analysis, there were no takers.[13] The line in the sand over which no responsible journalist could cross was only drawn after Hearst made the outrageous claim that corruption and bad behavior on the part of public officials could lead to legitimate assassinations of the perpetrators. Shortly after the editorial expressing this opinion appeared, President McKinley was shot down in Buffalo, New York. The Yellow Press had, in many ways, finally reached the zenith of its role as gossipmonger, social critic, and disturbing influence.

In spite of the fact that they were lumped together by those who condemned the Yellow Press, Joseph Pulitzer and William Randolph Hearst were very different people. As an eastern European Jewish immigrant, Pulitzer probably realized that he would never become part of the power-brokering establishment in New York City, regardless of his success and his great wealth. When he finally approached Columbia College about the possibility of establishing a journalism school on its campus, his dream was put on hold for well over a decade before he finally forced the issue. But Pulitzer did rely on New York society in a way Hearst did not.

In the influential circles in the city, Hearst was considered to be an appalling character. Most considered his newspaper a reflection of his character. The young student who had sent a chamber pot to the president of Harvard now regularly sent literary chamber pots to the citizenry of New York and often in the most provocative of ways. While Pulitzer worked with the newcomers to his city, Hearst rashly exploited them and their city. And when Pulitzer retreated to his yacht to deal with his strained nerves and increasing problems with blindness, Hearst was burning yet one more midnight candle[14] in the cause of personal ambition.

456 DAVID R. SPENCER

It can be argued with some conviction that Pulitzer was the creator and Hearst was the follower. In spite of continuing debates over the influence of the two on late nineteenth- and early twentieth-century journalism, it is a fact of life that while Hearst was busily spending a good chunk of his mother's money long before he arrived in New York, Pulitzer was turning the journalistic community on its head with an approach to fact gathering and storytelling that would later be dubbed New Journalism.

For the reporter involved in the execution of the New Journalism, the city was theater. Stories had color and life, and if they did not, those attributes could be created. The reporter roamed the streets and back alleys of the metropolis, seeking out what Pulitzer anointed as the human interest tale. Peoples' trials and triumphs became the meat of the material that appeared under gaudy and often suggestive headlines. It was no longer good enough to report that a man bit a dog after the dog bit him. What happened during the attack, from the first crunch to the last bloodletting, in many ways defined the New Journalism.

In that world, it was also fair to create the news or at least the factors leading up to the news of the day. Pulitzer's paper was filled with endless crusades to stamp out corruption and poverty. The publisher's victims were numerous, and among the leading villains of the day were the Standard Oil Company, the New York Central Railway, the telephone monopoly, slum landlords, crooked contractors, sexual exploiters, and the railway lobbyists of 1887. And if a reader was in danger of being turned away by stories of the ill health of the nation, there was the amusement of the stunt to provide the proper distraction. In the fall of 1888, *World* reporter Elizabeth Cochrane (Nellie Bly) boarded a steamship in Jersey City to begin what would be a seventy-two-day journey around the world, beating that of the fictional Phineas Fogg of Jules Verne's exceptionally popular novel *Around the World in Eighty Days*. Needless to say, Pulitzer ensured that his journal covered every vital moment of the adventure, which captured the hearts and souls[15] of many a resident of New York City and beyond.

For Pulitzer, the use of sensationalism was a means to an end. Hearst treated it as an end in itself. Pulitzer regarded himself as a champion for those with little or no voice in the community. Although the gory tales that appeared on page one sold his newspapers, they were actually designed to lead his readers to the more thoughtful commentary contained in the editorials inside. For Pulitzer, the editorial page was the heart of the Victorian newspaper[16] and the page that mattered most.

But try as he might to excuse the rabble that appeared on page one, Pulitzer had unleashed a journalism that would eventually engulf the city and the country and place in the hands of William Randolph Hearst a weapon that ultimately brought discredit to the institution of journalism in the United States. Until Hearst arrived on the scene in 1890s' New York, virtually every journalist working in the city was controlled by what appeared in Pulitzer's journal. Reporters lived in fear that they would miss an important story in *The World*. It was well known along the newspaper alley of Park Row that early editions of *The World* were snapped up by competitive journals and that *World* stories were often rewritten for consumption in those newspapers. The fearsome Charles Chapin, who would later become the subject of scandal himself, ran Pulitzer's empire in a bloodless and unfeeling manner. He eventually died in Sing Sing Prison,[17] serving a life term for the murder of his wife.

Pulitzer had created the model and Charles Chapin set the tone for what appeared on page one. In 1884, James L. Wilson and his wife were brutally murdered in Winnetka, Illinois. At the time, Chapin was cutting his teeth on sensationalist stories for the *Chicago*

Tribune. He learned his lessons well and eventually took his knowledge to New York and Pulitzer before his downfall. Chapin had noted that a similar murder had taken place in Lincoln, Illinois, some four months previously. Melville Stone, publisher of the *Chicago Morning News*, charged his reporters with not only covering a crime but also investigating it. The lessons of this so-called detective journalism were not lost on the young Chapin. He, too, conducted his own investigation into the Wilson murders and came to the conclusion that they were linked to the Lincoln case. Chapin also abandoned the inverted pyramid style of reporting for a series of articles on the case in which the readers were led along by a series of tantalizing facts that moved, step by step, in a logical order. In the end, in spite of his colorful rhetoric calling for justice in these cases, Chapin was unable to identify the murderer. But his experiences would soon hold him in good stead in the hurly-burly world[18] of New York journalism.

Until Hearst's significant faux pas in the McKinley case, journalism in New York had been resilient, existing for over a half century. When Lincoln Steffens returned to New York after a stint in Europe, where he attended university, the culture was alive and well. He noted in his biography that reporters were never allowed to get too comfortable in their role. In order to fight complacency, they were regularly shifted from department to department. Yesterday's police reporter could become tomorrow's art and music critic. As Steffens noted,[19] "When a reporter no longer saw red at a fire, when he was so used to police news that a murder was not a human tragedy but only a crime, he could not write police news for us." When he finally became an editor with the *New York Commercial Advertiser*, Steffens gave this charge to a young reporter about to go out and cover a murder:

> Here, Cahan, is a report that a man has murdered his wife, a rather bloody, hacked up crime. We don't care about that. But there's a story in it. That man loved that woman well enough once to marry her, and now he has hated her enough to cut her all to pieces. If you can find out just what happened between that wedding and this murder, you will have a novel for yourself and a short story for me. Go on now, take your time and get this tragedy[20] as a tragedy.

There was little doubt that the reporting of tragedy did much for a newspaper's circulation at that time in history. Previously, both Ellen (Helen) Jewitt and Mary Rogers had captured the fancy of New York readers in a way that neither would have preferred. Now, it was up to another woman, Nellie Bly, to put a female name on the masthead of one of the city's major newspapers, *The World New York*. Bly had started a modest newspaper career in Pittsburgh, reporting primarily on what was known in those days as women's issues. She had also convinced her editor to send her on a trip to Mexico, where, in return for the newspaper's generosity, she would report on life in that country. But when she returned to Pittsburgh, she was once again forced to return to the women's section of the journal. Fed up with these restrictions, she resigned and made her way to New York in search of a career in which her abilities as a reporter, regardless of gender, would be respected. Her quest took her to Pulitzer's offices on Park Row and a meeting with his editor, Col. John Cockerill.

Since *The World* dealt in controversy for most its existence, access to the home office was difficult if not impossible for anyone who had not been invited or who was not expected to be there. Bly was such a person, yet she doggedly worked her way through the strict security apparatus in the building to end up in Cockerill's presence. He was impressed with her determination but was more reserved about her story possibilities. She proposed taking a steamer to Europe and then posing as an immigrant to the United States on the return voyage in order to explore the hazards experienced by the unfortunates housed in the steerage section of the ship. Cockerill was not about to make any commitment, but he paid Nellie $25 to keep her from approaching other newspapers. He asked her to return on September 22, 1887, and she did.

Cockerill's reaction to the immigrant story was lukewarm at best. He had other ideas for making a journalistic splash and testing Nellie Bly's courage and stamina at the same time. He pointed her to a 120-acre site located in the East River. Its official name was Blackwell's Island, and it housed several city institutions, including the Women's Lunatic Asylum. Cockerill suggested that the young investigative reporter pose as a person with a mental problem in order to get herself committed to the hospital. Her mission was to investigate the continuing rumors that all was not well in the behavior of certain individuals, including physicians, who were employed at the hospital. Bly regarded the challenge as a way to get into the newspaper, and whatever concerns she may have had about her own health and welfare were superseded by the knowledge that she was about to embark on a journalism career in the heart of American journalism, New York City.

Blackwell's Island and whatever went on there had come to the attention of most of the newspapers in New York at one time or another. In August of that year, 1887, two nurses went to the *New York Times* with tales of abuse at the hospital. The Blackwell's Island facility was not the only institution that had been accused of mistreating patients. *The World* itself had penned two editorials, one on July 3 and the other on July 9, calling for an investigation into tales that inmates on Ward's Island, just north of Blackwell's, were also the victims of abuse. The story began to take on a life of its own when two guards were charged with manslaughter in the death of an inmate[21] whom they described as a lunatic.

If a story was dramatic, it made page one in Pulitzer's *World*. And if such New York events as the Festival of Connection, marking the opening of the Brooklyn Bridge, were considered to be worthy of front-page treatment, one can only guess the reaction in the editorial chambers of Pulitzer's fiefdom when Nellie Bly began to bang out her story of horror[22] at Blackwell's Island. The story had it all and proved, if anyone doubted, that truth can be stranger than fiction.

Bly began her odyssey by booking herself into Matron Irene Stenard's Temporary Home for Women on Second Avenue. She used the name Nellie Brown at Cockerill's suggestion, just in case a forgotten monogram should appear on an article of clothing. After having dined, she began a confusing and rambling conversation with some of the others in the working-class boardinghouse. She then feigned becoming more and more delusional, at which point some of the other guests began to fear for their lives. The proper authorities were called the following morning, and Nellie Brown was on her way[23] to Bellevue Hospital for observation after a short stop in the courtroom of Judge Patrick Duffy.

Duffy was intrigued by the lost soul and suggested that New York's journalistic community might be of some assistance in attempting to define who this person really was and from whence she came. Nellie told the judge and the congregated reporters that she came from Cuba and that her real name was Nellie Moreno. The *New York Sun* took up the challenge by treating her tale as an unresolved mystery. Other newspapers followed suit, but *The World* remained silent on the issue. Nellie was finally on her way to a stay on Blackwell's Island that she would never forget.

When "Ten Days in a Madhouse" hit the front pages of Pulitzer's the *World New York*, it was an instant sensation. But was it sensational? The opening insert, which later became the first chapter in the book version of the story, was simply entitled "A Delicate Mission," hardly the kind of graphic design that would later appear in Hearst's *New York Journal*. The title of the second chapter was no more provocative: Bly modestly entitled it "Preparing for the Ordeal." In fact, Bly's reporting had almost a matter-of-fact approach. Describing how the story came to be told, Bly carefully pieced together her experiences:

> I succeeded in getting committed to the insane ward at Blackwell's Island, where I spent ten days and nights and had an experience which I shall never forget. I took upon myself to enact the part of a poor, unfortunate crazy girl, and felt it my duty not to shirk any of the disagreeable results that should follow. I became one of the city's insane wards for that length of time, experienced much, and saw and heard more of the treatment accorded to this helpless class of our population, and when I had seen and heard enough, my release was promptly secured. I left the insane ward with pleasure and regret—pleasure that I was once more able to enjoy the free breath of heaven; regret that I could not have brought with me some of the unfortunate women who lived and suffered with me, and who, I am convinced, are just as sane[24] as I was and am now myself.

Even when she told of torture and relentless abuse of the inmates, the text of her columns had almost a distant feeling:

> Miss Tillie Mayard suffered more than any of us from the cold, and yet she tried to follow my advice to be cheerful and try to keep up for a short time. Superintendent Dent brought in a man to see me. He felt my pulse and my head and examined my tongue. I told them how cold it was, and assured them that I did not need medical aid, but that Miss Mayard did, and they should transfer their attentions to her. They did not answer me, and I was pleased to see Miss Mayard leave her place and come forward to them. She spoke to the doctors and told them she was ill, but they paid no attention to her. The nurses came and dragged her back to the bench, and after the doctors left they said, "After awhile, when you see that the doctors will not notice you, you will quit running up to them." Before the doctors left me I heard one say—I cannot give it in his exact words—that my pulse and eyes were not that of an insane girl, but Superintendent Dent assured him that in cases such as mine such tests failed. After watching me for awhile he said my face was the brightest he had ever seen for a lunatic. The nurses had on heavy undergarments and coats, but they refused to give us shawls. Nearly all night long I listened to a woman cry about the cold and beg for God to let her die. Another one yelled "Murder!" at frequent intervals and "Police!" at others until my flesh felt creepy.[25]

Bly's caper was a Pulitzer classic. The publisher told friends and colleagues that he admired her courage and the down-to-earth, populist approach[26] she took to reporting. However, not all persons in the journalistic community were turned on by Pulitzer's social agenda. Upton Sinclair, who was to have a little experience in exposé journalism himself, thought that Pulitzer and eventually Hearst were only taking up popular causes to increase circulation, which in turn was reflected in higher advertising rates, in order to become richer and richer. For Sinclair and like-minded individuals, the newspaper game was little more than an extension of the marketing mentality[27] that gripped New York at the time. But it was not to be turned back just yet. Nellie Bly had opened the floodgates, and more startling revelations were to follow.

If Sinclair was concerned that Pulitzer was doing little more than reviving the legacies of Benjamin Day and James Gordon Bennett, he must have been horrified by what he saw when William Randolph Hearst took over the minor league *New York Journal*. The paper, with an average pre-Hearst circulation of some seventy-seven thousand, once thrived on reporting tales of the seamier side of big-city living. It was known in New York circles as the chambermaid's delight. Retreating from the tabloid approach, the newspaper's management decided to reform the journal, but it began a serious slide in circulation. It apparently could not compete with Pulitzer's journal, with its nearly half a million daily readers.

Pulitzer left most of the less savory side of the world to front-page reporting. Hearst has no such restrictions. He took on Pulitzer in Pulitzer's own backyard. When his rival began crusades to help the poor and homeless, Hearst not only copied his initiatives but also usually expanded on them. When Pulitzer's employees were passing out bread[28] to starving New Yorkers, Hearst was giving away full meals and warm clothing.

There was always a school of thought in New York journalism circles that Hearst, as opposed to Pulitzer, was nothing more than a big kid at heart and that his newspaper world was his kindergarten. Certainly, much of the evidence in his behavior, which was later used in Orson Welles's *Citizen Kane*, tends to bear this out. One of Hearst's fetishes was to play fast and loose with New York's police force. As his biographer Ben Procter wrote, "Crime and passion, no matter how bizarre and grotesque, were the most pervasive themes in every *Journal* paper. Hearst seemed to be especially fascinated with police work,[29] with sleuthing and the vagaries of the criminal mind." And as with all of his passions, Hearst pushed his obsession to the limit. He gathered his reporters around him one day in 1897 and announced that they were the founding members of his special "Murder Squad." Their mandate was to investigate and solve heinous crimes before New York's finest came up with the answers.

One can only imagine the horror experienced by three young New Yorkers as they attempted to beat the city's summer heat with a dip in the East River on the last weekend in June 1897. They were accustomed to sharing their swimming hole with fish, garbage, and marine traffic, but a headless body was one find too many. To William Randolph Hearst and the Murder Squad, however, it was a gift from heaven, so to speak. The Sunday news edition of *The New York Journal* laid out four screaming headlines on page one.

In large, bold type, the leading headline barked out, "BEHEADED, CAST INTO THE RIVER." The second announced, "DISMEMBERED TRUNK OF A MAN FOUND BY THREE BOYS WHO WERE SWIMMING." Set in a descending size, the third read, "HE HAD BEEN MURDERED AND HIS CUNNING SLAYER SOUGHT TO FOREVER HIDE HIS CRIME." And finally, yet one more of Hearst's obsessions appeared via a headline that revealed,

"SCIENCE HAS RECONSTRUCTED THE LIVING MAN FROM WHAT REMAINS OF THE DEAD ONE—PROBABLY DECAPITATED WHILE STILL ALIVE." Of course, two very obvious liberties in terms of accurate reporting were taken in these announcements. First, since the murderer had yet to be captured, how could one possibly know how cunning the criminal really was, and second, there was no way of knowing whether the unfortunate victim had his head removed while still living. The headlines were little more than Hearst hyperbole.

The body, which was wrapped in a decorated oilcloth, was that of a Turkish bath masseur named William Guldensuppe. His identity would not be revealed for another four days. For the Hearst Murder Squad, the monetary value of the oilcloth was important. As one short headline noted, "THIS MAY BE A CLEW [sic]," and it would prove to be so. It would eventually connect the victim with Augusta Nack, a married woman who had ended their romance to take up with a barber named Martin Thorn. He should have known better.

The Monday edition of the newspaper was no less relentless in the coverage of the crime. Page one carried a graphic drawing of the victim's remains, showing in detail where the knife used to dismember the unfortunate Guldensuppe entered his body. The story revealed for the first time that along with his head, the victim was also missing his legs and arms, which were later discovered at separate locations along the river. When it came time to inter the bath masseur, it would be a challenge to reassemble him in death.

Along with the sketch of the body, Hearst's artists also drew pictures of the ropes used to tie the oilcloth together around the corpse. At the center of the visual treatment of the tale was a detailed sketch of the location where part of the discovery took place, at Cliff Avenue and 176th Street. For those readers captured by the lure of such a mystery, the saga continued on into the second page of the Monday edition. Again, the oilcloth with its unique diagrams was reproduced, as was a picture of the location on the river at Eleventh Street where the three young boys made the original discovery. And for those unaffected by squeamishness, a realistic drawing of Guldensuppe's slashed hand, with three deep knife wounds, accompanied the other drawings. Nothing was left to the imagination, unless it was Hearst's imagination.

By Tuesday, Hearst and his gang were in full coverage hysteria. The entire first two pages of their paper were devoted to the affair, with considerably large volumes of text supplemented by drawings related to the crime. The front-page headlines announced that the clothes belonging to the victim had been discovered, as was a valise that the newspaper claimed belonged to Guldensuppe, although no concrete evidence to link the findings and the victim was published. Hearst even hired a palmist to read the dead man's fingerprints for clues to his personality.

Day by day, coverage of the event took up more and more space in the first section of *The Journal*. Hearst even extended the story by inviting readers with missing relatives to contact him and his investigative team of journalists, delivering a faint hope of finding those who had gone astray. And then, Hearst dangled the temptation of a reward in front of his readers. In a can't-miss location on page one, he offered a $1,000 reward to anyone who could offer evidence that would result in solving the mystery.

When Wednesday arrived, the screaming headline on page one read simply, "DISCOVERED BY THE *JOURNAL*." So, what was discovered? First, Hearst's private police force had confirmed that the body found in the river was that of William Guldensuppe. Second and more important, they revealed that Augusta Nack had at one time left her husband to take up an illicit affair with the masseur. It also appeared that Nack had acquired yet one more devoted paramour, the barber Martin Thorn. Could she be involved, asked the newspaper? When the front-page story noted that she was under police surveillance, the least *The Journal* could do was to turn its attention away from the deceased to concentrate on the living. It was Nack's turn to lose any sense of privacy in the world governed by William Randolph Hearst. To ensure that no one could beat his *Journal* in revealing more of this lurid crime,[30] Hearst rented out the entire building where the major suspect lived and placed guards around all the entrances to prevent rival reporters from gaining access to the soon to be accused or her living accommodations. It would only be a matter of time, one would suspect, before Nack and the unfortunate Thorn[31] were paraded in front of a judge.

Throughout the summer, *The Journal* kept the drumbeats sounding. Day by day, the case grew more and more bizarre. Recognizing that it was very likely that the state of New York was reserving a place for her in the electric chair, Augusta Nack ultimately confessed her role in the crime but pointed to Thorn as the perpetrator. She told lawyers that she really loved William Guldensuppe but that Thorn had a better income, one that would help her enjoy a life of comfort. The prosecution bought her story. Nack, who was actually the person who dismembered the unfortunate Guldensuppe in a bathtub in New Jersey after Thorn had dispatched him with a barber's razor, finally entered Auburn Prison[32] for a fifteen-year term early in 1898.

Thorn was not as fortunate. He was charged with first-degree murder and sentenced to meet his maker in the electric chair at Sing Sing Prison. Virtually every major New York newspaper followed Thorn's trial, conviction, and sentencing. Even the august *New York Times* devoted a column to the barber's demise on August 1, 1898. Apparently, Thorn walked coolly to the electric chair, followed by his spiritual master, one Father Hanselman. The *Times* reported that Thorn held his head erect while carrying a crucifix in one hand. At 11:17 that morning, the first jolt of 1,750 volts passed through his body, to be followed by a second charge of 400 volts at 4 amperes. He was dead in less than a minute. Following the customary autopsy, his remains were claimed by men named Hippe and Hinchliffe. They were his employers.[33]

In comparison, Pulitzer's coverage of the Guldensuppe-Nack-Thorn affair was quite placid. In fact, the first mention of the case did not appear until page five of the June 30 edition of the newspaper. The story was less than a column long and featured six headlines, none of which indicated the scandal that was about to unfold. The lead, bold headline simply read, "DEEP MURDER MYSTERY," and the article recounted the discovery of the body in the East River and noted that the mysterious oilcloth was the only clue to the perpetrators. The second paragraph, quoted here, lacked any sense of emotion and was quite routine:

> The facts are briefly these: the upper part of the headless body of a man was found in the East River on Saturday. It bore unmistakable marks of assassination. On Sunday the lower part of the same body, but legless, was found in the woods eight miles away. Both fragments were wrapped in oil cloth of a peculiar pattern. The head has not yet been found but a diligent search is in progress. There is only one mark on the body by which it may be identified. It bears a scar on one finger.[34]

Unlike the Hearst publication, Pulitzer's paper contained no drawings in the initial story. That would change in subsequent coverage. Finally, on Friday, July 2, *The World* made the Guldensuppe murder a front-page story, supplemented by a medium-sized drawing of Nack appearing in Jefferson Market Court. Pulitzer's coverage of this spectacular case did not have the sideshow impact that Hearst had created. Hearst also pursued certain other aspects of the case, such as the rare experience of being able to report on a devious female murderer. In typical Hearst fashion, he gave her a day in court before the justice system was able to do so. The Sunday, August 1, 1897, edition of *The Journal* supplement *American Magazine* carried a full-length interview with the accused Nack in her cell in the New York jail, the Tombs, complete with extensive illustrations.

In subsequent editions, Hearst seemed to lose interest in the story, preferring to deal with political and social issues that were just as caustic as a good murder tale. As the tempo of rebellion increased in Cuba and as the legal profession in New York retreated behind closed doors to work on the Guldensuppe murder, the focus of sensationalism began to shift. And slowly but surely, Pulitzer would be dragged into Hearst's orbit, the prospect of which he detested. But with survival on his mind, when the opportunity to go head to head with Hearst presented itself in the form of the Spanish-American War, Pulitzer was about to show his mettle.

There is plenty of evidence that suggests Hearst's approach to selling newspapers was not significantly different from P. T. Barnum's approach to entertainment. The great circus and museum man had been dead some six years when Martin Thorn took his razor blade to the Murray Hill masseur, but there is little doubt that the worship of extravagance that he preached for many a year had an impact on the overall social structure of the city of New York. Both Benjamin Day and James Gordon Bennett were no strangers to the kind of hoaxes that Barnum sold as legitimate entertainment. Let us not forget that New York willingly bought into Day's fictional series[35] about life on the moon. It remained for Hearst, as we will see in the next few pages and the following chapter, to prove just how profitable planned exaggeration could be.

As noted in the previous chapter on the use of graphics, Hearst's Sunday supplement of August 8, 1897, had carried the tragic tale of Garrett E. Anderson and his wife. Anderson was a well-known Wall Street broker who had ventured to the deserts of Arizona. The Andersons had started out on a journey of a mere twenty miles across the sands to meet their son at a place called Caverock Station. It took some time before the couple, not to mention their horse, realized that they had gone too far and were undoubtedly lost. The rest of the real-life script could have easily been turned into a movie had such a technology existed at the time.

Anderson fell ill from the scorching heat, and the horse refused to move. Mrs. Anderson realized that unless the party was found and found quickly, death would be imminent. Eventually, a Phoenix-based freighter named John Moore came upon the couple and their wagon. By this time, the day was ebbing into evening. Moore agreed to help the Andersons return to the point from which they had started. Moving slowly to prevent any more heat-driven fatigue and illness, the party took from sunset until eleven o'clock in the evening to make the trip. But alas, the stock-broker was no match for what Hearst's reporters called the Arizona Hell Patch, and he died on the way to rescue.

The coverage of this story rated a full first page, and beyond that, the Hearst reporters convinced Mrs. Anderson, in spite of the untimely death of her husband, to write her own tale of grief. Not only did the widow compose one fairly long remembrance under the provocative headline "HOW I PASSED THROUGH THE VALLEY OF THE

SHADOW OF DEATH," she also telegraphed a supplement expanding on the role of John Moore in the tragedy. Moore as well was convinced to relate his view of the incident. Under the title "Death in an American Desert," he noted, "The desert kills, and no man knows why or how. The traveler faints from thirst with his canteen at his lips, his horse drops dead with his muzzle in the trough at the station." Certainly, if this view of the life-threatening qualities of the desert was accepted, few would venture into such an environment.

Along with tragedy, crime became a constant staple in *The New York Journal* of 1897, and it didn't even have to take place in New York. A small railroad in the center of America—the Missouri, Kansas and Texas, known affectionately as "the Katy"—had the dubious distinction of having more holdups per mile of track than any other railway in the country in the closing years of the century. The owners of the line, tiring of the constant interruptions to their service and the threat to their passengers, decided to fight fire with fire. As proof of their success, they mounted photographs of the high-waymen that the company had helped dispatch into the other world, men with colorful handles such as Chicken Elmer Lewis, Skeeter Baldwin, and Cherokee Bill, as well as the only female member of the gang of bandits, Jennie Metcalf, also known as "the Queen of the Rustlers."

Although most of the bandits had left this earth by acquiring a bullet to the brain, there were exceptions, the most notable of which was Cherokee Bill, the youngest member of the gang at age twenty-one. He had the misfortune to get caught alive. Cherokee Bill was reputed to be a person of mixed heritage whose various bloodlines came from African Americans, Creek Indians, and downright mean white folks. He had allegedly bolted from a Sunday school class when he was only fifteen, which launched him on a career of robbing, killing, and pillaging. When his luck finally ran out, he was sentenced to meet his maker at the end of a rope. Asked if he had any last words before the trap was sprung, Cherokee Bill replied, "I came here to die,[36] not to talk."

If murder and robbery were not enough to capture the imagination of his readers, Hearst knew that infidelity on the largest scale possible was a guaranteed winner. His reporters uncovered the marital shenanigans of a man they dubbed "the Modern Blue-beard." The paramour, whose real name was David A. Bates, of Chicago, juggled no less than seven different households with seven different brides, putting to shame those globe-trotting sailors who claimed they had a girl in every port. This generous lover[37] had apparently supported his seven women on a mere $60 a month, which led *The Journal* to refer to him as "A VERITABLE GENIUS ON THE ART OF LOVE MAKING AND MATRIMONY." However, when Bates was negligent in paying a doctor's fee, he set into motion a chain of events that eventually led to the discovery of his unusual lifestyle. No one could accuse him of cowardice: wives four and five lived next door to each other, completely unaware of anything being amiss.

Finally, one cannot leave any discussion of Hearst's extravagances without a mention of his almost demonic worship of things scientific. He devoted a full page, art included, to worshipping at the feet of the inventor Nikola Tesla. Electrical items were beginning to appear with some regularity in the industrial world, and it was only a matter of time before the world could take advantage of this new and inexpensive source of energy. Both Thomas Edison and George Westinghouse were expanding their manufacturing empires through electrical development. At that point, no one really knew whether AC or DC current would come to dominate the electrical industries.

Tesla had come up with the proposition that electricity could be transmitted through the air to all parts of the world. To this end, he had invented a large, eight-foot disc with brass electrodes that he claimed could transmit electrical energy. Tesla told *The Journal* he was confident that one day his device would be able to project electricity as far away as Mars. However, at the moment, the inventor was content to work out the details of sending electrical bursts to ships in the middle of the ocean. *Journal* reporter Julius Chambers called Tesla "the Wizard of Science," a man who had, by his own admission, "ENSLAVED EARTH'S MIGHTIEST FORCE FOR THE USE OF MAN." In spite of *The Journal's* obviously very biased worship of Tesla, he did prove to be a central figure in many of the electrically based inventions that first saw the light of day in the late nineteenth and early twentieth centuries.

If stories of unfortunate death, especially of elite persons, along with gross infidelity, train robbing, and an unquestioning worship of things scientific proved insufficient to keep Hearst busy, then something quite spectacular, such as a war, might help him stay in front of the circulation battles that were plaguing the New York newspaper market. Perhaps Hearst was not the catalyst who sparked the Spanish-American War, but he certainly exploited it to the fullest. Sensationalism and the Yellow Press were about to step out into the world at large.

Notes

1. *Gilman did not bend:* Denise D. Knight, "Charlotte Perkins Gilman, William Randolph Hearst and the Practice of Ethical Journalism," *American Journalism*, 11, no. 4 (Fall 1994): 337.
2. *This is the secret:* Ibid., pp. 337–8.
3. *She responded:* Ibid., p. 339n22.
4. *Place of comfort:* Fedler, p. 155.
5. *Revisionist histories:* Stephen Vaughan and Bruce Evensen, "Democracy's Guardians: Hollywood's Portrayal of Reporters, 1930–1945," *Journalism Quarterly* 68, no. 4 (Winter 1991): 829.
6. *Grabbing suspects:* Fedler, pp. 155–60.
7. *No room left:* John, P. Ferré, "The Dubious Heritage of Media Ethics: Cause and Effect Criticism in the 1890's," *American Journalism* 5, no. 4 (1988): 191.
8. *Left the premises:* Ibid., p. 195.
9. *Needed a diversion:* Ibid., p. 195–6.
10. *Benjamin Day:* Mott, pp. 310–11.
11. *Pure-minded and clean:* Ferré, pp. 196–7.
12. *List of crimes:* Ibid., pp. 197–8.
13. *No takers:* Ibid., p. 200.
14. *Midnight candle:* Burrows and Wallace, p. 1214.
15. *Hearts and souls:* Mott, pp. 436–8.
16. *Heart of the Victorian newspaper:* Ibid., p. 438; also see John D. Stevens, *Sensationalism and the New York Press* (New York: Columbia University Press, 1991), p. 68.
17. *Sing Sing Prison:* James McGrath Morris, *The Roseman of Sing Sing* (New York: Fordham University Press, 2003), p. 3.
18. *Hurly-burly world:* Ibid., pp. 44–8.
19. *Steffens noted:* Lincoln Steffens, *The Autobiography of Lincoln Steffens* (New York: Harcourt, Brace and World, 1931), pp. 314–15.
20. *Get this tragedy:* Ibid., p. 317.
21. *Death of an inmate:* Brooke Kroeger, *Nellie Bly* (New York: Times Books (Random House), 1994), pp. 85–7.
22. *Story of horror:* Burrows and Wallace, pp. 1152–3.
23. *On her way:* Kroeger, p. 92.
24. *Just as sane:* Nellie Bly, *Ten Days in a Mad House* (New York: Ian L. Munro, n.d.), chap. 1,

available at "Ten Days in a Madhouse," A Celebration of Women Writers, http://digital
.library.upenn.edu/women/bly/madhouse/madhouse.html.

25. *My flesh felt creepy:* Bly, chap. 12.
26. *Populist approach:* Brian, p. 125.
27. *Marketing mentality:* Upton Sinclair, *The Brass Check* (Urbana and Chicago: University of Illinois Press, 2003), p. xix.
28. *Passing out bread:* Burrows and Wallace, p. 1214.
29. *Fascinated with police work:* Ben Procter, *William Randolph Hearst: The Early Years* (New York: Oxford University Press, 1998), pp. 98–9.
30. *More of this lurid crime:* Ibid., p. 99.
31. *Nack and the unfortunate Thorn: Evening Journal and Advertiser;* see the coverage from Sunday, June 27, 1897, to August 1, 1897, for a more detailed look at *The Journal's* coverage of this event.
32. *Auburn Prison:* Procter, p. 114.
33. *His employers: New York Times,* August 2, 1898.
34. *Scar on one finger: World New York,* June 30, 1897.
35. *Day's fictional series:* Burrows and Wallace, pp. 643–44.
36. *I came here to die: New York Journal and Advertiser,* August 8, 1897.
37. *This generous lover:* Ibid.

Chapter 31

GENE ROBERTS and HANK KLIBANOFF

"A FIGHTING PRESS"

IF **MYRDAL'S RESEARCH HAD RELIED UPON** Frank Luther Mott's biblically revered 1941 textbook on the profession, *American Journalism*, he might have missed altogether the only newspapers that were covering race in any meaningful way. Mott devoted a mere half sentence to the Negro press—a passing reference to Frederick Douglass.[1]

Before World War II, Negro newspapers drew such little notice from their white counterparts that even when they clearly had the inside track on a story of national importance, the white press tended to ignore it. When A. Philip Randolph warned in 1941 that "a wave of bitter resentment, disillusionment and desperation was sweeping over the Negro masses" and that it might erupt into "blind, reckless and undisciplined outbursts of emotional indignation," accounts of his statements in the Negro newspapers were largely ignored by the white press. When Randolph a year later decried the lack of Negro employment in defense industries and insisted that 10,000 Negroes— later upped to 100,000—would march on Washington in a protest guided by a Gandhian commitment to nonviolence, he got little coverage in the white press.[2]

But all the warnings, all the harbingers, all the reports exploded onto the pages of Negro newspapers. Across the South, almost without limitation, Negroes had access to black weeklies that ridiculed white hypocrisy, spoke out bitterly against racial injustice, reinterpreted the mainstream press, and covered Negro social and religious organizations in detail. "It is," Myrdal said, "a fighting press,"[3] and he was in awe of the fact that Negro newspapers enjoyed—strangely—the kind of freedom of expression that might have meant death to the lone Negro who dared to make such utterances in some parts of the South.

Myrdal understood that white newspapers were written for whites and Negro papers for Negroes. He could see that Negroes were most likely to appear in white newspapers only if they committed a crime against whites and that Negro institutions and organizations were seldom covered, except in a smattering of southern dailies with "black star" editions that were distributed only in Negro neighborhoods.

But how could the Negro press attack white power with such impunity? Myrdal theorized that whites simply didn't read Negro newspapers and were unaware of their militancy, even of their existence. Perhaps, he mused, the negro press was tolerated because of something more fundamental in the American outlook, a "certain abstract feeling among all Americans for the freedom of the press which, even in the South, covers the Negro newspapers."[4]

Whatever the reasons, the Negro press clearly understood that its audience wanted racial inequities in America examined and denounced. This had been the case since March 16, 1827, when the country's first Negro newspaper, *Freedom's Journal*, had gone on New York streets to oppose slavery and push for full rights for Negro Americans. "We want to plead our own case," said its publishers, John B. Russwurm and the Reverend Samuel E. Cornish, in the first issue. "Too long have others spoken for us."[5]

In its short life—three years—it set two enduring standards: henceforth, most Negro newspapers in the United States would live hard and die young. By 1951, there had been 2,700 Negro papers, fewer than 175 of which were still around. On average, they died after nine years of publication.[6]

But the more important standard was the legacy of protest. The earliest newspapers, both Negro and white, were primarily advocates and special pleaders. But long after white papers had turned to coverage of general-interest news, their Negro counterparts remained loud, clear instruments of protest, by turns educative and provocative. And for virtually all of their history into the 1950s, they had the race story all to themselves.

That so many Negro newspapers were coming and going for 120 years on the mass of land between the Atlantic and Pacific Oceans, Mexico, and Canada is itself remarkable. More extraordinary is that white people did not know about it.

By the late 1800s and early 1900s, interest was growing among Negroes in newspapers that would reflect their lives, tell their stories, and give them political insight and social guidance. Literacy was up, and so, in a small way, was the income available to purchase newspapers. Churches and religious organizations became involved in publishing and found support from various northern welfare and missionary groups working in the South. As more Negroes became eligible to vote, newspapers fed a new hunger for political coverage.[7]

Very quickly, papers that would become the most insistent and most effective advocates of civil rights were created. In Baltimore in 1907, a Sunday school superintendent, John H. Murphy, Sr., whose full-time job was as a whitewasher, created the *Baltimore Afro-American*. He vowed on the paper's masthead to "stay out of politics except to expose corruption and condemn injustice, race prejudice and the cowardice of compromise."

In Chicago, Robert S. Abbott, a Georgia-born lawyer whose tar-black skin caused him to be ridiculed and rejected by other Negroes, pumped a little money and a lot of gumption into creating the *Chicago Defender* in 1905[8]—which a decade later claimed a stunning 230,000 circulation.[9]

The Norfolk *Journal and Guide*, which would come to have a circulation and influence far beyond its home base, began as a fraternal publication. Taken over in 1909 by P. B. Young, Sr., the *Journal and Guide* espoused a conservatism that reflected Young's close association with the gradualist Booker T. Washington; the paper, like Young himself, became more progressive in the years following the latter's death. And in 1910, the presses started rolling at *The Pittsburgh Courier*.

Those and other Negro newspapers began publishing at a time, unlike any other, when four of the most dynamic, strong-willed, and persuasive black leaders in the nation's history shared a common stage, even as they divided Negro thought. Each came with his own journalistic base and retinue, each had his own devoted following, and each helped crystallize the debate that Negro editors would wrestle with for the next seventy-five years.

Booker T. Washington's accommodationist views were evident in his own newspaper, the *New York Age*, and other ostensibly independent papers that he infused with thousands of dollars to spread his gospel.[10] W. E. B. Du Bois, as much as anyone, led the break from Washington and toward a more confrontational strategy. The Massachusetts-born sociologist's crisp, aggressive editorial attacks against discrimination were the hallmark of *The Crisis*, the NAACP's monthly magazine. It began in 1910 with a circulation of 1,000; within three years, 30,000 copies were being circulated; and by 1920, it was selling 95,000 copies each month.[11]

The most relentless advocate for mass action was A. Philip Randolph, co-author of the monthly *Messenger*. The socialist pitch of this self-described "magazine of scientific radicalism" may not have had widespread appeal among the Negro masses, but its strident criticism of black leaders who weakened in the face of white persuasion was popular well beyond the Negro trade unions that viewed it as their official mouthpiece.[12] And the angry separatist push of Marcus Garvey, who had been a printer before he became an advocate, was touted in his own newspapers, most prominently *The Negro World*, which routinely lacerated other notable blacks.

Though operating at odds that frequently became intensely personal, these four men pushed the outer limits of the debate and defined the journalistic tone for the more mainstream press. The *Defender*, the *Afro-American*, the *Journal and Guide*, and the *Courier* survived without conforming to the white press's notions about separating objective news from subjective editorials.

Readers of Negro newspapers, in the North and South, got a heavy dose of news, opinion, and polemic, sometimes blended together. In presenting a constant flow of reports about the brutality, mayhem, and deprivation caused by race discrimination, the Negro press sought not to take its readers' minds off their troubles, as one analyst pointedly put it, but precisely to keep their minds on them.[13]

World War I presented a dilemma for Negro editors. They wanted to support the war effort, and did, but they were troubled that the need to "make the world safe for democracy" was undercutting the push to make the United States a battleground in the fight for equal opportunity. The pressure on Negro editors to support the war effort without reservation came not merely from the cresting wave of national patriotism; the war was generating thousands of jobs for Negroes, many of them in the backyards of the most important Negro newspapers of the North.

Sacks full of letters flowed into the newsrooms of northern Negro papers, many of them barely literate scrawlings from southern readers seeking subscriptions and more information about jobs, housing, bus schedules, and all the golden opportunities ballyhooed in each week's editions. At the same time, readers' demand increased for more coverage of Negro soldiers at war. Circulation rose, largely and ironically because of a war the Negro press felt reluctant to support unconditionally.

There was one exception to the latitude white leaders gave the Negro press: when the newspapers criticized the government for taking the nation to war abroad when it hadn't resolved problems at home, they paid a price. In World War I, Negro newspapers were not spared by the freshly adopted federal antisedition laws. After the editor of a paper in San Antonio criticized the army for hanging thirteen Negro soldiers and sentencing forty-one others to life imprisonment following a 1917 Houston uprising that had killed seventeen white people, the editor was convicted of disloyalty and sent to Leavenworth for two years.[14] In the summer of 1918, Randolph and Chandler Owen, co-editors of the *Messenger*, spent two days in jail on charges of treason; copies of their magazine were confiscated, and they lost their second-class mailing privileges because of their antiwar speeches and articles.[15]

Bridling at any suggestion that criticism of race discrimination in the United States might hurt the war effort,[16] Negro editors kept their spotlight aimed on unequal treatment, particularly against Negro troops at home and abroad. They treated aberrant, disloyal, or mutinous behavior by black soldiers as the natural consequence of race discrimination.[17]

All the newspapers found a common result from their coverage: readers wanted more—from the front lines, the sidelines, and in between the lines. Negro papers, with few limits on the infusion of drama and parochialism, filled their pages with personal and effusive stories about the essential importance, valor, and loyalty of Negro soldiers. The war was a marketing bonanza.

The black press came out of World War I reasserting its role as crusader, muscling its way into the white political domain, and still encouraging one of the greatest mass movements in the nation's history: the migration of southern Negroes to the North. Circulation grew prodigiously, to more than a million copies each week.[18]

By the early 1920s, northern Negro papers, sent by mail, bus, and train, had reached deep into the South. The *Chicago Defender*, with a circulation of more than 150,000, was selling more than two thirds of its copies outside Chicago.[19] Over the next several decades, the major Negro newspapers developed networks of bureaus, zoned editions, and national editions, making it possible to pick up the *Defender* just as readily in Alabama or Mississippi. The *Afro-American* fought for dominance in Maryland, North Carolina, South Carolina, and Virginia, often competing head to head with Norfolk's *Journal and Guide*, the largest of the southern weeklies. *The Pittsburgh Courier* sold widely across the South and was easily the largest of all the Negro papers.

Negroes in the southern and border states had no shortage of indigenous race newspapers as well; indeed, most Negro newspapers were published in the South. The southern press sometimes tiptoed around local issues and customs, but on national and regional matters, they were no less militant than their northern counterparts.

The existing papers were achieving higher circulations, and newer ones were reaching the streets every day.[20] The close of the war also produced several national Negro news services, the largest and most enduring of which was the Associated Negro Press. A cooperative whose members provided news to the service and shared its expenses, the ANP could never truly call itself a wire service: the items it gathered from correspondents across the nation were distributed to its clients by mail.

With growth came influence and, for the newspaper publishers, a measure of prosperity. An examination of the social and economic trends in the South in the early 1920s concluded that the Negro press had become "the greatest single power in the Negro race."[21]

Its explosive gains in circulation had explanations that went beyond race-angled political crusades and campaigns for self-improvement. The papers, however inconsistently, were full of voices; Negro papers gave more of their space to columnists than did the white press.

Thomas Sancton, a white New Orleans writer who later became managing editor of *The New Republic*, was impressed by the Negro newspapers. "In some of their columns, fierceness is apparent in every sentence. In others, it lies beneath a calm and subtle prose, and sometimes dullness," he observed in 1943.

"The white reader will not find dullness very often. Almost everything in the Negro press will be new to him, or if not new, written in a strange new key. Sometimes these columnists are inaccurate with facts and careless in their attitudes. But the white reader must be careful about what he allows to anger him, for there is a vast amount of raw, solid fact which they handle well within the bounds of accuracy, and which the white reader simply has got to gulp down and let it educate him. . . . There are a lot of white columnists and reporters who are drawing pay today on writing they did in the 1920s, and their weariness is inescapable. The white reader doesn't find this weariness in the Negro columnists. They live and write at the beginning of a new era for their people, and they are swept along by it."[22]

The bread and butter of Negro newspapers were stories touting some new achievement by Negroes in business, literature, the arts, or something much less momentous. The reports, which fairly screamed at readers, tended to be skimpy on facts and heavy on hyperbole. "The appointments of Negroes to minor positions in the federal and state governments are reported as great achievements," the black sociologist E. Franklin Frazier complained. "In the Negro press, police magistrates become judges. As the result of the exaggeration of the achievements of Negroes, myths grow up about the accomplishments of Negroes. Myths grow up concerning the importance of books written by Negroes. A Negro student who makes a good record in a northern university may be reported to be a genius. The awarding of a doctorate to a Negro by a northern university is still reported as if it had great significance."[23]

For all their interest in bettering the opportunities for their race, Negro publishers found, as did their white counterparts, that stratospheric circulation and the influence that went with it could more easily be theirs in exchange for muckraking, for stories of sensational crimes (especially race crimes and race-sex crimes), and for coverage of lynchings and riots—all captured in bold, uppercase, jugular-squeezing, groin-grabbing headlines.[24] There was ongoing concern among Negro leaders that the Negro weeklies, stricken by a sensationalist fever, had succumbed to the same maladies of carelessness, inadequate corroboration, distortion, and flamboyance as the white Hearst dailies had.[25]

The *Chicago Defender* frequently went overboard in its early years, particularly when providing southern Negroes one-sided and alluring portraits of Chicago and the North as the Promised Land. When it was competitive on race stories with the white dailies, the *Defender* was not reluctant to stretch the truth in some stories and just plain fabricate others—in ways that Abbott's otherwise admiring biographer, Roi Ottley, concluded were not harmless. During racial confrontations, the *Defender* would design, for the front page, box scores showing how many Negroes had been injured and killed versus how many whites; it was a technique some segregationist southern newspapers would adopt during racial battles nearly fifty years later. "It produced a feeling that the score must be kept even—that is, on an eye-for-an-eye basis," Ottley later wrote.[26]

In the era between the world wars, the black press broadened its coverage areas, but never to the point of neglecting lynchings and other sensational atrocities against Negroes. In one view, the coverage of lynchings was good copy to throw at a readership that tended to be lower class. In another, the coverage was partly responsible for the reduction in the violence.[27]

Typically, lynch stories were assigned not to local correspondents but to staff reporters operating out of Chicago, Cleveland, Kansas City, Baltimore, New York, and other cities. Spending long hours on buses and trains, the reporters moved across the South, working their way into backwater towns where white dominance frequently slipped into tyranny.

One of those journalists was Vincent Tubbs, a *Baltimore Afro-American* reporter whose career climb to correspondent in the South Pacific in World War II began in Dallas when he was six and stood on a box to feed the printing press that was the source of his father's livelihood. By the time Tubbs was twenty-six, he had graduated from Morehouse College and worked for four Negro newspapers, each bigger and better than the previous one.

Tubbs got an early taste of the competitive nature of the Negro papers along the eastern seaboard. While he was serving as bureau chief of the Richmond edition of the Norfolk *Journal and Guide* for $25 a week, the publisher of the paper, P. B. Young, heard that Tubbs had been seen with the Richmond bureau chief of the *Afro-American*. Tubbs had consorted with the enemy. "You're fired," the Norfolk publisher told him. The *Afro-American* quickly hired him and gave him a $5-a-week pay increase. "I was moving up," Tubbs said later. Part of moving up meant taking on the challenging assignment, in 1941, of "lynch reporter."

At his desk in Baltimore, the call might come from Sikeston, Missouri, from Texarkana, Arkansas, or from any number of remote spots he knew nothing about. There had been a lynching, he would be told, and off he'd go, always unsure whether he'd be able to find lodging, a ride, or anything resembling a friendly reception. The reporter would not be heard from again until he got the story—or didn't. "When I got on the train, I was on my own until I got back," Tubbs recalled years later. "I mean, there was no communication with anybody."

White journalists could drive themselves into town and not draw suspicion. Not Negro reporters. Tubbs would have to get off the bus one town earlier than his destination, stash his city duds, throw on some local garb, muss himself up to blend with the local scenery, and hitchhike, Old Black Joe–like, to where the lynching had taken place. He'd hope to get in a couple of days of reporting, then slip out of town and hightail it either to a telephone where he could dictate his story or, if his deadline permitted, to the home office, where he'd write it.

It didn't always work. In the early 1940s, in Texarkana, Arkansas, Tubbs was caught in the act of reporting. The sheriff ordered him into his patrol car, quizzed him, then delivered him to the chief of police, deeper into the Dante's Hell of southern law enforcement. After another series of questions disclosed Tubbs's mission, the chief put it plainly.

"Do you see that street?" He pointed out the window. "That is the borderline between Texas and Arkansas. Texas that side, and Arkansas over here."

Sometimes a voice of authority is so clear that shouting would only diminish its power. Quietly, firmly, the chief concluded: "I'll give you five minutes, and I want you to be in Texas."

"Of course," Tubbs said in recalling that incident, "there was no dispute. In four minutes, I was in Texas."[28]

Motivated by the discrimination that had stunted his own opportunities for a pro baseball career, Wendell Smith, sports editor of *The Pittsburgh Courier*, made integration of baseball his mission. He had some influence. Pittsburgh was home to two highly regarded Negro baseball teams, and the *Courier* was the largest Negro newspaper in the nation. It was Smith who first mentioned a young player named Jackie Robinson to Branch Rickey, Sr., the president of the Brooklyn Dodgers.

Sam Lacy, a sportswriter for the *Chicago Defender* and later sports editor of the *Baltimore Afro-American*, combined vivid, persuasive writing with a strategic mind as he made personal appeals to the owners. Joe Bostic of the *People's Voice*, the Harlem newspaper founded by the pastor, and later congressman, Adam Clayton Powell, Jr., was the most aggressive of the group. His seething about discrimination was frequently reduced to mere angry cynicism.[29]

Though integration had the backing of some key white sportswriters, the Negro reporters pretty much operated alone. Typical of the opposition was this from *Sporting News*, the weekly statistical and informational bible of baseball: "There is not a single Negro player with major league possibilities."[30] Such arguments, it was plain, were smokescreens. Ultimately, as advocates of integration knew, the decision would rest with the baseball owners, who would look to their commissioner for guidance. There were no laws, rules, or regulations banning mixing on the diamond.

The *Courier*'s campaign was built on reporting stories of inequality, not on editorial harangues. Wendell Smith started out with his own poll of racial attitudes in the National League. He found that 80 percent of the league's players and managers had no objections to integration. Plenty of major leaguers, including southerners, hit the barnstorming road every off-season, playing in competitive games with Negroes.[31]

In 1942 and 1943, an owner here and there scheduled halfhearted tryouts for Negroes, including Jackie Robinson.[32] But in 1943, Sam Lacy, writing for the *Chicago Defender*, got the baseball owners to hear a personal appeal from him. Lacy was accustomed to setbacks, but he was not prepared for what happened next. His own paper, the *Defender*, picked him off clean. It decided to send the actor and former all-American football player Paul Robeson, instead of Lacy, to meet with the owners.

Fine actor and a credit to the race, Lacy thought, but Robeson had too many Communist ties at a time when Lacy and Wendell Smith had decided the Communist Party's efforts to integrate baseball were backfiring. The team owners listened to Robeson, then did nothing. Lacy quit the *Defender* and joined the *Baltimore Afro-American*.[33] Soon after the 1944 season, Lacy suggested to the owners that they establish a committee to examine the possibilities of integrating baseball. "It will be a step in the right direction," he wrote, adding that a step, when he really wanted to leap, was "a sort of compromise for me as a colored man in that it embraces the element of 'appeasement.' "[34]

The owners agreed to let Lacy address their group. He set forth his proposal, and the owners formed a Major League Committee on Baseball Integration, naming Lacy to it. But the committee foundered when Larry MacPhail, president of the New York Yankees, managed to prevent every scheduled meeting from taking place. One day Rickey went to the despondent Lacy. "Well, Sam, maybe we'll forget about Mr. MacPhail," Rickey said. "Maybe we'll just give up on him and let nature take its course.' "[35]

It was inconceivable at the time that there was a hidden meaning behind Rickey's words. But there was. From the front office of his baseball organization, Rickey had seen the tide starting to turn. Months before the end of the war, he had quietly begun making preparations. Looking for studies that might make the desegregation of his team easier, he had read widely in sociology, history, and race relations, including *An American Dilemma*. The crusade by the Negro press was providing the precise dynamic that Myrdal felt most essential for improvement of the blacks' lives: creating publicity. The Negro press was making Rickey's secret plan more plausible.

In the first months after the Japanese bombed Pearl Harbor, the mainstream press in the United States was focused on one overriding story: the mobilization of American armed forces and its factories into a war machine. But the nation's Negro papers were in a quandary. Should they support the war? Or sit on their hands? They had been in this position twenty-three years earlier. The betrayal that many Negro editors had felt after World War I, when they had given their support and gotten nothing in return, survived during World War II.

The pressure to withhold their advocacy of the war machinery, and to keep hammering away against discrimination on the home front, came from subscribers and the general Negro population. "It would surprise and startle the majority of white Americans if they knew what the so-called mass of Negroes is thinking," the editor of *The Philadelphia Tribune*, E. Washington Rhodes, said during the war. "The mass of Negroes is more radical than [Norfolk editor] P. B. Young and those of us who publish Negro newspapers. Anyone would tell you that a lot of Negroes are saying that they should not participate in this war."[36]

"We are on the spot," the Norfolk *Journal and Guide* wrote in the spring of 1942. "Our people cry out in anguish: This is no time to stick to a middle of the road policy; help us get some of the blessings of Democracy here at home first before you jump on the free-the-other-peoples bandwagon."[37]

Two weeks after Pearl Harbor, the *Chicago Defender* stated its case—and its dilemma: "The Negro press will not blemish its magnificent record of sound patriotism by indulging in subversive advocacy to the impairment of the national will. However, unless and until constitutional guarantees are suspended, the Negro press will continue to use its moral force against the mob in its criminal orgy, against such ultra violences as lynching, burning at [the] stake and judicial murder."[38]

That might not qualify as disloyalty, the Roosevelt administration felt, but it resembled its evil twin, divided loyalty. Paramount to Roosevelt was his "Double V" campaign, pursuing victory at war and victory in his 1944 reelection bid. The Negro press was important to both wings of that campaign. The combined circulation of the papers was rising, in part because of the war coverage, from 1,265,000 in 1940 to 1,613,255 million in 1943, to 1,809,000 in 1945.[39] Roosevelt understood that trying to run a war with the bitter opposition of a press that spoke to, and probably for, 13 million people, or 10 percent of the population, would be suicidal. Even more problematic was the issue of morale among Negro troops, who represented an even larger share, 16 percent, of the enlistments.[40]

From the Roosevelt administration, there was equal and opposite pressure on Negro newspapers to give their wholehearted support to the war effort and to back off their coverage of discrimination. The antisedition laws were still there, and so was the threat they would be used. The government had agencies, including the J. Edgar

Hoover–led FBI, that had the power to intimidate the Negro press, and seemed prepared to use it.

In the end, the Negro press's path was chosen for it by a cafeteria worker in Wichita, who wrote *The Pittsburgh Courier* an impassioned letter that evoked all the emotional conflicts and contradictions facing many Negro Americans. Bearing the title "Should I Sacrifice to Live Half American?" James G. Thompson's letter suggested that "we colored Americans adopt the double VV for a double victory. The first V for victory over our enemies from without, the second V for victory over our enemies from within. For surely those who perpetuate these ugly prejudices here are seeking to destroy our democratic form of government just as surely as the Axis forces."[41]

Readers' reaction was immediate, and the *Courier* swung into action. Its issue the week after Thompson's letter presented four Double V drawings; a week later, the paper announced a full-scale campaign. By the end of the first month, in each issue, the paper was running more than 340 column inches—roughly three full pages—of stories, photographs, and graphics.[42] And 200,000 people each week were buying it.

The counter–Double V campaign became a national cause for the Negro press—as well as a poke in the eye of the Roosevelt administration and a jab in the ribs to other federal authorities, such as Hoover. During the course of the war, Hoover launched investigations into the content of news stories in the Negro press, tried to interest Justice Department prosecutors in bringing sedition charges against some, and routinely sent his men to quiz editors about their criticisms of race discrimination, or of Hoover himself.[43]

Negro papers said they suffered inexplicable cutbacks and limits in newsprint supplies, as well as investigations by the Justice Department and the FBI, the Post Office, the Office of Facts and Figures, the Office of War Information, and the Office of Censorship.[44]

The enthusiasm of Negro columnists and editorial writers for the Double V campaign led them to become even bolder as the war progressed, pushing for an end to all segregation when peace came, if not sooner. Even the most liberal of white southern editors were shocked by the Negro press's expectations. After all, liberal editors became pariahs among many segregationists not by advocating racial integration but by opposing demagogic politicians, calling for better Negro schools, and campaigning against lynching and the poll tax. Sometimes they went a bit further, but they always stopped short of advocating an end to segregation. That, they believed, could invite racial cataclysm.

Virginius Dabney, the editor of the *Richmond Times-Dispatch*, who had himself argued editorially for equal pay for Negro teachers and an end to separate seating on wartime buses, couldn't believe what he was reading in the Negro press and decided to write national magazine articles calling for moderation. "Liberal minded whites concede that many grievances of the Negroes should be corrected, and they concede, further, that the Negro's disabilities are often the fault of whites," he wrote in *Saturday Review of Literature*. "But they cannot view with other than apprehension the speed with which Negro leadership, as exemplified in the Negro press, is pushing matters to a climax. Many Southerners who have long been conspicuous champions of Negro rights, and some Northerners as well, are saying that much can be done hereafter by evolutionary processes in providing better levels of living and more valid opportunities for the Negroes, but that the current effort to effect a drastic revolution overnight can only result in violence and bitterness, with the Negro suffering heavily, in the end."[45]

His fears were shared by Mark Ethridge, the Mississippi-born publisher of the Louisville *Courier-Journal*, who was widely recognized as the dean of the handful of liberal editors in segregated states. "Those Negro newspaper editors who demand 'all or nothing' are playing into the hands of the white demagogues," he said in a speech. "There is no power in the world—not even all the mechanized armies of the earth, Allied and Axis—which could now force the Southern white people to the abandonment of the principle of social segregation."[46]

Jonathan Daniels of the Raleigh *News & Observer* and Ralph McGill of *The Atlanta Constitution* muted their criticism of the Negro editors but said publicly that Negro progress could be made without ending segregation. McGill wrote in 1942 that the "Negro problem" was "economic almost entirely and not at all a 'social equality' problem." He added, "Anyone with an ounce of common sense must see . . . that separation of the two races must be maintained in the South."[47] Daniels wrote, also in 1942 as the war intensified, that "sometimes it is easier to ask people to give their lives than to give up their prejudices."[48]

Negro editors were dismayed by the reaction of the white liberal editors they regarded as their allies, but not enough to dampen their enthusiasm for full equality in the coming years. What the white editors did not see was that the Negro editors, perhaps without knowing it, were preparing new generations of their race for what would ultimately become the civil rights movement. The Negro press was ready for the future; it sensed it was on the cusp of one of the great stories in American history.

How long would it take the white press to share the vision?

Notes

1. Frank Luther Mott, *American Journalism: A History of Newspapers in the United States Through 250 Years, 1690 to 1940* (New York: Manville, 1941).
2. Lee Finkle, *Forum for Protest: The Black Press During World War II* (Rutherford, N.J.: Fairleigh Dickinson University Press, 1975), pp. 96–7, citing New York *Amsterdam News*, July 19, 1941. A search of *NYT* digital archives produced no story about such a warning in 1940–42. When Randolph criticized the lack of Negro employment, it ran in the Sports section of *The Times*.
3. Myrdal, *An American Dilemma*, p. 908.
4. Ibid., p. 910.
5. Edwin Emery and Michael Emery, *The Press and America: An Interpretive History of the Mass Media* (Englewood Cliffs, N.J.: Prentice-Hall, 1984), p. 174.
6. Armistead Scott Pride, "Negro Newspapers: Yesterday, Today and Tomorrow," *Journalism Quarterly* 28, no. 2, Spring 1951, p. 179.
7. Ibid., p. 180.
8. Roi Ottley, *The Lonely Warrior: The Life and Times of Robert S. Abbott* (Chicago: Henry Regnery, 1955), pp. 3, 7.
9. Emery and Emery, *The Press and America*, p. 308.
10. Roland E. Wolseley, *The Black Press, U.S.A.* (Ames: Iowa State University Press, 1990), p. 65. Du Bois claimed that Washington secretly funded some newspapers in exchange for their publication of views aligned with his.
11. Elliott M. Rudwick, *W. E. B. DuBois, Propagandist of the Negro Protest* (New York: Atheneum, 1978), passim.
12. Herbert Garfinkel, *When Negroes March* (Glencoe, Ill.: Free Press, 1959), pp. 30–1.
13. John H. Burma, "An Analysis of the Present Negro Press," *Social Forces* 26, October 1947, p. 173.

14. Patrick S. Washburn, *A Question of Sedition: The Federal Government's Investigation of the Black Press During World War II* (New York: Oxford University Press, 1986), p. 20, citing Gilbert C. Fite and H. C. Peterson, *Opponents of War, 1917–1918* (Madison: University of Wisconsin Press, 1957), pp. 89–90.
15. Washburn, *A Question of Sedition*, pp. 20–2.
16. Finkle, *Forum for Protest*, p. 46.
17. Henry Lewis Suggs, ed., *The Black Press in the South, 1865–1979* (Westport, Conn.: Greenwood Press, 1983), passim.
18. Detweiler, *The Negro Press in the United States*, pp. 6–7.
19. Ibid., p. 15, citing Negro Migration in 1916–17, U.S. Department of Labor, Division of Negro Economics, 1919, Washington, pp. 29–30.
20. E. Franklin Frazier, *Black Bourgeoisie: The Rise of a New Middle Class in the United States* (New York: Collier Books, 1962), p. 148, citing U.S. Department of Commerce, "Negro Newspapers and Periodicals in the United States, 1943," *Negro Statistical Bulletin*, no. 1 (August 1944). The Commerce report showed there were 164 black weekly newspapers, of which 144 reported the year of their establishment; 67.4 percent of those were less than twenty-five years old.
21. Edwin Mims, *The Advancing South* (New York: Doubleday, Page, 1926), p. 268. Myrdal, in *The American Dilemma*, p. 924, concluded that Mims had "rightly . . . characterized" the influence of the black press. Mims was a Vanderbilt professor of English who imbued one student, the future Atlanta editor Ralph McGill, with a love of poetry that led McGill to alter his plans to become a physician.
22. Thomas Sancton, "The Negro Press," *The New Republic*, April 26, 1943, p. 559.
23. Frazier, *Black Bourgeoisie*, p. 150–1.
24. Myrdal noted that sensationalism in the black press was more likely to be found in cities with sensationalist Hearst papers.
25. Walter White, *A Man Called White* (New York: Viking Press, 1948), pp. 206–7.
26. Ottley, *The Lonely Warrior*, pp. 173–87.
27. Sancton, "The Negro Press," p. 557.
28. Vincent Tubbs, oral history, August 21, 1971, AAJP, pp. 4, 6.
29. Jules Tygiel, *Baseball's Great Experiment: Jackie Robinson and His Legacy* (New York: Oxford University Press, 1983), passim.
30. Ibid., p. 32, citing *Sporting News*, November 1, 1945.
31. Ibid., p. 33.
32. Ibid., pp. 39–40.
33. David Falkner, *Great Time Coming: The Life of Jackie Robinson from Baseball to Birmingham* (New York: Simon and Schuster, 1995), pp. 99–100.
34. Tygiel, *Baseball's Great Experiment*, p. 42, based on Lacy article in *Afro-American*, February 28, 1948.
35. Ibid.
36. Finkle, *Forum for Protest*, p. 80, citing quotation in Council for Democracy, "Negro Press Conference," May 7–8, 1943 (typescript, Schomburg Collection), I: 7, 26.
37. Ibid., p. 64, citing *Journal and Guide*, April 25, 1942.
38. Washburn, *A Question of Sedition*, pp. 63–4, citing "Freedom of the Negro Press," *Chicago Defender*, December 20, 1941.
39. Burma, "An Analysis of the Present Negro Press," p. 172.
40. Thomas Sancton, "Something's Happened to the Negro," *The New Republic*, February 8, 1943, p. 178.
41. Washburn, *A Question of Sedition*, pp. 55–6, citing *The Pittsburgh Courier*, January 31, 1942.
42. Ibid., p. 55.
43. Ibid., pp. 66–91.
44. White, *A Man Called White*, pp. 207–8; Washburn, *A Question of Sedition*, pp. 8, 103–7, 137. The agency investigations have been confirmed over the years, but the War Production Board at the time denied it had made illegal newsprint cutbacks. White says the agency did but that Roosevelt stopped the practice.
45. Virginius Dabney, "Press and Morale," *Saturday Review of Literature*, July 4, 1942, p. 25.

46.   Myrdal, *An American Dilemma*, p. 663.
47.   Ralph McGill, *AC*, October 24, 1942, cited in John T. Kneebone, *Southern Liberal Journalists and the Issue of Race, 1920–1944*, p. 201.
48.   Charles W. Eagles, *Jonathan Daniels and Race Relations: The Evolution of a Southern Liberal* (Knoxville: University of Tennessee Press, 1982), p. 97.

FURTHER READING

Ambrose, Stephen E. *Undaunted Courage. Meriwether Lewis, Thomas Jefferson, and the Opening of the American West*. New York: Touchstone, 1996.

Bailyn, Bernard. *The Ideological Origins of the American Revolution*. Cambridge, MA: Belknap Press of Harvard University Press, 1992.

Bailyn, Bernard and John B. Hench (eds). *The Press and the American Revolution*. Worcester, MA: American Antiquarian Society, 1980.

Baldasty, Gerald J. *The Commercialization of News in the Nineteenth Century*. Madison, WI: University of Wisconsin Press, 1992.

Barnouw, Erik. *A Tower in Babel: A History of Broadcasting in the United States to 1933*. New York: Oxford University Press, 1966.

Becker, Carl. *The Declaration of Independence: A Study in the History of Political Ideas*. New York: Vintage Books, 1970.

Beard, Charles. *An Economic Interpretation of the Constitution of the United States*. New York: Free Press, 1935/1986.

Benjamin, S.G.W. "A Group of Pre-Revolutionary Editors. Beginnings of Journalism in America." *Magazine of American History*, 17: 1–28 (January 1887).

Bent, Silas. *Newspaper Crusaders: A Neglected Story*. New York: Whittlesey House, 1939.

Bernstein, Carl and Bob Woodward. *All the President's Men*. New York: Simon & Schuster, 1974.

Blanchard, Margaret A. "The Ossification of Journalism History: A Challenge for the Twenty-First Century." *Journalism History*, 25(3): 107–12 (Autumn 1999).

Bleyer, Willard Grosvenor. *Main Currents in the History of American Journalism*. Boston, MA: Houghton Mifflin, 1927.

Blondheim, Menahem. *News Over the Wires*. Cambridge, MA: Harvard University Press, 1994.

Brennen, Bonnie and Hanno Hardt (eds). *Picturing the Past: Media, History & Photography*. Urbana, IL: University of Illinois Press, 1999.

Brown, Walt. *John Adams and the American Press. Politics and Journalism at the Birth of the Republic*. London: McFarland, 1995.

Brown, Richard D. *Knowledge is Power: The Diffusion of Information in Early America 1700–1865*. New York: Oxford University Press, 1989.

Buchstein, Frederick D. "The Anarchist Press in American Journalism." *Journalism History*, 1: 43–5 (1974).

Burns, Eric. *Infamous Scribblers. The Founding Fathers and the Rowdy Beginnings of American Journalism*. New York: Public Affairs, 2006.

Carey, James. "The Problem of Journalism History." *Journalism History* 1(1): 3–5, 27 (1974).

Carey, James. "Technology and Ideology: The Case of the Telegraph." In *Communication As Culture. Essays on Media and Society*, 201–31. Boston, MA: Unwin Hyman, 1989.

Carlebach, Michael J. *The Origins of Photojournalism in America*. Washington, DC: Smithsonian Institute, 1992.

Charney, Mitchell V. *News By Radio*. New York: Macmillan, 1948.

Clark, Charles E. "The Newspapers of Provincial America." In John B. Hench (ed). *Three Hundred Years of the American Newspaper*, 367–389. Worcester, MA: American Antiquarian Society, 1991.

Covert, Catherine L. and John D. Stevens. *Mass Media Between the Wars: Perceptions of Cultural Tension, 1918–1941*. Syracuse, NY: Syracuse University Press, 1984.

Czitrom, Daniel J. *Media and the American Mind: From Morse to McLuhan*. Chapel Hill, NC: University of North Carolina Press, 1983.

Darton, Robert. "Writing News and Telling Stories." *Daedalus*, 104: 175–94 (Spring 1975).

Detweiler, Frederick G. *The Negro Press in the United States*. Chicago, IL: University of Chicago Press, 1922.

Dicken-Garcia, Hazel. *Journalistic Standards in Nineteenth-Century America*. Madison, WI: University of Wisconsin Press, 1989.

Douglas, Susan J. *Inventing American Broadcasting: 1899–1922*. Baltimore, MD: The Johns Hopkins University Press, 1987.

Fairfield, Roy P. (ed). *The Federalist Papers: A Collection of Essays Written in Support of the Constitution of the United States: From the Original Text of Alexander Hamilton, James Madison, John Jay*. Baltimore, MD: Johns Hopkins University Press, 1981.

Franklin, Benjamin. "Apology for Printers." *Pennsylvania Gazette*, 3–16, June 10, 1730.

Filler, Louis. *The Muckrakers: Crusaders for American Liberalism*. Chicago, IL: Henry Regnery, 1968.

Halberstam, David. *The Fifties*. New York: Villard Books, 1993.

Hallin, Daniel C. *The Uncensored War: The Media and Vietnam*. New York: Oxford University Press, 1986.

Hardt, Hanno. "Newsworkers, Technology, and Journalism History." *Critical Studies in Mass Communication*, 7(4): 346–65 (1990).

Hardt, Hanno and Bonnie Brennen. "Communication and the Question of History." *Communication Theory*, 3(2): 130–71 (1993).

Hardt, Hanno and Bonnie Brennen (eds). *Newsworkers: Toward A History of the Rank and File*. Minneapolis, MN: University of Minnesota Press, 1995.

Hudson, Frederic. *Journalism in the United States from 1690–1872*. New York: Harper & Brothers, 1873.

Irwin, Will. "The American Newspaper." *Collier's* (January–July) 1911.

Kielbowicz, Richard B. "Newsgathering by Printers' Exchanges Before the Telegraph." *Journalism History*, 9:2: 42–8 (Summer, 1982).

Kobre, Sidney. "The Revolutionary Colonial Press—A Social Interpretation." *Journalism Quarterly*, 20: 193–204 (1943).

Kobre, Sidney. *The Yellow Press and Gilded Age Journalism*. Tallahassee, FL: Florida State University, 1964.

La Popelinière, Lancelot-Voisin. *L'Histoire des histoires; L'Idée de l'histoire accomplie*. Paris: Fayard, 1599/1989.

Leab, Daniel. *A Union of Individuals. The Formation of the American Newspaper Guild, 1933–1936*. New York: Columbia University Press, 1970.

Lee, Alfred McClung. *The Daily Newspaper in America: The Evolution of a Social Instrument*. New York: Macmillan, 1937.

Levy, Leonard. *Emergence of a Free Press*. New York: Oxford University Press, 1985.

Lule, Jack. "Historiographical Essay: Telling the Story of Journalism, Journalism History and Narrative Theory." *American Journalism*, 7(4): 259–74 (1990).

Mailer, Norman. *The Armies of the Night: History as a Novel, the Novel as History*. New York: New American Library, 1968.

Marvin, Carolyn. *When Old Technologies Were New*. New York: Oxford University Press, 1988.

Marzolf, Marion. "American Studies: Ideas for Media Historians." *Journalism History*, 5(1): 13–16 (1978 cover).

McPherson, James Brian. *Journalism at the End of the American Century, 1965–Present*. Westport, CT: Praeger, 2006.

Mencken, H.L. "Reflections on Journalism." In *A Second Mencken Chrestomathy*, 357–60. New York: Knopf, 1995.

Mindich, David T. *Just the Facts. How "Objectivity" Came to Define American Journalism*. New York: New York University Press, 1998.

Murphy, James and Sharon M. Murphy. *Let My People Know: American Indian Journalism*. Norman, OK: University of Oklahoma Press, 1981.

Nerone, John. "The Mythology of the Penny Press." *Critical Studies in Mass Communication*, 4: 376–404 (1987).

Nerone, John. "Theory and History." *Communication Theory* 3(2): 148–57 (1993).

Nerone, John. *Violence Against the Press: Policing the Public Sphere in U.S. History*. New York: Oxford University Press, 1994.

Nevins, Alan. "American Journalism and Its Historical Treatment." *Journalism Quarterly*, 36(4): 411–22, 519 (1959).

Nord, David Paul. "A Plea for Journalism History." *Journalism History*, 15(1): 8–15 (1988).

Nord, David Paul. "Newspapers and American Nationhood, 1776–1826." In John B. Hench (ed.). *Three Hundred Years of the American Newspaper*, 391–405. Worcester, MA: American Antiquarian Society, 1991.

Nye, Russell B. "Freedom of the Press and the Antislavery Controversy." *Journalism Quarterly*, 22: 1–11 (1945).

Park, Robert. *The Immigrant Press and Its Control*. New York: Harper, 1922.

Roberts, Gene and Hank Klibanoff. *The Race Beat. The Press, the Civil Rights Struggle, and the Awakening of a Nation*. New York: Knopf, 2006.

Robinson, James Harvey. *The New History; Essays Illustrating the Modern Historical Outlook*. New York: Macmillan, 1922.

Ross, Edward Alsworth. "The Suppression of Important News." In Willard Grosvenor Bleyer (ed.) *The Profession of Journalism: A Collection of Articles on Newspaper Editing and Publishing, Taken From the Atlantic Monthly*, 79–96. Boston: *Atlantic Monthly*, 1918.

Ross, Ishbel. *Ladies of the Press. The Story of Women in Journalism by an Insider*. New York: Harper, 1936.

Rosten, Leo C. *The Washington Correspondents*. New York: Harcourt, Brace, 1937.

Schiller, Daniel. *Objectivity and the News: the Public and the Rise of Commercial Journalism*. Philadelphia, PA: University of Pennsylvania Press, 1981.

Schudson, Michael. *Discovering the News. A Social History of American Newspapers*. New York: Basic Books, 1978.

Schudson, Michael. "The Politics of Narrative Form: The Emergence of News Conventions in Print and Television." *Daedalus* 3(4): 97–112 (1982).

Schudson, Michael. "A Revolution in Historiography?" *Critical Studies in Mass Communication*, 4: 405–8 (1987).

Seldes, George. *Lords of the Press*. New York: Julian Messner, 1938.

Sims, Norman. *True Stories. A Century of Literary Journalism*. Evanston, IL: Northwestern University Press, 2007.

Sloan, William David and James D. Startt. *The Media in America* (3rd edn). Northport, AL: Vision Press, 1996.

Smith, Jeffery A. *Printers and Press Freedom: The Ideology of Early American Journalism*. New York: Oxford University Press, 1988.

Spencer, David. *The Yellow Journalism. The Press and America's Emergence as a World Power*. Evanston, IL: Northwestern University Press, 2007.

Starr, Paul. *The Creation of the Media: Political Origins of Modern Communications*. New York: Basic Books, 2004.

Stashower, Daniel. *The Boy Genius and the Mogul: The Untold Story of Television*. New York: Broadway Books, 2002.

Steffens, Lincoln. "The Business of a Newspaper." *Scribner's*, 22: 447–67 (October 1897).

Thomas, Isaiah, and Marcus A. McCorison. *The History of Printing in America: with a Biography of Printers & an Account of Newspapers*. New York: Weathervane Books, 1810/1970.

Villard, Oswald Garrison. *The Disappearing Daily: Chapters in American Newspaper Evolution*. New York: Knopf, 1944.

Williams, Talcott. *The Newspaperman*. New York: Scribner's, 1925.

Wingate, Charles F., (ed). *Views on Journalism*, 1875 (Reprint available from Whitefish, MT: Kessinger Publishing (Aug 2009)).

Yodelis Smith, MaryAnn. "The Method of History." In Guido H. Stempel III and Bruce H. Westley (eds). *Research Methods in Mass Communication*, 305–19. Englewood Cliffs, NJ: Prentice Hall, 1981.

Zinn, Howard. *A People's History of the United States*. New York: Harper Perennial, 1990.

INDEX

9 780415 801874